Listening to Western

Music

seventh edition

Listening to Western
Music

 Craig Wright
Yale University

SCHIRMER
CENGAGE Learning™

Australia · Brazil · Japan · Korea · Mexico · Singapore · Spain · United Kingdom · United States

**Listening to Western Music,
Seventh Edition**
Craig Wright

Publisher: Clark Baxter

Senior Development Editor: Sue
Gleason Wade

Assistant Editor: Elizabeth Newell

Editorial Assistant: Marsha Kaplan

Managing Media Editor: Kathryn Schooling

Brand Manager: Lydia LeStar

Marketing Communications Manager:
Linda Yip

Senior Content Project Manager:
Lianne Ames

Art Director: Faith Brosnan

Manufacturing Planner: Mary Beth
Hennebury

Senior Rights Acquisition Specialist:
Mandy Groszko

Production Service: Thistle Hill Publishing
Services

Text Designer: Shawn Girsberger

Cover Designer: Hanh L. Luu

Cover Image: shutterstock.com © Zheltyshev

Compositor: Cenveo Publisher Services/
Nesbitt Graphics, Inc.

For product information and technology assistance, contact us at
Cengage Learning Customer & Sales Support, 1-800-354-9706.

For permission to use material from this text or product,
submit all requests online at **www.cengage.com/permissions.**
Further permissions questions can be emailed to
permissionrequest@cengage.com.

Library of Congress Control Number: 2012945799

Western Student Edition:

ISBN-13: 978-1-133-95391-3

ISBN-10: 1-133-95391-3

Schirmer
20 Channel Center Street
Boston, MA 02210
USA

Cengage Learning is a leading provider of customized learning solutions
with office locations around the globe, including Singapore, the United
Kingdom, Australia, Mexico, Brazil, and Japan. Locate your local office at
international.cengage.com/region.

Cengage Learning products are represented in Canada by
Nelson Education, Ltd.

For your course and learning solutions, visit **www.cengage.com.**

Purchase any of our products at your local college store or at our
preferred online store **www.cengagebrain.com.**

Instructors: Please visit **login.cengage.com** and log in to access
instructor-specific resources.

Printed in the United States of America
1 2 3 4 5 6 7 16 15 14 13 12

Brief Contents

Contents

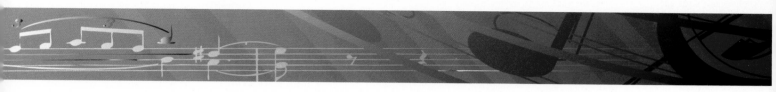

About the Author

Craig M. Wright received his Bachelor of Music degree at the Eastman School of Music in 1966 and his Ph.D. in musicology from Harvard University in 1972. He began his teaching career at the University of Kentucky and for the past forty years has been teaching at Yale University, where he is currently the Henry L. and Lucy G. Moses Professor of Music. At Yale, Wright's courses include his perennially popular introductory course, Listening to Music, also part of the offerings of Open Yale Courses, and his large lecture course Exploring the Nature of Genius. He is the author of numerous scholarly books and articles on composers ranging from Leoninus to Bach. Wright has also been the recipient of many awards, including a Guggenheim Fellowship, the Einstein and Kinkeldey Awards of the American Musicological Society, and the Dent Medal of the International Musicological Society. In 2004, he was awarded the honorary degree Doctor of Humane Letters from the University of Chicago. And in 2010 he was elected a member of the American Academy of Arts and Sciences, joining fellow inductee banjo player Steve Martin. Wright has also published *Listening to Music, Chinese Edition* (Schirmer Cengage Learning/Three Union Press, 2012), translated and simplified by Profs. Li Xiujung (China Conservatory, Beijing) and Yu Zhigang (Central Conservatory, Beijing), both of whom worked with Wright at Yale; *The Essential Listening to Music* (Schirmer Cengage Learning, 2012); and *Music in Western Civilization, Media Update* (Schirmer Cengage Learning, 2010), with coauthor Bryan Simms. He is currently at work on a volume titled *Mozart's Brain: Exploring the Nature of Genius.*

Preface

Listening to Western Music is not just the title of this book. Its aim is to teach students to listen to Western music so that they, too, might become transfixed by its expressive power.

Most music appreciation textbooks treat music not as an opportunity for personal engagement through listening but as a history of music. Students are required to learn something of the technical workings of music (what a tonic chord is, for example) and specific facts (how many symphonies Beethoven wrote), but are not asked to become personally engaged in the act of listening to music. What listening does take place is passive, not active. *Listening to Western Music,* however, is different. Through a variety of means within the covers of this book and beyond them, students are required to engage in a dialogue with the composer, thereby sharing the composer's vision of the world.

 ## New to This Edition

Although the goals of active listening have not changed, this edition of *Listening to Western Music* incorporates several improvements:

- For the first time, in this edition the complete musical selections are available for students to keep, as *downloads.*

- Craig Wright is now hosting a Facebook page—**Listening to Music with Craig Wright**—where readers will find discussions and blogs about what's happening with music today, and a mechanism for communicating directly with the author.

- Fourteen musical works are new to the Seventh Edition, spanning eras from medieval to modern. Four improved recordings replace previous versions.

- Many new references to popular culture enliven the entire text.

- Chapters 1 through 3 on the elements of music have been streamlined and rewritten for greater student appeal.

- Checklists of Musical Style have returned to the text by popular demand. Checklists for all eras appear in Chapter 4 as a preview and recur at the end of each era, to summarize composers, genres, and treatment of the elements of music during each era.

- "What to Listen For" pointers appear at the beginning of each Listening Guide.

- Nineteenth-century nationalism has been incorporated into Chapter 21 on early Romantic music and Chapter 26 on late Romantic orchestral music.

- Chapter 5 now includes a section focusing on the Agincourt Carol.

- Chapter 13 includes a new box: "Mozart: The Gold Standard of Genius."

- Haydn's Trumpet Concerto in E♭ major, performed by Wynton Marsalis, now appears in Chapter 15.

- Chapter 18 now includes Beethoven's *Ode to Joy,* from Symphony No. 9, as well as a new box: "Where Did Beethoven Compose?"

- Chapter 21 includes a different movement from Berlioz's *Symphonie fantastique:* "March to the Scaffold."

- Chapter 22 now includes several new pieces of Romantic piano music: "Eusebius," "Florestan," and "Chopin" from *Carnaval* by Robert Schumann, and Chopin's Nocturne in E♭ major.

- Chapter 24 has new coverage of Wagner's *Die Walküre* and two new selections: "Ride of the Valkyries" and "Wotan's Farewell."

- Chapter 25 includes a new box: "Great Opera for the Price of a Movie."

- Chapter 26 now includes coverage of Brahms's *Ein Deutsches Requiem,* as well as the orchestral song, represented by Mahler's *Ich bin der Welt abhanden gekommen.*

- Chapter 27 now includes Ravel's *Bolero.*

- Chapter 31 includes a new Ives selection, *Variations on America,* as well as new coverage of Modernist composer Augusta Read Thomas and *The Rub of Love.*

An alternative volume—*Listening to Music,* comprising Chapters 1–32 of *Listening to Western Music* plus seven additional chapters on American popular and global music—continues to be available for those who prefer a text that includes more coverage of popular and global music.

 # Pedagogical Aids

Listening Exercises

Listening to Western Music is the only music appreciation text on the market to offer detailed Listening Exercises within the book and online, keyed to important musical selections. Using these, students will embrace hundreds of specific passages of music and make critical decisions about them. All Listening Exercises are available in interactive form within CourseMate; Part I includes them in the print text as well.

The exercises begin in Part I by developing basic listening skills—recognizing rhythmic patterns, distinguishing major keys from minor, and differentiating various kinds of textures. The exercises then move on, in online form at CourseMate, to entire pieces in which students are required to become participants in an artistic exchange—the composer communicating with the listener, and the listener reacting over a long span of time. Ultimately, equipped with these newly developed listening skills, students will move comfortably to the concert hall, listening to classical and popular music with greater confidence and enjoyment. Although this book is for the present course, its aim is to prepare students for a lifetime of musical listening pleasure.

Listening Guides

In addition to the Listening Exercises, nearly 100 Listening Guides appear regularly throughout the text to help the novice enjoy extended musical compositions.

Within each guide are an introduction to the piece's genre, form, meter, and texture, as well as a "What to Listen For" reminder and a detailed "time log" that allows the listener to follow along as the piece unfolds. The discussion in the text and the Listening Guides have been carefully coordinated, minute by minute, second by second, with times on the CDs, in streaming music, and in downloads. Students may prefer to engage these Listening Guides as Active Listening Guides at the CourseMate website.

Because many pieces contain internal tracks to facilitate navigation to important points in the composition, the timings in both Listening Guides and in-text Listening Exercises have been carefully keyed to help students find and keep their place. The sample Listening Guide on the next page illustrates how these keys work. First, gold and blue disc symbols representing the 5-CD and 2-CD sets, respectively, appear at the upper right of the Listening Guide and Listening Exercise. Brown discs containing the word "intro" represent the Introduction to Listening CD bound into the textbook.

The first number below each symbol and before the slash indicates the appropriate CD number, and the number or numbers after the slash indicate track or tracks. (Intro CD references contain only track numbers.) Students can thus choose the correct CD and locate the tracks that they need, regardless of which CD set they own. Within all the Listening Guides, track number reminders appear in small squares, color-coded in gold for the 5-CD set, in blue for the 2-CD set, and in brown for the Intro CD.

For pieces with multiple tracks, there are two timing columns. Those on the left are total elapsed times from the beginning to the end of the piece; these times apply to the streaming music and downloads. Those to the right of the track number reminders and next to the comments are the timings that appear on a CD player's or computer media player's display.

The numbers in the discs indicate the 5-CD set and the 2-CD set. The numbers beneath them tell, first, the specific CD number within that set and, second, the appropriate tracks on that CD. Here, one needs CD 2, tracks 18–19, from the 5-CD set, or CD 1, tracks 21–22, from the 2-CD set. If students are using the eBook, clicking on the disc icons will allow them to hear the entire piece streaming.

Listening Guide

Joseph Haydn, The "Emperor" Quartet (1797), Opus 76, No. 3

⑤   ②

2/18–19 1/21–22

Second Movement, *Poco adagio cantabile* **(rather slow, song-like)**

Genre: String quartet

Form: Theme and variations

WHAT TO LISTEN FOR: The trick here is to recognize "the emperor" by his tune, no matter how ingeniously Haydn disguises him in different musical costumes.

THEME

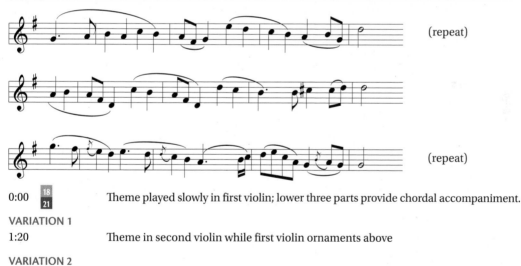

(repeat)

(repeat)

0:00 [18/21]   Theme played slowly in first violin; lower three parts provide chordal accompaniment.

VARIATION 1
1:20   Theme in second violin while first violin ornaments above

VARIATION 2
2:29   Theme in cello while other three instruments provide counterpoint against it

VARIATION 3
3:47 [19/22] 0:00 Theme in viola; other three instruments enter gradually.

VARIATION 4
5:04   1:17   Theme returns to first violin, but now accompaniment is more contrapuntal than chordal.

In this track number reminder, the top number indicates that the piece is now playing track 19 from the 5-CD set, and the bottom number indicates track 22 from the 2-CD set. The timing column on the right shows time elapsed within the track, as it would appear on a CD player. The first timing column, on the left, shows total elapsed times from the beginning of the piece, as they would appear in streaming music or a download.

🔊)) Listen to streaming music in an Active Listening Guide at CourseMate or in the eBook.

🔊)) Take online Listening Exercise 16.2 and receive feedback at CourseMate or in the eBook.

Each Listening Guide reminds students that they may watch and listen to the music streaming in an Active Listening Guide at CourseMate. If they are using the eBook, clicking on the loudspeaker icons allows them to play the Active Listening Guide or take the online Listening Exercise directly from their book.

Nearly 200 additional Supplementary Listening Guides, including those from previous editions, may be downloaded from CourseMate, the Instructor's Companion Site, and the instructor's PowerLecture. These may be used with *any* recording, because they were created without time cues.

 # Ancillaries for Students

Introduction to Listening CD

Packaged with each new copy of the book, and not sold separately, this CD contains all of the music discussed in Chapters 1 through 3 on the elements of music, as well as a guide to instruments of the orchestra, which presents the instruments and then tests students' ability to recognize the instruments by themselves and in various combinations.

2-CD Set

This set includes a core repertoire of music discussed in the book. In CourseMate, each selection may also be streamed by itself or in the context of an Active Listening Guide that demonstrates visually what students hear.

5-CD Set

This set includes all of the classical Western repertoire discussed in the book. In CourseMate, each selection may also be streamed by itself or in the context of an Active Listening Guide that demonstrates visually what students hear.

Streaming and Downloads

The content of all the CDs is also available streaming at CourseMate and in the eBook, and as album downloads, accessible via access code at the Sony Music storefront.

Active Listening Guides

The Active Listening Guides at CourseMate feature full-color interactive and streaming listening guides for every selection on the CD sets, along with listening quizzes, background information, and printable PDF Listening Guides.

CourseMate

The text website, CourseMate, offers several challenging and interesting features. First, it allows for chapter-by-chapter self-study in which students may take a quiz to explore their knowledge of the topics presented in the chapter, as well as study appropriate flashcards, topic summaries, and demonstrations.

In addition, CourseMate contains links to

- A video walkthrough of "How to Use CourseMate," presented by Professor Casey J. Hayes, Franklin College, with an introduction by Craig Wright

- The eBook

- Interactive versions of all the text's Listening Exercises

- Active Listening Guides for all text selections

- A video of a performance of Britten's *Young Person's Guide to the Orchestra*, in whole and by instrument families

- Video demonstrations of keyboard instruments

- Sixteen iAudio podcasts on difficult musical concepts

- An interactive music timeline

- A checklist of musical styles with integrated musical style comparisons
- Musical elements, genres, and forms tutorials
- Supplementary Listening Guide documents for music beyond that provided with the text
- A complete online course taught at Yale by the author and featuring in-class performances and demonstrations
- Online playlists from iTunes and YouTube, cued with marginal notes in the text

eBook

Also available is a multimedia-enabled eBook, featuring page design identical to that in the print book and links to all CourseMate content, including streaming music, Active Listening Guides, and links to iTunes and YouTube playlists.

 # For Instructors

CourseMate's Engagement Tracker

Engagement Tracker functions as an electronic gradebook for instructors. They can use it to assess student performance, preparation, and the length of time of each student's engagement. Engagement Tracker's tools allow the instructor to:

- Automatically record quiz scores
- Export all grades to an instructor's own Excel spreadsheet
- See progress for individuals or the class as a whole
- Identify students at risk early in the course
- Uncover which concepts are most difficult for the class and monitor time on task

PowerLecture with ExamView® and JoinIn on TurningPoint®

This feature includes the Instructor's Manual, Supplementary Listening Guides, ExamView® computerized testing (including musical clips), JoinIn on TurningPoint®, and Microsoft® PowerPoint® slides with lecture outlines, music clips, and images, which can be used as offered, or customized by importing personal lecture slides or other material. ExamView allows instructors to create, deliver, and customize tests and study guides (both print and online) in minutes with its easy-to-use assessment and tutorial system. It offers both a Quick Test Wizard and an Online Test Wizard that guide instructors step by step through the process of creating tests (up to 250 questions using up to twelve question types), while its "what you see is what you get" capability allows users to see the test they are creating on the screen exactly as it will print or display online. ExamView's complete word-processing capabilities allow users to enter an unlimited number of new questions or edit existing questions. JoinIn content (for use with most "clicker" systems) delivers instant classroom assessment and active learning opportunities such as in-class polling, attendance taking, and quizzing.

WebTutor™ for Blackboard and WebCT

This web-based teaching and learning tool is rich with study and mastery tools, communication tools, and course content. Use WebTutor™ to provide virtual office hours, post syllabi, set up threaded discussions, track student progress with the quizzing material, and more. For students, WebTutor™ offers real-time access to a full array of study tools, including flashcards (with audio), practice quizzes, online tutorials, and web links. Instructors can customize the content by uploading images and other resources, adding web links, or creating their own practice materials. WebTutor™ also provides rich communication tools, including a course calendar, asynchronous discussion, "real-time" chat, and an integrated email system—in effect, a complete online course. For information, contact your Cengage sales representative.

Online Instruction

Craig Wright has prepared a teaching packet for a multiweek online course using the briefer *Essential Listening to Music*. The packet provides a syllabus; content for each class, including external links; and PowerPoint® presentations. For access to this packet, you may contact the author directly via Facebook, at **Listening to Music with Craig Wright**.

 # Acknowledgments

Times are changing—and rapidly—with everything pushed by technological innovation. When we started this project some twenty-five years ago, I made the then-radical decision to dispense with vinyl records, in favor of tapes. Now tapes are gone and CDs are following them. Today music streams from the clouds.

One thing, however, hasn't changed: my enthusiasm for discussing with colleagues the best ways to introduce classical music to students who know little about music. What are the best pieces in both the popular and the classical realm to use as teaching exemplars? What can students be reasonably expected to hear? What is the best terminology to use? Profs. Keith Polk (University of New Hampshire) and Tilden Russell (Southern Connecticut State University) have gently taken me to task for using the term *ternary form* where *rounded binary* is more correct; they are right, yet for fear of overloading the beginning student with too many new formal concepts, here I simplify and call both rounded binary and ternary forms just ternary. So, too, I am indebted to Profs. Anne Robertson and Robert Kendrick of the University of Chicago for their input on matters large and small. Six former students—Profs. David Metzer (University of British Columbia), Jess Tyre (SUNY at Potsdam), Marica Tacconi (Pennsylvania State University), Lorenzo Candelaria (University of Texas, Austin), Laura Nash (Fairfield University), and Nathan Link (Centre College)—continue to provide me with valuable criticism and suggestions. Several colleagues made suggestions for specific improvements in content, for which I am grateful, namely, Profs. James Ladewig (University of Rhode Island), Carlo Caballero (University of Colorado, Boulder), Bryan Simms (University of Southern California), and Scott Warfield (University of Central Florida). My conversations with composer Augusta Read Thomas (University of Chicago) were a special privilege, and her music is now featured here in Chapter 31.

I am especially indebted to the following reviewers, who provided invaluable in-depth feedback: Francy Acosta, University of Chicago; Eric Bonds, University of Mississippi; Homer Ferguson, Arizona State University; Carla Gallahan, Troy University; Cliff Ganus, Harding University; Joice Gibson, Metropolitan State College, Denver; James Ieraci, Burlington County College; Elliott Jones, Santa Ana College; Lea Kibler, Clemson University; Nora Kile, University of Tennessee at Chattanooga; Spencer Lambright, Middle Tennessee State University; Mildred Lanier, Jefferson State Community College; Mark Latham, Butte Community College; Linda Li-Bleuel, Clemson University; Chauncey Maddren, Los Angeles Valley College; Francis Massinon, Austin Peay State University; Manuel Pena, Fresno State University; Daniel Robbins, Truckee Meadows Community College; and Christopher A. Wolfe, Community College of Baltimore County.

The engineering of the audio was accomplished at the Yale Recording Studio by the capable hands of Eugene Kimball. And Benjamin Thorburn generated the new musical autography for this book.

Julia Doe, also at Yale, proofread the manuscript, contributed ideas for improved content and style throughout, and developed many of the ancillary materials that appear in CourseMate.

Prof. Timothy Roden (Ohio Wesleyan University), the author of much of the web material, Instructor's Manual, and Test Bank, has corrected errors and saved me from myself on numerous occasions.

Sarah Dye (Martin University) has updated the PowerPoint® slides accompanying this edition.

As always, it has been a privilege to work with publisher Clark Baxter and his experienced team at Schirmer Cengage Learning—Sue Gleason, Jeanne Heston, Katie Schooling, Liz Newell, Marsha Kaplan, and Lianne Ames—as well as Angela Urquhart and Andrea Archer at Thistle Hill Publishing Services, Tom and Lisa Smialek, original developers of the Active Listening Tools, and especially Tom Laskey, Director of A&R, Custom Marketing Group, at SONY, who has helped usher this book into the era of downloads. My heartiest thanks to all of you!

Finally, I thank my wife (Sherry Dominick) and four children (Evan, Andrew, Stephanie, and Chris), who did their best to keep the paterfamilias aware of popular culture, musical and otherwise, and up to speed with the ever-changing face of technology.

f Join me on Facebook at **Listening to Music with Craig Wright**, where you'll find discussions and blogs about what's happening with music today, and a mechanism for communicating directly with me.

Craig Wright
Yale University

Listening to Western Music

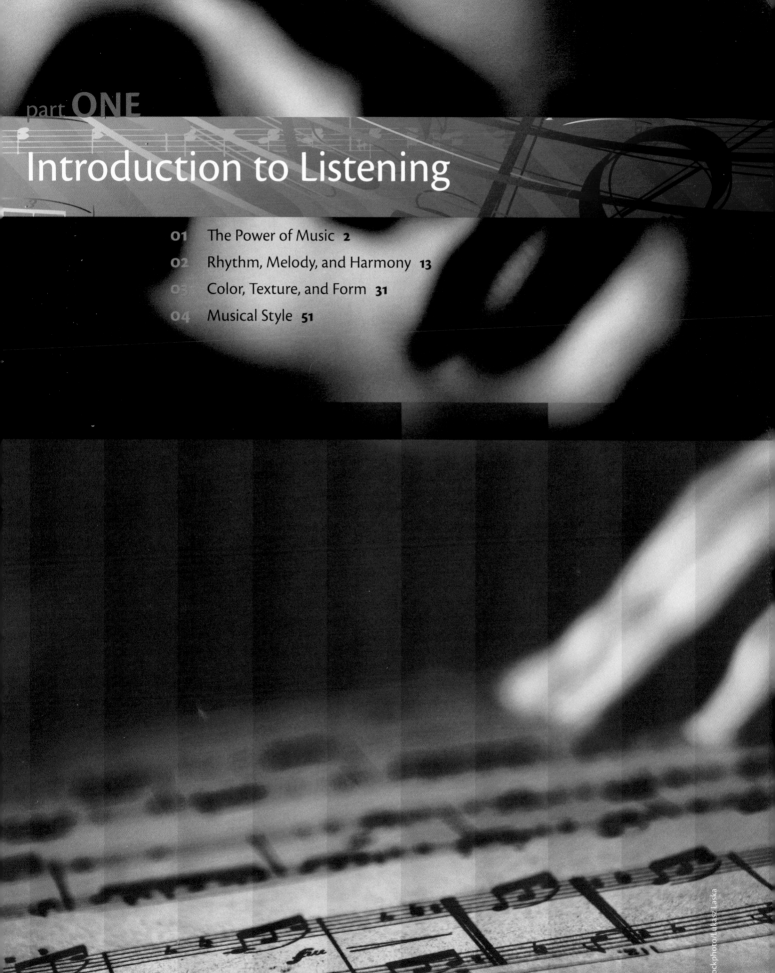

part **ONE**

Introduction to Listening

chapter ONE
The Power of Music

Why do we listen to music? Does it keep us in touch with the latest musical trends, help get us through our morning exercise, or relax us in the evening? Each day almost everyone in the industrialized world listens to music, whether intentionally or not. The global expenditure for commercial music is somewhere between $30 and $40 billion annually, more than the gross domestic product of 100 of the 181 countries identified by the World Bank. In 2011, nearly 1.3 billion singles were downloaded, and the number is increasing annually at the rate of about 10 percent. Look at most smartphones, and what do we see? At least one app for music (and many synced songs), but none for ballet or painting, for example. Turn on the radio, and what do we hear? Drama or poetry? No, usually just music; the radio is basically a transmission device for *music*.

But why is music so appealing? What is its attraction? Does it perpetuate the human species? Does it shelter us from the elements? No. Does it keep us warm? Not unless we dance. Is music some sort of drug or aphrodisiac?

Oddly, yes. Neuroscientists at Harvard University have done studies showing that when we listen to music we engage processes in the brain that are "active in other euphoria inducing stimuli such as food, sex, and drugs of abuse."[1] These same researchers have explained the neural processes through which listening to particular pieces of music can give us goose bumps. A chemical change occurs in the human brain as blood flow increases in some parts and decreases in others. Although listening to music today may or may not be necessary for survival, it does alter our chemical composition and our mental state. In short, it is pleasurable and rewarding.

Music is also powerful. "To control the people, control the music," Plato said, in essence, in his *Republic*. Thus governments, religions, and, more recently, corporations have done just that. Think of the stirring band music used to get soldiers to march to war. Think of the refined sounds of Mozart played in advertisements for luxurious products. Think of the four-note "rally" motive played at professional sports events to energize the crowd. Sound perception is the most powerful sense we possess, likely because it *was* once essential to our survival—who is coming from where? Friend or foe? Flight or fight? Horror films frighten us, not when the images on the screen become vivid, but when the music starts to turn ominous. In short, sounds rationally organized in a pleasing or frightening way—music—profoundly affect how we feel and behave.

Watch a video of Craig Wright's Open Yale Course class sessions 1 and 2, "Introduction" and "Introduction to Instruments and Musical Genres," at CourseMate for this text.

Music and Your Brain

The word *music* descends from the Greek word for "Muses," nine ladies who presided over the arts in classical mythology. Briefly defined, **music** is the rational organization of sounds and silences passing through time. Tones must be arranged in some consistent, logical, and (usually) pleasing way before we can call these sounds "music" instead of just noise. A singer or an instrumentalist generates music by creating **sound waves**, vibrations that reflect slight differences in air pressure. Sound waves radiate out in a circle from the source, carrying with them two types of essential information: pitch and volume. The speed of vibration within the sound wave determines what we perceive as high and low pitches; and the width (or amplitude) of the wave reflects its volume. When music reaches the brain, that organ tells us how we should feel and respond to the sound. We tend to hear low, soft tones as relaxing and high, loud ones as tension filled.

To learn more about music and the brain, see a video of "Music and the Mind" in the YouTube playlist at CourseMate for this text.

---

[1] Anne Blood and Robert Zatorre, "Intensely Pleasurable Responses to Music Correlate with Activity in Brain Regions Implicated in Reward and Emotion," *Proceedings of the National Academy of Sciences,* Vol. 98, No. 20 (Sept. 25, 2001), pp. 11818–11823.

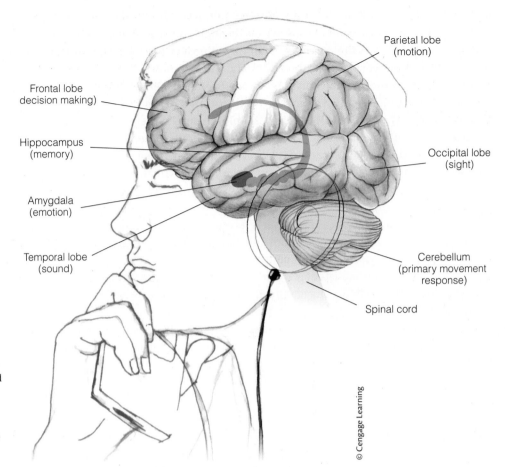

Parietal lobe
(motion)

Frontal lobe
decision making)

Hippocampus
(memory)

Amygdala
(emotion)

Temporal lobe
(sound)

Occipital lobe
(sight)

Cerebellum
(primary movement
response)

Spinal cord

© Cengage Learning

Figure 1.1

The processing of music in our brain is a hugely complex activity involving many areas and associated links. The first recognition and sorting of sounds, both musical and linguistic, occurs largely in the primary auditory cortex in both the left and right temporal lobes.

To watch the brain operate as it improvises music, see "Your Brain on Improv" in the YouTube playlist at CourseMate for this text.

Tune in to an iAudio podcast about learning how to listen at CourseMate for this text.

Given all the love songs in the world, we might think that music is an affair of the heart. But both love and music are domains of a far more complex vital organ: the brain (Fig. 1.1). When sound waves reach us, our inner ear transforms them into electrical signals that go to various parts of the brain, each analyzing a particular component of the sound: pitch, color, loudness, duration, direction of source, relation to familiar music, and so on. Most processing of sound (music as well as language) takes place in the temporal lobe. If we are imagining how the next line of a song will go, that decision is usually reached in the frontal lobe. If we are playing an instrument, we engage the motor cortex (parietal lobe) to move our fingers and the visual center (occipital lobe) to read the notes. As the music proceeds, our brain constantly updates the information it receives, hundreds of times per second. At a speed of 250 miles per hour, associative neurons integrate all the data into a single perception of sound. To sum up: Sound waves enter the brain as electrochemical impulses that cause chemical changes in the body; the human response can be to relax or, if the impulses come strongly at regular intervals, to get up and dance—to entrain with the rhythm.

 ## Listening to Whose Music?

Today, most music we hear isn't "live" music but recorded sound. Sound recording began in the 1870s with Thomas Edison's phonograph machine, which first played metal cylinders and then vinyl disks, or "records." During the 1930s, magnetic tape recorders appeared and grew in popularity until the early 1990s, when they were superseded by a new technology: digital recording. In digital recording, all the components of musical sound—pitch, tone color, duration, volume, and more—are analyzed thousands of times per second, and that information is stored on compact discs as sequences of binary numbers. When it's time to play the music, these digital data are reconverted to electrical impulses that are then changed back into sound waves that are intensified and pushed through speakers or headphones. Most recorded music now is no longer stored and sold on CDs, but distributed electronically as MP3 or M4A files. This holds true for popular and classical music alike.

Popular or Classical?

Most people prefer **popular music**, designed to please a large portion of the general public. Pop CDs and downloads outsell classical recordings by about twenty to one. But why are so many people, and young people in particular, attracted to popular music? Likely it has to do with beat and rhythm (both discussed in Ch. 2). A regular beat elicits a synchronized motor response in the central nervous system; people almost can't help but move in time to music with a good beat.

Most of the music discussed in this book, however, is what we call "classical" music, and it, too, can be a powerful force. The term *classical music* originated in the early nineteenth century to characterize music thought to be of high quality and worthy of repeated hearing. Indeed, hearing the "classics" played by a mass of acoustic instruments—a symphony orchestra—can be an overwhelming experience. Classical music is often regarded as "old" music, written by "dead white men." This isn't entirely true: No small amount of it has been written by women, and many composers, of both genders, are very much alive and well today. In truth, however, much of the classical music that we hear—the music of Bach, Beethoven, and Brahms, for example—*is* old. That is why, in part, it is called "classical." In the same vein, we refer to clothes, furniture, and cars as "classics" because they have timeless qualities of expression, proportion, and balance. Broadly defined, **classical music** is the traditional music of any culture, usually requiring long years of training; it is "high art" or "learned," timeless music that is enjoyed generation after generation.

Popular and Classical Music Compared

Today Western classical music is taught in conservatories around the world, from Paris to Beijing to Singapore. Western pop music enjoys even greater favor, having drowned out local popular music in many places. But what are the essential differences between the music we call popular and the music we call classical, or "art," music? Cutting to the quick, we list five ways in which these friendly neighbors differ:

- Popular music often uses electric enhancements (via electric guitars, synthesizers, and so on) to amplify and transform vocal and instrumental sounds. Much of classical music uses **acoustic instruments** that produce sounds naturally.

- Popular music is primarily vocal, involving **lyrics** (accompanying text that tells listeners what the music is about and thus implies what they are supposed to feel). Classical music is more often purely instrumental, performed on a piano or by a symphony orchestra, for example, which grants the listener more interpretive freedom.

- Popular music has a strong beat that makes us want to move in sync with it. Classical music often subordinates the beat in favor of melody and harmony.

© Lynn Goldsmith/CORBIS

Figure 1.2

Classical music requires years of technical training on an instrument and knowledge of often complicated music theory. Some musicians are equally at home in the worlds of classical and jazz, a genre of popular music. Juilliard School of Music–trained Wynton Marsalis can record a classical trumpet concerto one week and an album of New Orleans–style jazz the next. He has won nine Grammy awards—seven for various jazz categories and two for classical albums. To hear Marsalis perform Joseph Haydn's trumpet concerto, listen to the downloads, streaming music in Ch. 15 at CourseMate, or either of these CDs in the collection accompanying this text: **2** 1/17 or **5** 2/14.

- Popular tunes tend to be short and involve exact repetition. Classical compositions can be long, sometimes thirty to forty minutes in duration, operas and ballets even longer, and most repetitions are somehow varied.

- Popular music is performed by memory, not from a written score (have you ever seen music stands at a rock concert?), and each performer can interpret the work as he or she sees fit (hence the proliferation of "cover songs"). Classical music, even if played by memory, is normally generated from a written score, and there is usually one commonly accepted mode of interpretation—the piece exists, almost frozen in place, as a work of art.

 # How Does Classical Music Work?

Explaining how classical music works requires an entire book—this one. But some preliminary observations are in order.

Genres of Classical Music

Genre in musical terminology is simply a fancy word for "type of music." The types of popular music, of course, are almost endless: rap, hip-hop, blues, R&B, country, grunge, and Broadway show tunes among them. *Genre* implies not only where you might hear it performed (a bar, a jazz club, an arena, or a stadium, for example) but also how you might be expected to dress and act when you arrive. A fan goes to hear Beyoncé at the MGM Grand Garden Arena in Las Vegas dressed casually, ready to dance and make a lot of noise. That same person, however, would likely attend a concert of the Boston Symphony Orchestra in Symphony Hall attired in suit and tie, and prepared to sit quietly. Among the most prominent genres of classical music are dramatic works mounted in opera houses and large theaters. Most classical genres, however, are purely instrumental. Some are performed in large concert halls accommodating 2,000 to 3,000 listeners, whereas others are heard in smaller (chamber) halls seating perhaps 200 to 600 (Fig. 1.3). Again, genre dictates where one goes to hear music, what one hears, what one wears, and how one behaves.

Opera Houses and Theaters	Concert Halls	Chamber Halls
Opera	Symphony	Art song
Ballet	Concerto	String quartet
	Oratorio	Piano sonata

The Language of Classical Music

If a friend told you, "My house burned down last night," you'd probably react with shock and sadness. In this case, verbal language conveys meaning and elicits an emotional reaction.

Music, too, is a means of communication, one older than spoken language; spoken language, many biologists tell us, is simply a specialized subset of music. Over the centuries, composers of classical music have created a language that can convey shock and sadness as effectively as do the words of poetry or prose. This language of music is a collection of audible gestures that express meaning through sound. We need not take lessons to learn how to understand the language of music at a basic level, for we intuit much of it already. The reason is simple: We have been listening to the language of Western music every day since infancy. We intuit, for example, that music getting faster and rising in pitch communicates growing

Figure 1.3

Some concerts require a large hall seating 2,000 to 3,000 listeners (such as the Schermerhorn Symphony Center, Nashville, Tennessee, shown in the chapter opener). For other performances, a smaller venue with 200 to 600 seats is more appropriate, as we see here at the chamber music hall of the Royal Conservatory of Music in Brussels, Belgium.

excitement because we have heard these gestures frequently, as in chase scenes in films and on TV. Still another piece might sound like a funeral march. Why? Because the composer is communicating this idea to us by using a slow *tempo*, regular *beat*, and *minor key*. Understanding terms such as these will allow us to discuss the language of music accurately and thereby appreciate it more fully, which is another aim of this book.

 # Where and How to Listen

CDs for Your Book

The Introduction to Listening (Intro) CD bound into your book, as well as the 2-CD set, 5-CD set, and Popular/Global CD that are available for purchase, contains the highest-quality recordings commercially available, in terms of both musical artistry and engineering excellence. You can play them on your computer or your car stereo, of course, or even load them onto your smartphone. But access to quality audio equipment (a separate player, amplifier, and speakers) will help produce the best home audio experience.

Streaming Music

All music on the CDs is also available streaming on the text's CourseMate website and in its interactive eBook.

Downloads

By now, most people you know have a digital media library containing hundreds, perhaps thousands, of pieces of music. The difficulty doesn't lie in obtaining this music, but in organizing the countless downloads present.

This textbook offers downloads for all of the music on the CDs, which makes this as good a time as any for you to start a classical playlist. Devote a section in your listening library exclusively to classical music and arrange the pieces within it by composer. Most of the classical pieces you will buy, despite what iTunes says, will not be "songs." Songs have lyrics, and a great deal of classical music, as mentioned, is purely instrumental: instrumental symphonies, sonatas, concertos, and the like.

If you wish to do more than just listen, however, go to YouTube, which will allow you to see the performers, thereby humanizing the listening experience. Much music is available on YouTube, but a lot of it is of poor quality. For the classical repertoire, seek out big-name artists (Luciano Pavarotti and Renée Fleming among them) and top-of-the-line orchestras (the New York Philharmonic or the Chicago Symphony Orchestra, for example).

Live in Concert

Pop megastars now make more money from live concerts than from recording royalties; so, too, with classical musicians. Indeed, for classical musicians and listeners alike, nothing is better than a live performance. First comes the joy of witnessing a classical artist at work, delivering his or her craft with technical perfection. Second, and more importantly, the sound will be magnificent because, unlike that of most pop concerts, the classical sound is usually pure, unamplified acoustical music.

Unlike pop concerts, too, performances of classical music can be rather formal affairs. For one thing, people dress "up," not "down." For another, throughout the event the classical audience sits quietly, saying nothing to friends or to the performers on stage. No one sways, dances, or sings along to the music. Only at the end of each composition does the audience express itself, clapping respectfully.

Classical concerts weren't always so formal, however. In fact, at one time they were more like professional wrestling matches. In the eighteenth century, for example, the audience talked during performances and yelled words of encouragement to the players. People clapped at the end of each movement of a symphony and often in the middle of the movement as well. After an exceptionally pleasing performance, listeners would demand that the piece be repeated immediately in an **encore**. If, on the other hand, the audience didn't like what it heard, it might express its displeasure by throwing fruit and other debris at the stage. Our modern, more dignified classical concert was a creation of the nineteenth century, when musical compositions came to be considered works of high art worthy of reverential silence.

Attending a classical concert requires familiarizing yourself with the music in advance. These days, this is easy. Go to YouTube and type in the titles of the pieces on the program. Enter "Beethoven Symphony 5," for example. Several recorded versions will appear, and you can quickly compare different interpretations of the same piece. Should you need information about the history of the work and its composer, try to avoid Wikipedia, which is often unreliable. Instead, go to the more authoritative Oxford Music Online's Grove Music Online (most colleges and universities have an online subscription) and search under the name of the composer.

Regardless of how you listen—with CDs, downloads, online, or live—be sure to focus solely on the music. This text is here to help you do exactly that, more effectively.

 # Getting Started:
No Previous Experience Required

"I'm tone deaf, I can't sing, and I'm no good at dancing." Most likely this isn't true of you. What *is* true is that people are more or less good at processing sounds, whether musical or linguistic. Mozart, who had perfect pitch, could hear a piece just once and reconstruct several minutes of it note for note. But you don't need to be a Mozart to enjoy classical music. In fact, you likely know and enjoy a great deal of classical music already. A Puccini aria ("O, mio babbino caro") sounds prominently in the best-selling video game Grand Theft Auto, no doubt for ironic effect. The seductive

"Habanera" from Bizet's opera *Carmen* (see Ch. 25) underscores the characters' secret intentions in an early episode of *Gossip Girl*. Beethoven's Symphony No. 7 suggests a royal triumph at the climax of the Academy Award–winning film *The King's Speech*, and Mozart's Requiem Mass is used to promote Nikes. Beneath the surface of everyday life, classical music quietly plays on and in our mind.

Take the Classical Music Challenge

To test the power of classical music to move you, try a simple comparison. Go to YouTube and watch a video of your favorite female singer (Adele, Taylor Swift, Beyoncé, whomever you prefer). Then select a recent clip of soprano Renée Fleming (Fig. 1.4) singing the Puccini aria "O, mio babbino caro." Whose artistry impresses you the most and why? Or listen to Coldplay's latest hit, for example, next to a rendition of Richard Wagner's famous "Ride of the Valkyries" (at YouTube, in this text's downloads, in the streaming music for Ch. 24 at CourseMate, or on ② 2/8–9 or ⑤ 4/13–14) to compare the sound of a rock band with that of a full symphony orchestra. Which piece gives you chills, and which one just leaves you cold? Are you inspired by the classical clips?

If you weren't moved, try listening to two other famous examples of classical music. The first is the beginning of Ludwig van Beethoven's Symphony No. 5, perhaps the best-known moment in all of classical music. Its "short-short-short-long" (SSSL) gesture (duh-duh-duh-DUHHH) is as much an icon of Western culture as the "To be, or not to be" soliloquy in Shakespeare's *Hamlet*. Beethoven (Fig. 1.5; see Ch. 18 for his biography) wrote this symphony in 1808 when he was thirty-seven and had become almost totally deaf. (Like most great musicians, the nearly deaf Beethoven could hear with an "inner ear"—he could create and rework melodies in his head without relying on external sound.) Beethoven's **symphony**—an instrumental genre for orchestra—is actually a composite of four separate instrumental pieces, each called a **movement**. A symphony is played by an **orchestra**, and because the orchestra plays symphonies more than any other musical genre, it is called a **symphony orchestra**. The orchestra for which Beethoven composed his fifth symphony was made up of about sixty players, including those playing string, wind, and percussion instruments.

Beethoven begins his symphony with the musical equivalent of a punch in the nose. The four-pitch rhythm (SSSL) comes out of nowhere and hits hard. This SSSL figure is a musical **motive**, a short, distinctive musical unit that can stand by itself. After this "sucker punch," we regain our equilibrium, as Beethoven takes us on an emotionally wrenching, thirty-minute, four-movement symphonic journey dominated by his four-note motive.

Turn now to this opening section (downloads, this chapter's streaming music at CourseMate, or ⓘintro/1) and to its Listening Guide below. Here you will see written music, or musical notation, representing the principal musical events. This notation may seem alien to you (the essentials of musical notation will be explained in Ch. 2). But don't panic. Millions of people enjoy classical music every day without ever looking at a shred of written notation. For the moment, simply play the music and follow along according to the minute and second counter on your music player. If you prefer a more animated version of this Listening Guide (and all other guides in this book), go online to CourseMate and select Ch. 1, Active Listening Guides, Beethoven Symphony No. 5.

Figure 1.4

Renée Fleming arrives for opening night at The Metropolitan Opera House at Lincoln Center in New York on September 21, 2009.

© Landov

Compare a song by your favorite female artist on YouTube with "O, mio babbino caro," sung by Renée Fleming, in the YouTube playlist at CourseMate for this text.

Hear an example of the power of Beethoven's music—his Piano Concerto No. 5—in the iTunes playlist at CourseMate for this text.

Figure 1.5

Ludwig van Beethoven

© Snark/Art Resource, NY

Ludwig van Beethoven, Symphony No. 5 in C minor (1808)

First movement, *Allegro con brio* (fast with gusto)

(intro)
1

WHAT TO LISTEN FOR: The ever-changing appearance of the four-note motive as the force of the music waxes and wanes

0:00	1	Opening "short-short-short-long" motive
0:22		Music gathers momentum and moves forward purposefully.
0:42		Pause; French horn solo
0:46		New, lyrical melody sounds forth in strings and is then answered by winds.
1:08		Rhythm of opening motive returns.
1:17		Opening motive is reshaped into more heroic-sounding melody.

🔊 Listen to streaming music in an Active Listening Guide at CourseMate or in the eBook.

Figure 1.6

Strauss attempts to replicate in music the coming of a superhero, who ascends with the rising sun.

© Cengage Learning

Finally, for the grandest of all sounds, popular or classical, we turn to the beginning of an orchestral work by Richard Strauss, *Also sprach Zarathustra* (*Thus Spoke Zarathustra*). Strauss's musical work is based on a philosophical novel of this same name by Friedrich Nietzsche (1844–1900). Here, Strauss attempts to replicate in music the coming of Nietzsche's superhero, who ascends with the rising of the sun.

How do you depict the advent of a superhero and a sunrise (Fig. 1.6) through music? Strauss tells us. The music should ascend in pitch, get louder, and grow in warmth (more instruments). Moreover, the leading instrument should be the trumpet, the sound of which has traditionally been associated with heroic deeds. The climax should be signaled by the great volume of the full orchestra, in this case the large Romantic orchestra of the late nineteenth century. Simple as these techniques may be, they are the means through which Strauss conveys musical meaning.

Strauss could not have foreseen how his classical creation would later be exploited in popular culture. In recent times, *Also sprach Zarathustra* has been used to accompany a film as well as countless radio and TV commercials in which the aim is to astound you, the consumer, with the power, durability, and brilliance of the product. In contrast to Beethoven's composition, Strauss's piece isn't a symphony in four movements, but rather a one-movement work for orchestra called a **tone poem** (see Ch. 21). If you think orchestral music is dull, think again! For sheer sonic force, Strauss's stunning opening is unmatched by any other music, classic or popular.

See a video of Strauss's theme in Stanley Kubrick's film *2001* in the YouTube playlist at CourseMate for this text.

Listening Guide

Richard Strauss, *Also sprach Zarathustra* **(1896)**

WHAT TO LISTEN FOR: A gradual transition from the nothingness of murky darkness, to shafts of light (trumpets), and finally to the incandescent power of the full symphony orchestra

0:00	**2**	Rumbling of low string instruments, organ, and bass drum
0:14		Four trumpets ascend, moving from bright to dark (major to minor key).
0:26		A drum (timpani) pounds forcefully.
0:30		Four trumpets ascend again, moving from dark to light (minor to major key).
0:44		A drum (timpani) pounds forcefully again.
0:50		Four trumpets ascend a third time.
1:06		Full orchestra joins in to add substance to an impressive succession of chords.
1:15		Grand climax by full orchestra at high pitches

 Listen to streaming music in an Active Listening Guide at CourseMate or in the eBook.

Listening Exercise 1.1

intro
1–2

To take this Listening Exercise online and receive feedback, go to CourseMate or the eBook.

Musical Beginnings

This first Listening Exercise asks you to review two of the most powerful "beginnings" in all of classical music.

Beethoven, Symphony No. 5 (1808)—Opening

1. **1** (0:00–0:05) Beethoven opens his Symphony No. 5 with the famous "SSSL" motive and then immediately repeats it. Does the repetition present the motive at a higher or a lower pitch level?
   a. higher
   b. lower

2. (0:22–0:44) In this passage Beethoven constructs a musical transition that moves us from the opening motive to a more lyrical second theme. Which is true about this transition?
   a. The music seems to get faster and builds in volume.
   b. The music seems to get slower.

(continued)

3. (0:38–0:42) How does Beethoven add intensity to the conclusion of the transition?
   a. A pounding drum (timpani) is added to the orchestra, and then a French horn plays a solo.
   b. A French horn plays a solo, and then a pounding drum (timpani) is added to the orchestra.

4. (0:46–1:00) Now a more lyrical new theme begins in the violin section and is echoed by the winds. But has the opening motive (SSSL) really disappeared?
   a. Yes, it is no longer present.
   b. No, it can be heard above the new melody.
   c. No, it lurks below the new melody.

5. (1:17–1:26) *Student choice* (no "correct" answer): How do you feel about the end of the opening section, compared to the beginning?
   a. less anxious and more self-confident
   b. less self-confident and more anxious

Strauss, *Also sprach Zarathustra* (1896)—Opening

6. [2] (0:00–0:13) Which is true about the opening sounds?
   a. The instruments are playing several different sounds in succession.
   b. The instruments are holding one and the same note.

7. (0:14–0:20) When the trumpets enter and ascend, does the low, rumbling sound disappear?
   a. yes
   b. no

8. (0:14–0:22 and again at 0:30–0:40 and 0:49–0:57) When the trumpets rise, how many different notes do they play?
   a. one
   b. two
   c. three

9. (1:18) At the very last chord, a new sound is added for emphasis—to signal that this is indeed the last chord of the climax. What instrument is making that sound?
   a. a piano
   b. an electric bass
   c. a cymbal

10. *Student choice*: You've now heard two very different musical openings, by Beethoven and Strauss. Which do you prefer? Which grabbed your attention more? Think about why.
    a. Beethoven
    b. Strauss

Key Words

music (3)	lyrics (5)	orchestra (9)
sound waves (3)	genre (6)	symphony orchestra (9)
popular music (5)	encore (8)	motive (9)
classical music (5)	symphony (9)	tone poem (11)
acoustic instrument (5)	movement (9)	

For a complete review of this chapter, see the Main Points, Chapter Quiz, Flashcards, and Glossary in CourseMate.

Join us on Facebook at **Listening to Music with Craig Wright**

chapter **TWO**

Rhythm, Melody,
and Harmony

© istockphoto/Gord Horne

Music is an unusual art. You can't see it or touch it. But it has matter—compressed air yielding sounding pitches—and these pitches are organized in three ways: as rhythms, as melodies, and as harmonies. Rhythm, melody, and harmony, then, are the three primary elements—the *what*—of music.

 ## Rhythm

Rhythm is arguably the most fundamental element of music. Its primacy may result from our experience *in utero*; we heard the beat of our mother's heart before we were aware of any sort of melody or tune. Similarly, our brain reacts powerfully and intuitively to a regularly recurring, strongly articulated "beat" and a catchy, repeating rhythmic pattern. Pop music derives its power primarily from the way it stimulates in the brain a direct, physical response to rhythm. We move, exercise, and dance to its pulse (Fig. 2.1).

The basic pulse of music is the **beat**, a regularly recurring sound that divides the passing of time into equal units. **Tempo** is the speed at which the beat sounds. Some tempos are fast (*allegro)* or very fast (*presto*) and some are slow (*lento*) or very slow (*grave*). A moderate tempo (*moderato*) falls somewhere in the range of 60 to 90 beats per minute. Sometimes the tempo speeds up, producing an *accelerando,* and sometimes it slows down, creating a **ritard**. But, oddly, we humans don't like undifferentiated streams of anything, whether they proceed rapidly or slowly. We organize passing time into seconds, minutes, hours, days, years, and centuries. We subconsciously group the clicking of a seatbelt warning chime into units of two or three "dings." So, too, with the undifferentiated stream of musical beats, our psyche demands that we organize them into groups, each containing two, three, four, or more pulses. The first beat in each unit is called the **downbeat**, and it gets the greatest **accent**, or stress. Organizing beats into groups produces **meter** in music, just as arranging words in a consistent pattern of emphasis produces meter in poetry. In music each group of beats is called a **measure** (or **bar**). Although music has several different kinds of meter, about 90 percent of the music we hear falls into either a duple or a triple pattern—**duple meter** or **triple meter**. We mentally count "ONE-two" or "ONE-two-three." A quadruple pattern exists as well, but in most ways our ear perceives this as simply a double duple.

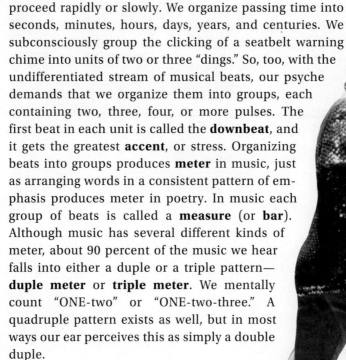

Watch a video of Craig Wright's Open Yale Course class session 3, "Rhythm: Fundamentals," at CourseMate for this text.

See Michael Jackson respond to and redefine the beat in the YouTube playlist at CourseMate for this text.

To see the power of rhythm in taking control of the body, watch Christopher Walken in action in the YouTube playlist at CourseMate for this text.

Figure 2.1

The fluid dance patterns of Michael Jackson show how rhythm can animate the body.

© Phil Dent/Redferns/Getty Images

Rhythmic Notation

About eight hundred years ago—in thirteenth-century Paris to be precise (see Ch. 5)—musicians began to devise a system to notate the beats, meters, and rhythms of their music. They created symbols that stood for long or longer, and short or shorter, durations. Over the centuries these signs developed into the notational symbols that we use today, as seen here.

Listen to an example of Beethoven's use of rhythm in his Symphony No. 7, in the iTunes playlist at CourseMate for this text.

EXAMPLE 2.1

(whole note) 𝅝 = 𝅗𝅥 𝅗𝅥 (2 half notes = 4 beats)

(half note) 𝅗𝅥 = 𝅘𝅥 𝅘𝅥 (2 quarter notes = 2 beats)

(quarter note) 𝅘𝅥 = 𝅘𝅥𝅮 𝅘𝅥𝅮 (2 eighth notes = 1 beat)

(eighth note) 𝅘𝅥𝅮 = 𝅘𝅥𝅯 𝅘𝅥𝅯 (2 sixteenth notes = ½ beat)

To help the performer keep the beat when playing, the smaller note values—specifically, those with flags on the vertical stem—are beamed, or joined together, in groups of two or four.

EXAMPLE 2.2

 becomes

Listen to an iAudio podcast about the basics of hearing meters at CourseMate for this text.

Today the symbol that usually represents, or "carries," one beat in music is the quarter note (𝅘𝅥). Normally, it moves along at roughly the rate of the average person's heartbeat. As you might suspect from its name, the quarter note is shorter in length than the half and the whole notes, but longer than the eighth and the sixteenth notes. Signs, called **rests**, indicate the absence of sound for different lengths of time.

Listen to an iAudio podcast about tempo at CourseMate for this text.

If music proceeded only with beats organized into meter, it would be dull indeed—like the endless sound of a bass drum (ONE-two, ONE-two, or ONE-two-three, ONE-two-three). In fact, what we hear in music by way of duration is **rhythm**, the division of time into compelling patterns of long and short sounds. Rhythm emerges from, and rests upon, the durational grid set by the beat and the meter. No one actually plays just the beat, except perhaps a drummer; rather, we hear a mass of musical rhythms, and our brain extracts the beat and the meter from them. To see how this works, let's look at a patriotic song, "Yankee Doodle," from the time of the American Revolution. It is in duple ($\frac{2}{4}$) meter.

EXAMPLE 2.3

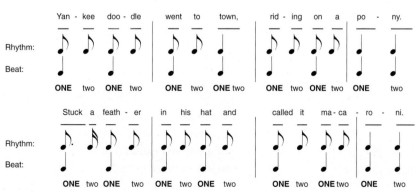

Here's another patriotic song, "America" (first known in England and Canada as "God Save the King"—or "Queen"), arranged the same way. It is in triple ($\frac{3}{4}$) meter.

EXAMPLE 2.4

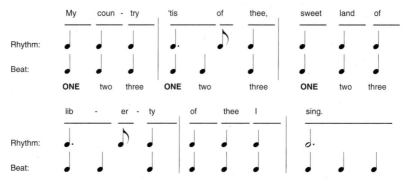

The numbers $\frac{2}{4}$ and $\frac{3}{4}$ aren't fractions, but rather **meter signatures** (also called **time signatures**). A meter signature tells the performer how the beats of the music are grouped to form a meter. The bottom number of the signature (usually a 4 representing the quarter note) indicates what note value receives the beat, and the top number tells how many beats are in each measure. The small vertical lines in the preceding examples are called **bar lines**; they help performers keep the music of one measure, or bar, separate from the next, and thus they help to keep the beat. Although this terminology of music theory might seem intimidating, the important question is this: Can you hear the downbeat and then recognize a duple meter (as in a ONE-two, ONE-two march) contrasted with a triple meter (as in a ONE-two-three, ONE-two-three waltz)? If so, you're well on your way to grasping the rhythmic element of music.

Figure 2.2

In action, Marin Alsop (1956–), conductor of the Baltimore Symphony Orchestra

Hearing Meters

One way you can improve your ability to hear a given meter is to establish some sort of physical response to the music: Tap your foot, stomping hard on the downbeat and softly on the weak beats; or conduct with your hand, using a conductor's pattern (down-up, or down-over-up), as shown in Example 2.5.

EXAMPLE 2.5

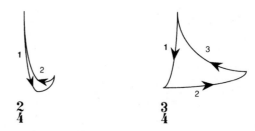

One final observation about meters and conducting patterns: Almost all music that we hear, especially dance music, has a clearly identifiable meter and a strong downbeat. But not all music *starts* with the downbeat. Often a piece will begin with an upbeat. An upbeat at the very beginning of a piece is called a pickup. The **pickup** is usually only a note or two, but it gives a little momentum or extra push into the first downbeat, as can be seen at the beginning of two other patriotic songs.

EXAMPLE 2.6

Oh	beau-	ti-	ful	for	spa-	cious	skies
two	**ONE**	two	**ONE**	two	**ONE**	two	**ONE** two

Oh	say	can	you	see		by	the	dawn's	ear -	ly	light
three	**ONE**	two	three	**ONE**	two	three		**ONE**	two	three	**ONE** two

Syncopation

Surprisingly, much classical music *doesn't* have a strong rhythmic component; rather, the beauty of the music rests in the melody and harmony. Popular music, on the other hand, is often irresistible, not only because of a strong beat but also because of a catchy rhythm, one created by syncopation. In most music, the accent, or musical emphasis, falls directly on the beat, with the downbeat getting the greatest emphasis of all. **Syncopation**, however, places the accent either on a weak beat or between beats—literally, it's "off beat." This unexpected, offbeat moment in the music creates the catchy "hook" of the tune, the part that pops up when you least expect it and sticks in your head.

A short example of syncopation can be heard in bar 2 of the chorus of The Beatles' song "Lucy in the Sky with Diamonds." The arrows show the moments of syncopation.

EXAMPLE 2.7

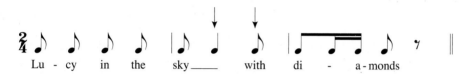

A far more complex example of syncopation can be found in the popular theme song to *The Simpsons.*

Example 2.8

If you are a fan of jazz, Latin music, or hip-hop, you must like syncopation, because those styles are full of it.

Listening Guide

The Basics of Rhythm

0:00	3	Music without strong sense of beat, meter, or rhythm	intro
0:34		Music with strong sense of beat, meter, and rhythm	3
1:01		Succession of undifferentiated beats	
1:15		Beats grouped into succession of strong-weak units, each forming measure (bar) in duple meter	
1:26		Beats grouped into succession of strong-weak-weak units, each forming measure (bar) in triple meter	
1:38		Duple-meter piece starting on downbeat (strong beat)	
1:57		Triple-meter piece starting on downbeat	
2:13		Triple-meter piece starting with pickup	

(continued)

| 2:25 | Regular duple meter concluding with one measure of syncopation |
| 2:35 | Regular duple meter concluding with two measures of syncopation |

 Listen to streaming music in an Active Listening Guide at CourseMate or in the eBook.

Listening Exercise 2.1

intro
4

To take this Listening Exercise online and receive feedback, go to CourseMate or the eBook.

Hearing Meters

Now it's your chance to be the conductor! On your Intro CD, track 4, you have ten short musical excerpts, each played once. (You can replay them as many times as you wish.) First, tap your foot with the beat, placing special emphasis on the downbeat. If you have only one weak beat between downbeats, the music is duple; if you have two, the music is triple. Then conduct using the duple or triple pattern. Your downbeat motion with your hand should always be in sync with the strongest tap of your foot. If you do this correctly, the completion of each full conductor's pattern will equal one measure. In this exercise all pieces are in duple $\left(\frac{2}{4}\right)$ or triple $\left(\frac{3}{4}\right)$ meter. There are five examples in duple meter and five in triple.

1. (0:00) Meter: _____ Mouret, *Rondeau* from *Suite de symphonies*
2. (0:26) Meter: _____ Chopin, Waltz in E♭ major
3. (0:45) Meter: _____ Beethoven, Variations on "God Save the King"
4. (1:00) Meter: _____ Prokofiev, *Romeo and Juliet*
5. (1:20) Meter: _____ Prokofiev, *Romeo and Juliet*
6. (2:04) Meter: _____ Bach, Brandenburg Concerto No. 5, 1st movement
7. (2:26) Meter: _____ Mozart, *A Little Night Music,* 1st movement
8. (2:46) Meter: _____ Haydn, Symphony No. 94, 3rd movement
9. (3:05) Meter: _____ Bizet, Habanera, from *Carmen*
10. (3:41) Meter: _____ Handel, Minuet from *Water Music*

 # Melody

Watch a video of Craig Wright's Open Yale Course class session 5, "Melody: Notes, Scales, Nuts, and Bolts," at CourseMate for this text.

Listen to an example of a familiar beautiful melody, "Ave Maria," in the iTunes playlist at CourseMate for this text.

A **melody**, simply put, is the tune. It's the part we sing along with, the part we like, the part we're willing to listen to again and again. TV promos try to entice us to buy CD sets of "The Fifty All-Time Greatest Melodies"—yet there are no similar collections devoted to rhythms or harmonies. Josh Groban, Andrea Bocelli, Katy Perry, Adele, and Renée Fleming sing the melody. They, and it, are the stars.

Every melody is composed of a succession of pitches, usually energized by a rhythm. **Pitch** is the relative position, high or low, of a musical sound. We traditionally assign letter names (A, B, C, and so on) to identify specific pitches. When an instrument produces a musical tone, it sets into motion vibrating sound waves that travel through the air to reach the listener's ears. A faster vibration will produce a higher pitch, and a slower one a lower pitch. Pressing the lowest key on the piano sets a string vibrating back and forth 27 cycles (times) per second, while the highest key does the same at a dizzying 4,186 times per second. Low pitches lumber along and sound "fuzzy," whereas high ones are fleetingly clear. A low note can convey sadness, a high one excitement (we don't usually hear a high-pitched piccolo as sad, for example). In Western music, melodies move along from one discrete pitch to another. In other musical cultures—Chinese, for example—melody often "slides," and much of its beauty resides *between* the pitches.

Have you ever noticed, when singing a succession of tones up or down, that the melody reaches a tone that sounds like a duplication of an earlier pitch, but higher or lower? That duplicating pitch is called an **octave**, for reasons that will become clear shortly, and it's usually the largest distance between notes that we encounter in a melody. Pitches an octave apart sound similar because the frequency of vibration of the higher pitch is precisely twice that of the lower. The ancient Greeks, from whom much of our Western civilization derives, knew of the octave and its 2:1 ratio, and they divided it into seven pitches using other ratios. Their seven pitches plus the eighth (the octave) yielded the white keys of the modern keyboard. When early musicians reached the repeating pitch, the octave, they began to repeat the A, B, C letter names for the pitches. Eventually, five additional notes were inserted. Notated with symbols called **flats** (♭) and **sharps** (♯), they correspond to the black keys of the keyboard.

EXAMPLE 2.9

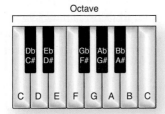

When a tune moves from one pitch to another it moves across a melodic **interval**. Some of these distances are small, others large. Melodies with large leaps are usually difficult to sing, whereas those with repeated or neighboring pitches are easier. Example 2.10 is the beginning of a well-known melody based on a large interval; both phrases of the tune begin with an ascending leap of an octave. To hear the octave, try singing "Take me . . ." to yourself.

EXAMPLE 2.10

Take me out to the ball game, take me out to the crowd

Now, here's the opening to Beethoven's famous *Ode to Joy* from his Symphony No. 9 (1823), in which almost all of the pitches are adjacent. It is known and beloved around the world because it is tuneful and singable. Try it—you'll recognize the melody. If you're not comfortable with the words, try singing the syllable "la" to each pitch. You can also hear it in the downloads, streaming music for Chapter 18 at CourseMate, and at (intro)/5.

EXAMPLE 2.11

Praise to Joy the God de-scend-ed, Daugh-ter of E - ly - si - um.

Ray of mirth and rap-ture blend-ed, God-dess to thy shrine wel-come.

"Take Me out to the Ball Game" and Beethoven's *Ode to Joy* are very different in both intervallic structure and mood. Indeed, in using all possible combinations of

Watch a video of Craig Wright's Open Yale Course class session 6, on what makes a great melody, "Melody: Mozart and Wagner," at CourseMate for this text.

rhythms and pitches, an almost endless number of melodies can be created. But can you explain what makes melodies like these memorable and others quickly forgettable? If you can, you've solved one of the biggest mysteries of music: What makes a great melody?

Melodic Notation

The type of notation used above for "Take Me out to the Ball Game" and *Ode to Joy* is helpful if we need only to be reminded of how a melody goes, but it isn't precise enough to allow us to sing it if we don't already know it. When the melody goes up, how *far* up does it go? Around the year 1000 C.E., even before the advent of rhythmic notation, church musicians added precision to pitch notation in the West. They started to write black and, later, white circles on horizontal lines and spaces so that the exact distance between these notes could be judged immediately. This gridwork of lines and spaces came to be called a **staff**. The higher on the staff a note is placed, the higher its pitch.

EXAMPLE 2.12

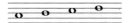

Later, the note heads were given stems and flags to show different durations and rhythms. Example 2.13A shows low, slow pitches that become gradually higher and faster, while Example 2.13B shows the reverse:

EXAMPLE 2.13A

EXAMPLE 2.13B

In notated music the staff is always provided with a **clef** sign to indicate the range of pitch in which the melody is to be played or sung. One clef, called the **treble clef**, designates the upper range and is appropriate for high instruments such as the trumpet and the violin, or a woman's voice. A second clef, called the **bass clef**, indicates the lower range and is used for lower instruments such as the tuba and the cello, or a man's voice.

EXAMPLE 2.14

Treble clef   Bass clef

For a single vocal part or a single instrument, a melody could easily be placed on either of these two clefs. But for two-handed keyboard music with greater range, both clefs are used, one on top of the other. The performer looks at this combination of clefs, called the **great staff** (also **grand staff**), and relates the notes to the keys beneath the fingers. The two clefs join at middle C (the middlemost C key on the piano).

EXAMPLE 2.15

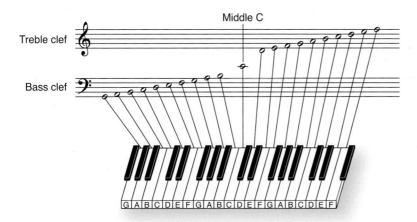

Each musical pitch can be represented by a particular line or space on the great staff as well as by a letter name (like C). We use only seven letter names (in ascending order A, B, C, D, E, F, and G) because, as we've seen, melodies were made up of only seven pitches within each octave. As a melody reaches and extends beyond the range of a single octave, the series of letter names is repeated (see Ex. 2.15). The note above G, then, is an A, which lies exactly one octave above the previous A. Here "Twinkle, Twinkle, Little Star" is notated on the great staff with the pitches doubled at the octave, as might happen when male and female voices sing together, the women an octave higher than the men.

EXAMPLE 2.16

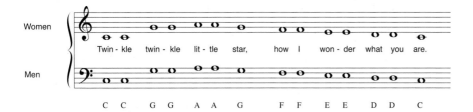

Listening Exercise 2.2

To take this Listening Exercise online and receive feedback, go to CourseMate or the eBook.

Hearing Melodies

Hearing melodies may be the single most important part of listening to music. To remember a melody, it helps to form a mental image of it, and perhaps make a quick sketch of the basic melodic contour. To familiarize you with this process, Listening Exercise 2.2 asks you to identify the melodic contour of ten famous classical melodies. Each is first performed as the composer originally intended and then played again in a more deliberate fashion to allow you to focus on the individual pitches. For each excerpt, select the pattern of notes that most accurately represents the pitches of the melody—the higher the note on the staff, the higher the pitch. Don't worry about rhythm for this exercise.

1. (0:00) Beethoven, Symphony No. 5, 1st movement

a.   b.   c.

(continued)

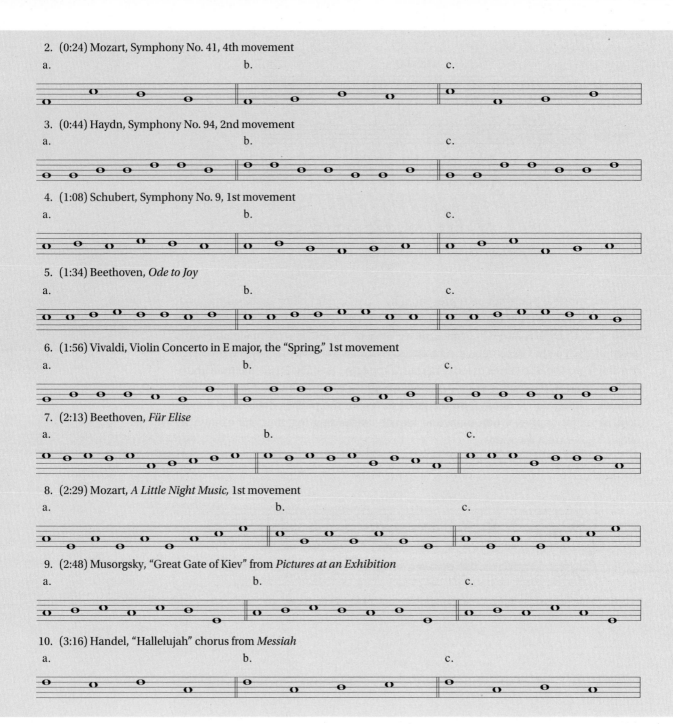

2. (0:24) Mozart, Symphony No. 41, 4th movement

a.   b.   c.

3. (0:44) Haydn, Symphony No. 94, 2nd movement

a.   b.   c.

4. (1:08) Schubert, Symphony No. 9, 1st movement

a.   b.   c.

5. (1:34) Beethoven, *Ode to Joy*

a.   b.   c.

6. (1:56) Vivaldi, Violin Concerto in E major, the "Spring," 1st movement

a.   b.   c.

7. (2:13) Beethoven, *Für Elise*

a.   b.   c.

8. (2:29) Mozart, *A Little Night Music,* 1st movement

a.   b.   c.

9. (2:48) Musorgsky, "Great Gate of Kiev" from *Pictures at an Exhibition*

a.   b.   c.

10. (3:16) Handel, "Hallelujah" chorus from *Messiah*

a.   b.   c.

Scales, Modes, Tonality, and Key

Listen to an iAudio podcast on hearing major and minor at CourseMate for this text.

When we listen to music, our brain hears a succession of pitches spaced out on a grid. That grid is a **scale**, a fixed pattern of tones within the octave that ascends and descends. Think of the scale as a ladder with eight rungs, or steps, between the two fixed points, low and high, formed by the octave. You can go up or down the ladder. But oddly, not all the steps are an equal distance apart. Five are a full step apart, but two are only a half step. For example, the distance between A and B is a full step, but between B and C it's only a half step—that's just the way the ancient Greeks built their musical ladder, an asymmetrical construction that Western musical culture retains to the present day.

The position of the two half steps tells us two important things: what kind of scale is in play and where we are within that scale. Since the seventeenth century, almost all Western melodies have been written following one of two seven-note scale patterns: the major one and the minor one. The **major scale** follows a seven-pitch pattern moving upward 1–1–½–1–1–1–½. The **minor scale** goes 1–½–1–1–½–1–1. Once the eighth pitch (octave) is reached, the pattern can start over again. Example 2.17 shows a major and minor scale, first on the pitch C and then on the pitch A.

EXAMPLE 2.17

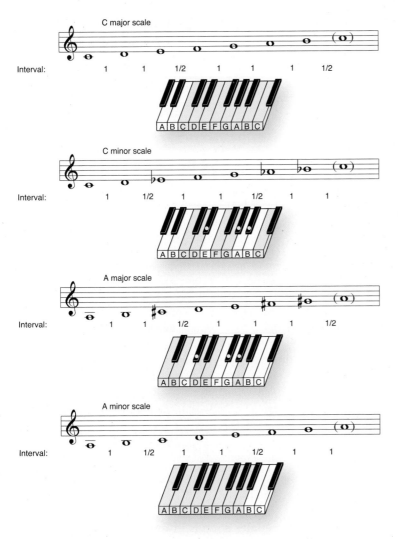

The choice of the scale (whether major or minor)—as well as our ability to hear the difference—is crucial to our enjoyment of music. To Western ears, melodies based on major scales sound bright, cheery, and optimistic, whereas minor ones come across as dark, somber, even sinister. Go back to the end of Ch. 1 and compare the bright, heroic sound of Richard Strauss's *Also sprach Zarathustra,* built on a major scale, with the almost threatening sound of Beethoven's Symphony No. 5, written in a minor one. Switching from major to minor, or from minor to major, is called a change of **mode**. Changing the mode affects the mood of the music. To prove the point, listen to the following familiar tunes (your instructor can play them for you). In each the mode has been changed from major to minor by inserting a flat into the scale near the last pitch (C), thereby switching from the beginning of the major scale (1–1–½) to that of the minor (1–½–1). Notice how this alteration sucks all the happiness, joy, and sunshine out of these formerly major melodies.

Hear the difference between major and minor in CourseMate's Elements of Music melody demo.

EXAMPLE 2.18

Joy to the world, the Lord is come

You are my sun - shine, my on - ly sun - shine

Hap- py birth - day to you

Listening Exercise 2.3

intro
7

To take this Listening Exercise online and receive feedback, go to CourseMate or the eBook.

Hearing Major and Minor

On your Intro CD, track 7, you will find ten musical excerpts that will help you begin to differentiate major from minor. Pieces in major usually sound bright, cheerful, and sometimes bland, whereas those in minor seem darker, more somber, mysterious, perhaps even exotic. In the blanks below, indicate whether each melody is in major or minor. Five are in major and five in minor.

1. (0:00) Mode: _____ Musorgsky, "Polish Ox-Cart" from *Pictures at an Exhibition*

2. (0:28) Mode: _____ Musorgsky, "Great Gate of Kiev" from *Pictures at an Exhibition*

3. (0:45) Mode: _____ Musorgsky, "Goldenburg and Schmuyle" from *Pictures at an Exhibition*

4. (1:05) Mode: _____ Tchaikovsky, "Dance of the Reed Pipes" from *The Nutcracker*

5. (1:23) Mode: _____ Tchaikovsky, "Dance of the Reed Pipes" from *The Nutcracker*

6. (1:39) Mode: _____ Mouret, Rondeau from *Suite de symphonies*

7. (1:53) Mode: _____ Handel, Minuet from *Water Music*

8. (2:07) Mode: _____ Prokofiev, "Dance of the Knights" from *Romeo and Juliet*

9. (2:29) Mode: _____ Vivaldi, Violin Concerto, "Spring," 1st movement

10. (2:39) Mode: _____ Vivaldi, Violin Concerto, "Spring," 1st movement

Finally, a third, special scale sometimes sounds in music: a **chromatic scale**, which makes use of all twelve pitches, equally divided, within the octave. *Chromatic* (from the Greek *chroma*, "color") is a good name for this pattern because the additional five pitches do indeed add color to the music (Ex. 2.19). Unlike the major and minor scales, the chromatic scale is not employed for a complete melody, but only for a moment of twisting intensity. Irving Berlin incorporates the chromatic scale at the beginning of his holiday favorite "White Christmas" (Ex. 2.20).

EXAMPLE 2.19

Chromatic scale

EXAMPLE 2.20

I'm dream - ing of a white Christ - mas

When listening to any music, we take pleasure, consciously or not, in knowing where we are. Here again the steps of the scale play a crucial role, orienting us during the listening experience. Virtually all the melodies we've heard since birth have been in major or minor, so these two patterns are deeply ingrained. Intuitively, our brain recognizes the mode and hears one pitch as central and the others as gravitating around it. That central, or home, pitch is called the tonic. The **tonic** is the first of the seven pitches of the scale and, consequently, the eighth and last as well. Melodies almost always end on the tonic, as can be seen in the familiar tunes given in Example 2.18, all of which happen to end on the tonic pitch C. The organization of music around a central pitch, the tonic, is called **tonality**. We say that such and such a piece is written in the tonality, and similarly the **key**, of C or of A (musicians use the terms *tonality* and *key* almost interchangeably). Composers—classical composers in particular—like to move temporarily from the home scale and home tonality to another, just for the sake of variety. Such a change is called a **modulation**. In any musical journey, we enjoy traveling away from our tonic "home," but we experience even greater satisfaction arriving back there. Again, almost all music, pop or classical, ends on the tonic pitch (Fig. 2.3).

Courtesy NASA/JPL

Figure 2.3

Planets rotate around and are pulled toward the sun, just as outlying pitches are pulled toward the tonic pitch.

Listen to an iAudio podcast on measures and phrases at the text website.

Hearing Melodies and Phrases

Melodies, just like sentences, are usually a composite of smaller segments called "phrases." When listening to a piece of music, whether a classical symphony or a popular song, we tend to follow along with the phrases. For the most part, we do this intuitively—we instinctively hear where a phrase begins and where it ends. Beethoven's *Ode to Joy* is composed of four symmetrical phrases, but so are "Take Me out to the Ball Game" and each of the verses of Adele's chart-busting "Rolling in the Deep." Indeed, much music is symmetrical in terms of its phrasing, being a composite of 2 + 2, 4 + 4, or 8 + 8 measures—that's why it sounds so solid and secure. Whether in architecture, poetic meter, or music, a symmetrical structure makes us feel comfortable. In Louis Armstrong's "Willie the Weeper" (1927) the regularity of the phrase structure is energized by the wild, joyful abandon of the performance. This, too, is "classical" music: classic New Orleans jazz.

© Michael Ochs Archives/CORBIS

Figure 2.4

Louis Armstrong at the age of thirty-two

Listening Exercise 2.4

intro

8

To take this Listening Exercise online and receive feedback, go to CourseMate or the eBook.

Counting Measures and Phrases

Louis Armstrong was born in poverty in New Orleans in 1901 but went on to become the most famous jazz musician of the twentieth century (Fig. 2.4). Armstrong's powerful, "in-your-face" style of trumpet playing can be heard prominently in this 1927 recording of the song "Willie the Weeper." Your task here is to count the number of measures, or bars, in each musical phrase.

Armstrong's "Willie the Weeper" is in a straightforward duple meter ($\frac{2}{4}$ time). First, listen for a bit and tap your foot with the beat, which here goes slightly faster than your heartbeat. Every two of your taps forms one measure. Start counting the number of measures in each phrase. (The timings indicate the beginning of

(continued)

the phrase, and a new solo instrument plays for the duration of each phrase.) After the four-measure introduction, every phrase is either eight or sixteen measures in length, so fill in the blanks accordingly (write "8" or "16"). The answer for the first phrase is provided.

(0:00–0:03) Four-measure introduction
(0:04–0:24) Full band. Number of measures: <u>16</u>
(0:25–0:45) Full band varies the tune. Number of measures: ___
(0:46–0:56) Trombone and tuba solo. Number of measures: ___
(0:57–1:06) Trombone and tuba repeat. Number of measures: ___
(1:07–1:27) Trombone solo. Number of measures: ___
(1:28–1:48) Extraordinary clarinet solo. Number of measures: ___

(1:49–1:58) Armstrong plays trumpet solo. Number of measures: ___
(1:59–2:08) Piano solo. Number of measures: ___
(2:09–2:28) Guitar solo. Number of measures: ___
(2:29–2:48) Armstrong plays trumpet solo. Number of measures: ___
(2:49–end)   Trumpet, trombone, and clarinet improvise around tune. Number of measures:_____

Figure 2.5

Claude Monet, *Waterlily Pond: Pink Harmony* (1900). Monet's painting of this famous bridge at Giverny, France, reveals not only the harmonious qualities of nature but also the painter's ability to harmonize various colors into a blend of pastels.

© Lauros/Giraudon/The Bridgeman Art Library

Harmony

Western music is exceptional among musical cultures of the world in its emphasis on harmony. Other cultures (African, for example) emphasize rhythm, and still others (Chinese, Japanese, and Korean, for example) pay special attention to melodic subtleties. But only Western music consistently creates **harmony**: the simultaneous sounding of one or more pitches that support and enhance a melody. The pitches of the melody are almost always higher than those of the accompanying harmony. At the piano, for example, our "higher" right hand usually plays the melody and our left the harmony (see Ex. 2.21). Although a melody can stand by itself, an accompanying harmony adds a richness to it, just as the dimension of depth adds a rich backdrop to a painting (Fig. 2.5).

EXAMPLE 2.21

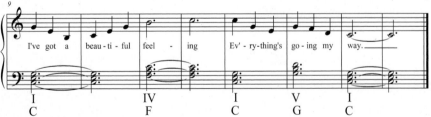

By definition, every harmony must be harmonious. From this truism we can see that harmony has two meanings. First, *harmony* means "a general sense that things work or sound well together"; second, *harmony* specifically denotes an exact musical accompaniment, as when we say "the harmony changes here to another chord."

Building Harmony with Chords

Chords are the building blocks of harmony. A **chord** is simply a group of two or more pitches that sound at the same time. The basic chord in Western music is the **triad**, so called because we construct it using three pitches arranged in a very specific way.

Let's start with a C major scale beginning with the tonic note C. To form a triad, we take one, skip one, take one, skip one, and take one—in other words, we select the pitches C, E, G (skipping D and F) and sound them together.

EXAMPLE 2.22

Watch a video of Craig Wright's Open Yale Course class session 7, "Harmony: Chords and How to Build Them," at CourseMate for this text

Triads can be constructed in a similar fashion on every pitch of the scale. But given the irregularity of the scale, not all intervals within the triad are the same distance apart; some triads will be major and others minor. A major triad has its middle pitch a half step closer to its top pitch than to its bottom one; conversely, a minor triad has its middle pitch a half step closer to its bottom pitch than its top one. While this may seem complicated, the difference between a major and a minor triad is immediately audible. To hear it, go to a piano and build a triad on middle C and then one on the D above, using the "take and skip" method. Major triads sound bright; minor ones dark. Example 2.23 shows triads built on every note of the C major scale. Each is assigned a Roman numeral to indicate on which pitch of the scale it is built. These triads provide all the basic chords necessary to harmonize a melody in C major.

EXAMPLE 2.23

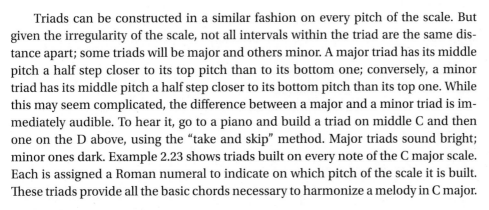

Why do we need more than one chord to harmonize a melody? And why is it necessary for the chords of the harmony to change? The answer lies in the fact that the pitches of a melody continually change, sometimes moving through all the notes of a scale. A single triadic chord, however, can be fully harmonious, or consonant, only with the three notes of the scale that it contains. To keep the harmony consonant with the melody, then, chords must change.

As chords change in a purposeful fashion beneath a melody, they create what is called a **chord progression**. The individual chords in a chord progression seem to "pull" each other along, one giving way to the next, with all ultimately gravitating toward the powerful tonic triad. The end of a chord progression is called a **cadence**. Usually at a cadence, a triad built on degree V of the scale, called the **dominant** triad, will yield to the tonic triad. This is a powerful harmonic move, one conveying a strong feeling of conclusion, as if to say, "The End."

To sum up: In Western music melodies are supported by an enriching, chordal accompaniment—a harmony. The harmony gains force and enriches the melody as the chords move in a purposeful progression. To avoid unwanted dissonance, it is necessary to change chords in a harmony.

Consonance and Dissonance

One reason the human spirit craves music is that this art expresses, through sounds alone, all of the emotional content of life itself. Just as our lives are full of consonance and dissonance, so, too, is our music.

Listen to an iAudio podcast on consonance and dissonance at CourseMate for this text.

Listen to an iAudio podcast on hearing the bass line at CourseMate for this text.

Watch a video of Craig Wright's Open Yale Course class session 8, "Bass Patterns: Blues and Rock," at CourseMate for this text.

Listen to an iAudio podcast on chord changes at CourseMate for this text.

You've undoubtedly noticed, when pressing the keys of the piano at one time or another, that some combinations of keys produce a harsh, jarring sound, whereas others are pleasing and harmonious. The former chords are characterized by **dissonance** (pitches sounding momentarily disagreeable and unstable) and the latter by **consonance** (pitches sounding agreeable and stable). Generally speaking, chords that contain pitches very close to one another, just a half or a whole step apart, sound dissonant. On the other hand, chords built with the somewhat larger interval of a third (C joined to E, for example) are consonant, as is the case for each triad in Example 2.23. But culture, and even personal taste, play a role in dissonance perception, too; what might be a hot, spicy, distasteful dissonance to one listener might be a delight to another. While some, for example, find the loud, aggressive distortion of heavy metal bands such as Metallica intolerable, others thrive on it.

Whatever the music, though, dissonance adds a feeling of tension and anxiety, while consonance produces a sense of calm and stability. Dissonant chords are unstable, and thus they seek out—want to move to—consonant resolutions. The continual flux between dissonant and consonant chords gives Western music a sense of drama, as a piece moves between moments of tension to longed-for resolution. We humans try not to end the day with an unresolved argument; nor do we end our music with unresolved dissonance.

Hearing the Harmony

If you were asked to listen to a new song by your favorite pop artist and sing it back, you'd undoubtedly sing back the melody. Because the tuneful melody is invariably the line with the highest pitches, we've become trained, subconsciously, to focus on the top part of any musical texture. To hear and appreciate harmony, however, we've got to "get down" with the bass. Chords are usually built on the bass note, and a change in the bass from one pitch to another may signal a change of chord. The bass is the foundation of the chord and determines where the harmony is going, more so than the higher melody. Some pop artists, such as Esperanza Spalding (see Fig. 3.4), Paul McCartney, and Sting, control both the upper melody and the lower harmony simultaneously. While they sing the tune, they play electric bass, setting the bass pitches for the lead guitar to fill out as accompanying triads.

To begin to hear the harmony beneath a melody, let's explore two alluring pieces, one from the world of popular music, the other a well-known classical favorite. First, a bit of soul music called doo-wop. **Doo-wop** emerged in the 1950s as an outgrowth of the gospel hymns sung in African-American churches in urban Detroit, Chicago, Philadelphia, and New York. Often doo-wop was improvised a cappella on the street because it was direct and repetitive—the accompanying singers could easily hear and form a harmony against the melody. And because the lyrics sung by the accompanying singers were often little more than "doo wop, doo wah," the name "doo-wop" stuck to describe these songs. Finally, doo-wop harmony used a short chord progression, most commonly a sequence of triads moving I-VI-IV-V-(I) that repeated over and over again (for these four repeating chords, see the Listening Guide below). In music any element (rhythm, melody, or harmony) that continually repeats is called an **ostinato** (from the Italian word meaning "obstinate thing"). In the doo-wop song "Duke of Earl," we hear the bass voice lead, not with "doo, doo, doo," but with "Duke, Duke, Duke," setting the foundation for the chords that sound as the other voices enter. The tempo is moderately fast, and each of the four chords lasts for four beats. Every time the vocal harmony sings the word "Earl," the chords change. The I-VI-IV-V-(I) chord progression lasts for about nine seconds and then repeats over and over again. As you listen to this doo-wop classic, sing along with the bass, no matter what your vocal range. Anyone can hear this harmony change.

Harmony (Chord Changes)

Gene Chandler, "Duke of Earl" (1962)

WHAT TO LISTEN FOR: A harmony that repeats as a four-bar ostinato

	I	VI	IV	V	(I)

0:00	**9**	Bass leads with:
		Duke, Duke, Duke, Duke of Earl, Duke, Duke, Duke of Earl, Duke, Duke, Duke of Earl
		I -------------------------------VI--------------------------------IV--------------------------V
0:09		Other voices and instruments enter, filling out harmony.
0:18		Voice of Gene Chandler enters with lyrics.
0:27		Further statement of harmonic pattern
0:37		Each chord now holds for two bars rather than one.
0:54 (and 1:03)		Each chord again holds for one bar.
1:13		Each chord again holds for two bars rather than one.
1:32 (and 1:41)		Each chord again holds for one bar.

For the rest, you're on your own!

 Listen to streaming music in an Active Listening Guide at CourseMate or in the eBook.

Finally, for a similar, but slightly more complex, piece from the classical repertoire, we turn to the famous Pachelbel Canon. Johann Pachelbel (1653–1706), who lived in Germany and was a mentor to musicians in the Bach family, composed this piece for four musical lines. The top three, here played by violins, are performed as a **canon** (a "round" in which one voice starts out and the others duplicate it exactly, as in "Three Blind Mice"). Below the three-part canon is a harmonic ostinato, a bass line of eight notes, each supporting a chord. So popular has Pachelbel's harmony become that it has been "borrowed" by The Beatles ("Let It Be"), U2 ("With or Without You"), Celine Dion (chorus of "To Love You More"), and many other pop artists. For more on Pachelbel's Canon, see Ch. 9, "Pachelbel and His Canon."

See an amusing rant by comedian Rob Paravonian about the excessive popularity of Pachelbel's famous eight-bar harmony, in the YouTube playlist at CourseMate for this text.

Listening Exercise 2.5

To take this Listening Exercise online and receive feedback, go to CourseMate or the eBook.

Hearing the Bass Line and Harmony

Johann Pachelbel, Canon in D major (c. 1685)

When we listen to music, most of us naturally concentrate on the highest-sounding part, which is where the melody is usually found. To hear harmony, however, we need to focus on the lowest-sounding line, the bass. Here, as with most bass lines, the lowest part establishes the foundation for the harmony (chords) above each of its pitches. In this piece the harmony (bass with chords) enters first, and then the canon (round) gradually unfolds. Focus now on the bass and answer the following questions.

(continued)

1. The bass enters first. At what point does the first violin enter to signal the beginning of the canon?
   - a. 0:00
   - b. 0:13
   - c. 0:21

2. Listen again to the beginning. How many pitches do you hear before the violin enters and the bass begins to repeat? In other words, how many pitches are in the bass pattern?
   - a. 4
   - b. 6
   - c. 8

3. Are all the pitches within the pattern of the bass held for the same duration?
   - a. yes
   - b. no

4. Therefore, the rate of harmonic change in Pachelbel's Canon is what?
   - a. regular
   - b. irregular

5. Which diagram most accurately reflects the pitches (the pattern) of the bass line?

   a.   b.   c.

   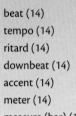

6. Listen now to more of the composition. The bass is highly repetitious, as the pattern recurs again and again. Each statement of the pattern lasts approximately how long?
   - a. 12 seconds
   - b. 15 seconds
   - c. 20 seconds

7. A melody, harmony, or rhythm that repeats again and again in music is called what?
   - a. chord progression
   - b. consonance
   - c. tempo
   - d. ostinato

8. Now listen up to 1:54 of the recording. Does the bass pattern ever change?
   - a. yes
   - b. no

9. From the beginning of the piece (0:00) to this point (1:54), how many times do you hear the pattern?
   - a. 8
   - b. 10
   - c. 12
   - d. 14

10. Listen all the way to the end of the work. Does Pachelbel ever vary his bass and his harmonic pattern?
    - a. yes
    - b. no

Key Words

beat (14)	melody (18)	chromatic scale (24)
tempo (14)	pitch (18)	tonic (25)
ritard (14)	octave (19)	tonality (key) (25)
downbeat (14)	flat (♭) (19)	modulation (25)
accent (14)	sharp (♯) (19)	harmony (26)
meter (14)	interval (19)	chord (26)
measure (bar) (14)	staff (20)	triad (26)
duple meter (14)	clef (20)	chord progression (27)
triple meter (14)	treble clef (20)	cadence (27)
rest (15)	bass clef (20)	dominant (27)
rhythm (15)	great staff (grand staff) (20)	dissonance (28)
meter signature (time signature) (16)	scale (22)	consonance (28)
bar lines (16)	major scale (23)	doo-wop (28)
pickup (16)	minor scale (23)	ostinato (28)
syncopation (17)	mode (23)	canon (29)

For a complete review of this chapter, see the Main Points, Chapter Quiz, Flashcards, and Glossary in CourseMate.

Join us on Facebook at **Listening to Music with Craig Wright**

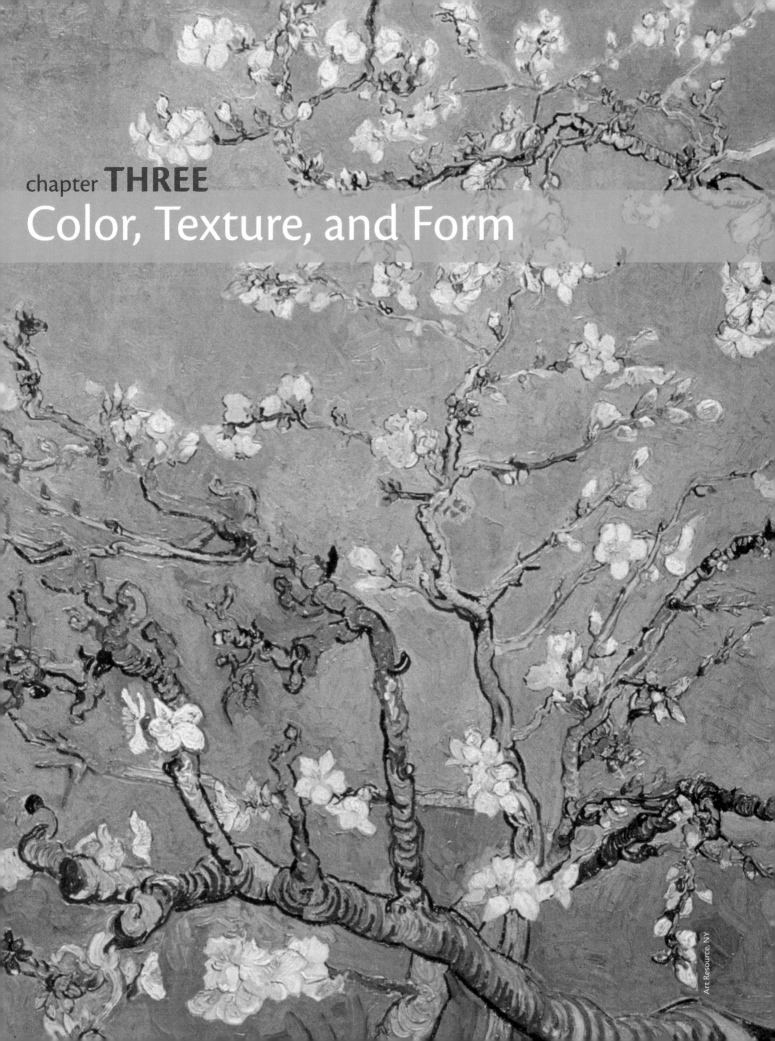

chapter **THREE**
Color, Texture, and Form

f rhythm, melody, and harmony are the *what* of music, then color, texture, and form are the *how*. These are the surface details of musical sound that catch our attention and evoke an emotional response, as when a brilliant trumpet suddenly shines forth or a silvery flute floats effortlessly on high. Color, texture, and form, then, refer not so much to the musical idea itself but instead to the way the musical idea is presented.

Listen to an iAudio podcast on dynamics at CourseMate for this text.

Dynamics

Musical **dynamics** (louds and softs) also influence our reaction to music. Heroic themes are usually played loudly and mournful ones quietly, for example, to create the desired mood and effect. Because Italian musicians once dominated the Western musical world, most of our musical terminology is drawn from that language, as can be seen in Table 3.1.

Table 3.1

Term	Musical Symbol	Definition
fortissimo	*ff*	very loud
forte (FOUR-tay)	*f*	loud
mezzo forte	*mf*	moderately loud
mezzo piano	*mp*	moderately soft
piano	*p*	soft
pianissimo	*pp*	very soft

Changes in dynamics need not be sudden and abrupt. They can be gradual and extend over a long period of time. A progressive increase in the volume of sound is called a **crescendo**, whereas a gradual decrease is called either a **decrescendo** or a **diminuendo**. An impressive crescendo sounds at the beginning of Richard Strauss's *Also sprach Zarathustra* (intro /2, downloads, and streaming music for Ch. 1 in CourseMate) as the full orchestra enters and gains force. Spectacular moments such as these remind us that in music, as in marketing and communications, the medium (here, powerful dynamics and color) can be the message. When such music is heard as background for a TV commercial, the viewer is supposed to conclude, "This product *sounds* great!"

Color

Simply stated, **color** in music is the tone quality of any sound produced by a voice or an instrument. **Timbre** (pronounced TAM-ber) is another term for the tone quality of musical sound. We can all hear that a clarinet produces a much different tone quality than does a trombone. Similarly, the voice of pop singer Rihanna has a different timbre than that of opera star Renée Fleming, even when the two produce the same pitch.

The Voice

How many different voices can you recognize? Perhaps as many as a hundred. Each of us has a uniquely constructed set of vocal cords (two folds of mucous membrane within the throat). When we talk or sing, we send air through them, creating vibrations that reach the ear as sounds of a distinctive timbre. We need hear only a few notes to recognize that this is Bublé singing, for example, and not Bono.

Musical voices are classified by range into four principal parts. The two women's vocal parts are the **soprano** and the **alto**, and the two men's parts the **tenor** and the **bass**. (Men's vocal cords are longer and thicker than women's, and for that reason the sound of the mature male voice is lower.) Midway between the soprano and the alto voice is the **mezzo soprano**, and between the tenor and the bass is the **baritone**. When many voices join together, they form a **chorus**.

Musical Instruments

Why Do Musical Instruments Sound the Way They Do?

Have you ever wondered why a flute or violin sounds the way it does—why it has a distinctive timbre? The answer rests in a basic law of musical acoustics.

When a string vibrates or air rushes through a column in a wind instrument—even in a Coke bottle—more than one sound is produced. We hear a basic sound, called the *fundamental*. However, a string, for example, vibrates not only in its full (fundamental) length but simultaneously in parts of the string (halves, thirds, quarters, and so on), and these fractional vibrations produce many very, very faint sounds, called **overtones** (Fig. 3.1). Generally, the larger the fraction (one-half rather than one-quarter, for instance), the louder the sound of the overtone. But each type of instrument—be it trumpet or oboe—projects a distinctive pattern of overtone volume depending on the instrument's material and design. The degree of prominence of particular overtones blending with the fundamental gives an entire family of instruments (see "Instrument Families" below) its distinctive sound. Figure 3.2 shows the overtone series of the G string of a violin. Notice how there is no straight-line descent as the overtones sound all at once. Overtone 7 is faint, but overtone 8 asserts itself strongly. The proportions of the overtones—just like the mix of various coffees in the "holiday blend" at Starbucks—give each instrument its unique color.

Instrument Families

Musical instruments come in groups, or families—instruments of one general type having the same basic shape and made of the same materials. The Western **symphony orchestra** is a large performing ensemble that includes four such groups:

Watch a video of Craig Wright's Open Yale Course class session 2, "Introduction to Instruments and Musical Genres," at CourseMate for this text.

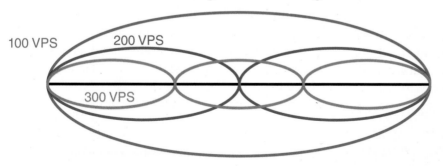

Full Length of Violin String

100 VPS   200 VPS

300 VPS

■ = Full string vibrating
■ = String vibrating in halves
■ = String vibrating in thirds
VPS = Vibrations per second

Figure 3.1

The diagram demonstrates that when a string (fundamental) vibrates, subsets of it also vibrate, thereby producing other faintly heard pitches called overtones.

Figure 3.2

The overtone series of a violin playing the G string, arranged to show degree of loudness. It is the particular mix of the faint overtones that gives each type of instrument its distinctive sound.

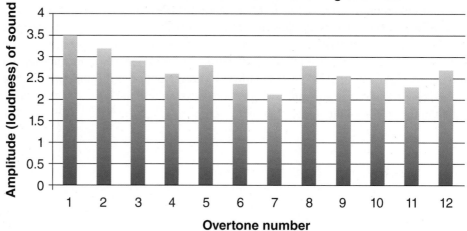

First Twelve Overtones of the G String of a Violin

Download the musician Sting's narration of Sergei Prokofiev's *Peter and the Wolf*, which uses instruments to evoke different characters, from the iTunes playlist at CourseMate for this text.

strings, woodwinds, brasses, and percussion. In addition, a fifth group of instruments exists, the keyboard instruments (piano, organ, and harpsichord), which are not normally part of the symphony orchestra.

STRINGS

If you travel to Beijing to hear a traditional Chinese orchestra, most of the instruments (erhu, pipa, and qinqin, for example) will be string instruments. If you attend the Bonnaroo Arts & Music Festival in Manchester, Tennessee, the rock bands there play electric bass and a variety of guitars—all string instruments. Visit the Country Music Hall of Fame in nearby Nashville, Tennessee, and you'll likely hear a fiddle and perhaps a mandolin added to the guitar ensemble. Watch the London Symphony Orchestra on stage at the Barbican Centre, and you'll notice the majority of its performers playing, again, string instruments. In sum, string instruments, whether plucked or bowed, dominate musical ensembles around the world.

VIOLIN GROUP

The violin group—violins, violas, cellos, and double basses—constitutes the core of the Western symphony orchestra. A large orchestra can easily include as many as a hundred members, at least sixty of whom play one of these four instruments.

The **violin** (Fig. 3.3) is chief among the string instruments. It is also the smallest—it has the shortest strings and therefore produces the highest pitch. The tune usually sounds in the highest part of the musical texture, so in an orchestra the violin generally plays the melody. Violins are often divided into groups known as firsts and seconds. The seconds play a part slightly lower in pitch and are subordinate in function to the firsts. (For the sound of the violin, listen to this chapter's streaming music at CourseMate or (intro)/11 at 0:00.)

The sound of the violin—indeed, that of all orchestral string instruments—is produced when the player pulls a bow across one of four strings. The strings are held tightly in place by four tuning pegs at one end of the instrument and by a tailpiece at the other, and they are slightly elevated above the wooden body by means of a supporting bridge. Different pitches are produced when a finger of the left hand shortens, or "stops," a string by pressing it down against the fingerboard. Again, the shorter the string, the higher the pitch.

Figure 3.3

This photo of the American group The Brentano String Quartet shows the relative size of the violin (center), viola (left), and cello (right).

Christian Steiner/Courtesy Brentano String Quartet

The **viola** (Fig. 3.3, left) is about six inches longer than the violin, and it produces a somewhat lower sound. If the violin is the string counterpart of the soprano voice, then the viola has its parallel in the alto voice. Its tone is darker, richer, and more somber than that of the brilliant violin. (For the sound of the viola, listen to (intro)/11 at 1:37.)

You can easily spot the **cello** (Fig. 3.3, right) in the orchestra because the player sits with the instrument placed between his or her legs. The pitch of the cello is well below that of the viola. It can provide a low bass sound as well as a lyrical melody. When played in its middle range by a skilled performer, the cello can produce an indescribably rich, expressive tone. (For the sound of the cello, listen to (intro)/11 at 2:10.)

The **double bass** (Fig. 3.4) gives weight and power to the bass line in the orchestra. Because at first it merely doubled the notes of the cello an octave below, it was called the double bass. As you can see, the double bass is the largest, and hence lowest sounding, of the string instruments. Its job in the orchestra, and even in jazz bands, is to help set a solid base/bass for the musical harmony. (For the sound of the double bass, listen to (intro)/11 at 2:50.)

The members of the violin group all generate pitches in the same way: A bow is drawn across a tight string. This produces the familiar penetrating string sound. In addition, a number of other effects can be created by using different playing techniques.

- **Vibrato.** By shaking the left hand as it stops the string, the performer can produce a sort of controlled "wobble" in the pitch. This adds richness to the tone of the string because, in fact, it creates a blend of two or more pitches. (For an example of a violin playing without vibrato and then with vibrato, listen to (intro)/11 at 0:31 and 0:51.)

- **Pizzicato.** Instead of bowing the strings, the performer plucks them. With this technique, the resulting sound has a sharp attack, but it dies away quickly. (For an example of pizzicato, listen to (intro)/11 at 1:13.)

- **Tremolo.** The performer creates a musical "tremor" by rapidly repeating the same pitch with quick up-and-down strokes of the bow. Tremolo creates a feeling of heightened tension and excitement when played loudly, and a velvety, shimmering backdrop when performed quietly. (For an example of tremolo, listen to (intro)/11 at 1:24.)

- **Trill.** The performer rapidly alternates between two distinctly separate but neighboring pitches. Most instruments, not just the strings, can play trills. (For an example of a trill, listen to (intro)/11 at 1:30.)

THE HARP

Although originally a folk instrument, the **harp** (Fig. 3.5) is sometimes added to the modern symphony orchestra. Its role is to lend its distinctive color to the orchestral sound and sometimes to create special effects, the most striking of which is a rapid run up or down the strings, called a **glissando**. When the notes of a triad are played in quick succession, up or down, an **arpeggio** results, a term derived from the Italian word for harp (*arpa*). (For the sound of the harp and an example of a glissando, listen to (intro)/11 at 3:35 and 3:44.)

Figure 3.4

Grammy Award–winning jazz double bass player Esperanza Spalding with her instrument. (She also plays electric bass.) The double bass is equally at home in a small jazz combo and in a large classical orchestra.

Figure 3.5

The harp's unique special effect is its glissando, a rapid run up and down the strings that seems to fill the atmosphere with energized sound.

Instruments of the Orchestra: Strings

intro
11

0:00	**11**	Violin plays major scale.
0:13		Violin solo: Tchaikovsky
0:31		Violin plays without vibrato: Haydn.
0:51		Violin plays vibrato: Haydn.
1:13		Violin plays pizzicato.
1:24		Violin plays tremolo.
1:30		Violin plays trill.
1:37		Viola plays major scale.
1:49		Viola solo: Haydn
2:10		Cello plays major scale.
2:30		Cello solo: Haydn
2:50		Double bass plays major scale.
3:13		Double bass solo: Haydn
3:35		Harp plays arpeggio.
3:44		Harp solo: Tchaikovsky

◀)) Listen to streaming music in an Active Listening Guide at CourseMate or in the eBook.

WOODWINDS

The name "woodwind" was originally given to this family of instruments because they emit sound when air is blown through a wooden tube or pipe. Today, however, some of these "wooden" instruments are made entirely of metal. Flutes, for example, are constructed of silver, and sometimes of gold or even platinum. As with the violin group, there are four principal woodwind instruments in every modern symphony orchestra: flute, oboe, clarinet, and bassoon (Fig. 3.6). In addition, each of these has a close relative that is larger or smaller in size and that possesses a somewhat different timbre and range. The larger the instrument or length of pipe, of course, the lower the sound.

© Conn-Selmer, Inc.

The lovely, silvery tone of the **flute** is probably familiar to you. The instrument can be rich in the lower register and light and airy at the top. It is especially agile, capable of playing tones rapidly and moving quickly from one range to another. (For the sound of the flute, listen to this chapter's streaming music at CourseMate or intro/12 at 0:00.) The smaller cousin of the flute is the **piccolo**.

Figure 3.6

(from left to right) A flute, two clarinets, an oboe, and a bassoon. The flute, clarinet, and oboe are about the same length. The bassoon is nearly twice their size.

(*Piccolo* comes from the Italian *flauto piccolo,* meaning "little flute.") It can produce higher notes than any other orchestral instrument. And though the piccolo is very small, its sound is so piercing that it can always be heard, even when the full orchestra is playing loudly. (For the sound of the piccolo, listen to intro/12 at 0:38.)

The **clarinet** produces sound when the player blows air under a single reed fitted to the mouthpiece. The tone of the clarinet is an open, hollow sound. It can be mellow in its low notes but shrill in its high ones. It also has the capacity to slide or glide smoothly between pitches, which allows for a highly expressive style of playing. (For the sound of the clarinet, listen to (intro)/12 at 0:54.) A lower, larger version of the clarinet is the bass clarinet.

The **oboe** is equipped with a double reed—two reeds tied together with an air space in between. When the player blows air between them and into the instrument through the double reed, the vibrations create a nasal, slightly exotic sound. Invariably, the oboe gives the pitch at the beginning of a symphony concert. Not only was the oboe the first nonstring instrument to be added to the orchestra, but also it is a difficult instrument to tune (regulate the pitch). Thus, it's better to have the other instruments tune to it than to try to have it adjust to them. (For the sound of the oboe, listen to (intro)/12 at 1:24.) Related to the oboe is the **English horn**. Unfortunately, it is wrongly named, for the English horn is neither English nor a horn. It is simply a larger (hence lower-sounding) version of the oboe that originated on the continent of Europe.

The **bassoon** functions among the woodwinds much as the cello does among the strings: It adds weight to the lowest sound or acts as a soloist. When playing moderately fast or rapid passages as a solo instrument, it has a dry, almost comic tone. (For the sound of the bassoon, listen to (intro)/12 at 1:54.) There is also a double bassoon, called the **contrabassoon**, which can play notes lower than any other orchestral instrument.

Strictly speaking, the single-reed **saxophone** is not a member of the symphony orchestra, though it can be added on occasion. Its sound can be mellow and expressive but also, if the player wishes, husky, even raucous. The expressiveness of the saxophone makes it a welcome member of most jazz ensembles.

See a video of all the orchestral instruments in Benjamin Britten's *Young Person's Guide to the Orchestra*, as well as keyboard videos, in the Book-Level Resources at CourseMate for this text.

Listening Guide

Instruments of the Orchestra: Woodwinds

(intro) 12

0:00	12	Flute plays major scale.
0:11		Flute solo: Debussy
0:38		Piccolo plays major scale.
0:47		Piccolo solo: Tchaikovsky
0:54		Clarinet plays major scale.
1:02		Clarinet solo: Berlioz
1:24		Oboe plays major scale.
1:33		Oboe solo: Tchaikovsky
1:54		Bassoon plays major scale.
2:05		Bassoon solo: Stravinsky

Listen to streaming music in an Active Listening Guide at CourseMate or in the eBook.

BRASSES

Like the woodwind and string groups of the orchestra, the brass family consists of four primary instruments: trumpet, trombone, French horn, and tuba (Fig. 3.7). Brass players use no reeds but instead blow into their instruments through

Figure 3.7

Members of the Canadian Brass, with the French horn player at the left and the tuba player at the right

Figure 3.8

Three mouthpieces for brass instruments

a cup-shaped **mouthpiece** (Fig. 3.8). By adjusting valves or moving a slide, the performer can make the length of pipe on the instrument longer or shorter, and hence the pitch lower or higher.

Everyone has heard the high, bright, cutting sound of the **trumpet**. Whether in a football stadium or an orchestral hall, the trumpet is an excellent solo instrument because of its agility and penetrating tone. Sometimes the trumpeter is required to play with a **mute** (a plug placed in the bell of the instrument) to lessen its piercing sound. (For the sound of the trumpet, listen to this chapter's streaming music at CourseMate or intro/13 at 0:00.)

Although distantly related to the trumpet, the **trombone** (Italian for "large trumpet") plays in the middle range of the brass family. Its sound is large and full. Most important, the trombone is the only brass instrument to generate sounds by moving a slide in and out to produce higher or lower pitches. Needless to say, the trombone can easily slide from pitch to pitch, sometimes for comical effect. (For the sound of the trombone, listen to intro/13 at 0:35.)

The **French horn** (sometimes just called "horn") was the first brass instrument to join the orchestra, back in the late seventeenth century. Because the French horn, like the trombone, sounds in the middle range of the brasses, these two instruments are often almost impossible to distinguish. The French horn, however, has a slightly mellower, more "veiled" sound than does the clearer, "in your face" trombone. (For the sound of the French horn, listen to intro/13 at 0:59.)

The **tuba** is the largest and lowest sounding of the brass instruments. It produces a full, though sometimes muffled, tone in its lowest notes. Like the double bass of the violin group, the tuba is most often used to set a base, or foundation, for the melody. (For the sound of the tuba, listen to intro/13 at 1:39.)

Listening Guide

Instruments of the Orchestra: Brasses

intro
13

0:00	13	Trumpet plays major scale.
0:09		Trumpet solo: Mouret
0:22		Trumpet solo with mute: Mouret
0:35		Trombone plays major scale.
0:45		Trombone solo: Copland
0:59		French horn plays major scale.
1:17		French horn solo: Copland
1:39		Tuba plays major scale.
2:00		Tuba solo: Copland

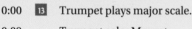 Listen to streaming music in an Active Listening Guide at CourseMate or in the eBook.

PERCUSSION

Want to make your own percussion instrument? Just find a metal trash can and strike its side with your hand. Percussion instruments are simply resonating objects that sound when hit or scraped with an implement in one fashion or another. Some percussion instruments, like the timpani (kettledrums), produce a specific pitch, while others generate sound that, while rhythmically precise, has no recognizable musical pitch.

The **timpani** (Fig. 3.9) is the percussion instrument most often heard in classical music. Whether struck in single, detached strokes or hit rapidly to produce a thunder-like roll, the function of the timpani is to add depth, tension, and drama to the music. Timpani usually come in pairs, one instrument tuned to the tonic and the other to the dominant. Playing only these pitches, the timpani feature prominently at the beginning of Strauss's *Also sprach Zarathustra* (downloads, streaming music for Ch. 1 at CourseMate, or intro/2 at 0:26).

The rat-a-tat-tat of the **snare drum**, the dull thud of the **bass drum**, and the crashing ring of the **cymbals** are sounds well known from marching bands and jazz ensembles, as well as the classical orchestra. None of them produces a specific musical tone. (To hear all three in a row, listen to this chapter's streaming music at CourseMate or intro/14 at 0:11.)

The job of all percussion instruments is to sharpen the rhythmic contour of the music. They add density to the sounds of other instruments and, when played loudly, can heighten the suspense and lend a sense of climax to a piece. Indeed, calling for a single cymbal crash at the top of a musical line is tantamount to holding up a sign: "EMOTIONAL CLIMAX."

© Tim Wimborne/Reuters/CORBIS

Figure 3.9

Tympanist Jonathan Haas of the American Symphony Orchestra

Listen to an iAudio podcast on identifying the different instruments at CourseMate for this text.

Listening Guide

Instruments of the Orchestra: Percussion

0:00 **14**	Timpani	0:19	Bass drum
0:11	Snare drum	0:31	Cymbal

 Listen to streaming music in an Active Listening Guide at CourseMate or in the eBook.

intro

14

KEYBOARD INSTRUMENTS

Keyboard instruments, which are unique to Western music, boast highly intricate mechanisms. The **pipe organ** (Fig. 3.10), the most complex of all musical instruments, traces its origins back to ancient Greece. When the player depresses a key, air rushes into a pipe, thereby generating sound. The pipes are arranged in separate groups, each producing a full range of musical pitches with one particular timbre (the sound of the trumpet, for example). When the organist wants to add distinctive musical color to a piece, he or she simply pulls a knob, called a **stop**. The most colorful, forceful sound occurs when all the stops have been activated (thus the expression "pulling out all the stops"). The several keyboards of the organ make it possible to play several colorful lines at once, each with its own timbre. There is even a keyboard for the feet to play. The largest fully functioning

Figure 3.11

A two-manual harpsichord built by Pascal Taskin (Paris, 1770), preserved in the Yale University Collection of Musical Instruments, New Haven, Connecticut

Figure 3.10

A three-manual (keyboard) pipe organ with only small pipes visible. Notice the stops (small circular objects on either side of the manual keyboards) and the pedal keyboard below.

View a video demonstration of the organ, harpsichord, and piano in the Book-Level Resources at CourseMate.

Figure 3.12

Pianist Lang Lang

pipe organ in the world is in the Cadet Chapel of the U.S. Military Academy at West Point, New York. It has 270 stops and 18,408 pipes. (To hear an organ, listen to Bach's Organ Fugue in G minor in the downloads, the streaming music for Ch. 10 at CourseMate, or ②1/11 or ⑤1/26.)

The **harpsichord** (Fig. 3.11) appeared in northern Italy as early as 1400 but reached its heyday during the Baroque era (1600–1750). When a key is depressed, it drives a lever upward that in turn forces a pick to pluck a string, thereby creating a bright, jangling sound. The harpsichord has one important shortcoming, however: The lever mechanism does not allow the performer to control the force with which the string is plucked. Each string always sounds at the same volume, no matter how hard the player strikes the key. (To hear a harpsichord, listen to Pachelbel's Canon in D major in the downloads, the streaming music for Ch. 9, or (intro)/10 at 0:00.)

The **piano** (Fig. 3.12) was invented in Italy around 1700, in part to overcome the sound-producing limitations of the harpsichord. The strings of a piano are not plucked; they are hit by soft hammers. A lever mechanism makes it possible for the player to regulate how hard each string is struck. Touch lightly and a soft sound results; bang hard and you hear a loud one. Thus the original piano was called the *pianoforte,* the "soft-loud." During the lifetime of Mozart (1756–1791), the piano replaced the harpsichord as the favorite domestic musical instrument. By the nineteenth century every aspiring household had to have a piano, whether as an instrument for real musical enjoyment or as a symbol of affluence.

Figure 3.13

Seating plan of a symphony orchestra

Percussion   Timpani   Trombones   French horns   Trumpets   Harps   Clarinets   Bassoons   Tuba   Piano   Flutes   Oboes   Double basses   Second violins   First violins   Conductor   Violas   Cellos

Today, the piano reigns supreme in the home and concert hall. But it has one natural predator that someday may make it extinct: the **electric keyboard**. This computer-driven synthesizer can, with the push of a button, change the overtones (see Fig. 3.2) in play and thereby alter the sound we hear from piano to harpsichord, or to organ, or to any instrument.

The Symphony Orchestra

The modern Western symphony orchestra is one of the largest and certainly the most colorful of all musical ensembles. When at full strength, the symphony orchestra can include upward of one hundred performers and nearly thirty different instruments, from the high, piping piccolo down to the rumbling contrabassoon. A typical seating plan for an orchestra is shown in Figure 3.13. To achieve the best balance of sound, strings are placed toward the front and the more powerful brasses at the back.

Surprisingly, when the orchestra originated in the seventeenth century, it had no separate conductor: The group was small enough for one of the instrumentalists to lead as he played. But around the time of Beethoven (1770–1827), when the orchestra was already two hundred years old and had expanded to include some sixty players, it became necessary to have someone stand before it and direct. Indeed, the **conductor** functions something like a musical traffic cop: He or she makes sure that the cellos don't overshadow the violins and that the oboe yields to the clarinet at the proper moment so the melody can be heard. The conductor reads from an **orchestral score** (a composite of all the parts) and must be able to immediately pick out any incorrectly played pitches and rhythms (Fig. 3.14). To do this, he or she must have an excellent musical ear.

Watch a video of Craig Wright's Open Yale Course class session 12, "Guest Conductor: Saybrook Orchestra," at CourseMate for this text.

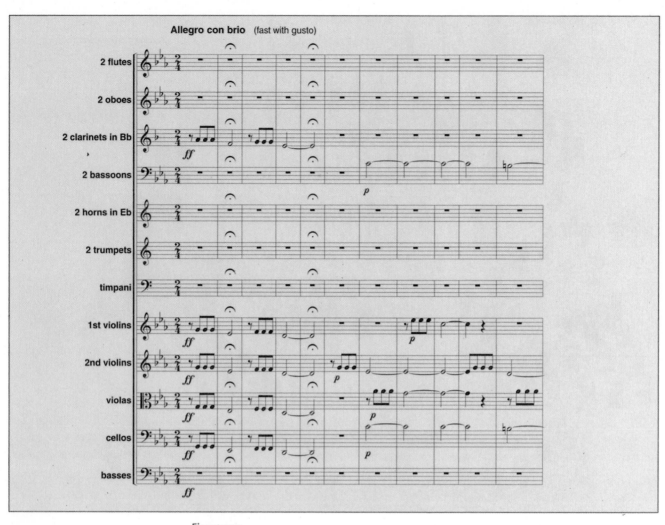

Figure 3.14

The orchestral score of the beginning of Beethoven's Symphony No. 5, first page, with instruments listed

Listening Exercise 3.1

15

To take this Listening Exercise online and receive feedback, go to CourseMate or the eBook.

Hearing the Instruments of the Orchestra: Identifying a Single Instrument

By listening to the Intro CD, tracks 11–14, you have heard all of the principal instruments of the Western symphony orchestra. Now it is time to test your ability to identify these instruments. The Intro CD, track 15, contains demonstrations of ten solo instruments. Write the name of the correct instrument in the blank by choosing one from the right-hand column.

1. (0:00) _Flute_   Bassoon (Rimsky-Korsakov)
2. (0:14) _Cello_   Flute (Tchaikovsky)
3. (0:38) _Clarinet_   Clarinet (Rimsky-Korsakov)
4. (0:52) _d.b._   French horn (Brahms)
5. (1:13) _oboe_   Cello (Saint-Saëns)
6. (1:30) _bassoon_   Oboe (Tchaikovsky)
7. (1:48) _Trombone_   Trombone (Ravel)
8. (2:09) _F.H._   Double bass (Beethoven)
9. (2:34) _violin_   Tuba (Berlioz)
10. (2:50) _tuba_   Violin (Tchaikovsky)

To take this Listening Exercise online and receive feedback, go to CourseMate or the eBook.

Hearing the Instruments of the Orchestra: Identifying Two Instruments

Now things get more difficult. Can you identify two instruments playing at once and determine which one is playing in a higher range? To keep you on track, a few instruments have been filled in. Choose from among the following instruments for the remaining blanks below: ~~violin~~, viola, cello, ~~double bass~~, flute (heard twice), clarinet, oboe (heard twice), ~~bassoon~~, ~~trumpet~~, and ~~trombone~~.

		First Instrument	**Second Instrument**	**Higher Instrument**
(0:00)	Brahms	French horn	1. *trumpet*	2. *trumpet*
(0:40)	Mahler	3. *db*	4. *clarinet*	5. *clarinet*
(1:08)	Lully	6. *bassoon*	clarinet	7. *clarinet*
(1:29)	Bach	8. *flute*	bassoon	9. *flute*
(1:44)	Bach	10. *trombone*	11. *flute*	12. *flute*
(2:00)	Telemann	13. *oboe*	viola	14. *viola*
(2:27)	Bartók	15. *cello*	16. *oboe*	17. *oboe*
(2:52)	Bach	18. *violin*	19. *viola*	20. *violin*

To take this Listening Exercise online and receive feedback, go to CourseMate or the eBook.

Hearing the Instruments of the Orchestra: Identifying Three Instruments

Ready for the ultimate test? Now you need to identify three instruments. Choose from among the following instruments for the blanks below: ~~violin~~, ~~viola~~, ~~cello~~, ~~flute (twice)~~, clarinet, bassoon, ~~trumpet (twice)~~, trombone, ~~French horn~~, and tuba.

		First Instrument	**Second Instrument**	**Third Instrument**
(0:00)	Tchaikovsky	1. *bassoon*	French horn	2. *flute*
(0:18)	Tchaikovsky	3. *tuba*	4. *French horn*	5. *trumpet*
(0:40)	Lully	6. *flute*	bassoon	7. *clarinet*
(1:00)	Bach	8. *trumpet*	French horn	9. *trombone*
(1:44)	Beethoven	10. *violin*	11. *viola*	12. *cello*

Finally, identify the highest and lowest sounding of the three instruments in four of the excerpts.

		Highest	Lowest
(0:40)	Lully	13. *flute*	14. *bassoon*
(0:00)	Tchaikovsky	15. *flute*	16. *bassoon*
(0:18)	Tchaikovsky	17. *trumpet*	18. *tuba*
(1:44)	Beethoven	19. *violin*	20. *cello*

Texture

When a painter or weaver arranges material on a canvas or loom, he or she creates a texture: **Texture** is the density and arrangement of artistic elements. Look at Vincent van Gogh's *Branch of an Almond Tree in Blossom* (1890; chapter-opening photo). Here the painter has used lines and spaces to create a texture heavy at the bottom but light at the top, projecting an image that is well grounded but airy. So, too, a composer creates effects with musical lines—also called parts or voices, even though they might not be sung. There are three primary textures in music, depending on the number of voices involved: monophonic, homophonic, and polyphonic.

Listen to an iAudio podcast on distinguishing the textures at CourseMate for this text.

Monophony is the easiest texture to hear. As its name—literally, "one sounding"—indicates, **monophony** is a single line of music, with no harmony. When you sing by yourself, or play the flute or trumpet, for example, you are creating monophonic music. When a group of men (or women) sings the same pitches together, they are singing in **unison**. Unison singing is monophonic singing. Even when men and women sing together, doubling pitches at the octave, the texture is still monophonic. When we sing "Happy Birthday" with our friends at a party, for example, we are singing in monophony. Monophonic texture is the sparsest of all musical textures. Beethoven uses it for the famous duh-duh-duh-DUHHH opening of his Symphony No. 5 (downloads, streaming music for Ch. 1, and intro/1 at 0:00) to create a lean, sinewy effect.

Homophony means "same sounding." In this texture the voices, or lines, all move together to new pitches at roughly the same time. The most common type of homophonic texture is tune plus chordal accompaniment. Notice in Example 3.1 how the melody, which by itself would be monophonic, now joins with vertical blocks of chords to create homophonic texture. Holiday carols, hymns, folk songs, and almost all pop songs have this sort of tune-plus-chordal-accompaniment texture when sung with harmony. Can you hear in your mind's ear a band playing "The Star-Spangled Banner"? That's homophonic texture.

EXAMPLE 3.1 HOMOPHONY

As we might suppose from its name, "many sounding," **polyphony** requires two or more lines in the musical fabric. In addition, the term *polyphonic* implies that each of the lines will be free and independent, often entering at different times. Thus polyphonic texture has a strong linear (horizontal) thrust, whereas in homophonic texture the fabric is structured more vertically as blocks of accompanying chords (compare the arrows in Ex. 3.1 and Ex. 3.2). In polyphonic texture the voices are of equal importance, moving against one another to create what is called **counterpoint**, the harmonious opposition of two or more independent musical lines. (Musicians use the terms *polyphony* and *counterpoint* interchangeably.) Finally, there are two types of counterpoint: free and imitative. In free counterpoint the voices are highly independent and go their separate ways; much jazz improvisation is done in free counterpoint. In imitative counterpoint, on the other hand, a leading voice begins, followed by one or more other voices that duplicate what the first voice presented. If the followers copy exactly, note for note, what the leader plays or sings, then a **canon** results. Think of "Three Blind Mice," "Are You Sleeping?" ("Frère Jacques"), and "Row, Row, Row Your Boat," and remember how each voice enters in turn, imitating the first voice from beginning to end (see Ex. 3.2). These are all short canons, or rounds, a type of strictly imitative counterpoint popular since the Middle Ages. A much longer canon, as we have seen in Listening Exercise 2.5, plays out in the upper three lines of Johann Pachelbel's well-known Canon in D major (downloads, streaming music for Ch. 9, and intro/10 at 0:12).

EXAMPLE 3.2 POLYPHONY

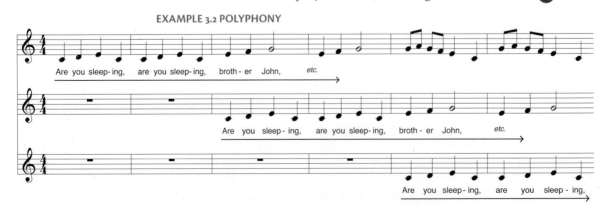

Of course, composers are not limited to just one of these three musical textures in a given piece—they can move from one to another, as George Frideric Handel does brilliantly in the justly famous "Hallelujah" chorus from his oratorio *Messiah*.

Listening Guide

George Frideric Handel, *Messiah,* **"Hallelujah" chorus (1741)**

WHAT TO LISTEN FOR: Handel's skillful manipulation of the musical texture to achieve variety and generate excitement

0:06	**18**	"Hallelujah! Hallelujah!"	Homophony
0:23		"For the Lord God Omnipotent reigneth"	Monophony
0:30		"Hallelujah! Hallelujah!"	Homophony
0:34		"For the Lord God Omnipotent reigneth"	Monophony
0:40		"Hallelujah! Hallelujah!"	Homophony
0:44		"For the Lord God Omnipotent reigneth" together with "Hallelujah"	Polyphony
1:09		"The Kingdom of this world is become"	Homophony
1:27		"And He shall reign for ever and ever"	Polyphony
1:48		"King of Kings and Lord of Lords" together with "Hallelujah"	Homophony
2:28		"And He shall reign for ever and ever"	Polyphony
2:40		"King of Kings and Lord of Lords" together with "Hallelujah"	Homophony
2:48		"And He shall reign for ever and ever"	Polyphony
2:55		"King of Kings and Lord of Lords" together with "Hallelujah"	Homophony

Listen to streaming music in an Active Listening Guide at CourseMate or in the eBook.

Listening Exercise 3.4

To take this Listening Exercise online and receive feedback, go to CourseMate or the eBook.

Hearing Musical Textures

On your Intro CD, track 19, you have ten excerpts that exemplify the three basic textures of music. Monophonic texture, you will find, is easy to hear because it has only one line of music. More difficult is differentiating homophonic texture and polyphonic texture. Homophonic texture usually uses blocks of chords that accompany and support a single melody. Polyphonic texture, on the other hand, embodies many active, independent lines. Identify the texture of each of the excerpts by writing an M, H, or P in the appropriate blank.

1. (0:00) _____P_____ Bach, *The Art of Fugue,* Contrapunctus IX
2. (0:44) _____M_____ Beethoven, Symphony No. 5, 1st movement
3. (0:52) _____M_____ Musorgsky, "Promenade" from *Pictures at an Exhibition*
4. (1:02) _____H_____ Musorgsky, "Promenade" from *Pictures at an Exhibition*
5. (1:12) _____P_____ Bach, Organ Fugue in G minor
6. (2:03) _____M_____ Debussy, *Prelude to The Afternoon of a Faun*
7. (2:22) _____P_____ Josquin Desprez, *Ave Maria*
8. (2:48) _____H_____ Dvořák, Symphony No. 9, "From the New World," 2nd movement
9. (3:17) _____P_____ Louis Armstrong, "Willie the Weeper"
10. (3:41) _____H_____ Copland, "A Gift to Be Simple" from *Appalachian Spring*

 # Form

Form in music is the arrangement of musical events. In architecture, sculpture, and painting, objects are situated in physical space to create a pleasing design. Similarly, in music a composer places important sonic events in an order that produces a compelling pattern as sounds pass by in time.

To create form in music, a composer employs one of four processes: statement, repetition, contrast, and variation. A **statement**, of course, is the presentation of an important musical idea. **Repetition** validates the statement by reiterating it. Nothing would be more bewildering for a listener than a steady stream of ever-new music. How would we make sense of it? Recurring musical ideas function as formal markers or signposts; each restatement is an important musical event—and a reassuring return to stability.

Contrast, on the other hand, takes us away from the familiar and into the unknown. Contrasting melodies, rhythms, textures, and moods can be used to provide variety and even to create conflict. In music, as in life, we need novelty and excitement; contrast invigorates us, making the eventual return to familiar ideas all the more satisfying.

Variation stands midway between repetition and contrast. The original melody returns but is altered in some way. For example, the tune may now be more complex, or new instruments may be added against it to create counterpoint. The listener has the satisfaction of hearing the familiar melody, yet is challenged to recognize how it has been changed.

If we look at the exterior of a building or stand before a painting inside a museum, we perceive the form of the object all at once. Not so with music. Music unfolds over time, and we have to use our memory to reconstruct and understand what we have heard. To help us remember, musicians have developed a system to visualize forms by using letters to represent musical units. The first statement of a musical idea is designated **A**. Subsequent contrasting sections are labeled **B**, **C**, **D**, and so on. If the first or any other musical unit returns in varied form, then that variation is indicated by a superscript number—A^1 and B^2, for example. Subdivisions of each large musical unit are shown by lowercase letters **a**, **b**, and so on. How this system works will become clear in the examples used throughout this book.

Listen to an iAudio podcast on distinguishing forms at CourseMate for this text.

 ## Strophic Form

Strophic form is the most familiar of all musical forms because our hymns, carols, folk songs, and pop tunes invariably make use of it. In **strophic form** the composer sets the words of the first poetic stanza (strophe) and then uses the same entire melody for all subsequent stanzas. In his famous *Wiegenlied (Lullaby)*, for instance, Johannes Brahms repeats a single musical idea for each strophe of the poem, as demonstrated in the Listening Guide below. Many pop songs throughout history have employed a slight twist on this procedure—each strophe beginning with a verse of new text and ending with a **chorus** (a textual **refrain** that repeats). A chart topper from the Civil War era, "The Battle Hymn of the Republic," may serve as a representative example of this common form. In this rallying cry for the Union forces, with text by Julia Ward Howe, each strophe (verse + chorus) is set to the same music:

Strophe 1

> (Verse) Mine eyes have seen the glory of the coming of the Lord:
> He is trampling out the vintage where the grapes of wrath are stored;
> He hath loosed the fateful lightning of His terrible swift sword:
> His truth is marching on.
>
> (Chorus) Glory, glory, hallelujah! Glory, glory, hallelujah!
>
> Glory, glory, hallelujah! His truth is marching on.

Strophe 2

> I've seen him in the watchfires
> Of a hundred circling camps,
> They have builded him an altar
> In the evening dews and damps;

I can read his righteous sentence
By the dim and flaring lamps;
His day is marching on.

(Chorus) Glory, glory, hallelujah! Glory, glory, hallelujah!

Glory, glory, hallelujah! His truth is marching on.

There are many YouTube clips with different arrangements and video backdrops for the hymn. Explore and find your favorite. A quick search of YouTube also confirms that strophic form is alive and well in the popular genres of today, from indie to rock to hip-hop. In Jay-Z and Alicia Keys's "Empire State of Mind," he raps the verse, and she then sings the refrain. This entire complex is repeated two more times, with music the same for each new strophe of text. Check out this hit (being mindful of "explicit content"), or explore and find your own example. Now listen to the first two strophes of the equally well known *Wiegenlied (Lullaby)* of Johannes Brahms. Each strophe, again, is sung to the same music, but in this case there is no chorus.

Listening Guide

Johannes Brahms, *Wiegenlied* (*Lullaby*, 1868)

(intro)
20

WHAT TO LISTEN FOR: An exact repeat of the music of strophe 1 for strophe 2

0:00	20	Gut' Abend, gut Nacht,	Good evening, good night
		Mit Rosen bedacht,	Covered with roses,
		Mit Näglein besteckt	Adorned with carnations,
		Schlüpf unter die Deck':	Slip under the covers.
		Morgen früh, wenn Gott will,	Tomorrow early, if God so wills,
		Wirst du wieder geweckt.	You will awake again.
0:48		Gut' Abend, gut Nacht,	Good evening, good night
		Von Englein bewacht,	Watched over by angels,
		Die zeigen im Traum	Who in dreams show
		Dir Christkindleins Baum:	You the Christ child's tree.
		Schlaf nun selig und süss,	Now sleep blissful and sweetly,
		Schau im Traum's Paradies.	Behold Paradise in your dreams.

◀)) Listen to streaming music in an Active Listening Guide at CourseMate or in the eBook.

A slightly varied version of strophic form, modified strophic form, can be heard in Clara Schumann's "Liebst du um Schönheit" ("If You Love for Beauty"); downloads, streaming music for Ch. 20 at CourseMate, and (intro)/21.

Theme and Variations

The working of **theme and variations** form is obvious: One musical idea continually returns but is varied in some fashion by a change in the melody, harmony, texture, or timbre. In classical music, the more variations the composer writes, the more obscure the theme becomes; the listener is increasingly challenged to hear the new as an outgrowth of the old. Theme and variations form can be visualized in Figure 3.15 and the following scheme:

Statement of theme   Variation 1   Variation 2   Variation 3   Variation 4
    A   **A**^{1} **A**^{2} **A**^{3} **A**^{4}

When Mozart was a young man, he lived briefly in Paris, where he heard the French folksong "Ah, vous dirai-je Maman." We know it today as "Twinkle, Twinkle, Little Star." Upon this charming tune (**A**) he later composed a set of variations for piano (discussed in full in Ch. 15, "Theme and Variations").

Neale Cousland/Shutterstock.com

Figure 3.15

The Opera House in the harbor of Sydney, Australia. Here we see a theme (a rising, pointed arch) that displays a new variation each time it appears in a different position.

Wolfgang Amadeus Mozart, Variations on "Twinkle, Twinkle, Little Star" (c. 1781)

(intro)

22

WHAT TO LISTEN FOR: How the theme is altered within each new variation

0:00	**22**	**A**	Tune played without ornamentation; melody above, harmony below
0:30		**A¹**	Variation 1: Tune above decorated with florid, fast-moving figurations
0:59		**A²**	Variation 2: Tune above undecorated; florid, fast-moving figurations now in bass
1:29		**A³**	Variation 3: Tune above decorated with graceful arpeggios

🔊 Listen to streaming music in an Active Listening Guide at CourseMate or in the eBook.

Binary Form

As the name indicates, **binary form** consists of two contrasting units, **A** and **B** (see Fig. 3.16, left). In length and general shape, **A** and **B** are constructed to balance and complement each other. Variety is usually introduced in **B** by means of a dissimilar mood, key, or melody. Sometimes in binary form, both **A** and **B** are immediately repeated, note for note. Musicians indicate exact repeats by means of the following sign: ‖: :‖ Thus, when binary form appears as ‖:A:‖‖:B:‖ it is performed **AABB**. Joseph Haydn created a perfect example of binary form in music for the second movement of his Symphony No. 94, and then wrote a set of variations upon this theme (discussed in full in Ch. 15, "Theme and Variations").

Figure 3.16

(left) The essence of binary form, or **AB** form, can be seen in this Japanese wood carving. Here the two figures are distinctly different yet mutually harmonious. (right) Ternary form, or **ABA** form, can clearly be seen in the architecture of the cathedral of Salzburg, Austria, where Mozart and his father frequently performed.

Digital Image © 2009 Museum Associates/LACMA/Art Resource, NY

© Richard Klune/CORBIS

Joseph Haydn, Symphony No. 94, the "Surprise" (1792)

(intro)

23

Second movement, *Andante* (moving)

WHAT TO LISTEN FOR: A charming **A** theme followed by a complementary **B**

0:00	**23**	**A** presented by strings
0:17		**A** repeated with surprise *sforzando* at end
0:33		**B** presented by strings
0:50		**B** repeated with flutes added to melody

🔊 Listen to streaming music in an Active Listening Guide at CourseMate or in the eBook.

Ternary Form

If the most prevalent form in pop songs is strophic form, in classical music it is **ternary form** (Fig. 3.16, right); the musical journey home-away-home (**ABA**) has satisfied composers and listeners for centuries. In the "Dance of the Reed Pipes" from Peter Tchaikovsky's famous ballet *The Nutcracker,* the **A** section is bright and cheery because it makes use of the major mode as well as silvery flutes. However, **B** is dark and low, even ominous, owing to the minor mode and the insistent ostinato (repeated pattern) in the bass.

Listening Guide

Peter Tchaikovsky, *The Nutcracker,* "Dance of the Reed Pipes" (1891)

24

WHAT TO LISTEN FOR: The bright, dancing music of **A**, then the change to the dark, minor **B**, and the return to an abbreviated **A**

0:00	24		Flutes play melody above low string pizzicato.
0:35		**A**	English horn and then clarinet add counterpoint.
0:51			Melody repeats with violins now adding counterpoint.
1:22		**B**	Change to minor mode: Trumpets play melody above two-note bass ostinato.
1:36			Violins join melody.
1:57		**A**^{1}	Return to flute melody (with violin counterpoint) in major mode

Listen to streaming music in an Active Listening Guide at CourseMate or in the eBook.

Rondo Form

Rondo form involves a simple principle: A refrain (**A**) alternates with contrasting music. Usually in a rondo, there are at least two contrasting sections (**B** and **C**). Perhaps because of its simple but pleasing design, rondo form has been favored by musicians of every age—medieval monks, classical symphonists such as Mozart and Haydn, and even contemporary pop artists like Sting (see "A Rondo by Sting" in Ch. 15). Although the principle of a recurring refrain is a constant, composers have written rondos in several different formal patterns, as seen below. The hallmark of each, however, is a refrain (**A**).

ABACA   ABACABA   ABACADA

Figure 3.17

The chateau of Chambord, France, has a formal design equivalent to **ABACABA** structure, a pattern often encountered in music in rondo form.

A   B   B   A   C   A   B   A

© Charles & Josette Lenars/CORBIS

You may already be familiar with a rondo composed by Jean-Joseph Mouret (1682–1738), made famous as the theme music for *Masterpiece Theatre* (now *Masterpiece*), America's longest-running prime-time drama series, on PBS. Here, the refrain (**A**), played by full orchestra with a brilliant trumpet and drums, alternates with two contrasting ideas (**B** and **C**) to form a neatly symmetrical pattern.

Listening Guide

Jean-Joseph Mouret, Rondeau from *Suite de symphonies* (1729)

intro

25

WHAT TO LISTEN FOR: The regular appearance of theme **A** played by a brilliant trumpet

0:00	25	**A**	Refrain played by full orchestra, including trumpet and drums, and then repeated (at 0:12)
0:24		**B**	Quieter contrasting section played by strings and woodwinds
0:37		**A**	Refrain returns but without repeat.
0:50		**C**	New contrasting section played by strings and woodwinds
1:22		**A**	Refrain returns and is repeated (at 1:35).

Listen to streaming music in an Active Listening Guide at CourseMate or in the eBook.

Key Words

dynamics (32)	vibrato (35)	counterpoint (44)
forte (32)	pizzicato (35)	canon (44)
piano (32)	tremolo (35)	form (46)
crescendo (32)	trill (35)	statement (46)
decrescendo (diminuendo) (32)	glissando (35)	repetition (46)
color (32)	arpeggio (35)	contrast (46)
timbre (32)	mouthpiece (38)	variation (46)
soprano (33)	mute (38)	strophic form (46)
alto (33)	stop (39)	chorus (refrain) (46)
tenor (33)	conductor (41)	theme and variations (47)
bass (33)	orchestral score (41)	binary form (48)
mezzo soprano (33)	texture (43)	‖:‖ (indication to performer to repeat the music) (48)
baritone (33)	monophony (44)	
chorus (33)	unison (44)	ternary form (49)
overtones (33)	homophony (44)	rondo form (49)
symphony orchestra (33)	polyphony (44)	

For a complete review of this chapter, see the Main Points, Chapter Quiz, Flashcards, and Glossary in CourseMate.

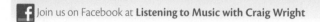

Join us on Facebook at **Listening to Music with Craig Wright**

When listening to music, we try, consciously or not, to make sense of what we hear. Walking into a coffee shop, for example, we often hear a piece of music, classical or popular, that we can immediately identify. For pieces we don't recognize, we try to make an educated guess as to the style of the music, and perhaps the composer. Is it rap or reggae? Romantic or Baroque? Blige or Beyoncé? In our high-tech age, we even have applications, such as Shazam, that will identify an unknown song. Another popular service, Pandora, will find and play tunes similar to the ones we like. How does it do this? Pandora makes use of something called the Musical Genome, which quickly scans an audio file for some four hundred markers of melody, rhythm, harmony, timbre, texture, and form. In other words, using the elements of music, the application seeks to identify a song's musical DNA—expressed as style—and find a match.

Style in music, then, is the distinctive sound created by a composer, an artist, or a performing group, as expressed through the elements of music. Every composer has a personal style, one that makes his or her work different from that of all other creators. Take a work by Mozart (1756–1791), for example. A trained listener will recognize it as a piece from the Classical period (1750–1820) because of its generally symmetrical melodies, light texture, and dynamic ebb and flow. A truly experienced ear will identify Mozart as the composer, perhaps by recognizing the sudden shifts to minor keys, the intensely chromatic melodies, or the colorful writing for the woodwinds, all fingerprints of Mozart's personal musical style.

Each period in the history of Western classical music likewise has a distinct musical style. That is, the music of one period has a common set of characteristics; the same practices and procedures appear in many, many works of that epoch. A great number of Masses from the Renaissance (1450–1600) exhibit short bursts of imitative counterpoint and are sung by voices alone, without instrumental accompaniment. A symphony from the Romantic period (1820–1900), on the other hand, will typically exhibit long, nonimitative melodies, chromatic harmonies, languid rhythms, and uniformly dense orchestral textures.

Historians have divided the history of music into eight style periods:

Middle Ages: 476–1450	Romantic: 1820–1900
Renaissance: 1450–1600	Impressionist: 1880–1920
Baroque: 1600–1750	Modern: 1900–1985
Classical: 1750–1820	Postmodern: 1945–present

Figure 4.1

Portions of the East Wing of the National Gallery of Art in Washington, built in 1978 to a design by I. M. Pei, stand in contrast to the U.S. Capitol in the background. Pei's building, with its flat surfaces and unadorned geometric shapes, is representative of the modern style in architecture, while the Capitol reflects the neoclassical style of the eighteenth century.

Of course, human activity—artistic or otherwise—cannot be so neatly categorized. Historical periods, in some ways, are like the ages of humankind. When does an infant become a child or the child an adult? Similarly, musical styles do not change overnight; they evolve and overlap. Composers can stand midway between periods. Beethoven (1770–1827), for example, straddles the Classical and Romantic eras, being somewhat conservative in his choice of harmonies but radically progressive in his use of rhythm and form. Despite such contradictions, historians of music, like historians of art, find it useful to discuss style in terms of historical periods (Fig. 4.1). This practice makes it possible to explore the ceaseless continuum of human creativity in terms of shorter, more easily understood units.

© Arcaid (Richard Bryant)/Alamy

The following Checklists of Musical Style analyze the style of each historical period in terms of the fundamental elements of music: melody, harmony, rhythm, and so on. The appropriate Checklist for each period recurs at the end of that period in later chapters.

Interactive Checklists of Musical Style may also be found at CourseMate for this text.

Checklists of Musical Style by Periods

Middle Ages: 476–1450

REPRESENTATIVE COMPOSERS

Anonymous (the most prolific of all)	Leoninus	Machaut
Hildegard of Bingen	Perotinus	Countess of Dia

PRINCIPAL GENRES

Gregorian chant	*troubadour* and *trouvère* songs	carol
polyphonic Mass	popular song	instrumental dance

Melody	Moves mostly by step within narrow range; rarely uses chromatic notes of the scale.
Harmony	Most surviving medieval music, notably Gregorian chant and *troubadour* and *trouvère* songs, is monophonic—consisting of a single melodic line without harmonic support.
	Medieval polyphony (Mass, motet, and carol) has dissonant phrases ending with open, hollow-sounding, consonant chords.
Rhythm	Gregorian chant as well as *troubadour* and *trouvère* songs sung mainly in notes of equal value without clearly marked rhythms; medieval polyphony is composed mostly in triple meter (in honor of the Holy Trinity, theorists said) and uses repeating rhythmic patterns.
Color	Mainly vocal sounds (choir or soloists) within the church; popular music might include instruments like trumpet, trombone, fiddle, or harp.
Texture	Mostly monophonic—Gregorian chant and *troubadour* and *trouvère* songs are monophonic melodies.
	Medieval polyphony (two, three, or four independent lines) is mainly contrapuntal.
Form	Gregorian chant has no one large-scale form, but each phrase of text generally receives its own phrase of music; strophic form in *troubadour* and *trouvère* songs and the carol; rondo form in the French chanson.

Renaissance: 1450–1600

REPRESENTATIVE COMPOSERS

Anonymous (now less prolific)	Palestrina
Josquin Desprez	Weelkes

PRINCIPAL GENRES

polyphonic Mass	instrumental dances (pavane and galliard)
sacred motet	secular song and madrigal

Melody	Mainly stepwise motion within moderately narrow range; still mainly diatonic, but some intense chromaticism found in madrigals from end of period.
Harmony	More careful use of dissonance than in Middle Ages as the triad, a consonant chord, becomes the basic building block of harmony.

Rhythm	Duple meter is now as common as triple meter; rhythm in sacred vocal music (Mass and motet) is relaxed and without strong downbeats; rhythm in secular music (madrigal and instrumental dance) is usually lively and catchy.
Color	Although more music for instruments alone has survived, the predominant sound remains that of unaccompanied (a cappella) vocal music, whether for soloists or for choir.
Texture	Mainly polyphonic: imitative counterpoint for four or five vocal lines is heard throughout Masses, motets, and madrigals; occasional passages of chordal homophonic texture are inserted for variety.
Form	Strict musical forms are not often used; most Masses, motets, madrigals, and instrumental dances are through composed—they have no musical repetitions and hence no standard formal plan.

Early and Middle Baroque: 1600–1690

REPRESENTATIVE COMPOSERS

Monteverdi	Lully	Corelli
Strozzi	Pachelbel	Vivaldi
Purcell		

PRINCIPAL GENRES

opera	sonata	dance suite
overture	concerto grosso	
chamber cantata	solo concerto	

Melody	Less stepwise movement, larger leaps, wider range, and more chromaticism reflect influence of virtuosic solo singing; melodic patterns idiomatic to particular musical instruments emerge.
Harmony	Stable, diatonic chords played by *basso continuo* support melody; standard chord progressions begin to emerge at end of the seventeenth century; modes are gradually limited to just two: major and minor.
Rhythm	Relaxed, flexible rhythms of the Renaissance gradually replaced by repetitive rhythmic patterns and a strongly articulated beat.
Color	Musical timbre becomes enormously varied as traditional instruments are perfected (e.g., harpsichord, violin, and oboe) and new combinations of voices and instruments are explored; string-dominated orchestra begins to take shape; sudden shifts in dynamics (terraced dynamics) reflect dramatic quality of Baroque music.
Texture	Chordal, homophonic texture predominates; top and bottom lines are strongest as *basso continuo* creates powerful bass to support melody above.
Form	Arias and instrumental works often make use of *basso ostinato* procedure; ritornello form emerges in the concerto; binary form regulates most movements of the sonata and dance suite.

Late Baroque: 1690–1750

REPRESENTATIVE COMPOSERS

Pachelbel	Vivaldi	Bach
Corelli	Mouret	Handel

PRINCIPAL GENRES

French overture	solo concerto	prelude
dance suite	church cantata	fugue
sonata	opera	
concerto grosso	oratorio	

Melody	Melody is marked by progressive development, growing longer and more expansive; idiomatic instrumental style influences vocal melodies; melodic sequence becomes prevalent.

Harmony	Functional chord progressions govern harmonic movement—harmony moves purposefully from one chord to the next; *basso continuo* continues to provide strong bass.
Rhythm	Exciting, driving, energized rhythms propel the music forward with vigor; "walking" bass creates feeling of rhythmic regularity.
Color	Instruments reign supreme; instrumental sounds, especially of violin, harpsichord, and organ, set musical tone for the era; one tone color used throughout a movement or large section of a movement.
Texture	Homophonic texture remains important, but denser, polyphonic texture reemerges in the contrapuntal fugue.
Form	Binary form in sonatas and dance suites; *da capo* aria (ternary) form in arias; fugal procedure used in fugues; ritornello form in concertos.

Classical: 1750–1820

REPRESENTATIVE COMPOSERS

Mozart	Beethoven
Haydn	Schubert

PRINCIPAL GENRES

symphony	string quartet	opera
sonata	solo concerto	

Melody	Short, balanced phrases create tuneful melodies; melody more influenced by vocal than instrumental style; frequent cadences produce light, airy feeling.
Harmony	The rate at which chords change (harmonic rhythm) varies dramatically, creating a dynamic flux and flow; simple chordal harmonies made more active by "Alberti" bass.
Rhythm	Departs from regular, driving patterns of Baroque era to become more stop-and-go; greater rhythmic variety within a single movement.
Color	Orchestra grows larger; woodwind section of two flutes, oboes, clarinets, and bassoons becomes typical; piano replaces harpsichord as principal keyboard instrument.
Texture	Mostly homophonic; thin bass and middle range, hence light and transparent; passages in contrapuntal style appear sparingly and mainly for contrast.
Form	A few standard forms regulate much of Classical music: sonata–allegro, theme and variations, rondo, ternary (for minuets and trios), and double exposition (for solo concerto).

Romantic: 1820–1900

REPRESENTATIVE COMPOSERS

Beethoven	Chopin	Dvořák
Schubert	Liszt	Tchaikovsky
Berlioz	Verdi	Musorgsky
Mendelssohn	Wagner	Mahler
Robert Schumann	Bizet	Puccini
Clara Schumann	Brahms	

PRINCIPAL GENRES

symphony	tone poem (symphonic poem)	solo concerto
program symphony	opera	character piece for piano
dramatic overture	art song (*Lied*)	ballet music
concert overture	orchestral song	

Melody	Melody is more flexible and irregular in shape than in the Classical period; long, singable lines with powerful climaxes and chromatic inflections for expressiveness.
Harmony	Greater use of chromaticism makes the harmony richer and more colorful; sudden shifts to remote chords for expressive purposes; prolonged dissonance conveys feelings of anxiety and longing.
Rhythm	Rhythms are free and relaxed, occasionally obscuring the meter; tempo can fluctuate greatly (tempo *rubato*) and sometimes slows to a crawl to allow for "the grand gesture".
Color	The orchestra becomes enormous, reaching upward of one hundred performers: trombone, tuba, contrabassoon, piccolo, and English horn added to the ensemble; experiments with new playing techniques for special effects; dynamics vary widely to create extreme levels of expression; piano becomes larger and more powerful.
Texture	Predominantly homophonic but dense and rich because of larger orchestras and orchestral scores; sustaining pedal on the piano also adds to density.
Form	No new forms created; rather, traditional forms (strophic, sonata–allegro, and theme and variations, for example) used and extended in length; traditional forms also applied to new genres such as tone poem and art song.

Impressionist: 1880–1920

REPRESENTATIVE COMPOSERS

Debussy   Ravel

PRINCIPAL GENRES

tone poem (symphonic poem)   orchestral song   character piece for piano
string quartet   opera   ballet music

Melody	Varies from short dabs of sound to long, free-flowing lines; melodies are rarely tuneful or singable but instead twist and turn rapidly in undulating patterns.
Harmony	Purposeful chord progressions replaced by static harmony; chords frequently proceed in parallel motion; use of nontraditional scale patterns (whole-tone, pentatonic) confuses sense of tonal center.
Rhythm	Usually free and flexible with irregular accents, making it difficult to determine meter; rhythmic ostinatos used to give feeling of stasis rather than movement.
Color	More emphasis on woodwinds and brasses and less on violins as primary carriers of melody; more soloistic writing to show that the color of the instrument is as important as, or more important than, the melody line it plays.
Texture	Can vary from thin and airy to heavy and dense; sustaining pedal of the piano often used to create a wash of sound; glissandos run quickly from low to high or high to low.
Form	Traditional forms involving clear-cut repetitions less frequent, although ternary form is not uncommon; composers try to develop a form unique and particular to each new musical work.

Modern: 1900–present

REPRESENTATIVE COMPOSERS

Stravinsky   Prokofiev   Copland
Schoenberg   Shostakovich   Thomas
Bartók   Ives

| symphony | string quartet | ballet music |
| solo concerto | opera | choral music |

Melody	Wide-ranging disjunct lines, often chromatic and dissonant, angularity accentuated by use of octave displacement.
Harmony	Highly dissonant, marked by chromaticism, new chords, and tone clusters; dissonance no longer must move to consonance but may move to another dissonance; sometimes two conflicting, but equal, tonal centers sound simultaneously (polytonality); sometimes no audible tonal center is present (atonality).
Rhythm	Vigorous, often asymmetrical rhythms; conflicting simultaneous meters (polymeter) and rhythms (polyrhythm) make for temporal complexity.
Color	Color becomes agent of form and beauty in and of itself; composers seek new sounds from traditional, acoustical instruments and innovative singing techniques from electronic instruments and computers, and from noises in environment.
Texture	As varied and individual as the men and women composing music.
Form	A range of extremes: sonata–allegro, rondo, theme and variations benefit from Neo-classical revival; twelve-tone procedure allows for almost mathematical formal control; forms and processes of classical music, jazz, and pop music begin to influence one another in exciting new ways.

Postmodern: 1945–present

REPRESENTATIVE COMPOSERS

| Varèse | Glass | Adams |
| Cage | Reich | Tan |

PRINCIPAL GENRES

no common genres; each work of art creates a genre unique to itself

Nearly impossible to generalize in terms of musical style; major stylistic trends not yet discernible.

Barriers between high art and low art removed; all art judged to be of more or less equal value— symphony orchestras now play video game music.

Experimentation with electronic music and computer-generated sound.

Previously accepted fundamentals of music, such as discrete pitches and division of octave into twelve equal pitches, often abandoned.

Narrative music (pictorial) music and "goal-oriented" music rejected.

Chance music permits random "happenings" and noises from the environment to shape a musical work.

Introduction of visual and performance media into the written musical score.

Instruments from outside the tradition of Western classical music (e.g., electric guitar, sitar, kazoo) prescribed in the score.

Experimentation with new notational styles within musical scores (e.g., sketches, diagrams, prose instructions).

Join us on Facebook at **Listening to Music with Craig Wright**

part TWO
The Middle Ages and Renaissance, 476–1600

400	500	600	700	800	900	1000	1100	1200	1300	1400

MIDDLE AGES

476 Fall of Rome to Visigoths

c. 530 Benedict of Nursia founds monastic order

c. 700 *Beowulf*

Hildegard of Bingen (1098–1179), musician, poet, visionary

c. 1170–1230 Leoninus and Perotinus develop polyphony in Paris

c. 1360 Guillaume de Machaut (c. 1300–1377) composes Messe de *Nostre Dame* at Reims

1066 William the Conqueror invades England

800 Charlemagne crowned Holy Roman Emperor

c. 880 Vikings invade Western Europe

c. 1150 Beatriz of Dia and other troubadours flourish in southern France

c. 1160 Gothic Cathedral of Notre Dame begun in Paris

c. 1390 Geoffrey Chaucer (c. 1340–1400) writes *Canterbury Tales*

1415 King Henry V and his English soldiers defeat French at battle of Agincourt

Historians use the term *Middle Ages* as a catchall phrase to refer to the thousand years of history between the fall of the Roman Empire (476) and the dawn of the Age of Discovery (mid-1400s, culminating in the voyages of Christopher Columbus). It was a period of monks and nuns, of knightly chivalry and brutal warfare, of sublime spirituality and deadly plagues, and of soaring cathedrals amidst abject poverty. Two institutions vied for political control: the Church and the court. From our modern perspective, the medieval period appears as a vast chronological expanse dotted by outposts of dazzling architecture, stunning stained glass, and equally compelling poetry and music.

Renaissance means literally "rebirth." Historians use the term to designate a period of intellectual and artistic flowering that occurred first in Italy, then in France, and finally in England, during the years 1350–1600. Music historians apply the term more narrowly to musical developments in those same countries during the period 1450–1600. The Renaissance was an age in which writers, artists, and architects looked back to classical Greece and Rome to find models for personal and civic expression. It was an important period for music as well. Among the most significant musical developments of the Renaissance was a newfound desire to use music to amplify the meaning of a given text. Finally, attributing creativity to human accomplishment as well as to God, Renaissance composers began to fashion secular music for the home as well as traditional religious music for the church.

1450	1475	1500	1525	1550	1575	1600

RENAISSANCE

1473 Pope Sixtus IV leads revival of Rome and begins Sistine Chapel

1486 Josquin Desprez (c. 1450–1521) joins Sistine Chapel choir

1492 Christopher Columbus's first voyage

c. 1495 Leonardo da Vinci (1452–1519) begins *Last Supper*

1501 Ottaviano Petrucci publishes first book of polyphonic music (Venice)

1554 Palestrina (1525–1594) joins Sistine Chapel choir

1501–1504 Michelangelo (1475–1564) sculpts statue of David

1558–1603 Elizabeth I Queen of England

1517 Martin Luther (1483–1546) posts Ninety-five Theses

1599–1613 Shakespeare's plays performed at Globe Theater

1528 Pierre Attaingnant publishes first book of polyphonic music north of the Alps (Paris)

1601 Madrigal collection *The Triumphes of Oriana* published to honor Elizabeth I

1534 King Henry VIII of England establishes Church of England

1545 Council of Trent begins

Medieval Music, 476–1450

For the harried inhabitant of the twenty-first century, it is difficult to imagine a life revolving around quiet prayer. But in the Middle Ages a large portion of the population (monks and nuns) defined their lives with two simple tasks: work and prayer. They worked to feed their bodies, and they prayed to save their souls. Indeed, the Middle Ages was a profoundly spiritual period, because life on earth was uncertain and often brief. If you got an infection, you likely died (there were no antibiotics); if insects ate your crops, you likely starved (no insecticides); if your village caught fire, it likely burned to the ground (no fire department). With seemingly little control over their own destiny, people turned to an outside agent (God) for help. And they did so mainly through organized religion—the Roman Catholic Church, the dominant spiritual and administrative force in medieval Europe.

 ## Music in the Monastery

Most medieval society was overwhelmingly agricultural; thus religion was centered in rural monasteries (for monks) and convents (for nuns). The clergy worked in the fields and prayed in the church. Religious services usually began well before dawn and continued at various other times throughout the day in an almost unvarying cycle. Set forth by the influential Italian monk Benedict of Nursia (c. 485–547), founder of the Benedictine Order of monks and nuns, these times of prayer had names such as Matins, coming early in the morning, and Vespers, at twilight. The most important service of the day was **Mass**, a symbolic reenactment of the Last Supper, celebrated at about nine o'clock in the morning.

Gregorian Chant

The music for these services was what we today call **Gregorian chant** (or **plainsong**)— a unique collection of thousands of religious songs, sung in Latin, that carry the theological message of the Church. Although this music bears the name of Pope Gregory the Great (c. 540–604), this pontiff actually wrote very little of it. Instead, Gregorian chant was created by many people, male and female, before, during, and long after Gregory's reign.

Watch a video of Craig Wright's Open Yale Course class session 15, "Gregorian Chant and Music in the Sistine Chapel," at CourseMate for this text.

To record chant and to pass it from one community to the next, medieval monks and nuns created a wholly new medium of communication: **musical notation**. At first the system used only a few dashes and dots, called *notae* (Latin for "notes"), which suggested the upward and downward motion of the melody. But exactly how *far* up or down did the pitch go? To represent the melodic distance, church musicians around the year 1000 began to put the notes on a grid of lines and spaces that were identified by letter names: space A, line B, space C, and so forth. Initially created to preserve the repertoire of Gregorian chant, this combination of symbols (notes) on a grid (the staff) formed the basis of the musical pitch notation that we still use today.

Gregorian chant is like no other music. It has a timeless, otherworldly quality that no doubt arises from its lack of meter and regular rhythms. True, some notes are longer or shorter than others, but pitches do not recur in obvious patterns that would allow us to clap our hands or tap our feet. Because all voices sing in unison, Gregorian chant is monophonic music. There is no instrumental accompaniment, nor, as a rule, are men's and women's voices mixed. For all these reasons, Gregorian chant has a consistently uniform, monochromatic sound, one far more conducive to meditation than to dancing. The faithful are not to hear the music per se, but rather to use the music as a vehicle to enter a spiritual state, to reach communion with God.

Example 5.1 shows most of a lengthy chant, *Viderunt omnes* (*All the Ends of the Earth*), sung during Mass on Christmas Day. We know that it dates from the fifth century C.E., but we know nothing about its creator. In fact, almost all medieval chant was composed by anonymous figures; this was a religious age in which creative individuals did not step forward to take credit for their accomplishments—the honor belonged to God. Notice here that, although the pitches are clearly indicated, no rhythmic information is provided. The notes are generally of one basic value, something close to our eighth note in length. Notice also the presence two kinds of singing: syllabic and melismatic. A passage of **syllabic singing** has only one or two notes for each syllable of text—as at "jubilate" ("sing joyfully"); in contrast, one of **melismatic singing** has many syllables—as on the final syllable of "terra" ("earth").

EXAMPLE 5.1

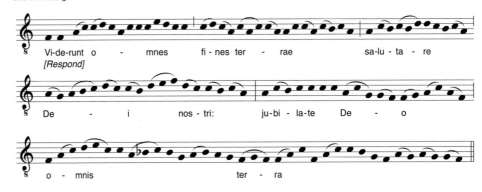

Vi-de-runt o — mnes fi - nes ter - rae sa-lu - ta - re
[Respond]

De — i nos - tri: ju-bi - la-te De - o

o - mnis ter - ra

All the ends of the earth have seen the salvation of our God; sing joyfully to God, all the earth.

Listening Guide

Anonymous, Gregorian chant, *Viderunt omnes* (fifth century)

Genre: Chant

Texture: Monophonic

WHAT TO LISTEN FOR: The restful, undulating melody that generally climbs up quickly by triadic intervals and then descends luxuriantly by step

| 0:00 | 1 | Soloist:
Choir: | Viderunt omnes
fines terrae salutare Dei nostri;
jubilate Deo omnis terra. | All the ends of the earth have seen
the salvation of our God; sing joyfully
to God, all the earth. |

Listen to streaming music in an Active Listening Guide at CourseMate or in the eBook.

The Chant of Hildegard of Bingen (1098–1179)

One of the most remarkable contributors to the repertoire of Gregorian chant was Hildegard of Bingen (1098–1179; Fig. 5.1), from whose fertile pen we received seventy-seven chants. Hildegard was the tenth child of noble parents who gave her to the Church as a tithe (a donation of a tenth of one's worldly goods). She was educated by Benedictine nuns and then, at the age of fifty-two, founded her own convent near the small town of Bingen, Germany, on the west bank of the Rhine. Over time, Hildegard manifested her extraordinary intellect and imagination as a playwright, poet, musician, naturalist, pharmacologist, and visionary. Today a Google search for "Hildegard of Bingen" will generate more than a million hits, perhaps a testimony to her widely varied interests. Ironically, the first "Renaissance man" was really a medieval woman: Hildegard of Bingen.

Hildegard's *O rubor sanguinis (O Redness of Blood)* possesses many qualities typical of her chants, and of chant generally (Ex. 5.2). First, it sets a starkly vivid text, which Hildegard herself created. Honoring St. Ursula and a group of 11,000 Christian women believed slain by the Huns in the fourth or fifth century, the poem envisages martyred blood streaming in the heavens and virginal flowers unsullied by serpentine evil. Each phrase of text receives its own phrase of music, but the phrases are not of the same length. Notice again the differentiation between syllabic singing (see "quod divinitas tetigit") and melismatic singing (see the twenty-nine notes for "num" of "numquam"). Even today some pop singers such as Christina Aguilera, Mariah Carey, and the late Whitney Houston are referred to as "melismatic singers" owing to their penchant for spinning out just one syllable with many, many notes.

EXAMPLE 5.2: Hildegard of Bingen, *O rubor sanguinis*

O — — ru - bor san - gui - nis — / qui — de ex - cel - so —
— il - lo — flu - - - - xi - sti / quod — di - vi - ni - tas te - ti - git: /
tu flos — es — / quem hy - - ems de — fla - - tu ser - pen - - tis — / num -
- - - - - - - - - - quam — le - sit.

Hildegard's chant *O rubor sanguinis* is sweeping, yet solidly grounded tonally, as each phrase ends with the first (tonic) or fifth (dominant) degree of the scale, with D or A (colored red in Ex. 5.2). Notice, too, that after an initial jump (D to A), the chant proceeds mostly in stepwise motion (neighboring pitches). This was, after all, choral music to be sung by the full community of musically unsophisticated nuns or monks, so it had to be easy. Finally, as with most chants, this piece has no overt rhythm or meter. The unaccompanied, monophonic line and the absence of pulsating rhythm allow a restful, meditative mood to develop. Hildegard did not see herself as an "artist" as we think of one today, but, in the spirit of medieval anonymity, as a mere vessel through which divine revelation came to earth (Fig. 5.2). Indeed, she styled herself simply "a feather floating on the breath of God."

Figure 5.1

A twelfth-century illumination depicting Hildegard of Bingen receiving divine inspiration, perhaps a vision or a chant, directly from the heavens. To the right, her secretary, the monk Volmar, peeks in at her in amazement.

Figure 5.2

(upper frame) A vision of Hildegard revealing how a fantastic winged figure of God the Father, the Son, and the Mystical Lamb killed the serpent Satan with a blazing sword. (lower frame) Hildegard (center) receives the vision and reports it to her secretary (left). This manuscript dates from the twelfth century.

Hildegard of Bingen, Gregorian chant, *O rubor sanguinis* (c. 1150)

Genre: Chant

Texture: Monophonic

WHAT TO LISTEN FOR: A transcendental experience. Does the absence of a beat relax you? Does Hildegard's chant seem to carry you away?

0:00		O rubor sanguinis,	O redness of blood,
0:14		qui de excelso illo fluxisti,	which flowed down from on high,
0:29		quod divinitas tetigit;	touched by divinity;
0:36		Tu flos es	You are the flower
0:41		quem hyems de flatu serpentis numquam lesit.	that the wintry breath of the serpent never wounded.
0:57		(Note the long melisma on "numquam.")	

Listen to streaming music in an Active Listening Guide at CourseMate or in the eBook.

Music in the Cathedral

Gregorian chant arose primarily in secluded monasteries and convents around Western Europe. The future of art music within the Church, however, rested not in rural monasteries, but in urban cathedrals. Every cathedral served as the "home church" of a bishop, who could minister to the largest flock by locating himself within one of Europe's rapidly expanding urban centers. During the twelfth century, cities such as Milan, Paris, and London, among others, grew significantly as trade and commerce increased. Much of the commercial wealth generated in the cities was used to construct splendid new cathedrals that served as both houses of worship and municipal civic centers. So substantial was this building campaign that the period 1150–1350 is often called the "Age of the Cathedrals." It started in northern France, with cathedrals possessing elements of what we now call the Gothic style: pointed arches, high ceiling vaults, flying buttresses, and richly colored stained glass.

Figure 5.3

The cathedral of Notre Dame of Paris, begun c. 1160, was one of the first to be built in the new Gothic style of architecture. Organum was composed there as the building was being constructed.

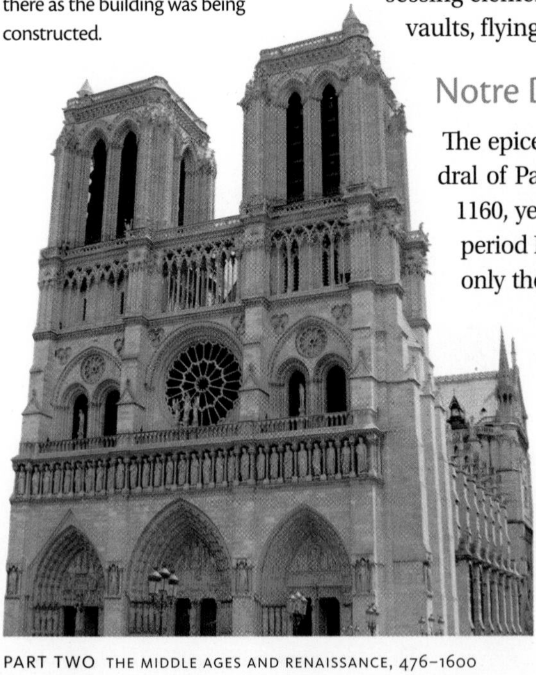

Catapult/Getty Images

Notre Dame of Paris

The epicenter for the new Gothic style in northern France was Paris. The cathedral of Paris (Fig. 5.3), dedicated to Notre Dame (Our Lady), was begun about 1160, yet not completed until more than a hundred years later. Throughout this period Notre Dame was blessed with a succession of churchmen who were not only theologians and philosophers but poets and musicians as well. Foremost among these were Master Leoninus (flourished 1169–1201) and Master Perotinus, called the Great (fl. 1198–1236). Leoninus wrote a great book of religious music (called, in Latin, the *Magnus liber organi*). Perotinus revised Leoninus's book and also composed many additional pieces of his own. In so doing, they helped create a new style of music called **organum**, the name given generally to early church polyphony. The novelty here rested in the fact that the composers added one, two, or three voices on top of the existing chant. In this musical development, we see an early instance of a creative spirit breaking free of the ancient authority (the chant) of the Church.

Perotinus: Organum *Viderunt omnes*

The surviving documents from Paris suggest that Perotinus the Great served as director of the choir at Notre Dame of Paris. To lend special splendor to the celebration of Mass on Christmas morning in the year 1198, Perotinus composed a four-voice organum for Mass, *Viderunt omnes* (*All the Ends of the Earth*; see Ex. 5.1). He took the centuries-old chant and added three new voices above it (Fig. 5.4). Compared to the new upper voices, the old borrowed chant moved very slowly, drawing out or holding each pitch. Because of this, the sustaining line with the chant came to be called the **tenor** voice (from the Latin *teneo*, French *tenir*, "to hold"). As you listen to the work of Perotinus, you will clearly hear the sustaining chant that provides a harmonic support for the upper voices, just as a massive pillar in a Gothic church might support the delicate movement of the arches above (see Fig. 5.5). Equally audible are the sprightly rhythms in triple meter, a novel sound.

Ms. Pluteus 29, Biblioteca laurenziana, Florence/Photo © Craig Wright

Figure 5.4

Perotinus's four-voice *Viderunt omnes* for Christmas Day. Note how the chant in the tenor voice (staffs 4, 8, and 12) provides a long-note foundation for the three voices above.

Earlier in the Middle Ages, when almost all written music was monophonic chant, there was little need to specify rhythm—all pitches were roughly the same length, and the singers could easily stick together as they moved from one note to the next. When as many as three or four separate parts sang together in organum, however, more direction was needed. How else would the singers know when to change pitches to make good harmony? Thus, during the thirteenth and fourteenth centuries musicians devised a system called **mensural notation** (measured notation) to specify musical rhythm as well as pitch precisely. To the note heads indicating pitch, musicians added various sorts of stems and flags to specify duration. These stems and flags are still with us today in our half, quarter, and eighth notes.

Listening Guide

Master Perotinus the Great, organum built on Gregorian chant *Viderunt omnes* (1198)

⑤

1/3

Genre: Organum

Texture: Polyphonic

WHAT TO LISTEN FOR: The jaunty triple meter. All early polyphony written in rhythmic notation was composed in triple meter to do honor, the theorists of the time tell us, to the Holy Trinity.

Because Perotinus sustains the chant in long notes in his setting of *Viderunt omnes* (see Ex. 5.1), a composition of great length—eleven to twelve minutes—results. Thus, only the beginning of his organum is given here. The singers relate that all the ends of the earth have seen ("Viderunt") the Christian Savior.

0:00	③	Syllable "Vi-" of "Viderunt"; all voices hold on open sound of fifth and octave.
0:06		Upper three voices proceed in rocking triple meter as tenor sustains first note of chant with all voices singing the "Vi-" syllable.
0:47		Tenor changes to next pitch, and all change to syllable "-de-" of "Viderunt."
1:10		Tenor changes to next pitch, and all change to syllable "-runt" of "Viderunt."
2:06		End of word "Viderunt"

(Continuing organum not included in this text's music compilation)

 Listen to streaming music in an Active Listening Guide at CourseMate or in the eBook.

Figure 5.5

Interior of the cathedral of Reims, looking from floor to ceiling. The pillars carry the eye up to the ribbed vaults of the roof, creating a feeling of great upward movement, just as the Mass of Machaut, with four superimposed voices, has a new sense of verticality.

© Craig Wright

Notre Dame of Reims

Thirteenth-century Paris was the first home of the new Gothic polyphony, but by the fourteenth century its primacy, in both music and architecture, was challenged by Reims (pronounced "Rance"). The city of Reims, 100 miles east of Paris in the Champagne region of France, boasted a cathedral as impressive as and, indeed, larger than the one that graced Paris. In the fourteenth century, Reims benefited from the service of a poetically and musically talented churchman, Guillaume de Machaut (c. 1300–1377). Judging by his nearly 150 surviving works, not only was Machaut (pronounced "ma-SHOW") the most important composer of his day, he was equally esteemed as a poet. Today, historians of literature place him on a pedestal next to his slightly younger English counterpart, Geoffrey Chaucer (c. 1340–1400), author of *The Canterbury Tales.* Indeed, Chaucer knew and borrowed heavily from the poetic works of Machaut.

Machaut: *Messe de Nostre Dame*

Machaut's *Messe de Nostre Dame (Mass of Our Lady)* is deservedly the best-known work in the entire repertoire of medieval music. Its length of twenty-five minutes is impressive, as is the novel way it applies music to the text of the Mass (Table 5.1). Before Machaut's time, composers writing polyphony for the Mass had set only one or two sections of the **Proper of the Mass** (chants whose texts changed to suit the feast day in question). Machaut was the first composer to set what is called the **Ordinary of the Mass**—five sung portions of the Mass, specifically, the *Kyrie, Gloria, Credo, Sanctus,* and *Agnus Dei*—with texts that did not change from day to day. From Machaut's work onward, composing a Mass meant setting the five texts of the Ordinary and finding some way to shape them into an integrated whole. Bach, Mozart, Beethoven, and Stravinsky were just a few of the later composers to follow Machaut's lead in this regard.

Table 5.1 Musical Portions of the Mass

Proper of the Mass	Ordinary of the Mass
Texts change with each new feast or saint's day.	Texts are the same each day.
1. Introit (an introductory chant for the entry of the celebrating clergy)	
	2. Kyrie (a petition for mercy)
	3. Gloria (a hymn of praise to the Lord)
4. Gradual (a reflective chant)	
5. Alleluia or Tract (a chant of thanksgiving or penance)	
	6. Credo (a profession of faith)
7. Offertory (a chant for the offering)	
	8. Sanctus (an acclamation to the Lord)
	9. Agnus Dei (a petition for mercy and eternal peace)
10. Communion (a chant accompanying communion)	

To construct his Mass, Machaut proceeded as follows. First, he took a chant in honor of the Virgin and placed it in long notes in the tenor voice. Above the foundational tenor, Machaut composed two new lines called the *superius* and the *contratenor altus,* and from these we get our terms *soprano* and *alto;* below the tenor, he composed a *contratenor bassus,* whence our term *bass.* Unlike Perotinus, who bunched his voices around middle C, Machaut spread his voices out over two and a half octaves, becoming the first composer to exploit nearly the full vocal range of a chorus. Yet as you will hear, this polyphony is often dissonant and biting. The exciting moments in Machaut's Mass come when the composer stretches out the dissonances into open, consonant chords (see the asterisk in Ex. 5.3). These chords sound especially rich in an echo-filled medieval cathedral, where the open sonorities can swirl and endlessly rebound around bare stone walls.

EXAMPLE 5.3

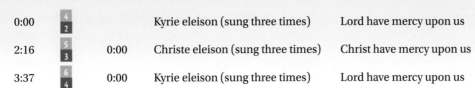

Listening Guide

Guillaume de Machaut, *Kyrie* of *Messe de Nostre Dame* (c. 1360)

Form: Ternary

Texture: Polyphonic and monophonic

WHAT TO LISTEN FOR: The alternating polyphony and chant and, within the polyphony, the alternation of dissonance and consonance, with consonance coming largely at the ends of phrases

0:00	4/2		Kyrie eleison (sung three times)	Lord have mercy upon us
2:16	5/3	0:00	Christe eleison (sung three times)	Christ have mercy upon us
3:37	6/4	0:00	Kyrie eleison (sung three times)	Lord have mercy upon us

Listen to streaming music in an Active Listening Guide at CourseMate or in the eBook.

Take online Listening Exercise 5.1 and receive feedback at CourseMate or in the eBook.

Music at the Court

Figure 5.6

Beatriz, Countess of Dia, who flourished during the mid-twelfth century, as depicted in a manuscript of troubadour and *trouvère* poetry.

For a modern evocation of royal life at the medieval French castle of Chinon in the twelfth century, watch the greeting of Eleanor of Aquitaine (Katharine Hepburn) by King Henry II (Peter O'Toole) in the YouTube playlist at CourseMate for this text.

Outside the walls of the cathedral was yet another musical world: one of popular song and dance centered at the court. If the music of the Church was calculated to move the soul toward spiritual reflection, that of the court was meant to move the body to sing and dance. The court emerged as a center for the patronage of the arts during the years 1150–1400, as kings, dukes, counts, and lesser nobles increasingly assumed responsibility for defending the land and regulating social behavior. The court embraced forms of public entertainment not permitted by Church authorities. Here, itinerant actors, jugglers, jesters, and animal acts provided welcome diversions at banquets and feasts. Minstrels wandered from castle to castle, playing instruments and bringing with them the latest tunes, along with the news and gossip of the day.

Troubadours and *Trouvères*

France was the center of this new courtly art, though French customs quickly spread to Spain, Italy, and Germany as well. The poet-musicians who flourished in the courts of southern France were called **troubadours** and those in the north **trouvères**. These names are distant ancestors of the modern French word *trouver* ("to find"). Indeed, the troubadours and *trouvères* were "finders," or inventors, of a new genre of vocal expression called the **chanson** (French for "song"). In all, the troubadours and *trouvères* created several thousand chansons. Most are monophonic love songs that extol the courtly ideals of faith and devotion, whether to the ideal lady, the just seigneur (lord), or the knight crusading in the Holy Land. The origins of the troubadours and *trouvères* were varied. Some were sons of bakers and drapers, others were members of the nobility, many were clerics who had left the rigors of the Church, and not a few were women.

In the Middle Ages, women were not allowed to sing in church, except in convents, owing to the biblical command of St. Paul ("A woman must be silent in the church"). But at court, women often recited poetry, sang, and played musical instruments. A few, such as Beatriz, Countess of Dia (Fig. 5.6), were composers in their own right. Beatriz lived in southern France in the mid-twelfth century. She was married to Count William of Poitiers but fell in love with a fellow troubadour, Raimbaut d'Orange (1146–1173). In her chanson *A chantar m'er (I Must Sing)* Beatriz complains of unrequited love (presumably hers toward Raimbaut) and does so from a woman's perspective. The seven-phrase melody displays a clear music form: **ABABCDB** (the use of letters to indicate musical form is explained in Ch. 3, "Form"). As with the chant of the Church, troubadour song has no clearly articulated meter and rhythm, but is sung in pitches of more or less equal duration.

Listening Guide

Countess of Dia, Troubadour song, *A chantar m'er* (c. 1175)

Genre: Troubadour chanson

5

1/7

WHAT TO LISTEN FOR: Although the vielle (medieval fiddle) heard here has been added by modern performers and is not called for in the original manuscript, it nonetheless sets up a lovely, often dissonant, harmonic interplay with the voice.

0:00   [7]   Improvised introduction played on vielle (medieval fiddle)

0:26   Solo voice enters and sings first of five strophes

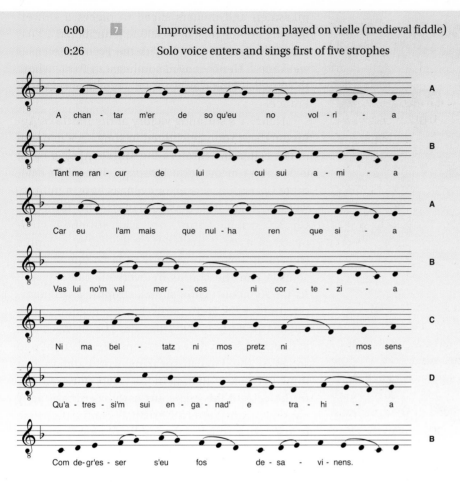

I must sing of that which I'd rather not,

So bitter do I feel toward him

Whom I love more than anything.

But with him kindness and courtliness get me nowhere,

Neither my beauty, nor my worth, nor my intelligence.

In this way am I cheated and betrayed,

Just as I would be if I were ugly.

🔊 Listen to streaming music in an Active Listening Guide at CourseMate or in the eBook.

A Battle Carol for the English Court

Although England was geographically separate from continental Europe, there, too, medieval music was patronized primarily by the Church and the court. The most important English court, of course, was that of the king, and the most illustrious English king in the late Middle Ages was Henry V (1386–1422). Immortalized in three plays by Shakespeare (*Henry IV*, Parts I and II, and *Henry V*), Henry was an irresponsible youth who grew to become an able administrator and fearsome warrior. His reign occurred during the **Hundred Years' War**, the name given to a century-long series of military conflicts between the French and English that took place on French soil. Henry's greatest victory was near the small town of Agincourt on October 25, 1415. His army of a mere 10,000 fast-moving

The Stapleton Collection/Art Resource, NY

Figure 5.7

A remarkably accurate depiction of the Battle of Agincourt, showing the English archers on the left cutting down the French cavalry on the right. The artist clearly shows the English flag, with lions rampant (left), and the French one, with *fleurs de lis* (right).

pikesmen and archers sliced to pieces a slower-moving French host of 40,000 as it lumbered across a muddy field (Fig. 5.7). With the French defenses weakened, Henry moved southeast to Paris, where this English king was eventually crowned regent of France.

Henry V's stunning victory at the **Battle of Agincourt** was soon celebrated in song, in a genre of music called the carol. In the Middle Ages, a **carol** was a song in the local language that might celebrate Christmas, Easter, or even, as here, a military victory. Most carols make use of strophic form (see Ch. 3, "Strophic Form"), and each strophe is composed of a verse (new text) followed by a chorus (repeating text). The verse is sung by one or more soloists and the chorus by everyone (all singers). As the Agincourt carol shows, strophic form incorporating verse and chorus has been common in English popular music since the Middle Ages and still regulates the flow of perhaps 75 percent of pop songs in the English-speaking world today—just think of Adele's "Rolling in the Deep," for example. In the case of the Agincourt carol, as occasionally happens with Western Christmas carols, the verse is in English (medieval "middle English") and the chorus in Latin.

Listening Guide

Anonymous, Agincourt Carol (c. 1415)

Genre: Carol

Form: Strophic

WHAT TO LISTEN FOR: The narrative quality of the verses as they tell the tale of King Henry's victory and the louder, celebratory sounds of the chorus as all singers rejoice as one

0:00	8	Deo gratias, Anglia, redde pro Victoria! [England, render thanks to God for this victory!]	Chorus

Strophe 1

0:13	Our king went forth to Normandy With grace and might of chivalry; There God for him wrought marv'lously Wherefore England may call and cry. Deo gratias.	Verse
	Deo gratias, Anglia, redde pro Victoria!	Chorus

Strophe 2

0:57	He sette a sege, forsothe to say,	Verse
	To Harflu [Harfleur] towne with ryal array;	
	That toune he wan and made affray	
	That Fraunce shal rewe tyl domesday. Deo gratias.	
	Deo gratias, Anglia, redde pro Victoria!	Chorus

Strophe 3

1:40	Then went hym forth, owre king comely,	Verse
	In Agincourt feld he faught manly;	
	Thorw grace of Gode most marvelously,	
	He had both feld and victory. Deo gratias.	
	Deo gratias, Anglia, redde pro Victoria!	Chorus

Strophe 4

2:23	Ther lordys, erles and barone	Verse
	Were slayne and taken and that full soon,	
	And summe were broght into Lundone [London]	
	With joye and blisse and gret renone. Deo gratias.	
	Deo gratias, Anglia, redde pro Victoria!	Chorus

Strophe 5

3:06	Almighty God he keep owre kynge,	Verse
	His peple, and all his well-syllynge,	
	And give them grace without ending;	
	Then may we call and savely syng: Deo gratias.	
	Deo gratias, Anglia, redde pro Victoria!	Chorus

 Listen to streaming music in an Active Listening Guide at CourseMate or in the eBook.

Medieval Musical Instruments

In the late Middle Ages, the principal musical instrument of the monastery and cathedral was the large pipe organ. In fact, the organ was the only instrument admitted by Church authorities. At court, however, a variety of instrumental sounds could be heard. Some, such as the trumpet and early trombone, were rightly identified as loud (*haut*). Others, such as the harp, lute, flute (recorder), fiddle (*vielle*), and small portable organ, were classified as soft (*bas*).

Figure 5.8 shows a group of angels playing musical instruments of the late Middle Ages. Moving from left to right we see a straight-pipe trumpet, early trombone, small portative organ, harp, and vielle. The **vielle** (pronounced like the letters "V-L") was a distant ancestor of the modern violin. It usually had five strings tuned in a way that made it very easy to play block chords, the same way that guitars today can easily produce basic triads, or "bar chords." In fact, in medieval society the easily portable vielle served the function of our modern guitar: Not only could it play a melody, it could also provide a basic chordal accompaniment for songs and dances. To hear the sound of the vielle, return to *A chantar m'er* (in this chapter), where it provides a solo introduction and then an accompaniment to the voice.

Figure 5.8

Hans Memling (c. 1430–1491), musical angels painted for the walls of a hospital in Bruges, Belgium. The depiction of the instruments is remarkably detailed.

© Scala/Art Resource, NY

Key Words

Mass (61)	organum (64)	Ordinary of the Mass (66)	Hundred Years' War (69)
Gregorian chant (plainsong) (61)	tenor (65)	troubadour (68)	Battle of Agincourt (70)
musical notation (61)	mensural notation (65)	*trouvère* (68)	carol (70)
syllabic singing (62)	Proper of the Mass (66)	chanson (68)	vielle (71)
melismatic singing (62)			

For a complete review of this chapter, see the Main Points, Chapter Quiz, Flashcards, and Glossary in CourseMate.

f Join us on Facebook at **Listening to Music with Craig Wright**

Checklists of Musical Style

Middle Ages: 476–1450

REPRESENTATIVE COMPOSERS

Anonymous (the most prolific of all)	Leoninus	Machaut
Hildegard of Bingen	Perotinus	Countess of Dia

> A complete Checklist of Musical Style for the Middle Ages can be found at CourseMate for this text.

PRINCIPAL GENRES

Gregorian chant	troubadour and *trouvère* songs	carol
polyphonic Mass	popular song	instrumental dance

Melody	Moves mostly by step within narrow range; rarely uses chromatic notes of the scale.
Harmony	Most surviving medieval music, notably Gregorian chant and troubadour and *trouvère* songs, is monophonic—consisting of a single melodic line without harmonic support.
	Medieval polyphony (Mass, motet, and carol) has dissonant phrases ending with open, hollow-sounding, consonant chords.
Rhythm	Gregorian chant as well as troubadour and *trouvère* songs sung mainly in notes of equal value without clearly marked rhythms; medieval polyphony is composed mostly in triple meter (in honor of the Holy Trinity, theorists said) and uses repeating rhythmic patterns.
Color	Mainly vocal sounds (choir or soloists) within the church; popular music might include instruments like trumpet, trombone, fiddle, or harp.
Texture	Mostly monophonic—Gregorian chant and troubadour and *trouvère* songs are monophonic melodies.
	Medieval polyphony (two, three, or four independent lines) is mainly contrapuntal.
Form	Gregorian chant has no large-scale form, but each phrase of text generally receives its own phrase of music; strophic form in troubadour and *trouvère* songs and the carol; rondo form in the French chanson.

chapter SIX

Renaissance Music, 1450–1600

Figure 6.1

Andrea Palladio's Villa Rotunda (c. 1550) near Vicenza, Italy, clearly shows the extent to which classical architecture was reborn during the Renaissance. Elements of ancient Greek and Roman style include the columns with capitals, triangular pediments, and central rotunda.

Figure 6.2

Michelangelo's giant statue of David (1501–1504) expresses the heroic nobility of man in near-perfect form. Like Leonardo da Vinci, Michelangelo made a careful study of human anatomy.

Renaissance means literally "rebirth." Historians use the term broadly to designate a period of intellectual and artistic flowering that occurred first in Italy, then in France, and finally in England, during the years 1350–1600. Music historians, however, apply the term more narrowly to musical developments in those same countries during the period 1450–1600. The Renaissance was an age in which writers, artists, and architects turned to the classical world of ancient Greece and Rome to find models for civic and personal expression. How should city government operate? What should a building look like (Fig. 6.1)? What about the sculpture erected within it? How should a poet construct a poem? How ought an orator fashion a speech, or a musician a song? The remains of classical antiquity, some of which were just then being unearthed, provided the answer.

For musicians, however, the process of "rebirth" posed a unique problem: No actual music from Greek and Roman times survived to be rediscovered! Renaissance intellectuals instead turned to the writings of Greek philosophers, dramatists, and music theorists, which contained accounts of how ancient music was constructed and performed. In this way, Renaissance musicians came to realize that the ancients had one primary article of faith regarding music: It had enormous expressive power.

To recapture the lost power of music, Renaissance musicians worked to forge a wholly new alliance between text and music, one in which music underscored and enhanced the meaning of the text in an overt, mimetic way. If the verse depicted birds soaring gracefully in the sky, the accompanying music should be in a major key and ascend into a high range; if the text lamented the pain and sorrow of sin, the music ought to be in a minor key, full of dark and dissonant chords. Compared to medieval compositions, those of the Renaissance contained a greater range of expression within each piece, as well as from one piece to the next. A similar development occurred in Renaissance visual arts, which now likewise allowed for a greater range of emotional expression. Compare, for example, the highly contrasting moods of two images created within a few years of each other—the serene confidence of Michelangelo's *David* (Fig. 6.2) and the painful anguish of Mathias Grünewald's *Saint John and the Two Marys* (Fig. 6.3).

Attending the rebirth of the arts and letters of classical antiquity was a

Figure 6.3

The expressive grief of the Virgin, Saint John, and Mary Magdalene mark this portion of an altarpiece (1510–1515) painted by Mathias Grünewald.

renewed interest in humankind itself. We have come to call this enthusiastic self-interest humanism. Simply said, **humanism** is the belief that people are something more than mere conduits for gifts descending from heaven, that they have the ability to create many things good and beautiful as well as the capacity to enjoy them. The culture of the Middle Ages, as we have seen, was fostered by the Church, which emphasized a collective submission to the Almighty, hiding the human form beneath layers of clothing. In medieval art, only the images of kings, divinities, and saints were generally depicted, and life on this earth was viewed as a temporary station on the road to Heaven or Hell. The culture of the Renaissance, by contrast, rejoiced in the human form in all its fullness, expressed in works such as Michelangelo's *David*. The Renaissance also introduced a new genre of painting—the portrait—which depicted worldly individuals enjoying the good life (Fig. 6.4). Renaissance humanists looked outward at the world with wonder and indulged a passion for invention and discovery. Today, when college students take courses in the "humanities," they study these arts, letters, and historical events that have enriched the human spirit over the centuries.

True to the humanistic spirit of the time, the genius of the Renaissance asserted a personal identity and carried a distinctive name, such as "Leonardo," "Michelangelo," or "Josquin"—this in contrast to the faceless, often anonymous, master of the Middle Ages. If artistic inspiration still came from God, it could be shaped in personal ways by an innovative creator. In this environment, the best Renaissance artists attained "star power," which gave them independence, recognition, and something more: money. Now a gifted artist might vie for the highest-paying commission, just as a sought-after composer might play one patron against another for the highest salary. And money, in turn, primed the pump of creativity and led to greater productivity. The prolific Michelangelo left an estate worth some $10 million in terms of today's money.

If artists were paid more in the Renaissance, it was because art was now thought to be more valuable. For the first time in the Christian West, there emerged the concept of a "work of art": the belief that an object might not only serve as a religious symbol but also be a creation of purely aesthetic value and enjoyment. Music in the Renaissance was composed by proud artists who aimed to give pleasure. Their music conversed not with eternity, but with the listener. It was judged good or bad only to the degree that it pleased fellow human beings. Music and the other arts could now be freely evaluated, and composers and painters could be ranked according to their greatness. Artistic judgment, appreciation, and criticism entered Western thought for the first time in the humanistic Renaissance.

Figure 6.4

Leonardo da Vinci's portrait of Cecilia Gallerani, called *The Lady with the Ermine* (1496). Cecilia was the mistress of the duke of Milan, Leonardo's patron, and she clearly enjoyed the finer things in life, including clothing, jewelry, and exotic animals like the ermine, or mink, that she holds.

Watch a video of Craig Wright's Open Yale Course class session 15, "Gregorian Chant and Music in the Sistine Chapel," at CourseMate for this text.

Josquin Desprez (c. 1455–1521) and the Renaissance Motet

Figure 6.5

The only surviving portrait of Josquin Desprez

Josquin Desprez (pronounced "josh-CAN day-PRAY") was one of the greatest composers of the Renaissance or, indeed, of any age (Fig. 6.5). He was born somewhere near the present border between France and Belgium about 1455 and died in the same region in 1521. Yet, like so many musicians of northern France, Josquin was drawn to Italy to pursue professional and monetary gain. Between 1484 and 1504, he worked for various dukes in Milan and Ferrara, and in Rome in the **Sistine Chapel**, the pope's private chapel in the Vatican (Fig. 6.6). Evidence suggests that Josquin had a temperamental, egotistical personality, one typical of many artists of the Renaissance. He would fly into a rage when singers tampered with his music; he composed only when he, not his patron, wished; and he demanded a salary twice that of composers only slightly less gifted. Yet Josquin's contemporaries recognized his

Figure 6.6

Interior of the Sistine Chapel. The high altar and Michelangelo's *Last Judgment* are at the far end; the balcony for the singers, including Josquin Desprez, is at the lower right. Josquin carved his name on the door to this balcony, and the graffito remains there to this day.

genius. Martin Luther said of him: "Josquin is master of the notes, which must express what he desires; other composers can do only what the notes dictate." And Florentine humanist Cosimo Bartoli compared him to the great Michelangelo (1475–1564):

> Josquin may be said to have been a prodigy of nature, as our Michelangelo Buonarroti has been in architecture, painting, and sculpture; for just as there has not yet been anyone who in his compositions approaches Josquin, so Michelangelo, among those active in his arts, is still alone and without a peer. Both Josquin and Michelangelo have opened the eyes of all those who delight in these arts or are to delight in them in the future.

Josquin composed in all of the musical genres of his day, but he excelled in writing motets, some seventy of which survive under his name. The Renaissance **motet** can be defined as a composition for a polyphonic choir, setting a Latin text on a sacred subject, and intended to be sung either at a religious service in a church or at home in private devotion. While composers of the Renaissance continued to set the prescribed text of the Mass, they increasingly sought more dramatic texts in the Old Testament of the Bible—specifically, in the expressive Psalms and the mournful Lamentations. A vivid text cried out for an equally vivid musical setting, allowing the composer to fulfill a mandate of Renaissance humanism: Use music to heighten the meaning of the word.

Josquin's motet *Ave Maria* (*Hail Mary*; c. 1485) honors the Virgin Mary and employs the standard four voice parts: soprano, alto, tenor, and bass (S, A, T, and B in Ex. 6.1). As the motet unfolds, the listener hears the voices enter in succession with the same musical motive. This process is called **imitation**, a polyphonic procedure whereby one or more voices duplicate, in turn, the notes of a melody.

Download another example by Josquin—*Miserere mei Deus*—from the iTunes playlist at CourseMate for this text.

EXAMPLE 6.1

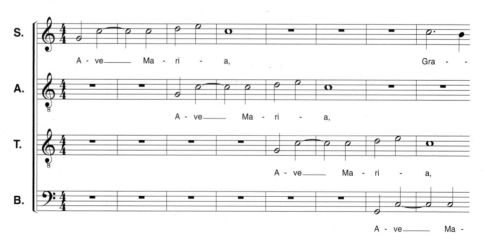

Josquin also sometimes has one pair of voices imitate another—the tenor and bass, for example, imitating what the alto and soprano have just sung.

EXAMPLE 6.2

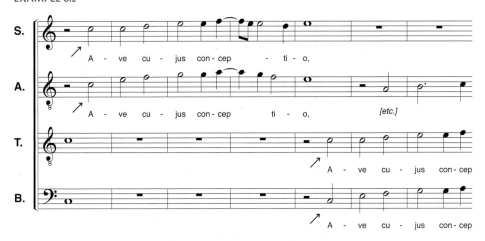

Josquin builds his *Ave Maria* much as a humanistic orator would construct a persuasive speech. The work begins with a salutation to the Virgin, sung in imitation. Thereafter, a key word, "Ave" ("Hail"), sparks a succession of salutes to the Virgin, each making reference to one of her principal feast days during the church year (Conception, Nativity, Annunciation, Purification, and Assumption). Along the way the music overtly mimics the text; for example, on the words "Coelestria, terrestria, nova replet laetitia" ("Fills heaven and earth with new joy") Josquin raises the pitch of all voices excitedly. Then he takes this gesture one step further, literally jumping for joy, by leaping upward an octave on the Latin *laetitia* ("joy"). At the end of the motet comes a final exclamation, "O Mater Dei, memento mei. Amen" ("O Mother of God, be mindful of me. Amen"). These last words are set to striking harmonies, with each syllable of text receiving a new chord. The chordal, homophonic treatment allows this final phrase to stand out with absolute clarity. Here Josquin reaffirms the key principle of musical humanism: Text and music must work together to persuade and move the listener. They must persuade the Virgin Mary as well, for they plead with her to intercede on behalf of the needy soul at the hour of death.

Finally, notice in our recording of Josquin's *Ave Maria* that no instruments accompany the voices. This unaccompanied mode of performance is called **a cappella** singing, and it was a hallmark of the Sistine Chapel during the Renaissance. This tradition continues to the present day: The pope's choir at the Sistine Chapel still sings all its religious music—chant, Masses, and motets—without organ or any other instruments. If you belong to an a cappella singing group, you, too, are perpetuating this venerable style of performance.

Hear another beautiful motet by Josquin, and follow the score, in the YouTube playlist at CourseMate for this text.

Listening Guide

Josquin Desprez, Motet, *Ave Maria* (c. 1485)

Genre: Sacred motet

Texture: Mostly imitative counterpoint (polyphony)

5   2
1/9   1/5

WHAT TO LISTEN FOR: Opening using imitation; five sections exalting the events in the life of the Virgin; and a final plea for salvation

0:00	9 / 5	All four voices present each two-word phrase in turn.	Ave Maria, gratia plena. Dominus tecum, virgo serena.	Hail Mary, full of grace. The Lord be with you, serene Virgin.
0:46		Soprano and alto are imitated by tenor and bass; then all four voices work to peak on "laetitia" ("joy").	Ave cujus conceptio, Solemni plena gaudio, Coelestia, terrestria, Nova replet laetitia.	Hail to you whose conception, With solemn rejoicing, Fills heaven and earth With new joy.

(continued)

1:20	Imitation in pairs; soprano and alto answered by tenor and bass	Ave cujus nativitas Nostra fuit solemnitas, Ut lucifer lux oriens, Verum solem praeveniens.	Hail to you whose birth Was to be our solemnity, As the rising morning star Anticipates the true sun.
1:58	More imitation by pairs of voices; soprano and alto followed by tenor and bass	Ave pia humilitas, Sine viro foecunditas, Cujus annuntiatio, Nostra fuit salvatio.	Hail pious humility, Fruitful without man, Whose annunciation Was to be our salvation.
2:26	Chordal writing; meter changes from duple to triple.	Ave vera virginitas, Immaculata castitas, Cujus purificatio Nostra fuit purgatio.	Hail true virginity, Immaculate chastity, Whose purification Was to be our purgation.
3:03	Return to duple meter; soprano and alto imitated by tenor and bass	Ave praeclara omnibus Angelicis virtutibus, Cujus fuit assumption Nostra glorificatio.	Hail shining example Of all angelic virtues, Whose assumption Was to be our glorification.
3:58	Strict chordal writing; clear presentation of text	O Mater Dei, Memento mei. Amen.	O Mother of God, Be mindful of me. Amen.

◀)) Listen to streaming music in an Active Listening Guide at CourseMate or in the eBook.

◀)) Take online Listening Exercise 6.1 and get feedback at CourseMate or in the eBook.

The Counter-Reformation and Palestrina (1525–1594)

To hear music in the style of Palestrina sung in one of the Roman churches in which he worked, listen to The Tallis Scholars, Allegri, "Miserere," in the YouTube playlist at CourseMate for this text.

Figure 6.7

Portrait of Giovanni Palestrina, the first important composer of the Church to have been a layman rather than a member of the clergy

© Scala/Art Resource, NY

On October 31, 1517, an obscure Augustinian monk named Martin Luther nailed to the door of the castle church at Wittenberg, Germany, ninety-five complaints against the Roman Catholic Church—his famous Ninety-five Theses. With this defiant act Luther began what has come to be called the Protestant Reformation. Luther and his fellow reformers sought to bring an end to corruption within the Roman Catholic Church, typified by the practice of selling indulgences (forgiving sin in exchange for money). By the time the Protestant Reformation had run its course, most of Germany, Switzerland, and the Low Countries, and all of England, as well as parts of France, Austria, Bohemia, Poland, and Hungary, had gone over to the Protestant cause. The established Roman Catholic Church was shaken to its very foundations.

In response to the Protestant Reformation, the leaders of the Church of Rome gathered in northern Italy to discuss their own reform in what proved to be an almost two-decades-long conference, the **Council of Trent** (1545–1563). Here began the **Counter-Reformation**, a conservative, sometimes austere, movement that changed not only religious practices, but also art, architecture, and music. Nudity in religious art was covered over, and offending books, sometimes along with their authors, were burned. In the realm of musical composition, the reformers of the Church of Rome were particularly alarmed by the incessant entry of voices in musical imitation; they feared that excessively dense counterpoint was burying the word of the Lord. As one well-placed bishop said mockingly:

In our times they [composers] have put all their industry and effort into the writing of imitative passages, so that while one voice says "Sanctus," another says "Sabaoth," still another says "Gloria tua," with howling, bellowing, and stammering, so that they more nearly resemble cats in January than flowers in May.

One important composer who got caught up in this debate about the appropriate style for church music was Giovanni Pierluigi da Palestrina (1525–1594; Fig. 6.7). In 1555, Palestrina composed a *Missa Papae Marcelli (Mass for Pope Marcellus)* that conformed to all the requirements for proper church music prescribed by the Council of Trent. His polyphonic Mass was devoid of a strong beat and "catchy" rhythms, and it privileged simple counterpoint over complex, imitative polyphony, all qualities that allowed the text to project with great clarity. Although the fathers of the Council of Trent had once considered banning all polyphony from the services of the Church, they now came to see that this somber, serene style of religious music could be a useful vehicle to inspire the faithful to greater devotion. For his role in securing a place for composed polyphony within the established Church, Palestrina came to be called, perhaps with some exaggeration, the "savior of church music."

To download Allegri's "Miserere," go to the iTunes playlist at CourseMate for this text.

Male Choirs: The Castrato

As mentioned in our discussion of medieval music (Ch. 5), women were allowed to sing in the early Roman Catholic Church in convents (Fig. 6.8) but not in any public church. Similarly, women were not permitted to appear in public in theatrical productions within territories under strict Church control. Thus, most church choirs in the Middle Ages and Renaissance were exclusively male. But who, then, sang the soprano and alto parts when polyphony was performed? The most common practice was to assign these parts to adult males who sang in what is called "head voice," or **falsetto**. Alternatively, choirboys might be used, but they were expensive to house and educate. Finally, beginning in 1562, the **castrato** (castrated male) voice was introduced into the papal chapel, mainly as a money-saving measure. A single castrato could produce as much volume as two falsettists or three or four boys. Castrati were renowned for their power and their great lung capacity, which allowed them to execute unusually long phrases in a single breath. Surprisingly, castrati sopranos remained a hallmark of the papal chapel until 1903, when they were officially banned by Pope Pius X. The voice of one castrato, Alessandro Moreschi, known as the "Last Castrato," was captured on a phonograph recording between 1902 and 1904 and is readily available for listening today.

In our recording of sections of Palestrina's *Missa Papae Marcelli*, women take the soprano line, while male falsettists and women share the alto part. To make their sound as close as possible to that of a choirboy, the women sing with almost no vibrato.

All-male choir with choirboys for the soprano part, as depicted in a sixteenth-century Italian fresco

Hear Alessandro Moreschi, the "Last Castrato," in the YouTube playlist at CourseMate for this text.

Figure 6.8

Although public church choirs in the Middle Ages and Renaissance were all-male ensembles, women could be heard at home and at court. And women, too, sang in churches, specifically in convents, where they performed all of the chant and, when required, polyphony. In this illumination from a fifteenth-century English manuscript, nuns sing from their choir stalls.

Palestrina proudly claimed that his *Missa Papae Marcelli* was written "in a new manner." By this he meant that he had set the text of the Mass with exceptional clarity, allowing the music to inspire the listener to greater piety and devotion. To see how Palestrina imposed this clarity of expression through music, let us explore two contrasting sections of this work. The first is the *Gloria* of the Mass, a lengthy hymn of praise in honor of the majestic Christ; here Palestrina commands the singers to declaim the text triumphantly, mostly in block chords, with the rhythm of the music emphasizing the accents in the Latin text. Who could possibly miss the meaning of the words as the singers seemingly spit out the text? By contrast, the *Agnus Dei* of the Mass commemorates the tender, merciful Lamb of God; now Palestrina deploys imitation with peacefully overlapping lines, but even here each phrase of text is kept separate from the next and remains clearly audible. What Palestrina proved to the prelates of the Council of Trent remains true for us today: Clarity of expression and beauty are not mutually exclusive.

Listening Guide

Giovanni Pierluigi da Palestrina, *Gloria* and *Agnus Dei* of the *Missa Papae Marcelli* (1555)

1/10–11

Genre: Sacred Mass

Texture: Mostly homophonic in *Gloria;* mostly polyphonic in *Agnus Dei*

WHAT TO LISTEN FOR: In the *Gloria*, how the mainly homophonic texture allows for a clear text declamation, and in the *Agnus Dei*, how the mainly polyphonic texture gives the feeling of multiple lines of Gregorian chant sounding simultaneously

Gloria Part I

0:00 [10]	Priest chants opening phrase.	Gloria in excelsis Deo,	Glory to God in the highest,
0:10	Six-voice choir completes phrase.	et in terra pax hominibus bonae voluntatis.	and on earth peace to men of good will.
0:26	Four similar Latin phrases clearly declaimed	Laudamus te. Benedicimus te. Adoramus te. Glorificamus te.	We praise you. We bless you. We worship you. We glorify you.
0:44	Loud choral exclamation	Gratias agimus tibi propter magnam gloriam tuam.	We give thanks to you because of your great glory.
1:04	Varying combinations of four of six voices address the Lord.	Domine Deus, rex caelestis Deus Pater omnipotens	Lord, God, king of heaven God the almighty Father
		Domine, Fili unigenite, Jesu Christe;	Lord, only begotten Son, Jesus Christ;
		Domine Deus,	Lord God,
		Agnus Dei,	Lamb of God,
2:20	Full cadence	Filius Patris.	Son of the Father.

Agnus Dei Part I

0:00 [11]	All six voices enter in turn in imitation.	A - gnus De - - [i]	Lamb of God,
0:50	Imitation quietly continues with new phrase.	qui tol - lis pec - - ca - ta	Who takes away the sins [of the earth]

mi - se - re - re no - [bis]

 Listen to streaming music in an Active Listening Guide at CourseMate or in the eBook.

Palestrina's serene music best captures the somber, restrained spirit of the Counter-Reformation, embodying in its quiet simplicity all that Roman Catholic authority thought proper church music should be. After his death in 1594, the legend of Palestrina, "savior of church music," continued to grow. Later composers such as Bach (Mass in B minor, 1733) and Mozart (Requiem Mass, 1791) incorporated elements of Palestrina's style into their religious compositions. Even in our universities today, courses in counterpoint for advanced music students usually include some practice in composing in the pure, contrapuntally correct style of Palestrina. Thus the spirit of the Counter-Reformation, distilled into a set of contrapuntal rules, continues to influence musicians long after the Renaissance came to an end.

Listen to the *Gloria* from Palestrina's *Missa Papae Marcelli*, and follow the score, in the YouTube playlist at CourseMate for this text.

Download another selection by Palestrina, "Con che soavità," from the iTunes playlist at CourseMate for this text.

Popular Music in the Renaissance

The motets and Masses of Josquin and Palestrina represent the "high" art of the Renaissance—learned music for the Church. But popular music existed as well and, unlike with much of the popular music of the Middle Ages, we have a good general sense of how it sounded. During the Middle Ages, most popular musicians, like pop musicians today, worked without benefit of written musical notation. In fact, most people in the Middle Ages couldn't read—text or music—and manuscripts (by definition copied by hand) were exceedingly expensive.

All this began to change, however, when Johann Gutenberg invented printing by movable type around 1460. Printing revolutionized the world of information in the late fifteenth century no less than the computer did in the late twentieth century. Hundreds of copies of a book could be produced quickly and cheaply once the type had been set. The first printed book of music appeared in Venice in 1501, and to this important event can be traced the origins of today's music industry. The standard press run for a printed book of music then was usually 500 copies. Mass production put the music book within reach of the banker, merchant, lawyer, and shopkeeper. "How to" manuals encouraged ordinary men and women to learn to read musical notation so they could sing and play an instrument at home. The learned amateur had arrived.

Germanisches Nationalmuseum

Figure 6.9

The band of municipal musicians employed by the city of Nuremberg, Germany, as painted by Georg Eberlein, c. 1500, after a mural by Albrecht Dürer in the Nuremberg Town Hall. The core instruments are the two early trombones and two shawms; also visible are a cornetto (left), recorder, and drum.

Dance Music

Our fascination with dance didn't begin with *Dancing with the Stars*. Dancing had existed, of course, since the beginning of time, although almost none of its music survives because it was passed along orally and not in written form. During the Renaissance, however, musicians came to benefit from the growth of literacy. Publishers now issued collections of dance music in notation, rightly assuming that many among the newly emergent middle class could read the notes and were ready to dance at home. Not wishing to miss a single sale, they issued volumes for wind instruments, keyboard instruments, "and any other instruments that might seem appropriate." A favorite ensemble—something akin to the Renaissance dance band—included an early trombone and a predecessor of the modern oboe, called the **shawm**. Its piercing tone made the melody easy to hear.

By far the most popular type of dance of the mid-sixteenth century was the **pavane**, a slow, gliding dance in duple meter performed by couples holding hands. It was often followed by a contrasting **galliard**, a fast, leaping dance in triple meter. (For a painting believed to show Queen Elizabeth I leaping in a galliard, see Fig. 6.11.) Around 1550 the French publisher Jacques Moderne issued a collection of twenty-five anonymous dances that included several pavanes and galliards. Moderne titled this collection *Musicque de joye*—listen and you'll understand why.

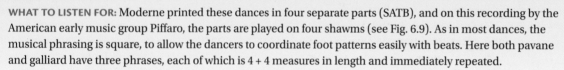

Listening Guide

Jacques Moderne, publisher, *Musicque de joye* (c. 1550)

Anonymous, Pavane and Galliard

Genre: Instrumental dance

Texture: Homophonic

WHAT TO LISTEN FOR: Moderne printed these dances in four separate parts (SATB), and on this recording by the American early music group Piffaro, the parts are played on four shawms (see Fig. 6.9). As in most dances, the musical phrasing is square, to allow the dancers to coordinate foot patterns easily with beats. Here both pavane and galliard have three phrases, each of which is 4 + 4 measures in length and immediately repeated.

Pavane (slow duple meter)			Galliard (fast triple meter)		
0:05 `12`	Phrase 1		1:43 `13`	0:04	Phrase 1
0:21	Phrase 1 repeated but with top line ornamented		1:54	0:11	Phrase 1 repeated
0:37	Phrase 2		2:02	0:19	Phrase 2
0:53	Phrase 2 repeated but with top line ornamented		2:10	0:27	Phrase 2 repeated
1:09	Phrase 3		2:17	0:34	Phrase 3
1:26	Phrase 3 repeated but with top line ornamented		2:25	0:42	Phrase 3 repeated

🔊 Listen to streaming music in an Active Listening Guide at CourseMate or in the eBook.

Figure 6.10

Singers of a four-part madrigal during the mid-sixteenth century. Women were very much a part of this secular, nonreligious music making.

© Giraudon/The Bridgeman Art Library International

The Madrigal

About 1530, a new kind of popular song took Europe by storm: the madrigal. A **madrigal** is a piece for several solo voices (usually four or five) that sets a vernacular poem, most often about love, to music (Fig. 6.10). The madrigal arose in Italy but soon spread to northern European countries. So popular did the madrigal become that by 1630, some 40,000 pieces had been printed by publishers eager to satisfy public demand. The madrigal was a truly social art, one that both men and women could enjoy.

Of all the musical genres of the Renaissance, the madrigal best exemplifies the humanist requirement that music express the meaning of the text. In a typical madrigal, each word or phrase of poetry receives its own musical gesture. Thus, when the madrigal text says "chase after" or "follow quickly," the music becomes fast, and one voice chases after another in musical imitation. For words such as "pain," "anguish," "death," and "cruel fate," the madrigal composer almost invariably employs a twisting chromatic scale or a biting dissonance. This practice of depicting the text by means of a descriptive musical gesture, whether subtly or jokingly as a musical pun, is called **word painting**. Word painting became all the rage with madrigal composers in Italy and England. Even today such musical clichés as a falling melody for "fainting" and a dissonance for "pain" are called **madrigalisms**.

Although the madrigal was born in Italy, popular favor soon carried it over the Alps to Germany, Denmark, the Low Countries, and to the England of Shakespeare's day. A single madrigal with English text will allow us to explore the "one to one" relationship between music and word that defined this new musical genre.

In 1601, musician Thomas Morley published a collection of twenty-four madrigals in honor of Virgin Queen Elizabeth (1533–1603), which he entitled *The Triumphes of Oriana*. (Oriana, a legendary British princess and maiden, was a poetic nickname of Queen Elizabeth.) Among these madrigals was *As Vesta Was from Latmos Hill Descending* composed by royal organist Thomas Weelkes (1576–1623). The text of the madrigal, likely fashioned by Weelkes himself, is a rather confused mixture of images from classical mythology: The Roman goddess Vesta, descending the Greek mountain of Latmos, spies Oriana (Elizabeth) ascending the hill; the nymphs and shepherds attending the goddess Diana desert her to sing the praises of Oriana. The sole virtue of this doggerel is that it provides frequent opportunity for word painting in music. As the text commands, the music descends, ascends, runs, mingles imitatively, and offers "mirthful tunes" to the maiden queen. Elizabeth herself played lute and harpsichord, and loved to dance (Fig. 6.11). Weelkes saw fit to end his madrigal with cries of "Long live fair Oriana." Indeed, the fair queen did enjoy a long and glorious reign of some forty-five years—thus our term "Elizabethan Age."

Madrigals such as Weelkes's *As Vesta Was from Latmos Hill Descending* were popular because they were fun to sing. Vocal lines were written within a comfortable range, melodies were often triadic, rhythms were catchy, and the music was full of puns. When Vesta descends the mountain, so, too, her music moves down the scale; when Oriana (Queen Elizabeth) ascends, her music does likewise; when Diana, the goddess of virginity, is all alone—you guessed it, we hear a solo voice. With sport like this to be had, no wonder the popularity of the madrigal endured beyond the Renaissance. In fact, in the seventeenth century the madrigal spawned another genre of popular vocal music called the glee, and groups to sing it proliferated. Today, the practices of the early English madrigal and glee remain with us in the form of a cappella madrigal groups and university glee clubs.

Figure 6.11

A painting believed to show Queen Elizabeth dancing a galliard with Robert Dudley, Earl of Leicester, in 1575. The exact nature of the relationship between Dudley and the Virgin Queen is still a matter debated by historians.

By kind permission of Viscount De L'Isle from his private collection at Penshurst Place, Kent, England (http://www.penshurstplace.com)

Listening Guide

Thomas Weelkes, *As Vesta Was from Latmos Hill Descending* (1601)

5   2
1/14   1/6

Genre: Madrigal

Texture: Changes according to dictates of text

WHAT TO LISTEN FOR: One to one relationship between text and music in which the music acts out, like a mime, each word or phrase of the text

0:00 [14] [6]	Opening homophonic chords give way to falling pitches on "descending."	As Vesta was from Latmos Hill descending,
0:12	Imitation falls, then rises on word "ascending."	She spied a maiden Queen the same ascending,

(*continued*)

0:32	Simple repeating notes suggest simple country swains.	Attended on by all the shepherds' swain;
0:49	All voices come "running down amain."	To whom Diana's darlings came running down amain,
1:13	Two voices exemplify "two by two," then three "three by three."	First two by two, then three by three together,
1:23	Solo voice highlights "all alone."	Leaving their goddess all alone, hasted thither;
1:35	Imitative entries suggest "mingling."	And mingling with the shepherds of her train,
1:42	Light, rapid singing produces "mirthful tunes."	With mirthful tunes her presence did entertain.
1:58	Stark chords announce final acclamation.	Then sang the shepherds and nymphs of Diana:
2:10	Long life to the queen is declaimed endlessly.	Long live fair Oriana.

Listen to streaming music in an Active Listening Guide at CourseMate or in the eBook.

Take online Listening Exercise 6.2 and receive feedback at CourseMate or in the eBook.

Key Words

Renaissance (74)	Council of Trent (78)	galliard (82)
humanism (75)	Counter-Reformation (78)	madrigal (82)
Sistine Chapel (75)	falsetto (79)	word painting (83)
motet (76)	castrato (79)	madrigalism (83)
imitation (76)	shawm (82)	
a cappella (77)	pavane (82)	

For a complete review of this chapter, see the Main Points, Chapter Quiz, Flashcards, and Glossary in CourseMate.

 Join us on Facebook at **Listening to Music with Craig Wright**

Checklists of Musical Style

Renaissance: 1450–1600

REPRESENTATIVE COMPOSERS

Anonymous (now less prolific)   Palestrina
Josquin Desprez   Weelkes

A complete Checklist of Musical Style for the Renaissance can be found at CourseMate for this text.

PRINCIPAL GENRES

polyphonic Mass   instrumental dances (pavane and galliard)
sacred motet   secular song and madrigal

Melody   Mainly stepwise motion within moderately narrow range; still mainly diatonic, but some intense chromaticism found in madrigals from end of period

Harmony	More careful use of dissonance than in Middle Ages as the triad, a consonant chord, becomes the basic building block of harmony
Rhythm	Duple meter is now as common as triple meter; rhythm in sacred vocal music (Mass and motet) is relaxed and without strong downbeats; rhythm in secular music (madrigal and instrumental dance) is usually lively and catchy
Color	Although more music for instruments alone has survived, the predominant sound remains that of unaccompanied (a cappella) vocal music, whether for soloists or for choir
Texture	Mainly polyphonic: imitative counterpoint for four or five vocal lines is heard throughout Masses, motets, and madrigals; occasional passages of chordal homophonic texture are inserted for variety
Form	Strict musical forms are not often used; most Masses, motets, madrigals, and instrumental dances are through composed—they have no musical repetitions and hence no standard formal plan

part THREE

The Baroque Period, 1600–1750

1600	1610	1620	1630	1640	1650	1660	1670

BAROQUE

● 1607 Claudio Monteverdi's opera *Orfeo* premiers in Mantua

1618–1648 Thirty Years' War in Europe

● 1626 Saint Peter's Basilica completed

● 1643 Louis XIV becomes king of France

● 1650s Barbara Strozzi publishes chamber cantatas in Venice

● c. 1660 Antonio Stradivari begins to make violins in Cremona

● 1669 King Louis XIV begins construction of Versailles

The dominant style of architecture, painting, sculpture, music, and dance in the period 1600–1750 is called Baroque. It originated first in Rome, as a way to glorify the Counter-Reformation Catholic Church, and then spread beyond Italy to Spain, France, Germany, Austria, the Low Countries, and England. The artists who created Baroque art worked mainly for the pope and important rulers throughout Europe. Thus, Baroque art is akin to the "official" art of the ruling establishment. Whereas the music of the Renaissance was marked by classical balance and rational restraint, that of the Baroque era is full of grandeur, extravagance, drama, and overt sensuality. This is as true for the music of Claudio Monteverdi at the beginning of the Baroque period as it is for that of Bach and Handel at the end. Finally, during the Baroque period, several new musical genres emerge: opera, cantata, and oratorio enter the realm of vocal music, and sonata and concerto appear among the instrumental types.

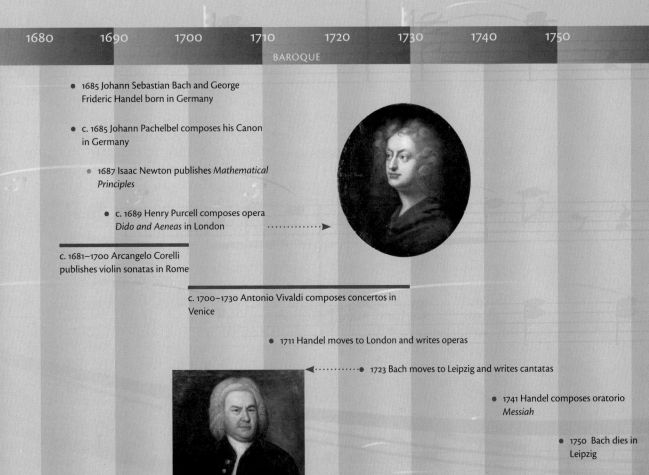

| 1680 | 1690 | 1700 | 1710 | 1720 | 1730 | 1740 | 1750 |

BAROQUE

● 1685 Johann Sebastian Bach and George Frideric Handel born in Germany

● c. 1685 Johann Pachelbel composes his Canon in Germany

● 1687 Isaac Newton publishes *Mathematical Principles*

● c. 1689 Henry Purcell composes opera *Dido and Aeneas* in London ·············▶

c. 1681–1700 Arcangelo Corelli publishes violin sonatas in Rome

c. 1700–1730 Antonio Vivaldi composes concertos in Venice

● 1711 Handel moves to London and writes operas

◀··········● 1723 Bach moves to Leipzig and writes cantatas

● 1741 Handel composes oratorio *Messiah*

● 1750 Bach dies in Leipzig

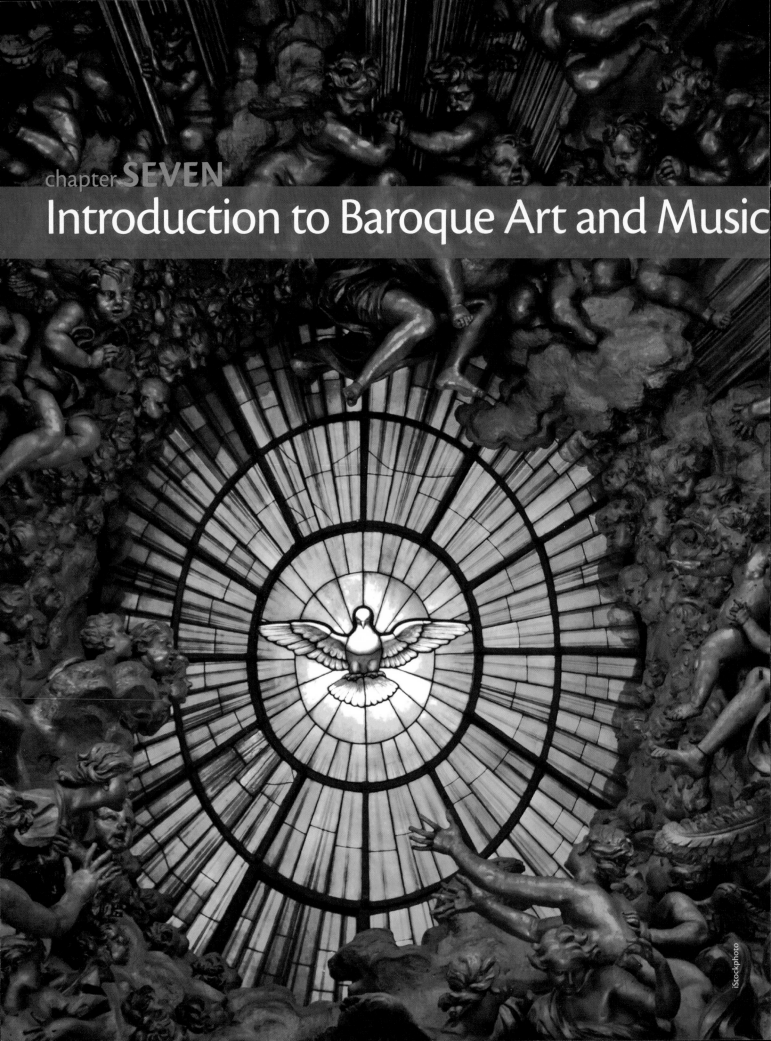

chapter **SEVEN**

Introduction to Baroque Art and Music

iStockphoto

Music historians agree, with unusual unanimity, that Baroque music first appeared in Italy in the early seventeenth century. Around 1600, the older equal-voiced choral polyphony of the Renaissance receded in importance as a new, more flamboyant, soloistic style gained in popularity. Eventually, the new style was given a new name: Baroque.

Baroque is the term used to describe the arts generally during the period 1600–1750. It is taken from the Portuguese word *barroco*, referring to a pearl of irregular shape then used in jewelry and fine decorations. Critics applied the term *baroque* to indicate excessive ornamentation in the visual arts and a rough, bold instrumental sound in music. Thus, originally, *baroque* had a negative connotation: It signified distortion, excess, and extravagance. Only during the twentieth century, with a newfound appreciation of the painting of Peter Paul Rubens (1577–1640) and the music of J. S. Bach (1685–1750), among others, has the term *baroque* come to assume a positive meaning in Western cultural history.

Baroque Architecture and Music

What strikes us most when standing before a monument of Baroque design, such as the basilica of Saint Peter in Rome or the palace of Versailles outside Paris, is that everything is constructed on the grandest scale. The plazas, buildings, colonnades, gardens, and fountains are all massive. Look at the ninety-foot-high altar canopy inside Saint Peter's, designed by Gian Lorenzo Bernini (1598–1680), and imagine how it dwarfs the priest below (Fig. 7.1). Outside the basilica, a circle of colonnades forms a courtyard large enough to encompass several football fields (Fig. 7.2). Or consider the French king's palace of Versailles, constructed during the reign of Louis XIV (1643–1715), so monumental in scope that it formed a small independent city, home to several thousand court functionaries (see Fig. 9.2).

Figure 7.1

The high altar at Saint Peter's Basilica, Rome, with baldachin by Gian Lorenzo Bernini. Standing more than ninety feet high, this canopy is marked by twisted columns and curving shapes, color, and movement, all typical of Baroque art. With 164,000 square feet, St. Peter's is by far the largest church in the world.

© Scala/Art Resource, NY

Figure 7.2

Saint Peter's Square, designed by Bernini in the mid-seventeenth century. The expanse is so colossal it seems to swallow people, cars, and buses.

© Bob Krist/Corbis

Figure 7.3

Church of the monastery of Saint Florian, Austria (1686–1708). The powerful pillars and arches set a strong structural framework, while the painted ceiling and heavily foliated capitals provide decoration and warmth.

© Interfoto/Alamy

The music composed for performance in such vast expanses could also be grandiose. While at first the Baroque orchestra was small, under King Louis XIV it sometimes swelled to more than eighty players. Similarly, choral works for Baroque churches sometimes required twenty-four, forty-eight, or even fifty-three separate lines or parts. These compositions for massive choral forces epitomize the grand or "colossal" Baroque.

Once the exteriors of the large Baroque palaces and churches were built, the artists of the time rushed in to fill these expanses with abundant, perhaps even excessive, decoration. It was as if the architect had created a large vacuum, and into it raced the painter, sculptor, and carver to fill the void. Examine again part of the interior of St. Peter's (see chapter-opening photo) and notice the brilliant but irregular design of the glass, as well as the riot of decoration in the surrounding sculptures. Or consider the Austrian monastery of Saint Florian (Fig. 7.3); massive columns are present, yet the frieze connecting them is richly decorated, as is the ceiling above. Here elaborate scrolls and floral capitals add warmth and humanity to what would otherwise be a vast, cold space.

Similarly, when expressed in the music of the Baroque era, this love of energetic detail within large-scale compositions took the form of a highly ornamental melody set upon a solid chordal foundation. Sometimes the decoration almost seems to overrun the fundamental harmonic structure of the piece. Notice in Example 7.1 the abundance of melodic flourishes in just a few measures of music for violin by Arcangelo Corelli (1653–1713). Such ornaments were equally popular with the singers of the early Baroque period, when the cult of the solo virtuoso first emerged.

EXAMPLE 7.1

Arcangelo Corelli's sonata for violin and *basso continuo*, Opus 5, No. 1. The bass provides the structural support, while the violin adds elaborate decoration above.

 ## Baroque Painting and Music

Many of the principles at work in Baroque architecture are also found in Baroque painting and music. Baroque canvases are usually large and colorful. Most important, they are overtly dramatic. Drama in painting is created by means of contrast: Bold

Figure 7.4

Rubens's *The Horrors of War* (1638) is a reaction to the Thirty Years' War (1618–1648), which ravaged Europe at this time. Here Mars, the god of war (center, wearing a military helmet), is pulled to the right by Fury and to the left by a mostly naked Venus, goddess of love. Beneath these figures, the populace suffers, a music book is trampled, and a lute lies broken.

colors are pitted against one another; bright light is set against darkness; and lines are placed at right angles to one another, which suggests tension and energetic movement. Figure 7.4 shows Peter Paul Rubens's *The Horrors of War*. The large canvas swirls with a chaotic scene that is extravagant yet sensual, typical qualities of Baroque art. Barely visible in the right lower foreground is a woman with a broken lute, which symbolizes that harmony (music) cannot exist beside the discord of war. Figure 7.5 paints an even more horrific scene: the woman Judith visiting revenge upon the Assyrian general Holofernes, as depicted by Artemisia Gentileschi (1593–1652). Here the play of light and dark creates a dramatic effect, the stark blue and red colors add intensity, while the head of the victim, set at a right angle to his body, suggests an unnatural motion. Baroque art sometimes delights in the pure shock value of presenting gruesome events from history or myth in a dramatic way.

Music of the Baroque is also highly dramatic. We observed in the music of the Renaissance (1450–1600) the humanistic desire to have music sway, or affect, the emotions, as ancient Greek drama had once done. In the early seventeenth century, this desire culminated in an aesthetic theory called the Doctrine of Affections. The **Doctrine of Affections** held that different musical moods could and should be used to influence the emotions, or affections, of the listener—be it rage, revenge, sorrow, joy, or love. Not surprisingly, the single most important new genre to emerge in the Baroque period was opera. Here the drama of the stage joined with music to form a powerful new medium.

Figure 7.5

Judith Beheading Holofernes (c. 1615) by Artemisia Gentileschi. The grisly scene of Judith slaying the tyrant general was painted several times by Gentileschi, perhaps as a vivid way of demonstrating her abhorrence of aggressive male domination.

Characteristics of Baroque Music

Perhaps more than any other period in the history of music, the Baroque (1600–1750) gave rise to a remarkable variety of musical styles, ranging from the expressive monody of Claudio Monteverdi (1567–1643) to the complex polyphony of J. S. Bach (1685–1750). Indeed, the music of the late Baroque is very different from that of the early

Baroque. The Baroque era also saw the introduction of many new musical genres—opera, cantata, oratorio, sonata, concerto, and suite—each of which is discussed in the following chapters. Yet despite the quick stylistic changes and all the new types of music created, two elements remain constant throughout the Baroque period: an expressive, sometimes extravagant, melody and a strong supporting bass.

Expressive Melody

Renaissance music, as we saw in Chapter 6, was dominated by polyphonic texture, in which the voices spin out a web of imitative counterpoint. The nature and importance of each of the lines are about equal, as the following graphic suggests:

An equal-voice choir was a useful medium to convey collective religious beliefs. To communicate raw individual emotion, however, a direct appeal by a soloist seemed more appropriate. In early Baroque music, then, all voices are not created equal. Rather, a polarity develops—the highest- and lowest-sounding lines shine forth, while the middle voices do little more than fill out the texture.

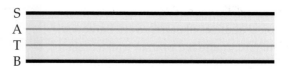

This new structure facilitated a new kind of solo singing called **monody** (from the Greek term meaning "solo song"). A single singer stepped forward, supported only by a bass line and a few accompanying instruments, to project a highly charged text. With the spotlight squarely on the soloist, a more elaborate, indeed showy, style of singing developed. Observe in Example 7.2 how the vocalist ascends rapidly (densely black notes) with a long and difficult melisma. The extravagance is heard in the quick shift from very long notes, to very short ones, and then back. Notice, too, that this heavenly flight underscores the word *paradiso* ("paradise"), the music reinforcing the meaning of the text.

EXAMPLE 7.2

Tan - ta bel - lez-za il pa-ra-di - - - - - - - - - - - - - so ha se - co.
(Wherever so much beauty resides contains paradise.)

Rock-Solid Harmony: The *Basso Continuo*

To prevent the high-flying melodies of the Baroque from spinning out of control, a strong harmonic framework was needed. The bass-driven, chordal support in Baroque music is called the **basso continuo** (continual bass), and it is played by one or more instruments. Figure 7.6 shows a woman singing to the accompaniment of a large plucked string instrument called the theorbo. This instrument has more low strings than its close cousin the lute, which allows it to not only strum chords but also play low bass notes. In the early Baroque (early to mid-seventeenth century), a theorbo or some other kind of bass lute often played the *basso continuo*. Figure 7.7 shows how the *basso continuo* had developed by the late Baroque (early eighteenth century). Here a solo singer, two violinists, and a violist are supported by a large double bass (to the left), which plays the bass line, and a harpsichord, which improvises chords built above that bass line. The singer, viola, and violins project an expressive melody while the other two instruments provide the *basso continuo*. Harpsichord and low string instrument formed the most common *basso continuo* in the Baroque, especially late Baroque, period. Indeed, it is the continual tinkling of the harpsichord, in step with a strong bass line, that signals the listener that the music being played comes from this era (downloads, streaming music for Ch. 9 at CourseMate, and (intro)/10, for example). Coincidentally, this top-bottom structure for monodic singing in Baroque music is similar to the structure used for pop songs today; in both styles, an expressive soloist sings above a rock-solid bass line, while a keyboardist (or guitar player), building on the bass line, improvises chords in the middle of the texture.

What chords did the Baroque harpsichordist play? These were suggested to the performer by means of **figured bass**—a numerical shorthand placed below the bass line. A player familiar with chord formations would look at the bass line, such as that given in Example 7.3A, and improvise chords along the lines of those given in Example 7.3B. These improvised chords, generated from the bass according to the numerical code, support a melody above. Here, too, a modern parallel is found. Figured bass is similar in intent to the alphanumerical code found in "fake sheets" used by jazz musicians and studio guitarists today, which suggests which chords to play beneath the written melody.

Figure 7.6

A *Woman Playing the Theorbo-Lute and a Cavalier* (c. 1658) by Gerard ter Borch. The bass strings are at the top of the instrument and off the fingerboard. The theorbo was often used to play the *basso continuo* in the seventeenth century.

EXAMPLE 7.3A   EXAMPLE 7.3B

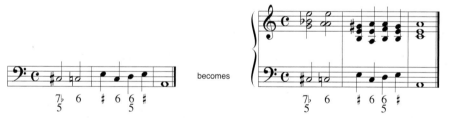

becomes

For an excellent demonstration of early Baroque violin music, accompanied by a *basso continuo* of harpsichord, cello, and Baroque guitar, go to Ciaccona, "Voices of Music," in the YouTube playlist at CourseMate for this text.

Figure 7.7

Antonio Visentini (1688–1782), *Concert at the Villa*. Notice how the double bass player at the left turns his head to read the bass (bottom) line in the score on the harpsichord; together they provide the *basso continuo*.

Elements of Baroque Music

Baroque music, as we have seen, is marked by grandeur, by passionate expression, and by drama. It is held together by a chordal framework and a strong bass line, both supplied by the *basso continuo.* In the music of the early Baroque in particular, the artistic expression of the voice and the richness of the harmony were especially intense. In the late Baroque, some of the excessively exuberant qualities of early Baroque music would be smoothed out and regularized by Bach and Handel (see Ch. 10 and 11). The following elements, however, are common to all Baroque music.

Melody: Expanding Types

In the Renaissance, melody was generic. It was all more or less of one kind—a direct, uncomplicated line that could be performed equally well by a voice or an instrument. But in the early Baroque period, beginning about 1600, two different melodic styles began to develop: a somewhat mechanical style, full of figural repetitions, in instrumental music; and a more dramatic, virtuosic style in singing. Baroque vocal music is marked by flourishes in which the voice luxuriates as it projects a single syllable as a melisma (see Ex. 7.2). Generally, Baroque melody does not unfold in short, symmetrical phrases, but expands lavishly over long musical spans. In a famous aria from Handel's oratorio *Messiah,* for example, the composer sets the word "exalted" with an appropriately extravagant melodic line (Ex. 7.4).

EXAMPLE 7.4

[Every valley] shall be ex - alt - - - - - - - - - - - - ed,

Harmony: The Beginning of Modern Chord Progressions and Keys

Contemporary pop songs are invariably supported by chordal harmonies that move in a predictable way. They follow certain sequences of chords, called chord progressions (see Ch. 2, "Building Harmony with Chords"), by now so familiar and ubiquitous that we scarcely give them notice. In fact, these sequences emerged in the Baroque era, particularly toward the end of the seventeenth century. Composers such as Arcangelo Corelli and Johann Pachelbel, for example, began to build their music around patterns of chords they would frequently repeat. The melody might continuously unfold and be endlessly new and different, but stock patterns—progressions such as I-VI-IV-V-I (see Ch. 2, "Building Harmony with Chords" for the meaning of these numbers)—would be heard over and over. So universal have these progressions become since the Baroque period that they have engendered a principle of U.S. copyright law: You can successfully sue someone for stealing your melody, but not for using your bass line.

Not only did stock harmonic patterns emerge in the Baroque era, but so, too, did our modern "two-key" (or "two-mode") system. During the Middle Ages and Renaissance, Western music had employed many different scales (called the "church modes"). During the seventeenth century, however, these were gradually reduced to just two patterns: major and minor. The two modes create sharply, indeed dramatically, different sounds, which can be used for expressive purposes. A composer could play the dark minor off against the bright major, for example, just as a painter might contrast light and dark (see Fig. 7.5) for dramatic effect.

Rhythm: Strong Beat and Persistent Rhythmic Patterns

Rhythm in Baroque music is generally characterized by uniformity rather than flexibility. The composer establishes a meter and certain rhythmic patterns at the outset of the piece, and then maintains them up to the very end. Moreover, in Baroque music—especially instrumental music—a strong recurring beat is usually clearly audible, which pushes the music forward and creates, in contemporary terms, a "groove." This tendency toward rhythmic clarity and drive becomes more and more pronounced as the Baroque period proceeds. It culminates in the rhythmically propulsive music of Vivaldi and Bach.

Texture: Homophony and Polyphony

Baroque composers approached musical texture in ever-changing ways. Texture in the early Baroque is overwhelmingly homophonic with the *basso continuo* providing a wholly chordal framework. Indeed, composers of the early seventeenth century rebelled against the predominantly polyphonic, imitative texture of the Renaissance. This initial hostility toward polyphony gradually diminished, however. In the late Baroque, composers such as Bach and Handel returned to contrapuntal writing, raising the technique to unsurpassed heights in a new genre: the fugue.

Dynamics: An Aesthetic of Extremes

Before the Baroque era, musicians did not put dynamic marks in their scores. That doesn't mean that music had no louds or softs, but simply that the performers intuited what they were to do without being told. In the early seventeenth century, however, composers began to dictate the desired dynamic level by inserting two very basic terms: *piano* (soft) and *forte* (loud). Sudden contrasts of dynamics were more prized than gradual crescendos and diminuendos, possibly because the harpsichord could play at only one, two, or, at most, three dynamic levels (see Ch. 3, "Keyboard Instruments"), and nothing in between. This practice of shifting the volume of sound suddenly from one level to another is called **terraced dynamics**. Terraced dynamics went hand in hand with clear contrasts between major and minor keys, as well as with abrupt changes in orchestration. By contrasting distinctly different dynamics, moods, and colors, composers of the Baroque created the one thing prized above all others in Baroque art: drama.

For a general demonstration of the variety of styles and sounds of Baroque music, watch Best Baroque Music Composers in the YouTube playlist at CourseMate for this text.

Key Words

Baroque (89)	monody (92)	figured bass (93)
Doctrine of Affections (91)	*basso continuo* (92)	terraced dynamics (95)

For a complete review of this chapter, see the Main Points, Chapter Quiz, Flashcards, and Glossary in CourseMate.

Join us on Facebook at **Listening to Music with Craig Wright**

Early Baroque Vocal Music

Opera

Given the popularity of opera today—and the fact that opera had existed in China and Japan since the thirteenth century—it is surprising that this genre of music emerged comparatively late in the history of Western European culture. Not until around 1600 did opera appear in Europe, and its native soil was Italy.

An **opera**, most basically, is a stage play (a drama) expressed through music. The term *opera* means literally "a work," and it first appeared in the Italian phrase *opera drammatica in musica*, "a dramatic work set to music." Opera demands singers who can act or, in some cases, actors who can sing. Indeed, in opera every word of the text (called the **libretto**) is sung. Such a requirement might strike us as unnatural. After all, we don't usually sing to our roommate, "Get out of the bathroom, I need to get to class this morning." But in opera, what we lose in credibility, we more than recoup in expressive power. Set to music, the text of a song, whether a pop hit or an opera aria, gains emotional force. Find a good drama, add music to the words, call the audience to attention with an opening instrumental piece (an **overture**), throw in a chorus and some instrumental mood music, and you've got a new medium: opera. This is how, in effect, the new genre of opera began. Ironically, its inventors thought they were resurrecting something old—ancient Greek drama.

The origins of Western opera can be traced to late sixteenth-century Italy—specifically, to progressive musicians and intellectuals in the cities of Florence, Mantua, and Venice (Fig. 8.1). Here, a number of visionary thinkers continued to pursue a goal of late Renaissance humanism—that of recapturing the expressive power of ancient Greek music. Florence in particular was home to several outstanding musical intellectuals, including Vincenzo Galilei (1533–1591), the father of the famous astronomer Galileo Galilei (1564–1642). The elder Galilei and his followers believed that the power of Greek drama owed much to the fact that every line was sung, not spoken. They aimed to bring ancient Greek drama to life through simply accompanied solo song. While various composers experimented with this new genre around 1600, it was not until 1607, with Claudio Monteverdi's *Orfeo,* that the first true opera emerged.

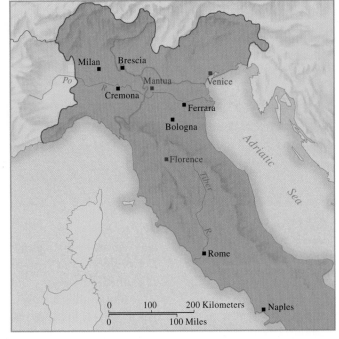

Figure 8.1

The major musical centers in northern Italy in the seventeenth century. Opera first developed in Florence, Mantua, and Venice.

Figure 8.2

Portrait of Claudio Monteverdi by Bernardo Strozzi (1581–1644). Strozzi also painted the singer and composer Barbara Strozzi (see "Barbara Strozzi: Professional Composer").

Claudio Monteverdi (1567–1643)

Claudio Monteverdi was a versatile musician who could manifest his enormous talents equally well in a madrigal, a Mass, a motet, or an opera (Fig. 8.2). He was born in the northern Italian town of Cremona in 1567 and moved to the larger city of Mantua (see Fig. 8.1) around 1590 to serve Duke Vincenzo Gonzaga as a singer and a performer on string instruments. In 1601, Monteverdi was appointed court director of music, and in this capacity, he composed two operas, *Orfeo* (1607) and *Arianna* (1608). But the duke failed to pay Monteverdi what he had promised. "I have never in my life suffered greater humiliation of the spirit than when I had to go and beg the treasurer for what was mine," said the composer some years later. Thus disenchanted with Mantua, Monteverdi accepted the much-coveted position of *maestro di cappella* at Saint Mark's in Venice (Fig. 8.3). Although called to Venice ostensibly to write church music for Saint Mark's, Monteverdi continued to compose opera. Among his important

 © Erich Lessing/Art Resource, NY

Figure 8.3

Piazza San Marco, Venice, Italy, painted by Gentile Bellini, c. 1500. Venice became the home to the first public opera houses. Yet opera composers, then as now, usually needed to have other employment to support themselves. Claudio Monteverdi was director of music at the central church of the city, the basilica of Saint Mark, seen in the center of this painting.

later works in this genre are *Il ritorno d'Ulisse* (*The Return of Ulysses*, 1640) and *L'incoronazione di Poppea* (*The Coronation of Poppea*, 1642). He died in Venice in 1643 after thirty years of faithful service.

Monteverdi's first opera—and the first important opera in the history of Western music—is his *Orfeo*. Because the goal of early opera was to replicate the power of ancient Greek drama, it was only natural that the libretto for *Orfeo* draw on a tale from classical Greek mythology. The leading character is Orfeo (Orpheus), the son of Apollo, the Greek god of the sun and of music. Orfeo, himself a demigod, finds love in the form of the beautiful Euridice, a mortal human. No sooner are they married than she is killed by a poisonous snake (see chapter-opening page, lower left) and carried off to Hades (the ancient world's version of hell). Orfeo vows to descend into the Underworld to rescue his beloved. This he nearly accomplishes by means of his divine musical powers, for Orfeo can make trees sway, calm savage beasts, and overcome demonic forces with the beauty of his song alone. The theme of *Orfeo,* then, is the divine power of music.

Monteverdi advances the drama in *Orfeo* mainly through **monody** (expressive solo singing to simple accompaniment), a medium thought to approximate the singing of the ancient Greek theater. The simplest type of monody was recitative. **Recitative**, from the Italian word *recitativo* (something recited), is musically heightened speech, through which the plot of the opera is communicated to the audience. Generally, recitative is performed without a perceptible meter or beat—you can't tap your foot to it. And because recitative attempts to mirror the natural rhythms of everyday speech, it is often made up of rapidly repeating notes followed by one or two long notes at the ends of phrases, as in the following example from Act II of *Orfeo*.

EXAMPLE 8.1

A l'a-ma - ra no-vel-la Ras-sem-bra l'in-fe - li - ce un mu - to sas-so
(At the bitter news the unhappy one resembles a mute stone)

Recitative in Baroque opera is accompanied only by the *basso continuo,* which consists, as we have seen, of a bass line and accompanying chords (Fig. 8.4). Such

Figure 8.4

Recitative from the beginning of the second act of Monteverdi's *Orfeo* (1607), from an early print of the opera. The vocal part of a messenger appears on the odd-numbered staffs above the slower-moving bass line of the *basso continuo* (even-numbered staffs).

sparsely accompanied recitative is called **simple recitative** (*recitativo semplice* in Italian). (In the nineteenth century, recitative accompanied by the full orchestra, called *recitativo accompagnato,* would become the norm.) A good example of simple recitative can be heard at the beginning of the vocal excerpt from Act II of *Orfeo,* discussed later in the Listening Guide.

In addition to recitative, Monteverdi made use of a more lyrical type of monody called aria. An **aria** (Italian for "song" or "ayre") is more passionate, more expansive, and more tuneful than a recitative. It also tends to have a clear meter and more regular rhythms. If a recitative tells what is happening on stage, an aria conveys what the character *feels* about these events. Similarly, whereas a recitative advances the plot, an aria usually halts the action to focus a spotlight on the emotional state of the singer. Finally, whereas a recitative often involves a rapid-fire delivery of text, an aria will work through text at a more leisurely pace; words are repeated to heighten their dramatic effect, and important vowels are extended by means of vocal melismas, as can be seen, for example, in Orfeo's aria "Possente spirto" ("Powerful Spirit").

EXAMPLE 8.2

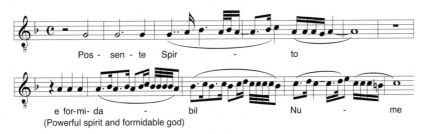

(Powerful spirit and formidable god)

An aria is an important, self-contained unit, both textually and musically. Whereas recitative is normally written in blank verse (has meter but no rhyme), an aria is usually composed with meter and rhyme—in other words, an aria text is a short, rhyming poem of one or more stanzas. The text of Orfeo's aria "Possente spirto" consists of three, three-line stanzas, each with a rhyme scheme **aba**. Moreover, the music for each stanza begins and ends in the same key (G minor). Finally, operatic arias are nearly always accompanied not merely by the *basso continuo* but also by all or part of the orchestra. Monteverdi gives special

© Erich Lessing/Art Resource, NY

Figure 8.5

Orfeo charms the guardians of Hades with his voice and lyre—a detail from a painting by Nicolas Poussin (1594–1665).

prominence to the violins, cornettos (see Fig. 6.9), and harps in "Possente spirto" to give added weight to the aria, as well as to show how music can charm even the guards of hell (Fig. 8.5).

Recitative and aria are the two main styles of singing in Baroque opera, and opera in general. In addition, a third style called **arioso** is a manner of singing halfway between aria and recitative. It is more declamatory than aria but has a less rapid-fire delivery than recitative. The lament that Orfeo sings on learning of the death of Euridice, "Tu se' morta" ("Thou Art Dead"; see Listening Guide below), is a classic example of arioso style.

Like all operas, *Orfeo* begins with a purely instrumental work that serves as a curtain raiser. Such instrumental introductions are usually called overtures, but Monteverdi called his musical preamble a toccata. The term **toccata** (literally, "a touched thing") refers to an instrumental piece, for keyboard or other instruments, requiring great technical dexterity of the performers. It is, in other words, an instrumental showpiece. Here the trumpet races up and down the scale while many of the lower parts rapidly articulate repeating pitches. Monteverdi instructs the toccata to be sounded three times. Brief though it may be, this toccata is sufficiently long to suggest the richness and variety of instrumental sounds available to a composer in the early Baroque period. Its theatrical function, of course, is to call the audience to attention, to signal that the action is about to begin.

Listening Guide

Claudio Monteverdi, *Orfeo* **(1607), Toccata**

			5
0:00	15	Trumpet highlights highest part.	1/15
0:32		Repeat of toccata with low strings added	
1:05		Repeat of toccata with full orchestra	

 Listen to streaming music in an Active Listening Guide at CourseMate or in the eBook.

See an authentic re-creation of a performance of Monteverdi's overture in the YouTube playlist at CourseMate for this text.

Although Monteverdi divided his *Orfeo* into five short acts, this ninety-minute opera was originally performed at Mantua without intermission—and the audience stood the entire time! The first dramatic high point occurs midway through Act II, when the hero learns that his new bride, Euridice, has been claimed by the Underworld. In the heartfelt arioso "Tu se' morta," Orfeo laments his loss and vows to enter Hades to reclaim his beloved. Listen especially to the poignant conclusion, in which Orfeo, by means of an ascending vocal line, bids farewell to earth, sky, and sun, and thus begins his journey to the land of the dead.

Listening Guide

Claudio Monteverdi, *Orfeo* **(1607), Act II**

Recitative, "A l'amara novella," and Arioso, "Tu se' morta"

5

1/16

Characters: Orfeo and two shepherds

Situation: The shepherds relate that, on the news of the death of Euridice, Orfeo fell into a stunned silence. He soon regains his powers of expression, laments her loss, and vows to reclaim her.

Recitative			Shepherd I	
0:00 [16]	Simple recitative (accompanied by *basso continuo* of bass lute)		A l'amara novella Rassembra l'infelice un muto sasso Che per troppo dolor no può dolersi.	At the bitter news The unhappy one resembles a mute stone Who is too sad to express sadness.
Recitative			**Shepherd II**	
0:17	Simple recitative (accompanied by *basso continuo* of harpsichord, bass viol, and bass lute)		Ahi, ben avrebbe un cor di tigre o d'orsa Chi non sentisse del tuo mal pietade, Privo d'ogni tuo ben, misero amante.	Ah, he must surely have a heart of a tiger or a bear, Who did not pity thy misfortune, Having lost all, unfortunate lover.
Arioso			**Orfeo**	
0:46	*Basso continuo* of organ and bass lute		Tu se' morta, mia vita, ed io respiro? Tu se' da me partita per mai più non tornare, ed io rimango? No, che se i versi alcuna cosa ponno,	Thou art dead, my life, but I still breathe? Thou hast left me, never to return, and yet I remain? No, if my verses possess any power,
1:59	Mention of descent into hell accompanied by fall in vocal line		N'andrò sicuro a'più profundi abissi E, intenerito il cor del re de l'ombre,	I will go undaunted into the deep abyss And, having softened the heart of the king of Hades,
2:22	Vision of Euridice climbing to heaven causes flourish in high register.		Meco trarrotti a riveder le stelle; O, se ciò negherammi empio destino, Rimarrò teco in compagnia di morte.	I will transport you to see again the stars. And, if cruel destiny works against me, I will remain with you in the company of death.
3:02	Growing conviction portrayed by chromatic ascent in vocal line		Addio terra, addio cielo e sole, addio!	Farewell earth, farewell heaven and sun, farewell!

🔊 Listen to streaming music in an Active Listening Guide at CourseMate or in the eBook.

Having descended to the shores of Hades, Orfeo now invokes all his musical powers to gain entry. In the aria "Possente spirto," he addresses Charon, the spirit that controls access to the kingdom of the dead. Orfeo's elaborate, florid vocal style, aided by an exotic instrumental accompaniment, soon disarms the frightful guard. After stanza 2, for example, we hear the **cornetto** (see Fig. 6.9), the now-extinct wind instrument of the Renaissance and Baroque that sounded something akin to a cross between a trumpet and a clarinet.

Watch a performance of the arioso "Tu se' morta" in the YouTube playlist at CourseMate for this text.

Listening Guide

Claudio Monteverdi, *Orfeo* (1607), Act III

Aria, "Possente spirto" (strophes 1 and 2 only)

Characters: Orfeo and Charon

Situation: Orfeo pleads through his music that Charon grant passage into Hades.

5
1/17

ARIA (Strophe 1)			Orfeo	
0:00 [17]	Florid singing, joined by violin flourishes, above *basso continuo*		Possente spirto e formidabil nume, Senza cui far passaggio a l'altra riva Alma da corpo sciolta in van presume.	Powerful spirit and formidable god, Without whom no soul, deprived of body, may presume to pass to Hades' shore.
1:30	Instrumental postlude played by *basso continuo* and two solo violins			*(continued)*

ARIA (Strophe 2)		Orfeo	
1:55	Florid singing continues, joined now by cornettos, above *basso continuo*.	Non viv'io, no, che poi di vita è priva Mia cara sposa, il cor non è più meco, E senza cor com'esser può ch'io viva?	I live no longer, since now my dear spouse is deprived of life, I have no heart within me, And without a heart how can I still be alive?
3:03	Instrumental postlude played by *basso continuo* and two solo cornettos		

 Listen to streaming music in an Active Listening Guide at CourseMate or in the eBook.

See all three strophes of the aria "Possente spirto" in the YouTube playlist at CourseMate for this text.

In the original Greek myth, Pluto, the lord of Hades, releases Euridice to Orfeo with one condition: He is to have faith that she is following behind him, and he must not look back before reaching earth's surface. When Orfeo yields to the temptation to turn around and embrace Euridice, she is reclaimed by Pluto forevermore. In his opera *Orfeo,* Monteverdi altered this tragic conclusion: Apollo intervenes, transforming his son Orfeo into a constellation that radiates eternal spiritual harmony with the beloved Euridice. In so doing, Monteverdi established what was to become a convention for seventeenth- and eighteenth-century opera: the *lieto fine,* or "happy ending."

Chamber Cantata

Seventeenth- and eighteenth-century Venice had much in common with modern Las Vegas. It was a tourist destination where gambling and prostitution flourished, and because the citizens were accustomed to wearing masks, "What happened in Venice stayed in Venice." In 1613, Claudio Monteverdi moved to this very worldly city on the sea to become director of music at the basilica of Saint Mark, then perhaps the most prestigious musical position in the world. But Monteverdi not only wrote religious music there; he also composed opera and a new genre: the chamber cantata.

A **chamber cantata** is a "sung thing" (from the Italian *cantata*) for solo voice and a few accompanying instruments, intended to be performed at home or a private chamber; thus it is a type of **chamber music**. While J. S. Bach's later church cantatas would deal with religious subjects (see Ch. 10), the chamber cantata usually described the worldly exploits of the heroes and heroines of classical mythology, or told a tale of unrequited love. A typical chamber cantata lasts eight to fifteen minutes and is usually divided into contrasting sections that alternate between recitative and aria. Thus a chamber cantata might be called a "mini opera," except it lacks costumes and scenery, and involves only a single (solo) character. The most prolific composer of chamber cantatas in the early Baroque was the Venetian Barbara Strozzi.

Barbara Strozzi (1619–1677) was steeped in the traditions of opera composer Claudio Monteverdi, for her teacher had been one of his pupils. Strozzi did not write operas, but excelled in composing chamber cantatas that she herself could sing in the fashionable homes of Venice's elite. Her cantata *L'amante segreto* (*The Secret Lover*) treats the eternal subject of unrequited love, but from a fresh perspective—the female point of view. The forlorn heroine is too timid to reveal her passion to the object of her desire, preferring to plead for a merciful death. The petition for death, "Voglio morire" ("I want to die"), comes in the form of a brief aria accompanied by a *basso continuo* (Ex. 8.3). The bass line of the *basso continuo* sounds a stepwise descent of four notes that repeats again and again.

Barbara Strozzi: Professional Composer

Until the twentieth century, very few women earned a living as professional composers. In the Middle Ages, for example, a few *trobairitz* (female troubadours) wrote chansons, but these women were all members of the lesser nobility and not financially dependent on the success of their creations. So, too, a few women composed during the late Renaissance and early Baroque, but most were cloistered nuns who received their sustenance from the Church. The reason for the scarcity of independent women composers in the Baroque era is simple: Only performance within the home was then thought to be an appropriate musical activity for ladies. Musical activities outside the home were deemed improper because they smacked of "professionalism." Women did not go to university, nor did they engage in income-earning professions or trades.

A few notable exceptions, however, could be found. Adriana Basile, an associate of Monteverdi at Mantua, carved out for herself a highly successful career as a virtuoso soprano, thereby laying claim to the title "the first diva." In 1678, Elena Piscopia became the first woman to receive a university degree, when she earned the title Doctor of Philosophy at the University of Padua, Italy, following a rigorous public examination carried out in Latin. We have seen the work of Artemisia Gentileschi (see Fig. 7.5), a Florentine

© Erich Lessing/Art Resource, NY

A portrait of Barbara Strozzi painted in the 1630s by Bernardo Strozzi, perhaps a relative

painter who was the first woman to be admitted to the prestigious Accademia del Disegno (Academy of Design) and who went on to become a court painter for King Charles I of England. And to this list of illustrious women artists and intellectuals should be added the name of Barbara Strozzi.

Barbara Strozzi was born out of wedlock in 1619, the daughter of a Venetian man of letters, Giulio Strozzi, who encouraged her musical development. Giulio Strozzi not only provided his daughter with lessons in composition but also organized domestic gatherings where her works could be heard. When Giulio Strozzi died in 1652, Barbara was left both destitute and desperate—she had four children but was unmarried. Over the next six years, she published six collections of cantatas, more than any other composer of the early Baroque. Each collection was dedicated to a member of the high nobility, and according to custom, the dedicatee paid for the honor. Barbara Strozzi may have been unique as a professional woman composer, but she had to deal with economic reality just like her male counterparts. Throughout the Baroque era, composers earned handsome sums from dedicatory fees paid by wealthy patrons, but nothing from royalties generated by sales of the music itself. Payment of royalties, to both male and female composers, would not come until the twentieth century.

EXAMPLE 8.3

A melody, harmony, or rhythm that repeats continually throughout a musical composition is an **ostinato.** When the repetition occurs in the bass, it is called a ***basso ostinato***. The term *ostinato* comes from an Italian word meaning "obstinate," "stubborn," or "pig-headed." In Baroque operas and cantatas, performers often sang laments accompanied by a *basso ostinato* that descended, as here, in stepwise motion. Such a descending bass consequently became a symbol for grief or lamentation, especially when presented in a minor key. At the first sounds of this figure, the listener would know, just as if a banner had been held up: Here comes an aria dealing with despair!

Barbara Strozzi, *L'amante segreto* (1651)

Aria, "Voglio morire," Part 1

5 2
1/18 1/7

Genre: Chamber cantata

Form: Ostinato

WHAT TO LISTEN FOR: The *basso continuo* of cello and harpsichord introduces the voice. The bass repeats continually, thereby forming a *basso ostinato*.

0:00	**18 / 7**	*Basso continuo* begins, with *basso ostinato* played by cello.
0:19		Soprano enters as *basso continuo* proceeds.
0:41		*Basso ostinato* extended by one note to accommodate cadence
0:45		*Basso continuo* alone
0:50		Soprano reenters; *basso continuo* proceeds to end.

Voglio morire,	I want to die,
più tosto ch'il mio mal venga a scoprire;	rather than have my pain discovered;
ò disgrazia fatale,	oh, fatal misfortune,
quanto più miran gl'occhi il suo bel volto	the more my eyes admire his beautiful face
più tien la bocca il mio desir sepolto.	the more my mouth keeps my desire hidden.

🔊 Listen to streaming music in an Active Listening Guide at CourseMate or in the eBook.

🔊 Take online Listening Exercise 8.1 and receive feedback at CourseMate or in the eBook.

Opera in London

Opera originated in Italy during the early seventeenth century. From there it spread over the Alps to German-speaking countries, to France, and eventually to England. But owing to the strong tradition of theater in England, epitomized by productions of Shakespeare's plays, the English had a love-hate affair with opera: Sometimes they wanted to hear it, and sometimes they did not. The first important opera written in English, Henry Purcell's *Dido and Aeneas,* dates from 1689. Chronologically, it falls outside the boundaries of the "early Baroque." But because English opera at this time was heavily influenced by earlier Italian opera, Purcell's opera belongs stylistically to the earlier period.

Henry Purcell (1659–1695)

Figure 8.6

Henry Purcell, by an anonymous painter

Henry Purcell (Fig. 8.6) has been called the "greatest of all English composers." Indeed, only the late Baroque composer George Frideric Handel (who was actually German born) and pop songwriter Paul McCartney can plausibly challenge Purcell for this title. Purcell was born in London, the son of one of the king's singers. In 1679, the younger Purcell obtained the position of organist at Westminster Abbey, and then, in 1682, he became organist for the king's Chapel Royal as well. But London has always been a vital theater town, and although an employee of the court, Purcell increasingly devoted his attention to works for the public stage.

Purcell's *Dido and Aeneas* was among the first operas written in the English language. Yet it was apparently created for neither the king's court nor a public theater, but for a private girls' boarding school in the London suburb of Chelsea. The girls presented one major stage production annually, something like the senior class play of today. In *Dido and Aeneas,* they sang the numerous choruses and danced in the equally frequent dance numbers. All nine solo parts save one (the role of Aeneas) were written for female voices. The libretto of the opera, one appropriate for a school curriculum steeped in classical Latin, is drawn from Virgil's *Aeneid.* Surely the girls had studied this epic poem in Latin class, and likely they had memorized parts of it. Thus, they likely knew the story of the soldier-of-fortune Aeneas, who seduces proud Dido, queen of Carthage, but then deserts her to fulfill his destiny—sailing on to found the city of Rome. Betrayed and alone, Dido vents her feelings in an exceptionally beautiful aria, "When I am laid in earth," and then expires. In Virgil's original story, Dido stabs herself with the sword of Aeneas (Fig. 8.7). In Purcell's opera, she dies of a broken heart: Her pain is poison enough.

© Scala/Art Resource, NY

Figure 8.7

A detail from the painting *The Death of Dido* by Guercino (1599–1666). The servant Belinda bends over the dying Dido, who has fallen on her formidable sword.

Dido's final aria is introduced by a brief example of simple recitative (accompanied by *basso continuo* only): "Thy hand, Belinda." Normally, simple recitative is a businesslike process that moves the action along through direct declamation. In this passage, however, recitative transcends its routine role. Notice the remarkable way Purcell sets the English language. He understood where the accents fell in the text of his libretto, and he knew how to replicate these effectively in music. In Example 8.4, the stressed words in the text generally appear in long notes and at the beginning of each measure. Equally important, notice how the vocal line descends a full octave, passing through chromatic notes along the way. (Chromaticism is another device composers use to signal pain and grief.) As the voice twists chromatically downward, we feel the pain of the abandoned Dido. By the end, she has slumped into the arms of her servant Belinda.

EXAMPLE 8.4

Thy hand, Be - lin - da! Dark - - ness shades me; on thy bo - som let me

rest. More I would, but Death in - vades me: Death is now a wel - come guest.

From the recitative "Thy hand Belinda," Purcell moves imperceptibly to the climactic aria "When I am laid in earth," where Dido sings of her impending death. Because this high point of the opera is a lament, Purcell chooses, in the Baroque tradition, to build it upon a *basso ostinato.* English composers called the *basso ostinato* the **ground bass**, because the repeating bass provided a solid foundation, or grounding, on which an entire composition could be built. The ground bass Purcell composed for Dido's lament consists of two sections (see the Listening Guide): (1) a chromatic stepwise descent over the interval of a fourth (G, F♯, F, E♭, D) and (2) a two-measure cadence returning to the tonic G (B♭, C, D, G).

In the libretto, Dido's lament consists of a brief one-stanza poem with an **aba** rhyme scheme:

> When I am laid in earth, may my wrongs create
> No trouble in thy breast.
> Remember me, but ah! Forget my fate.

Each line of text is repeated, as are many individual words and pairs of words alike. (Such repetition of text is typical of an aria but not of recitative.) In this case, Dido's repetitions

Watch a video of Craig Wright's Open Yale Course class session 14, "Ostinato Form in the Music of Purcell, Pachelbel, Elton John, and Vitamin C," at CourseMate for this text.

are perfectly appropriate to her emotional state—she can communicate in fragments, but cannot articulate her feelings in complete sentences. Here the listener cares less about grammatical correctness, however, and more about the emotion of the moment. No fewer than six times does Dido plead with Belinda, and with us, to remember her. And, indeed, we do remember, for this plaintive aria is one of the most moving pieces in all of opera.

Listening Guide

Henry Purcell, *Dido and Aeneas* (1689)

Recitative, "Thy hand, Belinda," and aria, "When I am laid in earth"

5   2

1/19–20   1/8–9

Characters: Dido, queen of Carthage; Belinda, her servant

Situation: Having been deserted by her lover, Aeneas, Dido sings farewell to Belinda (and to all) before dying of a broken heart.

WHAT TO LISTEN FOR: Dido's recitative, accompanied by *basso continuo,* giving way to her mournful aria, built on a *basso ostinato*

BRIEF RECITATIVE

0:00 19 8   Continuo played by large lute and cello   Thy hand, Belinda! Darkness shades me; on thy bosom let me rest. More I would, but Death invades me: Death is now a welcome guest.

ARIA

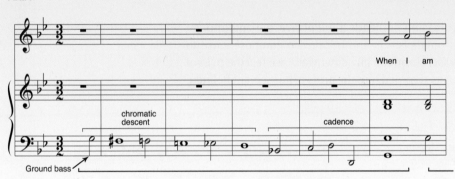

0:58 20 9	0:00	*Basso ostinato* alone in cellos and double basses
1:10	0:12	*Basso ostinato* with voice and strings
1:27	0:29	*Basso ostinato* repeats beneath voice.
1:44	0:46	*Basso ostinato* repeats beneath voice.
2:02	1:04	*Basso ostinato* repeats beneath voice.
2:17	1:19	*Basso ostinato* repeats beneath voice.
2:37	1:39	*Basso ostinato* repeats beneath voice.
2:53	1:55	*Basso ostinato* repeats beneath voice.

3:10	2:12	*Basso ostinato* repeats beneath voice.
3:29	2:31	*Basso ostinato* alone with strings
3:46	2:48	*Basso ostinato* alone with strings

 Listen to streaming music in an Active Listening Guide at CourseMate or in the eBook.

 Take online Listening Exercise 8.2 and receive feedback at CourseMate or in the eBook.

See a performance of this climactic aria in the YouTube playlist at CourseMate for this text.

Elton John and Basso Ostinato

For an up-to-date example of ostinato bass, we turn to an aria-lament by a more recent English composer, Elton John: "Sorry Seems to Be the Hardest Word" (1976; covered more recently by Ray Charles, Mary J. Blige, and Clay Aiken, among others). Although not built exclusively on an ostinato figure, this song has one striking affinity to the aria by Purcell—it, too, makes use of a *basso ostinato*, incorporating in the chorus a chromatically descending fourth as a way of setting a very, very sad text. The ostinato pattern begins on G, with a chromatically descending fourth followed by a one-measure cadence:

It's sad (so sad), it's a sad, sad situation
Bass
G   F#   F   E

And it's getting more and more absurd
          E♭   D   F#GAD
                              (cadence)

© DMI/Time Life Pictures/Getty Images

Elton John (Sir Reginald Dwight). Was the pop artist, who studied for five years at the Royal Academy of Music in London, where the music of Purcell is regularly taught, inspired by the famous aria of his equally well-coiffed countryman (see Fig. 8.6)?

Listen to Elton John, "Sorry Seems to Be the Hardest Word," in the iTunes playlist at CourseMate for this text.

This *basso ostinato*, as well as a slightly varied form of it, is then repeated several times for this and other lines of text. Compare Elton John's bass line with Purcell's *basso ostinato*, and note that both laments are set in the key of G minor.

Key Words

opera (97)	simple recitative (99)	chamber cantata (102)
libretto (97)	aria (99)	chamber music (102)
overture (97)	arioso (100)	ostinato (103)
monody (98)	toccata (100)	*basso ostinato* (103)
recitative (98)	cornetto (101)	ground bass (105)

For a complete review of this chapter, see the Main Points, Chapter Quiz, Flashcards, and Glossary in CourseMate.

 Join us on Facebook at **Listening to Music with Craig Wright**

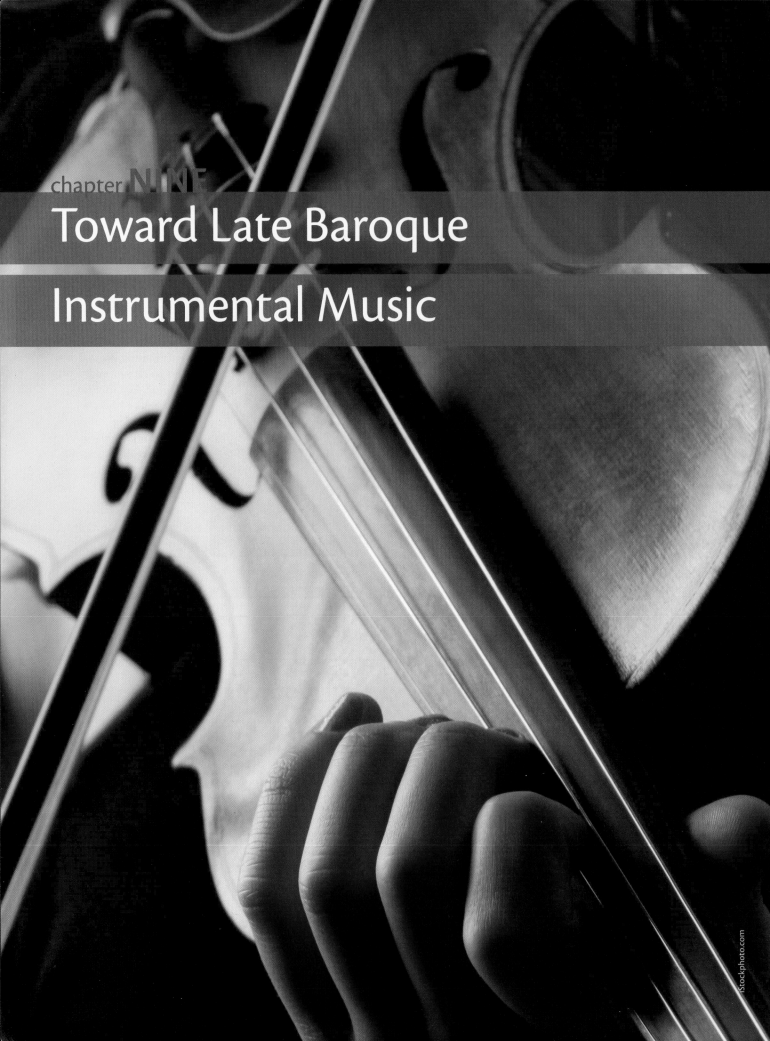

Toward Late Baroque

Instrumental Music

When we think of classical music today, we usually think of instrumental music and instrumental performing groups—a symphony orchestra or a string quartet, for example. The equation classical = instrumental, while certainly not entirely true, nonetheless has some validity; about 80 percent of the Western classical repertoire is instrumental. When and why did this happen? This shift occurred during the seventeenth century, when instrumental music came to rival, and indeed surpass, vocal music in popularity. Statistics prove this point. During the Renaissance, the number of prints of vocal music outsold those of instrumental music by almost ten to one; by the end of the seventeenth century, on the other hand, instrumental publications outnumbered vocal ones by about three to one.

The ascent of instrumental music can be attributed directly to the growing popularity of the violin and other instruments of the violin family. While the violin originated around 1520 as an instrument played solely by low-level professionals in taverns and dance halls, by 1650 it had become a favorite of talented amateurs in the home. Composers such as Corelli, Vivaldi, and (later) Bach responded to the growing demand for music for the violin and other string instruments by writing sonatas and concertos for them.

Accompanying the growth of instrumental music was the emergence of a distinctly instrumental sound. Composers increasingly recognized that the Baroque trumpet, for example, could easily leap an octave but could not run quickly up a scale and stay in tune. Accordingly, they began to write idiomatic (well-suited) music not only for voice but also for instruments, to take advantage of their special abilities and colors. **Idiomatic writing**, then, exploits the strengths and avoids the weaknesses of particular voices and instruments.

Finally, during the Baroque era, the vocabulary of expressive gestures that had developed for vocal music came to be applied to instrumental music as well. Composers realized that the Doctrine of Affections (see Ch. 7, "Baroque Painting and Music") was valid for instrumental music, too. By adopting devices used in vocal music, composers made it possible for purely instrumental music to express rage (with tremolos and rapidly racing scales, for example), despair (as with a swooning violin line above a lamenting bass), or a bright spring day (by such means as trills and other "chirps" high in the violins and flutes). Even without the benefit of a text, instrumental music could tell a tale or paint a scene. As we shall see, it was by means of such expressive devices that Antonio Vivaldi was able to depict the four seasons of the year with music.

 ## The Baroque Orchestra

The symphony orchestra as we know it today had its origins in seventeenth-century Italy and France. Originally, the term *orchestra* referred to the area for musicians in the ancient Greek theater, between the audience and the stage; eventually, it came to mean the musicians themselves. At the beginning of the seventeenth century, the orchestra was something of a musical Noah's ark—it included a large variety of instruments, but usually no more than one or two of each type. The small orchestra that accompanied Monteverdi's *Orfeo* (1607), for example, consisted of fourteen different instruments from the late Renaissance—viol, sackbut (trombone), trumpet, cornetto, theorbo, violin, organ, and so on. By the mid-seventeenth century, however, the core of the orchestra had begun to solidify around the four instruments of the violin family—violins, violas, cellos, and the related double bass. To this string nucleus were added woodwinds: first flutes and oboes, and then bassoons, usually in pairs. Occasionally, a pair of trumpets would be included to provide extra brilliance. When trumpets appeared, so, too, often did timpani, although the parts for these drums were usually not written out but simply improvised as the music seemed to require.

Figure 9.1

Detail of an orchestra playing for a Baroque opera, as seen in Pietro Domenico Olivero's *Interior of the Teatro Regio*, Turin (1740). From left to right are a bassoon, two French horns, a cello, a double bass, a harpsichord, and then violins, violas, and oboes. Notice that once again we see the cello and double bass player looking onto the score at the harpsichord, where they will find their bass line. These three instruments (along with the bassoon) formed the *basso continuo*, which creates the heavy bass typical of Baroque music.

Finally, by the end of the seventeenth century, a pair of French horns was sometimes added to the orchestra to give it more sonic resonance. Supporting the entire ensemble was the ever-present *basso continuo*, one usually consisting of a harpsichord to provide chords and one or two low string instruments to play the bass line (Fig. 9.1). The **orchestra** for Western classical music, then, can be described as an ensemble of musicians, organized around a core of strings, with added woodwinds and brasses, playing under a leader.

Most Baroque orchestras were small, usually with no more than twenty performers, and none of the parts was doubled—that is, no more than one instrumentalist was assigned to a single written line. Yet while the Baroque orchestra was usually small, exceptions did exist, especially toward the end of the seventeenth century. At some of the more splendid courts around Europe, the orchestra might swell to as many as eighty instrumentalists for special occasions. Foremost among these was the court of French king Louis XIV.

Of all the courts of Baroque Europe, that of King Louis XIV (reigned 1643–1715) was the most splendid. Louis styled himself the "Sun King," after Apollo, the god of the sun and of music. Outside Paris, near the small town of Versailles, Louis built himself a palace, the largest court complex ever constructed (Fig. 9.2). There, Louis not only shone forth in all his glory but also ruled absolutely: As he famously said, "I *am* the state" ("L'État, c'est moi").

Figure 9.2

This standard view of the front of Versailles gives a sense of the grandeur of the palace that King Louis XIV began there in 1669. His orchestra, like his palace, was the largest in Europe.

To direct music at the court, Louis XIV engaged another domineering figure, composer Jean-Baptiste Lully (1632–1687). Lully controlled the string-dominated court orchestra with such dictatorial powers that he might have said, "La musique, c'est moi." Not only did Lully write much of the music, he also selected the players, led rehearsals, and made sure all performers executed the notes exactly and in strict time. If necessary, Lully instilled discipline by force; in one instance, he hit a violinist with his large conducting stick, and in another, he broke a violin over the owner's back. Ironically, Lully's penchant for musical discipline killed him. Late in 1686, while thumping the floor with his conducting stick (the method of the day for keeping the beat within exceptionally large ensembles), he stabbed himself in the foot and died of gangrene a few weeks later.

Besides solidifying the place of the modern string-dominated orchestra as a model for the rest of Europe, Jean-Baptiste Lully can claim credit for creation of a new musical genre: the French overture. A **French overture**—so called because it then opened all of the musical-dramatic productions at the French court—consists of two sections. The first is set in a slow duple meter, with stately dotted rhythms suggesting a royal procession; the second is in a fast triple meter and features much imitation among the various musical lines. Although developed at the court of Louis XIV, the French overture spread to England and Germany. Handel wrote one, for example, to begin his *Messiah,* and Bach did likewise to open each of his orchestral suites.

Watch a video of Craig Wright's Open Yale Course class session 14, "Ostinato Form in the Music of Purcell, Pachelbel, Elton John, and Vitamin C," at CourseMate for this text.

Pachelbel and His Canon

Today most of us remember the name Johann Pachelbel (rhymes with "Taco Bell") because of a single musical composition, the famous "Pachelbel Canon" in D major. In his day, however, Pachelbel was known as a composer of much instrumental music, some of it for small orchestra but most for organ or harpsichord. Pachelbel's Canon is the first movement of a two-movement instrumental suite (on the suite, see Ch. 11, "Handel and the Orchestral Dance Suite"), with the second being a lively contrapuntal dance called a gigue. The odd thing about Pachelbel's Canon is that the listener doesn't hear the imitative canon, or at least doesn't focus on it. The three canonic voices are all in the same range and all played by a violin—the violin-dominated ensemble is all powerful here. Because the lines don't stand out from one another by range or color, the unfolding of the canon is difficult for the ear to follow.

Listen to comedian/musician Rob Paravonian rant about Pachelbel's Canon in the YouTube playlist at CourseMate for this text.

What we hear instead is the bass line churning inexorably in the low strings, which, together with the harpsichord, form the *basso continuo* (Ex. 9.1). A strong bass is typical of Baroque music generally, but Pachelbel's bass is unforgettable in part because it has a pleasing intervallic pattern to it (fourths alternate with steps) and because it gravitates strongly around the subdominant, dominant, and tonic chords. This eight-chord unit, then, is a good example of the kind of standard chord progression that began to emerge toward the end of the seventeenth century (see below, "Arcangelo Corelli"). Pachelbel knew he was on to a good thing, so he gives us this bass line twenty-eight times, a classic example of a *basso ostinato.* The allure of the bass is such that later classical composers made use of it (Handel, Haydn, and Mozart among them), as well as recent pop musicians, such as Blues Traveler, Vitamin C, and Coolio—one website lists more than fifty songs using this bass. The full composition, moreover, has served as background music in numerous TV commercials and films, and is often heard at weddings. Why such popularity? Likely the reason is a play of opposites that we find appealing: The regular, almost plodding bass provides a rock-solid foundation for the free flights of fancy that unfold in the soaring violins.

Hear Pachelbel's Canon with *basso continuo* consisting of small organ, cello, and lute—the instruments that might have been used originally—in the YouTube playlist at CourseMate for this text.

EXAMPLE 9.1

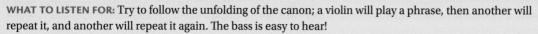

Listening Guide

Johann Pachelbel, Canon in D major (c. 1685)

Texture: Polyphonic

Form: Canon

WHAT TO LISTEN FOR: Try to follow the unfolding of the canon; a violin will play a phrase, then another will repeat it, and another will repeat it again. The bass is easy to hear!

0:00	**10**	*Basso continuo* begins.
0:12		Violin 1 enters.
0:24		Violin 2 enters in imitation.
0:35		Violin 3 enters in imitation.
0:57		Violin 1 followed by violins 2 and 3 at two-bar intervals
1:44		Violin 1 followed by violins 2 and 3 at two-bar intervals
2:30		Violin 1 followed by violins 2 and 3 at two-bar intervals
3:18		Violin 1 followed by violins 2 and 3 at two-bar intervals
4:04		Violin 1 followed by violins 2 and 3 at two-bar intervals

 Listen to streaming music in an Active Listening Guide at CourseMate or in the eBook.

During the 1680s, about the time he composed his Canon, Pachelbel worked in central Germany, where, among other things, he became the teacher of Johann Christoph Bach, the older brother and only known teacher of Johann Sebastian Bach. Pachelbel's use of counterpoint here (the three-voice canon) is suggestive of a return to favor of polyphony and contrapuntal texture in instrumental music generally at the end of the seventeenth century. The greatest proponent of late Baroque instrumental counterpoint, as we shall see in the next chapter, would be J. S. Bach himself.

Corelli and the Trio Sonata

The melody of Pachelbel's Canon is carried by three violins. As the Baroque era progressed, the popularity of the violin continued to grow and so, too, did the demand for string music that talented amateurs might play in the home. This demand, in turn, encouraged the growth of a new genre of instrumental music: the sonata. A **sonata** is a type of instrumental chamber music (music for the home with just one player per part). When the term *sonata* originated in early seventeenth-century Italy, it connoted "something sounded," in distinction to a cantata (see Ch. 8, "Chamber Cantata"), which meant "something sung." A Baroque sonata consists of a collection of movements, each with its own mood and tempo, but all in the same key. In the Baroque era, the movements usually carried such names as "allemande," "sarabande," "gavotte," or "gigue"—all names of dances. A Baroque sonata with dance movements was normally called a **chamber sonata** (*sonata da camera*) and consisted of four movements with alternating tempos: slow-fast-slow-fast.

In the Baroque era, sonatas were of two types: the solo sonata and the trio sonata. A **solo sonata** might be written either for a solo keyboard instrument, such as the harpsichord, or for a solo melody instrument, such as the violin. If for a solo melody instrument, three musicians were actually needed: the soloist and the two *basso continuo* performers. A **trio sonata** consists of three musical lines (two melody instruments plus bass). Yet here, too, the term is somewhat misleading, for when a harpsichord joins with the bass to form the *basso continuo*, four players actually perform. The sonata originated in Italy and then spread to the rest of Europe, in large measure through the published works of Arcangelo Corelli.

Arcangelo Corelli (1653–1713)

The composer-virtuoso who made the Baroque solo and trio sonatas internationally popular was Arcangelo Corelli. Corelli was born in 1653 near Bologna, Italy, then an important center for violin instruction and performance. By 1675, he had moved to Rome, where he remained for the duration of his life as a teacher, composer, and performer on the violin (Fig. 9.3). Corelli was one of the first superstars of the violin, and he remains today the only musician buried in Rome's Pantheon—as its name implies, a "hall for the gods" (hall of fame) of Italian culture.

Although Corelli's musical output was small, consisting of only five sets of sonatas and one of concertos, his works were widely admired. Such diverse composers as Johann Sebastian Bach in Leipzig, François Couperin (1668–1733) in Paris, and Henry Purcell in London either borrowed his melodies directly or more generally studied and absorbed his style.

The most remarkable aspect of Corelli's music is its harmony: It sounds modern to our ears. We have heard so much classical and popular music that we have come to possess an almost subconscious sense of how a succession of chords—a harmonic progression—should sound. Corelli, even before Pachelbel, was one of the first composers to write this kind of harmony. We call it "functional" harmony because each chord has a specific role, or function, in the overall succession of chords. Not only does the individual chord constitute an important sound in itself, but it also draws us toward the next, thereby helping to form a tightly linked chain of chords, which sounds directed and purposeful. The most basic link in the chain is the V-I (dominant-tonic) cadence (see Ch. 2, "Harmony"). In addition, Corelli often constructs bass lines that move upward chromatically by half step. This chromatic, stepwise motion pulls up and into the next-higher note, increasing the sense of direction and cohesiveness we feel in Corelli's music.

TRIO SONATA IN C MAJOR, OPUS 4, NO. 1 (1694)

The Trio Sonata in C major, Opus 4, No. 1, is a chamber sonata written by Corelli in 1694 for two violins and *basso continuo*, here played by a harpsichord and cello. Corelli called this sonata Opus 4, No. 1. (Composers frequently use opus, the Latin word meaning "work," to enumerate and identify their compositions; this was the first piece in Corelli's fourth published collection.) This chamber sonata is in four movements, the second and fourth of which are dance movements in binary form (**AB**), the most common musical form for Baroque dances. No one danced, however. These movements were stylized pieces that aimed to capture in music only the spirit of the dance in question. As one musician of the day observed, they are written "for the refreshment of the ear alone."

ColouriserAL/Lebrecht

Figure 9.3

Arcangelo Corelli looks placid enough in this print. But when playing the violin, according to a contemporary, "his eyes turn red as fire, his face becomes distorted, and his eyeballs roll as if in agony."

© Victoria & Albert Museum, London/The Bridgeman Art Library International

Figure 9.4

The violin came to be the most important string instrument of the orchestra during the Baroque period—up to that point it had been mainly a "low-class" instrument for playing dances in taverns. Compared to the earlier viol, the violin (from *violino* = "little viol") had only four strings, no frets, and a louder, more penetrating sound. The best of the Baroque violin makers was Antonio Stradivari (1644–1737), whose instruments today, as seen in this photo, have sold for as much as $4 million at auction.

Corelli begins sonata Opus 4, No. 1, with a *preludio* (prelude), which gives the players a chance to warm up and also establishes the general musical mood of the sonata. Notice that the prelude makes use of what is called a **walking bass**, a bass that moves at a moderate, steady pace, mostly in equal note values and often stepwise up or down the scale.

EXAMPLE 9.2

The second movement, a dance called the *corrente* (from the Italian *correre*, "to run"), is rather fast and in triple meter. Here the first violin engages in a rapid dialogue with the cello. The second violin is scarcely audible as it helps fill in the chords, literally playing "second fiddle" to the first violin. The short *adagio* ("slow" movement) serves merely as a bridge that links the *corrente* with the final movement—the brisk, duple-meter *allemanda* (literally, "the German dance"). This last movement, too, has a walking bass, but the tempo is so fast (*presto*) that it sounds more like a running or a sprinting bass.

Listening Guide

Arcangelo Corelli, Trio Sonata in C major, Opus 4, No. 1 (1694)

Ensemble: Two violins, cello, and harpsichord

WHAT TO LISTEN FOR: The contrast between the sedate, somber style of movements one and three, and the energetic abandon of movements two and four, the dance movements

PRELUDE

0:00	21		"Walking bass" descends stepwise below dotted rhythms in violins.
0:35			Bass now moves twice as fast.
0:45			Bass returns to original slow pace.

CORRENTE

1:18	22	0:00	**A** first violin and cello lead lively dance in triple meter.
1:32		0:14	Repeat of **A**
1:46		0:28	**B** begins with melodic sequences in cello and violins.
2:03		0:46	Rhythmic syncopation signals arrival of final cadence.
2:10		0:52	Repeat of **B**, including syncopation (1:10 on CD; 2:28 streaming)

ADAGIO

| 2:37 | 23 | 0:00 | Stationary chords in violins; only cello moves in purposeful fashion. |
| 4:13 | | 1:36 | Cadential chords prepare way to next movement. |

ALLEMANDA

4:29	24	0:00	**A:** Two violins move together above racing bass.
4:50		0:22	Repeat of **A** and pause
5:11		0:43	**B** begins and includes sudden shift to minor key (0:56 on CD; 5:24 streaming).
5:32		1:03	Repeat of **B**, including sudden shift to minor key (1:16 on CD; 5:45 streaming)

◀)) Listen to streaming music in an Active Listening Guide at CourseMate or in the eBook.

Vivaldi and the Baroque Concerto

The concerto was to the Baroque era what the symphony would later become to the Classical period: the showpiece of orchestral music. A Baroque concerto emphasizes abrupt contrasts within a unity of mood, just as striking change between the zones of light and darkness often characterizes a Baroque painting (see, for example, Fig. 7.5).

A **concerto** (from the Latin *concertare*, "to strive together") is a musical composition marked by a friendly contest or competition between a soloist and an orchestra. When only one soloist confronts the orchestra, the work is a **solo concerto**—featuring a solo violin, flute, or oboe, for example. When a small group of soloists works together, performing as a unit against the full orchestra, the piece is called a **concerto grosso**. A concerto grosso consists of two performing forces that work together: a larger group forming the basic orchestra, called the concerto grosso (big concert), and a smaller one of two, three, or four soloists, called the **concertino** (little concert). Playing together, the two groups constitute the full orchestra, called the **tutti** (meaning "all" or "everybody"). A typical concerto grosso had a concertino of two violins and continuo. The soloists were not highly paid masters imported from afar, but rather the regular first-chair players who, when they were not serving as soloists, joined with the others to form the tutti. The resulting contrast was desirable, said a contemporary, "so that the ear might be astonished by the alternation of loud and soft . . . as the eye is dazzled by the alternation of light and shade."

As written by Vivaldi and Bach, the solo concerto and the concerto grosso usually had three movements: fast-slow-fast. The serious first movement is composed in a carefully worked-out structure called ritornello form (see next section); the second movement is invariably more lyrical and tender; and the third movement, though often using ritornello form, tends to be lighter and more dancelike in mood. Both the solo concerto and the concerto grosso originated in Italy toward the end of the seventeenth century. The vogue of the concerto grosso peaked about 1730 and had all but ended around the time of Bach's death (1750). But the solo concerto continued to be cultivated during the Classical and Romantic periods, becoming increasingly a showcase in which a single soloist could display his or her technical mastery of an instrument.

Antonio Vivaldi (1678–1741)

No composer was more influential, and certainly none more prolific, in the creation of the Baroque concerto than Antonio Vivaldi (Fig. 9.5). Vivaldi, like Barbara Strozzi a native of Venice, was the son of a part-time barber and substitute musician at the basilica of Saint Mark (see Fig. 8.3). Young Vivaldi's proximity to Saint Mark's naturally brought him into contact with the clergy. Although he became a skilled performer on the violin, he also entered Holy Orders, ultimately being ordained a priest. Vivaldi's life, however, was by no means confined to the realm of the spirit. He concertized on the violin throughout Europe; he wrote and produced nearly fifty operas, which brought him a great deal of money; and he lived for fifteen years with an Italian opera star. The worldly pursuits of *il prete rosso* (the red-haired priest) eventually provoked a response from the authorities of the Roman Catholic Church. In 1737, Vivaldi was forbidden to practice his musical artistry in papally controlled lands, which then constituted a large portion of Italy. This ban affected his income as well as his creativity. He died poor and obscure in 1741 in Vienna, where he had gone in search of a post at the emperor's court.

From 1703 until 1740, Vivaldi worked in Venice at the *Ospedale della Pietà* (Hospice of Mercy), first as a violinist and music teacher, and then as musical director. The Hospice of Mercy was an orphanage for the care and education of young women. It was one of four such charitable institutions in Venice that accepted abandoned, mostly illegitimate, girls who, as several reports state, "otherwise would have been thrown in the canals." By 1700, music

Figure 9.5

Portrait of a violinist and composer believed by some to be the musician Antonio Vivaldi

Figure 9.6

Foreign visitors attend a concert performed by orphan girls assembled from various orphanages around Venice, as depicted by Gabriele Bella about 1750. The Hospice of Mercy was the most musically intense of the Venetian orphanages. Here girls who showed a special talent for music were placed within a prestigious ensemble of forty musicians. Their musical education included tutelage in singing, ear training, and counterpoint, as well as instruction on at least two musical instruments. Antonio Vivaldi was one of the teachers.

had been made to serve an important role in the religious and social life of the orphanage. Each Sunday afternoon, its orchestra of young women offered public performances for the well-to-do of Venice (see Fig. 9.6). Also attending these concerts were foreign visitors—Venice was already a tourist city—among them a French diplomat, who wrote in 1739:

> These girls are educated at the expense of the state, and they are trained solely with the purpose of excelling in music. That is why they sing like angels and play violin, flute, organ, oboe, cello, and bassoon; in short, no instrument is so big as to frighten them. They are kept like nuns in a convent. All they do is perform concerts, always in groups of about forty girls. I swear to you that there is nothing as pleasant as seeing a young and pretty nun, dressed in white, with a little pomegranate bouquet over her ears, conducting the orchestra with all the gracefulness and incredible precision one can imagine.

VIOLIN CONCERTO IN E MAJOR, OPUS 8, NO. 1, THE "SPRING" (EARLY 1700S)

During the early 1700s, Vivaldi composed literally hundreds of solo concertos for the all-female orchestras of the Hospice of Mercy in Venice. In 1725, he gathered twelve of the more colorful of these together and published them under the title "Opus 8." (This set of concertos was thus Vivaldi's eighth published work.) In addition, he called the first four of these solo concertos *The Four Seasons*. What Vivaldi meant by this was that each of the four concertos in turn represents the feelings, sounds, and sights of one of the four seasons of the year, beginning with spring. To avoid ambiguity regarding what sensations and events the music depicts at any given moment, Vivaldi first composed a poem (an "illustrative sonnet," as he called it) about each season. Then he placed each line of the poem at the point in the music where that particular event or feeling was to be expressed, even specifying at one point that the violins are to sound "like barking dogs." In so doing, Vivaldi showed that not only voices, but instruments as well, could create a mood and sway the emotions. Vivaldi also fashioned here a landmark in what is called instrumental program music—music that plays out a story or a series of events or moods (for more on program music, see Ch. 21).

It is fitting that *The Four Seasons* begins with the bright, optimistic sounds of spring. In fact, the "Spring" Concerto for solo violin and small orchestra is Vivaldi's best-known work. The fast first movement of this three-movement concerto is composed in ritornello form, a form that Vivaldi was the first to popularize. (The Italian word *ritornello* means "return" or "refrain"; in English we call this "rondo"— see Ch. 15, "Rondo Form.") In **ritornello form**, all or part of the main theme—the ritornello—returns again and again, invariably played by the tutti, or full orchestra. Between the tutti's statements of the ritornello, the soloist inserts fragments and extensions of this refrain in virtuosic fashion. Much of the excitement of a Baroque concerto comes from the tension between the reaffirming ritornello played by the tutti and the inventive flights of the soloist.

The jaunty ritornello theme of the first movement of the "Spring" Concerto has two complementary parts, the second of which returns more often than the first. Between appearances of the ritornello, Vivaldi inserts the music that represents his feelings about spring. He creates the songbirds of May by asking the violin to play rapidly and staccato (very short notes) in a high register. Similarly, he depicts the sudden arrival of thunder and lightning by means of a tremolo and shooting scales, then returns to the cheerful song of the birds. Next, in the slow second movement, a vision

© Scala/Art Resource, NY

of a flower-strewn meadow is conveyed by an expansive, tender melody in the violin. Finally, during the fast finale, a sustained droning in the lower strings invokes "the festive sounds of country bagpipes." The full text of Vivaldi's "program" for the first movement of the "Spring" Concerto is given in the Listening Guide.

Vivaldi's "Spring" Concerto is marked by a stylistic trait that is often prominent in his music: melodic sequence. A **melodic sequence** is the repetition of a musical motive at successively higher or lower degrees of the scale. Example 9.3 shows a sequence from the middle of the first movement of this work. In this sequence, the motive is played three times, with each repetition a step lower than the last.

EXAMPLE 9.3

Although melodic sequence can be found in music from almost all periods, it is especially prevalent in the late Baroque. It helps propel the music forward, and creates the energy we associate with Baroque style. However, because hearing the same melodic phrase time and again can become a tedious listening experience, Baroque composers usually follow the "three strikes and you're out" rule: The melodic unit appears, as in Example 9.3, three times, but no more.

Vivaldi composed more than 450 concertos and thus is known as "the father of the concerto." Though widely admired as both a performer and a composer in his day, he was largely forgotten within a few years of his death, a victim of rapidly changing musical tastes. Not until the revival of Baroque music in the 1950s were his scores resurrected from obscure libraries and dusty archives. Now Vivaldi's music is loved for its freshness and vigor, its exuberance and daring. A search of iTunes turns up more than 6,200 items for *The Four Seasons,* representing more than 300 recordings. So often is the "Spring" Concerto played that it has passed from the realm of art music into that of "classical pops"—a staple at Starbucks.

Listening Guide

Antonio Vivaldi, Violin Concerto in E major, Opus 8, No. 1 (the "Spring"; early 1700s)

First movement, *Allegro* (fast)

Meter: Duple

Texture: Mainly homophonic

Form: Ritornello

WHAT TO LISTEN FOR: The ritornello played by the tutti, alternating and contrasting with the descriptive music of the soloists

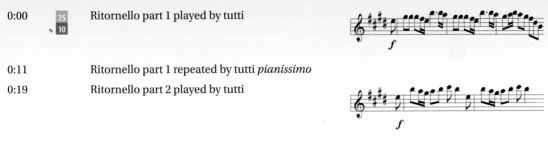

0:00	Ritornello part 1 played by tutti	
0:11	Ritornello part 1 repeated by tutti *pianissimo*	
0:19	Ritornello part 2 played by tutti	
0:27	Ritornello part 2 repeated by tutti *pianissimo*	

(continued)

0:36	Solo violin (aided by two violins from tutti) chirps on high.	"Spring with all its festiveness has arrived And the birds salute it with happy song"
1:10	Ritornello part 2 played by tutti	
1:18	Tutti softly plays running sixteenth notes.	"And the brooks, kissed by the breezes, Meanwhile flow with sweet murmurings"
1:42	Ritornello part 2 played by tutti	
1:50	Tutti plays tremolo, and violins shoot up scale.	"Dark clouds cover the sky Announced by bolts of lightning and thunder"
1:58	Solo violin plays agitated, broken triads while tutti continues with tremolos below.	
2:19	Ritornello part 2 played by tutti	
2:28	Solo violin chirps on high, adding ascending chromatic scale and trill.	"But when all has returned to quiet The birds commence to sing once again their enchanted song"
2:47	Ritornello part 1, slightly varied, played by tutti	
3:00	Solo violin plays rising sixteenth notes.	
3:16	Ritornello part 2 played by tutti	

Listen to streaming music in an Active Listening Guide at CourseMate or in the eBook.

Take online Listening Exercise 9.1 and receive feedback at CourseMate or in the eBook.

Key Words

idiomatic writing (109)	solo sonata (113)	concerto grosso (115)
orchestra (110)	trio sonata (113)	concertino (115)
French overture (111)	walking bass (114)	tutti (115)
sonata (112)	concerto (115)	ritornello form (116)
chamber sonata (113)	solo concerto (115)	melodic sequence (117)

For a complete review of this chapter, see the Main Points, Chapter Quiz, Flashcards, and Glossary in CourseMate.

Join us on Facebook at **Listening to Music with Craig Wright**

Early and Middle Baroque: 1600–1690

REPRESENTATIVE COMPOSERS

Monteverdi	Lully	Corelli
Strozzi	Pachelbel	Vivaldi
Purcell		

A complete Checklist of Musical Style for the early and middle Baroque can be found at CourseMate for this text.

PRINCIPAL GENRES

opera	sonata	solo concerto
overture	concerto grosso	dance suite
chamber cantata		

Melody	Less stepwise movement, larger leaps, wider range, and more chromaticism reflect influence of virtuosic solo singing; melodic patterns idiomatic to particular musical instruments emerge
Harmony	Stable, diatonic chords played by *basso continuo* support melody; standard chord progressions begin to emerge at end of the seventeenth century; modes are gradually limited to just two: major and minor
Rhythm	Relaxed, flexible rhythms of the Renaissance gradually replaced by repetitive rhythmic patterns and a strongly articulated beat
Color	Musical timbre becomes enormously varied as traditional instruments are perfected (e.g., harpsichord, violin, and oboe) and new combinations of voices and instruments are explored; string-dominated orchestra begins to take shape; sudden shifts in dynamics (terraced dynamics) reflect dramatic quality of Baroque music
Texture	Chordal, homophonic texture predominates; top and bottom lines are strongest as *basso continuo* creates powerful bass to support melody above
Form	Arias and instrumental works often make use of *basso ostinato* procedure; ritornello form emerges in the concerto; binary form regulates most movements of the sonata and dance suite

The Late Baroque: Bach

The music of the late Baroque period (1710–1750), represented by the two great figures Johann Sebastian Bach and George Frideric Handel, stands as a high-water mark in Western musical culture. The most noteworthy works of Bach and Handel are large-scale compositions full of dramatic power, broad gestures, and, often, complex counterpoint. At the same time, they convey to the listener a sense of technical mastery. Building on the innovations of previous Baroque composers, Bach and Handel could compose, seemingly without effort, in a variety of musical genres and forms. Subsequent composers—perhaps sensing their inability to compete, or that the listening public wanted something new—headed in another direction. Thus Baroque style culminated in, and ended with, the music of these two giants.

The early Baroque period witnessed the creation of many new musical genres, among them opera, the sonata, and the concerto grosso. The late Baroque, by contrast, is not a period of musical innovation, but one of refinement. Bach and his contemporaries did not, in the main, invent new genres or forms, but rather gave greater weight, length, and polish to those established by their musical forebears. Arcangelo Corelli (1653–1713), for example, had introduced functional harmony in his sonatas, but Bach and Handel expanded Corelli's harmonic template to create much longer, and often more compelling, works of art. Bach and Handel approached the craft of composition with unbounded self-confidence. Their music has a sense of rightness, solidity, and maturity about it. Each time we choose to listen to one of their compositions, we offer further witness to their success in bringing a hundred years of musical innovation to a glorious conclusion.

Aspects of Late Baroque Musical Style

How to characterize the music, and particularly the melody, of the late Baroque era? "Progressive expansion" might best describe the process involved. A composer sets forth an initial theme and then continually spins it out over an ever-lengthening line. The resulting melody is thus long and often asymmetrical, and may be propelled forward by melodic sequence, as exemplified by this passage in the overture to Bach's first orchestral suite.

EXAMPLE 10.1

Rhythm in late Baroque music is also ruled by the principle of progressive development. A piece typically begins with one prominent rhythmic idea (see Ex. 10.1), and it or a complementary one continues uninterrupted to the very end of the movement, pushed along by a strong, clearly audible beat. Indeed, beat and meter are more easily recognized in late Baroque music than in music of any other period. Thus, if an overture or concerto by Bach or Handel seems to "chug along" with irrepressible optimism and vitality, it is usually because of a strong beat, a clearly articulated meter, and a continually recurring rhythmic pattern.

Finally, the music of Bach and Handel is usually denser in texture than that of the early Baroque era. Recall that around 1600, composers of the early Baroque rebelled against what they perceived to be the excessively polyphonic style of Renaissance music; consequently, they created music that is mainly homophonic in texture. By the heyday of Bach and Handel, around 1725, however, composers had returned to polyphonic writing, primarily to add richness to the middle range of their sound. German composers of the late Baroque were particularly fond of counterpoint, perhaps owing to their traditional love of the organ, an instrument with several keyboards and thus well suited to playing multiple polyphonic lines at once. The gradual reintegration of counterpoint into the fabric of Baroque music culminates in the rigorously contrapuntal vocal and instrumental music of J. S. Bach.

Johann Sebastian Bach (1685–1750)

For a period of more than 200 years, roughly 1600 to 1800, nearly 100 musicians with the name of Bach worked in central Germany—the longest of all musical dynasties. In fact, the name Bach (German for "brook") was nearly a brand name, like our Kleenex and "to Google": "A Bach" meant "a musician." J. S. Bach (Fig. 10.1) was simply the most talented and industrious member of the clan. Although he received some instruction from his older brother, Johann Christoph, Bach was largely self-taught. To learn his craft, he studied, copied, and arranged the compositions of Corelli, Vivaldi, Pachelbel, and even Palestrina. He also learned to play the organ, in part by emulating others, once traveling 400 miles round trip on foot to hear a great performer. Bach's first position of importance was in the town of Weimar, Germany, where he served as organist to the court between 1708 and 1717. It was here that he wrote many of his finest works for organ and that his reputation for extraordinary improvisations on that instrument became the stuff of legend.

Of all instruments, the organ is the most suitable for playing polyphonic counterpoint. Most organs have at least two separate keyboards for the hands, in addition to one placed on the floor, which the performer plays with the feet (see Figs. 3.10 and 10.2). This gives the instrument the capacity to play several lines simultaneously. More important, each of these keyboards can be set to engage a different group (rank) of pipes, each with its own color, making it easier for the listener to hear individual musical lines. For these reasons, the organ is the instrument *par excellence* for playing fugues.

Fugue

Bach was the master of counterpoint—the art of combining completely independent melodies in imaginative ways—and rich, complex counterpoint lies at the heart of the fugue. Fugue is a contrapuntal form and procedure that flourished during the late Baroque era. The word *fugue* itself comes from the Latin *fuga*, meaning "flight." Within a fugue, one voice presents a theme and then "flies away" as another voice enters with the same theme. The theme in a fugue is called the **subject**. At the outset, each voice presents the subject in turn, and this successive presentation is called the **exposition** of the fugue. As the voices enter, they do not imitate or pursue each other exactly—this would produce a canon or a round such as "Three Blind Mice" (see Ch. 3, "Texture"). Rather, passages of exact imitation are interrupted by sections of free writing in which the voices more or less go their own ways. These freer sections, where the subject is not heard in its entirety, are called **episodes**. Episodes and further presentations of the subject alternate throughout the remainder of the fugue (see Fig. 10.3).

Fugues have been written for two to as many as thirty-two voices, but the norm is between two and five. These may be actual human voices in a chorus or choir, or they may simply be lines or parts played by a group of instruments. Fugues can also be composed for solo instruments like the piano, organ, or guitar, which have the capacity to play several "voices" simultaneously. Thus, a formal definition of a **fugue** might be as follows: a composition for two, three, four, or five parts, played or sung by voices or instruments, which begins with a presentation of a subject in imitation in each part (exposition), continues with

Figure 10.1

The only authentic portrait of Johann Sebastian Bach, painted by Elias Gottlob Haussmann in 1746. Bach holds in his hand a six-voice canon, or round, which he created to symbolize his skill as a musical craftsman.

Figure 10.2

The organ presently in the choir loft of Saint Thomas's Church, Leipzig. It was from this loft that Bach played and conducted.

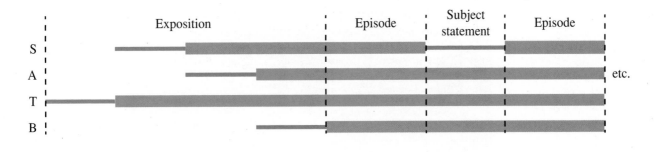

	Exposition	Episode	Subject statement	Episode
S				
A				etc.
T				
B				

——— = subject

▬▬▬ = counterpoint

Figure 10.3

An example of a typical formal plan of a fugue.

modulating passages of free counterpoint (episodes) and further appearances of the subject, and ends with a strong affirmation of the tonic key. Fortunately, the fugue is easier to hear than to describe: The unfolding and recurrence of a single subject make it easy to follow.

ORGAN FUGUE IN G MINOR (C. 1710)

The organ was Bach's favorite instrument, and in his day, he was known more as a performer and improviser on it than as a composer—his fame as a composer came, ironically, years after his death. Bach composed his G minor organ fugue early in his career, when he was in Weimar. It is written for four voices, which we will refer to as soprano, alto, tenor, and bass, and it begins with the subject appearing first in the soprano:

EXAMPLE 10.2

As fugue subjects go, this is a rather long one, but typical of the way Baroque composers liked to "spin out" their melodies. It sounds very solid in tonality because the subject is clearly constructed around the notes of the G minor triad (G, B♭, D), not only in the first measure but on the strong beats of the following measures as well. The subject also conveys a sense of gathering momentum, like a train pulling out of a station. It starts moderately with quarter notes and then seems to gain speed as eighth notes and finally sixteenth notes are introduced. This, too, is typical of fugue subjects. After the soprano introduces the subject, it is then presented, in turn, by the alto, the tenor, and the bass. The voices need not appear in any particular order; here, Bach simply decided to have them enter in succession from top to bottom.

When each voice has presented the subject and joined the polyphonic complex, Bach's exposition is at an end. Now a short passage of free counterpoint follows—the first episode—which uses only bits and pieces of the subject. Then the subject returns, but in a highly unusual way: It begins in the tenor, but continues and ends in the soprano. Thereafter, Bach's G minor fugue unfolds in the usual alternation of episodes and statements of the subject. The episodes sound unsettled and convey a sense of movement, modulating from one key to another. The subject, on the other hand, doesn't modulate. It is *in* a key—here the tonic G minor, or the dominant D

Hear a fugue based on Lady Gaga's pop song "Bad Romance" in the YouTube playlist at CourseMate for this text.

Watch a video of Craig Wright's Open Yale Course class session 13, "Fugue: Bach, Bizet, and Bernstein," at the text website.

Figure 10.4

Fugue (1925) by Josef Albers. Albers's design suggests the "constructivist" quality of the fugue, one full of repeating and reciprocal relationships. The black-and-white units seem to allude to subject and episode, respectively.

The Art Archive/Kunstmuseum Basel/Gianni Dagli Orti/Picture Desk © 2012 Artists Rights Society (ARS), New York / ADAGP, Paris

minor, or some other closely related major key. The tension between settled music (the subject) and unsettled music (the episodes) creates the exciting, dynamic quality of the fugue.

Because Bach wrote many fugues for organ, they often make use of a device particularly well suited to the organ—the pedal point. A **pedal point** is a note, usually in the bass, that is sustained (or repeated) for a time while harmonies change around it. Such a sustaining tone in the bass derives its name, of course, from the fact that on the organ the note is sounded by having the foot hold down a key on the pedal keyboard. After a pronounced pedal point (at 1:35 on our recording) and additional statements of the subject, Bach modulates back to the tonic key, G minor, for one final statement of the subject in the bass to end his fugue. Notice that, although this fugue is in a minor key, Bach puts the last chord in major. This is common in Baroque music, with composers preferring the brighter, more optimistic, sound of the major mode at the very end.

Finally, given all the complexities of the fugue and the fact that it is full of reciprocating, almost mathematical relationships (see Fig. 10.4), it is not surprising that the genre has traditionally appealed to listeners with scientific interests. Fugues are music for the rational processing part of the brain, rather than the emotional part.

Listening Guide

Johann Sebastian Bach, Organ Fugue in G minor (c. 1710)

5 / 1/26   2 / 1/11

Texture: Polyphonic

WHAT TO LISTEN FOR: After all voices appear in the exposition, the succession of episodes and subject statements that follows

The format of this listening guide is different. By means of a graph showing the two axes of music (pitch is vertical and duration horizontal) and numbers indicating bars or measures (which also mark the passing of time), the unfolding of Bach's complex fugue can be better understood. If you follow the piece correctly, you will know approximately which bar you are hearing!

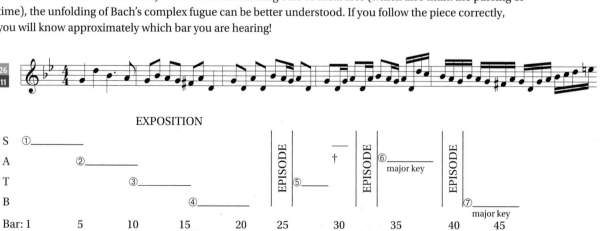

†This entry starts in the tenor and continues in the soprano.

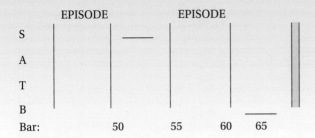

Bar: 50 55 60 65

🔊)) Listen to streaming music in an Active Listening Guide at CourseMate or in the eBook.

🔊)) Take online Listening Exercise 10.1 and receive feedback at CourseMate or in the eBook.

Bach's Orchestral Music

After nine years as organist in Weimar, Bach, then a young man with a wife and four children, was determined to improve his station in life. In 1717, he auditioned for the position of music director at the court of Cöthen, Germany, and was awarded the post. When he returned to Weimar to collect his family and possessions, the Duke of Weimar, displeased that the composer had "jumped ship," had Bach thrown in jail for a month. (Composers before the time of Beethoven were not like free agent baseball players today; they were little more than indentured servants who needed to obtain a release from one employer before entering the service of another.) When freed from jail, Bach fled to Cöthen, where he remained for six years (1717–1723).

At Cöthen, Bach turned his attention from organ music for the church to instrumental music for the court. It was here that he wrote the bulk of his orchestral scores, including more than a dozen solo concertos. The Prince of Cöthen had assembled something of an "all-star" orchestra, drawing many top players from the larger city of Berlin. He also ordered a large two-keyboard harpsichord from Berlin and sent Bach to fetch it. About this time, Bach began his *Well-Tempered Clavier* (see end of this chapter) for keyboard, and during these years, he completed six concertos of the concerto grosso type. This set has come to be called the Brandenburg Concertos.

THE BRANDENBURG CONCERTOS (1715–1721)

In 1721, still in Cöthen, Bach began to look for yet another job in the politically more important city of Berlin—specifically, at the court of Margrave Christian Ludwig of Brandenburg. To impress the margrave, Bach gathered together a half-dozen of his best concertos and sent them to his prospective employer. Although no job offer was forthcoming, Bach's autograph manuscript survives (Fig. 10.5), and in it are six superb examples of the concerto grosso.

The concerto grosso, as we have seen (Ch. 9, "Vivaldi and the Baroque Concerto"), is a three-movement work involving a musical give-and-take between a full orchestra (tutti) and a much smaller group of soloists (concertino), consisting usually of just two or three violins and continuo. In the first movement, the tutti normally plays a recurring musical theme, called the ritornello. The soloists in the concertino play along with the tutti; but when the ritornello stops, they go on to present their own musical material in a flashy, sometimes dazzling show of technical skill. Each of the six Brandenburg Concertos calls for a different group of soloists in the concertino. Together, these works constitute an anthology of nearly all instrumental combinations known to the Baroque era.

In Brandenburg Concerto No. 5, the razzle-dazzle projects from a concertino of solo violin, flute, and, most important, harpsichord. In principle, in a concerto

CHAPTER TEN THE LATE BAROQUE: BACH 125

Figure 10.5

The autograph manuscript of the opening of Bach's Brandenburg Concerto No. 5

grosso, the tutti plays the ritornello, and the soloists play motives derived from it. In practice, however, the separation between tutti and concertino, at least with Bach, is not so distinct. In Bach's more elaborate treatment of ritornello form, the line between the large (loud) ensemble and the small (soft) group of soloists is less obvious. Notice here also that Bach's ritornello (see the Listening Guide) possesses many characteristics of late Baroque melody: It is idiomatic to the violin (having many repeated notes); it is lengthy and somewhat asymmetrical (expanding out over many measures); and it possesses a driving rhythm that propels the music forward.

While the sound of violins initially dominates the ritornello in this opening movement, the solo harpsichord gradually steals the show. In fact, this work might fairly be called the first keyboard concerto. In earlier concertos, the harpsichord had appeared only as part of the *basso continuo,* not as a solo instrument. But here, toward the end of the movement, all the other instruments fall silent, leaving the harpsichord to sound alone in a lengthy section full of brilliant scales and arpeggios. Such a showy passage for soloist alone toward the end of a movement in a concerto is called a **cadenza**. One can easily imagine the great virtuoso Bach performing Brandenburg Concerto No. 5 in the Hall of Mirrors at Cöthen (Fig. 10.6), the principal concert hall

Figure 10.6

The Hall of Mirrors at the court of Cöthen, Germany, in which most of Bach's orchestral music was performed while he resided in that town. The bust on the pedestal at the right is of Bach.

of the court. There, seated at the large harpsichord he had brought from Berlin, Bach riffed away in this nearly three-minute cadenza, while patron, audience, and fellow performers alike listened in stunned silence to his bravura playing.

Finally, note the length of this movement: more than nine minutes! Typical of Bach's grand musical vision, his movement is three times longer than the usual concerto movement by Vivaldi.

Listening Guide

Johann Sebastian Bach, Brandenburg Concerto No. 5 in D major (c. 1720)

1/27–29

First movement

Genre: Concerto grosso

Texture: Polyphonic

Form: Ritornello

WHAT TO LISTEN FOR: The interplay between the tutti and the concertino, and also the high level of skill required of the performers at every moment. Bach suffered neither fools nor weak players lightly.

0:00	27		Tutti plays complete ritornello.
0:20			Concertino (violin, Baroque [wooden] flute, and harpsichord) enters.
0:45			Tutti plays ritornello part **A**.
0:50			Concertino varies ritornello part **B**.
1:10			Tutti plays ritornello part **B**.
1:37			Tutti plays ritornello part **B** in minor mode.
1:43			Concertino plays motives derived from ritornello, especially part **B**.
2:24			Tutti plays ritornello part **B**.
2:30			Concertino plays motives derived from ritornello part **B**.
3:20	28	0:00	Cello of tutti joins concertino; plays arpeggios in descending melodic sequence.
3:51		0:31	Double bass of tutti repeats single bass pitch (pedal point).
4:09		0:49	Tutti plays ritornello part **A**.
4:33		1:13	Concertino repeats much of music heard toward beginning (0:20).
4:58		1:38	Tutti plays ritornello parts **A** and **B**; sounds very solid.
5:08		1:48	Concertino plays motives derived from ritornello part **B**.
5:38		2:18	Tutti plays ritornello part **B**.
5:43		2:23	Harpsichord plays scales that race up and down keyboard.
6:22	29	0:00	Cadenza: long, brilliant passage for solo harpsichord
8:45		2:23	Left hand (bass) of harpsichord repeats one pitch (pedal point).
9:10		2:48	Tutti plays complete ritornello.

Listen to streaming music in an Active Listening Guide at CourseMate or in the eBook.

The fingers of the harpsichordist get a much-deserved rest in the slow second movement of Brandenburg Concerto No. 5. Now an elegiac mood envelops the music as the violin and flute engage in a quiet dialogue. The fast finale is dominated by fugal writing, a style in which Bach excelled above all other composers.

The Church Cantata

Watch a video of Craig Wright's Open Yale Course class session 16, "Baroque Music: The Vocal Music of Johann Sebastian Bach," at CourseMate for this text.

In 1723, Bach moved yet again, this time to assume the coveted position of cantor of Saint Thomas's Church and choir school in Leipzig, Germany (Fig. 10.7), a post he retained until his death in 1750. He seems to have been attracted to Leipzig, then a city of about 30,000 inhabitants, because of its excellent university, where his sons might enroll at no cost.

Although prestigious, the post of cantor of the Lutheran church of Saint Thomas was not an easy one. As a municipal employee of Leipzig, Bach was charged to organize the music for the four principal churches of the city, play organ at weddings and funerals, and sometimes even teach Latin grammar to the boys at the choir school of Saint Thomas. But by far the most demanding part of his job as cantor was to provide new music for the church each Sunday and religious holiday, a total of about sixty days a year. In those days in Germany, to be a choir director at a major church meant you had to compose much of the music yourself! If anyone was up for this challenge, however, it was Bach. During his time in Leipzig, the composer brought an important genre of music, the church cantata, to the highest point of its development.

The **cantata** (recall that it means "a sung thing") first appeared in Italy during the seventeenth century in the form we call the chamber cantata (see Ch. 8, "Chamber Cantata"), which engaged an aspect of love or a subject drawn from classical mythology. During the early eighteenth century, however, composers in Germany increasingly came to regard the cantata as an appropriate vehicle for religious music in the church. Bach and his contemporaries created the **church cantata**, a multimovement sacred work including arias, ariosos, and recitatives, performed by vocal soloists, a chorus, and a small accompanying orchestra. The church cantata became the musical soul of the Sunday service of the Lutheran Church, the Protestant religion that then dominated spiritual life in German-speaking lands.

Bach wrote almost 300 cantatas (five annual cycles) for the citizens of Leipzig, though only about 200 of these survive today. His musical forces consisted of about a dozen men and boy singers from the Saint Thomas choir school (see Fig. 10.7) and an equal number of instrumentalists from the university and town—there were still no women in either chorus or orchestra. The ensemble was placed in a choir loft above the west door (see Fig. 10.2), and Bach himself conducted the group while seated at the keyboard.

Figure 10.7

Leipzig, Saint Thomas's Church (center) and choir school (left) from an engraving of 1723, the year in which Bach moved to the city. Bach's large family occupied 900 square feet of the second floor of the choir school.

© Bettmann/Corbis

WACHET AUF, RUFT UNS DIE STIMME (AWAKE, A VOICE IS CALLING, 1731)

Bach was a devoted husband, a loving father to twenty children in all, and a respected burgher of Leipzig. Yet above all, he was a religious man who composed not only for self-expression but also for the greater glory of God and the spiritual edification of fellow Lutherans. Bach composed the cantata *Wachet auf, ruft uns die Stimme (Awake, a Voice Is Calling)* in 1731 for a Sunday immediately before the beginning of Advent (four Sundays before Christmas). The text, drawing upon the Gospel of Matthew (25:1–13), speaks opaquely of a bridegroom (Christ) who is arriving to meet the Daughters of Zion (the Christian community). Indeed, immediately before the cantata, a deacon read from the pulpit (Fig. 10.8, lower right) the full text of this gospel:

Then shall the kingdom of heaven be likened unto ten virgins, which took their lamps, and went forth to meet the bridegroom. And five of them were wise, and five were foolish. They that were foolish took their lamps, but took no oil with them. . . . And at midnight there was a cry made, Behold, the bridegroom cometh; go ye out to meet him. Then all those virgins arose, and trimmed their lamps. And the foolish said unto the wise, Give us of your oil; for our lamps are gone out. But the wise answered, saying, Not so; lest there be not enough for us and you: but go ye rather to them that sell, and buy for yourselves. And while they went to buy, the bridegroom came; and they that were ready went in with him to the marriage: and the door was shut. . . . Watch therefore, for ye know neither the day nor the hour wherein the Son of man cometh.

The message to every good Lutheran of Leipzig was clear: Get your spiritual house in order to receive the coming Christ. Thus Bach's cantatas were intended not as concert entertainment, but rather as religious instruction for his community—sermons in music.

Like most of Bach's cantatas, *Wachet auf* makes use of a **chorale**, a spiritual melody or religious folk song, of the Lutheran church. (In other denominations, such a melody is simply called a hymn.) Just as many people today know hymn tunes well, so most Lutherans of Bach's day knew their chorales by heart. Chorales, like hymns, were meant to be easy to remember; indeed, many of the melodies had begun life as folk songs and popular tunes. And, in keeping with their common origins, the musical forms of these chorales were generally straightforward. *Wachet auf* (see Listening Guide) has **AAB** form, and the seven musical phrases unfold in the following way: **A** (1, 2, 3) **A** (1, 2, 3) **B** (4–7, 3). The last phrase of section **A** returns at the end of **B** to round out the melody.

Bach uses the chorale *Wachet auf* to create a clear, large-scale structure, which is typical in his cantatas. Notice the formal symmetry across all seven movements of the work. The chorale is sung three times to three different stanzas of text, and these presentations appear at the beginning, middle, and end of the work. Between statements of the chorale tune come pairs of recitative and aria, each joyfully announcing the divine love that Christ would bring to the Christian community.

Figure 10.8

Looking across the parishioners' pews and toward the high altar at Saint Thomas's Church, Leipzig, as it was in the mid-nineteenth century. The pulpit for the sermon is at the right. In Bach's day, nearly 2,500 people would crowd into the church.

Movement						
1	**2**	**3**	**4**	**5**	**6**	**7**
Chorus chorale 1st stanza	Recitative	Aria (duet)	Chorus chorale 2nd stanza	Recitative	Aria (duet)	Chorus chorale 3rd stanza

Movement 1. Of the seven movements of the cantata *Wachet auf*, the most remarkable is the first, a gigantic chorale fantasy that displays a polyphonic mastery exceptional even for Bach. Here, Bach creates a multidimensional spectacle surrounding the coming of Christ. First, the orchestra announces Christ's arrival by means of a three-part ritornello (refrain) that conveys a sense of growing anticipation. Part **a** of the ritornello, with its dotted rhythm, suggests a steady march; part **b**, with its strong downbeat and then syncopations, imparts a tugging urgency; part **c,** with its rapid sixteenth notes, implies an unrestrained race toward the object of desire (Christ). Now the chorale melody enters high in the sopranos, the voice of tradition, or perhaps the voice of God. In long, steady notes placed squarely on downbeats, it calls the people to prepare themselves to receive God's Son. Beneath this the voices of the people—the

altos, tenors, and basses—scurry in rapid counterpoint, excited by the call to meet their Savior. Lowest of all is the bass of the *basso continuo*. It plods along, sometimes in a dotted pattern, sometimes in rapid eighth notes, but mostly in regularly recurring quarter notes falling on the beat. Are these, in Bach's mind, the steps of Christ? The masterful simultaneous handling of so many diverse musical lines shows why musicians, then and now, view Bach as the greatest contrapuntalist who ever lived.

Listening Guide

Johann Sebastian Bach, Cantata, *Wachet auf, ruft uns die Stimme* (1731)

First movement

Texture: Polyphonic

Form: **AAB**

5
1/30–31

WHAT TO LISTEN FOR: A multiplicity of musical elements all sounding simultaneously: an introductory ritornello, a chorale tune on high, mini-fugues in the lower voices, and a walking bass below

A section of chorale tune

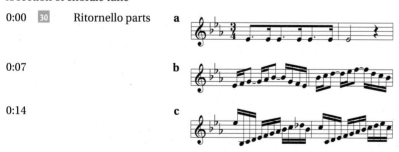

0:00	30	Ritornello parts	a
0:07			b
0:14			c

Chorale phrases sung by sopranos accompanied by horn, instrument of watchmen

0:28	Chorale phrase 1	Wachet auf, ruft uns die Stimme	Awake, a voice is calling
0:43	Ritornello part **a**		
0:50	Chorale phrase 2	Der Wächter sehr hoch auf der Zinne	From the watchmen from high in the tower
1:07	Ritornello part **b**		
1:14	Chorale phrase 3	Wach' auf, du Stadt Jerusalem!	Awake, Jerusalem!

Repeat of **A** section of chorale tune (0:00–1:30) with new text as required by repeat in chorale tune

| 1:31 | Ritornello parts **a**, **b**, and **c** | | |
| 2:00 | Chorale phrase 1 | Mitternacht heisst diese Stunde | Midnight is the hour |

2:15		Ritornello part **a**		
2:21		Chorale phrase 2	Sie rufen uns mit hellem Munde	They call us with a clarion voice
2:38		Ritornello part **b**		
2:46		Chorale phrase 3	Wo seid ihr klugen Jungfrauen?	Where are the Wise Virgins?

B section of chorale tune

3:05	31	0:00	Variation of ritornello parts **a**, **b**, and **c** leads to new keys.		
3:24		0:19	Chorale phrase 4	Wohl auf, der Bräutgam kommt	Get up, the Bridegroom comes
3:37		0:31	Ritornello part **a**		
3:42		0:36	Chorale phrase 5	Steht auf, die Lampen nehmt	Stand up and take your lamps
3:57		0:51	Altos, tenors, and basses enjoy extended imitative fantasy on "Alleluja."		
4:23		1:17	Chorale phrase 6	Alleluja	Alleluia
4:34		1:27	Ritornello part **a**		
4:44		1:37	Chorale phrase 7 begins	Macht euch bereit	Prepare yourselves
4:52		1:45	Ritornello part **a**		
4:58		1:52	Chorale phrase 7 ends	Zu der Hochzeit	For the wedding
5:07		2:00	Ritornello part **b**		
5:16		2:09	Chorale phrase 3	Ihr müsset ihm entgegen gehn!	You must go forth to meet him!
5:33		2:26	Ritornello parts **a**, **b**, and **c**		

🔊 Listen to streaming music in an Active Listening Guide at CourseMate or in the eBook.

What Did Mrs. Bach Do?

Actually, there were two Mrs. Bachs. The first, Maria Barbara, died suddenly in 1720, leaving the composer with four young children (three others had died in infancy). The second, Anna Magdalena, he married in 1722, and she would bear him thirteen more. Anna Magdalena Bach was a professional singer, earning about as much as her new husband at the court of Cöthen. When the family moved to Leipzig and the Saint Thomas Church, however, Anna Magdalena curtailed her professional activities. Women did not perform publicly in the Lutheran Church at this time; the difficult soprano lines in Bach's religious works were sung by choirboys. Consequently, Anna Magdalena put her musical skills to work as manager of what might be called "Bach Inc."

For almost every Sunday, J. S. Bach was required to produce a cantata, about twenty to twenty-five minutes of new music, week after week, year after year. Writing the music was only part of the high-pressure task. Rehearsals had to be set and music learned by the next Sunday. But composing and rehearsing paled in comparison to the amount of time needed to copy all the parts—these were the days before photocopy machines and software programs to notate music. Each of the approximately twelve independent lines of the full score had to be copied, entirely by hand, for each new cantata, along with sufficient copies (parts) for all the singers and players. For this, Bach turned to the members of his household—namely, his wife and children (both sons and daughters), his nephews, and other fee-paying private students who resided in the cantor's quarters at the Saint Thomas school (see Fig. 10.7). In 1731, the year he composed the cantata *Wachet auf, ruft uns die Stimme*, the roof was taken off the building and two more stories added to accommodate the Bach family and its "music industry."

When Bach died in 1750, he left his most valuable assets (his musical scores) to his eldest sons. The performing parts to many of his cantatas, however, he left to his wife, with the expectation that she would rent or sell them in the course of time, providing her with an old-age pension. In the end, however, the income from these cantata manuscripts did not prove sufficient—Bach's music was thought to be old-fashioned!—and Anna Magdalena Bach finished her days in 1760 in poverty, a ward of the city of Leipzig.

Movement 2. In this recitative, the Evangelist (the narrator) invites the daughters of Zion to the wedding feast; there is no use of chorale tune. In Bach's religious vocal music, the Evangelist is invariably sung by a tenor.

Movement 3. In this aria (duet) between the Soul (soprano) and Jesus (bass), the chorale tune is also not used. It is traditional in German sacred music of the Baroque era to assign the role of Christ to a bass.

Movement 4. For this meeting of Christ and the daughters of Zion (true believers), Bach fashioned one of his loveliest creations. Again the chorale tune serves as a unifying force, now carrying the second stanza of the chorale text. Once more Bach constructs a musical tapestry for chorus and orchestra, though a less complex one than the first movement. Here we hear only two central motives. One is the chorale melody sung by the tenors, who represent the watchmen calling on Jerusalem (Leipzig) to awake. The other is the exquisite melody played by all the violins and violas in unison—their togetherness symbolizing the unifying love of Christ for his people. This unison line is a perfect example of a lengthy, ever-expanding Baroque melody, and one of the most memorable of the entire era. Beneath it we hear the measured tread of the ever-present *basso continuo.* The bass plays regularly recurring quarter notes on the beat. As we have seen, a bass that moves at a moderate, steady pace, mostly in equal note values and often stepwise up or down the scale, is called a walking bass. The walking bass in this movement again enhances the text, underscoring the steady approach of the Lord. This movement was one of Bach's own favorites and the only cantata movement that he published—all the rest of his Leipzig cantata music was left in handwritten scores at the time of his death.

Listening Guide

Johann Sebastian Bach, *Wachet auf, ruft uns die Stimme*

Fourth movement

Texture: Polyphonic

Form: **AAB**

5   **2**
2/1   1/12

WHAT TO LISTEN FOR: Three-part polyphonic texture: melody in violins and violas, chorale tune in tenor voices, and walking bass

0:00	**1 12**	Violins and violas play flowing melody above walking bass.		
		Chorale phrases sung by the tenors		
0:43		Chorale phrases 1, 2, and 3	Zion hört die Wächter singen,	Zion hears the watchmen singing,
			Das Herz tut ihr vor Freuden springen,	The heart makes her spring up with joy.
			Sie wachet und steht eilend auf.	She awakes and quickly rises.
1:12		Flowing string melody repeated		
1:53		Chorale phrases 1, 2, and 3 repeated	Ihr Freund kommt vom Himmel prächtig,	Her splendid friend arrives from Heaven,
			Von Gnaden stark, von Wahrheit mächtig,	Mighty in grace, strong in truth,
2:22		Flowing string melody repeated	Ihr Licht wird hell, ihr Stern geht auf.	Her light grows bright, her star arises.
2:47		Chorale phrases 4, 5, and 6	Nun komm, du werte Kron,	Now come, you worthy crown,
			Herr Jesu, Gottes Sohn!	Lord, Jesus, Son of God!
			Hosanna!	Hosanna!
3:09		String melody continues in minor.		

3:28	Chorale phrases 7 and 3	Wir folgen all zum Freudensaal	We will follow all to the banquet hall
		Und halten mit das Abendmahl.	And share in the Lord's supper.
3:56	String melody concludes movement.		

🔊 Listen to streaming music in an Active Listening Guide at CourseMate or in the eBook.

🔊 Take online Listening Exercise 10.2 and receive feedback at CourseMate or in the eBook.

Movement 5. In this recitative for Christ (bass), the chorale tune is not used. Christ invites the anguished Soul to find comfort in Him.

Movement 6. In this aria (duet) for bass and soprano, again the chorale tune is not used. The form is ternary (**ABA**), which in an aria is often called *da capo* **form** because the performers, when reaching the end of **B**, "take it from the head" and repeat **A**. Here, Christ and the Soul sing a passionate love duet. A religious man who did not compose operas, Bach nonetheless heard many in nearby Dresden, a Catholic court center where opera flourished. In this ardent duet, devout Bach most closely approaches the world of the popular theater.

Movement 7. Bach's cantatas usually end with a simple four-voice homophonic setting of the last stanza of the chorale tune. In his closing movements, the composer always places the chorale melody in the soprano part, harmonizing and supporting it with the other three voices below. The instruments of the orchestra have no line of their own and merely double the four vocal parts. But more important, the members of the congregation join in the singing of the chorale melody. Martin Luther had ordained that the community should not merely witness but also participate in the act of worship. At this moment, all of the spiritual energy of Leipzig was concentrated into this one emphatic declaration of faith. The coming Christ reveals to all true believers a vision of life in the celestial kingdom.

Listening Guide

Johann Sebastian Bach, *Wachet auf, ruft uns die Stimme*

Seventh and last movement

5
2/2

Texture: Homophonic

Form: **AAB**

WHAT TO LISTEN FOR: To truly experience this music as Bach would have, think of music here as a medium that unites a community and reinforces a common set of values.

(continued)

0:00	[2]	Phrase 1	Gloria sei dir gesungen	May Glory be sung to you
		Phrase 2	Mit Menschen und englischen Zungen	With the tongues of man and angels
		Phrase 3	Mit Harfen und mit Zimbeln schon.	And harps and cymbals too.
0:24		Phrase 1	Von zwölf Perlen sind die Pforten,	The gates are of twelve pearls,
		Phrase 2	An deiner Stadt, wir sind Konsorten	In your city, we are consorts
		Phrase 3	Der Engel hoch um deiner Thron.	Of the angels high above your throne.
0:48		Phrase 4	Kein Aug hat je gespürt,	No eye has ever seen,
		Phrase 5	Kein Ohr hat je gehört	No ear has ever heard
		Phrase 6	Solche Freude.	Such joy.
		Phrase 7	Des sind wir froh,	Let us therefore rejoice,
			Io, io!	Io, io!
		Phrase 3	Ewig in dulci jubilo.	Eternally in sweet jubilation.

🔊 Listen to streaming music in an Active Listening Guide at CourseMate or in the eBook.

Figure 10.9

When Bach died in 1750, he was buried in an outlying parish church, and he and his music soon forgotten. But during the nineteenth century, the world came to realize that the citizens of Leipzig had had in their midst a musical genius. By then a theory had developed to the effect that the genius had a misshaped head. So in 1895, they dug up Bach to measure his skull to see if it was abnormally large or small (it was not), photographed his remains, and repositioned them beneath the high altar of his Saint Thomas Church (Saint Bach!).

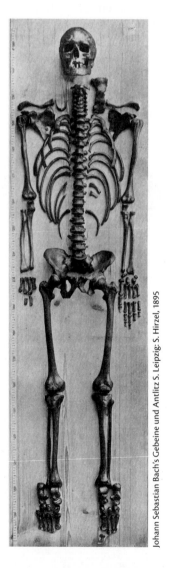

Johann Sebastian Bach's Gebeine und Antlitz S. Leipzig: S. Hirzel, 1895

In the last decade of his life, Bach gradually withdrew from the world to dwell in the contrapuntal realm of his own mind. He finished the best known of his large-scale contrapuntal projects, *The Well-Tempered Clavier* (1720–1742), a "clavier" simply being a general term for keyboard instruments. (It is called "Well-Tempered," or "Well-Tuned," because Bach was moving toward a tuning in which all the half steps were equidistant in pitch, something that had not been universally true before this time.) *The Well-Tempered Clavier* consists of two sets of twenty-four preludes and fugues. The **prelude** is a short preparatory piece that sets a mood and serves as a technical warm-up for the player before the fugue. In both sets of twenty-four, there is one prelude and fugue in each of the twelve major and twelve minor keys. Today every serious pianist around the world "cuts his or her teeth" on what is affectionately known as the "WTC."

Bach's last project was ***The Art of Fugue*** (1742–1750), an encyclopedic treatment of all known contrapuntal procedures set forth in nineteen canons and fugues. So closely did Bach identify with this project that he derived the four pitches of the final fugue subject (B♭-A-C-B♮ from the four letters of his name B-A-C-H (in the German system B = B♭ and H = B♮). *The Art of Fugue* was Bach's last musical effort; when he died in 1750 (the result of a stroke following unsuccessful cataract surgery), the work was left incomplete. Ironically, the same eye surgeon who operated on Bach also operated on Handel at the end of that composer's life—with a similarly unsuccessful result.

Key Words

subject (122)	pedal point (124)	chorale (129)
exposition (122)	cadenza (126)	*da capo* form (133)
episode (122)	cantata (128)	prelude (134)
fugue (122)	church cantata (128)	*The Art of Fugue* (134)

For a complete review of this chapter, see the Main Points, Chapter Quiz, Flashcards, and Glossary in CourseMate.

Join us on Facebook at **Listening to Music with Craig Wright**

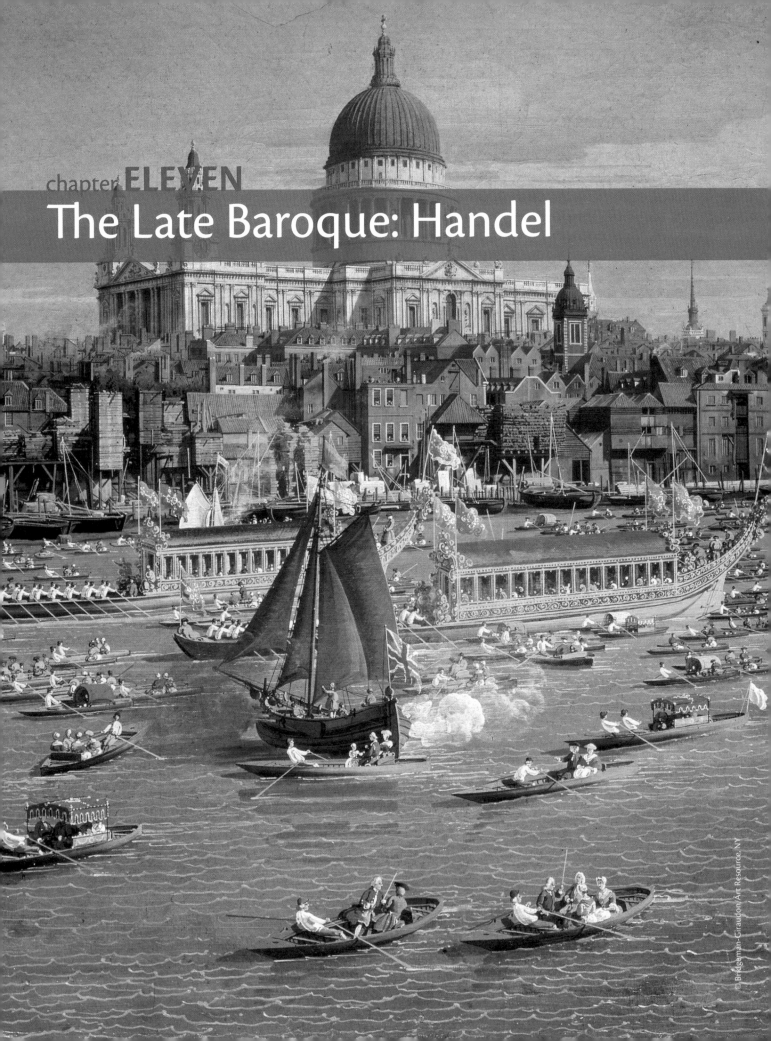

The Late Baroque: Handel

B ach and Handel were born in the same year, 1685, in small towns in central Germany. Other than that commonality, their careers could not have been more different. While Bach spent his life confined to towns in the region of his birth, the cosmopolitan Handel traveled the world—from Rome, to Venice, to Hamburg, to Amsterdam, to Dublin, and to London (see chapter opener). Though Bach was most at home playing organ fugues and conducting church cantatas from the choir loft, Handel was a musical entrepreneur working in the theater, by training and temperament a composer of opera. And though Bach fell into obscurity at the end of his life, retreating into a world of esoteric counterpoint, Handel's stature only grew larger on the international stage. During his lifetime, he became the most famous composer in Europe and a treasured national institution in England. In fact, owing to the eternal popularity of his *Messiah*, Handel is the first composer whose music never went out of fashion—and never had to be "rediscovered."

George Frideric Handel (1685–1759)

George Frideric Handel was born in the town of Halle, Germany, in 1685, and died in London in 1759 (Fig. 11.1). Although his father had decreed a program of study in law, the young Handel managed to cultivate his intense interest in music, sometimes secretly in the attic. At the age of eighteen, he left for the city of Hamburg, where he took a job as second violinist in the public opera (he was later promoted to continuo harpsichordist). But because the musical world around 1700 was dominated by things Italian, he set off for Italy to learn his trade and broaden his horizons. He moved between Florence and Venice, where he wrote operas, and Rome, where he composed mainly chamber cantatas. In 1710, Handel returned to North Germany to accept the post of chapel master to George, Elector of Hanover, but on the condition that he be given an immediate leave of absence to visit London. Although he made one final voyage back to his employer in Hanover in 1711 and many subsequent visits to the Continent, Handel conveniently "forgot" about his obligation to the Hanoverian court. London became the site of his musical activity and the place where he won fame and fortune.

In the early eighteenth century, London was the largest city in Europe, boasting a population of 500,000. It was also the capital city of a country in the process of forming an empire for international trade and commerce. London may not have possessed the rich cultural heritage of Rome or Paris, but it offered ample opportunity for financial gain. As a friend of Handel said famously: "In France and Italy there is something to learn, but in London there is something to earn."

Handel soon found employment in the homes of the aristocracy and took on the role of music tutor to the English royal family. As fate would have it, his continental employer, George of Hanover, became King George I of England in 1714, when the Hanoverians acceded to the English throne. (By law only a Protestant could wear the English crown, and "German George" was the nearest Protestant by lineage to be found.) Fortunately for Handel, the new king bore his truant countryman no grudge, and Handel became, in effect, royal court composer. For the court Handel produced such works as *Water Music* (1717) and *Music for the Royal Fireworks* (1749), as well as the Coronation Service (1727) for King George II and Queen Caroline, parts of which have been used at the coronation of every English monarch since then.

Handel and the Orchestral Dance Suite

The English royal family, which has historically suffered problems with its image, has sometimes given concerts of popular music to win favor with the public. Queen Elizabeth II, a direct descendant of King George I,

Figure 11.1

Thomas Hudson's portrait (1749) of Handel with the score of *Messiah* visible in the composer's left hand. Handel had a quick temper, could swear in four languages, and liked to eat.

Lebrecht Music and Arts

Figure 11.2

View of London, Saint Paul's Cathedral, and the Thames River by Canaletto (1697–1768). Notice the large barges. Crafts such as these could have easily accommodated the fifty musicians reported to have played behind the king as he moved upstream in 1717, listening to Handel's *Water Music*. On June 3, 2012, Queen Elizabeth II made a similar nautical journey up the Thames as part of her "Diamond Jubilee" celebration.

did so in 2012—inviting Elton John and Paul McCartney to her "Diamond Jubilee" celebration at Buckingham Palace and giving away free tickets to her subjects via lottery. Handel's *Water Music* was created for an earlier bit of royal image burnishing. In 1717, new King George was an unpopular monarch. He refused to speak a word of English, preferring his native German. He fought with his son, the Prince of Wales, even banning him from court. His subjects considered George dimwitted—"an honest blockhead," as one contemporary put it.

To improve his standing in the eyes of his subjects, the king's ministers planned a program of public entertainments, including an evening of music on the Thames River for the lords of Parliament and the lesser people of London (Fig. 11.2). Thus, on July 17, 1717, the king and his court left London, accompanied by a small armada of boats, and progressed up the Thames to the strains of Handel's orchestral music. An eyewitness describes this nautical parade in detail:

> About eight in the evening the King repaired to his barge, into which were admitted the Duchess of Bolton, Countess Godolphin, Madam de Kilmansech [the king's mistress], Mrs. Were and the Earl of Orkney, the Gentleman of the Bedchamber in Waiting. Next to the King's barge was that of the musicians, about 50 in number, who played on all kinds of instruments, to wit trumpets, horns, hautboys [oboes], bassoons, German flutes, French flutes [recorders], violins and basses; but there were no singers. The music had been composed specially by the famous Handel, a native of Halle [Germany], and His Majesty's principal Court Composer. His Majesty so greatly approved of the music that he caused it to be repeated three times in all, although each performance lasted an hour—namely twice before and once after supper. The evening weather was all that could be desired for the festivity, the number of barges and above all of boats filled with people desirous of hearing the music was beyond counting.

The score played for King George and the crowd of music lovers moving on the Thames River was, of course, Handel's *Water Music. Water Music* belongs to a genre called the **dance suite**: a collection of dances, usually from two to seven in number, all in one key and for one group of instruments, be it full orchestra, trio, or solo. (The term derives from the French word *suite*, meaning "a succession of things or pieces.") No one danced, of course, especially not during this naval parade. These were stylized, abstract dances intended only for the ear. It was the job of the composer, however, to bring each one to life—to tell the listener, by means of salient rhythms and stereotypical melodic gestures, which particular dance was being played. Among the dances found in a typical late-Baroque suite are the allemande (literally, "German dance"; a moderate or brisk, stately dance in duple meter), the sarabande (a slow, sensual dance of Spanish origin in triple meter), and the minuet (a moderate, elegant dance in triple meter).

Almost all dances of the Baroque period were composed in one musical form: binary form (**AB**), the two sections of which could be repeated. Some dance movements are followed by a second, complementary dance called a trio (**CD**) because it was originally played by only three instruments. When a minuet, for example, is followed by a trio and the minuet repeated, a large-scale ternary arrangement results:

AB|CD|AB. What make the dance movements of *Water Music* so enjoyable and easy to follow are their tuneful themes and formal clarity. Notice in the Minuet and Trio how Handel asks the French horns and trumpets first to announce both the **A** and **B** sections before passing this material on to the woodwinds and then the full orchestra. Here, instrumentation makes the form clearly audible.

Listening Guide

George Frideric Handel, *Water Music* (1717)

5
2/3–4

Minuet and Trio

Genre: Dance from dance suite

Form: Binary (**AB**) within larger ternary (**ABCDAB**)

WHAT TO LISTEN FOR: The jaunty sound of the minuet, presented here by various combinations of instruments, contrasted with the somber tones of the trio played by strings and continuo alone

MINUET (triple meter, major key)

0:00	3	**A**		French horns introduce part **A**.
0:12		**B**		Trumpets introduce part **B**.
0:29		**A**		Winds and continuo play **A**.
0:42				Full orchestra repeats **A**.
0:55		**B**		Winds and continuo play **B**.
1:08				Full orchestra repeats **B**.

TRIO (triple meter, minor key)

| 1:28 | 4 | **C** | 0:00 | Strings and continuo play part **C**. |
| 1:43 | | **D** | 0:15 | Strings and continuo play part **D**. |

MINUET

| 2:19 | | **A** | 0:51 | Full orchestra plays **A**. |
| 2:31 | | **B** | 1:03 | Full orchestra plays **B**. |

Listen to streaming music in an Active Listening Guide at CourseMate or in the eBook.

Handel and Opera

George Frideric Handel emigrated from Germany to England in 1710 not for the chance to entertain the king, and certainly not for the cuisine or the climate. Rather, he went to London to make money producing Italian opera. With the rare exception of a work such as Purcell's *Dido and Aeneas* (see Ch. 8, "Opera in London"), London had no opera at this time. The legacy of Shakespeare in England remained strong, and the occasional sonic interlude was about as much music as English audiences tolerated in their spoken plays. Handel aimed to change this. London audiences, he reasoned, were daily growing wealthier and more worldly, and would welcome the importation of a cosmopolitan "high art" form, namely, Italian opera. Guaranteeing himself a healthy share of the profits, Handel formed an opera company, the Royal Academy of Music, in which he served as composer, producer, and performer. He wrote the music, engaged highly paid soloists from Italy, led the rehearsals, and conducted the

Figure 11.3

In 1730, Handel tried (unsuccessfully) to hire the celebrated castrato Farinelli, whose life was chronicled in a film of the same name (1994). For the film, the now-extinct castrato voice was simulated by synthesizing a female soprano with a male falsetto voice.

Figure 11.4

Title page of an early English edition of Handel's opera *Julius Caesar*. The musicians form a *basso continuo*.

finished product from the harpsichord in the orchestra pit. His first opera, *Rinaldo*, premiered at the Queen's Theatre in 1711, the same theater in which Andrew Lloyd Webber's *Phantom of the Opera* first saw the light of day in 1986.

The type of Italian opera Handel produced in London is called **opera seria** (literally, serious, as opposed to comic, opera), a style that then dominated the operatic stage throughout continental Europe. These were long, three-act works that chronicled the triumphs and tragedies of kings and queens, gods and goddesses. Affirming the values of the "high born," they naturally appealed to the English upper crust. *Opera seria* tends to be theatrically static: Much of the action occurs off stage and is simply reported in the form of recitatives. The principal characters do not so much act as react to these unseen events, through arias that express stock emotions—hope, anger, hate, frenzy, and despair, to name a few.

In Handel's day, the leading male role was usually sung by a castrato—a castrated male with the vocal range of a female (Fig. 11.3; see Ch. 6, "Male Choirs: The Castrato"). Baroque audiences associated high social standing on stage with a high voice, male or female. From 1710 until 1728, Handel had great artistic and some financial success, producing two dozen examples of Italian *opera seria*. Foremost among these was *Giulio Cesare in Eggito* (*Julius Caesar in Egypt,* 1724), a recasting of the story of Caesar's conquest of the army of Egypt and Cleopatra's romantic conquest of Caesar (Fig. 11.4). Conforming to Baroque convention, the male hero (Julius Caesar) was portrayed by a castrato and sung in a high, "womanly" register.

But opera—then and now—is a financially risky business, and in 1728, Handel's Royal Academy of Music went bankrupt, a victim of the exorbitant fees paid to the star singers and the fickle tastes of English theatergoers. Handel continued to write operas into the early 1740s, but he increasingly turned his attention to a musical genre similar in construction to opera, but more lucrative: oratorio.

Handel and Oratorio

An **oratorio** is literally "something sung in an oratory," an oratory being a hall or chapel used specifically for prayer and sometimes prayer with music. Thus the oratorio in seventeenth-century Italy had something in common with today's gospel music: It was sacred music sung in a special hall or chapel, intended to inspire the faithful to greater devotion. By the time it reached Handel's hands, however, the oratorio had become close to an unstaged opera with a religious subject.

Both Baroque oratorio and opera begin with an overture, are divided into acts, and are composed primarily of recitatives and arias sung by characters. Both genres are also long, usually lasting two to three hours. But there are a few important differences between opera and oratorio, aside from the obvious fact that oratorio treats a religious subject. Oratorio, being a quasi-religious genre, is performed in a church, a theater, or a concert hall, but it makes no use of acting, staging, or costumes. Because the subject matter is almost always sacred, the oratorio affords more opportunity for moralizing, a dramatic function best performed by a chorus. Thus the chorus assumes greater importance in an oratorio. It sometimes serves as a narrator but more often functions, like the chorus in ancient Greek drama, as the voice of the people commenting on the action that has transpired.

By the 1730s, oratorio appeared to Handel as an attractive alternative to the increasingly unprofitable opera in London. He could do away with the irascible and expensive castrati and prima donnas. He no longer had to pay for elaborate sets and costumes. He could draw on the ancient English love of choral music, a tradition that extended well back into the Middle Ages. And he could exploit a new, untapped market—the faithful of the Puritan, Methodist, and growing evangelical sects in England, who had viewed the pleasures of foreign opera with distrust and even contempt. In contrast to the Italian opera, the oratorio was sung in English, contributing further to the appeal of the genre to a large segment of English society.

MESSIAH (1741)

Beginning in 1732 and continuing over a twenty-year period, Handel wrote upward of twenty oratorios. The most famous of these is his *Messiah*, composed in the astonishingly short period of three and a half weeks during the summer of 1741. It was first performed in Dublin, Ireland, the following April as part of a charity benefit, with Handel conducting. Having heard the dress rehearsal, the local press waxed enthusiastic about the new oratorio, saying that it "far surpasses anything of that Nature, which has been performed in this or any other Kingdom." Such a large crowd was expected for the work of the famous Handel that ladies were urged not to wear hoopskirts and gentlemen were admonished to leave their swords at home. In this way, an audience of 700 could be squeezed into a hall of only 600 seats.

Buoyed by his artistic and financial success in Dublin, Handel took *Messiah* back to London, made minor alterations, and performed it in Covent Garden Theater. In 1750, he offered *Messiah* again, this time in the chapel of the Foundling Hospital, an orphanage in London (Fig. 11.5), and again there was much popular acclaim for Handel, as well as profit for charity. This was the first time one of his oratorios was sung in a religious setting rather than a theater or a concert hall. The annual repetition of *Messiah* in the Foundling Hospital chapel during Handel's lifetime and long after did much to convince the public that his oratorios were essentially religious music to be performed in church.

In a general way, *Messiah* tells the story of the life of Christ. It is divided into three parts (instead of three acts): (I) the prophecy of His coming and His Incarnation; (II) His Passion and Resurrection, and the triumph of the Gospel; and (III) reflections on the Christian victory over death. Most of Handel's oratorios recount the heroic deeds of characters from the Old Testament; *Messiah* is exceptional because the subject comes from the New Testament, though much of the libretto is drawn directly from both the Old and New Testaments. Moreover, unlike Handel's other oratorios, the text features neither plot action nor "characters" in the dramatic sense. The drama of Christian "eschatology"—a fancy word suggesting the contemplation of death, resurrection, and heaven—is experienced in the mind of the listener.

Messiah has many beautiful and stirring arias, including "Ev'ry valley shall be exalted" and "O thou that tellest good tidings to Zion." Perhaps the loveliest of all, though, is the pastoral aria "He shall feed His flock," which comes at the end of Part I and alludes to the birth of Christ. A **pastoral aria** has several distinctive characteristics, all of which suggest the movement of simple shepherds attending the Christ Child: The melody glides along mainly in stepwise motion; the rhythms are repetitive, thereby allowing the triple meter to be easily heard; and the harmony changes slowly over a drone, in imitation of shepherds' bagpipes. Even the key of F major is suggestive, for F major was traditionally heard as a relaxed tonality, and composers from Bach to Beethoven and beyond employed its particular sound to evoke shepherds and pastoral scenes. (Before the mid-nineteenth century, each key was tuned a slightly different

Listen to a performance of "He shall feed his flock" in the YouTube playlist at CourseMate for this text.

Figure 11.5

The chapel of the Foundling Hospital, London, where *Messiah* was performed annually for the benefit of the orphans. Handel himself designed and donated the organ seen on the second story at the back of the hall.

way and had its own particular associations.) But let's not kill a beautiful melody with too much analysis and history. Just listen to what is arguably the most relaxing aria ever written, an anthem for peace.

Listening Guide

George Frideric Handel, *Messiah*, Aria, "He shall feed His flock" (1741)

Genre: Pastoral aria from an oratorio

2/5–6

Form: Strophic (two stanzas with vocal ornamentation applied to the second, some written by Handel, some added by the singer of this recording)

WHAT TO LISTEN FOR: Although the peaceful mood is constant throughout, an abrupt change of register—indeed, of singer (alto gives way to soprano)—comes at the second stanza.

He shall feed His flock like a shep - herd,

0:00	**5**		Instrumental introduction

STANZA 1

0:20			Undulating melody unfolds above slowly changing harmony.	He shall feed His flock like a shepherd And He shall gather the lambs with His arm.
0:50			Repeat of first lines with slight orna-mentation	
1:17			Modulation to minor key	And carry them in His bosom,
1:40			Return to tonic major key	And gently lead those that are with young.
2:01			Instruments lead modulation to higher range (dominant key).	

STANZA 2

2:13	**6**	0:00	Melody of stanza 1 in higher range; ornaments added to melodic line	Come unto Him all ye that labour, Come unto Him that are heavy laden and He will give you rest.
2:43		0:30	Repeat of first lines with increased ornamentation	
3:11		0:58	Modulation to minor key	Take His yoke upon you, and learn of Him
3:33		1:18	Return to tonic major	For He is meek and lowly of heart and ye shall find rest unto your souls.
3:56		1:41	Repeat of last lines with increased ornamentation	
4:42		2:27	Instruments conclude with reminis-cence of beginning.	

Listen to streaming music in an Active Listening Guide at CourseMate or in the eBook.

Despite the beauty of the arias, the true glory of *Messiah* is to be found in its nineteen choruses. Handel is arguably the finest composer for chorus who ever lived. As a world traveler with an unsurpassed ear, he absorbed a variety of musical styles from throughout Europe: In Germany, he acquired knowledge of the fugue and the Lutheran chorale; in Italy, he immersed himself in the styles of the oratorio and the chamber cantata; and during his years in England, he became familiar with the idioms of the English church anthem (essentially an extended motet). Most important, having spent a lifetime in the opera house, Handel had a flair for the dramatic.

Nowhere is Handel's choral mastery more evident than in the justly famous "Hallelujah" chorus that concludes Part II of *Messiah*. We have moved from peaceful, pastoral adoration to triumphant resurrection, and now a variety of choral styles are displayed in quick succession: chordal, unison, fugal, and fugal and chordal together. The opening word "Hallelujah" recurs throughout as a powerful refrain, yet each new phrase of text generates its own distinct musical idea. The vivid phrases speak directly to the listener, making the audience feel like a participant in the drama. So moved by this music was King George II, or so the story goes, that he rose to his feet in admiration at the great opening chords. This event established the tradition of the audience standing for the "Hallelujah" chorus—for no one sat while the king stood. Indeed, this movement would serve well as a royal coronation march, though in *Messiah*, of course, it is Christ the King who is being crowned.

Listening Guide

George Frideric Handel, *Messiah*, "Hallelujah" chorus (1741)

(intro) 18

Genre: Oratorio chorus

Form: Through-composed

WHAT TO LISTEN FOR: The masterful use of contrasting textures (monophonic, homophonic, and polyphonic) to create drama—for at the heart of drama lies contrast

0:00	**18**	Brief string introduction	
0:06		Chorus enters with two salient motives.	
0:14		Five more chordal exclamations of "Hallelujah" motive, but at higher pitch level	
0:23		Chorus sings new theme in unison answered by chordal cries of "Hallelujah."	
0:34		Music repeated but at lower pitch	
0:45		Fugue-like imitation begins with subject.	For the Lord God omnipotent reigneth
1:09		Quiet and then loud; set in chorale style	The kingdom of this world is become the Kingdom of our Lord . . .
1:27		New fugue-like section begins with entry in bass.	
1:48		Altos and then sopranos begin long ascent in long notes.	King of Kings and Lord of Lords
2:28		Basses and sopranos reenter.	And he shall reign for ever and ever

(continued)

2:40	Tenors and basses sing in long notes.	King of Kings and Lord of Lords
2:55	Incessant major tonic chord	King of Kings
3:20	Broad final cadence	Hallelujah

🔊)) Listen to streaming music in an Active Listening Guide at CourseMate or in the eBook.

🔊)) Take online Listening Exercise 11.1 and receive feedback at CourseMate or in the eBook.

Figure 11.6

Eighteenth-century London was a place of biting satire. Here, in William Hogarth's *The Oratorio Singer* (1732), the chorus of an oratorio is the object of parody. But there is an element of truth here: The chorus for the first performance of *Messiah*, for example, numbered about sixteen males, with choirboys (front row) taking the soprano part. Women, however, sang soprano and alto for the vocal solos.

The "Hallelujah" chorus is a strikingly effective work mainly because the large choral force creates a variety of exciting textures. In fact, however, Handel's chorus for the original Dublin *Messiah* was much smaller than those used today. It included about four singers on the alto, tenor, and bass parts and six choirboys singing the soprano (Fig. 11.6). The orchestra was equally slight. For the Foundling Hospital performances of the 1750s, however, the orchestra grew to thirty-five players. Then, over the next hundred years, the chorus progressively swelled to as many as 4,000 with a balancing orchestra of 500 in what were billed as "Festivals of the People"—a precursor of the *Messiah* sing-alongs that we have today.

And, just as the performing forces for his *Messiah* continually increased, so, too, did Handel's fortune and reputation grow. Toward the end of his life, he occupied a squire's house in the center of London; bought paintings, including a large and "indeed excellent" Rembrandt; and, on his death, left an enormous estate of nearly £20,000 (roughly $5 million), as the newspapers of the day were quick to report. More than 3,000 persons attended his funeral in Westminster Abbey on April 20, 1759, and a sculpture of the composer holding an aria from *Messiah* was erected above his grave (Fig. 11.7). As an enduring monument to Handel's music, *Messiah* was an apt choice, for it is still performed each year at Christmas and Easter by countless amateur and professional groups throughout the world.

Figure 11.7

Handel's funeral monument at Westminster Abbey. The composer holds the aria "I know that my Redeemer liveth" from *Messiah*. When Handel was buried, the gravedigger left room to cram in another body immediately adjacent. That space was later filled by the corpse of Charles Dickens.

Key Words

dance suite (138)   oratorio (140)   pastoral aria (141)

opera seria (140)

For a complete review of this chapter, see the Main Points, Chapter Quiz, Flashcards, and Glossary in CourseMate.

f Join us on Facebook at **Listening to Music with Craig Wright**

Checklists of Musical Style

Late Baroque: 1690–1750

REPRESENTATIVE COMPOSERS

Lully	Vivaldi	Bach
Pachelbel	Mouret	Handel
Corelli		

A complete Checklist of Musical Style for the late Baroque can be found at CourseMate for this text.

PRINCIPAL GENRES

French overture	solo concerto	oratorio
dance suite	church cantata	prelude
sonata	opera	fugue
concerto grosso		

Melody	Melody is marked by progressive development, growing longer and more expansive; idiomatic instrumental style influences vocal melodies; melodic sequence becomes prevalent
Harmony	Functional chord progressions govern harmonic movement—harmony moves purposefully from one chord to the next; *basso continuo* continues to provide strong bass
Rhythm	Exciting, driving, energized rhythms propel the music forward with vigor; "walking" bass creates feeling of rhythmic regularity
Color	Instruments reign supreme; instrumental sounds, especially of violin, harpsichord, and organ, set musical tone for the era; one tone color used throughout a movement or large section of a movement
Texture	Homophonic texture remains important, but denser, polyphonic texture reemerges in the contrapuntal fugue
Form	Binary form in sonatas and dance suites; *da capo* aria (ternary) form in arias; fugal procedure used in fugues; ritornello form in concertos

part. FOUR

The Classical Period, 1750–1820

1750	1755	1760	1765	1770	1775	1780	1785

CLASSICAL

1756–1763 Seven Years' War (French and Indian War)

● 1759 Voltaire publishes Enlightenment novel *Candide*

● 1761 Joseph Haydn takes first job at Esterházy court

● 1762 Rousseau publishes outline for just government in *The Social Contract*

1763–1766 Mozart family tours and performs around Western Europe

1773–1780 Mozart based mostly in Salzburg

● 1776 American Declaration of Independence signed in Philadelphia

● 1781 Mozart moves to Vienna and composes operas, symphonies, concertos, and quartets

During the years 1750–1820, music manifested a style called "Classicism," often termed "Neoclassicism" in the other fine arts. In art and architecture, for example, Neoclassicism aimed to reinstitute the aesthetic values of the ancient Greeks and Romans by incorporating balance and harmonious proportions while avoiding ornate decoration, all leading to a feeling of strength, quiet grace, and noble simplicity. When expressed in music, these same tendencies appeared as balanced phrases, uncluttered textures, and clear, easily audible musical forms. Although composers in cities such as Milan, Paris, and London all wrote symphonies and sonatas with these qualities, the music of this period is often referred to as the "Viennese Classical style." Vienna, Austria, was the capital city of the Holy Roman Empire and the most active center of Classical music in Central Europe. The three principal composers of the Classical era—Joseph Haydn (1732–1809), Wolfgang Amadeus Mozart (1756–1791), and Ludwig van Beethoven (1770–1827)—chose to make Vienna their home because of the city's vibrant musical life. In many ways, Mozart and Haydn created the Classical style, while Beethoven extended it. The majority of the works of Beethoven fall within the time frame of the Classical era, but they also sometimes exhibit stylistic characteristics of the succeeding Romantic period.

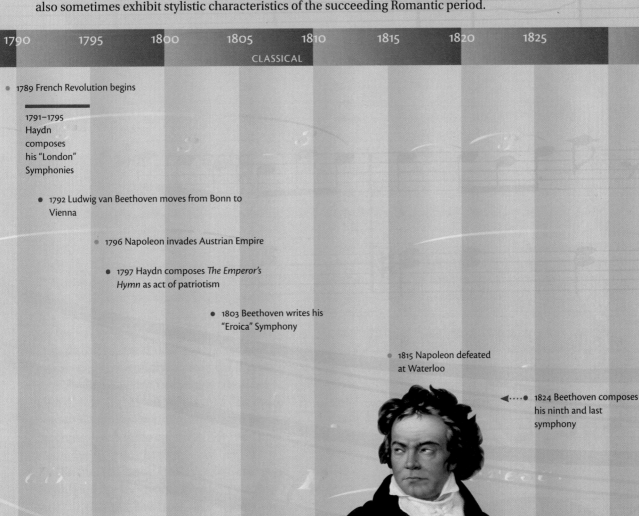

| 1790 | 1795 | 1800 | 1805 | 1810 | 1815 | 1820 | 1825 |

CLASSICAL

1789 French Revolution begins

1791–1795 Haydn composes his "London" Symphonies

1792 Ludwig van Beethoven moves from Bonn to Vienna

1796 Napoleon invades Austrian Empire

1797 Haydn composes *The Emperor's Hymn* as act of patriotism

1803 Beethoven writes his "Eroica" Symphony

1815 Napoleon defeated at Waterloo

1824 Beethoven composes his ninth and last symphony

chapter TWELVE
Classical Style

iStockphoto

"Classical" as a musical term has two separate, though related, meanings. We use the word *classical* to signify the "serious" or "learned" music of the West, as distinguished from folk music, popular music, and the traditional music of various ethnic cultures. We call this music "classical" because something about the excellence of its form and style makes it enduring, just as a finely crafted watch or a vintage automobile may be labeled a "classic" because it has a timeless beauty. Yet in the same breath, we may refer to "Classical" music (now with a capital C), and by this we mean the music of a specific historical period, 1750–1820, a period of the great works of Haydn and Mozart and the early masterpieces of Beethoven. The creations of these artists have become so identified in the public mind with musical proportion, balance, and formal correctness—with standards of musical excellence—that this comparatively brief period has given its name to all music of lasting aesthetic worth.

"Classical" derives from the Latin *classicus*, meaning "something of the first rank or highest quality." To the men and women of the eighteenth century, no art was more admirable and worthy of emulation than that of ancient Greece and Rome. Other periods in Western history also have been inspired by classical antiquity—the Renaissance heavily (see Fig. 6.1), the early Baroque less so, and the twentieth century to some degree—but no period more than the eighteenth century. Classical architecture, with its formal control of space, geometric shapes, balance, and symmetrical design, became the only style thought worthy for domestic and state buildings of consequence. European palaces, opera houses, theaters, and country homes all made use of it. While American ambassador to France, Thomas Jefferson also traveled to Italy and later brought Classical design to the United States (Figs. 12.1 and 12.2). Our nation's Capitol, many state capitols, and countless other governmental and university buildings abound with the well-proportioned columns, porticos, and rotundas of the Classical style.

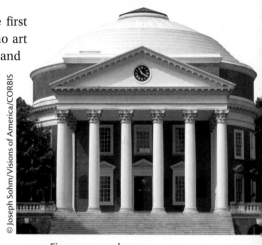

Figures 12.1 and 12.2

(top) The second-century Pantheon in Rome. (bottom) The library of the University of Virginia, designed by Thomas Jefferson in the late eighteenth century. Jefferson had visited Italy and studied the ancient ruins while serving as ambassador to France (1784–1789). The portico, with columns and triangular pediment, and the central rotunda are all elements of Classical style in architecture.

The Enlightenment

The Classical era in music, art, and architecture coincides with the period in philosophy and letters known as the **Enlightenment**. During the Enlightenment, also referred to as the Age of Reason, thinkers gave free rein to the pursuit of truth and the discovery of natural laws, formulated largely by Isaac Newton (1642–1727). Science now began to provide as many explanations for the mysteries of life as did religion. In many churches around Europe the medieval stained glass depicting saintly legends was replaced by clear glass that let in natural light: a literal example of "enlightenment." This was also the age of such scientific advances as the discovery of electricity and the invention of the steam engine. The first *Encyclopedia Britannica* appeared in 1771, and the French *Encyclopédie*—a twenty-four-volume set that aimed to replace medieval faith with modern, scientific reasoning—between 1751 and 1772. French encyclopedists Voltaire (1694–1778) and Jean-Jacques Rousseau (1712–1778) espoused the principles of social justice, equality, religious tolerance, and freedom of speech. These Enlightenment ideals subsequently became fundamental to democratic government and were enshrined in the American Constitution.

As might be expected, the notion that all persons are created equal and should enjoy full political freedom set the thinkers of the Enlightenment on a collision course with the defenders of the existing social order. The old political structure had been built on the superstitions of the Church, the privileges of the nobility, and the divine right of kings. Voltaire attacked the habits and prerogatives of both clergy and aristocracy, and championed middle-class virtues: honesty, common sense, and hard work. The extravagant gestures and powdered wigs of the frivolous courtier were easy targets for his pen. A more natural appearance, one appropriate to a tradesman, merchant, or manufacturer, now became the paradigm (Fig. 12.3). Spurred on by economic self-interest and the new principles of the Enlightenment, an expanding, more confident middle class in France and America rebelled against the monarchy and its supporters. The American colonists issued a Declaration of Independence in 1776, and French citizens stormed the Bastille in 1789 to seize weapons, thereby precipitating a civil war among classes. By the end of the eighteenth century, the Age of Reason gave way to the Age of Revolution.

Figure 12.3

Thomas Jefferson, by the French sculptor Houdon, done in Paris in 1789, the year of the French Revolution

Figure 12.4

A performance at the Burgtheater in Vienna in the late 1700s. The nobility occupied the frontmost seats on the floor, but the area behind them was open to all. So, too, in the galleries, the aristocracy bought boxes low and close to the stage, while commoners occupied higher rungs, as well as the standing room in the fourth gallery. Ticket prices depended, then as now, on proximity to the performers.

The Democratization of Classical Music: Public Concerts

Music was not exempt from the social changes sweeping eighteenth-century Europe and America. In fact, the century witnessed something of a democratization of classical music. The "audience base" for such music expanded greatly, extending now to the newly affluent middle class. In an earlier day, when art music was performed in only two venues (church and court), the average citizen heard very little of it. By midcentury, however, the bookkeeper, physician, cloth merchant, and stock trader collectively had enough disposable income to organize and patronize their own concerts. In Paris, then a city of 450,000 residents, one could attend, as was then said, "the best concerts every day with complete freedom." The most successful Parisian concert series was the *Concert spirituel* (founded in 1725), at which the West's first noncourt orchestra played a regular schedule of performances. The *Concert spirituel* advertised its offerings by means of flyers distributed in the streets. To make its performances accessible to several strata of society, it instituted a two-tiered price scheme for a subscription series (4 *livres* for boxes and 2 *livres* for the pit, roughly $200 and $100 in today's money). Children under fifteen were admitted for half price. Thus we can trace to the middle of the eighteenth century the commercialization of a shared musical experience. The institution of the "concert" as we know it today dates from this time.

Public concerts sprang up in London, in the Vauxhall Gardens—the eighteenth-century equivalent of Disney World—which drew as many as 4,500 paying visitors daily. Here, symphonies could be heard inside in the orchestra room or outside when the weather was good. When Leopold Mozart took his young son Wolfgang to concerts there in 1764, he was surprised to see that the audience was not segregated by class. Likewise in Vienna, the Burgtheater (City Theater; Fig. 12.4) opened in 1759 to any and all paying customers, as long as they were properly dressed and properly behaved. Although the allure was music, the hall itself became a place for a leveling of social classes. As their

numbers increased, the middle classes began to vie with the aristocracy for control of high culture—to have a say in the kind of music to be heard.

Watch a video of Craig Wright's Open Yale Course class session 17, "Mozart and His Operas," at CourseMate for this text.

The Rise of Popular Opera

Social reform in the eighteenth century affected not only the people who went to concerts but also those who went to the opera and even the characters who populated the stage. A new musical genre, comic opera, appeared and soon drove the established *opera seria* to the wings. Baroque *opera seria* had portrayed the deeds of heroic rulers and glorified the status quo, making it, in essence, an aristocratic art. By contrast, the new **comic opera**, called **opera buffa** in Italy, exemplified social change and championed middle-class values. Comic opera made use of everyday characters and situations; it typically employed spoken dialogue and simple songs in place of recitatives and lengthy *da capo* (**ABA**) arias; and it was liberally spiced with sight gags, bawdy humor, and social satire.

Like seditious pamphlets, comic operas appeared across Europe; among them were John Gay's *The Beggar's Opera* (1728) in England, Giovanni Pergolesi's *La serva padrona* (*The Maid Made Master,* 1733) in Italy, and Rousseau's *Le Devin du village* (*The Village Soothsayer,* 1752) in France. Even a "high-end" composer like Mozart embraced the more natural, down-to-earth spirit of the comic style. Mozart was not always treated fairly by his noble employers, and several of his operas are rife with anti-aristocratic sentiment. In *Don Giovanni* (1787), for example, the villain is a leading nobleman of the town. In *Le nozze di Figaro* (*The Marriage of Figaro,* 1786) a barber outwits a count and exposes him to public ridicule (see Fig. 12.7). So seriously did the king of France and the Holy Roman Emperor take the threat of such theatrical satire that they banned the play on which *Le nozze di Figaro* was based. Comic theater and comic opera, it seemed, not only reflected social change but could also inspire it.

The Advent of the Piano

Finally, the newly affluent middle class was not content merely to attend concerts and operatic performances; they also wished to make their own music at home. Most of this domestic music making revolved around an instrument that first entered public consciousness in the Classical period: the piano. Invented in Italy about 1700, the piano gradually replaced the harpsichord as the keyboard instrument of choice—and with good reason, for the piano could play at more than one dynamic level (hence the original name **pianoforte**, "soft-loud"). Compared with the harpsichord, the piano could produce gradual dynamic changes, well-shaped phrases, and—ultimately—more power.

Those who played this new domestic instrument were mostly amateurs, and the great majority of these were women (Fig. 12.5). A smattering of French, an eye for needlepoint, and some skill at the piano—these were signs of status and gentility that rendered a young woman suitable for marriage. For the nonprofessional woman to play in the home, however, a simpler, more homophonic style of keyboard music was needed, one that would not tax the presumed technical limitations of the performer. The spirit of democracy may have been in the air, but this was still very much a sexist age. It was assumed that ladies would not wish, as one publication said, "to

Figure 12.5

Marie Antoinette, in 1770 at the age of fifteen, seated at an early piano. In 1774, this Austrian princess became queen of France, but in 1793, at the height of the French Revolution, she was beheaded.

© Kunsthistorisches Museum, Vienna, Austria/The Bridgeman Art Library

bother their pretty little heads with counterpoint and harmony," but would be content with a tuneful melody and a few rudimentary chords to flesh it out. Collections such as *Keyboard Pieces for Ladies* (1768) were directed at these new musical consumers.

 # Elements of Classical Style

Fashions change. At the beginning of the eighteenth century, aristocratic men powdered their faces, painted on "beauty spots," and wore elaborate wigs (see George Frideric Handel, Fig. 11.1). By century's end a simpler, more natural style was in vogue (see Thomas Jefferson, Fig. 12.3). So, too, did musical style evolve during the eighteenth century. Compared with the relentless, ornate, and often grandiose sound of the Baroque era, Classical music is lighter in tone, generally simpler, and sometimes more folk-like, yet still full of high drama. It is even capable of humor and surprise, as when Joseph Haydn explodes with a thunderous chord in a quiet passage in his "Surprise" Symphony (1791). But what, in precise musical terms, creates the levity, grace, clarity, and balance characteristic of Classical music?

Melody

Perhaps most striking about the music of Haydn and Mozart is the fact that the melody is usually tuneful, catchy, even singable. Not only are melodies simple and short, but the phrases are balanced, often organized into matching antecedent-consequent, or "question-answer" pairs. **Antecedent** and **consequent phrases** are units that operate together: One opens, the other closes. To see how this works, think of the first two phrases (the first ten words) of "Twinkle, Twinkle Little Star," a folk song set by Mozart. During the eighteenth century the simple structure of the folk song came to influence the organization of melody in more learned music. As a result, classical melodies tend to be short, balanced phrases of 2 + 2 measures, or 3 + 3, or 4 + 4. The brevity of the phrases, and the frequent pauses at the end, allow for ample breathing space within the melodic line.

Example 12.1 is the theme from the second movement of Mozart's Piano Concerto in C major (1785). It is composed of two three-bar phrases—an antecedent and a consequent phrase. The melody is light and airy, yet perfectly balanced. It is also tuneful, indeed memorable; in fact, it has been turned into a popular movie theme often played in airports and shopping malls. Contrast this to the long, asymmetrical melodies of the Baroque that were often instrumental in character (see Ex. 10.1 and 10.2).

EXAMPLE 12.1

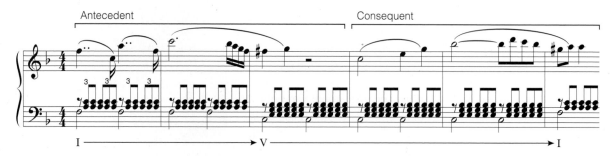

Harmony

After about 1750, all classical music assumed a more homophonic, less polyphonic character. The new tuneful melody was supported by a simple harmony. Note that in Example 12.1 only two chords—tonic (I) and dominant (V)—support Mozart's lovely melody. The heavy *basso continuo* of the Baroque era has disappeared entirely. The bass still generates the harmony, but it does not always move in the regular, constant fashion typified by the

Baroque walking bass. Rather, the bass might sit on the bottom of one chord for several beats, even several measures, then move rapidly, and then stop again. Thus, the rate at which chords change—the "harmonic rhythm," as it is called—is much more fluid and flexible in Classical music.

To avoid a feeling of inactivity when the harmony is static, Classical composers invented new patterns for accompaniment. Sometimes, as in Example 12.1, they simply repeat the accompanying chord in a uniform triplet rhythm. More common is the pattern called the **Alberti bass**, named after the minor Italian keyboard composer Domenico Alberti (1710–1740), who popularized this figure. Instead of playing the pitches of a chord all together, the performer spreads them out to provide a continual stream of sound. Mozart used an Alberti bass at the beginning of his famous C major piano sonata (1788).

EXAMPLE 12.2

Figure 12.6

Many major artists of the eighteenth century journeyed to Rome to absorb the ancient classical style, and what they created in painting and architecture we now call "Neoclassicism." Among such classically inspired painters was the Englishwoman Angelica Kauffmann (1741–1807), whose *The Artist [Angelica Kauffmann] in the Character of Design Listening to the Inspiration of Poetry* (1782) shows classical balance (two women and two columns). Not coincidentally, the complementary figures in this painting function as do antecedent–consequent phrases in Classical music: They are somewhat different, but they balance each other.

The Alberti bass serves essentially the same function as both the modern "boogie-woogie" bass and the process of "tapping" on a guitar (made famous by Eddie Van Halen). It provides an illusion of harmonic activity for those moments when, in fact, the harmony is not changing.

Rhythm

Rhythm, too, is more flexible in the hands of Haydn and Mozart than it was in the music of the Baroque era, animating the stop-and-go character of Classical melody and harmony. Rapid motion may be followed by repose and then further quick movement, but little of the driving, perpetual motion of Baroque musical rhythm is present.

Texture

Musical texture was also transformed in the latter half of the eighteenth century, mainly because composers began to concentrate less on writing dense counterpoint and more on creating charming melodies. No longer are independent polyphonic lines superimposed, layer upon layer, as in a Baroque fugue of Bach or a polyphonic chorus of Handel. This lessening of counterpoint made for a lighter, more transparent sound, especially in the middle range of the texture (see Ex. 12.1, in which chords repeat quietly in the middle between melody and bass). Mozart, after a study of Bach and Handel in the early 1780s, infused his symphonies, quartets, and concertos with greater polyphonic content, but this seems to have caused the pleasure-loving Viennese to think his music too dense!

 ## The Dramatic Quality of Classical Music

What is perhaps most revolutionary in the music of Haydn, Mozart, and their younger contemporary Beethoven is its capacity for rapid change and endless fluctuation. Recall that in earlier times, a work by Purcell, Vivaldi, or Bach would establish one "affect," or mood, to be rigidly maintained from beginning to end—the rhythm, melody, and harmony all progressing in a continuous, uninterrupted flow. Such a uniform approach to expression is part of the "single-mindedness" of Baroque art. Now, with Haydn, Mozart, and the young Beethoven, the mood of a piece might change radically within a few short phrases. An energetic theme in rapid notes may be followed by a second one that is slow, lyrical, and tender. Similarly, textures might change quickly from light and airy to dense and more contrapuntal, adding tension and excitement. For the first time, composers began to call for crescendos and diminuendos, gradual increases or diminishings of the dynamic level, so that the volume of sound might continually fluctuate. When skilled orchestras made use of this technique, audiences were fascinated and rose to their feet. Keyboard players, too, now took up the crescendo and diminuendo, assuming that the new multidynamic piano was at hand in place of the older, less flexible harpsichord. These rapid changes in mood, texture, color, and dynamics give to Classical music a new sense of urgency and drama. The listener feels a constant flux and flow, not unlike the continual swings of mood we all experience.

An Example of Classical Style

To experience the essence of the Classical style in music, let's turn to an aria from Mozart's comic opera *Le nozze di Figaro* (1786). Recall that the libretto of this opera was taken from a revolutionary play that criticized the aristocracy (see above, "The Rise of Popular Opera"). It was Mozart's idea to set this play to music, softening only slightly its call for a new social order.

Social tension is immediately apparent at the beginning of the opera. The main character is Figaro (Fig. 12.7), a clever, mostly honest barber and valet, who outwits his lord, the philandering, mostly dishonest Count Almaviva. We first meet Figaro as he discovers that he and his betrothed, Susanna, have been assigned a bedroom next to the Count's. The Count wishes to exercise his ancient *droit du seigneur*—a supposed law allowing the lord of the manor to claim sexual favors from a servant's fiancée. Figaro responds with a short aria "Se vuol ballare" ("If you want to dance"). Here he calls the Count by the diminutive "Contino," translated roughly as "Count, you little twerp," and vows to outsmart his master.

Example 12.3 shows the simplicity, clarity, and balance typical of the Classical style. The texture is light and homophonic—really only supporting chords—as if Figaro were accompanying himself on the guitar. (In those days, barbers often kept guitars in their shops so that waiting customers could pass the time.) The melody begins with a four-bar phrase that immediately repeats at a higher level of pitch. Formally, the aria consists of four sections: **A**, **B**, **C**, and **D**, with a return to **A** at the end. Section **A** has five, four-bar phrases, and so do sections **B** and **C**, while section **D** has twice that number. Although the sections are connected by a measure or two of purely instrumental music, the vocal sections of this aria thus have the proportions 20 + 20 + 20 + 40 + 20—a balanced, "classical" arrangement indeed.

Figure 12.7

Welsh baritone Bryn Terfel as the combative, cunning Figaro, a barber-valet who outsmarts his master, Count Almaviva

EXAMPLE 12.3

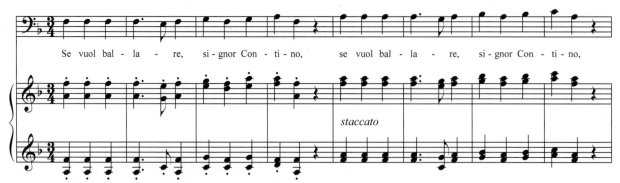

Se vuol bal - la - re, si - gnor Con - ti - no, se vuol bal - la - re, si - gnor Con - ti - no,

staccato

(If you want to dance, Count, you little twerp . . .)

The dynamic quality of Classical music—its capacity to encompass changes of mood—is also evident in Figaro's "Se vuol ballare." Figaro begins in a calm, measured manner, but the more he thinks about the Count's lechery and treachery, the more anxious he becomes. Musically, we hear Figaro's agitation grow throughout sections **A**, **B**, **C**, and **D**, each gaining in intensity. Only at the end does the valet regain his composure, as signaled by the return of **A**. Mozart casts the aria "Se vuol ballare" within the context of a dance, specifically, the courtly minuet. Here dance serves as a metaphor for a shuffling of social order—if the Count wants to "dance" (fool around), Figaro, the servant, will call the tune.

Listening Guide

Wolfgang Amadeus Mozart Aria, "Se vuol ballare" ("If you want to dance")
From the comic opera *Le nozze di Figaro* (1786)

5
2/7

Character: Figaro, a clever barber and valet to Count Almaviva

Situation: Figaro has learned that the Count intends to seduce his fiancée, Susanna, and Figaro vows to outwit him.

WHAT TO LISTEN FOR: How Mozart depicts through music Figaro's growing agitation and return to composure at the end

0:00 7	Section **A**: Music begins with style of courtly minuet.	Se vuol ballare, Signor Contino, Il chitarrino Le suonerò.	If you want to dance, Count, you little twerp, I'll sound the guitar. (I'll call the tune.)
0:28	Section **B**: Music becomes slightly more agitated with fluttering strings.	Se vuol venire Nella mia scuola, La capriole Le insegnerò.	If you want to come To my dancing school, I'll teach you How to caper.
0:55	Section **C**: Music becomes much more agitated with racing strings.	Saprò . . . ma piano Meglio ogni arcane	I know . . . but quietly All his secrets
1:13	Music assumes dark, sinister tone, changing to minor.	Dissimulando Scoprir potrò.	Better by trickery I can discover.

(I can discover all his secrets better by trickery.)

1:25	Section **D**: Tempo increases and meter changes to duple.	L'arte schermendo, L'arte adoprando, Di qua pungendo, Di là scherzando, Tutte le maccine	Sometimes concealing, Sometimes revealing, Punching here, Feigning there, All your schemes

(continued)

1:45	Mozart slows down music.	Rovescierò.	I'll turn against you.
1:52	Music of section **A** returns.	Se vuol ballare,	If you want to dance,
		Signor Contino,	Count, you little twerp,
		Il chitarrino	I'll sound the guitar.
		Le suonerò.	(I'll call the tune.)
2:18	Orchestral conclusion		

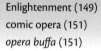 Listen to streaming music in an Active Listening Guide at CourseMate or in the eBook.

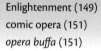 Take online Listening Exercise 12.1 and receive feedback at CourseMate or in the eBook.

Key Words

Enlightenment (149)	*pianoforte* (151)	consequent phrase (152)
comic opera (151)	antecedent phrase (152)	Alberti bass (153)
opera buffa (151)		

For a complete review of this chapter, see the Main Points, Chapter Quiz, Flashcards, and Glossary in CourseMate.

Join us on Facebook at **Listening to Music with Craig Wright**

Classical Composers:

Haydn and Mozart

When we think of the music of the Classical era, we tend to focus on three towering figures: Haydn, Mozart, and Beethoven. There were, of course, other important composers working in Europe at this time. At the very beginning of the Classical period, Haydn was greatly influenced by Carl Philipp Emanuel Bach, then residing in Berlin, just as Mozart was inspired by this Bach's half-brother Johann Christian Bach, living in London. (Both Bachs were sons of Baroque master Johann Sebastian Bach.) In the 1790s, the symphonies of Mozart were not as well known in Paris and London as those of Haydn's pupil, Ignace Pleyel. Mozart once played a piano competition against Muzio Clementi, whose sonatas are still studied by beginning pianists today. Haydn's younger brother Michael, who worked in Salzburg with Mozart, composed a Symphony in G (1783) that was long thought (mistakenly) to be Mozart's. As this confusion suggests, many musicians active during the Classical era possessed compositional skills approaching those of the three great masters. The best compositions of Haydn, Mozart, and Beethoven, however, belong in a class all their own.

Vienna: A City of Music

New Orleans jazz, Hollywood film music, and the Broadway musical—these names all suggest that a particular locale became the epicenter for the development of a distinctive kind of music. So, too, with the Viennese Classical style. The careers of Haydn, Mozart, Beethoven, and the young Franz Schubert all unfolded in Vienna, and from Vienna radiated their powerful musical influence. For that reason, we often refer to them collectively as the **Viennese School** and say that their music epitomizes the "Viennese Classical style."

Vienna was then the capital of the old Holy Roman Empire, a huge expanse covering much of Western and Central Europe (Fig. 13.1). In 1790, the heyday of Haydn and Mozart, Vienna had a population of 215,000, which made it the fourth-largest city in Europe, after London, Paris, and Naples. Surrounded by vast farmlands ruled by an aristocratic gentry, it served as a cultural mecca, especially during the winter months when there was little agricultural work to be supervised. Vienna boasted a greater percentage of noblemen among its population than did London or Paris, and here the aristocratic hold on high culture loosened only gradually—but loosen it did. Haydn was a court employee, but Mozart and Beethoven became independent operators. And while Viennese nobles still patronized music, they often enjoyed it with middle-class citizens at public concerts. The city had theaters for German and Italian opera, concerts in the streets on fine summer nights, and ballroom dances where as many as 2,000 couples might sway to a minuet or a waltz by Mozart or Beethoven.

Figure 13.1

A map of eighteenth-century Europe showing the Holy Roman Empire and the principal musical cities, including Vienna, Austria

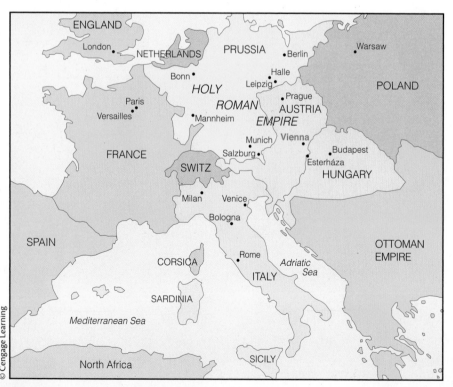

With so much musical patronage to offer, Vienna attracted musicians from throughout Europe. Haydn moved there from Lower Austria, Mozart from Upper Austria, his rival Antonio Salieri from Italy, and Beethoven from Bonn, Germany. Later, in the nineteenth century, in addition to native-born Franz Schubert, outsiders such as Anton Bruckner, Johannes Brahms, and Gustav Mahler spent many of their most productive years there. Even today, with an annual expenditure of about $150 million, Vienna spends more per capita on its opera, for example, than any city in the world.

Franz Joseph Haydn (1732–1809)

Joseph Haydn was the first of the great composers to move to Vienna, and his life offers something of a "rags-to-riches" story (Fig. 13.2). Haydn was born in 1732 in a farmhouse in Rohrau, Austria, about twenty-five miles east of Vienna. His father, a wheelwright, played the harp but could not read music. When the choir director of Saint Stephen's Cathedral in Vienna happened to be scouting for talent in the provinces, he heard the boy soprano Haydn sing and, impressed by his musicianship, brought him back to the cathedral in Vienna. Here Haydn remained as a choirboy, studying the rudiments of composition and learning to play the violin and keyboard. After nearly ten years of service, his voice broke, and he was abruptly dismissed—replaced, ironically, by his younger brother Michael. For most of the 1750s, Joseph Haydn eked out a "wretched existence," as he called it, working as a freelance musician around Vienna. He gave keyboard lessons, played in street bands, and sang or played violin or organ at three churches each Sunday, moving quickly from one to the next. In 1761, Haydn's years of struggle ended when he was engaged as director of music at the Esterházy court.

The **Esterházy family** was the richest and most influential among the German-speaking aristocrats of Hungary, with extensive landholdings southeast of Vienna and a passionate interest in music. At the family seat at Esterháza (see Fig. 13.1), Prince Nikolaus Esterházy (1714–1790) constructed a palace (Fig. 13.3) influenced by that of King Louis XIV at Versailles. Here he maintained an orchestra, a chapel for singing religious music, and a theater for opera. As was typical of the period, Prince Nikolaus engaged Haydn to be a musical servant at the court, required to wear a valet's uniform (see Fig. 13.2). Haydn also was obliged to sign a contract of employment, one that suggests the subservient place of the composer in eighteenth-century society:

> [He] and all the musicians shall appear in uniform, and the said Joseph Haydn shall take care that he and all the members of the orchestra follow the instructions given, and appear in white stocking, white linen, powdered, and with either a pigtail or a tiewig....
>
> The said [Haydn] shall be under obligation to compose such music as his Serene

Figure 13.2

Portrait of Joseph Haydn (c. 1762–1763) wearing a wig and the blue livery of the Esterházy court

Figure 13.3

The palace of the Esterházy family southeast of Vienna, where Joseph Haydn lived until 1790. The elements of Neoclassical architectural style include the triangular pediment over the entryway, the columns, and the Ionic capitals atop the flat columns.

Courtesy of Professor Daniel Heartz/University of California, Berkeley Department of Music

© Imagno/Hulton Archive/ Getty Images

Highness may command, and neither to communicate such compositions to any other person, nor to allow them to be copied, but he shall retain them for the absolute use of his Highness, and not compose for any other person without the knowledge and permission of his Highness.

Haydn was thus prohibited from circulating his music without the express permission of his patron. But somehow his symphonies, quartets, and sonatas began to make their way to Vienna and other foreign capitals. In the 1770s, they surfaced in Amsterdam, London, and Paris in unauthorized editions—the eighteenth-century equivalent of today's illicit "file sharing." Because no international copyright law existed in those years, a publisher could simply print a work from a copyist's score without the composer's knowledge or consent and without paying royalties. When Haydn signed another contract with Prince Nikolaus in 1779, there was no such "exclusive use" provision, and he began to sell his works to various publishers, sometimes consigning the same piece to two or three at the same time!

For a period of nearly thirty years, Haydn served Nikolaus Esterházy at his remote court, writing symphonies, operas, and string trios in which the prince himself might participate. A London newspaper, *The Gazeteer*, perhaps exaggerated Haydn's isolation when it wrote in 1785:

> There is something very distressing [that] this wonderful man, who is the Shakespeare of music, and the triumph of the age in which we live, is doomed to reside in the court of a miserable German [Austrian] prince, who is at once incapable of rewarding him, and unworthy of the honour . . . . Would it not be an achievement equal to a pilgrimage, for some aspiring youths to rescue him from his fortune and transplant him to Great Britain, the country for which his music seems to be made?

As it turns out, that is precisely what happened. Prince Nikolaus died in 1790, leaving Haydn a pension for life and freedom to travel. Heeding the call of an enterprising impresario (concert producer)—and the promise of a substantial fee—Haydn journeyed to London in 1791. For this capital, then the richest of all European cities, he wrote his last twelve symphonies, fittingly called the **London Symphonies** (Nos. 93–104). With Haydn conducting from the keyboard, these were first performed in the Hanover Square Rooms (see Fig. 15.2), London's newest and largest public concert hall. Haydn stayed in London during 1791–1792 and returned again for the concert season in 1794–1795. He was presented to the king and queen, received an honorary doctorate from Oxford, and was generally accorded the status of a visiting celebrity, as a letter written within two weeks of his arrival attests:

> Everyone wants to know me. I had to dine out six times up to now, and if I wanted, I could have an invitation every day; but first I must consider my health and second my work. Except for the nobility, I admit no callers 'til 2 o'clock in the afternoon.

In the summer of 1795, Haydn returned to Vienna a wealthy man. From his activities in London, he had netted 24,000 Austrian gulden, the equivalent about $1.2 million U.S. today—not bad for the son of a wheel maker. Haydn also returned from England with an abiding love of the oratorios of Handel; among his last completed works are his own two oratorios, *The Creation* (1798) and *The Seasons* (1801). When he died on May 31, 1809, at the age of seventy-seven, he was the most respected composer in Europe.

Haydn's long life, commitment to duty, and unflagging industry resulted in an impressive number of musical compositions: 106 symphonies, about 70 string quartets, nearly a dozen operas, 52 piano sonatas, 14 Masses, and 2 oratorios. He began composing before the death of Bach (1750) and did not put down his pen

Take a tour of an Esterházy palace constructed during Haydn's tenure there, in the YouTube playlist at CourseMate for this text.

until about the time Beethoven set to work on his Symphony No. 5 (1808). Thus, Haydn not only witnessed but, more than any other composer, helped to create the mature Classical style.

Despite his accomplishments, Haydn did not rebel against the modest station assigned to him in traditional eighteenth-century society: "I have associated with emperors, kings, and many great people," he said, "and I have heard many flattering things from them, but I would not live in familiar relations with such persons; I prefer to be close to people of my own standing." And though keenly aware of his own musical gifts, he was quick to recognize talent in others, especially Mozart: "Friends often flatter me that I have some genius, but he [Mozart] stood far above me."

Wolfgang Amadeus Mozart (1756–1791)

Indeed, who, except possibly Bach, could match Mozart's diversity, breadth of expression, and perfect formal control? Wolfgang Amadeus Mozart (Fig. 13.4) was born in 1756 in the mountain town of **Salzburg**, Austria, then a city of about 20,000 residents. His father, Leopold Mozart, was a violinist in the orchestra of the archbishop of Salzburg and the author of a best-selling introduction to playing the violin. Leopold was quick to recognize the musical gifts of his son, who by the age of six was playing the piano, violin, and organ, as well as composing. In 1762, the Mozart family coached off to Vienna, where Wolfgang and his older sister Nannerl displayed their musical wares before Empress Maria Theresa (1717–1780). They then embarked on a three-year tour of Northern Europe that included extended stops in Munich, Brussels, Paris, London, Amsterdam, and Geneva (Fig. 13.5). In London, Wolfgang sat on the knee of Johann Christian Bach (1735–1782) and improvised a fugue. And here, at the age of eight, he wrote his first two symphonies. Eventually, the Mozarts made their way back to Salzburg. But in 1768, they were off again to Vienna, where the now twelve-year-old Wolfgang staged a production of his first opera, *Bastien und Bastienne,* in the home of the famous Dr. Franz Anton Mesmer (1734–1815), the inventor of the theory of animal magnetism (hence, "to mesmerize"). The next year father and son visited the major cities of Italy, including Rome, where, on July 8, 1770, the pope dubbed Wolfgang a Knight of the Order of the Golden Spur (Fig. 13.6). Although the aim of all this globe-trotting was to acquire fame and fortune, the result was that Mozart, unlike Haydn, was exposed at an early age to a wealth of musical styles—French Baroque, English choral, German polyphonic, and Italian vocal. His extraordinarily keen ear absorbed them all, and ultimately, they increased the breadth and substance of his music.

A period of relative stability followed: For much of the 1770s, Mozart resided in Salzburg, where he served as organist, violinist, and

Figures 13.4 and 13.5

(top) An unfinished portrait of Mozart painted by his brother-in-law Joseph Lange during 1789–1790. (bottom) The child Mozart at the keyboard, with his sister Nannerl and his father Leopold, in Paris in 1764 during their three-year tour of Europe.

© Alinari/The Bridgeman Art Library

©British Library Board, London/The Bridgeman Art Library

composer to the archbishop. But the reigning archbishop, Colloredo, was a stern, frugal man who had little sympathy for Mozart, genius or not (the composer referred to him as the "Archboobie"). Mozart was given a place in the orchestra, a small salary, and his meals. Like the musicians at the court of Esterházy, those at Salzburg ate with the cooks and valets. For a Knight of the Golden Spur who had hobnobbed with kings and queens across Europe, this was humble fare indeed, and Mozart chafed under this system of aristocratic patronage. After several unpleasant scenes in the spring of 1781, the twenty-five-year-old composer goaded the archbishop into firing him and set out to make his living as a freelance musician in Vienna.

Mozart chose Vienna partly because of the city's rich musical life and partly because it was a comfortable distance from his overbearing father. In a letter to his sister written in the spring of 1782, Wolfgang spells out his daily regimen in the Austrian capital:

> My hair is always done by six o'clock in the morning and by seven I am fully dressed. I then compose until nine. From nine to one I give lessons. Then I lunch, unless I am invited to some house where they lunch at two or even three o'clock . . . . I can never work before five or six o'clock in the evening, and even then I am often prevented by a concert. If I am not prevented, I compose until nine. Then I go to my dear Constanze.

Against the advice of his father, Wolfgang married his "dear Constanze" (Weber) in the summer of 1782. But, alas, she was as romantic and impractical as he, though less given to streaks of hard work. In addition to his composing, teaching, and performing, Mozart now found time to study the music of Bach and Handel, play chamber music with his friend Joseph Haydn, and join the **Freemasons** (the Masons of today). Although still very much a practicing Catholic, he was attracted to this fraternity of the Enlightenment because of its belief in tolerance and universal brotherhood. His opera *Die Zauberflöte* (*The Magic Flute*, 1791) is viewed by many as a hymn in praise of Masonic ideals.

Figure 13.6

Young Mozart proudly wearing the collar of a Knight of the Order of the Golden Spur, an honor conferred upon him for his musical skills by Pope Clement XIV in July 1770

Watch "Mozart" presented to the Emperor Joseph II and improvising, from the film *Amadeus*, in the YouTube playlist at CourseMate for this text.

Mozart: The Gold Standard of Genius

The CBS program *60 Minutes* describes the world's number one chess player, Magnus Carlson, as "the Mozart of Chess." Tennis great Roger Federer is referred to as "the Mozart of tennis." Even painter Pablo Picasso was called "the Mozart of painting." But when it comes to genius, why is Mozart the standard against whom all others are compared? To answer this question, we must inquire into the nature of genius. Is it enough to possess an immense gift for cognitive processing? In other words, must a genius add up figures at a grocery checkout as fast as a computer, like Kim Peek, the real-life subject of the film *Rainman*, or play (and win) ten games of chess simultaneously while blindfolded, as can the twenty-one-year-old Carlson? Or must a genius create something truly significant—a painting, a poem, a symphony, a new drug, or a scientific theory—that changes the lives of others? Suppose you could do both: process information with lightning speed *and* produce innovative creations that influence society. Then, presumably, you would be a candidate for the A list of geniuses, at the top of which sits Mozart.

Indeed, according to these measures of genius, Mozart had it all. He was precocious, composing at the age of five, and his cognitive skills were extraordinary. As a child, he could identify the notes played in any chord, judge the pitch of an instrument within a quarter of a tone, or pick out a wrong note in a musical score while crawling on his back across a table. At the age of fourteen, he heard a motet sung in the Sistine Chapel in Rome and wrote it down by memory, note for note. This motet was about two minutes long and in several voices. How much music can we remember on first hearing—four or five seconds of the melody? Obviously, Mozart could store and process a great deal of music in his "mind's ear." And not just music, but other sounds as well. Mozart was a superb mimic, and he learned to speak several foreign languages almost upon first hearing. Little wonder that the great German poet Goethe (1749–1832) referred to him as "the human incarnation of a divine force of creation."

But with the gifts of genius came peculiarities of personality—almost by definition, geniuses are rarely "normal." Mozart fidgeted constantly with both hands and feet, and he often made childish jokes and puns. Until the age of ten or so, he was terrified by the sound of a trumpet, and out-of-tune instruments brought physical pain to his ears. Was he slightly autistic? At parties he often seemed to be in his own world, and his financial affairs were sometimes chaotic. Never did he attend school or receive a systematic education beyond the art of music, though his letters reveal him to be highly intelligent. Other than a passing interest in mathematics and game theory, Mozart's sole occupation—indeed, obsession—was music. What

This still from the spectacularly good Academy Award–winning film *Amadeus* (1985) shows "Mozart" composing at a billiard table. Mozart did in fact keep a billiard table in his bedroom. But in most other ways, the portrayal of Mozart in *Amadeus* is largely fictitious. Mozart was not an irresponsible idiot-savant who died penniless, but a highly intelligent entrepreneur whose income fluctuated wildly from year to year; moreover, he was not poisoned by his rival, composer Antonio Salieri (1750–1825). However, *Amadeus* does pose an intriguing question in brilliant fashion: What does a mediocre or even somewhat gifted person (Salieri) do when faced with an absolute genius (Mozart)?

allowed him to create so many masterpieces? Among the factors were a prodigious memory and enormous powers of concentration, two characteristics common to all top-tier geniuses. While the external world around him might have been frenetic and unruly, he had the capacity to create in his mind a world of music that was all balance, order, and perfection. Once all had been arranged there, writing it down was easy.

The years 1785–1787 witnessed the peak of Mozart's success and the creation of many of his greatest works. He had a full complement of pupils, played several concerts a week, and enjoyed lucrative commissions as a composer. Piano concertos, string quartets, and symphonies flowed from his pen, as did his two greatest Italian operas, *The Marriage of Figaro* and *Don Giovanni.*

But *Don Giovanni*, a huge success when first performed in Prague in 1787, was little appreciated when mounted in Vienna in the spring of 1788. "The opera is divine, perhaps even more beautiful than *Figaro*," declared Emperor Joseph II, "but no food for the teeth of my Viennese." Mozart's music was no longer in vogue with the nobility. His style was thought to be too dense, too intense, and too dissonant. One publisher warned him: "Write in a more popular style or else I cannot print or pay for more of your music."

In his last year (1791), despite declining health, Mozart was still capable of creating the greatest sort of masterpieces. He composed a superb clarinet concerto and *The Magic Flute,* and began work on a Requiem Mass, one he was never to finish (it was completed by a pupil, Franz Süssmayr). Mozart died unexpectedly on December 5, 1791, at the age of thirty-five. The precise reason for his death has never been determined, though rheumatic fever and kidney failure, made worse by needless bloodletting, are the most likely causes. No single event in the history of music is more regrettable than the premature loss of Mozart. He left us about as much, or more, great music as Haydn, but did so in less than half the time!

Key Words

Viennese School (158)   Esterházy family (159)   London Symphonies (160)   Salzburg (161)   Freemasons (162)

For a complete review of this chapter, see the Main Points, Chapter Quiz, Flashcards, and Glossary in CourseMate.

 Join us on Facebook at **Listening to Music with Craig Wright**

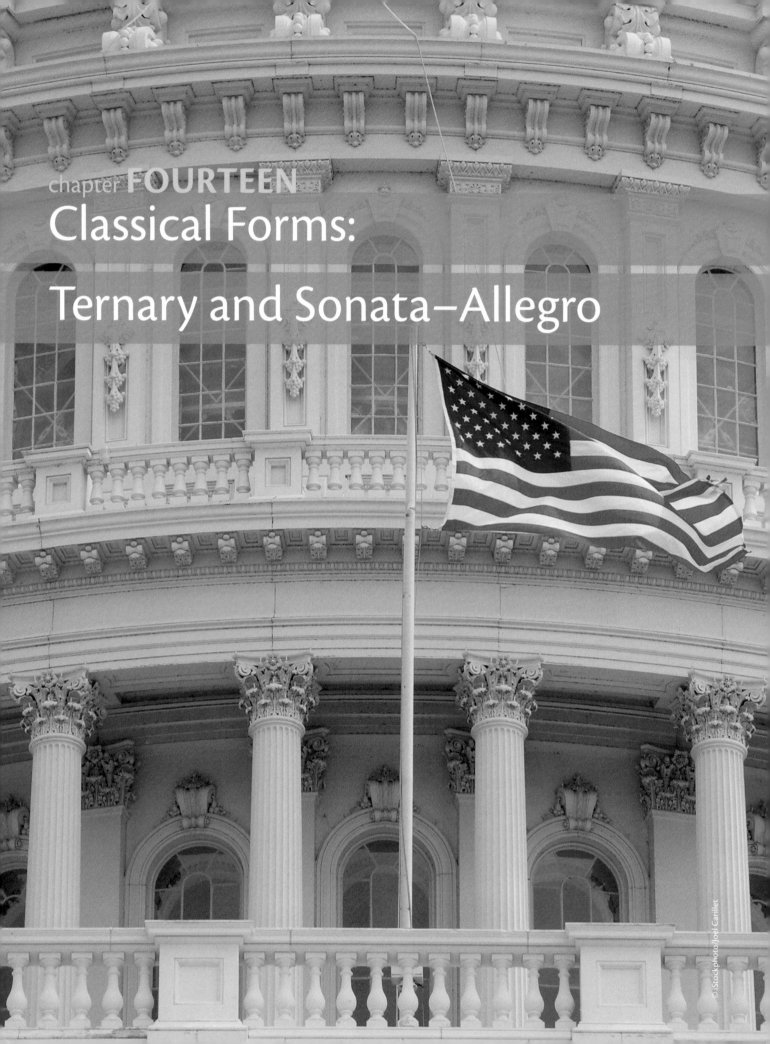

chapter **FOURTEEN**

Classical Forms:

Ternary and Sonata–Allegro

When we use the term *form* to describe a building, we refer to that structure's shape and the way it is positioned in physical space. The forms of Classical architecture were consistent and widespread; around 1800, for example, buildings looked much the same in Vienna and in Virginia (see the beginning of Ch. 12). Moreover, the forms of Classical architecture are still very much with us today. Consider, for example, the windows in the dance auditorium at the emperor's court in Vienna (Fig. 14.1), where Mozart and his wife often waltzed. Windows of precisely this design still can be found in the U.S. Capitol (see this chapter's opening photo), the concert hall of your author's university, and even his living room. Look for others next time you walk around your campus.

The musical forms of the Classical period were similarly uniform and well traveled. A few musical designs shaped most Classical music, no matter who the composer or where the concert. Indeed, in the Classical period, more than any other in the history of music, a small number of forms—ternary, sonata–allegro, rondo, and theme and variations—regulated almost all art music. Some of these forms, like rondo, predated the Classical period, and some, such as sonata–allegro, were created during it. And as in architecture, these forms have proved timeless, serving composers down to the present day.

But how do composers make a "form" out of music—something you hear but cannot see? They do so, as mentioned in Chapter 3, by arranging musical events into patterns over the course of a work, making use of four basic procedures: statement, repetition, contrast, and variation.

© Erich Lessing/Art Resource, NY

Figure 14.1

A ball at the Redoutensaal (dancing hall) in the emperor's palace in Vienna, c. 1800. Mozart, Haydn, and, later, Beethoven composed minuets and "German dances" for these events, which sometimes attracted nearly 4,000 fee-paying dancers. The orchestra can be seen in the gallery to the left. The Redoutensaal still provides a venue for concerts and balls today.

Watch a video of Craig Wright's Open Yale Course class session 9, on ternary and sonata–allegro forms, at CourseMate for this text.

Ternary Form

In **ternary (ABA) form**, the idea of statement–contrast–repetition is obvious. Think of this design as a kind of musical "home–away–home" if you wish. To demonstrate the point in the simplest possible terms, consider again the French folk song known to us as "Twinkle, Twinkle, Little Star." Wolfgang Amadeus Mozart came to know the melody when he toured France as a youth, and he composed a setting for keyboard that begins as in Example 14.1.

EXAMPLE 14.1

(continued)

Notice that both units (**A** and **BA**) are repeated (see repeat sign ⫯). Observe also that **A** is in the tonic, **B** emphasizes a contrasting key (here the dominant), and the returning **A** is again in the tonic (these harmonies are indicated by the roman numerals I and V). If a piece in ternary form is in a minor key, the contrasting **B** section is usually in what is called the **relative major**.* Of course, most pieces in ternary form are more complex than "Twinkle, Twinkle." Most have more contrast of melody, key, and/or mood between the **B** section and the surrounding units of **A**.†

Minuet and Trio in Ternary Form

Dance music generally has a clear beat and a symmetrical form, so that the mind and body can more easily grasp and perform the steps. During the Baroque and Classical eras, most dances were written in simple forms, such as binary and ternary (see Ch. 3, "Binary Form" and "Ternary Form"). The latter provides the structure of the **minuet**, a stately dance in triple meter (Fig. 14.2). The minuet began life in the Baroque era as a popular dance, but during the Classical period composers appropriated it for use within the high-art genres of the symphony and the string quartet. In this case "dance music" became domesticated as "listening music."

When the minuet appeared as a movement of a symphony or quartet, it was usually presented in a two-part set. Because the second minuet of the pair had originally been played by only three instruments, it was called the **trio**, a name that persisted into the nineteenth century, no matter how many instruments were required. Once the trio was finished, convention dictated a return to the first minuet, now performed without repeats. Because the trio also was composed in ternary form, an **ABA** pattern was heard three times in succession. (In the following, the **ABA** structure of the trio is represented by **CDC**, to distinguish it from the minuet.) And, because the trio was different from the surrounding minuet, the entire minuet–trio–minuet movement formed an **ABA** arrangement.

<table>
<tr><td>**A** (minuet)</td><td>**B** (trio)</td><td>**A** (minuet)</td></tr>
<tr><td>‖: A :‖: BA :‖</td><td>‖: C :‖: DC :‖</td><td>**ABA**</td></tr>
</table>

Mozart's *Eine kleine Nachtmusik (A Little Night Music)*, written in the summer of 1787, is among his most popular works. It is a **serenade**, a light, multi-movement piece for strings alone or small orchestra, intended for an evening's entertainment and often performed outdoors. Although we do not know the precise occasion for which Mozart composed it, we might well imagine *Eine kleine Nachtmusik* providing the musical backdrop for a torch-lit party in a formal

Figure 14.2

Couples in the late eighteenth century dancing the stately minuet. In some areas of Europe at this time, women were forbidden to dance the minuet because it was thought to involve excessive body contact!

© Bettmann/CORBIS

---

* Relative keys are keys that share the same key signature—E♭ major and C minor (both with three flats), for example.

† *Note for instructors:* On the designation "ternary form" for this and other pieces, see the Preface of this book at Acknowledgments.

Viennese garden. The *Menuetto* appears as the third of four movements in this serenade and is a model of grace and concision.

EXAMPLE 14.2

As you can see, the contrasting **B** section interjects rapid motion but is only four measures long, and the return to **A** does not reproduce the full eight bars of the original but only the last four—thus, this pattern might be viewed as **ABA′**. Formal symmetry, of course, is reflected here also in a simple equation: **A** (8 bars) = **B** (4 bars) + **A′** (4 bars). In the trio that follows, a lighter texture is created as the first violin plays a solo melody quietly above a soft accompaniment in the lower strings (**C**). The **D** section of the trio is distinguished by a *forte* stepwise run up and down the scale, and then the quiet melody of **C** returns to complete the ternary form. Finally, the minuet appears once again, but now without repeats.

Listening Guide

Wolfgang Amadeus Mozart, *Eine kleine Nachtmusik* **(A Little Night Music, 1787)**

Third movement, Minuet and Trio

5   2

2/11   1/16

Genre: Serenade

Form: Ternary

WHAT TO LISTEN FOR: The formal divisions between sections—both within the minuet (**ABA**) and from the minuet to trio (at 0:38) and back (at 1:33); also, the much thinner texture of the trio

(continued)

MINUET				Number of Bars
0:00	11 16	A	Strong violin melody with active bass	8
0:09			Repeat of A	
0:19		B	Softer violin scales	4
0:24		A′	Return of violin melody	4
0:28			Repeat of B and A′	
TRIO				
0:38		C	Soft, stepwise melody in violin	8
0:49			Repeat of C	
1:00		D	Louder violins	4
1:05		C	Return of soft stepwise melody	8
1:17			Repeat of D and C	
MINUET				
1:33		A	Return of A	8
1:43		B	Return of B	4
1:48		A′	Return of violin melody A′	4

◀)) Listen to streaming music in an Active Listening Guide at CourseMate or in the eBook.

We have said that Classical music is symmetrical and proportional. Notice here how both minuet and trio are balanced by a return of the opening music (**A** and **C**) and how all the sections are either four or eight bars in length. This can be verified by conducting and counting while listening.

If Mozart's *Menuetto* represents the minuet in its most succinct form, the minuet of Haydn's Symphony No. 94 (the "Surprise" Symphony) offers a more typically symphonic presentation of this ternary design. Here Haydn extends ternary form, mainly because he was writing for a full orchestra rather than the small string ensemble of Mozart's serenade. (It is axiomatic in music that the larger the performing force, the more extended the musical form.) Notice at the end of **B** how Haydn builds up great expectation—and holds us back by means of a static pedal point (at 0:50)—before delivering the longed-for return home to **A**. This is the central "emotional event" of the movement.

Listening Guide

Franz Joseph Haydn, Symphony No. 94, the "Surprise" Symphony (1791)

5

Third movement, Minuet and Trio

2/12–13

Genre: Symphony

Form: Ternary

WHAT TO LISTEN FOR: The divisions between the various sections of the form, as indicated by changes of theme, instrumentation, and volume

MINUET [ ] = repeats

0:00	12		A	Rollicking dance in triple meter begins.
0:17				Repeat of A

0:34	[1:21]	**B**	Imitation and lighter texture
0:43	[1:30]		Strong harmonic movement
0:50	[1:37]		Bass sits on dominant pedal point.
0:56	[1:43]	**A′**	Return of **A**
1:03	[1:50]		Pause on dominant chord
1:13	[1:59]		Gentle rocking over tonic pedal point
TRIO			
2:08 13	0:00	**C**	Light descending scales for violins and bassoon
2:16	0:08		Repeat of **C**
2:26	0:17 [0:37]	**D**	Two-voice counterpoint for 1st and 2nd violins
2:35	0:27 [0:47]	**C**	Bassoon reentry signals return of **C**.
MINUET			
3:06	0:58	**A**	Return to minuet
3:22	1:14	**B**	Return of **B**
3:43	1:35	**A′**	Return of **A**

◀)) Listen to streaming music in an Active Listening Guide at CourseMate or in the eBook.

Having now mastered ternary form (**ABA**), let's proceed to a greater challenge: hearing sonata–allegro form.

 ## Sonata–Allegro Form

Most stories, plays, and films have a stereotypical form: setup, complication, resolution. So, too, with sonata–allegro form, which, like a great play, has the potential for dramatic presentation (**A**), conflict (**B**), and resolution (**A**). Sonata–allegro form is the most complex of all musical structures, and it tends to result in the longest pieces. Yet it is also the most important: In the Classical era, more movements of symphonies, quartets, and the like were written in this form than in any other, and its popularity endured throughout the nineteenth century as well.

But first, an important distinction: the difference between the *genre* called sonata and the *form* called sonata–allegro. A sonata is a *genre* of music usually featuring a solo instrument; sonata–allegro, however, is a *form* giving structure to a single movement of any one of several genres: sonata, string quartet, serenade, symphony, even a one-movement overture. To see how this works, consider the movements in two different compositions in two different genres, Mozart's serenade *Eine kleine Nachtmusik* and Haydn's Symphony No. 94. Each work comprises four movements, and each movement has its own form. We get the term **sonata–allegro form** from the fact that most sonatas employ this form in the first movement, and the first movement almost always goes fast, or "allegro."

Mozart, *Eine kleine Nachtmusik* (1787)

Movement	1	2	3	4
Tempo	Fast	Slow	Lively	Fast
Form	Sonata-allegro	Rondo	Ternary	Rondo

Haydn, Symphony No. 94 (1791)

Movement	1	2	3	4
Tempo	Fast	Slow	Lively	Fast
Form	Sonata–allegro	Theme and variations	Ternary	Sonata–allegro

The Shape of Sonata–Allegro Form

To get a sense of what might happen in a typical first movement of a sonata, string quartet, symphony, or serenade, look at Figure 14.3. Although not every sonata–allegro movement follows this ideal scheme, the diagram provides a useful overall model for the listener.

SONATA–ALLEGRO FORM

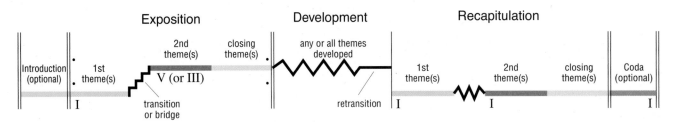

Figure 14.3

Sonata–allegro form

In its broad outline, sonata–allegro form looks much like ternary form. It consists of an **ABA** plan, with the **B** section providing contrast in mood, key, and thematic treatment. The initial **A** in sonata–allegro form is called the exposition, the **B** the development, and the return to **A** the recapitulation. In the early Classical period, the exposition **(A)** and the development and recapitulation **(BA)** were each repeated, as in ternary form. But Haydn and Mozart gradually dropped the repeat of the development and recapitulation, and composers of the Romantic period eventually dispensed with the repeat of the exposition. Let's examine each of these sections in turn and learn what we are likely to hear.

EXPOSITION

In the **exposition**, the composer presents the main themes (or musical personalities) of the movement. It begins with the first theme or theme group and is always in the tonic key. Next comes the **transition**, or **bridge** as it is sometimes called, which carries the music from the tonic to the dominant (from tonic to relative major if the movement is in a minor key) and prepares for the arrival of the second theme. Often the transition is composed of rapid figural patterns—scales, arpeggios, and melodic sequences—giving us a feeling of movement. The second theme typically contrasts in character with the first; if the first is rapid and assertive, the second may be more languid and lyrical. The exposition usually concludes with a closing theme (or group of themes), often simply oscillating between dominant and tonic chords—not much is happening harmonically, so we must be near the end. After the final cadence, the exposition is repeated in full. We've now met all the "characters" in the piece; let's see how things develop.

DEVELOPMENT

If sonata-allegro is a dramatic musical form, most of the drama comes in the **development**. As the name indicates, a further working out, or "developing," of the thematic material occurs here. The themes can be extended and varied, or wholly transformed; a character we thought we knew can turn out to have a completely different personality. Dramatic confrontation can occur, as when several themes sound together, fighting for our attention. The contrapuntal possibilities lurking within a theme might emerge, with the composer using that idea as the subject of a brief fugue. (A fugue within a movement of a sonata is called a **fugato**.) Not only are developments dramatic, they are unstable and unsettling with the harmony typically modulating quickly from one key to the next. Only toward the end of the development, in the passage called the **retransition**, is tonal order restored, often by means of a stabilizing pedal point on the dominant note. When the dominant chord (V) finally gives way to the tonic (I), the recapitulation begins.

RECAPITULATION

After the turmoil of the development, the listener greets the return of the first theme and the tonic key of the exposition with relief and satisfaction—we've returned to the familiar. Though the **recapitulation** is not an exact, note-for-note repetition of the exposition, it nonetheless presents the same musical events in the same order. The only change that regularly occurs in this restatement is the rewriting of the transition, or bridge. Because the movement must end in the tonic, the bridge does not modulate to a new key as before, but stays at home in the tonic. Thus, the recapitulation imparts to the listener not only a feeling of return to familiar surroundings but also an increased sense of harmonic stability, as all themes are now heard in the tonic key. We've gone on a great musical (and emotional) journey and are now back home safe and sound.

The following two elements are optional to sonata–allegro form, functioning something akin to a preface and an epilogue.

INTRODUCTION

About half the mature symphonies of Haydn and Mozart have brief introductions before the exposition begins. (That the introduction is not part of the exposition is shown by the fact that it is never repeated.) These "curtain raisers" are, without exception, slow and stately, and usually filled with ominous or puzzling chords designed to get the listener wondering what sort of musical drama he or she is about to experience.

CODA

As the name **coda** (Italian for "tail") indicates, this is a section added to the end of the movement to wrap things up. Like tails, codas can be long or short. Haydn and Mozart wrote relatively short codas in which a motive might simply be repeated again and again in conjunction with repeating dominant-tonic chords. Beethoven, however, was inclined to compose lengthy codas, sometimes introducing new themes even at the end of the movement. But no matter how long the coda, most will end with a final cadence in which the harmonic motion slows down to just two chords, dominant and tonic, played over and over, as if to say "the end, the end, the end, THE END." The more these repeat, the greater the feeling of conclusion.

Hearing Sonata–Allegro Form

Why all this attention to sonata–allegro form? First, because it is absolutely central to the core repertoire of Classical music and beyond. Haydn, Mozart, Beethoven, Schubert, Tchaikovsky, Brahms, Mahler, and Shostakovich all used it. And second, because sonata–allegro form is the most complex and difficult of the classical forms to follow. A sonata–allegro movement tends to be long, lasting anywhere from four minutes in a simple composition from the Classical period, to twenty minutes or more in a full-blown movement of the Romantic era.

How does one tame this musical beast? First, be sure to memorize the diagram of sonata–allegro form in Figure 14.3. Equally important, think carefully about the four distinctive styles of writing

See a fascinating interaction between Mozart's *Eine kleine Nachtmusik* and the musical style of Bobby McFerrin in the YouTube playlist at CourseMate for this text.

Figure 14.4

Jazz artist and improv singer Bobby McFerrin conducting the St. Paul Chamber Orchestra. McFerrin has conducted orchestras around the world and issued several recordings of Mozart, including his *Eine kleine Nachtmusik,* heard in the Listening Guide.

© Steve Kagan/Time Life Pictues/Getty Images

found in sonata–allegro form: thematic, transitional, developmental, and cadential (ending). Each has a characteristic sound. A thematic passage has a clearly recognizable theme, often a singable tune. The transition is full of motion, with melodic sequences and rapid chord changes. The development sounds active, perhaps confusing; the harmonies shift quickly, and the themes, while recognizable, often pile one on top of another in a dense contrapuntal texture. Finally, a cadential passage, coming at the end of a section or the end of the piece, sounds repetitious because the same chords are heard again and again in a harmony that seems to have stopped moving forward. Each of these four styles has a specific function within sonata–allegro form: to state, to move, to develop, or to conclude.

To test our ability to follow along in a movement composed in sonata–allegro form, we turn to the first movement of Mozart's *Eine kleine Nachtmusik.* The following Listening Guide is not typical of this book. It is unusually lengthy so that it may lead you through the challenging task of hearing sonata–allegro form. First, read the description in the center column; then listen to the music, stopping where indicated to rehear each of the principal sections of the form. Likely, this movement, one of the favorites in the classical repertoire, will seem like an old friend. Its sophisticated sounds have been used as background music in countless radio and TV commercials to suggest that a particular product is "high end"—we associate expensive items with Classical elegance.

Listening Guide

Wolfgang Amadeus Mozart, *Eine kleine Nachtmusik* **(1787)**

First movement, *Allegro* (fast)

Genre: Serenade

Form: Sonata–allegro

WHAT TO LISTEN FOR: The various structural divisions of sonata–allegro form

5   2

2/8–10 1/13–15

EXPOSITION

First Theme Group [ ] = repeats

0:00 **8** [1:37]   The movement opens aggressively with a leaping, fanfare-
      13   like motive. It then moves on to a more confined, pressing
                      melody with sixteenth notes agitating beneath, and ends
                      with a relaxed, stepwise descent down the scale, which is
                      repeated with light ornamentation.

STOP: LISTEN TO THE FIRST THEME GROUP AGAIN

Transition

0:30   [2:08]   This starts with two quick turns and then races up the   0:30 [2:08]   Rapid scales
                 scale in repeating sixteenth notes. The bass is at first static, 0:40 [2:18]   Bass moves
                 but when it finally moves, it does so with great urgency,   0:45 [2:21]   Cadence and pause
                 pushing the modulation forward to a cadence. The stage
                 is then cleared by a brief pause, allowing the listener an
                 "unobstructed view" of the new theme that is about to enter.

STOP: LISTEN TO THE TRANSITION AGAIN

Second Theme

0:48   [2:24]   With its *piano* dynamic level and separating rests, the second theme sounds soft and delicate. It is soon overtaken by a light, somewhat humorous closing theme.

STOP: LISTEN TO THE SECOND THEME AGAIN

Closing Theme

1:01   [2:37]   The light quality of this melody is produced by its repeating note and the simple rocking of dominant-to-tonic harmony below. Toward the end, more substance is added when the music turns *forte*, and counterpoint appears in the bass. The bass's closing theme is then repeated, and a few cadential chords are tacked on to bring the exposition to an end.

1:07	[2:44]	Loud; counterpoint in bass
1:14	[2:51]	Closing theme repeated
1:33	[3:09]	Cadential chords

STOP: LISTEN TO THE CLOSING THEME AGAIN

1:37–3:12   The exposition is now repeated.

DEVELOPMENT

3:13 0:00   Just about anything can happen in a development, so the listener had best be on guard. Mozart begins with the fanfare-like first theme again in unison, as if this were yet another statement of the exposition. But abruptly the theme is altered and the tonal center slides up to a new key. Now the closing theme is heard, but soon it, too, begins to slide tonally, down through several keys that sound increasingly remote and bizarre. From this arises a unison scale (all parts move up stepwise together) in a dark-sounding minor key. The dominant note is held, first on top in the violins and then in the bass (0:33). This is the retransition. The mode changes from dark minor to bright major, and the first theme returns forcefully in the tonic key, signaling the beginning of the recapitulation.

3:13	0:00	First theme developed
3:17	0:04	Quick modulation
3:20	0:07	Closing theme developed
3:29	0:16	More modulations
3:37	0:24	Rising scale in unison
3:46	0:33	Retransition: held note (dominant) in violins and then bass

STOP: LISTEN TO THE DEVELOPMENT AGAIN

RECAPITULATION

3:48 0:00   It is this "double return" of both the tonic key and the first theme that makes the arrival of this and all recapitulations so satisfying. We expect the recapitulation to more or less duplicate the exposition, and this one holds true to form. The only change comes, as usual, in the transition, or bridge, where the modulation to the dominant is simply omitted—there's no need to modulate to the dominant, since tradition demands that the second theme and the closing theme appear in the tonic.

3:48	0:00	Loud return of first theme
4:18	0:30	Transition much abbreviated
4:32	0:44	Second theme
4:45	0:57	Closing theme
4:59	1:11	Closing theme repeated
5:17	1:29	Cadential chords

CODA

5:26   1:31   After the cadential chords that ended the exposition are heard again, a brief coda begins. It makes use of a fanfare motive strongly resembling that of the opening theme, but this one is supported below by a pounding tonic chord that drives home the feeling that the movement has come to an appropriate end.

 Listen to streaming music in an Active Listening Guide at CourseMate or in the eBook.

What we have just heard is an example of sonata–allegro form in miniature. Rarely has this design been produced in less time, or space, and almost never as artfully.

In the Classical era, sonatas, quartets, symphonies, and serenades typically began with a movement in sonata–allegro form. So, too, did operas. That is, a Classical opera often commenced with an overture, performed by full orchestra, composed in sonata–allegro form. A case in point is Mozart's overture to *Don Giovanni* (1787). (The full opera will be discussed in Ch. 17.) Mozart begins this dramatic overture with a slow introduction in a minor key that incorporates some of the musical motives we hear later in the opera. This slow, ominous beginning soon changes to a fast tempo and a major key at the start of the exposition. Because this is an overture to an opera, and not a symphony, the exposition is not repeated.

Listening Guide

Wolfgang Amadeus Mozart, Overture to the opera *Don Giovanni* (1787)

5

2/23–26

Genre: Opera overture

Form: Sonata-allegro

WHAT TO LISTEN FOR: Radically contrasting musical moods (and major and minor modes)—as befitting an opera that is hugely dramatic and exciting—all unfolding within the tight confines of sonata–allegro form

INTRODUCTION

0:00	23	Slow, sinister chords give way to twisting chromaticism and finally to writhing scales, all of which suggest the evil nature of Don Giovanni.

EXPOSITION

1:57	24	0:00	First theme moves ahead rapidly.
2:20		0:23	Transition starts with scalar theme presented in melodic sequence.
2:30		0:33	Transition continues with unstable chords that build tension.
2:35		0:38	Transition ends with strong cadence.
2:39		0:41	Second theme marked by scalar descent and "birdlike fluttering" in woodwinds
3:00		1:02	Light closing theme

DEVELOPMENT

3:18	25	0:00	Themes from exposition are heard in unexpected order (material discussed in Listening Exercise 14.1).
4:15		0:57	Retransition: gradual return to first theme

RECAPITULATION

4:23	26	0:00	Themes return in same order as in exposition (material discussed in Listening Exercise 14.1).

CODA

5:43	1:19	No loud cadential chords to produce "big bang" ending; rather, orchestral fadeout designed to coincide with raising of curtain and beginning of first scene.

◀)) Listen to streaming music in an Active Listening Guide at CourseMate or in the eBook.

◀)) Take online Listening Exercise 14.1 and receive feedback at CourseMate or in the eBook.

A discussion of another Classical movement in sonata–allegro form (Mozart's Symphony No. 40 in G minor, first movement) can be found in Chapter 16, along with a Listening Guide.

Finally, if you like the overture to *Don Giovanni*, you'll love the opera (see Ch. 17, "Mozart and Opera"). The central character, Don Giovanni, is full of frightening ambiguities and, in many ways, served as the model for the Phantom in *Phantom of the Opera* (see Fig. 17.2).

Key Words

ternary (**ABA**) form (165)	sonata–allegro form (169)	retransition (171)
relative major (166)	exposition (170)	recapitulation (171)
minuet (166)	transition (bridge) (170)	coda (171)
trio (166)	development (170)	
serenade (166)	fugato (171)	

For a complete review of this chapter, see the Main Points, Chapter Quiz, Flashcards, and Glossary in CourseMate.

Join us on Facebook at **Listening to Music with Craig Wright**

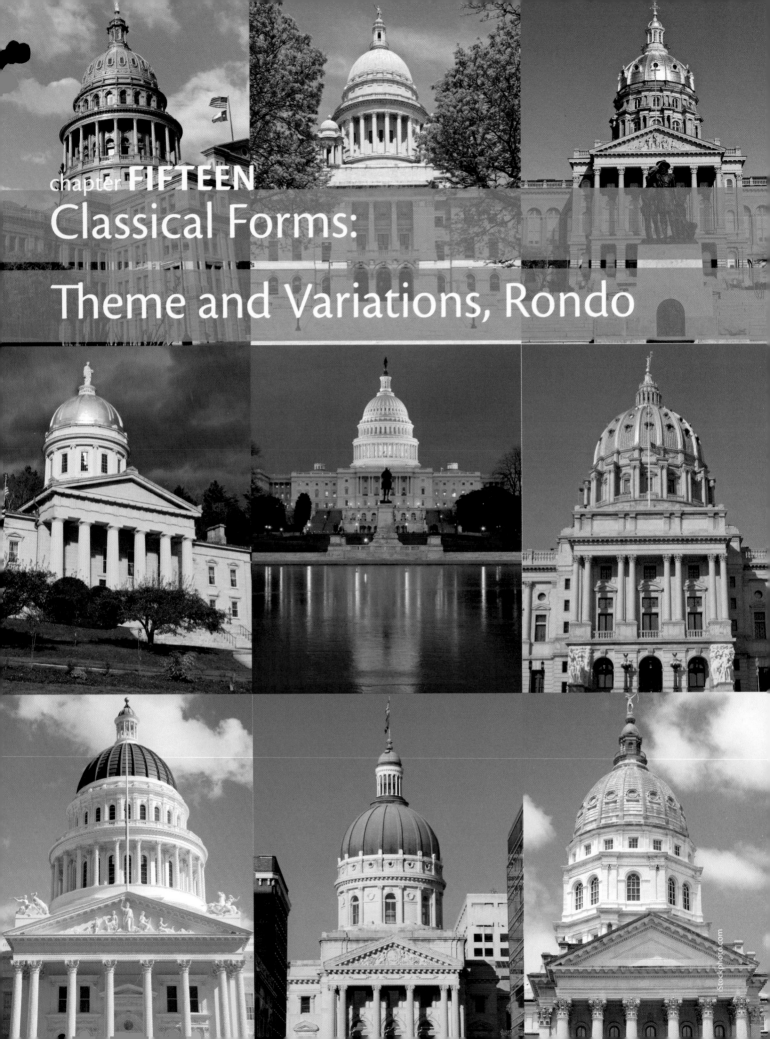

chapter **FIFTEEN**

Classical Forms:

Theme and Variations, Rondo

According to the tenets of Classical architecture, buildings had distinct forms that reflected their unique societal functions. We can still view this legacy in the Classical-style structures that surround us today. The circular rotunda of a state capitol (see chapter opener), for example, is very different from the rectangular front of the city or state courthouse. Likewise with musical structure in the Classical period: Several important forms dominated, and each had its own role to play. In addition to ternary and sonata–allegro, theme and variations and rondo form appear frequently in the music of the Classical era. A piece in theme and variations form might show how inventive a composer could be with a popular tune, whereas a rondo was often called upon to send the audience home in a cheerful mood. Each of these forms might exist as a movement within a multimovement sonata or symphony, or stand alone as a one-movement, independent piece.

Theme and Variations

In the film *Amadeus,* Mozart is shown composing variations on a theme of another composer (Salieri), tossing them off effortlessly like a magician pulling handkerchiefs from his sleeve. The capacity, indeed need, of a great artist for substantive change or modification is called the "transformational imperative"; Leonardo da Vinci continually transforms one and the same face, just as Shakespeare endlessly riffs on a metaphor for a sunrise. In music, it is not an image or a vision that is varied, but usually a melody. **Theme and variations** occurs when a melody is altered, decorated, or adorned in some way by changing pitch, rhythm, harmony, or even (major or minor) mode. The object is still recognizable but somehow doesn't seem to sound the same.

As we've seen in Chapter 3, we can visualize this musical process with the following scheme:

Statement of theme	Variation 1	Variation 2	Variation 3	Variation 4
A	**A^1**	**A^2**	**A^3**	**A^4**

For theme and variations to work, the theme must be well known or at least easy to remember. Traditionally, composers have chosen to vary folk songs and, especially, patriotic songs, such as "God Save the King" or "America." Such tunes are popular in part because they are simple, and this, too, is an advantage for the composer. Melodies that are spare and uncluttered can more easily be dressed in new musical clothing.

Broadly speaking, a musical variation can be effected in either of two ways: (1) by changing the theme itself, or (2) by changing the context around that theme (the accompaniment). Sometimes these two techniques are used simultaneously. The two examples that follow—one by Mozart and one by Haydn—illustrate a number of techniques for varying a melody and its context. In a set of variations, whether in the fine arts or music, the further one moves from the initial theme, the more obscure it becomes (Fig. 15.1). For the listener, the primary task is to keep track of the tune as it is altered in increasingly complex ways.

Mozart: Variations on "Twinkle, Twinkle, Little Star" (c. 1781)

In the Classical period, it was common for a composer-pianist to improvise in concert a set of variations on a well-known tune, perhaps one requested by the audience. Contemporary reports tell us that Mozart was especially skilled in this art of

Watch a video of Craig Wright's Open Yale Course class session 10, "Sonata–Allegro and Theme and Variations," at CourseMate for this text.

Figure 15.1

Henri Matisse's classically inspired series of bronze sculptures of the head of his model, Jeannette Vaderin, executed in 1910, allows us to visualize the process of theme and variations. The image becomes progressively more abstract and distant from the original as we move left to right.

spontaneous variation. In the early 1780s, Mozart wrote down a set of such improvised variations built on the French folk song "Ah, vous dirai-je, Maman," which we know as "Twinkle, Twinkle, Little Star." With such a well-known tune as this, it is easy to follow the melody, as it is increasingly ornamented and altered in the course of twelve variations. (Only the first eight bars of the theme are given here; for the complete melody, see Ex. 14.1; the music through the first five variations can be heard on (intro)/22, as well as in this text's downloads and the streaming music for Ch. 3 in CourseMate.)

EXAMPLE 15.1A "TWINKLE, TWINKLE, LITTLE STAR," BASIC THEME (0:00)

Variation 1 ornaments the theme and almost buries it beneath an avalanche of sixteenth notes. Would you know that "Twinkle, Twinkle" lurks herein (see the asterisks) if you didn't have the tune securely in your mind?

EXAMPLE 15.1B VARIATION 1 (0:30)

In variation 2, the rushing ornamentation is transferred to the bass, and the theme surfaces again rather clearly in the upper voice. In this instance, the accompaniment is changed substantially, but the theme very little.

EXAMPLE 15.1C VARIATION 2 (0:59)

In variation 3, triplets (three notes in the time of two) in the right hand alter the theme, which is now recognizable only by its general contour.

EXAMPLE 15.1D VARIATION 3 (1:29)

After the same technique has been applied to the bass (variation 4; 2:00), a thematic alteration again occurs in variation 5. Here the rhythm of the melody is "jazzed up" by placing part of it off the beat, in syncopated fashion.

EXAMPLE 15.1E VARIATION 5 (2:29)

Of the remaining seven variations, some change the tune to minor, while others add Bach-like counterpoint against it. The final variation presents this duple-meter folk tune reworked into a triple-meter waltz! Yet throughout all of Mozart's magical embroidery, the theme remains clearly audible, so well ingrained is "Twinkle, Twinkle" in our musical memory.

Haydn: Symphony No. 94 (the "Surprise" Symphony, 1792), Second Movement

Mozart composed his set of variations on "Twinkle, Twinkle, Little Star" as a freestanding, independent piece. Joseph Haydn (1732–1809) was the first composer to take theme and variations form and use it for a movement within a symphony. To be sure, Haydn was an innovative artist—he could "surprise" or "shock" as no other composer of the Classical period. In his "Surprise" Symphony, the shock comes in the form of a sudden *fortissimo* chord inserted, as we shall see, into the second movement in the middle of an otherwise serene theme. When Haydn's Symphony No. 94 was first heard in London in 1792 (Fig. 15.2), the audience cheered this second movement and demanded its immediate repetition. Ever since, this surprising movement has been Haydn's most celebrated composition.

The famous opening melody of the second movement (*Andante*) is written in binary form, a simple **AB** arrangement. Here **A** is an eight-bar antecedent (opening) phrase, and **B** an eight-bar consequent (closing) one—a prime example of Classical balance. Notice how the beginning of the theme (see Listening Guide) is shaped by laying out in succession the notes of a tonic triad (I) and then a dominant chord (V). The triadic nature of the tune accounts for its folk song–like quality and makes it easy to remember during the variations that follow. These first eight bars (**A**) are stated, then repeated quietly. And just when all is ending peacefully, the full orchestra, including a thunderous timpani, comes crashing in with a *fortissimo* chord (see asterisk), as if to shock the drowsy listener back to attention. What better way to show off the latent dynamic power of the larger Classical orchestra? The surprise *fortissimo* chord leads into the **B** section of the theme, which also is repeated. With the simple yet highly attractive binary theme now in place, Haydn proceeds to compose four variations on it, adding a superb coda at the end. In his memoirs, dictated in 1809, Haydn explains that he included the surprise blast as something of a publicity stunt, "to make a début in a brilliant manner" and thereby call further attention to his concerts in London.

Figure 15.2

The Hanover Square Rooms in London, the hall in which Haydn's "Surprise" Symphony was first performed in 1792. Designed for an audience of 800 to 900, nearly 1,500 crowded in for the performances of these London Symphonies.

Private Collection/The Bridgeman Art Library

Joseph Haydn, Symphony No. 94, the "Surprise" Symphony (1791)

Second movement, *Andante* (moving)

Genre: Symphony

Form: Theme and variations

WHAT TO LISTEN FOR: The seemingly endless number of ways in which a master composer such as Haydn can vary a very simple tune

23

THEME

0:00   **23**   **A** First part of theme

0:17   **A** repeated softly with second violins adding chords to accompaniment, then *fortissimo* chord at end

0:33   **B** Second part of theme

0:50   **B** repeated with flute and oboe added

VARIATION 1

1:06   **A** played by second violins while first violins and flute add counterpoint above

1:24   **A** repeated

1:41   **B** with counterpoint continuing above in first violins and flutes

1:57   **B** repeated

VARIATION 2

2:14   **A** played loud and in minor key, shift (2:23) to rich major chord

2:30   **A** repeated (variation of **B** omitted)

2:46   Full orchestra develops **A** in minor key.

3:14   First violins alone, playing in unison

VARIATION 3

3:23   **A** ornamented rapidly by oboe

3:39   **A** repeated; melody in strings with oboe and flute ornamenting above

3:56   **B** now in strings with oboe and flute ornamenting above

4:13   **B** repeated

VARIATION 4

4:29   **A** loud, in full orchestra, with violins playing running arpeggios

4:45   **A** repeated with theme rhythmically varied

5:03   **B** varied further by violins

5:20   **B** repeated loudly by full orchestra

5:37   Transition to coda, pause (5:45)

CODA

5:51   Reminiscences of theme in its original form

🔊 Listen to streaming music in an Active Listening Guide at CourseMate or in the eBook.

Listening to this theme and variations movement by Haydn requires hearing discrete units of music. Each block (variation) is marked by some new treatment of the theme or the accompaniment. In the Classical period, all the units are usually the same size—that is, have the same number of measures. The variations become progressively more complicated as more ornamentation and transformation are applied, but each unit remains the same length. The addition of a coda after the last variation gives extra weight to the end, so the listener feels that the set of variations has reached an appropriate conclusion. If such extra bars were not appended, the audience would be left hanging, expecting yet another variation to begin.

The Art Archive/Eileen Tweedy/Picture Desk

Figure 15.3

A portrait of Joseph Haydn at work. His left hand is trying an idea at the keyboard while his right is ready to write it down. Haydn said about his compositional process: "I sat down at the keyboard and began to improvise. Once I had seized upon an idea, my whole effort was to develop and sustain it."

Rondo Form

Of all musical forms, the rondo is perhaps the easiest to hear, because a single, unvaried theme (the refrain) returns again and again. The rondo is also one of the oldest forms, having existed since the Middle Ages. The Baroque era made frequent use of rondo structure (see Ch. 9) and even contemporary pop songs occasionally employ this form (see "A Rondo by Sting" near the end of this chapter). A true Classical **rondo** must have at least three statements of the refrain (**A**) and at least two contrasting sections (at least **B** and **C**). Often the placement of the refrain creates symmetrical patterns such as **ABACA**, **ABACABA**, or even **ABACADA**. Haydn and Mozart infused the rondo with musical processes found in sonata–allegro form—specifically, transitional and developmental writing. They thereby created a more elastic, flexible rondo in which the refrain (**A**) and, more often, the contrasting sections (**B**, **C**, or **D**) might develop and expand dramatically.

The rondo is typically light, quick, and jovial in nature. Classical composers most often chose the rondo form for the last movement, the **finale** (Italian for "end") of a sonata, quartet, or symphony. The carefree tune and the easily grasped digressions lend to the rondo finale an "upbeat" feeling, the musical equivalent of a happy ending.

Figure 15.4

A natural trumpet fabricated in Germany around 1800. Such an instrument could play a full scale only in the higher part of the register—and even then only with difficulty.

Haydn: Trumpet Concerto in E♭ major (1796), Third Movement (Finale)

Listening to Haydn's Trumpet Concerto in E♭ major makes us think about the construction of the trumpet—and the French horn as well—around the turn of the nineteenth century. Prior to 1800 both the trumpet and horn were natural instruments, without valves (Fig. 15.4). They could play successive intervals of an octave and fifth, and even those of a triad, by "overblowing" (as you can overblow an octave on a recorder, for example). But even great virtuosos had difficulty playing all the notes of a scale perfectly in tune. Moreover, because *over*blowing produces only higher pitches, not lower ones, the trumpet could play very few low notes.

To remedy these deficiencies, a Viennese trumpeter and friend of Haydn, Anton Weidinger (1767–1852), came up with a new design for his instrument. He had the brass of the trumpet

Courtesy Yale University Collection of Musical Instruments; Collection purchase, 1957; Accession No. 3650.1957 pierced with holes that could be covered with movable keypads, anticipating the approach used on woodwinds today. In 1796 Haydn wrote a concerto for Weidinger and his new trumpet. Judging from the reviews of the first performance, the sound of Weidinger's instrument was muffled and unpleasant. In fact, this "covering keypad" approach was soon abandoned; the trumpet thereafter remained "natural" until around 1830, when a wholly new valve-type mechanism was invented for it—and the French horn as well (see Fig. 19.2). Yet, because his concerto exploits the full range of our modern instrument, Haydn must have intuited that Weidinger was headed in the right direction and that technology would catch up with his innovative idea.

Not only has the trumpet changed since Haydn's day, so, too, have trumpeters. Yes, the jaunty, irrepressible rondo theme dominates the movement, and its placement creates an **ABABACABA** form. But notice toward the end how the driving orchestra reaches a point of arrival and then holds a single chord (at 4:09). Haydn surely intended this sustained chord to be a platform from which the soloist would launch into a flashy cadenza, as this was the custom of his day. However, Haydn left no music for it. He assumed that any good performer could, and would want to, improvise one. Today such improvisation by classical performers is a lost art, and our soloist, Wynton Marsalis, simply leaves a few seconds of silence. If you are so inclined, when you get to that spot, hum a few bars to fill in—Haydn's spirit would appreciate the gesture!

Listening Guide

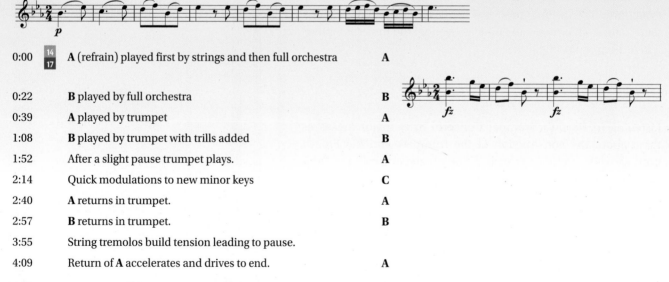

Joseph Haydn, Trumpet Concerto in E♭ major (1796)

Third movement, *Allegro* (fast)

Genre: Concerto

Form: Rondo

WHAT TO LISTEN FOR: Who can miss the constant return of the rondo theme as it gradually forms an **ABABACABA** structure?

0:00	**A** (refrain) played first by strings and then full orchestra	A
0:22	**B** played by full orchestra	B
0:39	**A** played by trumpet	A
1:08	**B** played by trumpet with trills added	B
1:52	After a slight pause trumpet plays.	A
2:14	Quick modulations to new minor keys	C
2:40	**A** returns in trumpet.	A
2:57	**B** returns in trumpet.	B
3:55	String tremolos build tension leading to pause.	
4:09	Return of **A** accelerates and drives to end.	A

◀)) Listen to streaming music in an Active Listening Guide at CourseMate or in the eBook.

◀)) Take online Listening Exercise 15.1 and receive feedback at CourseMate or in the eBook.

Although rondo form has existed in what we call "classical music" since the Middle Ages, it appears often in the realm of folk and popular music as well. For example, the pop tune "Every Breath You Take," composed by Sting and recorded in 1983 by his New Wave group The Police, produces a rondo pattern (**ABACABA**) that in its symmetrical, indeed palindromic, shape would do any Classical composer proud. This song has now been around for nearly thirty years and been the object of more than fifty "covers" extending to almost every pop idiom. It has even crossed over into the classical-pop repertoire, having been recorded by both the London Philharmonic and the Royal Philharmonic Orchestra. "Every Breath You Take" accounts for between a quarter and a third of Sting's music publishing income, generating by itself many thousands of dollars every day. What the rest of us wouldn't give for just one moment of equally lucrative inspiration!

Sting, a.k.a. Sir Gordon Sumner

© George De Sota/Getty Images

Every breath you take …	**A**
Can't you see …	**B**
Every move you make …	**A**
Since you've gone …	**C**
[Instrumental interlude to **A** music]	**A**
Can't you see …	**B**
Every move you make …	**A**

To hear "Every Breath You Take," go to the iTunes and YouTube playlists at CourseMate for this text.

Form, Mood, and The Listener's Expectations

When today we attend a concert of classical music—of a symphony orchestra, for example—most of the music on the program will have been played by that orchestra and in that hall many times over the years. The overtures, symphonies, and concertos that we like to hear belong to the **canon** (standard repertoire, or "chestnuts") of Western classical music. By contrast, when concertgoers stepped into a hall in the late eighteenth century, they expected all of the music to be new and up to date—why would anyone want to hear old music? But while the late-eighteenth-century audience didn't know the pieces in advance, listeners did come with certain expectations, not only about the musical form but also about the mood of the music. For the Classical period, we might summarize these as follows:

Four-Movement Symphony				
Movement	1	2	3	4
Tempo	Fast	Slow	Lively	Fast
Form	Sonata– allegro	Large ternary, theme and variations, or rondo	Minuet and trio in ternary form	Sonata–allegro, theme and variations, or rondo
Mood	Serious and sub-stantive despite fast tempo	Lyrical and tender	Usually light and elegant, some-times spirited	Bright, lighthearted, sometimes humorous

Ludwig van Beethoven (1770–1827) and later composers of the Romantic era (1820–1900) modified somewhat this conventional format; the third movement, for example, was often treated as a boisterous scherzo (see Ch. 18, "Symphony 5 in C minor") rather than an elegant minuet. Yet the Classical model of what was good and worthy of repeated performance—the Classical canon—continued to gain force among music listeners. Succeeding generations not only wanted to hear "new" mu-sic but increasingly demanded a return to certain tried-and-true works of Haydn, Mozart, and their later contemporary Beethoven. Oddly, a similar sort of canon has developed for pop music today; at pop concerts the audience gets most revved up hearing the featured artist's best-known songs. When the canon sounds at either venue, classical or popular, the crowd feels a collective sense of excitement: This is what we came for!

Key Words

theme and variations (177)
rondo (181)

finale (181)

canon (of Western music) (183)

For a complete review of this chapter, see the Main Points, Chapter Quiz, Flashcards, and Glossary in CourseMate.

Join us on Facebook at **Listening to Music with Craig Wright**

chapter **SIXTEEN**

Classical Genres:

Instrumental Music

n music, the term **genre** simply means the type or class of music to which we listen. The string quartet is a genre of music, as are the opera aria, country music ballad, twelve-bar blues piece, military march, and rap song. When we listen to a piece of music, we come armed with expectations of how it will sound, how long it will last, and how we should behave. We may even go to a special place, such as an opera house or a bar, and dress a certain way—in gown and diamond earrings or black leather jacket and nose rings, for example. It all depends on the genre of music we expect to hear. If you change the genre, you change the audience, and vice versa.

In the age of Haydn and Mozart, there were five main genres of art music: the instrumental genres of symphony, string quartet, sonata, and concerto, and the vocal genre of opera. Whereas the sonata, concerto, and opera emerged during the Baroque era, the symphony and string quartet were entirely new to the Classical period. Thus we begin our exploration of Classical genres with the instrumental symphony and quartet.

The Advent of the Symphony and the Symphony Orchestra

A **symphony** is a multimovement composition for orchestra lasting about twenty-five minutes in the Classical period to nearly an hour in the Romantic era. The origins of the symphony go back to the late-seventeenth-century Italian opera house, where an opera began with an instrumental *sinfonia* (literally, "a harmonious sounding together"). Around 1700, the typical Italian *sinfonia* was a one-movement instrumental work in three sections: fast–slow–fast. Soon, Italian musicians and foreigners alike took the *sinfonia* out of the opera house and expanded it into three separate and distinct movements. A fourth movement, the minuet, was inserted by composers north of the Alps beginning in the 1740s. Thus, by midcentury the symphony had assumed its now-familiar, four-movement format: fast–slow–minuet–fast (see Ch. 15, "Form, Mood, and the Listener's Expectations"). Although the movements of a symphony are usually independent with regard to musical themes, all are written in a single key (or set of closely related keys).

The public favor the symphony came to enjoy was tied to progressive social changes that swept Europe during the Enlightenment, including the appearance of public concerts (see Ch. 12, "The Democratization of Classical Music"). The center of musical life in such cities as London, Paris, and, to a lesser degree, Vienna gradually shifted from the aristocratic court to the newly constructed or refurbished public concert hall. Among these halls were the Hanover Square Rooms in London (see Fig. 15.2), where Haydn's London Symphonies premiered, and the Burgtheater (City Theater) in Vienna (see Fig. 12.4), where many of Mozart's symphonies and concertos were first heard. All but a few of Haydn's last twenty symphonies were composed for public performance in Paris and London, and Mozart wrote no symphonies for a court patron during the last ten years of his life. His famous G minor symphony (1788) was intended for a casino in central Vienna (Fig. 16.1)—that's where the people were and that's where the money was to be found.

The audiences at these public concerts in the capital cities of Europe increasingly came to hear the symphony and the large ensemble that played it. A symphony usually opened and closed each concert. So dominant did the genre of the "symphony" become that it was linked forever with the concert "hall" and the performing "orchestra," thus creating our terms *symphony hall* and *symphony orchestra*.

Erich Lessing/Art Resource, NY

Figure 16.1

The New Market in Vienna in the late 1700s. The building on the far right (today the Ambassador Hotel) housed the casino, and it was here that Mozart's G minor symphony was apparently first performed in 1788. Even today, famous musicians, from Yo Yo Ma to Bobby Brown, perform in casinos, because that's where the money is!

The Classical Symphony Orchestra

As the symphony orchestra moved from private court to public auditorium, the ensemble increased in size to satisfy the demands of its new performance space—and expanding audience. During the 1760s and 1770s, the ensemble at the court of Haydn's patron, Prince Nikolaus Esterházy, was never larger than twenty-five, and the audience at this court often consisted of only the prince and his staff (Fig. 16.2). But when Haydn went to London in 1791, his concert promoters provided him with an orchestra of nearly sixty players in the Hanover Square Rooms. Although this hall normally accommodated 800 to 900 persons, for one concert in the spring of 1792 nearly 1,500 eager listeners crowded in to hear Haydn's latest works.

Mozart's experience in Vienna was similar. For the public concerts he mounted in the Burgtheater in the mid-1780s, he engaged an orchestra of thirty-five to forty players. But in a letter of 1781, he mentions an orchestra of eighty instrumentalists, including forty violins, ten violas, eight cellos, and ten double basses. While this was an exceptional ensemble brought together for a special benefit concert, it shows that at times a very large group could be assembled. It also reveals that a large number of string players could be assigned to play just one string part—as many as twenty might "double" each other on the first violin line, for example.

To balance the growth in the string section, and to increase the variety of color in the orchestra, more winds were added. Now, instead of just one oboe or one bassoon, pairs of them were usually included. And a new woodwind, the clarinet, was welcomed into the orchestra. By the 1790s, a typical symphony orchestra in a large European city might include the instrumentalists listed below. Compared to the Baroque orchestra, this ensemble of up to forty players was larger, more colorful, and more flexible. Moreover, within the Classical orchestra, each instrumental family had a specific assignment. The strings presented the bulk of the musical material; the woodwinds added richness and colorful counterpoint; the French

Figure 16.2

A watercolor of 1775 shows Haydn leading the small orchestra at the court of the Esterházy princes during a performance of a comic opera. The composer is seated at the keyboard (lower left), surrounded by the cellos. The higher strings and woodwinds are seated in two rows at the desk.

Deutsches Theatermuseum, Munich/The Bridgeman Art Library

horns sustained a sonorous background; and the trumpets and percussion provided brilliance when a magnificent sound was needed.

Strings	first violins, second violins, violas, cellos, double basses (about 27 players in all)
Woodwinds	2 flutes, 2 oboes, 2 clarinets, 2 bassoons
Brasses	2 French horns, 2 trumpets (for festive pieces)
Percussion	2 timpani (for festive pieces)

Mozart: Symphony No. 40 in G minor (1788), K. 550

In his short lifetime, Mozart wrote 41 symphonies and more than 650 compositions in all. To help us keep track of this enormous amount of music, a nineteenth-century musicologist, Ludwig von Köchel, published a list of Mozart's works in approximately chronological order, assigning each a **Köchel (K) number**. The need for such a numbering system is obvious when we realize that Mozart actually wrote two symphonies in G minor: a short, early one (which accompanies the opening of the film *Amadeus*), K. 183; and a longer, later symphony in G minor, K. 550, to which we now turn.

Mozart's celebrated Symphony in G minor, K. 550, requires all the full instrumental sound and disciplined playing the late-eighteenth-century orchestra could muster. This is not a festive composition (hence no trumpets and drums), but rather an intensely brooding work that suggests tragedy and despair. While we might be tempted to associate the minor key and despondent mood with a specific event in Mozart's life, apparently no such causal relationship exists. This was one of three final symphonies that Mozart produced in the incredibly short span of six weeks during the summer of 1788, and the other two are sunny, optimistic works. Rather than responding to a particular crisis, it is more likely that Mozart invoked the tragic muse in this G minor symphony by drawing on a lifetime of disappointments and a premonition—as his letters attest—of an early death.

FIRST MOVEMENT (*MOLTO ALLEGRO*)

Exposition. Although Mozart begins his G minor symphony with a textbook example of Classical phrase structure (four-bar antecedent, four-bar consequent phrases), an unusual sense of urgency is created by the repeating, insistent eighth-note figure at the beginning (Ex. 16.1). This urgent motive is immediately grasped by the listener and becomes the most memorable theme in the work. Embedded in the motive is a falling half step (here E♭ to D), a tight interval used throughout music history to denote pain and suffering.

EXAMPLE 16.1

Less immediately audible, but still contributing equally to the sense of urgency, is the accelerating rate of harmonic change. At the outset, chord changes are set beneath the melody at an interval of one chord change every four measures, then one every two bars, then one every measure, then two chord changes per measure, and finally four. Thus, the "harmonic rhythm" is moving sixteen times faster at the end of this section than at the start. This is how Mozart creates the sense of drive and urgency we all feel yet may be unable to explain. After this quickening start, the first theme begins once again but soon veers off its previous course, initiating the transition. Transitions take us somewhere, usually by means of running scales, and this one is no exception. What is unusual is that a new motive is inserted, one so distinctive we might call it a "transition theme" (see the example in the following Listening Guide). As if to reciprocate for an extra theme here, Mozart dispenses with one toward the end of the exposition, at the point where we would expect a closing theme to appear. Instead, as closing material, he uses the persistent motive and rhythm from the beginning of the first theme, which rather nicely rounds off the exposition. Finally, a single, isolated chord is heard, one that first leads back to a repeat of the exposition and then, after the second statement of the exposition, launches into the development.

Development. Here Mozart employs only the first theme (and then only the first four bars) but subjects it to a variety of musical treatments. He first pushes it through several distantly related keys, next shapes it into a fugue subject for use in a fugato, then sets it as a descending melodic sequence, and finally inverts the direction of the half-step motive.

EXAMPLE 16.2

The retransition (journey back to the main theme and tonic key) is suddenly interrupted by *sforzandi* (loud attacks). But soon a dominant pedal point sounds in the bassoons, and above it, the flute and clarinets cascade like a musical waterfall down to the tonic pitch. This use of colorful, solo woodwinds in the retransition is a hallmark of Mozart's symphonic style.

Recapitulation. As expected, the recapitulation offers the themes in the same order in which they appeared in the exposition. But now the transition theme, which Mozart has left untouched since its initial appearance, receives extended treatment, creating something akin to a second development section as it charges through one new key after another, only to end up right back in the original tonic minor. When the lyrical second theme finally reappears, now in the minor mode, its mood is altered to somber and plaintive. Because the repeating figure of the first theme rounds off the recapitulation by way of a closing theme, only the briefest coda is needed to end this passionate, haunting movement.

Listening Guide

Wolfgang Amadeus Mozart, Symphony No. 40 in G minor (1788), K. 550

First movement, *Molto allegro* (very fast)

Genre: Symphony

Form: Sonata–allegro

WHAT TO LISTEN FOR: While the divisions within sonata–allegro form are important to hear, in this movement Mozart seems to emphasize the anxiety, even despair, we all sometimes experience.

5   2
2/15–17 1/18–20

EXPOSITION [ ] = REPEAT

0:00	[1:49]	Urgent, insistent first theme
0:21	[2:10]	First theme begins to repeat but is cut short.
0:30	[2:18]	Transition
0:36	[2:23]	Rapid, ascending scales
0:44	[2:32]	Strong cadence ending transition; pause to clear air
0:47	[2:35]	Lyrical second theme, major key contribute to brighter mood.

(continued)

0:57	[2:44]		Second theme repeated with new orchestration
1:07	[2:54]		Crescendo leads to closing material (taken from first theme); abrupt stop

DEVELOPMENT

3:34	16 19	0:00	First theme modulates through several distant keys.
3:51		0:17	First theme used as fugue subject in fugato in basses and then violins
4:12		0:38	First theme reduced to just opening motive
4:32		0:58	*Sforzandi* (loud attacks) give way to retransition.
4:39		1:05	Retransition: dominant pedal point in bassoons as music cascades downward

RECAPITULATION

4:45	17 20	0:00	First theme returns.
5:06		0:21	First theme begins to repeat but is cut off by transition.
5:15		0:30	Transition theme returns but is greatly extended.
5:41		0:56	Rapid, ascending scales
5:49		1:04	Cadence and pause
5:52		1:07	Second theme now in (tonic) minor
6:01		1:16	Second theme repeated with new orchestration
6:12		1:27	Return of crescendo, which leads to closing material (taken from first theme)

CODA

6:51		2:05	Begins with rising chromatic scale
6:56		2:10	Opening motive returns, then three final chords.

◀)) Listen to streaming music in an Active Listening Guide at CourseMate or in the eBook.

◀)) Take online Listening Exercise 16.1 and receive feedback at CourseMate or in the eBook.

SECOND MOVEMENT (*ANDANTE*)

After the feverish excitement of the opening movement, the slow, lyrical *Andante* comes as a welcome change of pace. What makes this movement exceptionally beautiful is the extraordinary interplay between the light and dark colors of the woodwinds against the constant tone of the strings. If no thematic contrast and confrontation can be found here, there is, nonetheless, heartfelt expression brought about by Mozart's masterful use of orchestral color.

THIRD MOVEMENT (*MENUETTO: ALLEGRETTO*)

We expect the aristocratic minuet to provide elegant, graceful dance music. But much to our surprise, Mozart returns to the intense, somber mood of the opening movement. This he does, in part, by choosing to write in the tonic minor key—a rare minuet in minor. This again demonstrates how the minuet had changed from "dance music" to "listening music."

FOURTH MOVEMENT (*ALLEGRO ASSAI*)

The finale starts with an ascending "rocket" that explodes in a rapid, *forte* flourish—and only carefully rehearsed string playing can bring off the brilliant effect of this opening gesture. The contrasting second theme of this sonata–allegro form movement is typically Mozartean in its grace and charm, a proper foil to the explosive opening melody. Midway through the development, musical compression takes hold: There is no retransition, only a pregnant pause before the recapitulation; the return dispenses with the repeats built into the first theme; and a coda is omitted.

This musical foreshortening at the end produces the same psychological effect experienced at the very beginning of the symphony—a feeling of urgency and acceleration.

ᗷ The String Quartet

The symphony is the ideal genre for the public concert hall, for it aims to please a large listening public. The **string quartet**, on the other hand, typifies chamber music—music for the small concert hall, the private chamber, or the simple enjoyment of the performers themselves (Fig. 16.3). Like the symphony, the string quartet normally has four movements, all unified by a common key. But unlike the symphony, which might have a dozen violinists joining on the first violin line, the string quartet features only one player per part: first violinist, second violinist, violist, and cellist. Such an intimate ensemble has no need for a conductor; all performers function equally and communicate directly among themselves in a spirit of disciplined collegiality. No wonder the German poet Johann Wolfgang von Goethe (1749–1832) compared the string quartet to "a conversation among four intelligent people."

Joseph Haydn is rightly called "the father of the string quartet." In the 1760s and 1770s, he began to compose music for four string instruments requiring a new, more agile kind of interaction. From the old Baroque trio sonata Haydn removed the *basso continuo,* replacing it with a more melodically active bass played by a nimble cello alone. And he enriched the middle of the texture by adding a viola, playing immediately above the cello. If Baroque music had a top- and bottom-heavy texture (see Ch. 7, "Characteristics of Baroque Music"), the newer Classical string quartet style shows a texture covered evenly by four instruments, each of which participates more or less equally in a give and take of theme and motive. Haydn's string quartet could not have pulled off the "big bang" special effect of his "Surprise" Symphony (see Ch. 15, "Haydn: Symphony No. 94")—it didn't have the firepower. But Haydn's symphony orchestra could not have effectively played all the rapidly moving notes in Example 16.3, from his "Emperor" Quartet—it wasn't agile enough.

The chance to play string quartets together gave rise to a lasting friendship between Haydn and Mozart. During 1784–1785, the two men met in Vienna, sometimes at the home of an aristocrat, and other times in Mozart's own apartment. In their quartet, Haydn played first violin, and Mozart viola. As a result of this experience, Mozart was inspired to dedicate a set of his best works in this genre to the older master, which he published in 1785 (Fig. 16.4). Yet in this convivial, domestic music-making, Haydn and Mozart merely joined in the fashion of the day. For whether in Vienna, Paris, or London, aristocrats and members of the well-to-do middle class were encouraged to play quartets with friends, as well as to engage professional musicians to entertain their guests.

Haydn: The "Emperor" Quartet (1797), Opus 76, No. 3, Second Movement

Haydn's "Emperor" Quartet, written in Vienna during the summer of 1797, numbers among the best works of the string quartet genre. It is known as the "Emperor" because it makes liberal use of "The Emperor's Hymn," a melody that Haydn composed in response to the military and political events of his day.

In 1796, the armies of Napoleon invaded the Austrian Empire, which ignited a firestorm of patriotism in Vienna, the Austrian capital. But the Austrians were at a musical disadvantage: The French now had the "Marseillaise," and the English had their "God Save the King," but the

Figure 16.3

A representation of a string quartet at the end of the eighteenth century. The string quartet was at first an ensemble for playing chamber music in the home. Not until 1804 did a string quartet appear in a public concert in Vienna, and not until 1814 in Paris.

Figure 16.4

Title page of six string quartets by Mozart dedicated to Haydn (1785). Mozart offers them to Haydn as "six children," asking Haydn to be their "father, guide, and friend."

bpk, Berlin/Art Resource, NY

Figure 16.5

Franz II (1765–1835), last Holy Roman Emperor and first emperor of Austria. Haydn composed "The Emperor's Hymn" in his honor.

Austrians had no national anthem. To this end, the ministers of state approached Haydn, who quickly fashioned one to the text "Gott erhalte Franz den Kaiser" ("God Preserve Franz the Emperor"), in honor of the reigning Austrian Emperor Franz II (Fig. 16.5). Called "The Emperor's Hymn," it was first sung in theaters throughout the Austrian realm on the emperor's birthday, February 12, 1797. Later that year, Haydn took the tune and worked it into a string quartet.

In truth, when Haydn fashioned quartet Opus 76, No. 3, he made use of his imperial hymn mainly in the slow, second movement, where it serves as the basis of a theme and variations set. The theme (see the example in the following Listening Guide) is first presented by the first violin and harmonized in simple chords. Four variations follow in which the theme is ornamented but never altered. All four instruments are given equal opportunity to hold forth with the tune. Even the cello, more flexible and lyrical than the double bass of the orchestra, can participate as an equal partner. Example 16.3 shows how in the Classical string quartet the melodic profile of each of the lines is more or less the same—musical democracy at its finest.

EXAMPLE 16.3

Listening Guide

Joseph Haydn, The "Emperor" Quartet (1797), Opus 76, No. 3

Second Movement, *Poco adagio cantabile* (rather slow, song-like)

Genre: String quartet

Form: Theme and variations

⑤ ②
2/18–19   1/21–22

WHAT TO LISTEN FOR: The trick here is to recognize "the emperor" by his tune, no matter how ingeniously Haydn disguises him in different musical costumes.

THEME

| 0:00 | | Theme played slowly in first violin; lower three parts provide chordal accompaniment. |

VARIATION 1

| 1:20 | | Theme in second violin while first violin ornaments above |

VARIATION 2

| 2:29 | | Theme in cello while other three instruments provide counterpoint against it |

VARIATION 3

| 3:47 | 0:00 | Theme in viola; other three instruments enter gradually. |

VARIATION 4

| 5:04 | 1:17 | Theme returns to first violin, but now accompaniment is more contrapuntal than chordal. |

🔊)) Listen to streaming music in an Active Listening Guide at CourseMate or in the eBook.

🔊)) Take online Listening Exercise 16.2 and receive feedback at CourseMate or in the eBook.

The popularity of "The Emperor's Hymn" did not end with the defeat of Napoleon in 1815 or the death of Emperor Franz II in 1835. So alluring is Haydn's melody that with altered text it became a Protestant hymn ("Glorious Things of Thee Are Spoken"), as well as the national anthem of Austria (1853) and Germany (1922). It was also Haydn's own favorite piece, and he played a piano arrangement of it every night before retiring. In fact, "The Emperor's Hymn" was the last music Haydn played before he died in the early hours of May 31, 1809.

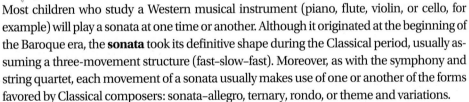 ## The Sonata

Most children who study a Western musical instrument (piano, flute, violin, or cello, for example) will play a sonata at one time or another. Although it originated at the beginning of the Baroque era, the **sonata** took its definitive shape during the Classical period, usually assuming a three-movement structure (fast–slow–fast). Moreover, as with the symphony and string quartet, each movement of a sonata usually makes use of one or another of the forms favored by Classical composers: sonata–allegro, ternary, rondo, or theme and variations.

According to publishers' inventories from the end of the eighteenth century, more sonatas were printed than any other type of music. The explanation for the sudden vogue of the sonata in the Classical era is tied to the equally sudden popularity of the piano. Indeed, the word *sonata* has become so closely associated with the piano that unless the work is otherwise qualified as "violin sonata," "cello sonata," or the like, we usually assume that "sonata" refers to a three-movement work for piano.

Who played this flood of new sonatas for the piano? Amateur musicians, mostly women, who practiced and performed for polite society in the comfort of their own homes. (Oddly, men in this period usually played not the piano, but string instruments such as the violin or cello.) As we have seen (Ch. 12, "Advent of the Piano"), in Mozart's time, the ability to play the piano, to do fancy needlework, and to utter a few selected words of French was thought by male-dominated society all that was necessary to be a cultured young lady. To teach the musical handicraft, instructors were needed. Mozart, Haydn, and Beethoven all served as piano teachers in fashionable circles early in their careers. The piano sonatas they composed for their many pupils were not intended to be played in public concert halls. Rather, sonatas were to provide students with material that they might practice to develop technique and that they might play as musical entertainment in the home. Even among the thirty-two splendid piano sonatas that Beethoven composed, only one was ever performed at a public concert in Vienna during his lifetime.

Watch a video of Craig Wright's Open Yale Course class session 18, "Piano Music of Mozart and Beethoven," at CourseMate for this text.

(An example of a Classical piano sonata by Beethoven, his *"Pathétique"* Sonata, is found on ⑤3/1–3 and ② 1/23–25, as well as in this text's downloads and the streaming music for Ch. 18 in CourseMate. It is discussed in detail in Ch. 18, "Piano Sonata, Opus 13, the *'Pathétique'* Sonata.")

The Concerto

With the genre of the concerto, we leave the salon or private chamber and return to the public concert hall. The Classical concerto, like the symphony, was a large-scale, multi-movement work for instrumental soloist and orchestra intended for a public audience. While the symphony might have provided the greatest musical substance at a concert, audiences were often lured to the hall by the prospect of hearing a virtuoso performer play a concerto. Then, as now, listeners were fascinated with the virtuosity and derring-do that a stunning technical display might bring. Gone was the Baroque tradition of the concerto grosso, in which a group of soloists (concertino) stepped forward from the full orchestra (tutti) and then receded back into it. From this point forward, the concerto was a **solo concerto**, usually for piano but sometimes for violin, cello, French horn, trumpet, or woodwind. In the new concerto, a single soloist commanded all the audience's attention.

Mozart composed twenty-three piano concertos, many among the best ever written, securing his claim to fame as the originator of the modern piano concerto. Mozart's motivation, however, was not enduring fame, but money. After cutting himself loose from the patronage of the archbishop of Salzburg in 1781 and establishing residence in Vienna, Mozart no longer had an annual salary on which to rely. The Viennese were eager to hear brilliant passagework and dazzling displays of keyboard virtuosity on the newly popular piano. The piano concerto was for Mozart the perfect vehicle for such a display. At each of the public concerts he produced, Mozart offered one or two of his latest concertos. But he had to do more: He was responsible for renting the hall, hiring the orchestra, leading rehearsals, attracting an audience, and selling tickets from his apartment (Fig. 16.6)—all this in addition to composing the music and appearing as solo virtuoso. When all went well, however, Mozart could make a killing, as a music journal of March 22, 1783, reported:

> Today the celebrated Chevalier Mozart gave a musical concert for his own benefit at the Burgtheater in which pieces of his own music, which was already very popular, were performed. The concert was honored by the presence of an extraordinarily large audience and the two new concertos and other fantasies which Mr. Mozart played on the Forte Piano were received with the loudest approval. Our Monarch [Emperor Joseph II], who contrary to his custom honored the entire concert with his presence, joined in the applause of the public so heartily that one can think of no similar example. The proceeds of the concert are estimated at sixteen hundred gulden.

Sixteen hundred gulden was the equivalent of about $150,000 today, and more than five times the annual salary of Mozart's father. With a take such as this, young Mozart could, at least for a time, indulge his expensive tastes.

Mozart: Piano Concerto in A major (1786), K. 488

We derive our term *concerto* from the Italian word *concertare*. It means above all else "to strive together," but it also resonates with a sense of "to struggle against." In a piano concerto, the piano and orchestra engage in a spirited give-and-take of thematic material—because of its size, the piano can compete on an equal footing with the orchestra (Fig. 16.7).

Internationale Stiftung Mozarteum (ISM), Salzburg, Austria

Figure 16.6

One of the few surviving tickets to a concert given by Mozart in Vienna. These were sold in advance, not from a ticket agency, but from Mozart's own apartment.

Figure 16.7

Mozart's own piano, preserved in the house of his birth in Salzburg, Austria. The keyboard spans only five octaves, and the black-and-white color scheme of the keys is reversed, both typical features of the late-eighteenth-century piano. Mozart purchased the instrument in 1784, two years before he composed his A major piano concerto.

bpk, Berlin/Art Resource, NY

Mozart composed his Piano Concerto in A major of 1786 for one of his star pupils, Barbara Ployer.

FIRST MOVEMENT (ALLEGRO)

As with all of Mozart's concertos, this one is in three movements (there is never a minuet in a concerto). And, as is invariably the case, the first movement is written in sonata–allegro form. Here, however, the form is expanded to meet the special demands and opportunities of the concerto. What results is **double exposition form** (Fig. 16.8), in which the orchestra plays one exposition and the soloist then plays another. First, the orchestra presents the first, second, and closing themes, all in the tonic key. Then the soloist enters and, with orchestral assistance, offers the piano's version of the same material, but modulating to the dominant before the second theme. After the piano expands the closing theme, part of the first theme group returns, a throwback to the ritornello principle of the old Baroque concerto grosso.

Then a surprise: Just when we expect this second exposition to end, Mozart inserts a lyrical new melody in the strings. This is another feature of the Classical concerto—a melody held back for last-minute presentation, a way of keeping the listener "on guard" during the second exposition.

DOUBLE EXPOSITION FORM

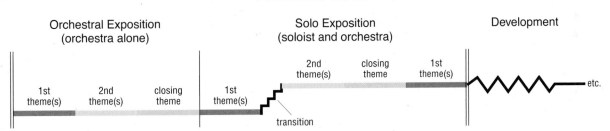

Orchestral Exposition
(orchestra alone)

1st theme(s)   2nd theme(s)   closing theme

Solo Exposition
(soloist and orchestra)

1st theme(s)   transition   2nd theme(s)   closing theme   1st theme(s)

Development

etc.

Figure 16.8

Double exposition form

The development here is concerned exclusively with exploiting the new theme that appeared at the end of the second exposition. The recapitulation compresses the two expositions into one, presenting the themes in the same order as before, but now all in the tonic key. Finally, toward the end of the movement, the orchestra suddenly stops its forward motion and comes to rest on a single chord for several moments. Using this chord as a springboard, the pianist plunges headlong into a flight of virtuosic fancy: the **cadenza**. Normally, Mozart, like Haydn, didn't write out his cadenzas—it was left to the performer (Mozart himself) to improvise one on the spot by mixing rapid runs, arpeggios, and snippets of previously heard themes into a fantasy-like improvisation, just as a talented jazz musician might improvise an extended solo. But because this concerto was intended for his pupil Barbara Ployer, Mozart notated what he thought she should play, and thus his cadenza survives today. Toward the end of this virtuosic razzle-dazzle, Mozart calls for a trill, the traditional signal to the orchestra that it is time to re-enter the competition. From here to the end, the orchestra holds forth, making use of the original closing theme. There is much to absorb in the long Listening Guide that follows, but the glorious music of Mozart will amply reward the attentive listener.

Graphische Sammlung, Zentralbibliothek Zürich

Figure 16.9

A young woman performs a keyboard concerto in 1777. When Mozart moved to Vienna in 1781 he was forced to earn a living, so he gave composition lessons (mostly to men) and piano lessons (mostly to women). Among his best female students was Barbara Ployer (1765–1811), for whom he wrote the Piano Concerto in A major (K. 488) discussed here.

Wolfgang Amadeus Mozart, Piano Concerto in A major (1786)

First movement, *Allegro* (fast)

Genre: Concerto

Form: Sonata–allegro

WHAT TO LISTEN FOR: The harmonious give-and-take—"concerto"—between soloist and orchestra

5

2/20–22

EXPOSITION 1 (orchestra)

0:00	**20**	Strings present first theme.
0:16		Woodwinds repeat first theme.
0:34		Full orchestra presents first theme, part **b**.
0:59		Strings present second theme, part **a**.
1:15		Woodwinds repeat second theme, part **a**.
1:30		Strings present second theme, part **b**.
1:35		Strings present closing theme, part **a**.
2:02		Woodwinds present closing theme, part **b**.

EXPOSITION 2 (piano and orchestra)

2:11	Piano enters with first theme.
2:40	Orchestra plays first theme, part **b**.
3:11	Piano plays second theme, part **a**.
3:27	Woodwinds repeat second theme, part **a**.
3:44	Piano plays and ornaments second theme, part **b**.
3:53	Piano and orchestra in dialogue play closing theme, part **a**.
4:24	Piano trill heralds return of first theme, part **b**.
4:39	Strings quietly offer lyrical new theme.

DEVELOPMENT

5:05	**21**	0:00	Woodwinds transform new theme as piano interjects scales and then arpeggios.
5:35		0:30	Woodwinds offer new theme in imitative counterpoint.
5:49		0:44	Pedal point on dominant note in low strings signals beginning of retransition.
6:04		0:59	Piano takes over dominant pedal point.
6:18		1:13	Piano flourish above sustained dominant chord leads to recapitulation.

RECAPITULATION

6:30	**22**	0:00	Orchestra plays first theme, part **a**.
6:47		0:17	Piano repeats first theme, part **a**.
7:00		0:30	Orchestra plays first theme, part **b**.
7:10		0:40	Scales in piano signal beginning of transition.
7:30		1:00	Piano plays second theme, now in tonic, part **a**.

7:46	1:16	Woodwinds repeat second theme, part **a**.
8:02	1:32	Piano plays second theme, part **b**.
8:06	1:36	Piano and orchestra divide closing theme, part **a**.
8:35	2:05	Piano plays new theme.
8:48	2:18	Woodwinds play new theme while piano offers scales and arpeggios against it.
9:17	2:47	Trill in piano announces return of first theme, part **b**.
9:46	3:16	Orchestra stops and holds chord.
9:50	3:20	Cadenza for piano
10:53	4:23	Trill signals reentry of orchestra.
11:05	4:35	Orchestra plays closing theme, parts **a** and **b**.
11:27	4:57	Final cadential chords

 Listen to streaming music in an Active Listening Guide at CourseMate or in the eBook.

SECOND MOVEMENT (*ANDANTE*)

The essence of this movement rests in Mozart's exquisitely crafted lines and coloristic harmonies. This is the only work the Viennese master ever wrote in the remote key of F# minor, and the daring harmonic changes it contains prefigure those of the Romantic era. Musicians who have lived with Mozart's music from childhood to old age continue to be profoundly moved by this extraordinary movement. It is at once sublimely beautiful and distantly remote, its ending as cold and desolate as death itself.

THIRD MOVEMENT (*PRESTO*)

The sublime pessimism of the *Andante* is suddenly shattered by a boisterous rondo refrain in the piano. As Mozart was well aware, this movement, not the previous slow one, had the kind of music the fun-loving Viennese would pay to hear. And in this rondo, his subscribers got more than they bargained for; the soloist and orchestra do not simply "speak in turn," but rather banter back and forth in the most playful and pleasing way. "Anything you can do, I can do better," "No you can't," "Yes I can," the antagonists seem to say. In Mozart's contest between interactive forces, there is no winner—except the listener.

To get a sense of the "physicality" involved in performing a Mozart concerto for piano and orchestra, check the YouTube playlist at CourseMate for this text.

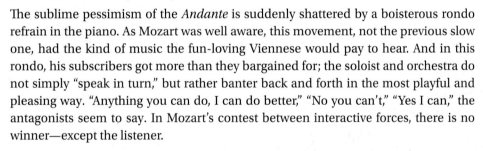

Key Words

genre (186)	Köchel (K) number (188)	solo concerto (194)
symphony (186)	string quartet (191)	double exposition form (195)
sinfonia (186)	sonata (193)	cadenza (195)

For a complete review of this chapter, see the Main Points, Chapter Quiz, Flashcards, and Glossary in CourseMate.

 Join us on Facebook at **Listening to Music with Craig Wright**

When we consider the genres of vocal music of the Classical period, we turn first and foremost to opera. Although Mozart, Haydn, and Beethoven did write wonderful Masses for the Roman Catholic liturgy, even these sacred works came under the sway of opera, being full of virtuosic arias and rousing choruses. In the Classical era, as today, the public was smitten with opera because, in addition to beautiful music, it had glamour, star appeal, and all the excitement of the theater.

Opera is drama, yes, but drama propelled by music. In the Classical period, opera maintained the essential features it had developed during the Baroque era. It still began with an overture, was divided into two or three acts, and made use of a succession of arias and recitatives, along with an occasional choral number. And, of course, it still was performed in a theater large enough to accommodate both an orchestra and elaborate stage sets.

A central development in the eighteenth century was the rise of comic opera (*opera buffa*), a powerful voice for social change during the Enlightenment (see Ch. 12, "The Rise of Popular Opera"). The statue-like gods and emperors of the old Baroque *opera seria* gradually departed the stage, making room for more natural, realistic characters drawn from everyday life—a barber and a maid, for example. Where Baroque opera posed magnificently, Classical opera moves fluidly. Arias and recitatives flow easily from one to another, and the mood of the music changes rapidly to reflect the quick-moving, often comic, events on stage.

Comic opera introduces a new element into the opera house, the **vocal ensemble**, which allows the plot to unfold more quickly. Instead of waiting for each character to sing in turn, three or more characters can express their own particular emotions simultaneously, singing together. One might sing of her love, another of his fear, another of her outrage, while a fourth pokes fun at the other three. If an author attempted this in a spoken play (everyone talking at once), an incomprehensible jumble would result. In opera, however, the end product is both harmonious and dramatically compelling. Composers often placed vocal ensembles at the ends of acts to help spark a rousing conclusion, one in which all the principals might appear together on stage. The vocal ensemble typifies the more democratic spirit, and better dramatic pacing, of the late eighteenth century.

Watch a video of Craig Wright's Open Yale Course class session 17, "Mozart and His Operas," at CourseMate for this text.

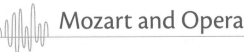

Mozart and Opera

The master of Classical opera, and of the vocal ensemble in particular, was Wolfgang Amadeus Mozart (1756–1791). While Haydn wrote more than a dozen operas and conducted others (see Fig. 16.2), he lacked Mozart's instinct for what was effective in the theater and what was not. Beethoven wrote only one opera, *Fidelio,* and he labored mightily on it, working through several revisions over the course of nearly ten years. Neither Haydn nor Beethoven had Mozart's talent for lightning-quick changes in mood or his capacity to give each character a distinctly personal set of musical attributes. Mozart's music is inherently dramatic and perfectly suited to the stage.

Mozart wrote Italian *opera seria* of the old Baroque sort, modern *opera buffa,* as well as German comic opera, which was called *Singspiel.* Like a Broadway musical, a **Singspiel** is made up of spoken dialogue (instead of recitative) and songs. Mozart's best work of this type is *Die Zauberflöte* (*The Magic Flute,* 1791). But, more important, Mozart created a new kind of opera that mixed serious and comic elements to powerful effect. His *Le nozze di Figaro* (*The Marriage of Figaro,* 1786) is a domestic comedy that nonetheless examines betrayal, adultery, love, and, ultimately, absolution; his *Don Giovanni* (1787) sets hilarious moments of comic buffoonery within a story of rape, murder, and, ultimately, damnation. In these two masterpieces, both set to texts (libretti) by Lorenzo da Ponte (Fig. 17.1), Mozart's quickly changing music evokes laughter and tears in almost equal measure.

Mozart: *Don Giovanni* (1787), K. 527

Don Giovanni has been called not only Mozart's greatest opera but also the greatest opera ever written. It tells the tale of an amoral philanderer, a Don Juan, who seduces and murders his way across Europe before being pursued and finally dragged down to hell by the ghost of a man whom he has killed. Because the seducer and mocker of public law and morality is a nobleman, *Don Giovanni* is implicitly critical of the aristocracy, and Mozart and da Ponte danced quickly to stay one step ahead of the imperial censor before production. Mozart's opera was first performed on October 29, 1787, in Prague, Czech Republic, a city in which his music was especially popular. As fate would have it, the most notorious Don Juan of the eighteenth century, Giacomo Casanova (1725–1798), was in the audience that first night in Prague. It turns out that he had a small hand in helping his friend da Ponte shape the libretto.

The overture to *Don Giovanni*, as we have seen (⑤ 2/23–26; downloads; and streaming music for Ch. 14 in CourseMate), is a perfect example of sonata–allegro form. It begins with a slow introduction that incorporates several themes or motives important later in the opera. Just as an author may postpone writing a preface until after the book is finished, so a composer typically saves the overture for the end of the creative process. In this way, the overture can not only prefigure important themes in the opera but also characterize the overall tone of the work. Mozart, as was his tendency, postponed much of the writing of *Don Giovanni* until the last minute, and the overture was not completed until the night before the premiere, the copyist's ink still wet on the pages as the music was handed to the orchestra.

The rape and murder perpetrated by Don Giovanni isn't funny. The comedy in *Don Giovanni* is delivered not by the Don, but rather by his worldly wise servant, Leporello, who points out the contradictions (the basis of all humor) in his master's life and in society in general. As the curtain rises, we find the reluctant accomplice Leporello keeping watch outside the house of Donna Anna, while inside his master is attempting to satisfy his sexual appetite. Grumbling as he paces back and forth, Leporello sings about how he would gladly trade places with the fortunate aristocrat, in "Notte e giorno faticar" ("I would like to play the gentleman" ⑤ 2/27; also in downloads and streaming music for Ch. 17 in CourseMate). Immediately, Mozart works to establish Leporello's musical character. He sets this opening aria in F major, a traditional key for the pastoral in music, showing that Leporello is a rustic fellow; he gives him a narrow vocal range without anything fancy; and he has him sing quick, repeated notes, almost as if stuttering. This last technique, called "patter song," is a stock device used to depict low-caste, inarticulate characters in comic opera.

As Leporello concludes his complaint, the masked Don Giovanni rushes onstage, chased by the virtuous Donna Anna. Here the strings rush up the scale and the music modulates up a fourth (at 1:40) to signify that we are now dealing with the highborn. The victim of Don Giovanni's unwelcome sexual advances, Donna Anna wants her assailant captured and unmasked (Fig. 17.2). While the gentleman and lady carry on a musical tug-of-war in long notes above, the cowering Leporello patters away fearfully below. This excellent example of vocal ensemble makes clear the conflicting emotions of each party.

Now Donna Anna's father, the Commandant, enters to confront Don Giovanni. Mozart's music tells us that this bodes ill—there is a troubling tremolo in the strings, and the mode (and mood) shifts from major to minor (3:04). Our fear

Figure 17.1

The man who wrote the librettos for Mozart's most important operas of the 1780s, including *Don Giovanni*, was Lorenzo da Ponte. Da Ponte was an Italian priest who, after the death of Mozart and a stay in London, immigrated to America in 1805. Once there, he ran a dry goods store in Sunbury, Pennsylvania, and worked as a trader, distiller, and occasional gunrunner during the War of 1812. Eventually, he moved to New York City, becoming the first professor of Italian literature at Columbia University in 1825. In 1826, he sponsored a performance of *Don Giovanni*, the first opera by Mozart to be heard in America.

To see the entirety of this action-packed first scene, go to the YouTube playlist at CourseMate for this text.

is immediately confirmed as the Don, first refusing to duel, draws his sword and attacks the aging Commandant. In the brief exchange of steel, Mozart depicts the rising tension by means of ascending chromatic scales and tight, tense chords (3:50). At the very moment Don Giovanni's sword pierces the Commandant, the action stops and the orchestra holds on to a painful **diminished chord** (4:00)—a tension-filled chord composed entirely of minor thirds. Mozart then clears the air of discord with a simple texture and accompaniment as Don Giovanni and Leporello gaze in horror on the dying Commandant.

Now comes a magical moment that perhaps only Mozart could have created (5 2/28; 4:06 in downloads and in streaming music for Ch. 17 in CourseMate)—a vocal ensemble in which three very different sentiments are conveyed simultaneously: surprise and satisfaction (Don Giovanni), the desire to flee (Leporello), and the pain of a violent death (Commandant). At the end, the listener can *feel* the Commandant die, his life sinking away through the slow descent of a chromatic scale (0:56; 5:02 in downloads and streaming music). In its intensity and compression, only the opening scene of Shakespeare's *King Lear* rivals the beginning of *Don Giovanni*.

Tristram Kenton/Lebrecht Music & Arts

Figure 17.2

Don Giovanni (Roderick Williams) tries to seduce Donna Anna (Suzannah Glanville) at the beginning of a 2005 British production of Mozart's *Don Giovanni*. Note the similarity in approach to *The Phantom of the Opera* by Andrew Lloyd Webber. Lloyd Webber drew heavily from Mozart's *Don Giovanni*. For example, the opera composed by the Phantom in Act II is called *Don Juan [Giovanni] Triumphant*, which tells this timeless tale of seduction from Don Juan's point of view.

Listening Guide

Wolfgang Amadeus Mozart, Opera, *Don Giovanni* (1787), K. 527

5
2/27–28

Act I, Scene 1

Characters: Don Giovanni, a rakish lord; Leporello, his servant; Donna Anna, a virtuous noblewoman; the Commandant, her father, a retired military man

WHAT TO LISTEN FOR: Leporello's simple aria followed by a vocal ensemble, leading to a duel and another vocal ensemble

ARIA

Leporello

0:00 27	The pacing Leporello grumbles as he awaits his master Don Giovanni.	Notte e giorno faticar, per chi nulla sa gradir, piova e il vento sopportar, mangiar male e mal dormir. Voglio far il gentiluomo e non volgio più servir . . .	On the go from morn 'til night for one who shows no appreciation, sustaining wind and rain, without proper food or sleep. I would like to play the gentleman and no more a servant be . . .
		(Leporello continues in this vein.)	
1:40	Violins rush up the scale and music modulates upward as Don Giovanni and Donna Anna rush in.		

(continued)

VOCAL ENSEMBLE (TRIO)

1:46 — Donna Anna tries to hold and unmask Don Giovanni while Leporello cowers on the side.

Donna Anna

Non sperar, se non m'uccidi,
ch'io ti lasci fuggir mai.

Do not hope you can escape
unless you kill me.

Don Giovanni

Donna folle, indarno gridi,
chi son io tu non saprai.

Crazy lady, you scream in vain,
you will never know who I am.

Leporello

Che tumulto, oh ciel, che gridi
il padron in nuovi guai.

What a racket, heavens,
what screams, my master in a new scrape.

Donna Anna

Gente! Servi! Al traditore!
Scellerato!

Everyone! Help! Catch the traitor!
Scoundrel!

Don Giovanni

Taci et trema al mio furore!
Sconsigliata!

Shut up and get out of my way!
Fool!

Leporello

Sta a veder che il malandrino mi
farà recipitar . . . .

We will see if this malefactor will be
the ruin of me . . . .

(The trio continues in this manner with liberal repeats of text and music.)

3:04 — String tremolo and shift from major to minor as the Commandant enters

VOCAL ENSEMBLE (TRIO)

3:11 — The Commandant comes forward to fight; Don Giovanni first refuses, then duels; Leporello tries to flee.

Commandant

Lasciala, indegno!
Battiti meco!

Let her go, villain!
Fight with me!

Don Giovanni

Va! non mi degno di pugnar teco!

Away, I wouldn't deign to fight with you!

Commandant

Così pretendi da me fuggir!

So you think you can get away thus?

Leporello (aside)

Potessi almeno di qua partir!

If I could only get out of here!

Don Giovanni

Misero! Attendi se vuoi morir!

You old fool! Get ready then, if you
wish to die!

3:50 — Musical duel (running scales and tense diminished chords)

4:00 — Climax on intense diminished chord (the Commandant falls mortally wounded), then pause

VOCAL ENSEMBLE (TRIO)

4:06 **28** **0:00** — Don Giovanni and Leporello look upon dying Commandant; "ticking" sound in strings freezes time.

Commandant

Ah, soccorso! son tradito.
L'assassino m'ha ferito,
e dal seno palpitante
sento l'anima partir.

Ah, I'm wounded, betrayed.
The assassin has run me through,
and from my heaving breast
I feel my soul depart.

Don Giovanni

Ah, gia cade il sciagurato,
affannoso e agonizzante,
già del seno palpitante
Veggo l'anima partir.

Ah, already the old fool falls,
gasping and writhing in pain,
and from his heaving breast
I can see his soul depart.

Leporello

Qual misfatto! qual eccesso!	What a horrible thing, how stupid!
Entro il sen dallo spavento	I can feel within my breast
palpitar il cor mi sento.	my heart pounding from fear.
Io non so che far, che dir.	I don't know what to say or do.

5:02	0:56	Slow, chromatic descent as last breath seeps out of the Commandant

🔊 Listen to streaming music in an Active Listening Guide at CourseMate or in the eBook.

When we next meet the unrepentant Don Giovanni, he is in pursuit of the country girl Zerlina. She is the betrothed of another peasant, Masetto, and the two are to be married the next day. Don Giovanni quickly dismisses Masetto and turns his charm on the naive Zerlina. First, he tries verbal persuasion carried off in simple recitative (the harpsichord is still used to accompany simple recitatives in Classical opera, a vestige of the older Baroque practice). Zerlina, he says, is too lovely for a country bumpkin like Masetto. Her beauty demands a higher state: She will become *his* wife!

Simple recitative now gives way to more passionate expression in the charming duet "Là ci darem la mano" ("Give me your hand, o fairest"). During this duet, Don Giovanni persuades Zerlina to extend her hand (and the prospect of a good deal more). He begins with a seductive melody (**A**) cast squarely in the Classical mold of two four-bar antecedent–consequent phrases (see the following Listening Guide). Zerlina repeats and extends this, but she still sings alone and untouched. The Don becomes more insistent in a new phrase (**B**), and Zerlina, in turn, becomes flustered, as her quick sixteenth notes reveal. The initial melody (**A**) returns but is now sung together by the two principals, their voices intertwining—musical union accompanies the act of physical touching that occurs on stage. Finally, as if to further affirm this coupling through music, Mozart adds a concluding section (**C**) in which the two characters skip off, arm in arm ("Let's go, my treasure"), their voices linked together in parallel-moving thirds to show unity of feeling and purpose. These are the means by which a skilled composer like Mozart can underscore, through music, the drama unfolding on the stage.

To see the entirety of this scene, both recitative and duet, go to the YouTube playlist at CourseMate for this text.

Listening Guide

Wolfgang Amadeus Mozart, Opera, *Don Giovanni* (1787), K. 527

Act I, Scene 7

Characters: Don Giovanni and the peasant girl Zerlina

Situation: Don Giovanni apparently succeeding in the seduction of Zerlina

WHAT TO LISTEN FOR: The stylistic distinction between recitative and aria (duet), and gradual unification of the voices signaling a uniform desire

5

2/29–30

RECITATIVE

Don Giovanni

0:00	29	Alfin siam liberati, Zerlinetta gentil, da quel scioccone.	At last, gentle Zerlina, we are free of that clown.
		Che ne dite, mio ben, sò far pulito?	And say, my love, didn't I handle it well?

Zerlina

	Signore, è mio marito.	Sir, he is my fiancé.

(continued)

Chi? Colui?	Who? Him?
Vi par che un onest'uomo,	Do you think that an honorable man,
un nobil cavalier, qual io mi vanto,	a noble cavalier as I believe I am,
possa soffrir che quel visetto d'oro,	could let such a golden face,
quel viso inzuccherato	such a sweet beauty,
da un bifolcaccio vil sia strapazzato?	be profaned by that clumsy oaf?

Zerlina

Ma, signor, io gli diedi parola di sposarlo.	But sir, I have already given my word to marry him.

Don Giovanni

Tal parola non vale un zero.	Such a promise counts for nothing.
Voi non siete fatta per esser paesana;	You were not made to be a peasant girl,
un altra sorte vi procuran quegli	a higher fate is in store for those
occhi bricconcelli, quei labretti sì belli,	mischievous eyes, those beautiful lips,
quelle dituccia candide e odorose,	those milky, perfumed hands,
par me toccar giuncata e fiutar rose.	so soft to touch, scented with roses.

Zerlina

Ah! . . . Non vorrei . . .	Ah! . . . I do not wish . . .

Don Giovanni

Che non vorreste?	What don't you wish?

Zerlina

Alfine ingannata restar.	In the end to be deceived.
Io sò che raro colle donne voi altri	I know that rarely are you noblemen
cavalieri siete onesti e sinceri.	honest and sincere with women.

Don Giovanni

Eh, un'impostura della gente plebea!	A vile slander of the low classes!
La nobiltà ha dipinta negli occhi l'onestà.	Nobility can be seen in honest eyes.
Orsù, non perdiam tempo; in questo	Now let's not waste time. I will marry you
istante io ti voglio sponsar.	immediately.

Zerlina

Voi?	You?

Don Giovanni

Certo, io. Quell casinetto è mio.	Certainly I. That villa over there is mine.
Soli saremo, e là, gioiello mio,	We will be alone, and there, my little jewel,
ci sposeremo.	we will be married.

ARIA (DUET)

Don Giovanni

Là ci da-rem la mano, là mi di-rai di sì; ve-di, non è lon-ta-no, par-tiam, ben__ mio, da__ qui.

0:00 30 A	Là ci darem la mano,	Give me your hand, o fairest,
	là mi dirai di sì	whisper a gentle "yes."
	Vedi, non è lontano:	See, it's not far:
	partiam, ben mio, da qui.	let's go, my love.

Zerlina

0:20	Vorrei, e non vorrei,	I'd like to but yet I would not.
	mi trema un poco il cor;	My heart will not be still.
	felice, è ver, sarei,	'Tis true I would be happy
	ma può burlarmi ancor.	yet he may deceive me still.

Don Giovanni

Vie - ni, mio bel di - let - to!

0:45	**B**	Vieni, mio bel diletto!	Come with me, my pretty one!

Zerlina

Mi fa pietà Masetto!   May Masetto take pity!

Don Giovanni

Io cangierò tua sorte!   I will change your fate!

Zerlina

Presto, non son più forte.   Quick then, I can no longer resist.

1:15	**A'**	Repeat of first eight lines, but with Don Giovanni's and Zerlina's parts moving closer together
1:43	**B'**	Repeat of next four lines
2:09	**C**	Change of meter to dance-like as principals skip off together

Together

(Zerlina) An - diam, an-diam, mio be-ne, a ri-sto-rar le pe-ne d'un' in - no - cen-tea - mor!

(Don Giovanni) An - diam, an-diam, mio be-ne, a ri-sto-rar le pe-ne d'un' in - no - cen-tea - mor!

Andiam, andiam mio bene,   Let's go, let's go, my treasure,
a ristorar le pene   to soothe the pangs
d'un innocente amor!   of innocent love!

🔊 Listen to streaming music in an Active Listening Guide at CourseMate or in the eBook.

In the end, the frightful ghost of the dead Commandant confronts Don Giovanni and orders him to repent. Ever defiant, Don Giovanni cries, "No, no," and is dragged down to hell to the sounds of Mozart's most demonic music. It is the admixture of divine beauty and sinister power that makes *Don Giovanni* a masterpiece of the highest order. No wonder Andrew Lloyd Webber paid homage to it in his long-running *Phantom of the Opera*.

See the exciting conclusion of *Don Giovanni* in the YouTube playlist at CourseMate for this text.

Key Words

vocal ensemble (199)	*Singspiel* (199)	diminished chord (201)

For a complete review of this chapter, see the Main Points, Chapter Quiz, Flashcards, and Glossary in CourseMate.

Join us on Facebook at **Listening to Music with Craig Wright**

chapter **EIGHTEEN**

Beethoven: Bridge to Romanticism

Ludwig van Beethoven (1770–1827) Composing his 'Missa Solemnis' (oil on canvas), Stieler, Joseph Carl (1781–1858) (after)/Private Collection/The Bridgeman Art Library

No composer looms larger as an iconic figure than Ludwig van Beethoven. When we imagine the "musician as struggling artist," who comes first to mind? The angry, defiant, disheveled Beethoven. Isn't it the bust of Beethoven, rather than that of the elegant Mozart or the stalwart Bach, that sits atop Schroeder's piano in the comic strip *Peanuts* (Fig. 18.1)? Doesn't Beethoven's music triumphantly accompany "the king's speech" in the 2010 Academy Award–winning film of that name? Isn't Beethoven among the iconic "3 B's" of classical music (Bach, Beethoven, and Brahms)? And why is our first listening example (intro/1) the beginning of Beethoven's Symphony No. 5? Because he and it serve as a useful reference point that everyone recognizes. Beethoven is, in short, deeply ingrained in our culture.

But Beethoven was lucky. The period of his maturity (the early nineteenth century) was the first to create the image of the great artist as an angry, self-absorbed loner who suffers for art. Beethoven was all these and more; thus, his contemporaries made him something of a poster boy for "artist as eccentric genius." Oblivious to the world, he walked about Vienna humming and scribbling music in a notebook. Although Beethoven's last compositions were understood only by a few, he was well known to the masses of his day. He had elevated the stature of the artist and of art itself. He had transformed the image of the composer from Classical servant to Romantic visionary (Fig. 18.2). When he died in March of 1827, 20,000 citizens of Vienna turned out for the funeral. Schools closed, and the army mobilized to control the crowd. An artist—and a musician, no less—had become a cult figure.

Today Beethoven's music continues to enjoy great popular favor. Statistics show that his symphonies, sonatas, and quartets are played in concert and on the radio more than those of any other classical composer, slightly more than Mozart's. If Mozart's sublime music seems to communicate universal truths, Beethoven's seems to tell us about Beethoven, his struggles, and ultimately the struggles of all of us. As was true of his own personality, Beethoven's music is full of extremes: sometimes tender and sometimes violent. And just as Beethoven the composer triumphed over personal adversity—his growing deafness—so his music imparts a feeling of struggle and ultimate victory. It has a sense of rightness, even morality, about it. It seems to speak to the humanity in all of us.

Historians have traditionally divided Beethoven's music into three periods: early, middle, and late. In many regards, his work belongs to the tradition of the Classical Viennese style. Beethoven employs Classical genres (symphony, sonata, concerto, string quartet, and opera) and Classical forms (sonata–allegro, rondo, and theme and variations). Yet even in compositions from his early period, Beethoven projects a new spirit in his music, one that foreshadows the musical style of the Romantic era (1820–1900). An intense, lyrical expression is heard in his slow movements, while his allegros abound with pounding rhythms, strong dynamic contrasts, and startling orchestral effects. Although Beethoven largely stays within the bounds of Classical forms, he pushes their confines to the breaking point, so great is his urge for personal expression. Though a pupil of Haydn and a lifelong admirer of Mozart, he nevertheless elevated music to new heights of both lyricism and dramatic power. For this reason, he can rightly be called the prophet of Romantic music.

Figure 18.1

Sitting atop Schroeder's piano in the cartoon strip *Peanuts*, a bust of Beethoven, icon of classical music

Figure 18.2

Sitting atop Franz Liszt's piano, a bust of Beethoven as he appeared to listeners around 1840. Here Beethoven looms godlike over the scene as Liszt and other artists of the day look up with reverential respect. For the nineteenth century, Beethoven came to personify the divinely inspired genius, perhaps because Beethoven himself said that he "conversed with God."

Lebrecht Music & Arts

 ## The Early Years (1770–1802)

Like Bach and Mozart before him, Beethoven came from a family of musicians. His father and grandfather were performers at the court at Bonn, Germany, on the Rhine River, where Beethoven was baptized on December 17, 1770. Seeing great musical talent in his young son, Beethoven's father, a violent alcoholic, forcibly made him practice at the keyboard at all hours, day and night. Soon he tried to exploit his son as a child prodigy, a second Mozart, telling the world that the diminutive boy was a year or two younger than he actually was. Throughout his life, Beethoven was convinced that he was born in 1772, two years after his actual birth date.

In 1787 Beethoven went to Vienna, then the musical capital of the world, with the aim of studying with Mozart. But the mortal illness of Beethoven's mother in Bonn required this eldest son to return home, and not until 1792, a year after Mozart's death, did he move to Vienna permanently. As one of his financial backers said at the time, "You are going to Vienna in fulfillment of your long-frustrated wishes . . . you will receive the spirit of Mozart from the hands of Haydn."

Upon his arrival in Vienna, Beethoven not only took composition lessons from Joseph Haydn but also bought new clothes, located a wig maker, and found a dancing instructor. His aim was to gain entrée into the homes of the wealthy of the Austrian capital. And this he soon achieved, owing not to his woeful social skills but to his phenomenal ability as a pianist.

Beethoven played louder, more forcefully, and even more violently than any pianist the Viennese nobility had ever heard. He possessed an extraordinary technique—even if he did hit occasional wrong notes—and this he put to good use, especially in his fanciful improvisations. As a contemporary witness observed, "He knew how to produce such an impression on every listener that frequently there was not a single dry eye, while many broke out into loud sobs, for there was a certain magic in his expression."

The aristocracy was captivated. One patron put a string quartet at Beethoven's disposal, another made it possible for the composer to experiment with a small orchestra, and all showered him with gifts. He acquired well-to-do pupils; he sold his compositions ("I state my price and they pay," he said with pride in 1801); and he requested and eventually received an annuity from three noblemen so that he could work undisturbed. The text of this arrangement included the following provisions:

It is recognized that only a person who is as free as possible from all cares can consecrate himself to his craft. He can only produce these great and sublime works which ennoble Art if they form his sole pursuit, to the exclusion of all unnecessary obligations. The undersigned have therefore taken the decision to ensure that Herr Ludwig van Beethoven's situation shall not be embarrassed by his most necessary requirements, nor shall his powerful Genius be hampered.

What a contrast between Beethoven's contract and the one signed by Haydn four decades earlier (see Ch. 13)! Music was no longer merely a craft, and the composer a servant. It had now become an exalted Art, and the great creator a Genius who must be protected and nurtured—a new, Romantic notion of the value of music and the importance of the creator. Beethoven did his best to encourage this belief in the exalted mission of the composer as artist. He claimed that he spoke with God. And when one noble patron demanded that he play for a visiting French general, Beethoven stormed out of the salon and responded by letter: "Prince, what you are, you are through the accident of birth. What I am, I am through my own efforts. There have been many princes and there will be thousands more. But there is only one Beethoven!" What Beethoven failed to realize, of course, is that he, too, owed his success partly to "the accident of birth." Coming from a long line of musicians, he had been born with a huge musical talent.

Figure 18.3

A fanciful, yet in many ways accurate, depiction of Beethoven in the midst of creative chaos. Beethoven's domestic surroundings were always in disarray. In many ways, he served as the model for the nineteenth-century concept of genius: a solitary, lonely figure who suffered for, and lived only for, his art.

Piano Sonata, Opus 13, the *"Pathétique"* Sonata (1799)

The bold originality in Beethoven's music can be heard in one of his most celebrated compositions, the **"Pathétique" Sonata**. A Classical sonata, as we have seen (Ch. 16), is a multimovement work for solo instrument or solo instrument with keyboard accompaniment. This particular sonata, for solo piano, is identified as Beethoven's Opus 13, denoting that it is the thirteenth of 135 works that Beethoven published. But Beethoven himself also supplied the sonata with its descriptive title—*"Pathétique"* ("Plaintive")—underscoring the passion and pathos he felt within it. Its great drama and intensity derive in large part from the juxtaposition of extremes, specifically those of dynamics (from *fortissimo* to *pianissimo*), tempo (*grave* to *presto*), and range (from very high to very low). The piece also demands of the pianist more technical skill and stamina than had any piano sonata of Mozart or Haydn. Displaying his virtuosity, Beethoven frequently performed the *"Pathétique"* in the homes and palaces of the Viennese aristocracy.

Watch a video of Craig Wright's Open Yale Course class session 18, "Piano Music of Mozart and Beethoven," at CourseMate for this text.

FIRST MOVEMENT

Contemporaries recount how Beethoven the pianist played with "superhuman" speed and force, and how he banged the keys so hard on one occasion that he broke six strings. The crashing C minor chord that opens the *"Pathétique"* Sonata suggests Beethoven's sometimes violent approach to the instrument. After this startling opening gesture, Beethoven the dramatist takes over, juxtaposing music of wildly differing moods: The *sforzando* chord is immediately followed by the quietest sort of lyricism, only to be interrupted by another chordal thunderbolt (Ex. 18.1). This slow introduction is probably a written-out version of the sort of improvisation that gained Beethoven great fame in Vienna.

EXAMPLE 18.1

The dramatic introduction leads to a racing first theme that rises impetuously in the right hand (Ex. 18.2). The sense of anxiety felt by the listener is amplified by the throbbing bass, where the left hand of the pianist plays broken octaves (the alternation of two tones an octave apart), reminiscent of the rumbling thunder of an approaching storm.

EXAMPLE 18.2

The remainder of the movement now plays out as a contest between the impetuous, racing themes and the stormy chords. But while much passion and intensity is found here, Classical formal control is also present. The crashing chords come back at the beginning of both the development and the coda of this movement in sonata–allegro form. Thus, the chords establish firm formal boundaries that serve as auditory signposts for the listener, signaling the progress of the piece. For Beethoven, these chordal repeats set limits to his compositional imagination, keeping the music under control. Beethoven's music often conveys a feeling of struggle: Classical forms gave Beethoven something to struggle against.

Listening Guide

Ludwig van Beethoven, Piano Sonata, Opus 13, the "*Pathétique*" Sonata (1799)

First movement, *Grave; Allegro di molto e con brio* (grave; very fast and with gusto)

5   2

3/1–3   1/23–25

Genre: Sonata

Form: Sonata–allegro

WHAT TO LISTEN FOR: If conflict lies at the heart of drama, the contrasts between loud and soft, fast and slow, high and low, and violent and tender create it here.

INTRODUCTION

0:00	**1** **23**	Crashing chords alternate with softer, more lyrical ones.
0:33		Softer chords are continually cut off by crashing chords below.
0:50		Melody builds to climax and then rapid descent.

EXPOSITION [ ] = repeats

1:24   [3:08]   **First theme:** Rising agitated melody in right hand against broken octaves in left

| 1:43 | [3:27] | Transition modulates to new key, thinner texture. |
| 1:56 | [3:40] | **Second theme:** Bass, followed by treble, initiates "call and response." |

2:29	[4:12]	**Closing theme, part 1:** Right and left hands race in opposite directions.
2:49	[4:32]	**Closing theme, part 2:** Rapid scales in right hand above simple chords in left
2:56	[4:39]	Reminiscence of first theme

DEVELOPMENT

4:54	2 24	0:00	Crashing chords and softer chords from introduction
5:30		0:36	First theme extended and varied
6:11		1:17	Rapid, twisting descent played by right hand leads to recapitulation.

RECAPITULATION

6:17	3 25	0:00	**First theme:** Rising agitated melody in right hand
6:28		0:11	Transition
6:38		0:21	**Second theme:** Call and response between bass and treble
7:05		0:48	**Closing theme, part 1:** Hands move rapidly in opposite directions.
7:25		1:08	**Closing theme, part 2:** Scale runs in right hand
7:31		1:14	Reminiscence of first theme

CODA

| 7:49 | 1:32 | Recall of chords from introduction |
| 8:21 | 2:04 | Reminiscence of first theme leads to drive to final cadence. |

Listen to streaming music in an Active Listening Guide at CourseMate or in the eBook.

Take online Listening Exercise 18.1 and receive feedback at CourseMate or in the eBook.

SECOND MOVEMENT

Eyewitnesses who heard Beethoven at the piano remarked on the "legato" quality of his playing and contrasted it with Mozart's lighter, more staccato style. Beethoven himself said in 1796 that "one can sing on the piano, so long as one has feeling." We can hear Beethoven sing through the legato melodic line that dominates the slow second movement of the "*Pathétique*" Sonata. Indeed, the expression mark he gave to the movement is *cantabile* (songful). The singing quality of the melody seems to have appealed to pop-star "piano man" Billy Joel, who borrowed this theme for the chorus (refrain) of his song "This Night" on the album *Innocent Man*.

Listen to "This Night" in the iTunes and YouTube playlists at CourseMate for this text.

THIRD MOVEMENT

A comparison of the second and third movements of the "*Pathétique*" Sonata shows that musical form does not always determine musical mood. Although both the *Adagio* and the fast finale are in rondo form, the former is a lyrical hymn and the latter a passionate, but slightly comical, chase. The finale has hints of the crashing chords and stark contrasts of the first movement, but the earlier violence and impetuosity have been softened into a mood of impassioned playfulness.

The eighteenth-century piano sonata had been essentially private music of a modest sort—music a composer-teacher like Mozart or Haydn would write for a talented amateur pupil, to be played as entertainment in the home. Beethoven took the modest, private piano sonata and infused it with the technical bravura of the public stage. The louder sound, wider range, and greater length of Beethoven's thirty-two piano sonatas made them appropriate for the increasingly large concert halls—and larger and louder pianos—of the nineteenth century. Beginning in the Romantic period, Beethoven's piano sonatas became a staple of the professional virtuoso's repertoire. But there was a downside: Sonatas originally written for amateurs to play were now becoming too difficult. The virtuoso had begun to run off with the amateur's music, a development that would continue throughout the nineteenth century.

Beethoven Loses His Hearing

Beethoven cut a strange, eccentric figure as he wandered the streets of Vienna, sometimes humming, sometimes mumbling, and sometimes jotting on music paper. Dogs barked and street kids, knowing nothing about genius, occasionally threw stones. Adding to the difficulties of his somewhat unstable personality was the fact that Beethoven was gradually losing his hearing—a serious handicap for any person, but a tragic condition for a musician. Can you imagine a blind painter?

Beethoven first complained about his hearing and a ringing in his ears (tinnitus) in the late 1790s, and he suffered considerable anguish and depression. His increasing deafness did not stop him from composing—most people can hear simple melodies inside their heads, and the gifted Beethoven could generate complex melodies and harmonies in his "inner ear" without need of external sound. However, his condition caused him to retreat even further from society and all but ended his career as a pianist, because he could no longer gauge how hard to press the keys. By late 1802, Beethoven recognized that he would ultimately suffer a total loss of hearing. In despair, he wrote something akin to a last will and testament, today called the **Heiligenstadt Testament** after the Viennese suburb in which he penned it. In this confessional document for posterity, the composer admits that he considered suicide: "I would have ended my life; it was only *my art* that held me back." Beethoven emerged from this personal crisis with renewed resolve to fulfill his artistic destiny—he would now "seize Fate by the throat."

 # The "Heroic" Period (1803–1813)

Watch a video of Craig Wright's Open Yale Course class session 20, "The Colossal Symphony: Beethoven, Berlioz, Mahler, and Shostakovich," at CourseMate for this text.

It was in this resurgent, defiant mood that Beethoven entered what we call his **"heroic" period** of composition (1803–1813; also simply termed his "middle period"). His works became longer, more assertive, and full of grand gestures. Simple, often triadic, themes predominate, and these are repeated, sometimes incessantly, as the music swells to majestic proportions. When these themes are played *forte* and given over to the brass instruments, a heroic, triumphant sound results.

Beethoven wrote nine symphonies in all, six of them during his "heroic" period. These symphonies are few in number in part because they are so much longer and more complex than those of Mozart or Haydn. They set the standard for the epic symphony of the nineteenth century. Most noteworthy are the "Eroica" (Third), the famous Fifth Symphony, the Sixth (called the "Pastoral" because it evokes the ambiance of the Austrian countryside), the Seventh, and the monumental Ninth. In these, Beethoven introduces new orchestral colors by bringing new instruments into the symphony orchestra: the trombone (Symphony Nos. 5, 6, and 9), the contrabassoon (Symphony Nos. 5 and 9), the piccolo (Symphony Nos. 5, 6, and 9), and even the human voice (Symphony No. 9).

Symphony No. 3 in E♭ major ("Eroica," 1803)

As its title suggests, Beethoven's **"Eroica" ("Heroic") Symphony** epitomizes the grandiose, heroic style. More than any other single orchestral work, it changed the historical direction of the symphony. Its length, some forty-five minutes, is nearly twice that of a typical symphony by his teacher Haydn. Its sound assaults the ear with rhythmic gestures and startling orchestral effects that were shocking to early-nineteenth-century listeners. Most novel for Beethoven, the work has biographical content, for the hero of the "Eroica" Symphony, at least originally, was Napoleon Bonaparte.

Austria and the German states were at war with France in the early nineteenth century. Yet German-speaking Beethoven was much taken with the enemy's revolutionary call for liberty, equality, and fraternity. Napoleon Bonaparte became his hero, and the composer dedicated his third symphony to him, writing on the title page "intitolata Bonaparte." But when news that Napoleon had declared himself emperor reached Beethoven, he flew into a rage, saying, "Now he, too, will trample on all the rights of man and indulge his ambition." Taking up a knife, he scratched so violently to erase Bonaparte's name from the title page that he left a hole in the paper (Fig. 18.4). When the work was published, Napoleon's name had been removed in favor of the more general title "Heroic Symphony: To Celebrate the Memory of a Great Man." Beethoven was not an imperialist; he was a revolutionary.

Symphony No. 5 in C minor (1808)

At the center of Beethoven's symphonic output stands his remarkable Symphony No. 5 (Fig. 18.6; see also Ch. 1). Its novelty rests in the way the composer conveys a sense of psychological progression, from darkness to light, over the course of four movements. An imaginative listener might perceive the following sequence of events: (1) a fateful encounter with dark, elemental forces; (2) a period of quiet soul-searching; followed by (3) a further wrestling with the elements; and, finally, (4) a triumphant victory over the forces of Fate. Beethoven himself is said to have remarked with regard to the famous opening motive of the symphony: "There Fate knocks at the door!"

The rhythm of the opening—perhaps the best-known moment in all of classical music—animates the entire symphony. Not only does it dominate the opening *Allegro,* but it reappears in varied form in the three later movements as well, binding the symphony into a unified whole (Ex. 18.3). Nowhere else in classical music does such a large work grow so organically from a single musical idea.

Figures 18.4 and 18.5

(top) The title page of the autograph of Beethoven's "Eroica" Symphony: *Sinfonia grande intitolata Bonaparte.* Note the hole where Beethoven took a knife and scratched out the name "Bonaparte." As a young officer, Napoleon Bonaparte seized control of the government of France in 1799. He established a new form of republican government that emphasized the revolutionary ideals of liberty, equality, and humanity. After Napoleon elevated himself to emperor in 1804, Beethoven changed the title of his Symphony No. 3 from "Bonaparte" to "Eroica." (bottom) The portrait by Jacques-Louis David shows the newly crowned Napoleon in full imperial regalia. Liberator had become oppressor.

Figure 18.6

Interior of the Theater-an-der-Wien, Vienna, where Beethoven's Symphony No. 5 premiered on December 22, 1808. This all-Beethoven concert lasted four hours, from 6:30 until 10:30 P.M., and presented eight new works, including his Symphony No. 5. During the performance of the symphony, the orchestra sometimes halted because of the difficulties in playing Beethoven's radically new music. Notice the horses on stage. Beethoven lived during a time of transition, when theaters were used for both public spectacles and music-only concerts.

EXAMPLE 18.3

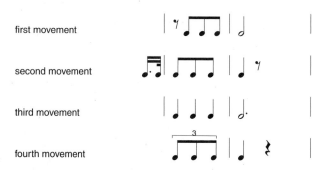

FIRST MOVEMENT

Bam! The listener is jolted to attention, forced to sit up and take notice by a sudden explosion of sound. And what an odd beginning to a symphony—a blast of three short notes and a long one, followed by the same three shorts and a long, all now a step lower. The movement can't quite get going. It starts and stops, then seems to lurch forward and gather momentum. And where is the melody? This three-shorts-and-a-long pattern is more a motive or musical cell than a melody. Yet it is striking by virtue of its power and compactness. As the movement unfolds, the actual pitches of the motive prove to be of secondary importance. Beethoven is obsessed with its rhythm. He wants to demonstrate the enormous latent force lurking within even the most basic rhythmic atom, a power waiting to be unleashed by a composer who understands the secrets of rhythmic energy.

To control the sometimes violent forces that will emerge, the music unfolds within the traditional confines of sonata–allegro form. The basic four-note motive provides all the musical material for the first theme area:

EXAMPLE 18.4

The brief transition played by a solo French horn is only six notes long and is formed simply by adding two notes to the end of the basic four-note motive. As expected, the transition carries us tonally from the tonic (C minor) to the relative major (E♭ major):

EXAMPLE 18.5

The second theme offers a moment of escape from the rush of the "Fate" motive, but even here the pattern of three shorts and a long lurks beneath like a ticking time bomb:

EXAMPLE 18.6

The closing theme, too, is none other than the motive once again, now presented in a more heroic guise:

EXAMPLE 18.7

In the development, the opening motive returns, recapturing, and even surpassing, the force it had at the beginning. Beethoven now inverts the motive—he makes it go up as well as down, though the rhythmic shape remains the same:

EXAMPLE 18.8

As the motive rises, so does the musical tension. A powerful rhythmic climax ensues and then gives way to a brief imitative passage. Soon Beethoven reduces the six-note motive of the transition to merely two notes, and then just one, passing these figures around *pianissimo* between the strings and winds:

EXAMPLE 18.9

Beethoven was a master of the process of thematic condensation—stripping away all extraneous material to get to the core of a musical idea. Here, in this mysterious *pianissimo* passage, he presents the irreducible minimum of his motive: a single note. In the midst of this quiet, the original four-note motive tries to reassert itself *fortissimo,* but is rebuffed. Its explosive force, however, cannot be held back. A thunderous return of the opening pitches signals the beginning of the recapitulation.

Although the recapitulation offers a repeat of the events of the exposition, Beethoven has a surprise in store. No sooner has the motive regained its momentum than an oboe interjects a tender, languid, and wholly unexpected solo. A deviation from the usual path of sonata–allegro form, this brief oboe cadenza allows for a momentary release of excess energy. The recapitulation then resumes its expected course.

What is not expected is the enormous coda that follows. It is even longer than the exposition! A new form of the motive appears, and it, too, is subjected to development. In fact, this coda constitutes essentially a second development section, so great is Beethoven's single urge to exploit the latent power of this one simple musical idea.

Listening Guide

Ludwig van Beethoven, Symphony No. 5 in C minor (1808)

First movement, *Allegro con brio* (fast with gusto)

Genre: Symphony

Form: Sonata–allegro

WHAT TO LISTEN FOR: Explosive power created by the manipulation of the rhythm of a single musical cell

5 2
3/4–6 1/26–28

EXPOSITION [ ] = repeats

0:00	4 26	[1:27]	Two statements of "Fate" motive

0:06	[1:33]	Motive builds momentum in crescendo, working up to climax and three chords, the last of which is held.
0:22	[1:49]	Transition begins and builds to climax using rhythmic motive.
0:43	[2:11]	End of transition played by solo French horn

0:46	[2:14]	Quiet second theme in new major key (relative major), motive below

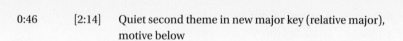

1:01	[2:27]	Crescendo
1:07	[2:35]	Loud string passage prepares arrival of closing theme.
1:17	[2:44]	Closing theme

DEVELOPMENT

2:54	5 27	0:00	Motive played *fortissimo* by horn and strings, then passed back and forth between woodwinds and strings
3:16		0:22	Another crescendo or "Beethovenian swell"
3:22		0:28	Rhythmic climax in which motive is pounded incessantly
3:30		0:36	Short passage of imitative counterpoint using transition motive
3:40		0:46	Two notes of transition motive passed back and forth

3:51	0:57	Single note passed back and forth between winds and strings; gets quiet
4:03	1:09	Basic four-note motive tries to reassert itself loudly.
4:11	1:17	Motive reenters insistently.

RECAPITULATION

4:17	0:00	Return of motive
4:26	0:09	Motive gathers momentum and cadences with three chords.
4:37	0:20	Unexpected oboe solo

4:51	0:34	Motive returns and moves hurriedly to climax.
5:15	0:58	Quiet second theme with motive below
5:31	1:14	Crescendo leading to closing theme
5:51	1:34	Closing theme

CODA

5:59	1:42	Motive pounded *fortissimo* on one note, then again a step higher
6:15	1:58	Imitative counterpoint
6:30	2:13	Rising quarter notes form new four-note pattern.

6:40	2:23	New four-note pattern alternates between strings and woodwinds.
7:00	2:42	Pounding on single note, then motive as at beginning
7:21	3:04	Succession of I–V–I chords brings movement to abrupt end.

◀)) Listen to streaming music in an Active Listening Guide at CourseMate or in the eBook.

◀)) Take online Listening Exercise 18.2 and receive feedback at CourseMate or in the eBook.

SECOND MOVEMENT

After the pounding we experienced in the explosive first movement, the calm of the noble *Andante* comes as a welcome change of pace. The mood is at first serene, and the melody is expansive—in contrast to the four-note motive of the first movement, the opening theme here runs on for twenty-two measures. The musical form is also a familiar one: theme and variations. But this is not the simple, easily audible theme and variations of Haydn and Mozart (see Ch. 15). There are two themes: the first lyrical and serene, played mostly by the strings; and the second quiet, then triumphant, played mostly by the brasses (Fig. 18.7). By means of this "double" theme and variations, Beethoven demonstrates his ability to add length and complexity to a standard Classical form. He also shows how it is possible to contrast within one movement two starkly opposed expressive domains—the intensely lyrical (theme 1) and the brilliantly heroic (theme 2).

Figure 18.7

Original autograph of Beethoven at work on the second movement of his Symphony No. 5. The many corrections in different-colored inks and red pencil suggest the turmoil and constant evolution involved in Beethoven's creative process. Unlike Mozart, to whom finished musical ideas came quickly, Beethoven's art was a continual struggle.

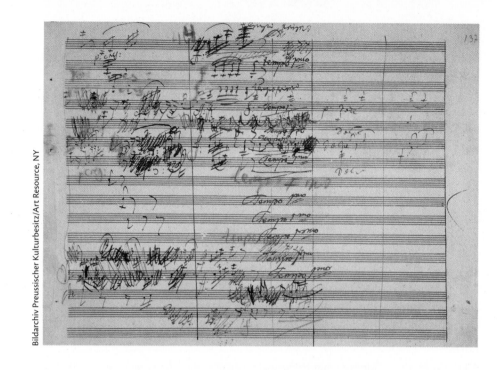

Bildarchiv Preussischer Kulturbesitz/Art Resource, NY

Listening Guide

Ludwig van Beethoven, Symphony No. 5 in C minor (1808)

Second movement, *Andante con moto* (moving with purpose)

Genre: Symphony

Form: Theme and variations

WHAT TO LISTEN FOR: The emotional counterpoint that results from engaging in succession two themes very different in mood

3/7–8

THEMES

0:00	7	Violas and cellos play beginning of theme 1.

0:24	Woodwinds play middle of theme 1.

0:36	Violins play end of theme 1.

0:52	Clarinets, bassoons, and violins play theme 2.

1:14	Brasses play theme 2 in fanfare style.
1:30	Mysterious *pianissimo*

VARIATION 1

1:58		Violas and cellos vary beginning of theme 1 by adding sixteenth notes.	

p

2:18		Woodwinds play middle of theme 1.
2:31		Strings play end of theme 1.
2:48		Clarinets, bassoons, and violins play theme 2.
3:10		Brasses return with fanfare (theme 2).
3:26		More of mysterious *pianissimo*

VARIATION 2

3:52	**8**	0:00	Violas and cellos overlay beginning of theme 1 with rapidly moving ornamentation.

p

4:27	0:35	Pounding repeated chords with theme below in cellos and basses
4:44	0:52	Rising scales lead to fermata (hold).
5:04	1:12	Woodwinds play fragments of beginning of theme 1.
5:50	1:58	Fanfare (theme 2) now returns in full orchestra.
6:36	2:44	Woodwinds play beginning of theme 1 detached and in minor key.

VARIATION 3

7:17	3:25	Violins play beginning of theme 1 *fortissimo*.
7:43	3:51	Woodwinds play middle of theme 1.
7:52	4:00	Strings play end of theme 1.

CODA

8:08	4:17	Tempo quickens as bassoons play reminiscence of beginning of theme 1.
8:23	4:31	Violins play reminiscence of theme 2.
8:34	4:41	Woodwinds play middle of theme 1.
8:48	4:55	Strings play end of theme 1.
9:11	5:19	Ends with repetitions of rhythm of very first measure of movement

🔊 Listen to streaming music in an Active Listening Guide at CourseMate or in the eBook.

THIRD MOVEMENT

In the Classical period, the third movement of a symphony or quartet was usually a graceful minuet and trio (see Ch. 14). Haydn and his pupil Beethoven wanted to infuse this third movement with more life and energy, so they often wrote a faster, more rollicking piece and called it a **scherzo**, meaning "joke." And while there is nothing particularly humorous about the mysterious and sometimes threatening sound of the scherzo of Beethoven's Symphony No. 5, it is certainly far removed from the elegant world of the courtly minuet.

The formal plan of Beethoven's scherzo, **ABA′**, derives from the ternary form of the minuet, as does its triple meter. The scherzo, **A**, is in the tonic key of C minor, while the trio, **B**, is in C major. The return to **A** shows how Beethoven does things differently than other Classical composers: Instead of an exact repeat, he reworks this scherzo, interjecting an element of mystery and suspense as the strings tiptoe around with ghost-like pizzicatos.

Ludwig van Beethoven, Symphony No. 5 in C minor (1808)

Third movement, Allegro (fast)

Genre: Symphony

Form: Ternary

WHAT TO LISTEN FOR: How this sometimes mysterious, sometimes pounding scherzo and trio differ radically from the more elegant minuet and trio of Mozart's *Eine kleine Nachtmusik* (downloads; streaming music in CourseMate, Ch. 14; 2 1/16 and 5 2/11)

SCHERZO A

| 0:00 | 9 | | Cellos and basses creep in with theme 1 and pass it on to higher strings. |

0:09		Repeat
0:20		French horns *fortissimo* enter with theme 2.
0:40		Cellos and basses return with theme 1.
0:55		Crescendo
1:03		Full orchestra again plays theme 2 *fortissimo*.
1:25		Development of theme 1
1:52		Ends with theme 2 *fortissimo*, then *piano*

TRIO B

| 1:59 | 10 | 0:00 | Cellos and basses present subject of fugato. |

			Violas and bassoons enter with subject.
			Second violins enter with subject.
			First violins enter with subject.
2:14		0:15	Repeat of imitative entries
2:36		0:37	Subject enters imitatively again: Cellos and basses, violas and bassoons, second violins, first violins, and then flutes are added.
3:04		1:05	Subject enters imitatively again in same instruments and flutes extend it.

SCHERZO A′

3:30		1:31	Quiet return of theme 1 in cellos and basses
3:39		1:40	Pizzicato (plucked) presentation of theme 1 in cellos accompanied by bassoons
3:50		1:51	Ghost-like return of theme 2 in short notes in winds and pizzicato in strings

BRIDGE TO FOURTH MOVEMENT

4:47		2:48	Long note held *pianissimo* in strings with timpani beating softly below
5:02		3:03	Repeating three-note pattern emerges in first violins.
5:23		3:24	Great crescendo leads to fourth movement.

 Listen to streaming music in an Active Listening Guide at CourseMate or in the eBook.

Now, a stroke of creative genius on Beethoven's part: He links the third and fourth movements by means of a musical bridge. Holding a single pitch (a dominant pedal point) as quietly as possible, the violins create an eerie sound, while the timpani beats menacingly in the background. A three-note motive grows from the violins and is repeated over and over as a wave of sound begins to swell from the orchestra. Here Beethoven is concerned only with volume, not melody, rhythm, or harmony. With enormous force, the wave finally crashes down, and from it emerges the triumphant beginning of the fourth movement—one of the grandest special effects in all of music.

FOURTH MOVEMENT

When Beethoven arrived at the finale, he was faced with a nearly impossible task. The last movement of a symphony had traditionally been a light sendoff. How to write a conclusion that would relieve the tension of the preceding musical events, yet provide an appropriate, substantive balance to the weighty first movement? To this end, he created a finale that is longer and beefier than the first movement. To bulk up his orchestra, Beethoven adds three trombones, a contrabassoon (low bassoon), and a piccolo (high flute), the first time any of these instruments had been called for in a symphony. He also writes big, bold, and, in most cases, triadic themes, assigning these most often to the powerful brasses. In these instruments and themes, we hear the "heroic" Beethoven at his best. The finale projects a feeling of affirmation, a sense that superhuman will has triumphed over adversity.

Listening Guide

Ludwig van Beethoven, Symphony No. 5 in C minor (1808)

Fourth movement, *Allegro* (fast)

Genre: Symphony

Form: Sonata–allegro

5

3/11–13

WHAT TO LISTEN FOR: See if you don't experience a change in mood as you listen to Beethoven's triumph over Fate. Do you not feel a sense of surging exhilaration from beginning to end?

EXPOSITION

| 0:00 | 11 | Full orchestra with prominent brasses plays first theme. |

| 0:33 | French horns play transition theme. |

| 0:59 | Strings play second theme. |

| 1:25 | Full orchestra plays closing theme. |

(Repeat of exposition omitted)

DEVELOPMENT

| 1:56 | 12 | 0:00 | Loud string tremolo (fluttering) |
| 2:01 | | 0:05 | Strings and woodwinds pass around fragments of second theme in different keys. |

(continued)

2:24	0:28	Double basses begin to play countermelody against second theme.
2:31	0:36	Trombones play countermelody.
2:59	1:04	Woodwinds and brasses play countermelody above dominant pedal point in cellos and basses.
3:15	1:20	Climax and pause on dominant triad
3:35	1:40	Ghost-like theme from scherzo (third movement) with four-note rhythm

RECAPITULATION

4:09	0:00	Full orchestra plays first theme *fortissimo*.
4:42	0:33	French horns play transition theme.
5:13	1:04	Strings play second theme.
5:38	1:29	Woodwinds play closing theme.

CODA

6:09	2:00	Violins play second theme.
6:19	2:10	Brasses and woodwinds play countermelody from development.
6:32	2:23	V–I, V–I chords sound like final cadence.
6:40	2:31	Bassoons, French horns, flutes, clarinets, and then piccolo continue with transition theme.
7:07	2:58	Trill high in piccolo
7:23	3:14	Tempo changes to *presto* (very fast).
7:47	3:38	Brasses recall first theme, now twice as fast.
7:55	3:46	Prolonged, almost excessive, V–I, V–I final cadence

◀)) Listen to streaming music in an Active Listening Guide at CourseMate or in the eBook.

Beethoven's Symphony No. 5 reveals his genius in a paradox: From minimal material (the basic cell) he derives maximum sonority. Present everywhere is a feeling of raw, elemental power propelled by the newly enlarged orchestra. Beethoven was the first to recognize that massive sound could be a potent psychological weapon. Mood and emotions could be manipulated by sonority alone. No wonder that during World War II (1939–1945) both sides, Fascist as well as Allied, used the music of this symphony to symbolize triumph—in Morse code, short-short-short-long is the letter "V," as in "Victory."

Where Did Beethoven Compose?

Most composers today compose at the piano. It gives them a chance to sound out a musical idea immediately, and sometimes the tactile experience of running the fingers over various chords can stimulate musical inspiration. Some earlier composers created at the keyboard as well (see Haydn seated with pen in hand in Fig. 15.3). Mozart and Beethoven generally did not compose at a keyboard, and certainly did not write down their music there. In the summers, Beethoven often composed outdoors while he walked through the woods around Vienna; as ideas came to him, he scribbled them in a music notebook. If it was hot, he would strip down to his underwear and walk on, his clothes tied to a pole slung over his shoulder. As to Beethoven's indoor composition, the floor plan of his final residence, a rather large apartment in Vienna, gives us a sense of how he worked. The apartment had an entry chamber and an entry hall with family portraits, a room for the storage of books and music, as well as rooms for servants and for food preparation. The main music room contained a bookshelf and two grand pianos, each a gift from a manufacturer and each situated before a window (Fig. 18.8). Oddly enough, Beethoven's bed was also in this always messy room (and it was here that he died in 1827). When Beethoven wrote music, however, he went next door into a composing room, where he sat at a desk, putting down his ideas in a score. In truth, Beethoven could compose almost anywhere he was able to think. Teenager Gerhard von Breuning, who frequently observed Beethoven in his last years, tells the following story: "Once in a restaurant in Vienna he started to order a meal but then began to write furiously in his music book. The waiter, not wishing to disturb the master, brought no food. After an extended period, Beethoven put down his pen and asked for the bill, not realizing that he had eaten nothing." Now that's focus! Obviously Beethoven could compose anywhere he could concentrate. And because he was deaf, external noise did not bother him.

The Final Years (1814–1827)

By 1814, Beethoven had lost his hearing entirely and had withdrawn from society. His music, too, took on a more remote, inaccessible quality, placing heavy demands on performer and audience alike. In these late works, Beethoven requires the listener to connect musical ideas over extended spans of time—to engage in long-term listening to music in which the ties between melodies or rhythms are not immediately obvious. This is music that seems intended not for the audience of Beethoven's day, but rather for future generations. Most of Beethoven's late works are piano sonatas and string quartets—intimate, introspective chamber music. But two pieces, the Mass in D major (*Missa Solemnis,* 1823) and the Symphony No. 9 (1824), are large-scale compositions for full orchestra and chorus. In these latter works, Beethoven strives once again to communicate directly to a broad spectrum of humanity.

Symphony No. 9 in D minor (1824)

Beethoven's Symphony No. 9, his last, was the first symphony in the history of music to include a chorus; in the fourth and final movement, the composer turned to choral voices to add an immediate, human appeal. Here a chorus sings a poem in honor of universal brotherhood, *An die Freude* (**Ode to Joy**), written by Friedrich von Schiller (1759–1805). For more than twenty years, Beethoven had struggled to craft just the right melody for this text. Example 18.10 gives the final result: Beethoven's complete melody with Schiller's poem in English. Observe the direct, four-square phrase structure of the melody: antecedent, consequent, extension, consequent, or **abcb** form. Notice also that nearly every pitch is adjacent to the next; there are almost no leaps. Everyone can sing this melody—and that was exactly Beethoven's wish.

Erich Lessing/Art Resource, NY

Figure 18.8

A historically accurate depiction of Beethoven's music room as drawn by J. N. Hoechle three days after the composer's death. In truth, this room contained two grand pianos. Note the mess still on the piano and the fact that the instrument is filled with broken strings.

EXAMPLE 18.10

(a) Praise to Joy the God de-scend-ed, Daugh-ter of E - ly - si-um.

(b) 5 Ray of mirth and rap-ture blend-ed, God-dess, to thy shrine wel-come.

(c) 10 By thy ma-gic is u - nit-ed what tra - di - tion kept a - part. All ___

(b) 15 ___ hu-mans are peo-ple plight - ed where thy gen-tle spi - rit darts.

Having fashioned this simple but inspiring melody, Beethoven used it as the centerpiece of the final movement of the symphony. Here *Ode to Joy* becomes the thematic foundation of a magnificent set of variations. Beethoven first sets the melody for instruments alone, beginning with the low strains of the double basses and cellos. The theme is repeated three more times, gathering force as it moves to successively higher registers. In each variation, Beethoven changes the surrounding context, rather than the melody itself. This passage demonstrates how Beethoven, like no composer before him, exploited the power of pure sound, detached from the usual concerns of rhythm or harmony. The essential idea hasn't changed; it simply gets louder and more compelling as more and more instruments enter. When the full orchestra with brilliant brasses presents the theme a fourth time, we all feel the power of an overwhelming sonic force.

Listening Guide

Ludwig van Beethoven, *An die Freude (Ode to Joy)* **from Symphony No. 9 (1824)**

(intro) 5

Genre: Symphony

Form: Theme and variations

WHAT TO LISTEN FOR: How Beethoven employs his favorite *modus operandi* for theme and variations form: start low and quietly, finish high and loud

0:00 **5** Theme begins quietly in cellos and double basses.

0:32 Parts **c** and **b** of the theme are repeated, as in subsequent variations.

VARIATION 1

0:48 Theme moves higher to second violins; bassoon plays beautiful counterpoint.

VARIATION 2

1:38 Theme moves higher to first violins; lower strings provide accompaniment.

VARIATION 3

2:22 Theme moves to high woodwinds and prominent brasses; full orchestra plays loudly.

◀)) Listen to streaming music in an Active Listening Guide at CourseMate or in the eBook.

With this *fortissimo* statement of the theme, the orchestra has done all it can do alone. Beethoven now bids the chorus to join in, singing Schiller's liberating text. From here to the end of the movement, chorus and orchestra speak with one exalted voice, pressing the tempo, volume, and the range of the pitches to the limits of the performers' abilities. Their message is Beethoven's message: Humanity will be unified and victorious if it strives together, as it does here, to create great art. In the course of time, Beethoven's hope has been realized: *Ode to Joy* has been sung at every Olympic Games since 1956, was performed to celebrate the fall of the Berlin Wall, and currently serves as the official anthem of the European Union.

Beethoven and the Nineteenth Century

Beethoven was a cult figure during his own lifetime, and his image continued to tower over all the arts throughout the nineteenth century. He had shown how personal expression might push against and break free from the confines of Classical form. He had expanded the size of the orchestra by calling for new instruments and had doubled the length of the symphony. He had given music "the grand gesture," stunning effects like the crashing introduction of the "*Pathétique*" Sonata or the gigantic crescendo leading to the finale of Symphony No. 5. Most important, he had shown that pure sound—sound divorced from melody and rhythm—could be glorious in and of itself. The power and originality of his works became the standard against which composers, indeed all artists, of the Romantic era measured their worth. The painting shown earlier in this chapter (see Fig. 18.2) depicts Franz Liszt at the piano surrounded by other writers and musicians of the mid-nineteenth century. A larger-than-life bust gazes down from Olympian heights. It is Beethoven, the prophet and high priest of Romanticism.

Key Words

"Pathétique" Sonata (209)	"heroic" period (middle period) (212)	scherzo (219)
Heiligenstadt Testament (212)	"Eroica" ("Heroic") Symphony (213)	*Ode to Joy* (223)

For a complete review of this chapter, see the Main Points, Chapter Quiz, Flashcards, and Glossary in CourseMate.

Join us on Facebook at **Listening to Music with Craig Wright**

Checklist of Musical Style

Classical: 1750–1820

A complete Checklist of Musical Style for the Classical period can be found at CourseMate for this text.

REPRESENTATIVE COMPOSERS

Mozart	Beethoven
Haydn	Schubert

PRINCIPAL GENRES

symphony	string quartet	opera
sonata	solo concerto	

Melody	Short, balanced phrases create tuneful melodies; melody more influenced by vocal than instrumental style; frequent cadences produce light, airy feeling
Harmony	The rate at which chords change (harmonic rhythm) varies dramatically, creating a dynamic flux and flow; simple chordal harmonies made more active by "Alberti" bass
Rhythm	Departs from regular, driving patterns of Baroque era to become more stop-and-go; greater rhythmic variety within a single movement
Color	Orchestra grows larger; woodwind section of two flutes, oboes, clarinets, and bassoons becomes typical; piano replaces harpsichord as principal keyboard instrument
Texture	Mostly homophonic; thin bass and middle range, hence light and transparent; passages in contrapuntal style appear sparingly and mainly for contrast
Form	A few standard forms regulate much of Classical music: sonata–allegro, theme and variations, rondo, ternary (for minuets and trios), and double exposition (for solo concerto)

part. **FIVE**

Romanticism, 1820–1900

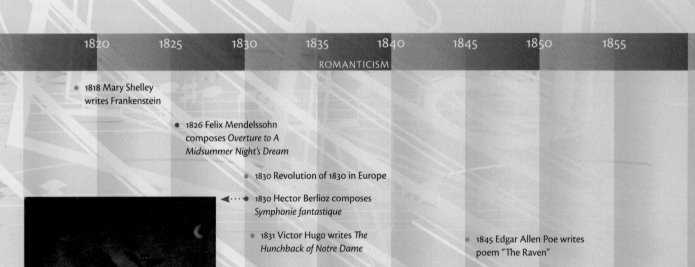

1820	1825	1830	1835	1840	1845	1850	1855

ROMANTICISM

● 1818 Mary Shelley writes Frankenstein

● 1826 Felix Mendelssohn composes *Overture to A Midsummer Night's Dream*

● 1830 Revolution of 1830 in Europe

◄···● 1830 Hector Berlioz composes *Symphonie fantastique*

● 1831 Victor Hugo writes *The Hunchback of Notre Dame*

● 1845 Edgar Allen Poe writes poem "The Raven"

● 1848 Revolution of 1848 in Europe

● 1848 Karl Marx writes *The Communist Manifesto*

● 1853 Giuseppe Verdi composes opera *La traviata*

1853–1876 Richard Wagner works on his cycle *Der Ring des Nibelungen*

Today we think of a "romantic" as an idealistic person, a dreamer, sometimes fearful, always hopeful, and perpetually in love. This view resonates with and emerges from the values of the Romantic era (1820–1900), when reason gave way to passion, objective analysis to subjective emotion, and "the real world" to a realm of the imagination and of dreams. If a single theme dominated the era, it was love; indeed, from the word *romance*, we derive the term *romantic*. Nature and the natural beauty of the world also fascinated the Romantics. But the Romantic vision had its dark side as well, and these same artists expressed a fascination with the occult, the supernatural, and the macabre. This was the age not only of Robert Schumann's piano reverie "Dreaming" but also of Mary Shelley's nightmare novel *Frankenstein*.

What was music in the Romantic era? To critic Charles Burney, writing in 1776, music was "an innocent luxury, unnecessary, indeed, to our existence." But to Beethoven, writing in 1812, music was the most important of the arts "that would raise men to the level of gods." Clearly, the very concept of music—its purpose and meaning—had undergone a profound change in these thirty-six years. No longer seen merely as entertainment, music now could point the way to previously unexplored realms of the spirit. Beethoven led the way, and many others—Berlioz, Wagner, and Brahms among them—followed in his footsteps. When the German author E. T. A. Hoffmann wrote that Beethoven's Symphony No. 5 "releases the flood gates of fear, of terror, of horror, of pain, and arouses that longing for the eternal which is the essence of Romanticism," he prophesied for much Romantic music to come.

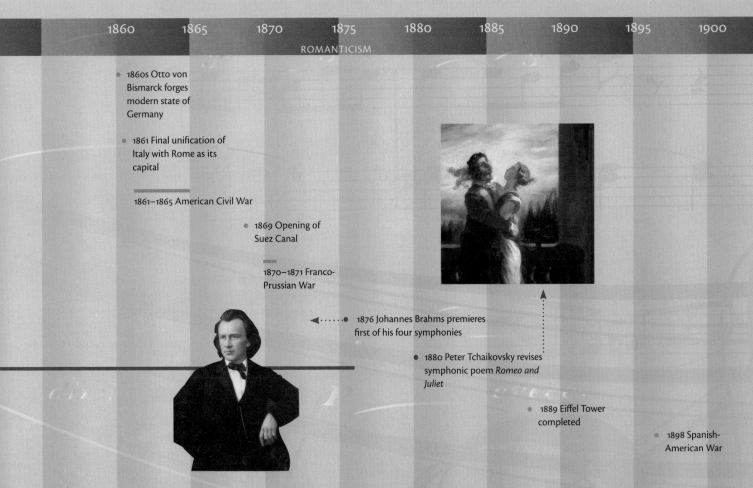

| 1860 | 1865 | 1870 | 1875 | 1880 | 1885 | 1890 | 1895 | 1900 |

ROMANTICISM

1860s Otto von Bismarck forges modern state of Germany

1861 Final unification of Italy with Rome as its capital

1861–1865 American Civil War

1869 Opening of Suez Canal

1870–1871 Franco-Prussian War

1876 Johannes Brahms premieres first of his four symphonies

1880 Peter Tchaikovsky revises symphonic poem *Romeo and Juliet*

1889 Eiffel Tower completed

1898 Spanish-American War

chapter **NINETEEN**

Introduction to Romanticism

The mature music of Beethoven, with its powerful crescendos, pounding chords, and grand gestures, announces the arrival of the Romantic era in music. The transition from musical Classicism to Romanticism in the early nineteenth century coincides with similar stylistic changes in the novels, plays, poetry, and paintings of the period. In all the arts, revolutionary sentiments were in the air: a new desire for liberty, bold action, passionate feeling, and individual expression. Just as the impatient Beethoven finally cast off the wigs and powdered hair of the eighteenth century, many other Romantic artists gradually cast aside the formal constraints of the older Classical style.

Romantic Inspiration, Romantic Creativity

Romanticism is often defined as a revolt against the Classical adherence to reason and tradition. Whereas artists of the eighteenth century sought to achieve unity, order, and balance, those of the nineteenth century leaned toward self-expression, striving to communicate with passion no matter what bizarre imbalance might result. If Classical artists drew inspiration from the monuments of ancient Greece and Rome, those of the Romantic era looked to the human imagination and the wonders of nature. The Romantic artist exalted instinctive feelings—not those of the masses, but individual, personal ones. As the American Romantic poet Walt Whitman said, "I celebrate myself, and sing myself."

If a single feeling or sentiment pervaded the Romantic era, it was love. Indeed, "romance" is at the very heart of the word *romantic*. The loves of Romeo and Juliet (as seen in the chapter-opening photo) and of Tristan and Isolde, for example, captured the public's imagination in the Romantic era. The endless pursuit of an unattainable love became an obsession that, when expressed as music, produced the sounds of longing and yearning heard in so many Romantic works.

Nature, too, worked her magic on the minds of the Romantics (Fig. 19.1). Beethoven proclaimed in 1821, "I perform most faithfully the duties that Humanity, God, and Nature enjoin upon me." In his "Pastoral" Symphony (Symphony No. 6), the first important Romantic "nature piece," Beethoven seeks to capture both nature's tranquil beauty and its destructive fury. Schubert's "Trout" Quintet, Schumann's *Forest Scenes,* and Strauss's "Alpine" Symphony are just a few of the many musical works that continue this tradition.

Yet love and nature were only two of several emotions prized by the Romantics. Despair, frenzy, and heavenly exaltation were others expressed in music and poetry. Just how the range of expression was broadened in Romantic music can be seen in the "expression marks" that came into being at this time: *espressivo* (expressively), *dolente* (sadly), *presto furioso* (fast and furious), *con forza e passione* (with force and passion), *misterioso* (mysteriously), and *maestoso* (majestically). Not only do these directives explain to the performer how a passage ought to be played, they also reveal what the composer wished the listener to feel while experiencing the music.

Figure 19.1

The Dreamer, by German Romantic artist Casper David Friedrich (1774–1840). The painting suggests two forces dear to the hearts of the Romantics: the natural world and the world of dreams. Here timeless nature, creator and destroyer of all things human, surrounds a dreamer lost in solitary contemplation. Notice how the tree to the left is squarely centered within the "window" on the left, as if an altar has been erected in honor of nature.

© The Art Gallery Collection/Alamy

Just as Romantic music is regarded as the emotional core of classical music generally, so the poetry of the English Romantics (Wordsworth, Keats, Byron, and Shelley) is commonly seen as the heart and soul of poetry in the English language. The eccentric behavior of many of these creators inspired the notion that artists are somehow above "the common cloth," and therefore need not conform to societal norms. Were the musicians and poets of the period free spirits blindly following their creative muse, or were they just self-centered and irresponsible—or both? Composers Berlioz, Wagner, and Liszt led lives that were considered scandalous, as did poets George Gordon Lord Byron (1788–1824) and Percy Bysshe Shelley (1792–1822). Byron—famous today for having swum the Hellespont and having died young while fighting for Greek independence—had a string of affairs and illegitimate children, as well as an incestuous relationship with his half-sister. Shelley was expelled from Oxford, abandoned his first wife (who later drowned herself in the center of London), and ran off with (and eventually married) Mary Godwin (1797–1851). In the summer of 1816, Percy and Mary, along with best friend Byron, lived as neighbors in the Swiss Alps, where, as an evening entertainment, she conceived her gothic novel *Frankenstein*.

Ultimately, Percy Shelley died at age thirty when caught in a sudden storm while sailing on the Italian coast. Shelley's poem "Love's Philosophy" (1819), written for Mary, suggests the "lunar" spell under which these wild English Romantics had fallen.

> The fountains mingle with the river
> And the rivers with the ocean,
> The winds of heaven mix for ever
> With a sweet emotion;
> Nothing in the world is single;
> All things by a law divine

John Opie/The Bridgeman Art Library/Getty Images
Amelia Curran/The Bridgeman Art Library/Getty Images

Mary Godwin and Percy Bysshe Shelley

> In one spirit meet and mingle.
> Why not I with thine?—
>
> See the mountains kiss high heaven
> And the waves clasp one another;
> No sister-flower would be forgiven
> If it disdained its brother;
> And the sunlight clasps the earth
> And the moonbeams kiss the sea:
> What is all this sweet work worth
> If thou kiss not me?

The Romantic synthesis of love and nature is typified by the final quatrain "And the sunlight clasps the earth/And the moonbeams kiss the sea:/What is all this sweet work worth/If thou kiss not me?"

The Musician as "Artist," Music as "Art"

With the Romantic era came the idea that music transcended mere entertainment and that the composer was more than a hired employee. Bach had been a municipal civil servant, devoted and dutiful, in the town of Leipzig. Haydn and Mozart had served and been treated as domestics in the homes of the great lords of Europe. But Beethoven began to break the chains of submission. He was the first to demand, and receive, the respect and admiration due a great creative spirit. For the composer Franz Liszt (1811–1886), who deeply admired Beethoven, the duty of the artist was nothing less than "the upbringing of mankind." Never was the position of the creative musician loftier than in the mid-nineteenth century.

Just as the musician was elevated from servant to artist, so the music he or she produced was transformed from entertainment to art. Classical music had been created for the immediate gratification of patron and audience, with little thought given to its lasting value. With the mature Beethoven and the early Romantics, this attitude began to change. Symphonies, quartets, and piano sonatas sprang to life, not to give immediate pleasure to listeners, but to satisfy a deep-seated creative urge within the composer. They became extensions of the artist's inner personality. These works might not be understood by the creator's contemporaries, but they would be understood by posterity, by future generations of listeners. The idea of "art for art's sake"—art free of all immediate functional concerns—was born of the Romantic spirit.

Romantic Ideals Change the Listening Experience

The newly exalted position of the composer and his art soon brought a more serious tone to the concert hall. Prior to 1800, a concert was as much a social event as a musical experience. People talked, drank, ate, played cards, flirted, and wandered about. Dogs ran freely on the ground floor, and armed guards roamed the theater to maintain at least some order. When people turned to the music, they were loud and demonstrative. They hummed along with the melody and tapped the beat to music they liked. If a performance went well, people applauded, not only at the ends of the pieces but also between movements. Sometimes they demanded an immediate encore; at other times they hissed their disapproval.

Around 1840, however, a sudden hush came over the concert hall—rendering it more like a church or temple. With the revered figure of the Romantic artist-composer now before them, the audience sat in respectful silence. A concertgoer who was not distracted socially became a listener who was engaged emotionally. More was expected of the audience, because symphonies and sonatas were longer and more complex. But the audience, in turn, expected more from the music. The concert was no longer an entertaining event, but an emotionally satisfying encounter that would leave the attentive listener exhausted yet somehow purified and uplifted by the artistic experience.

Romanticism has kept its grip on the Western imagination. Belief in the artist as superhero, reverence for the object as a "work of art," and expectations of silence and even formal dress at a concert all developed in the Romantic period. What's more, the notion that a particular group of pieces merited repeated hearings gained currency at this time. Prior to 1800, almost all music was disposable: It was written as entertainment for the moment and then forgotten. But the generation following Beethoven began to consider his finest symphonies, concertos, and quartets, as well as those of Mozart and Haydn, as worthy of preservation and repeated performance (see Ch. 15). These and the best works of succeeding generations came to form a **canon**—indeed, a museum— of classical music, and they constitute the core of today's concert repertoire. The term *classical music* itself was a creation of the early nineteenth century. Thus, what we think about the composer, how we view the work of art, what we can expect to hear at a concert, and even how we dress and behave during the performance are not eternal ideals, with us since time immemorial, but rather values created during the Romantic period.

 # The Style of Romantic Music

Why is film music today almost always written in the Romantic style? Why are collections of "classical favorites" or "classical moods" filled mostly with music, not of the Classical period, but of the Romantic era? Why has *The Phantom of the Opera*, whose story and music are quintessentially Romantic, been seen by more than 130 million people around the world? In brief, because Romantic music hits an emotional "sweet spot." We love its long, surging melodies and rich harmonies—rendered all the more powerful when delivered by the large and colorful Romantic orchestra. The sound is lush, often sensuous, yet contains little of the aggressive dissonance of more modern music. The Romantic style is luxurious and consonant, and our psyche cannot resist its pull.

The distinctive sound of the Romantic period is, in truth, heavily indebted to the music that preceded it. Indeed, the works of Romantic composers represent not so much a *revolution* against Classical ideals as an *evolution* beyond them. Throughout the nineteenth century, the Classical genres of the symphony, concerto, string quartet, piano sonata, and opera remain fashionable, though somewhat altered in shape.

The symphony now grows in length, embodying the widest possible range of expression, while the concerto becomes increasingly virtuosic, as a heroic soloist does battle against an orchestral mass. The Romantics introduced no new musical forms and only two new genres: the art song (see Ch. 20) and the tone poem (see Ch. 21). Instead, Romantic composers took the musical materials received from Haydn, Mozart, and the young Beethoven and made them more intensely expressive, more personal, more colorful, and, in some cases, more bizarre.

Romantic Melody

Listen to the love theme from *Romeo and Juliet* in the iTunes and YouTube playlists at CourseMate for this text.

The Romantic period saw the apotheosis of melody. Melodies become broad, powerful streams of sound intended to sweep the listener away. They go beyond the neat symmetrical units (two plus two, four plus four) inherent in the Classical style, becoming longer, rhythmically more flexible, and increasingly irregular in shape. At the same time, Romantic melodies continue a trend that had developed in the late eighteenth century, in which themes become vocal in conception, more singable or "lyrical." Countless melodies of Schubert, Chopin, and Tchaikovsky have been turned into popular songs and movie themes—Romantic music is perfectly suited to the romance of film—because these melodies are so profoundly expressive. Example 19.1 shows the well-known love theme from Tchaikovsky's *Romeo and Juliet*. As the brackets show, it rises and falls, only to rise higher again, a total of seven times, on the way to a *fortissimo* climax. (The melody can be heard on 🔵 5 3/19 at 2:58, or at 13:35 in the downloads or in the streaming music for Ch. 21 at CourseMate.)

EXAMPLE 19.1

Colorful Harmony

Part of the emotional intensity of Romantic music was generated by a new, more colorful harmony. Classical music had, in the main, made use of chords built upon only the seven notes of the major or minor scale. Romantic composers went further by creating **chromatic harmony**, adding chords constructed on the five remaining notes (the chromatic notes) within the full twelve-note chromatic scale. This gave more colors to their harmonic palette, allowing for the rich, sensuous sounds we associate with Romantic music. Example 19.2 shows a passage with quick-changing chromatic chords found in a nocturne of Chopin (discussed further in Ch. 22). Neither you nor the author can hear this passage simply by looking at it, although the many sharps and flats signal chromatic movement. To hear it, listen to 🔵 2 2/4 or 🔵 5 4/5, at 1:21, to your downloads for this book, or to the streaming music for Chapter 22 at CourseMate.

EXAMPLE 19.2

Chromatic harmony opened up the tonal landscape, encouraging bold shifts between distant chords—a chord built on a scale with one flat might soon be followed by one with seven flats, for example. These striking harmonic juxtapositions allowed composers to express a wider range of feeling. In Example 19.3, Chopin's rich chords from the same nocturne (at 1:04) are given and then reduced to their simplest forms.

EXAMPLE 19.3A

EXAMPLE 19.3B

F Major   Ab Major   Ab Minor   Eb Major

Finally, nineteenth-century composers lent a "romantic feel" to music by means of temporary dissonance. Longing, pain, and suffering traditionally have been expressed in music by dissonance. All musical dissonance, according to the rules of composition, must resolve to consonance. In Romantic music the dissonance is passing: It sounds and then resolves (in later, Modernist music it need not resolve). The longer the painful dissonance, the greater the desire for resolution. A delay in the resolution intensifies feelings of anxiety, longing, and searching, all sentiments appropriate to music that deals with love or loneliness. The very end of Gustav Mahler's orchestral song *Ich bin der Welt abhanden gekommen* (*I Am Lost to the World*; 5/2 at 2:46; 6:23 in downloads and in streaming music for Ch. 26 in CourseMate) offers an exquisitely beautiful example of dissonance-consonance resolution. Here, first violins and English horn (low oboe) in turn hold a dissonant pitch (see arrows) that resolves downward (see asterisks), dying away (*morendo*) to the final consonant tonic.

EXAMPLE 19.4

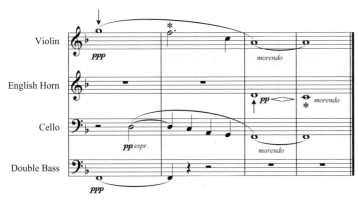

Romantic Tempo: *Rubato*

In keeping with an age that glorified personal freedom and tolerated eccentric behavior, tempo in Romantic music was cut loose from the restraints of a regular beat. The watchword here was *rubato* (literally "robbed"), an expression mark for the performer written into the score by the composer. A performer playing tempo **rubato** "stole" some time here and gave it back there, moving faster or slower in an intensely personal way. The free approach to tempo was often reinforced by fluctuating dynamic levels—ritards were executed with diminuendos, and accelerations with crescendos—as a way of explaining, even exaggerating, the flow of the music. Whatever excesses might result could be excused under license of artistic freedom.

Romantic Forms: Monumental and Miniature

Romantic composers established no new musical forms, but merely expanded those used in the Classical era. As nineteenth-century composers laid out broad and sweeping melodies, indulged in gigantic crescendos, and reveled in the luxurious sound of the enlarged orchestra, the length of individual movements increased dramatically. Mozart's G minor symphony (1788) lasts about twenty minutes, depending on the tempo of the conductor. But Berlioz's *Symphonie fantastique* (1830) takes nearly fifty-five minutes, and Mahler's Symphony No. 2 (1894) nearly an hour and a half. Perhaps the longest of all musical works is Richard Wagner's four-opera *Ring* cycle (1853–1876), which runs some *seventeen* hours over the course of four evenings.

Romantic musicians were not alone in their ever-expanding vision. Charles Darwin (*On the Origin of Species*, 1859) posited that the earth was not merely 7,000 years old, as the Bible suggested, but several million. Painters such as J. M. W. Turner and Casper David Friedrich depicted on canvas the slow, inexorable evolution of the earth. Look again at Friedrich's *The Dreamer* (see Fig. 19.1), in which vines overgrowing the ruins of a medieval church suggest the slow passing of the ages. The grand, protracted gestures we hear in the symphonies of Beethoven, Brahms, and Mahler are all part of the expansive spirit of the age.

Yet, paradoxically, Romantic composers were not interested only in the monumental; the miniature fascinated them as well. In works of only a minute or two, they tried to capture the essence of a single mood, sentiment, or emotion. Such a miniature was called a **character piece**. It was usually written for the piano and often made use of simple binary (**AB**) or ternary (**ABA**) form. Because the character piece passes by in the twinkling of an eye, it was sometimes given a whimsical title, such as bagatelle (a trifle), humoresque, arabesque, musical moment, caprice, romance, intermezzo, or impromptu. Schubert, Schumann, Chopin, Liszt, and Brahms all enjoyed creating these musical miniatures, perhaps as antidotes to their lengthy symphonies and concertos.

 # More Color, Size, and Volume

Perhaps the most striking aspects of Romantic music are the color and sheer volume of the sound. Sometimes all thematic and harmonic movement stops, and nothing but pure sound remains. Appropriate to an age that indulged in wild mood swings, Romantic composers prescribed greater dynamic extremes. Whereas the range in Classical music extended only from *pp* (*pianissimo*) to *ff* (*fortissimo*), now exaggerated "hyper-marks" such as *pppp* and *ffff* appear. To create sounds as loud as *ffff*, a larger orchestra or a bigger piano was needed. Composers demanded musical forces equal to the task of expressing the emotional extremes, changing moods, and extravagant gestures of the Romantic spirit.

The Romantic Orchestra

Technology has sometimes profoundly affected the history of music. Think, for instance, of the invention of the electrically amplified guitar, which made possible the sounds of rock virtuosos such as Jimi Hendrix and Eric Clapton. Think, too, of the more recent MP3 file, iPod, smartphone, and YouTube, which have made music instantly accessible anywhere around the world. Just as the digital revolution has altered our contemporary musical landscape, so did the technological advancements that led to the modern symphony orchestra transform nineteenth-century music.

Watch a video of Craig Wright's Open Yale Course class session 20, "The Colossal Symphony: Beethoven, Berlioz, Mahler, and Shostakovich," at the text website.

In many ways, the symphony orchestra that we hear today was a product of the nineteenth-century Industrial Revolution. Around 1830, some existing orchestral instruments received mechanical enhancements. The wood of the flute, for example, was replaced by silver, and the instrument was given a new fingering mechanism that added to its agility and made it easier to play in tune. Similarly, the trumpet and French horn were provided with valves that improved technical facility and accuracy of pitch in all keys (Fig. 19.2). The French horn in particular became an object of special affection during the Romantic period. Its rich, dark tone and its traditional association with the hunt of the forest—and by extension, all of nature—made it the Romantic instrument par excellence.

Entirely new instruments were added to the Romantic orchestra as well. Beethoven expanded its range both higher and lower. In his famous Symphony No. 5 (1808; see Ch. 18), he called for a piccolo (a high flute), trombones, and a contrabassoon (a bass bassoon)—the first time any of these had been heard in a symphony. In 1830, Hector Berlioz went even further, requiring an early form of the tuba, an English horn (low oboe), a cornet, and two harps in his *Symphonie fantastique.*

Berlioz, a composer who personified the Romantic spirit (see Ch. 21 opening photo), had a typically grandiose notion of what the ideal symphony orchestra should contain. He wanted no fewer than 467 performers, including 120 violins, 40 violas, 45 cellos, 35 double basses, and 30 harps! Such a gigantic instrumental force (Fig. 19.3) was never actually assembled, but Berlioz's utopian vision indicates the direction in which Romantic composers were headed. By the second half of the nineteenth century, orchestras with nearly a hundred players were not uncommon. Compare, for example, the number and variety of instruments required for a typical eighteenth-century performance of Mozart's Symphony in G minor (1788) with the symphony orchestra needed for Berlioz's *Symphonie fantastique* (1830) and for Gustav Mahler's Symphony No. 1 (1889). In the course of a hundred years, the orchestra had more than tripled in size. But it went no further: The symphony orchestra that we hear today is essentially that of the late nineteenth century.

Our reaction to the Romantic orchestra today, however, is very different from the response of nineteenth-century listeners. Modern ears have been desensitized by an overexposure to electronically amplified sound. But imagine the impact of an orchestra of a hundred players before the days of amplification. Apart from the military cannon and the steam engine, the nineteenth-century orchestra produced the loudest sonic level of any human contrivance. The big sound—and the big contrasts—of the nineteenth-century orchestra were new and startling, and audiences packed ever-larger concert halls to hear these impressive "special effects."

Figure 19.2

A modern French horn with valves, an invention of the 1820s. The valves allow the performer to engage different lengths of tubing instantly and thereby play a fully chromatic scale.

Hear Berlioz's colossal *Grande Messe des morts*, Op. 5 (Requiem), *Dies irae*, *Tuba mirum*, in the YouTube playlist at CourseMate for this text.

The Growth of the Symphony Orchestra

Mozart (1788)	Berlioz (1830)	Mahler (1889)
Symphony in G minor	***Symphonie fantastique***	**Symphony No. 1**
	Woodwinds	
1 flute	1 piccolo	3 piccolos
2 oboes	2 flutes	4 flutes
2 clarinets	2 oboes	4 oboes
2 bassoons	1 English horn	1 English horn
	2 B♭ clarinets	4 B♭ clarinets

Figure 19.3

A satirical engraving suggesting the public's impression that Berlioz's (center) vastly enlarged symphony orchestra would harm the audience and might lead to death (note coffin at lower right)!

(continued)

Take online Listening Exercise 19.1 at CourseMate or in the eBook.

*Number of string players estimated according to standards of the period.

Mozart (1788)	Berlioz (1830)	Mahler (1889)
Symphony in G minor	***Symphonie fantastique***	**Symphony No. 1**
Woodwinds		
	1 E♭ clarinet	2 E♭ clarinets
	4 bassoons	1 bass clarinet
		3 bassoons
		1 contrabassoon
Brasses		
2 French horns	4 French horns	7 French horns
	2 trumpets	5 trumpets
	2 cornets	4 trombones
	3 trombones	1 tuba
	2 ophicleides (tubas)	
Strings		
1st violins (8)*	1st violins (15)*	1st violins (20)*
2nd violins (8)	2nd violins (14)	2nd violins (18)
violas (4)	violas (8)	violas (14)
cellos (4)	cellos (12)	cellos (12)
double basses (3)	double basses (8)	double basses (18)
	2 harps	1 harp
Percussion		
	timpani	timpani (2 players)
	bass drum	bass drum
	snare drum	triangle, cymbals
	cymbals and bells	tam-tam
Total: 36	*Total: 89*	*Total: 129*

Figure 19.4

A large orchestra depicted at Covent Garden Theater, London, in 1846. The conductor stands toward the middle, baton in hand, with strings to his right and woodwinds, brass, and percussion to his left. It was typical in this period to place all or part of the orchestra on risers, which allowed the sound to project more fully.

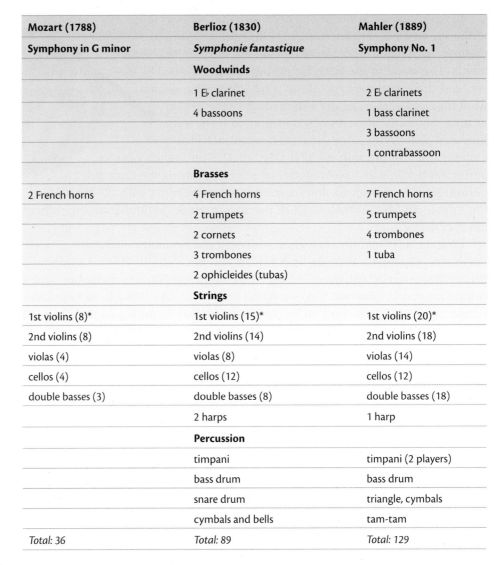

Erich Lessing/Art Resource, NY

The Conductor

As the streets of London became more congested with wagons in the mid-nineteenth century, traffic cops appeared, waving red and green flags and then lanterns at night. So, too, as the Romantic symphony orchestra became larger and more complex, a musical "traffic cop" was needed: the conductor waving a baton (Fig. 19.4). In Mozart's day, the leader of the orchestra was one of the performers, either a keyboardist or the first violinist, who led by moving his head and body. Beethoven, however, at least at the end of his life, stood before the orchestra with his back to the audience and waved his hands, gesturing how the music should go. Thereafter, conductors might lead with a rolled-up piece of paper, a violin bow, a handkerchief, or a wooden baton, the chosen object intending to clarify the meter and speed of the beat (Fig. 19.5). Sometimes the leader merely banged the beat on a music stand. Gradually during the nineteenth century, however, this director evolved from a mere time-beater into an interpreter, and sometimes a dictator, of the musical score. The modern conductor had arrived.

The Virtuoso

Appropriate for an era that glorified the individual, the nineteenth century was the age of the solo **virtuoso**. Of course, instrumental virtuosos had been on the scene before: Bach on the organ and Mozart on the piano, to name just two. Now, though, many musicians began to expend enormous energy striving to raise their performing skills to unprecedented heights. Pianists and violinists in particular spent long hours practicing technical exercises—arpeggios, tremolos, trills, and scales played in thirds, sixths, and octaves—to develop show-stopping hand speed on their instrument. Naturally, some of what these wizards played was lacking in musical substance, little more than tasteless displays designed to appeal immediately to the audiences that packed the ever-larger concert halls. Pianists even developed tricks to make it seem as if they had more than two hands (see Fig. 22.7). Franz Liszt (1811–1886) sometimes played at the keyboard with a lighted cigar between his fingers. The Italian Niccolò Paganini (1782–1840) secretly tuned the four strings of his violin in ways that would allow him to negotiate with ease extraordinarily difficult passages (Figs. 19.6 and 19.7). If one of his strings broke, he could play with just three; if three broke, he continued apace with just one. So great was his fame that Paganini became the "celebrity spokesperson" of the day, his picture appearing on napkins, ties, pipes, billiard cues, and powder boxes. As a composer later remarked, "The attraction of the virtuoso is like that of the circus performer; there's always the hope that something disastrous will happen." The daredevil quality of Paganini's virtuosic music can be seen in Example 19.5, which looks something like a roller coaster. Fortunately, as we shall see, some of these performing daredevils were also gifted composers.

Lebrecht Music & Arts

Historical/Corbis

Figure 19.5

Silhouette of composer Carl Maria von Weber conducting with a rolled sheet of music, to highlight the movement of his hand

Figures 19.6 and 19.7

(above) Niccolò Paganini. (below) Paganini sleeping while the devil teaches him to play the violin. Paganini's extraordinary powers on the violin led some to believe that he had made a deal with the devil. The highest string of his violin was said to be made of the intestine of his mistress, whom he had murdered with his own hands. None of this was true, and Paganini filed several libel suits to reclaim his honor.

EXAMPLE 19.5 Paganini, Caprice, Opus 1, No. 5

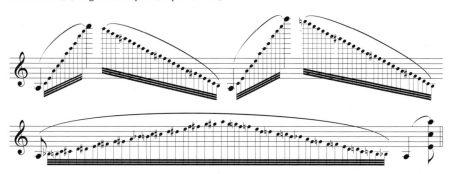

Interfoto/Alamy

Coda

While this introduction to musical Romanticism treats the major developments of the nineteenth century, there were others. The increased attention paid to literature in the Romantic era inspired new musical genres: the art song (*Lied*), the program symphony, and the related tone poem. The technological innovations that fostered the development of the large symphony orchestra also led to the fabrication of a much larger and more powerful piano, as well as a musical literature specifically written for it. Finally, political events, which resulted in the creation of modern nations such as Germany and Italy, caused musical reverberations in the form of nationalistic musical styles in both instrumental music and opera. All of these developments—the art song, program music, Romantic piano music, and musical nationalism—will be discussed in the following chapters.

Key Words

canon (231)	*rubato* (233)	virtuoso (237)
chromatic harmony (232)	character piece (234)	

For a complete review of this chapter, see the Main Points, Chapter Quiz, Flashcards, and Glossary in CourseMate.

 Join us on Facebook at **Listening to Music with Craig Wright**

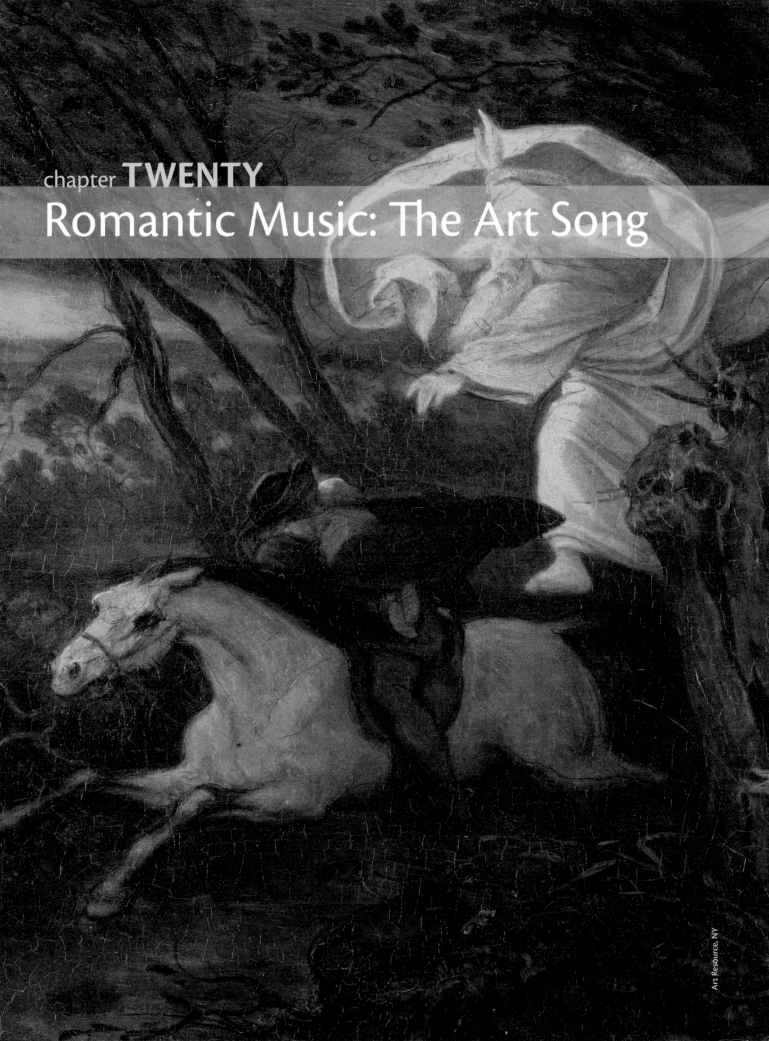

chapter **TWENTY**
Romantic Music: The Art Song

The decade 1803–1813 stands as perhaps the most auspicious in the history of Western music. In this short span of time were born the composers Hector Berlioz (1803), Felix Mendelssohn (1809), Frédéric Chopin (1810), Robert Schumann (1810), Franz Liszt (1811), Giuseppe Verdi (1813), and Richard Wagner (1813). Add to these the shining figures of Franz Schubert (born 1797) and Clara Schumann (born 1819), and this brilliant galaxy of Romantic musical stars is complete. We call them Romantics because they were part of—indeed, they created—the Romantic movement in music. Perhaps not surprisingly, they were all very unconventional people. Their lives typify all that we have come to associate with the Romantic spirit: self-expression, passion, a love of nature and literature, occasional excess, and sometimes even a bit of lunacy (see Ch. 19, "Love and Lunacy Among the Artists"). Not only did they create great art, but life, and how they lived it, also became an art.

 ## The Art Song

A hallmark of the Romantic age was a quickening interest in literature, especially poetry. Indeed, never were word and tone more closely allied than during the Romantic era. The Romantic poets viewed music as the purest of all the arts, owing to the abstract quality of sound. Composers, in turn, found musical resonance in the poetry of the day and transformed it into song, believing that music could intensify poetic sentiments by expressing things that words alone could not.

Songs inspired by great poetry have appeared throughout human history. But the near frenzy of poetic activity in the nineteenth century stirred Romantic composers to set poems to music in unprecedented numbers. This was, of course, the great age of the Romantic poets: Wordsworth, Keats, Byron, and Shelley in England; Hugo in France; and Goethe and Heine in Germany. Literally thousands of odes, sonnets, ballads, and romances poured from their pens, and many were quickly set as songs by young Romantic composers. In so doing, these musicians popularized a genre called the **art song**—a song for solo voice and piano accompaniment with high artistic aspirations. Because the art song was cultivated most intensely in German-speaking lands, it is also called the *Lied* (pl. *Lieder*), German for "song." Although many composers wrote art songs, none had greater success in the genre than Franz Schubert. His special talent was to fashion music that captured both the spirit and the detail of the text, creating a sensitive mood painting in which the voice, with help from the accompanying piano, expresses every nuance of the poem. Schubert said, "When one has a good poem the music comes easily, melodies just flow, so that composing is a real joy."

 ## Franz Schubert (1797–1828)

Franz Schubert was born in Vienna in 1797. Among the great Viennese masters—Haydn, Mozart, Beethoven, Schubert, Brahms, and Mahler—only he was native born to the city. Schubert's father was a schoolteacher, and the son, too, was groomed for that profession. Yet the boy's obvious musical talent made it imperative that he also have music lessons, so his father taught him to play the violin, and his older brother the piano. At the age of eleven, Schubert was admitted as a choirboy in the emperor's chapel, a group still famous today as the Vienna Boys' Choir.

After his voice changed in 1812, young Franz left the court chapel and enrolled in a teacher's college. He had been spared compulsory military service because he was below the minimum height of five feet and his sight was so poor that he was compelled to wear the spectacles now familiar from his portraits (Fig. 20.1). By 1815, he had become a teacher at his father's primary school. But he found teaching demanding and tedious, and so after three unpleasant years, Schubert quit his "day job" to give himself over wholly to music.

"You lucky fellow; I really envy you! You live a life of sweet, precious freedom, can give free rein to your musical genius, can express your thoughts in any way you like." This was Schubert's brother's view of the composer's newfound freedom. But as many Romantics would find, the reality was harsher than the ideal. Aside from some small income he earned from the sale of a few songs, he lacked financial support. Schubert, unlike Beethoven, had no circle of aristocrats to provide patronage. Consequently, he lived a vagabond life, helped along by the generosity of his friends, with whom he often lodged when he was broke. He spent his mornings passionately composing music, passed his afternoons in cafés discussing literature and politics, and often occupied his evenings performing his songs and dances for friends and admirers.

As Schubert was reaching artistic maturity, the era of the great aristocratic salon (entertainment room) was drawing to an end, its role now filled by the middle-class parlor or living room. Here, in less formal surroundings, groups of men and women with a common interest in music, novels, drama, or poetry would meet to read and discuss the latest developments in these arts. The gatherings at which Schubert appeared, and at which only his compositions were played, were called **Schubertiads** by his friends. It was in small, purely private assemblies such as these (Fig. 20.2), not in large public concerts, that most of his best songs had their first performances.

In 1822, disaster befell the composer: He contracted syphilis, a venereal disease tantamount to a death sentence before the discovery of antibiotics. His lyrical Symphony in B minor of that year, appropriately called the "Unfinished Symphony," was left incomplete. Yet during the years that preceded his premature death in 1828, Schubert created some of his greatest works: the song cycles *Die schöne Müllerin* (*The Pretty Maid of the Mill,* 1823) and *Winterreise* (*Winter Journey,* 1827), the "Wanderer" Fantasy for piano (1822), and the great C major symphony (1828). When Beethoven died in 1827, Schubert served as a torchbearer at the funeral. The next year he, too, was dead, the youngest of the great composers. The epitaph for his tombstone reads, "The art of music here entombed a rich treasure, but even fairer hopes."

In his brief life of thirty-one years, Franz Schubert wrote eight symphonies, fifteen string quartets, twenty-one piano sonatas, seven Masses for chorus and orchestra, and four operas—a sizable oeuvre by any standard. Most went unperformed. Unlike Beethoven, Schubert was not famous in his day; his reputation grew only posthumously. To the extent his music circulated, it did so through his art songs (*Lieder*). Indeed, he composed more than 600 works in this genre, many of them minor masterpieces. In a few cases, Schubert chose to set several texts together in a series. In so doing, he created what is called a **song cycle** (something akin to a "concept album")—a tightly structured group of individual songs that tell a story or treat a single theme. *Die schöne Müllerin* (twenty songs) and *Winterreise* (twenty-four songs), both of which portray the sad consequences of unrequited love, are Schubert's two great song cycles.

Figures 20.1 and 20.2

(top) Franz Schubert. (bottom) A small, private assembly known as a Schubertiad, named after the composer, at which artists presented their works. The singer before the piano is Johann Vogl, accompanied by Schubert at the piano, immediately to Vogl's left.

Wien Museum Karlsplatz, Vienna/The Bridgeman Art Library

An Evening at Baron von Spaun's: Schubert at the piano among his friends, including the operatic baritone Heinrich Vogl (1845–1900) (pen & ink on paper), Schwind, Moritz Ludwig von (1804–71)/Wien Museum Karlsplatz, Vienna, Austria/The Bridgeman Art Library

Erlkönig (1815)

To get an idea of Schubert's precocious musical talent, we need only listen to his song *Erlkönig* (*Elf King*), written when he was just eighteen. The text itself is a **ballad**—a vivid story told alternately in narrative verse and dramatic dialogue—from the pen of the famous German poet Johann von Goethe (1749–1832). It relates the tale of the evil King of the Elves and his malevolent seduction of a young boy. Legend had it that whoever was touched by the King of the Elves would die. This tale typifies the Romantic fascination with the supernatural and the macabre, which is evinced most famously in Mary Shelley's *Frankenstein* (1818), and was depicted as a painting (see chapter-opening image) by Schubert's close friend Moritz von Schwind, who had heard the composer perform the song at many Schubertiads.

According to a friend's account, Schubert was reading a book of Goethe's poetry, pacing back and forth. Suddenly, he sprang to a piano and, as fast as he could write, set Goethe's entire ballad to music. From there, Schubert and his friend hastened to the composer's college to play it for a few other friends. In his lifetime, *Erlkönig* became Schubert's best-known song, and one of only a few that earned him any money.

The opening line of the poem sets the frightening nocturnal scene: "Who rides so late through night and wind?" With his feverish son cradled in his arms, a father rides at breakneck speed to an inn in an attempt to save the child. Schubert captures both the general sense of terror in the scene and the detail of the galloping horse; he creates an accompanying figure in the piano that pounds on relentlessly just as fast as the pianist's right hand can make it go (Ex. 20.1).

EXAMPLE 20.1

The specter of death, the Elf King, beckons gently to the boy. He does so in seductively sweet tones, in a melody with the gentle lilt and folksy "um-pah-pah" accompaniment of a popular tune (Ex. 20.2).

EXAMPLE 20.2

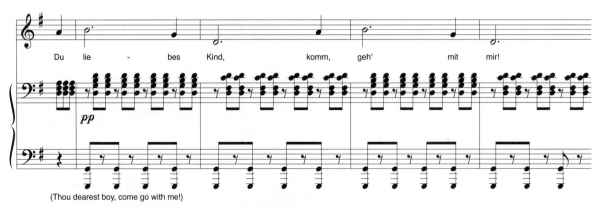

(Thou dearest boy, come go with me!)

The frightened boy cries out to his father in an agitated line that culminates in a tense, chromatic ascent (Ex. 20.3).

EXAMPLE 20.3

(Dear father, my father, say, did'st thou not hear the Elf King whisper promises in my ear?)

This cry is heard again and again in the course of the song, each time at a successively higher pitch and with increasingly dissonant harmonies. In this way, the music mirrors the boy's growing terror. The father tries to calm him in low tones that are steady, stable, and repetitive. At first the Elf King charms in sweet, consonant tones but then threatens in dissonant ones, as seduction gives way to abduction. Thus, each of the three characters in the story is portrayed with distinct musical qualities (though all are sung by a single voice). This represents musical characterization at its finest; the melody and accompaniment not only support the text but also intensify and enrich it. Suddenly, the end is reached: The hand of the Elf King (Death) has touched his victim. Anxiety gives way to sorrow as the narrator announces in increasingly somber (minor) tones, "But in his arms, his child was dead!"

Begin exploring how this art song by Schubert can be interpreted in very different ways by different performers, in the YouTube playlist at CourseMate for this text.

Listening Guide

Franz Schubert, *Erlkönig* (1815)

Genre: Art song

5
3/14

2
1/29

Form: Through-composed

WHAT TO LISTEN FOR: Onomatopoetic music—music that sounds out its meaning at every turn. In this art song, Schubert takes the changing expressive elements of the text (galloping horse; steady, reassuring tones of the father; sweet enticements of the Elf King; increasingly frantic cries of the boy) and provides each with characteristic music. Done today, such a treatment likely would generate cartoon music; done by a master songwriter like Schubert, it produces great art.

0:00   Piano introduction: pounding triplets in right hand and ominous minor-mode motive in left

Narrator

0:23	Wer reitet so spät	Who rides so late
	durch Nacht und Wind?	through night so wild?
	Es ist der Vater	A loving father
	mit seinem Kind.	with his child.
	Er hat den Knaben wohl	He clasps his boy close
	in dem Arm,	with his arm,
	er fasst ihn sicher,	he holds him tightly
	er hält ihn warm.	and keeps him warm.

(continued)

		Father	
0:56		Mein Sohn, was birgst du so bang dein Gesicht?	My son, what makes you hide your face in fear?
		Son	
1:04	With disjunct leaps but no agitation	Siehst, Vater, du den Erlkönig nicht? Den Erlenkönig mit Kron' und Schweif?	Father don't you see the Elf King? The Elf King with crown and shroud?
		Father	
1:20	In low, calming tones	Mein Sohn, es ist ein Nebelstreif.	My son, it's only some streak of mist.
		Elf King	
1:31	With seductive melody in major key	Du liebes Kind, komm, geh' mit mir! gar schöne Spiele spiel' ich mit dir; manch' bunte Blumen sind an dem Strand, meine Mutter hat manch' gülden Gewand.	You dear child, come along with me! I'll play some very fine games with you; where varied blossoms are on meadows fair, and my mother has golden garments to wear.
		Son	
1:54	Growing agitation depicted by tight chromatic movement in voice	Mein Vater, mein Vater, und hörest du nicht, was Erlenkönig mir leise verspricht?	My father, my father, do you not hear how the Elf King whispers promises in my ear?
		Father	
2:07	In low, steady pitches	Sei ruhig, bleibe ruhig, mein Kind, in dürren Blättern säuselt der Wind.	Be calm, stay calm, my child, Through wither'd leaves the wind blows wild.
		Elf King	
2:18	With happy, lilting tune in major key	Willst, feiner Knabe, du mit mir geh'n? Meine Töchter sollen dich warten schön, meine Töchter führen den nächtlichen Reih'n, und wiegen und tanzen und singen dich ein.	My handsome young lad, will you come with me? My beauteous daughters wait for you, With them you would join in the dance every night, and they will rock and dance and sing you to sleep.
		Son	
2:35	Intense chromatic notes, but now a step higher and with minor key suggesting panic	Mein Vater, mein Vater, und siehst du nicht dort Erlkönigs Töchter am düstern Ort?	My Father, my father, don't you see at all the Elf King's daughters over there in the dusk?
		Father	
2:48	Low register, but more leaps (agitation) than before	Mein Sohn, mein Sohn, ich seh' es genau, es scheinen die alten Weiden so grau.	My son, my son, the form you there see, is only the aging gray willow tree.
		Elf King	
3:05	Music starts seductively but then turns minor and menacing	Ich liebe dich, mich reizt deine schöne Gestalt; und bist du nicht willig, so brauch' ich Gewalt.	I love you, I'm charmed by your fine appearance; And if you're not willing, I'll seize you by force!

		Son	
3:17	Piercing cries in highest range	Mein Vater, mein Vater, jetzt fasst er mich an! Erlkönig hat mir ein Leids gethan!	My father, my father, now he's got me, the Elf King has seized me by his trick.
		Narrator	
3:31	With rising and then falling line	Dem Vater grauset's; er reitet geschwind, er hält in den Armen das ächzende Kind. Erreicht den Hof mit Müh' und Noth:	The father shudders, he rides headlong, holding the groaning child in his arms. He reaches the inn with toil and dread,
3:47	Piano slows down and stops, then recitative	in seinen Armen das Kind war todt!	but in his arms, his child was dead!

🔊 Listen to streaming music in an Active Listening Guide at CourseMate or in the eBook.

🔊 Take online Listening Exercise 20.1 and receive feedback at CourseMate or in the eBook.

Just as the tension in Goethe's poem rises incessantly, from the beginning to the very end, Schubert's music unfolds continually, without significant repetition. Such a musical composition featuring ever-changing melodic and harmonic material is called **through-composed**, and Schubert's *Erlkönig*, accordingly, is termed a through-composed art song. For lyric poems, as opposed to dramatic ballad stories, however, **strophic form** is often preferred. Here a single poetic mood is maintained from one stanza, or strophe, of the text to the next. Most folk songs and contemporary pop songs are written in strophic form, each strophe often consisting of a verse and chorus. For a familiar example of a nineteenth-century art song in strophic form, revisit the famous Brahms *Lullaby* (intro/20, downloads, and streaming music for Ch. 3 in CourseMate).

Robert Schumann (1810–1856)

Lyric poems almost always deal with love. Indeed, the subject of love dominates not only Schubert's *Lieder* but also those of Robert and Clara Schumann (Fig. 20.3), whose conjugal life story is itself something of an ode to love.

Robert Schumann was born not to music but to literature. His father was a novelist who introduced him to Romantic poetry and the ancient classics. But the father died young, and Robert's mother determined that her son should take a safe route to prosperity by studying law. Reluctantly, Schumann matriculated at the University of Heidelberg, but he attended not a single class, preferring to pass the time with poetry and music. In 1830, determined to become a virtuoso, Schumann moved, with his mother's grudging consent, to Leipzig. But after two years of lessons with the eminent Friedrich Wieck (1785–1873)—during which he practiced seven hours a day— all he had to show for his labors was a permanently damaged right hand, so he turned his attention to music criticism and composition.

While studying piano with Wieck, Schumann met and fell in love with Wieck's beautiful and talented daughter Clara. Her father vehemently opposed the union, however, forcing Robert to begin a legal battle to win Clara's hand. One of Wieck's objections was that Schumann could not support himself, let alone a wife. Inspired

Figure 20.3

Robert and Clara Schumann in 1850, from an engraving constructed from an early photograph

© Bettmann/CORBIS

by his love of Clara, and perhaps motivated to show that he could earn a living, Schumann turned to writing art songs, then probably the most marketable of musical genres. In 1840, he composed nearly 125 *Lieder*, including settings of poems by major Romantic poets such as Byron and Goethe, as well as a few by Shakespeare. That same year Robert won a legal victory over Clara's father, enabling the couple to marry.

The day Robert Schumann won his court victory for the hand of Clara, he wrote in his diary, "Happiest day and end of the struggle." In this euphoric mood, he completed a setting of eight poems by the German Romantic poet Adelbert von Chamisso (1781–1838) that speak of the hopes and desires of a young middle-class woman. Titled *Frauenliebe und leben* (*Women in Love and Life*), the eight poems form a unit, and Schumann set all eight to music as a song cycle. In the middle of the cycle comes "Du Ring an meinem Finger" ("You Ring on My Finger"), a five-strophe poem in which the newly betrothed gazes starstruck at her ring. Because strophe 3 is similar to, and strophe 5 identical with, strophe 1 (see Listening Guide below), Schumann chose not to opt for the expected strophic-form setting but to give the song an **ABACA** (rondo) musical form, providing identical music (**A**) for similar stanzas. The climax comes in strophe (section) **C**, in which the young voice climbs up the scale excitedly as she professes her undying love. Composure returns with the repeat of the lyrical refrain (**A**), which is followed by a soft piano epilogue.

Listening Guide

Robert Schumann, "Du Ring an meinem Finger" from *Frauenliebe und leben* (1840)

Genre: Art song

Form: Rondo (**ABACA**)

5

3/15

WHAT TO LISTEN FOR: A poignant depiction of young love; the alternation between excitement and gentle lyricism within the bounds of a rondo form

Du Ring an mei - nem Fin - ger, mein gol - de - nes Rin - ge - lein,

			Strophe 1	
0:00	15	**A**	Du Ring an meinem Finger,	You ring on my finger,
			Mein goldenes Ringelein,	My little golden ring,
			Ich drücke dich fromm an die Lippen,	I press you devoutly to my lips,
			Dich fromm an das Herze mein.	I press you devoutly to my heart.
			Strophe 2	
0:26		**B**	Ich hatt' ihn ausgeträumet,	I had dreamed of it.
			Der Kindheit friedlich schönen Traum,	A peaceful, beautiful dream of childhood,
			Ich fand allein mich, verloren	I found myself alone, lost
			Im öden, unendlichen Raum.	In barren, infinite space.
			Strophe 3	
0:52		**A**	Du Ring an meinem Finger,	You ring on my finger,
			Da hast du mich erst belehrt,	You have taught me for the first time,
			Hast meinem Blick erschlossen	Have opened my gaze to
			Des Lebens unendlichen, tiefen Wert.	The infinite deep meaning of life.
			Strophe 4	
1:18		**C**	Ich will ihm dienen, ihm leben,	I want to serve him, live for him,
			Ihm angehören ganz,	Belong to him entirely,
			Hin selber mich geben und finden	Give myself, find myself
			Verklärt mich in seinem Glanz.	Transformed in his radiance.

1:39	**A**	Du Ring an meinem Finger,	You ring on my finger,
		Mein goldenes Ringelein,	My little golden ring,
		Ich drücke dich fromm an die Lippen,	I press you devoutly to my lips,
		Dich fromm an das Herze mein.	I press you devoutly to my heart.

2:11   Brief coda for piano alone

 Listen to streaming music in an Active Listening Guide at CourseMate or in the eBook.

 # Clara Wieck Schumann (1819–1896)

Unlike her husband, Robert, a gifted composer but failed performer, Clara Wieck Schumann (see Fig. 20.3) was one of the great piano virtuosos of the nineteenth century. A child prodigy, she made her debut at the age of eleven in Leipzig, Germany, the city of her birth. She then undertook a concert tour of Europe during which she impressed and befriended several important composers of the Romantic era, including Mendelssohn, Berlioz, Chopin, and Liszt. In Austria, the emperor named her "Royal and Imperial Chamber Virtuosa"—the first time that official title had been given to a Protestant, a teenager, or a woman.

When she married Robert Schumann in 1840, Clara was an international star, and Robert a nobody. Nevertheless, she took up the dual roles of wife to Robert and mother to the eight children she soon bore him. She, too, tried her hand at musical composition, writing mostly art songs and character pieces for piano. But despite her unmistakable talent as a composer, Clara was ambivalent about the capacity of women, herself included, to excel as creative artists (see box "Where Were the Women?"). As her children grew more numerous, her compositions became fewer. Clara's most productive period as a composer of art songs coincided with the very early years of her marriage to Robert.

Clara's "Liebst du um Schönheit" ("If You Love for Beauty") makes a lovely companion piece to husband Robert's "Du Ring an meinem Finger." Composed in 1841, a year after her marriage, Clara's "Liebst du um Schönheit" is a setting of a four-stanza love poem by Joseph Eichendorff (1788–1857). In this wistful, playful text, the poet sets forth three reasons (stanzas 1–3) why the lady should *not* be loved—not for beauty, youth, or money (all three of which Clara actually possessed). In the last stanza, however, we learn for what she *should* be loved—for love alone. Although the melodic and accompanimental figures presented in the first strophe prevail in subsequent ones, Clara varies the musical setting on each occasion, thereby producing what is called **modified strophic form** (the music of each strophe changes slightly from one to the next). Here a form represented as **AA'A''A'''** results. Example 20.4 shows the melody of strophe 1 and how it is modified in strophe 2. The ever-evolving music gives this art song its remarkable freshness. Did Clara equal or surpass Robert as a composer of *Lieder*? You be the judge.

EXAMPLE 20.4

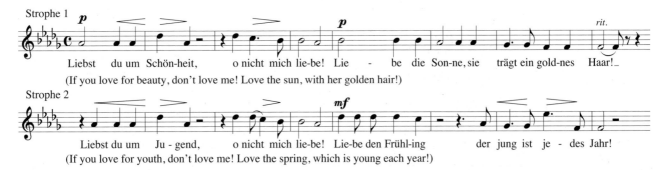

Strophe 1
Liebst du um Schön-heit, o nicht mich lie-be! Lie - be die Son-ne, sie trägt ein gold-nes Haar!
(If you love for beauty, don't love me! Love the sun, with her golden hair!)

Strophe 2
Liebst du um Ju - gend, o nicht mich lie-be! Lie-be den Früh-ling der jung ist je - des Jahr!
(If you love for youth, don't love me! Love the spring, which is young each year!)

You may have noticed that female composers are poorly represented in this book. We have explored the works of some—Hildegard of Bingen (Ch. 5) and Barbara Strozzi (Ch. 8), for example—and later we will meet those of Augusta Read Thomas (Ch. 31). But in general, although women have been actively engaged as performers of secular music since the Middle Ages, only rarely did they become composers. While the reasons for this may be many, one stands out above all others: opportunity.

Before the twentieth century, male-dominated society thought it neither proper nor even possible for women to be creative artists. As twentieth-century novelist Virginia Woolf points out in her essay *A Room of One's Own*, daughters were almost never given lessons—or encouragement—in creative writing, musical composition, or painting; and female authors were forced to disguise their gender through pen names such as George Sand (Aurore Dudevant) and George Elliot (Mary Ann Evans). Rules of the Paris Conservatory exemplify the barrier to women in musical composition. Founded in 1793, the institution did not admit women into classes in advanced music theory and composition until almost a century later; women might study piano, but according to a decree of the 1820s, they had to enter and leave by a separate door. Similarly, the state-sponsored Academy of Fine Arts in Paris did not admit women painters until 1897; even then, they were barred from nude anatomy classes, instruction crucial to the figural arts, because their presence was thought "morally inappropriate." Only in those exceptional cases in which a daughter received an intensive musical education at home did a woman have a fighting chance to become a musical creator.

But even among "home-schooled" women, opposition and self-doubt existed. As Clara Schumann wrote in her diary in 1839, "I once believed that I possessed creative talent, but I have given up this idea; a woman must not desire to compose. There has never yet been one able to do it. Should I expect to be that one?" And Fanny Mendelssohn Hensel (1805–1847), the gifted sister of composer Felix Mendelssohn, received this mandate from her father when she was fifteen and considering music as a profession: "What you wrote to me about your musical occupations, and in comparison to those of Felix, was rightly thought and expressed. But though music will perhaps become his profession, for you it can and must only be an ornament, never the core of your existence. . . . You must become more steady and collected, and prepare yourself for your real calling, the only calling for a young woman—*the state of a housewife!* [emphasis added]"

Fanny Mendelssohn in 1829, in a sketch by her husband-to-be, Wilhelm Hensel

Mary Evans Picture Library/The Image Works

Listening Guide

Clara Schumann, "Liebst du um Schönheit" (1841)

intro
21

Genre: Art song

Form: Modified strophic (**AA'A''A''**)

WHAT TO LISTEN FOR: The ever-so-slight changes in the vocal line and accompaniment from one stanza to the next; the musical freshness and sparkle that can perhaps be created only by a young person in love

			Strophe 1	
0:00 **21**	**A'**	Liebst du um Schönheit, o nicht mich liebe!	If you love for beauty, don't love me!
		Liebe die Sonne, sie trägt ein gold'nes Haar!	Love the sun, with her golden hair!
			Strophe 2	
0:34	**A'**	Liebst du um Jugend, o nicht mich liebe!	If you love for youth, don't love me!
		Liebe den Frühling, der jung ist jedes Jahr!	Love the spring, which is young each year!
			Strophe 3	
1:00	**A''**	Liebst du um Schätze, o nicht mich liebe!	If you love for money, don't love me!
		Liebe die Meerfrau, sie hat viel Perlen klar!	Love the mermaid, she has many pearls!

Strophe 4

| 1:27 | A''' | Liebst du um Liebe, o ja—mich liebe! | If you love for love, oh yes, love me! |
| | | Liebe mich immer, dich lieb' ich immerdar! | Love me for always, and I will love you eternally! |

| 2:04 | | Brief coda for piano alone | |

🔊)) Listen to streaming music in an Active Listening Guide at CourseMate or in the eBook.

🔊)) Take online Listening Exercise 20.2 and receive feedback at CourseMate or in the eBook.

Lives of Tragedy and Fidelity

Robert Schumann was something of a "streak" composer. During the 1830s, he wrote music for solo piano almost exclusively: sonatas, variations, and character pieces. In 1840, he composed almost nothing but art songs. In 1841, he wrote two of his four symphonies, and in 1842, he turned his attention to chamber music, which culminated in a highly regarded piano quintet. The year 1845 saw the composition of the brilliant Piano Concerto in A minor, but after that his creative output diminished.

From his earliest years, Robert Schumann had been afflicted with what psychiatrists now call bipolar disorder (likely exacerbated by doses of arsenic that he had taken as a young man to cure a case of syphilis). His moods swung from nervous euphoria to suicidal depression. In some years, he produced a torrent of music; in others, virtually nothing. As time progressed, Schumann's condition worsened. He began to hear voices, both heavenly and hellish, and one morning, pursued by demons within, he jumped off a bridge into the Rhine River. Nearby fishermen pulled him to safety, but from then on, by his own request, he was confined to an asylum, where he died of dementia in 1856.

Clara Schumann outlived Robert by forty years. She raised the children, and to pay the bills, she resumed her career as a touring piano virtuoso. Dressed in mourning black ("widow's weeds" as they were called), she played across Europe into the 1890s. After Robert's death, Clara never composed again and never remarried. Proving that life sometimes imitates art, Clara remained true to the pledge made in her song "Liebst du um Schönheit": "I will love you eternally." Today the Schumanns rest side by side in a small cemetery in Bonn, Germany, two souls exemplifying the spirit of the Romantic age.

Key Words

art song (240)	song cycle (241)	strophic form (245)
Lied (pl. *Lieder*) (240)	ballad (242)	modified strophic form (247)
Schubertiad (241)	through-composed (245)	

For a complete review of this chapter, see the Main Points, Chapter Quiz, Flashcards, and Glossary in CourseMate.

Join us on Facebook at **Listening to Music with Craig Wright**

chapter TWENTY-ONE

Romantic Music: Program Music, Ballet, and Musical Nationalism

The Romantic love of literature stimulated interest not only in the art song but also in program music. Indeed, the nineteenth century can fairly be called the "century of program music." True, earlier isolated examples of program music had appeared—in Vivaldi's *The Four Seasons,* for example (see Ch. 9). But Romantic composers believed that music could be more than pure, abstract sound—that music alone (without a text) could tell a story. Most important, they now had the power and color of the newly enlarged orchestra to help tell the tale.

Program music is instrumental music, usually written for symphony orchestra, that seeks to re-create in sound the events and emotions portrayed in some extramusical source: a story, legend, play, novel, or even historical event. The theory of program music rests on the obvious fact that specific musical gestures can evoke particular feelings and associations. A lyrical melody may spur memories of love, harshly dissonant chords might imply conflict, or a sudden trumpet call may suggest the arrival of the hero, for example. By stringing together such musical gestures in a convincing sequence, a composer might tell a story through music. Program music is fully harmonious with the strongly literary spirit of the nineteenth century.

Some Romantic composers, notably Johannes Brahms (1833–1897), resisted the allure of program music and continued to write what came to be called **absolute music**: symphonies, sonatas, quartets, and other instrumental music without extramusical or programmatic references. In these it was up to the listener to infer whatever meaning he or she wished. Most composers, however, desiring to convey a clear, coherent message, took advantage of the more overtly narrative character of program music. In 1850, Franz Liszt, a leading advocate of program music, said that a program gave the composer a "means by which to protect the listener against a wrong poetical interpretation and to direct his attention to the poetical idea of the whole."

The three most common types of program music are the following:

- **Program symphony:** a symphony with the usual three, four, or five movements, which together depict a succession of specific events or scenes drawn from an extramusical story or event. Examples include Berlioz's *Symphonie fantastique* (1830) and Liszt's "Faust" Symphony (1857).

- **Dramatic overture** (to an opera, a play, or even a festival): a one-movement work, usually in sonata–allegro form, that portrays through music a sequence of dramatic events. Many overtures became audience favorites and are today performed at concerts without the opera or play that originally inspired them. Examples include Rossini's overture to his opera *William Tell* (1829) and Mendelssohn's *Overture* (1826) to Shakespeare's play *A Midsummer Night's Dream*, as well as Tchaikovsky's *1812 Overture* (1882), written to commemorate Russia's victory over Napoleon.

- **Tone poem** (also called **symphonic poem**): a one-movement work for orchestra that gives musical expression to the emotions and events associated with a story, play, political event, or personal experience. Examples include Tchaikovsky's *Romeo and Juliet* (1869; revised 1880), Musorgsky's *Night on Bald Mountain* (1867), and Strauss's *Also sprach Zarathustra* (1896). In fact, the tone poem and the dramatic overture differ very little: Both are one-movement orchestral works with programmatic content intended for the concert hall.

Hector Berlioz (1803–1869) and the Program Symphony

Hector Berlioz was one of the most original figures in the history of music (Fig. 21.1). He was born in 1803 near the mountain city of Grenoble, France, the son of a local doctor. As a youth, Berlioz studied mainly the sciences and ancient Roman literature.

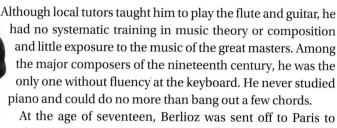

Scala/Art Resource, NY

Figure 21.1

Hector Berlioz at the age of twenty-nine

Although local tutors taught him to play the flute and guitar, he had no systematic training in music theory or composition and little exposure to the music of the great masters. Among the major composers of the nineteenth century, he was the only one without fluency at the keyboard. He never studied piano and could do no more than bang out a few chords.

At the age of seventeen, Berlioz was sent off to Paris to study medicine, his father's profession. For two years he pursued a program in the physical sciences, earning a degree in 1821. But Berlioz found the gore of the dissecting table repulsive and the allure of the concert hall irresistible. After a period of soul-searching, and the inevitable falling-out with his parents over the choice of career, he vowed to become "no doctor or apothecary but a great composer."

His dismayed father immediately cut off his living stipend, leaving young Berlioz to ponder how he might support himself while studying composition at the Paris Conservatory (the French national school of music). Other composers had relied on teaching as a means to earn a regular income, but Berlioz, with no particular skill at any instrument, was not qualified to give music lessons. Instead, he turned to music criticism, writing reviews and articles for literary journals. Berlioz was the first composer to earn a livelihood as a music critic, and criticism, not composition, remained his primary source of income for the rest of his life.

Perhaps it was inevitable that Berlioz would turn to writing about music, for in his mind, music and literature were always connected. As a student, Berlioz encountered the works of Shakespeare, and the experience changed his life: "Shakespeare, coming upon me unawares, struck me like a thunderbolt. The lightning flash of that discovery revealed to me at a stroke the whole heaven of art." Berlioz devoured Shakespeare's plays and based musical compositions on four of them: *The Tempest, King Lear, Hamlet,* and *Romeo and Juliet.* The common denominator in the art of both Shakespeare and Berlioz is range of expression. Just as no dramatist before Shakespeare had portrayed the full spectrum of human emotions on the stage, so no composer before Berlioz, not even Beethoven, had undertaken to create such a wide range of moods through sound.

Figure 21.2

A caricature of Berlioz conducting in mid-nineteenth-century Paris, in what became known as "monster concerts" because of the huge forces the composer required. Berlioz would have liked several hundred performers for the premiere of his *Symphonie fantastique* in 1830, but the printed program suggests that he had to settle for about 100.

To depict wild swings of mood in music, Berlioz called for enormous orchestral and choral forces—hundreds and hundreds of performers (Fig. 21.2). He also experimented with new instruments: the **ophicleide** (an early form of the tuba), the **English horn** (a low oboe), the harp (an ancient instrument that he brought into the symphony orchestra for the first time), the **cornet** (a brass instrument with valves, borrowed from the military band), and even the newly invented saxophone. In 1843, he wrote a textbook on **orchestration**—the art of arranging a composer's music for just the right instruments—still used today in colleges and conservatories around the world. The boy who could barely play the piano had become a master of the orchestra!

Berlioz's approach to musical form was equally innovative; he rarely used such standard forms as sonata–allegro or theme and variations. Instead, he preferred to create forms that flowed from the particular narrative of the story at hand. His French compatriots called his seemingly formless compositions "bizarre" and "monstrous," and thought him something of a madman. Subscribing to the adage "No man is a prophet in his own land," Berlioz took his progressive music to London, Vienna, Prague, and even Moscow, introducing such works as *Symphonie fantastique* and *Roméo et Juliette.* He died in Paris in 1869, isolated and embittered, the little recognition he received in his native France having come too late to boost his career or self-esteem.

Archives Charmet/The Bridgeman Art Library

Symphonie fantastique (1830)

Berlioz's most celebrated composition, then and now, is his *Symphonie fantastique,* perhaps the single most radical example of musical Romanticism. While the orchestration and form of the symphony are revolutionary, the most innovative aspect of the work is its programmatic content. Over the course of five movements, Berlioz tells a story in music and thereby creates the first program symphony. What's more, the history surrounding the creation of *Symphonie fantastique* is as fascinating, indeed fantastical, as the piece itself.

In 1827, a troupe of English actors came to Paris to present Shakespeare's *Hamlet* and *Romeo and Juliet.* Though he understood little English, Berlioz attended and was overwhelmed by the human insights, touching beauty, and sometimes brutal onstage action that characterize Shakespearean drama. Berlioz, however, not only fell in love with Shakespeare's work—he was also smitten with the leading lady who played Ophelia to Hamlet and Juliet to Romeo, one Harriet Smithson (Fig. 21.3). As a crazed young man might stalk a Hollywood starlet today, Berlioz wrote passionate letters and chased after Smithson. Eventually, his ardor cooled; for a time, he even became engaged to someone else. But the experience of an all-consuming love, the despair of rejection, and the vision of darkness and possible death furnished the stimulus—and story line—for an unusually imaginative symphony.

Symphonie fantastique is so called not because it is "fantastic" in the sense of "wonderful" (though it is), but because it is a fantasy. Through the course of a symphony, Berlioz fantasizes about his relationship with Harriet Smithson. The thread that binds the five disparate movements is a single melody that personifies the beloved. Berlioz called this theme his ***idée fixe*** ("fixed idea" or musical fixation); the melody is always present, like Harriet, an obsession in Berlioz's tortured mind. However, as his feelings about Harriet change from movement to movement, the composer transforms the fundamental melody, altering the pitches, rhythms, and instrumental color. To make sure the listener could follow this wild progression of emotional states, Berlioz prepared a written program to be read as the music was performed. His lurid fantasy involves unrequited love, attempted suicide by drug overdose, an imaginary murder, an execution, and a hellish revenge.

Yale Center for British Art, Paul Mellon Collection, USA/The Bridgeman Art Library

Figure 21.3

The actress Harriet Smithson became an obsession for Berlioz and the source of inspiration for his *Symphonie fantastique.* Eventually, Berlioz did meet and marry Smithson. Today they lie side by side in the cemetery of Montmartre in Paris.

FIRST MOVEMENT: REVERIES, PASSIONS

Program: A young musician . . . sees for the first time a woman who embodies all the charms of the ideal being he has imagined in his dreams. . . . The subject of the first movement is the passage from this state of melancholy reverie, interrupted by a few moments of joy, to that of delirious passion, with movements of fury, jealousy, and its return to tenderness, tears, and religious consolation.

A slow introduction ("this state of melancholy reverie") prepares the way for the first vision of the beloved, who is represented by the first appearance of the main theme, the *idée fixe:*

EXAMPLE 21.1

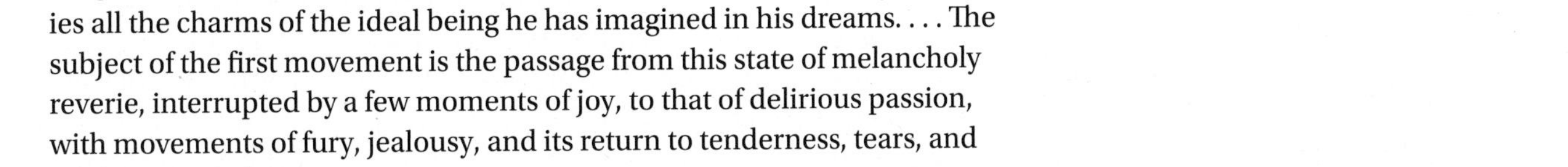

The movement unfolds in something akin to sonata–allegro form. The "reca-pitulation," however, does not so much repeat the *idée fixe* as transform the melody to reflect the artist's feelings of sorrow and tenderness.

SECOND MOVEMENT: A BALL

> Program: The artist finds himself . . . in the midst of the tumult of a party.

A lilting waltz now begins, but it is interrupted by the unexpected appearance of the *idée fixe* (the beloved has arrived), its rhythm changed to accommodate the triple meter of the waltz. Four harps add a graceful accompaniment when the waltz returns, and, toward the end, there is even a lovely solo for cornet. The sequence of waltz-*idée fixe*-waltz creates a ternary form.

THIRD MOVEMENT: SCENE IN THE COUNTRY

> Program: Finding himself one evening in the country, the artist hears in the distance two shepherds piping. . . . He reflects upon his isolation and hopes that soon he will no longer be alone.

The dialogue between the shepherds is presented by an English horn and an oboe, the latter played offstage to give the effect of a distant response. The unexpected appearance of the *idée fixe* in the woodwinds suggests that the artist has hopes of winning his beloved. But has she falsely encouraged him? In response to the lonely petition of an English horn, we now hear only the rumble of distant thunder in the timpani. The call for love goes unanswered.

FOURTH MOVEMENT: MARCH TO THE SCAFFOLD

> Program: Having realized that his love goes unrecognized, the artist poisons himself with opium. The dose of the narcotic, too weak to kill him, plunges him into a sleep accompanied by the most horrible visions. He dreams that he has killed the one he loved, that he is condemned, led to the scaffold, and now witnesses his own execution.

This drug-induced nightmare centers on the march to the scaffold, where the artist faces execution. The steady beat of the low strings and the muffled bass drum sound the steps of the procession. Near the end, the image of the beloved returns in the clarinet, only to be suddenly cut off by a *fortissimo* crash by the full orchestra. The guillotine has fallen and with it the lover's head.

Berlioz had envisioned an orchestra of 220 players for his *Symphonie fantastique* but had to settle for about 100 at its first definitive performance. The important thing, however, is not how many instrumentalists play but how they sound. Berlioz has orchestrated his score in a radically new and colorful way, one full of sonic special effects. In "March to the Scaffold," he re-creates the sounds of the French military bands that he heard as a boy during the Napoleonic Wars. Besides a rousing march tempo, we hear exceptionally heavy low brass instruments blare forth (at 2:04), a new sound for a symphony orchestra, one created by the addition of the ophicleide (tuba). More striking, at 2:11 Berlioz assigns to each and every note of a descending scale a different instrumental color. And he writes his climax—drum roll, please—with a crescendo and snare drum announcing the fall of the guillotine. So graphically does Berlioz orchestrate this moment that we hear the severed head of the lover fall and thud on the ground: a musical first (and last).

Listening Guide

Hector Berlioz, *Symphonie fantastique* (1830)

Fourth movement, "March to the Scaffold"

Genre: Program symphony

WHAT TO LISTEN FOR: Rousing marches and a vivid execution, all brought off by a brilliantly inventive orchestral sound

0:00   **16** **1**   Quiet intro and then loud first march (condemned led to the scaffold)

0:41   March theme repeats with bassoon counterpoint.

1:40   New, loud march theme (the crowd roars)

2:04   Low brass, including ophicleide (tuba)

2:11   Descending scales, each note with distinctive orchestration

2:22   New march theme and descending scales repeated and extended

3:44   End of new march theme goes faster (the crowd presses forward).

4:15   Clarinet plays *idée fixe* (lover's last vision of beloved).

4:23   Sudden crashing chord, then pizzicatos (head is severed and falls to ground)

4:26   Loud, brassy, final chords (the crowd cheers, for executions were once a spectator sport)

🔊 Listen to streaming music in an Active Listening Guide at CourseMate or in the eBook.

🔊 Take online Listening Exercise 21.1 and receive feedback at CourseMate or in the eBook.

FIFTH MOVEMENT: DREAM OF THE WITCHES' SABBATH

> Program: He sees himself at the witches' sabbath surrounded by a troop of frightful shadows, sorcerers, and monsters of all sorts, gathered for his funeral. Strange noises, groans, bursts of laughter, distant cries echoed by others. The beloved melody returns again, but it has lost its noble, modest character and is now only base, trivial, and grotesque. An outburst of joy at her arrival; she joins in the devilish orgy.

In this monstrous finale, Berlioz creates his personal vision of hell (Fig. 21.4). A crowd of witches and other ghouls is summoned to dance around the corpse of the artist on its way to the inferno. Eerie sounds are produced by the strings, using mutes, and by the high woodwinds and French horn, playing glissandos. A piercing clarinet enters with a horrid parody of the *idée fixe* as Harriet Smithson, now in the frightful garb of a wicked old hag, comes on stage:

EXAMPLE 21-2

She is greeted by a joyous *fortissimo* outburst by the full assembly as all proceed to dance to the now perverted *idée fixe*. Suddenly, the music becomes ominously quiet, and in one of the most strikingly original moments in all of classical music, great Gothic church bells are heard. Against this solemn backdrop sounds the burial hymn of the medieval Church, the **Dies irae**, played by ophicleides (tubas) and bassoons (Ex. 21.3). In more recent years, the *Dies irae* has been used to signal doom and gloom in three movie thrillers: *Nightmare Before Christmas*, *Sleeping with the Enemy*, and *The Shining*.

EXAMPLE 21.3

[Di - es i - rae di - es il - la sol - vet sae - clum in fa - vil - la]
[Day of anger, day of wrath, on which the ages will be changed to ash]

Not only is the orchestration sensational, but the musical symbolism is sacrilegious. Just as the painter Goya parodies the Catholic Mass in his *Witches' Sabbath*—making babies serve as communion wafers (see Fig. 21.4)—so Berlioz creates a mockery of one of the most venerable Gregorian chants of the Catholic Church. First, the *Dies irae* is played by the horns twice as fast (a process called rhythmic **diminution**). Then the sacred melody is transformed into a jazzed-up dance tune played by a shrill, high clarinet, the entire scene now becoming a blasphemous black mass. At one point Berlioz instructs the violins to play **col legno** (with the wood)—to strike the strings, not with the usual front of the bow, but with the wooden back, creating a noise evocative of the crackling of hellfire.

To the audience that first heard the *Symphonie fantastique* on December 5, 1830, all of this must have seemed incomprehensible: new instruments, novel playing effects, simultaneous melodies in different keys, and a form that is not traditional, like sonata–allegro or rondo, but rather grows out of the events in a program that reads like the screenplay for a horror movie. But it all works. Here again is an instance of a creator, a genius, breaking the rules and stepping outside the box of conventional art; yet he does so in a way that produces a wholly integrated, unified, and ultimately satisfying work. The separate effects may be revolutionary and momentarily shocking, but they are consistent and logical among themselves when heard within the total artistic concept. Had Berlioz never written another note of music, he would still be justly famous for this single masterpiece of Romantic invention.

Figure 21.4

Witches' Sabbath by Francisco de Goya (1746–1828) bears the same title as the finale of Berlioz's *Symphonie fantastique*. Both create images of the bizarre and macabre so dear to the hearts of Romantic artists.

The Witches' Sabbath (oil on canvas), Goya y Lucientes, Francisco Jose de (1746–1828)/Museo Lazaro Galdiano, Madrid, Spain/Giraudon/The Bridgeman Art Library

The Real End of the Program

In Berlioz's programmatic *Symphonie fantastique*, art imitates life—he constructs a musical narrative to mirror events (real and imagined) in his young life. How did the story of Berlioz and his beloved Harriet Smithson really end, then? In truth, Berlioz did meet and marry Harriet, but the two lived miserably together ever after. He complained about her increasing weight, she about his infidelities. Harriet died in 1854 and was buried in a small graveyard in Paris. In 1864, that cemetery was to be closed and the remains of all the deceased transferred to a new, larger burial ground. It fell to widower Berlioz to remove Harriet's corpse to the new cemetery, as he recounts in his memoirs:

One dark, gloomy morning I set forth alone for the sad spot. A municipal officer was waiting, to be present at the disinterment. The grave had already been opened, and on my arrival the gravedigger jumped in. The coffin was still entire, though it had been ten years underground; the lid alone was injured by the damp. The man, instead of lifting it out, tore away the rotten lid, which cracked with a hideous noise, and brought the contents of the coffin to light. He then bent down, took up the crowned, decayed head of the poor *Ophelia*—and laid it in a new coffin awaiting it at the edge of the grave.

Then, bending down a second time, he lifted with difficulty the headless trunk and limbs—a blackish mass to which the shroud still adhered, resembling a heap of pitch in a damp sack. I remember the dull sound . . . and the odor. (Hector Berlioz, *Memoirs*)

Berlioz had begun by playing Romeo to Harriet's Juliet, and ended by playing Hamlet to her Ophelia. He cast his music, and his life, in terms of Shakespearean drama. And so did the twentieth century. In 1969, during the centenary commemorating Berlioz's death, Romantic enthusiasts repositioned the remains of star-crossed Hector and Harriet. Today they lie side by side in the Parisian cemetery of Montmartre.

The Parisian painter Eugène Delacroix's depiction of the graveyard scene in *Hamlet* (1829)

Erich Lessing/Art Resource, NY

Peter Tchaikovsky (1840–1893): Tone Poem and Ballet Music

Lebrecht Music & Arts

Figure 21.5

Peter Tchaikovsky

The Romantic mania for program music continued throughout the nineteenth century, most notably in the tone poems of Peter Tchaikovsky (Fig. 21.5). As defined earlier in this chapter, a tone poem is a one-movement work for orchestra that captures the emotions and events of a story through music. Thus a tone poem is really no different from a program symphony, except that everything happens in just one movement. Because Tchaikovsky was not so much a symphonist as he was a musical narrator, he excelled in a genre (program music) that had a story to tell.

Peter Tchaikovsky was born in 1840 into an upper-middle-class family in provincial Russia. He showed a keen ear for music in his earliest years and by the age of six could speak fluent French and German. (An excellent musical ear and a capacity to learn foreign languages often go hand in hand—both involve processing patterns of sound.) As to his career, his parents determined that law would provide the safest path to success. But, like Robert Schumann before him, Tchaikovsky eventually realized that music, not law, fired his imagination, so he made his way to the Saint Petersburg Conservatory of Music. When he graduated in 1866, Tchaikovsky was immediately offered a position as professor of harmony and musical composition at the newly established Moscow Conservatory.

In truth, it was not his conservatory job in Moscow that supported Tchaikovsky during most of his mature years, but rather a private arrangement with an eccentric patroness, Madame Nadezhda von Meck (Fig. 21.6). This wealthy, music-loving widow furnished him with an annual income of 6,000 rubles (about $50,000 U.S. today) on the condition that she and the composer never meet—a requirement not always easily fulfilled, because the two sometimes resided at the same summer estate. In addition to this annuity, in 1881 Tsar Alexander III awarded Tchaikovsky an annual pension of 3,000 rubles in recognition of his importance to Russian cultural life. Now a man of independent means, Tchaikovsky traveled extensively in Western Europe, and even to America. He enjoyed the freedom that so many artists find necessary to inspire creative activity.

Tchaikovsky's creative output touched every genre of nineteenth-century classical music, including opera, song, string quartet, piano sonata, concerto, and symphony. But today concertgoers know Tchaikovsky best for his program music and ballets. For example, his programmatic *The 1812 Overture* (1882), which commemorates the Russian defeat of Napoleon in 1812, is heard in the United States on the Fourth of July, with Tchaikovsky's musical pyrotechnics usually accompanied by fireworks in the night sky. By the end of the nineteenth century, Tchaikovsky was the world's most popular orchestral composer, the "big name" brought from Europe to America when star appeal was needed to add luster to the opening of Carnegie Hall in 1891. He died suddenly in 1893, at the age of fifty-three, after drinking unboiled water during an epidemic of cholera.

Figure 21.6

Nadezhda von Meck was the widow of an engineer who made a fortune constructing the first railroads in Russia during the 1860s and 1870s. She used her money, in part, to support composers such as Tchaikovsky and, later, Claude Debussy.

Tone Poem *Romeo and Juliet* (1869; revised 1880)

Tchaikovsky was at his best when writing illustrative music for large orchestra, whether program music or music for ballet. He termed his most overtly programmatic works "overture," "overture fantasy," or "symphonic fantasy." Today we group all of these in the general category of tone poem, or symphonic poem, a title suggesting the literary flavor of these one-movement, programmatic pieces. Tchaikovsky, like Berlioz before him, found that Shakespeare's plays provided the richest source of extramusical inspiration. Of his three tone poems based on the works of Shakespeare—*Romeo and Juliet* (1869; revised 1880), *The Tempest* (1877), and *Hamlet* (1888)—the finest is *Romeo and Juliet*.

In *Romeo and Juliet*, Tchaikovsky aimed to capture the spirit, not the letter, of Shakespeare's play, and thus he crafted a free, not literal, representation of its principal dramatic events. In fact, the composer distills these into just three musical themes: the compassionate music of the kindly Friar Laurence, whose plan to unite the lovers goes fatally awry; the fighting music, which represents the feud between the Capulets and Montagues; and the love theme, which expresses the passion of Romeo and Juliet. Most important, whereas Shakespeare's drama unfolds as a continuous linear process, Tchaikovsky sets his themes within the confines of sonata–allegro form, which gives the music a recursive shape: presentation, confrontation, resolution.

The introduction begins with the music of Friar Laurence and concludes with a succession of mysterious chords strummed on a harp, as if Friar Laurence, like a medieval bard, were about to narrate a long, tragic tale. When the exposition begins, we hear angry percussive music, racing strings, and syncopated cymbal crashes, suggesting that we have entered the violent world of the Capulets and Montagues. Soon the fighting subsides and the love theme emerges, precisely where we would expect a lyrical second theme to appear in sonata–allegro form. As appropriate for a pair of lovers, the love theme is in two parts (Exs. 21.4 and 21.5), each of which grows and becomes more passionate when pushed upward in ascending melodic sequences.

EXAMPLE 21.4 Love Theme Part 1

viola and English horn

EXAMPLE 21.5 Love Theme Part 2

violins

pp

The brief development section pits the feuding families against the increasingly adamant pleas of Friar Laurence. The recapitulation, true to sonata form, begins with the feud music but moves quickly to an expanded, more ecstatic presentation of the love theme (part 2 first, then part 1), which is eventually cut off by a noisy return of the feuding clans. The beginning of the dramatic coda is announced by a foreboding *fortissimo* roll on the timpani. As we hear the steady drumbeats of a funeral procession and fragments of the broken love theme, we know that Romeo and Juliet are dead. A celestial, hymn-like passage (a transformation of the love theme) suggests that the lovers have been reunited in some higher realm, a feeling confirmed by the return of the love theme in high violins. All that remains is to bring the curtain down on the story of the star-crossed lovers, which Tchaikovsky does with seven *fortissimo* hammer-strokes for full orchestra, all on the tonic chord.

Shakespeare wrote *Romeo and Juliet* as a tragedy: "For never was a story of more woe/Than this of Juliet and her Romeo," say the final lines of the play. By incorporating a "celestial conclusion" into his coda—a hymn-like choir of angelic woodwinds followed by the transcendent love theme on high in the violins—Tchaikovsky has changed the final import of the play. True child of the Romantic age, he suggests that the love-death of Romeo and Juliet was, in fact, not a tragedy but a spiritual triumph.

Listening Guide

Peter Tchaikovsky, *Romeo and Juliet* (1869; revised 1880)

Genre: Tone poem

Form: Sonata–allegro

WHAT TO LISTEN FOR: As the music unfolds, focus on the three main sonic groups—Friar Laurence, the feuding Capulets and Montagues, and the love of Romeo and Juliet—and you'll be able to follow the story line of Tchaikovsky's version of this timeless tale.

3/17–20

INTRODUCTION

| 0:00 | 17 | Friar Laurence theme sounding organ-like in woodwinds |

p

0:37	Anguished, dissonant sound in strings and French horn
1:29	Harp alternates with flute solo and woodwinds.
2:11	Friar Laurence theme returns with new accompaniment.
2:36	Anguished sound returns in strings with French horn.
3:23	Harp strumming returns.
3:56	Timpani roll and string tremolos build tension; hints of Friar Laurence theme in woodwinds.
4:32	Anguished sound again returns, then yields to crescendo on repeating tonic chord.

(continued)

EXPOSITION

5:16	18	0:00	Feud theme in agitated minor; angry rhythmic motive in woodwinds, racing scales in strings

6:04	0:49	Crashing syncopations (with cymbal) running against scales
6:38	1:22	Gentle transition, with release of tension, to second theme
7:28	2:12	Love theme (part 1) played quietly by English horn and viola

7:50	2:33	Love theme (part 2) played quietly by strings with mutes

8:32	3:16	Love theme (part 1) returns with growing ardor in high woodwinds while French horn plays counterpoint against it.
9:34	4:18	Lyrical closing section in which cellos and English horn engage in dialogue against backdrop of gently plucked chords in harp

DEVELOPMENT

10:36	19	0:00	Feud theme against which horn soon plays Friar Laurence theme
10:56		0:20	String syncopations, again against Friar Laurence theme
11:20		0:44	Feud theme and Friar Laurence theme continue in opposition.
12:03		1:27	Cymbal crashes signal climax of development as trumpet blares forth with Friar Laurence theme.

RECAPITULATION

12:35	2:00	Feud theme in woodwinds and brasses against racing strings
12:58	2:23	Love theme (part 2) softly in woodwinds
13:35	2:58	Love theme (part 1) sounds ecstatically with all its inherent force and sweep.
14:14	3:38	Love theme begins again in strings, with counterpoint in brasses.
14:30	3:56	Fragments of love theme in strings, then brasses
14:55	4:20	Love theme begins again but is cut off by feud theme; syncopated cymbal crashes.
15:14	4:39	Feud theme and Friar Laurence theme build to a climax.
16:12	5:36	Timpani roll announces coda.

CODA

16:24	20	0:00	Timpani beats funeral march while strings play fragments of love theme.
17:19		0:55	Love theme (part 2) transformed into sound of heavenly chorale played by woodwinds
18:20		1:56	Transcendent love theme sounds from on high in violins.
18:55		2:31	Timpani roll and final chords

◀)) Listen to streaming music in an Active Listening Guide at CourseMate or in the eBook.

◀)) Take online Listening Exercise 21.2 and receive feedback at CourseMate or in the eBook.

Ballet Music

Ballet, like opera, calls to mind "high-end" culture. Indeed, the origins of ballet are tied to the history of opera, for ballet emerged from a hybrid of the two genres performed at the French royal court of Louis XIV (who reigned 1643–1715). Throughout the eighteenth century, no opera was complete without a ballet or two to provide a pleasant diversion. By the early nineteenth century, however, this dance spectacle had separated from opera and moved on stage as the independent genre we know today. A **ballet** is thus a dramatic dance in which the characters, using various stylized steps and pantomime, tell a story. While ballet first developed in France, during the nineteenth century it gained great popularity, and indeed an adopted homeland, in Russia. Even today, the terms *Russian* and *ballerina* seem inextricably linked.

Early in his career, Tchaikovsky realized that ballet required precisely the compositional skills that he possessed. Unlike Bach, Mozart, and Beethoven, Tchaikovsky was not a "developer"; he was not adept at teasing out intricate thematic relationships over long spans of time. Instead, his gift was to create one striking melody and mood after another, to fashion one vivid scene and then move on to the next. And this is precisely what **ballet music** requires—not symphonic invention or contrapuntal intricacy, but short bursts of tuneful melody and captivating rhythm, all intended to capture the emotional essence of the scene. *Short* is the operative word here; because dancing in a ballet is exhausting, neither the principals nor the *corps de ballet* hold center stage for more than three minutes at a time. Tchaikovsky's "short-segment" style proved perfect for the demands of ballet. From his pen flowed *Swan Lake* (1876), *Sleeping Beauty* (1889), and *The Nutcracker* (1892), arguably the three most popular works in the entire repertoire of grand Romantic ballet.

Who doesn't know some of the ballet music from *The Nutcracker* (1892), a holiday ritual as traditional as caroling and gift giving (Fig. 21.7)? The story, typical of Romantic-era narratives, springs from a fairy-tale fantasy. After a Christmas Eve celebration, an exhausted young girl, Clara, falls asleep and dreams (more Romantic dreams!) of people from exotic places and toys that come to life. Fantastical characters parade before us, not merely accompanied but literally brought to life by the music. In "Dance of the Reed Pipes," sleeping Clara imagines she sees shepherds dancing in a meadow. Because shepherds since time immemorial had played "pan pipes," Tchaikovsky orchestrates this scene in a way that features flutes. (The tableau is also called "Dance of the Toy Flutes.") In "Dance of the Sugar Plum Fairy," an instrument new to the orchestra, a keyed percussion instrument called the **celesta**, conjures up an appropriately elfin sound. But not only must ballet music create evocative moods; it must also project a strong, clear metrical pulse to animate—indeed, regulate—the steps of the dancers. If you can't hear the beat, you can't dance, tutu or not!

Robbie Jack/Corbis

Figure 21.7

A recent production of *The Nutcracker* by the Royal Ballet of London, showing a *pas de deux* (the dance equivalent of a musical duet) in "Dance of the Sugar Plum Fairy"

Watch part of a performance of *The Nutcracker* in the YouTube playlist at CourseMate for this text.

Listening Guide

Peter Tchaikovsky, "Dance of the Reed Pipes" from *The Nutcracker* (1891)

(intro)

24

SITUATION: In this portion of the ballet, Clara's dream takes her and the Handsome Prince to exotic places around the globe (China, Arabia, Russia, and Spain among them), and for each, Tchaikovsky creates music that sounds evocative of a foreign locale, at least to Western ears. While in China, we encounter a group of dancing shepherds playing reed pipes—hence the prominence of the flutes.

Genre: Ballet music

Form: Ternary

(continued)

0:00	24		Flutes play melody above low string pizzicato.
0:35	**A**	{	English horn and then clarinet add counterpoint.
0:51			Melody repeats with violins now adding counterpoint.
1:22	**B**		Change to minor mode: Trumpets play melody above two-note bass ostinato.
1:36			Violins join melody.
1:57	**A'**		Return to flute melody (with violin counterpoint) in major mode

◀)) Listen to streaming music in an Active Listening Guide at CourseMate or in the eBook.

Listening Guide

Peter Tchaikovsky, "Dance of the Sugar Plum Fairy" from *The Nutcracker* **(1891)**

SITUATION: The Sugar Plum Fairy charms the Handsome Prince at the Magic Castle, in a show-piece for any great *prima ballerina*.

3/21

Genre: Ballet music

Form: Ternary

0:00	21		Pizzicato strings set beat in duple meter.
0:08	**A**		Celesta enters with melody as bass clarinet plays amusing descending scale.
0:39	**B**		Tempo increases and scales rise.
1:01			Rippling glissandos and static harmony build expectation of return to opening music.
1:11	**A**		Celesta returns with opening melody.
1:45	Coda		Ballerina scampers away.

◀)) Listen to streaming music in an Active Listening Guide at CourseMate or in the eBook.

Finally, it is important to keep in mind that ballet music is not program music. Program music is purely instrumental music, in which sounds alone create the narrative. In ballet music, on the other hand, music is an adjunct: The movements, facial expressions, gestures, and costumes of the dancers tell the story.

Musical Nationalism

Today we are witnessing a globalization of music, and of culture generally. Companies such as Apple, Google, and Facebook covertly encourage the adoption of English as a universal language and overtly promote economic ties that jump borders. The various nations of Europe have formed a European Community, and we in the United States belong to the North America Free Trade Zone (NAFTA). University students are encouraged to spend a semester studying abroad. Everyone, it seems, is looking outward.

In the nineteenth century, however, things were diametrically different. People were looking inward, often for a force that would liberate them from political oppression. At a time when people of one language were frequently ruled by foreigners who spoke another, Europe's ethnic groups came to realize that their ethnicity might be an agent of liberation. Driven by the unifying force of group identity, the Greeks threw off the Turks and formed their own country (1820s), the French-speaking Belgians rebelled from the Dutch (1830s), and the Finns from the Russians (1860s). Similarly, the Italian city-states expelled their Austrian rulers to form a unified nation in 1861, and a decade later a hodgepodge of German-speaking principalities united into what we now call Germany. Prior to the nineteenth century, French, German, and Russian were the dominant languages of Europe; thereafter, literary works published in Czech, Hungarian, Norwegian, and Finnish, among other languages, were not uncommon.

Music played an important part in this ethnic awakening, sounding out cultural differences and providing a rallying point in a process called **musical nationalism**. National anthems, native dances, protest songs, and victory symphonies all evoked through music the rising tide of national identity. "The Star-Spangled Banner," the "Marseillaise" (French national anthem), and "Italian Brothers, Italy Has Arisen" (Italian national anthem), for example, were all products of this patriotic zeal. But how did a composer create music that sounded ethnic or national? He did so by incorporating indigenous folk songs, native scales, dance rhythms, and local instrumental colors. Ethnic sentiments could also be conveyed by the use of national subjects—the life of a national hero, for example—as the basis of an opera or a tone poem. Among Romantic compositions with overtly nationalistic titles are Liszt's *Hungarian Rhapsodies*, Rimsky-Korsakov's *Russian Easter Overture*, Dvořák's *Slavonic Dances*, Smetana's *Má vlast* (*My Fatherland*), and Sibelius's *Finlandia*. For all these composers, a musical signifier (a folk song, for example) served as a badge of both personal identity and national pride.

Russian Nationalism: Modest Musorgsky (1839–1881)

Russia was one of the first countries to develop its own national style of art music, one distinct and separate from the traditions of German orchestral music and Italian opera. An early use of Russian subject matter can be found in Mikhail Glinka's opera *A Life for the Tsar* (1836). As a review of the first performance reported: "All were enthralled with the sounds of the native, Russian national music. Everyone showed complete accord in the expression of enthusiasm that the patriotic content of the opera aroused." Glinka's nationalist spirit was passed to a group of young composers whom contemporaries dubbed "The Mighty Handful" or, less grandiosely, the **Russian Five**: Alexander Borodin (1833–1887), César Cui (1835–1918), Mily Balakirev (1837–1910), Nikolai Rimsky-Korsakov (1844–1908), and Modest Musorgsky (1839–1881). Like Glinka, they created a national art by taking the sophisticated traditions of Western classical music and incorporating therein simple elements of Russian folk and religious music. Of the "Russian Five," the most original and least Western in musical style was Modest Musorgsky (Fig. 21.8).

As with most members of the "Russian Five," Musorgsky (pronounced moo-SORG-ski) did not at first seem destined for a career in music. He was trained to be a military officer and for a period of four years was commissioned in the Russian army. He resigned his appointment in 1858 in favor of a minor post as a civil servant, which gave him more free time to indulge his avocation, musical composition. The next year he said, "I have been a cosmopolitan [Western classical composer], but now there's been some sort of regeneration. Everything Russian is becoming dear to me." Unfortunately, his brief, chaotic life was marked by increasing poverty, depression, and alcoholism, a development evident in the one surviving portrait of him (see Fig. 21.8). During his few periods of creative productivity, Musorgsky managed to compile a small body of work, which includes a boldly inventive tone poem, *Night on Bald Mountain* (1867, used prominently in Walt Disney's *Fantasia*); an imaginative set of miniatures (character pieces) called *Pictures at an Exhibition* (1874); and an operatic masterpiece, *Boris Godunov* (1874), based on the life of a popular sixteenth-century Russian tsar. Many of Musorgsky's works remained unfinished at the time of his death in 1881.

Figure 21.8

Modest Musorgsky

Tretyakov Gallery, Moscow, Russia/The Bridgeman Art Library

Pictures at an Exhibition (1874)

The genesis of *Pictures at an Exhibition* can be traced to the death of Musorgsky's close friend, the Russian painter and architect Victor Hartmann, who had died suddenly of a heart attack in 1873. As a memorial to Hartmann, friends mounted an exhibition of his paintings and drawings in Moscow the next year. Musorgsky was inspired to capture the spirit of Hartmann's works in a series of ten short pieces for piano. To provide unity within the sequence of musical pictures, the composer hit on the idea of incorporating a recurring interlude, which he called *Promenade*. This gave listeners the impression of enjoying a leisurely stroll into and through a gallery, moving from one of Hartmann's images to the next each time the *Promenade* music was heard.

PROMENADE

With the *Promenade* we enter not any gallery but one filled with purely Russian art. The tempo is marked "Fast but resolute, in the Russian manner"; the meter is irregular, as in a folk dance, with alternating five- and six-beat measures; and the melody is built on a **pentatonic scale**, which uses only five notes instead of the usual Western scale of seven—here B♭, C, D, F, and G (Ex. 21.6). Throughout the world, indigenous folk cultures use the pentatonic (five-note) scale. To Western ears, then, *Promenade,* like Russia itself, seems both familiar and strange.

To appreciate the power of the pentatonic scale around the globe, watch "World Science Fair 2009: Bobby McFerrin Demonstrates" in the YouTube playlist at CourseMate for this text.

EXAMPLE 21.6

Now begins a musical depiction of ten paintings. We focus our gaze on numbers 4 and 10.

PICTURE 4: *POLISH OX-CART*

In Hartmann's scene, a rickety ox-cart lumbers down a dirt road. Musorgsky suggests the side-to-side rocking of the cart with a two-note bass ostinato. Notice in this brief composition how music can project a sense of time and movement in a way that a painting cannot. In Musorgsky's setting, the viewer remains stationary as the cart appears in the distance (*pp*), moves closer and closer by means of a crescendo (reaching *fff*), and slowly disappears as the orchestra is gradually reduced to playing *ppp*. In addition, Musorgsky was aware of an important acoustical phenomenon: Larger sound waves (and hence lower pitches) travel farther than shorter waves (higher pitches). (This is why we hear the bass drum and tubas of an approaching marching band long before we hear the higher trumpets and clarinets; this is also why musicians write fewer pitches for the basses than violins, for example—it takes longer for bass sounds to "clear.") Thus, in *Polish Ox-Cart*, Musorgsky begins and ends with the very lowest sounds (orchestrated with tuba and double basses), to give the impression that the sound comes from a distance and then disappears into the distance at the end.

PICTURE 10: *THE GREAT GATE OF KIEV*

The stimulus for the majestic conclusion to *Pictures at an Exhibition* was Hartmann's design for a new and grandiose gate to the ancient city of Kiev, then part of Russia. Musorgsky arranges his thematic material to give the impression of a parade passing beneath the giant gate, in what is tantamount to rondo form (here **ABABCA**). The majestic vision of the gate (**A**) alternates with religious music for a procession of Russian pilgrims (**B**), and even the composer–viewer walks beneath the gate as the *Promenade* theme (**C**) appears, before a final return to a panoramic view of the gate (**A**), now with Hartmann's bells ringing triumphantly.

In this climactic final tableau, Ravel's setting for full orchestra (see below) gives more powerful expression to all of the local color and grandeur inherent in Musorgsky's original music for piano, just as Musorgsky's musical creation is a more powerful artistic statement than was Hartmann's original design (Fig. 21.9).

Figure 21.9

Victor Hartmann's vision *The Great Gate of Kiev*, which inspired the last of the musical paintings in Musorgsky's *Pictures at an Exhibition*. Note the bells in the tower, a motif featured prominently at the very end of Musorgsky's musical evocation of this design.

RIA Novosti/The Bridgeman Art Library

Listening Guide

Modest Musorgsky, *Pictures at an Exhibition* (1874; orchestrated by Maurice Ravel, 1922)

5   2

3/22–23, 4/1   2/2–3

PROMENADE

WHAT TO LISTEN FOR: The alternation of texture between monophony (brilliant trumpet) and homophony (full brasses). Also, try conducting with the music, and you'll notice how the meter continually shifts—a characteristic of folk music.

0:00	**22** **2**	Solo trumpet begins *Promenade* theme.
0:10		Full brasses respond.

0:18		Trumpet and full brasses continue to alternate.
0:33		Full strings and then woodwinds and brasses enter.
1:22		Brasses briefly restate *Promenade* theme.

PICTURE 4: *POLISH OX-CART*

WHAT TO LISTEN FOR: Musical effects create the impression of movement and distance. An ostinato figure depicts the rocking ox-cart, while changes in register and dynamic level suggest shifts in perspective.

0:00	**23**	Solo tuba plays ox-cart melody against backdrop of two-note ostinato.
0:47		Strings and full orchestra join in.
1:25		Full orchestra plays ox-cart theme (note rattle of tambourine and snare drum).
1:45		Tuba returns with ox-cart theme.
2:07		Diminuendo and fade-out

(continued)

PICTURE 10: *THE GREAT GATE OF KIEV*

WHAT TO LISTEN FOR: Three distinctly different kinds of music: **A** (brasses and full orchestra), **B** (woodwinds), and **C** (*Promenade* theme). **A** sounds Western; **B** and **C** more Russian. Most important, note how Musorgsky makes the gate theme (**A**) appear more grand with each appearance.

0:00	**A**	Gate theme in full brasses	
0:56	**B**	Pilgrims' hymn sounds in woodwind choir.	
1:23	**A**	Gate theme in brasses, with running scales in strings	
1:53	**B**	Pilgrims' hymn reappears in woodwinds.	
2:18	**X**	Exotic sounds	
2:41	**C**	*Promenade* theme returns in trumpet.	
3:07	**A**	Gate theme in full glory	

◀)) Listen to streaming music in an Active Listening Guide at CourseMate or in the eBook.

◀)) Take online Listening Exercise 21.3 and receive feedback at CourseMate or in the eBook.

Today *Pictures at an Exhibition* is best known in the brilliantly orchestrated version by Maurice Ravel (1875–1937), completed in 1922. (Perhaps by coincidence, the first attempts at making color motion pictures occurred about the same time.) Whether fulfilling Musorgsky's original intent or going beyond it, Ravel's version greatly enhances the impact of the music by replacing the "black-and-white" sounds of the piano with the radiant color of the full late-Romantic orchestra.

Key Words

program music (251)	cornet (252)	ballet music (261)
absolute music (251)	orchestration (252)	celesta (261)
program symphony (251)	*idée fixe* (253)	musical nationalism (263)
dramatic overture (251)	*Dies irae* (256)	Russian Five (263)
tone (symphonic) poem (251)	diminution (256)	pentatonic scale (264)
ophicleide (252)	*col legno* (256)	
English horn (252)	ballet (261)	

For a complete review of this chapter, see the Main Points, Chapter Quiz, Flashcards, and Glossary in CourseMate.

 Join us on Facebook at **Listening to Music with Craig Wright**

Romantic Music: Piano Music

95

Review the evolution of the piano in the keyboard videos at Book-Level Resources at CourseMate for this text.

Figure 22.1

A large concert grand piano once owned by Franz Liszt and now in the Liszt Museum in Budapest, Hungary. The instrument was made by the Chickering Piano Company of Boston (the largest U.S. piano manufacturer before the appearance of the Steinway Company) and shipped overseas to Liszt as a marketing tool: "If Liszt plays a Chickering, so, young American, should you!"

Craig Wright

We have all banged away on a piano at one time or another. Some of us were subjected to piano lessons, with endless finger exercises, accompanied by our mother's prediction: "Someday you'll thank me for this!" But did you ever stop to think how the piano came to be?

The first piano was constructed in Italy about 1700 as an alternative to the harpsichord; the objective was to create an instrument that could give more dynamics and shading to the musical line. Mozart was the first composer to use the piano exclusively, beginning about 1770. His instrument was small, with only 61 keys, a frame made of wood, and a weight of about 120 pounds (see Fig. 16.7). A century later, the piano had grown into the 88-key, 1,200-pound grand monster that we know today (Fig. 22.1).

Just as the new technologies of the nineteenth-century Industrial Revolution contributed to the growth in size and power of the symphony orchestra (see Ch. 19, "The Romantic Orchestra"), so, too, did these advancements influence development of the piano. About 1825, a cast-iron frame replaced the older wooden one, allowing for greater tension on the strings. This in turn permitted thicker steel strings, which greatly increased the volume of sound and the punishment the instrument could take. (Recall that the forceful Beethoven had frequently broken strings while playing the older wooden-frame piano—see Fig. 18.8.) The Romantic piano could not only support louder and more aggressive playing; it also facilitated a gentler, more lyrical style because its hammers were covered with felt, which allowed the instrument to "sing" with a mellow tone, in contrast to the "ping" of the pianos of Mozart's day. Moreover, foot pedals were added in the nineteenth century, which contributed to the pianist's ability to "shape" the music. On the right side was the **sustaining pedal**, which enabled strings to continue to sound after the performer had lifted his or her hand from the keys. On the left was the **soft pedal**, which softened the dynamic level by shifting the position of the hammers relative to the strings. Finally, in the 1850s, the Steinway Company of New York began **cross-stringing** the piano, overlaying the lowest-sounding strings across those of the middle register, and thereby giving the instrument a richer, more homogeneous sound. By the mid-nineteenth century, all the essential features of the modern piano were in place—the basic design of the piano has not changed in 150 years.

As the piano grew larger and more expressive, it became something of a home entertainment center. In the days before television and video games, the family could gather around the piano to while away the evening hours. Every aspiring middle-class home had to own a piano, both for family enjoyment and as a status symbol—the high-art instrument in the parlor signified to visitors that they had entered a cultured home. Parents made sure their children, especially the girls, received lessons; and publishers, eager to profit from the piano vogue, turned out reams of sheet music for pianists of all skill levels.

Spurred by the sudden popularity of the piano, a host of virtuoso performers descended upon the concert halls of Europe with fingers blazing. Playing rapid octaves, racing scales, and thundering chords, their music was often little more than displays of technical fireworks. Happily, however, several of the greatest piano virtuosos of the nineteenth century were also exceptional composers.

Robert Schumann (1810–1856)

We met Robert Schumann, as well as Clara Schumann and Franz Schubert, in our discussion of the nineteenth-century art song (Ch. 20). All three composers wrote extensively for the piano. Clara Schumann was one of the great virtuosos of the nineteenth century. Robert Schumann tried to become one, but his career on the instrument ended with a self-inflicted hand injury. Thereafter, he concentrated on composition and music criticism.

Carnaval (1834)

In 1834, Robert Schumann, then a young piano student in Leipzig, composed a collection of twenty-one short piano pieces that he collectively named *Carnaval*. In these "carnivalesque goings-on" as he called them, Schumann aimed to re-create in music the various colorful characters that he had seen around Mardi Gras, including traditional masked comic characters such as Pierrot (whom we will meet at length in Ch. 29). Yet Schumann also incorporates real people into the collection, depicting several acquaintances, as well as other musicians he admired. Indeed, the vignettes in *Carnaval* are, literally, musical **character pieces**; here the composer briefly sketches in sound the spirit of a clown, the personality of a friend, or the style of a composer. Among the personalities are "Chiarina" (Clara Schumann); "Estrella" (Ernestine von Fricken, Schumann's girlfriend before he became involved with Clara); and Schumann himself, who masquerades under two pseudonyms, "Eusebius" and "Florestan." Even composers Chopin and Paganini join the parade.

Robert Schumann, as we have seen, suffered from bipolar disorder and eventually ended his days in an asylum. His dual personality is perhaps already evident here at the age of twenty-four. As "Eusebius" he is meek and sensitive, while as "Florestan" he is assertive, even fiery. Schumann made use of these distinctive personas not only in his music but also in his work as a critic. In 1834, the year he composed *Carnaval*, Schumann started a high-end music magazine *Die neue Zeitschrift für Musik* (*The New Music Journal*). Writing for the magazine sometimes as "Eusebius" and sometimes as "Florestan," he introduced to the public up-and-coming artists, including the young Chopin. Indeed, his review of Chopin's music helped put the Polish composer on the map, famously ending: "Hats off gentlemen, a genius." The musical portrait of Chopin in *Carnaval* confirms Schumann's admiration for the rising composer, as well as his own skill as a musical mimic. This brief characterization sounds almost more like Chopin than Chopin himself!

Listening Guide

Robert Schumann, "Eusebius," "Florestan," and "Chopin" from *Carnaval* (1834)

4/2–4

Genre: Character pieces

WHAT TO LISTEN FOR: The melancholy, drooping melody of "Eusebius"; the frenetic leaps and erratic tempos of "Florestan"; and the beautifully wistful melody, supported by a regular, "guitar-strumming" bass, that characterizes "Chopin"

"Eusebius"

| 0:00 | 2 | Metrical uncertainty as seven eighth notes in melody sound against four in bass |
| 0:57 | | Melody doubled in octaves and then (1:32) repeated in its simpler form |

"Florestan"

| 0:00 | 3 | Fiery, assertive ascents, interrupted by moments of "uncertainty" (contrasting tempo) |
| 0:54 | | Music seems to fly off into space with no resolution. |

"Chopin"

| 0:00 | 4 | Chromatic harmonies, bold harmonic shifts, and haunting melody sound the essence of musical Romanticism. |
| 0:35 | | Music repeated quietly as if in nocturnal dream |

 Listen to streaming music in an Active Listening Guide at CourseMate or in the eBook.

Frédéric Chopin was born near Warsaw, Poland, of a French father and a Polish mother (Fig. 22.2). The father taught French—then the universal language of the elite—at a prestigious secondary school for the sons of Polish nobility. As a student there, Frédéric not only gained an excellent general education but also acquired aristocratic friends and tastes. In 1826, Chopin enrolled at the newly founded Warsaw Conservatory, where he studied piano and composition. During this period, he composed his first major work, a brilliant set of variations for piano and orchestra on Mozart's duet "Là ci darem la mano" ("Give Me Your Hand") from *Don Giovanni* (on the duet, see the end of Ch. 17). After this success, Warsaw seemed too small, too provincial, for a young man of Chopin's musical talents. So, in 1830, he departed to seek his fortune in Vienna and Paris. The next year, Poland's fight for independence was crushed by Russian troops; Chopin never returned to his homeland.

After an unsuccessful year in Vienna, the twenty-one-year-old Chopin arrived in Paris in September 1831. His inaugural concerts caught Parisians' fancy, and his imaginative playing soon became the stuff of legend. But Chopin was not cut out for the life of the public virtuoso. He was introverted, physically slight, and somewhat sickly. Consequently, he chose to play at private *musicales* (musical evenings) in the homes of the aristocracy and to give lessons for a fee only the very rich could afford. "I have been introduced all around the highest circles," he said within a year of his arrival. "I hobnob with ambassadors, princes, and ministers. I can't imagine what miracle is responsible for all this since I really haven't done anything to bring it about."

In October 1836, Chopin met Baroness Aurore Dudevant (1803–1876), a writer who, under the pen name of George Sand, poured forth a steady stream of Romantic novels roughly akin to our Silhouette Romances. Sand, a bisexual, was an ardent individualist with a predilection for wearing men's clothing and smoking cigars (see Sand seated behind Liszt in Fig. 18.2, and Fig. 22.3). Six years Chopin's senior, she became his lover and protector. Many of the composer's best works were written at Nohant, her summer residence 150 miles south of Paris. After their relationship ended in 1847, Chopin undertook a taxing concert tour of England and Scotland. While this improved his depleted finances, it weakened his delicate health. He died in Paris of tuberculosis at the age of thirty-nine.

Nocturne in E♭ major, Opus 9, No. 2 (1832)

Can music be painfully beautiful? If so, such music surely can be found in a Chopin nocturne. A **nocturne** (night piece) is a slow, dreamy genre of piano music that came into favor in the 1820s and 1830s. It suggests moonlit nights, romantic longing, and a certain wistful melancholy, all evoked through bittersweet melodies and softly strumming harmonies. (Robert Schumann did a wonderful imitation of a nocturne in his character piece "Chopin," discussed earlier in this chapter.) To set a nocturnal mood, Chopin usually lays out a very regular accompaniment, either as an arpeggio going up and down, or as chords going low-middle-high, both of which give the sense of a harp or guitar strumming in the night. Above this support he places a sensuous melody that plays around and against the very square accompaniment, as we see in his Nocturne in E♭ major (Ex. 22.1). Note that Chopin has carefully indicated how the pianist is to use the sustaining pedal to extend the lowest bass notes, and thereby create a richer, more sonorous sound. ("Ped." here means to depress the sustaining pedal; asterisk means to release it.)

Figure 22.2

A superbly Romantic portrait of Chopin by his friend Eugène Delacroix. It was originally painted with Chopin next to George Sand (see Fig. 22.3). But in 1870, a vandal slashed the double portrait, thereby (unintentionally) creating two canvases.

Figure 22.3

Novelist Aurore Dudevant (George Sand) by Eugène Delacroix. Both the painter Delacroix and the composer Chopin often stayed at her summer estate in Nohant in the south of France.

EXAMPLE 22.1

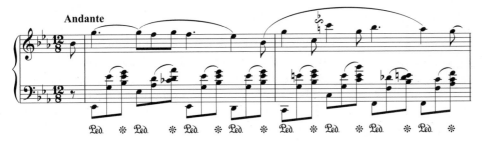

Where did Chopin derive this nocturnal style?—oddly enough, from the arias found in the Italian **bel canto** opera ("beautiful singing" opera; see Ch. 23) that he heard when he first arrived in Paris in 1831. In the Nocturne in E♭ major (Opus 9, No. 2; 1832) the beautiful song consists of two parts: presentation (**a**) and extension (**b**), which are heard three times. At the end, Chopin adds an elaborate, soprano-like cadenza that leads to the final tonic chord. Then, as this chord softly repeats, the nocturnal world dissolves.

Listening Guide

Frédéric Chopin, Nocturne in E♭ major, Opus 9, No. 2 (1832)

Genre: Nocturne

Form: Theme and variations

WHAT TO LISTEN FOR: The exquisite performance of Polish-born Arthur Rubinstein (1887–1982), universally recognized as the greatest interpreter of the music of his countryman Chopin

Theme

0:00	5/4	"Vocal" melody (**a**) set above solid "low-middle-high" chordal accompaniment
0:29		Melody **a** repeated with ornaments
0:58		Melody extended (**b**) through . . .
1:04		. . . bold harmonic shifts, and then . . .
1:20		. . . chromatic harmony

Variation 1

| 1:27 | Melody **a** returns but is now more ornate. |
| 1:56 | Extension **b** is lightly ornamented. |

Variation 2

| 2:24 | Melody **a** returns with new ornamentation. |
| 2:54 | Extension **b** elongated to reach climax |

Coda

| 3:49 | "Vocal" cadenza of rapidly repeating pattern sounding akin to a trill |
| 4:06 | Final strumming of accompaniment on tonic chord |

Listen to streaming music in an Active Listening Guide at CourseMate or in the eBook.

Franz Liszt (1811–1886)

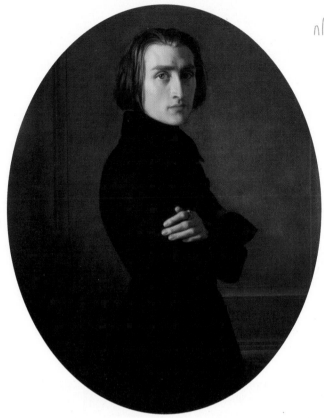

Figure 22.4

The young, charismatic Franz Liszt, the preeminent pianist of the Romantic era.

Figure 22.5

Countess Marie d'Agoult in 1843. She was a novelist in her own right, and some of the tracts on music that appeared under Liszt's name were probably penned by her. Like many female writers of the day, including George Sand and George Eliot, she wrote under a masculine *nom de plume*, Daniel Stern.

Although they were close friends and sometimes traveled together, pianists Frédéric Chopin and Franz Liszt could hardly have been less alike. Chopin was frail, sickly, and introspective. Liszt, on the other hand, was an extroverted showman, perhaps the most flamboyant artistic personality of the entire nineteenth century. Handsome, supremely talented, and equally self-confident, he strutted across the stage as the musical sex symbol of the Romantic era (Fig. 22.4). But he could also play the piano, and like no other. He was, as composer Hector Berlioz said, "A god for pianists."

Franz Liszt was born in Hungary to German-speaking parents. In 1822, his ambitious father took him to Vienna and then Paris to be the next child prodigy, the latest musical *Wunderkind*. But his father died suddenly, and the young pianist's career languished. Liszt's life took a dramatic turn on April 20, 1832, however, when he attended a concert given by the great violin virtuoso Niccolò Paganini (see Ch. 19, "The Virtuoso"). "What a man, what a violin, what an artist! Oh, God, what pain and suffering, what torment in those four strings." Liszt vowed to bring Paganini's technical virtuosity to the piano. Practicing four to five hours a day—unusual dedication for a prodigy—he taught himself to play on the piano what had never been played before: tremolos, leaps, double trills, glissandos, and simultaneous octaves in both hands, all at breathtaking speed. When he returned to the stage for his own concerts, he overwhelmed the audience. He had become the greatest pianist of his time, and perhaps of all time.

In 1833, Liszt's life took another unexpected turn. He met the Countess Marie d'Agoult (at his feet in Fig. 18.2, and in Fig. 22.5) and decided to give up the life of the performing artist in exchange for domestic security. Although she was already married and the mother of two children, Marie and Liszt eloped, first to Switzerland and then to Italy. Residing in these countries for four years, the couple had three children of their own. (Their youngest daughter would become the wife of Richard Wagner; see Fig. 24.3.)

Beginning in 1839, and continuing until 1847, Liszt once more took to the road as a touring virtuoso. He played more than a thousand concerts: from Ireland to Turkey, from Sweden to Spain, from Portugal to Russia. Everywhere he went, the handsome pianist was greeted with the sort of mass hysteria today reserved for rock stars. Audiences of 3,000 crowded into the larger halls (Fig. 22.6). Women tried to rip off his silk scarf and white gloves, and fought for a lock of his hair. **Lisztomania** swept Europe.

Despite their obvious sensationalism, Liszt's concerts in the 1840s established the format of our modern-day piano **recital**. He was the first to play entire programs from memory (not reading from music). He was the first to place the piano parallel with the line of the stage so that neither his back nor his full face, but rather his extraordinary side profile, was visible to the audience. He was the first to perform on the stage alone—up to that point, concerts traditionally had included numerous performers on the program. These solo appearances were called first "soliloquies" and then "recitals," suggesting they were something akin to personal dramatic recitations. As Liszt modestly claimed in his adopted French, "*Le concert, c'est moi!*"

But Liszt was a complex man with a many-faceted personality. He thought of himself not only as a showman–pianist but also as a serious composer. So, in 1847, he suddenly quit the lucrative concert circuit and settled in Weimar, Germany, to serve the ducal court as music director and composer-in-residence. Here he concentrated on writing orchestral music. All told, he composed a dozen tone poems, as well as two program symphonies and three piano concertos. In 1861, Liszt again surprised the world: He moved to Rome, entered Holy Orders in the Roman Catholic Church, and took up residence in the Vatican! "Abbé Liszt," as the composer now styled himself, had replaced Don Juan. While in Rome, Liszt wrote the bulk of his sixty religious works, including two oratorios. He died at the age of seventy-five in Bayreuth, Germany, where he had gone to hear the latest opera of his son-in-law, Richard Wagner.

Despite Liszt's interest in religious music and programmatic works for orchestra, his reputation as a composer—if not for quality then for sensationalism—rests mainly on such piano works as his *Hungarian Rhapsodies* and *Transcendental Etudes*. Liszt had large hands and unusually long fingers with very little web-like connective tissue between them (Fig. 22.7), which allowed him to make wide stretches with relative ease. He could play a melody in octaves when others could play only the single notes of the line. If others might execute a passage in octaves, Liszt could dash it off in more impressive-sounding tenths (octave plus third). So he wrote daredevil music full of virtuosic display.

To build sufficient technique to tackle Liszt's difficult showpieces, performers practiced a musical genre called the "etude." An **etude** is a short, one-movement composition designed to improve one or more aspects of a performer's technique (faster scales, more rapid note repetition, surer leaps, and so on). Before 1840, dozens of composers had published books of technical exercises that became the cornerstone of piano instruction for the burgeoning middle class. Chopin and Liszt took this development one step further. They added beautifully crafted melodies and unusual textures to what previously had been merely mind-numbing finger work, thereby demonstrating that an etude might embody artistry as well as mechanics.

Liszt's most difficult pieces of this sort are his twelve *Transcendental Etudes* (1851). As the title suggests, these works require transcendent, indeed superhuman, technical skill. Ironically, these etudes by Liszt are not useful studies for the average pianist—they are so difficult that the performer must already be a virtuoso to play them! As composer and critic Robert Schumann said, "The *Transcendental Etudes* are studies in storm and dread designed to be performed by, at most, ten or twelve players in the world."

Transcendental Etude No. 8, "Wilde Jagd" ("Wild Hunt," 1851)

Among the most technically difficult of Liszt's *Transcendental Etudes* is No. 8, "Wilde Jagd" ("Wild Hunt"). The title suggests a nocturnal chase in a supernatural forest of the sort often evoked in German Romantic literature. The similarly "supernatural" demands placed on the pianist are intended to develop skill in playing broken octaves in the left hand and simultaneous chromatic runs in both hands (Ex. 22.2). Occasionally, a lyrical melody shines forth in the dark forest of digital dangers. In these moments, the pianist must project the expressive melody while keeping the difficult accompaniment up to tempo, performing simultaneously the roles of poet and technical virtuoso. Today this etude serves as a "musical Mount Everest"—dozens of young virtuosos can be seen on YouTube trying to scale it.

Figure 22.6

Lisztomania (a term coined by the German Romantic poet Heinrich Heine), as depicted in 1842 at a concert in Berlin. A recital by Liszt was likely to cause the sort of sensation that a concert by a rock star might generate today. Women fought for a lock of his hair or a shred of his velvet gloves.

Figure 22.7

The aged Liszt, still dazzling audiences and destroying pianos. That Liszt was not only a lady killer but also a piano slayer was noted by a critic of the day: "He is as much a piano slayer as a piano player."

EXAMPLE 22.2

Franz Liszt, *Transcendental Etude* No. 8, "Wilde Jagd" (1851)

Genre: Etude

5

4/6

WHAT TO LISTEN FOR: An onslaught of technical display and the lovely melody that emerges from it

0:00　6　　　　Racing octaves followed by crashing chords with "short-long" rhythm

0:34　　　　Simultaneous chromatic scales in both hands (see Ex. 22.2)

0:40　　　　Racing octaves and crashing chords return.

1:11　　　　"Short-long" rhythm transformed into folk-like tune

1:41　　　　Lyrical melody appears in top of right hand (soprano line).

1:55	Lyrical melody moved an octave higher
2:28	Lyrical melody is set to more complex accompaniment and grows in intensity.
2:56	Racing octaves and crashing chords return and are developed harmonically.
3:59	Lyrical melody returns.
4:15	Lyrical melody rises in melodic sequence to climax.
4:24	Arpeggios ascend and then crashing chords descend to end.

◀)) Listen to streaming music in an Active Listening Guide at CourseMate or in the eBook.

Key Words

sustaining pedal (268)	character piece **(269)**	Lisztomania (272)
soft pedal (268)	nocturne (270)	recital (272)
cross-stringing (268)	*bel canto* (271)	etude (273)

For a complete review of this chapter, see the Main Points, Chapter Quiz, Flashcards, and Glossary in CourseMate.

f Join us on Facebook at **Listening to Music with Craig Wright**

The nineteenth century is often called the "golden age of opera." It is the century of Rossini, Bellini, Verdi, Wagner, Bizet, and Puccini. True, great opera composers had come before—Monteverdi, Handel, and Mozart, to name just three. But the nineteenth century saw the creation of much of the "core" repertoire presented today. Currently, about two-thirds of productions by the world's leading opera companies—the Metropolitan Opera in New York and La Scala in Milan, for example—are works created during the years 1820–1900.

Italy, of course, is the home of opera. The Italian language, with its evenly spaced, open vowels, is perfectly suited for singing, and the people of Italy seem to have an innate love of melody. Beginning about 1600, the first operas were created in Florence, Rome, Venice, and Mantua (see Ch. 8). For nearly two centuries, Italian opera dominated the international stage. When Handel wrote operas for London in the 1720s, for example, he composed Italian operas (see Ch. 11), as did Mozart when he created musical theater for the courts of Germany and Austria in the 1770s and 1780s (see Ch. 17).

In the early nineteenth century, the primacy of Italian opera was maintained almost single-handedly by Gioachino Rossini (1792–1868). Surprising as it may seem today, Rossini was the most celebrated composer in Europe during the 1820s, far exceeding even Beethoven in fame. Why this "Rossini fever," as it was called? Because Rossini wrote operas—not symphonies or string quartets—and opera was then the leading genre of musical entertainment. Indeed, during Rossini's lifetime, opera captured the popular imagination in much the way that film does today.

Rossini's best-known opera is a comic one, an *opera buffa*, titled *Il barbiere di Siviglia* (*The Barber of Seville*), which has never disappeared from the stage since its premiere in 1816. Even casual music lovers know a little of this enduring work in the form of the "Figaro, Figaro, Figaro" call from the opening aria of the resourceful barber, Figaro. Rossini could also write in a more serious style, as exemplified in his last opera, *William Tell* (1829). This stormy drama, too, has achieved a measure of immortality, the overture providing the theme music for the radio and film character of the Lone Ranger.

Watch a video of Craig Wright's Open Yale Course class session 19, "Romantic Opera: Verdi's *La Traviata*, Bocelli, Pavarotti, and Domingo," at CourseMate for this text.

Figure 23.1

The reigning opera diva Renée Fleming, of Rochester, New York, specializes in *bel canto* opera.

Italian *Bel Canto* Opera

Rossini and his younger contemporaries pioneered a style of opera in which they focused attention exclusively on the solo voice—on the art of beautiful, sometimes extravagant singing, called **bel canto**, a term coined by Rossini himself. After Rossini, the two most gifted of the early creators of *bel canto* opera were Gaetano Donizetti (1797–1848) and Vincenzo Bellini (1801–1835). In their works, the orchestra provides merely a simple harmonic support for the soaring, sometimes divinely beautiful, lines of the voice. Look at the opening of the famous aria "Casta diva" from Bellini's *Norma* (1831), in which the heroine sings a prayer to a distant moon goddess (Ex. 23.1). Here the orchestra functions like a giant guitar. Simple chords are fleshed out as arpeggios by the strings while an even simpler bass line is plucked below. All of the musical interest lies in the rapturous sound of the human voice as it spins out an expansive melody. One Italian newspaper of the day declared, "In the theatrical arts it is said that three things are required: action, action, action; likewise, three things are demanded for music: voice, voice, voice."

Kevin Mazur/WireImage/Getty Images

EXAMPLE 23.1

(Chaste goddess, who does bathe in silver light these hallowed, ancient trees)

Many divas can be seen and heard singing "Casta diva" at YouTube, including Renée Fleming in the YouTube playlist at CourseMate for this text.

Not surprisingly, by placing such importance on the voices of the leading singers, *bel canto* opera fostered a star system among the cast. Usually, the lyric soprano—heroine and **prima donna** (first lady)—held the most exalted position in the operatic pantheon. By the 1880s, she would also be called a **diva**, which, as in the aria "Casta diva," means "goddess." Indeed, the diva and her beautiful voice would rule Italian *bel canto* opera throughout the nineteenth century and even down to the present day.

Giuseppe Verdi (1813–1901)

The name Giuseppe Verdi is virtually synonymous with Italian opera. For six decades, from the time of *Nabucco* in 1842 until *Falstaff* in 1893, Verdi had almost no rival for the affections of the opera-loving public in Italy and throughout Europe. Even today the best-loved of his twenty-six operas are more readily available—in opera houses, TV productions, DVDs, and webcasts—than those of any other composer.

Verdi was born near Busseto in northern Italy in 1813, the son of a tavern keeper. He was no musical prodigy: At the age of eighteen, Verdi was rejected for admission to the Conservatory of Music in Milan because he was already too old and his piano technique faulty. Indeed, not before the age of twenty-nine did he finally achieve musical success, with the opera *Nabucco* (1842). A surprise hit when it premiered at La Scala Opera House in Milan (Fig. 23.2), *Nabucco* launched Verdi's career in Europe, and eventually North and South America as well.

Today Giuseppe Verdi would be characterized variously as a political "leftist," "rebel," or "revolutionary." He worked for the overthrow of the Austrian government, which then ruled much of Italy. By coincidence, the

Figure 23.2

La Scala Opera House about 1830. Verdi's first four and last two operas had their premieres at La Scala, then, as now, the foremost opera house in Italy.

Scala/Art Resource, NY

name "Verdi" ("Green" in Italian) had produced an acronym for **V**ittorio **E**manuele **R**e **d'I**talia, the people's choice to lead a new, free, unified Italy. Verdi willingly lent his name to the nationalist Green Party. During the 1840s, popular cries of "Viva Verdi" ("Long Live the Green [Nationalist] Party") echoed in support of Italian unification. Yet it was not only Verdi's name but also his music that connected the composer to Italian nationalism. In *Nabucco,* for example, Verdi honors a suppressed people (in this case, the Jews), who collectively sing against the rule of a cruel foreign power (the Babylonians). Sensitive listeners, however, heard such rousing choruses as contemporary "protest songs" intending to effect political change in Italy. But change did not come immediately; in 1849, much to Verdi's dismay, the nationalist revolution was dealt a setback, crushed by foreign troops.

Disillusioned with politics, in 1850 Verdi temporarily moved to Paris and turned his attention from national to personal drama. In quick order, he composed a trio of works without which no opera house today could function: *Rigoletto* (1851), *La traviata* (1853), and *Il trovatore* (1853). Upon his return to Italy in 1857, the number, but not the quality, of Verdi's operas declined. He composed only when the subject held special interest or the money was so great that he couldn't refuse. His opera *Aida* (1871), commissioned to celebrate the opening of the Suez Canal, brought him an astonishing fee—the equivalent of about $720,000 in today's dollars. Verdi had become wealthy, so he retired to his estate in northern Italy to lead the life of a country squire—or so he thought.

But like a performer who feels he owes the audience more, or has something more to prove to himself, Verdi returned to the theater, composing the critically acclaimed *Otello* (1887) and *Falstaff* (1893), both based on plays of Shakespeare. Of all artists, musical or otherwise, late-bloomer Verdi created quality works at the most advanced age: *Falstaff* was composed in his eightieth year.

Verdi's Dramaturgy and Musical Style

When the curtain goes up on a Verdi opera, the listener will find elements of dramaturgy—construction of the drama—and musical style that are unique to this composer. For Giuseppe Verdi, conflict lay at the root of every emotion, and he expressed conflict, whether national or personal, by juxtaposing self-contained, clearly contrasting units of music. A stirring march, a patriotic chorus, a passionate recitative, and a lyrical aria follow in quick succession, each with its own distinct mood. The composer aims not at musical and dramatic subtlety but rather at banner headlines of emotion. The psychic states of the characters are so clearly depicted, sometimes exaggerated, that the drama comes perilously close to melodrama, reliant on sentimentality and sensationalism at the expense of subtle character development. But it is never dull. Action, passion, and intensity—all the things that give an opera mass appeal—abound in his operas. In 1854, Verdi said, "There is one thing the public will not tolerate in the theater: boredom."

How does Verdi generate this feeling of intense passion and nonstop action? He does so by creating a new kind of recitative and a new style of aria. As before, recitative still narrates the action, and arias still express the characters' emotional states. But Verdi replaces simple recitative, accompanied only by *basso continuo*, with orchestrally accompanied **recitativo accompagnato**. This allows the action to flow smoothly from orchestrally accompanied aria to orchestrally accompanied recitative and back without a jarring change of texture. As for the aria, Verdi brings to it a new intensity. Yes, he is a composer squarely in the tradition of Italian *bel canto* opera. He focuses his attention on the solo voice and on a lyrical, beautiful vocal line. Indeed, no composer had a greater gift for writing simple, memorable melodies that the audience could whistle on their way out of the theater. Yet Verdi also adds intensity and passion to these arias by forcing

Figure 23.3

A photograph of Giuseppe Verdi, taken about 1885, on an early published score of his opera *La traviata*. Said a newspaper of the day about Verdi's appearance: "Medium build, not ugly but far from handsome, earnest and self-important."

Mary Evans Picture Library/The Image Works

the singers to scale the upper reaches of their range. The tenor is asked to go up to the B above middle C, while the soprano must sing two octaves (or even higher!) above middle C. The thrilling moments in which the hero (the tenor) or the heroine (the soprano) goes right to the top are literally the high points of any Verdi opera.

La traviata (1853)

We may measure the high intensity and passion in Verdi's operas by listening to a portion of his *La traviata* (1853). *La traviata* means literally *The Woman Gone Astray*. It tells the story of the sickly Violetta Valery, a courtesan, or high-class prostitute, who first resists and then succumbs to the love of a new suitor, the young Alfredo Germont. For a while, the couple retires from Paris to lead a quiet life in the country. But without explanation Violetta deserts Alfredo, in truth so that her scandalous reputation will not bring disgrace on his respectable family. The hot-tempered Alfredo now publicly insults Violetta, fights a duel with her new "protector," and is banished from France. When the nature of Violetta's sacrifice is revealed, Alfredo rushes back to Paris. But it is too late! She is dying of tuberculosis—her fate dictated by an operatic convention that requires the heroine to sing one last show-stopping aria and then die.

Verdi based the libretto of *La traviata* on a play that he had seen in Paris in 1852 called *Camille*, by Alexandre Dumas the younger. (His father, Alexandre Dumas senior, wrote *The Count of Monte Cristo* and *The Three Musketeers*.) *Camille* tells the story of the real-life figure Marie Duplessis (Fig. 23.4), the mistress of the playwright Dumas and, for a short time, of the composer-pianist Franz Liszt as well. Marie served as the model for Violetta in Dumas's play and, a year later, for the same character in Verdi's opera *La traviata*. Like many in this period, Marie died young of tuberculosis, at the age of twenty-three.

We join *La traviata* toward the end of the first act. A gala party is in progress in a fashionable Parisian salon, and here the dashing Alfredo has finally managed to cut Violetta away from the crowd to profess his love. He does so in the aria "Un dì felice" ("One Happy Day"), which is lovely, yet somber in tone. The seriousness of Alfredo's intent is underscored by the slow, square, even plodding accompaniment in the orchestra. When Violetta enters, she is supported by the same accompaniment, but the mood of the aria changes radically, becoming light and carefree. Witness Verdi's direct musical characterization at work: Alfredo's slow melody with a hint of minor is replaced by Violetta's flighty sound of high, rapidly moving pitches. Eventually, the two join together: he below, somberly proclaiming the mysteries of love; she above, making light of them. What started as a solo aria has become a duet, the voices—and hands—of the principals now intertwined. Once again, music enhances drama by replicating in its own language the action on stage.

Figure 23.4

Marie Duplessis. The end of her brief, scandalous life is the subject of Giuseppe Verdi's opera *La traviata*. So notorious had she become by the time of her death at age twenty-three that no less a figure than Charles Dickens said, "You would have thought her passing was a question of the death of a hero or a Joan of Arc."

See this scene in the YouTube playlist at CourseMate for this text.

Listening Guide

Giuseppe Verdi, *La traviata* (1853), "Un dì felice"

Characters: Alfredo, a young man of good standing; Violetta, a kept woman leading a wanton life in Paris

Situation: A party in a Parisian salon around 1850; Alfredo professes his love to Violetta, who at first rejects him.

4/7

ARIA		**Alfredo (tenor)**	
0:00 7		Un dì felice, eterea,	One happy day,
		Mi balaneste innante,	you appeared to me.
		E da quel dì tremante	And from this day, trembling,
		Vissi d'ignoto amor.	I have lived in that unspoken love,
		Di quell'amor ch'è palpito	in that love which animates
		Dell'universo intero,	the world,
	Shift to minor	Misterioso, altero,	mysterious, proud,
		Croce e delizia al cor.	pain and delight to the heart.
		Violetta (soprano)	
1:22	Violetta changes aria to lighter mood through faster tempo and shorter notes.	Ah, se ciò è ver, fuggitemi.	If that's true, leave me.
		Solo amistade io v'offro;	Only friendship I offer you.
		Amar non so, nè soffro	I don't know how to love or suffer
		Un cosi eroico amore.	such a heroic love.
		Io sono franca, ingenua;	I'm being honest and sincere.
		Altra cercar dovete;	You must find another.
		Non arduo troverete	It won't be difficult.
		Dimenticarmi allor.	Just leave me.
DUET		**Alfredo**	
1:48	Alfredo and Violetta together in rapturous duet	Oh amore!	Oh love!
		Misterioso, altero,	Mysterious, proud,
		Croce e delizia al cor.	pain and delight to the heart.
		Violetta	
		Non arduo troverete.	It won't be difficult.
		Dimenticarmi allor.	Just leave me.
2:50	Exuberant vocal flourishes for both	"Ah"	"Ah"

🔊 Listen to streaming music in an Active Listening Guide at CourseMate or in the eBook.

Alfredo kisses Violetta's hand and departs, leaving her alone on stage to ponder her future. She reveals, in a slow strophic aria, "Ah fors'è lui" ("Ah, perhaps he's the one"), that Alfredo may be the one true love she has long desired. But Violetta abruptly rejects the whole idea as impossible. Forget love, she says in an impassioned accompanied recitative: "Folly! Folly! What sort of crazy dream is this!" As Violetta's emotional barometer rises, so does her music, climaxing on the word "Gioir" ("Enjoy"). Recitative leads naturally to aria, and here follows "Sempre libera" ("Always free"), one of the great showpiece arias for soprano voice. Through this high-flying music, Verdi defines Violetta's dangerous, "live-for-the-moment" character. Her declaration of independence is momentarily broken by the distant voice of Alfredo, who again reminds her of the mysterious power of love. This, too, Violetta brushes aside as she emphatically repeats her pledge always to be free.

In this scene Verdi has moved quickly from slow aria, to recitative, to fast-concluding aria. Such a three-movement unit is a dramatic convention of Italian opera called a **scena** (a scenic plan made up of diverse movements). So, too, the fast aria at the end of the scena has a name: "cabaletta." A **cabaletta** is a fast-concluding aria in which the increased speed of the music allows one or more soloists to race off stage at the end of a scene or act. Here Violetta, vowing to remain free, dashes off as the

View Verdi's scena (starting at 1:20), with Russian soprano Anna Netrebko singing the role of Violetta, in the YouTube playlist at CourseMate for this text.

Figure 23.5

As writer Mark Evan Bonds has pointed out, the romantic comedy *Pretty Woman* (1990), starring Richard Gere and Julia Roberts, is a cinematic remake of the story of *La traviata*—respectable businessman meets call girl. An important difference, however, is that in Verdi's treatment, as often happens in opera, no Hollywood ending prevails: The tragic heroine dies at the end.

Everett Collection

curtain falls to end Act I. But, of course, our heroine does not remain free—she falls hopelessly in love with Alfredo, as Acts II and III reveal. Listen now to the final scene of Act I of Verdi's *La traviata*.

Listening Guide

Giuseppe Verdi, *La traviata* (1853), Act I, Scene 6

Characters: Violetta and Alfredo (outside her window)

5   2

4/8–12   2/5–7

Situation: Violetta at first believes Alfredo to be the passionate love she has long sought, but then rejects this notion, vowing to remain free.

First Strophe

0:00	8	Soprano sings first phrase.	Ah, fors'è lui che l'anima Solinga ne' tumulti	Ah, perhaps he's the one whom my lonely heart
0:35		First phrase repeated	Godea sovente pingere De' suoi colori occulti.	delighted often to paint with vague, mysterious colors.
0:59		Voice rises up in melodic sequence.	Lui, che modesto e vigile All'egre sogli ascese, E nuova febbre accese Destandomi all'amor!	He who, so modest and attentive during my illness, waited and with youthful fervor aroused me again to love!
1:27		Return of Alfredo's major-key refrain from previous aria	A quell'amor ch'è palpito Dell'universo intero, Misterioso, altero, Croce e delizia al cor.	To that love which animates the world, mysterious, proud, pain and delight to the heart.

Second Strophe

2:23	9	0:00	Return of first phrase	A me, fanciulla, un candido E trepido desire,	To me, a girl, this was an innocent, anxious desire,
2:57		0:34	First phrase repeated	Quest'effigiò dolcissimo Signor dell'avvenire.	this sweet vision, lord of things to come.
3:21		0:58	Voice rises up in melodic sequence.	Quando ne' cieli il raggio Di sua beltà vedea	When in the heavens I saw rays of his beauty

			E tutta me pascea Di quel divino error.	I fed myself completely on that divine error.
3:46	1:23	Return of Alfredo's major-key refrain from previous aria	Sentia che amore è il palpito Dell'universo intero, Misterioso altero,	I felt that love which animates the world, mysterious, proud,
4:44	2:21	Highly ornamental final cadence with lengthy trill	Croce e delizia al cor.	pain and delight to the heart.

Situation: Now abruptly changing her mind, Violetta vehemently vows to reject love and always to remain free.

RECITATIVE   Violetta

0:00	**10** **5**	Accompanied by orchestra	Follie! Follie! Delirio vano è questo! Povera donna, sola, abbandonata, in questo popoloso deserto che appellano Parigi. Che spero or più? Che far degg'io?	Folly! Folly! What sort of crazy dream is this! Poor woman, alone, abandoned in this populated desert that they call Paris. What hope have I? What can I do?
0:55		Flights of vocal fancy as she thinks of pleasure	Gioir! Di voluttà ne' vortici perir! Gioir!	Pleasure! Perish in a whirl of indulgence! Enjoy!
1:06		Introduction to cabaletta		

CABALETTA

1:17	**11** **6**	0:00	Sempre libera degg'io Folleggiare di gioia in gioia, Vo' che scorra il viver mio Pei sentieri del piacer. Nasca il giorno, o il giorno muoia, Sempre lieta ne' ritrovi, A diletti sempre nuovi Dee volare il mio pensier.	Always free I must remain to reel from pleasure to pleasure, running my life along the paths of joy. From dawn to dusk I'm always happy finding new delights that make my spirit soar.

Alfredo

1:58	0:41	Echoes of his previous aria	Amor è palpito Dell'universo intero, Misterioso, altero, Croce e delizia al cor.	Love that animates the world, mysterious, proud, pain and delight to the heart.

Violetta

2:34	1:17	Extravagant flourishes	Follie! Follie! Gioir! Gioir!	Folly! Folly! Enjoy! Enjoy!

CABALETTA RETURNS

3:03	**12** **7**	0:00	This time even more brilliant in its showy, superficial style	Sempre libera . . .	Always free . . .

🔊 Listen to streaming music in an Active Listening Guide at CourseMate or in the eBook.

🔊 Take online Listening Exercise 23.1 and receive feedback at CourseMate or in the eBook.

Key Words

For a complete review of this chapter, see the Main Points, Chapter Quiz, Flashcards, and Glossary in CourseMate.

Join us on Facebook at **Listening to Music with Craig Wright**

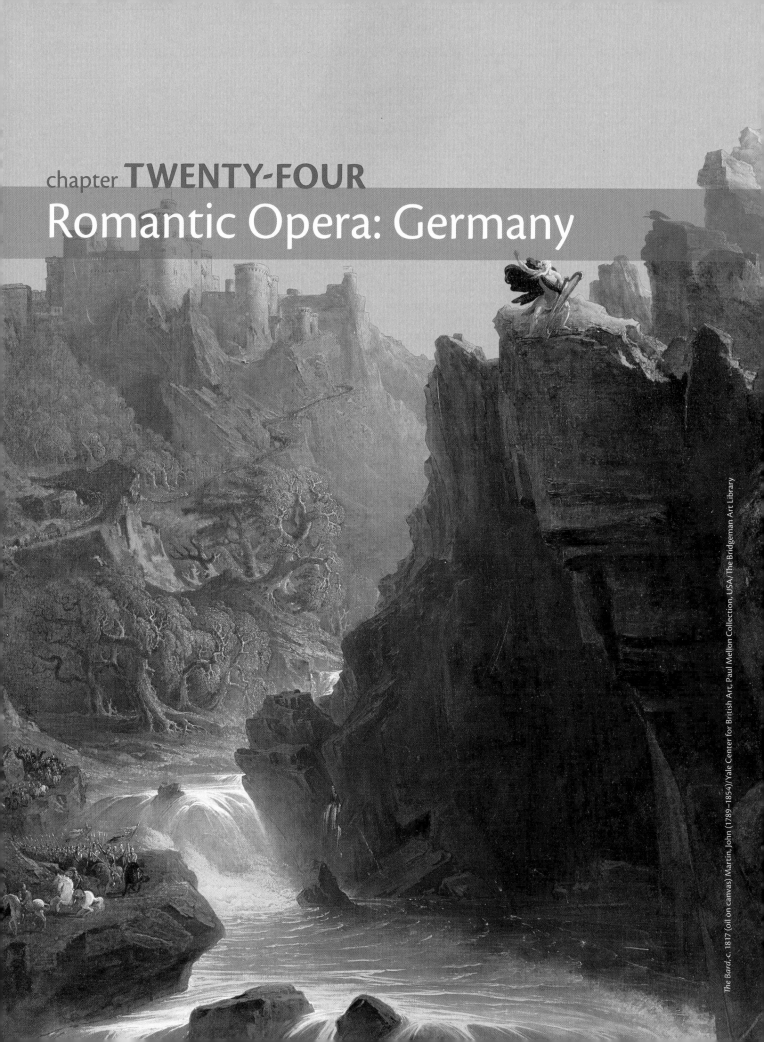

chapter **TWENTY-FOUR**
Romantic Opera: Germany

When we go to the opera today, we usually see supertitles in English but hear singing in one of two languages: Italian or German. Before 1820, opera was mainly an Italian affair. First created in Italy around 1600, it then, over the next 200 years, was exported to all parts of Europe. With the onset of the nineteenth century, however, other people, driven by an emerging sense of national pride (see "Musical Nationalism" in Ch. 21), developed idiomatic opera in their native tongues. Although Italian opera remained the dominant style, it now had to share the stage with newer forms of opera written in French, Russian, Czech, Swedish, and especially German—all languages found north of the Alps.

Germany and Nordic Fantasy Literature

Historical periods often seem to look back to earlier times for inspiration. The Renaissance and the Classical era, for example, embraced elements of Greek and Roman antiquity. The Romantic imagination, however, chose to model itself on the Middle Ages. A nostalgic fondness for a dimly understood "dark ages" developed early in the nineteenth century, especially in Nordic countries. In these years, philologists (scholars of language) began to rediscover and publish "lost" medieval sagas and epic poems: the Anglo-Saxon *Beowulf* (1815), the German *Song of the Nibelungs* (1820), and the Finnish *Kalevala* (1835) among them. These were not medieval historical records, but rather flights of fancy in which a bard told of dark castles, fair maidens, heroic princes, and fire-breathing dragons. They were also markers of nationalism in that each was written in an early form of an indigenous national language. Inspired by these stories were Romantic artists such as John Martin (1789–1854), whose *The Bard* (1817; chapter-opening page) set the image of a poet against the backdrop of a medieval landscape replete with castle above and knights below. Writers such as Alfred Tennyson (1809–1892) fantasized in serial novels. And composers, most notably Richard Wagner, constructed operas with mythical backdrops. The popularity of "fantasy literature" continues today. Think of the success of C. S. Lewis's *The Chronicles of Narnia*, J. R. R. Tolkien's *The Hobbit* and *The Lord of the Rings*, and J. K. Rowling's gothic *Harry Potter* series. These are wonderful authors in the literal sense, yet they all owe a debt of gratitude to the past master of the epic fantasy series: Richard Wagner.

Richard Wagner (1813–1883)

The discovery of a deeply rooted German literature went hand in hand with the development of a national tradition of German opera, one led by Richard Wagner (REEK-hard VAHG-ner). Before Wagner, German composers rarely wrote operas in their native language. Wagner, in contrast, not only set German librettos exclusively; he also wrote them himself, the only major operatic composer to fashion his own texts. Indeed, Wagner was a poet, philosopher, politician, propagandist, and visionary who believed that operas—*his* operas—would revolutionize society. Naturally, many of his contemporaries were skeptical, and even today opinion about Wagner is strongly divided. Some people are left cold, believing Wagner's music to be longwinded and his operatic plots devoid of realistic human drama. (In this camp was Mark Twain, who quipped famously: "Wagner's music is not nearly as bad as it sounds!") Some, knowing of Wagner's rabid anti-Semitism and Adolf Hitler's adoration of him, refuse to listen at all. (Wagner's music is still unofficially banned in Israel.) But others are converted into adoring Wagnerites at the first sound of the composer's heroic themes and powerful orchestral climaxes.

Who was this controversial artist who has engendered such mixed feelings within the musical public for more than a century? Although Richard Wagner studied a bit of music at the church where Bach had worked in Leipzig, Germany (Fig. 10.7), he was largely self-taught in musical matters. After a succession of jobs as opera director in several small German towns, Wagner moved to Paris in 1839 in the hope of seeing his first opera produced there. But instead of meeting acclaim in Paris, as had Liszt and Chopin before him, Wagner was greeted with thundering indifference. No one would produce his work. Reduced to poverty, he did a brief stint in debtor's prison.

When Wagner's big break came, it did not happen in Paris but back in his native Germany, in the city of Dresden. His opera *Rienzi* was given a hearing there in 1842, and Wagner was soon offered the post of director of the Dresden Opera. During the next six years, he created three additional German Romantic operas for the Dresden stage: *Der fliegende Holländer* (*The Flying Dutchman*, 1844), *Tannhäuser* (1845), and *Lohengrin* (1848). All three involve plots situated in some ill-defined time of the "Middle Ages." In the aftermath of the political revolution that swept much of Europe in 1848, Wagner was forced to flee Dresden, though in truth he took flight as much to avoid his creditors as to escape any repressive government.

Wagner found a safe haven in Switzerland, which was to be his home, on and off, for the next dozen years. Having read the recently published edition of the Germanic epic titled *Niebelungenlied* (*Song of the Nibelungs*), Wagner began to imagine a complex of music dramas on a vast and unprecedented scale. What he ultimately created was *Der Ring des Nibelungen* (*The Ring of the Nibelungs*), a set of four operas, now called the **Ring cycle**, intended to be performed over the course of four successive evenings. As with Tolkien's trilogy *The Lord of the Rings*, Wagner's Ring cycle involves wizards, goblins, giants, dragons, and sword-wielding heroes. Both sagas revolve around a much-coveted ring, which offers its possessor the power to rule the world, but also carries a sinister curse. And as with Tolkien's tale, Wagner's story is of epic length. *Das Rheingold,* the first opera, lasts two and a half hours; *Die Walküre* and *Siegfried* run nearly four and a half hours each; the finale, *Götterdämmerung* (*Twilight of the Gods*), goes on for no less than five and a half hours and ends with the destruction of the world of the gods. Wagner began the project in 1853 and did not finish until 1876, perhaps the grandest, longest-running project by a single creator in the history of art.

Not surprisingly, producers were reluctant to mount the operas of Wagner's Ring, given their massive scope and fantastical subject matter. They would, however, pay well for the rights to the composer's more traditional works. So, in the midst of his labors on the Ring cycle, the often penurious Wagner interrupted the project for a period of years to create *Tristan und Isolde* (1865) and *Die Meistersinger von Nürnberg* (*The Mastersingers of Nuremberg*, 1868). But these, too, were long and not easy to produce. The bulky scores piled up on his desk.

In 1864, Wagner was rescued from his plight by King Ludwig II of Bavaria, who paid off his debts, gave him an annual allowance, encouraged him to complete the *Ring* tetralogy, and helped him to build a special theater where his giant operas could be mounted according to the composer's own specifications (Fig. 24.2). This opera house, or Festival Theater as Wagner called it, was constructed at Bayreuth, a small town between Munich and Leipzig in southern Germany. The first **Bayreuth Festival** took place in August 1876 with three successive performances of the entire Ring cycle. Following Wagner's death in 1883, his remains were interred on the grounds of the Wagner villa in Bayreuth. Still controlled by the descendants of Wagner today,

Hulton-Deutsch Collection/Corbis

Figure 24.1

Richard Wagner in an 1871 photograph

Hear music from Wagner's *Götterdämmerung* in the iTunes playlist at CourseMate for this text.

Figure 24.2

Bayreuth Festival Theater, an opera house built especially to produce the music dramas of Richard Wagner—and only Wagner. When the first production of the complete Ring cycle was given here in 1876, many Americans of German descent were in attendance, including Theodore Steinway, founder of the Steinway Piano Company, and Gustav Schirmer, founder of the music publishing house from which the publisher of this book (Schirmer/Cengage) is descended.

INTERFOTO/Alamy

the Bayreuth Festival continues to stage the music dramas of Wagner—and only Wagner. Tickets currently cost upwards of $500 apiece, and the wait to obtain them can stretch between five and ten years. Yet each summer, nearly 60,000 Wagnerites make the pilgrimage to this theatrical shrine to one of art's most determined, and ruthless, visionaries.

Wagner's "Music Dramas"

With few exceptions, Wagner composed only opera, ignoring such concert hall genres as the symphony and the concerto. But he wanted his opera to be radically different, so he gave it a new name: "music drama." A **music drama** for Wagner was a musical work for the stage in which all the arts—poetry, music, acting, mime, dance, and scenic design—are of equal importance and function harmoniously together. Such an artistic union Wagner referred to as a ***Gesamtkunstwerk*** (total art work). Thus combined, the unified force of the arts would generate more realistic drama. No longer would the action grind to a halt in order to spotlight the vocal acrobatics of a prima donna, as often happened in Italian opera.

Indeed, Wagner's music drama differs from conventional Italian opera in three important ways. First, Wagner removed ensemble singing almost entirely; duets, trios, choruses, and full-cast finales became extremely rare. Second, Wagner did away with the traditional Italian "numbers opera," in which separate, closed units, such as aria and recitative, are strung together. Instead, he wrote an undifferentiated stream of solo singing and declamation, what is now called **endless melody**. In his vocal writing, Wagner avoided repetition, symmetry, and regular cadences—all things that can make a melody "catchy." He instead wanted his melodic line to spring forth directly from the rise and fall of the words. Third and finally, as Wagner decreased the importance of the traditional aria, he increased the role of the orchestra.

With Wagner, the orchestra is everything. It sounds forth the main musical themes, develops and exploits them, and thereby plays out the drama through purely instrumental music. As had Beethoven and Berlioz before him, Wagner continued to expand the size of the orchestra. The orchestra required for the Ring cycle, for example, is massive, especially with regard to the brasses: four trumpets, four trombones, eight horns (four doubling on tuba), and a contrabass (very low) tuba. If Wagner's music sounds powerful, it is the heavy artillery of the brasses that makes it so.

A bigger orchestra demanded, in turn, more forceful singers. To be heard above an orchestra of nearly a hundred players, large, specially trained voices were needed: the so-called Wagnerian tenor and Wagnerian soprano. The voice types that typically dominate the operatic stage today—with their power and wide vibrato—first developed in Wagner's music dramas.

Wagner's *Ring* and *Die Walküre* (*The Valkyrie*, 1856; first performed 1870)

Richard Wagner conceived his Ring cycle not only as a timeless fantasy adventure, but also as a timely allegory for nineteenth-century German society. Through his libretto, Wagner explores power, greed, heroism, and race—issues sure to resonate in the Germany of his day, then rapidly industrializing and striving to become a unified nation. The curse-bearing "ring" at the center of the cycle, for example, represents (capitalist) power; characters fight to possess it, for whoever wears the ring controls the world. Wagner had neither wealth nor power and jealously despised those who did. But his *Ring* contains a second theme that was important to Wagner's personal life: love. The composer, a Romantic visionary *par excellence*, found it impossible to write operas about love without being in love himself. (That the objects of his desire tended to be the wives of his unsuspecting patrons posed but a minor obstacle.) Bidding art to imitate life, Wagner set the issue of unconditional free love at the very heart of *Die Walküre*, the second of the four *Ring* dramas.

The plot of the *Ring* is long and maddeningly complicated. To simplify greatly: Wotan, the chief god, rules over a fantasy world of heroes and villains, of natural and supernatural creatures. Wotan is well intentioned, but suffers many human foibles. Like some politicians today, he lies, cheats, and breaks promises in an attempt to maintain traditional values as well as his personal power. Although married, he has sired many children of uncertain maternity, among them the Valkyries, nine high-flying, hard-riding goddesses. Wotan's favorite offspring is Brünnhilde, the Valkyrie after whom this drama is named. But Brünnhilde has disobeyed Wotan. She has encouraged an incestuous love between two of Wotan's other children, twin brother and sister Siegmund and Sieglinde, from whom the superhero Siegfried will be born. (We said this plot was complicated.) At the beginning of Act III, the Valkyries ride away furiously, carrying the bodies of fallen heroes toward a mountaintop. Fleeing Wotan's wrath, Brünnhilde soon joins them.

Of all the seventeen hours of music in the Ring cycle, "The Ride of the Valkyries" is the most famous and, arguably, the most exciting. Its popularity caused Wagner to create, as a surefire moneymaker, a purely instrumental version that could be performed in concert or even outdoors, and in this form the fame of the music spread. Indeed, "The Ride of the Valkyries" was among the pieces played at an all-Wagner concert in Central Park, New York, in September 1872, the first time Wagner's music was publicly performed in the United States. At the very beginning, Wagner calls the listener to attention by means of high trills in the woodwinds and a racing scale below. From this scale, the ever-surging Valkyries motive emerges, a rising arpeggio initiated by the strings but soon blaring forth in the brasses. Initially associated with warrior women, "The Ride of the Valkyries" has become the epitome of militaristic music in all its frightful glory.

Listening Guide

Richard Wagner, "Ride of the Valkyries," from *Die Walküre* (1856; orchestral version 1870)

4/13–14 2/8–9

Characters: The Valkyries

Situation: With music that pushes continually forward for more than five minutes, the warrior maidens, carrying the corpses of fallen heroes to Valhalla, the house of the gods, arrive at a mountaintop.

WHAT TO LISTEN FOR: How the hard-charging motive pushes the music continually forward, literally nonstop from beginning to end

0:00		Opening call to attention with trills in high strings and woodwinds
0:25		Entrance of the Valkyries motive in French horns and trombones

0:39		Entrance of the Valkyries motive in trumpets
0:53		Brasses continue to present and share all or parts of the motive.
1:13		Bass trombones present motive, adding gravity to the sound.
1:30		Valkyries vocal motive played by violins

(continued)

1:56		Brasses continue with Valkyries motive played *fortissimo*.
2:30		Dramatic descents in the strings and woodwinds
3:07		Bold, chromatic chord changes rising by half step
3:23	**14** **9** 0:00	Valkyries motive returns, quietly at first.
4:06	0:43	Cymbal sounds on the downbeat; tubas are audible beneath.
4:41	1:18	Valkyries vocal motive returns in strings.
5:11	1:58	Rising scale and sudden end

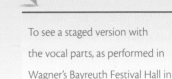

To see a staged version with the vocal parts, as performed in Wagner's Bayreuth Festival Hall in 1976, go to the YouTube playlist at CourseMate for this text.

🔊 Listen to streaming music in an Active Listening Guide at CourseMate or in the eBook.

Mary Evans Picture Library/The Image Works

Figure 24.3

Cosima Wagner (daughter of Franz Liszt and Marie d'Agoult), Richard Wagner, and Liszt at Wagner's villa in Bayreuth in 1880. At the right is a young admirer of Wagner, Hans von Wolzogen, who first coined the term *leitmotif*.

Wagner's associates (Fig. 24.3) came to call his Valkyries motive and others like it "leitmotifs." A **leitmotif** (signature-tune) is a brief, distinctive unit of music designed to represent a character, object, or idea, which returns repeatedly to show how the drama is unfolding. Wagner's leitmotifs are usually not sung but rather are played by the orchestra. In this way, an element of the subconscious can be introduced into the drama: The orchestra can give a sense of what a character is thinking even when he or she is singing about something else. By developing, extending, varying, contrasting, and resolving these representational leitmotifs, Wagner is able to play out the essence of the drama almost without recourse to his singers. In *Die Walküre*, Wagner employs more than thirty leitmotifs and, as one careful critic has noted, they sound 405 times, not including immediate repeats. The following three leitmotifs appear in the final scene of *Die Walküre*, "Wotan's Farewell":

Slumber

Magic fire

Renunciation of love

Having disobeyed Wotan, Brünnhilde must endure his punishment (Fig. 24.4). She is to be "demoted" from god to mortal and made to sleep upon a rock until some pedestrian male happens along and claims her as his wife. Brünnhilde recoils in horror, and Wotan agrees to surround her slumbering body with a ring of fire that only a deserving figure—a superhero—can penetrate. Clutching her in his arms, he bids farewell, knowing that they will never meet again.

Wotan is more than sad at the loss of Brünnhilde; he is destroyed, for among all his children, she is his favorite. At the heart of this climactic scene is one of the drama's central conflicts: Wotan is torn between love (Brünnhilde) and power (enforcing his authority). By choosing the latter, he loses not only Brünnhilde but also any illusion that he can really shape the world as he sees it. Wotan's inner conflict is compounded by the fact that he does not believe in the stricture against total sexual freedom that societal norms ask him to enforce. The intense physical attraction demonstrated on stage between father and daughter causes the audience to wonder: Had Wotan and Brünnhilde already extended to themselves license for incestuous true love? The composer suggests as much in this supercharged final scene.

© DeAgostini/ SuperStock

Figure 24.4

Wotan punishes Brünnhilde as the other Valkyries look on, a depiction of the original production of *Die Walküre* of 1870. Note Wotan's spear, on which are written the covenants that will govern society. Because she has encouraged free love, Brünnhilde has violated one of those rules.

Listening Guide

Richard Wagner, "Wotan's Farewell," from *Die Walküre* (1856; first performed 1870), first of two parts

4/15–16 2/10–11

Characters: Wotan, chief of the gods, and Brünnhilde, leader of the Valkyries

Situation: Wotan bids eternal farewell to his beloved daughter, Brünnhilde, at the outset of the final scene of the drama.

WHAT TO LISTEN FOR: The intense emotion of the moment, expressed through a huge bass-baritone voice and rich orchestral sound, and the leitmotifs as they enter in turn in the instruments

0:00   Brief introduction featuring "Slumber" leitmotif

Leb'wohl, du kühnes, herrliches Kind!	Farewell, brave, splendid child!
Du meines Herzens heiligster Stolz!	You, my heart's most holy possession!
Leb'wohl! Leb'wohl! Leb'wohl!	Farewell! Farewell! Farewell!

0:39   Wotan suddenly drops to *pianissimo* and becomes more passionate.

Muss ich dich meiden	Must I reject you
und darf nicht minnig	and must I no longer lovingly
mein Grüss dich mehr grüssen,	greet you with my greeting,
sollst du nun nicht mehr neben mir reiten	shall you no longer ride next to me
noch Met beim Mahl mir reichen;	or bring me my mead at dinner;
muss ich verlieren dich, die ich liebe	must I send you away, the one whom I love
du lachende Lust meines Auges?	you, laughing joy of my eyes?

(continued)

1:20   Magic fire leitmotif sounds in violins

Ein bräutliches Feuer soll dir nun brennen   A bridal fire shall now burn
wie nie einer Braut es gebrannt,   as one has never burned before,
Flammende Gluth umglühe den Fels;   a flaming threat shall flare round the rock;
mit zehrenden Schrecken   with withering terror
scheuch'es den Zagen;   it will frighten the weak;
der Feige fliehe Brünnhildes Fels!   the fainthearted will flee Brünnhilde's rock!

1:52   **16** 0:00   Renunciation of love leitmotif

       11

1:54   0:03   Denn einer nur freie die Braut   For one alone will win the bride
                 der freier als ich, der Gott!   one who is free like I, the god!

2:24   0:32   "Slumber" leitmotif returns in violins.

3:27   1:35   Orchestral climax led by surging strings,
                 then long, gradual fadeout

To see this scene portrayed with soloist James Morris, perhaps the finest of the most recent Wotans, go to the YouTube playlist at CourseMate for this text.

🔊)) Listen to streaming music in an Active Listening Guide at CourseMate or in the eBook.

🔊)) Take online Listening Exercise 24.1 and receive feedback at CourseMate or in the eBook.

Leitmotifs in *Star Wars*

The technique of the leitmotif, as developed by Richard Wagner, has been borrowed by many composers of Hollywood film music, among them Howard Shore, who wrote the scores for *The Lord of the Rings* trilogy, and John Williams, creator of the music for the *Star Wars* series. When Williams wrote the music for *Star Wars*, *The Empire Strikes Back*, and *The Return of the Jedi*, he composed for each main character (and theme or force) a particular musical motive. Below are two of Williams's leitmotifs, the first signifying the hero Luke Skywalker and the second (merely an insistent rhythm), the evil Darth Vader.

Williams sets these leading motives in the orchestra, thereby telling the audience what the character is thinking or what the future may hold. This technique owes much to the ideas of Wagner. For example, at the end of *Die Walküre* Wagner signals to the audience that Brünnhilde will be rescued by a hero (in the next opera) when a powerful trumpet leitmotif cuts the air; similarly, we learn that farm boy Luke Skywalker will become a Jedi warrior (in the next film) when the orchestra plays the heroic "Force" leitmotif in the background.

Luke's Theme

Darth Vader's Theme

In fact, *Star Wars*, conceived and created by George Lucas, has more than just leitmotifs in common with Wagner's music dramas. Both Wagner and Lucas started with a core of three dramas and added a fourth as a preface or "prequel" (*Das Rheingold* was prefixed to the *Ring*, and *The Phantom Menace* to *Star Wars*). Lucas, of course, has added two further episodes to his saga, bringing his total to six, but the leitmotifs remain the same. Both Wagner's cycle and Lucas's saga play out a series of epic battles between larger-than-life heroes and villains, mythical forces for good and evil, warring throughout cosmic time. Lucas's fantasy cycle has great visual effects; Wagner's has great music.

Richard Wagner was the first opera composer to end his important scenes, as here, not with the sound of voices, but with a long, climactic instrumental postlude. This gambit worked for Wagner, because he could call upon the glorious sweep of the huge nineteenth-century orchestra to transport the listener to a world where words are inconsequential. This is typical of the contradictions and controversies surrounding Wagner's life and art. Although today Wagner is known as one of the two or three greatest opera composers of all time, his most remarkable gift was, ironically, in writing for the orchestra. And, although he argued in prose for *Gesamtkunstwerk*, or equality among the arts, for the most crucial moments in his scores he always gave the final "word" to music alone.

Key Words

Ring cycle (287)	music drama (288)	endless melody (288)
Bayreuth Festival (287)	*Gesamtkunstwerk* (288)	leitmotif (290)

For a complete review of this chapter, see the Main Points, Chapter Quiz, Flashcards, and Glossary in CourseMate.

Join us on Facebook at **Listening to Music with Craig Wright**

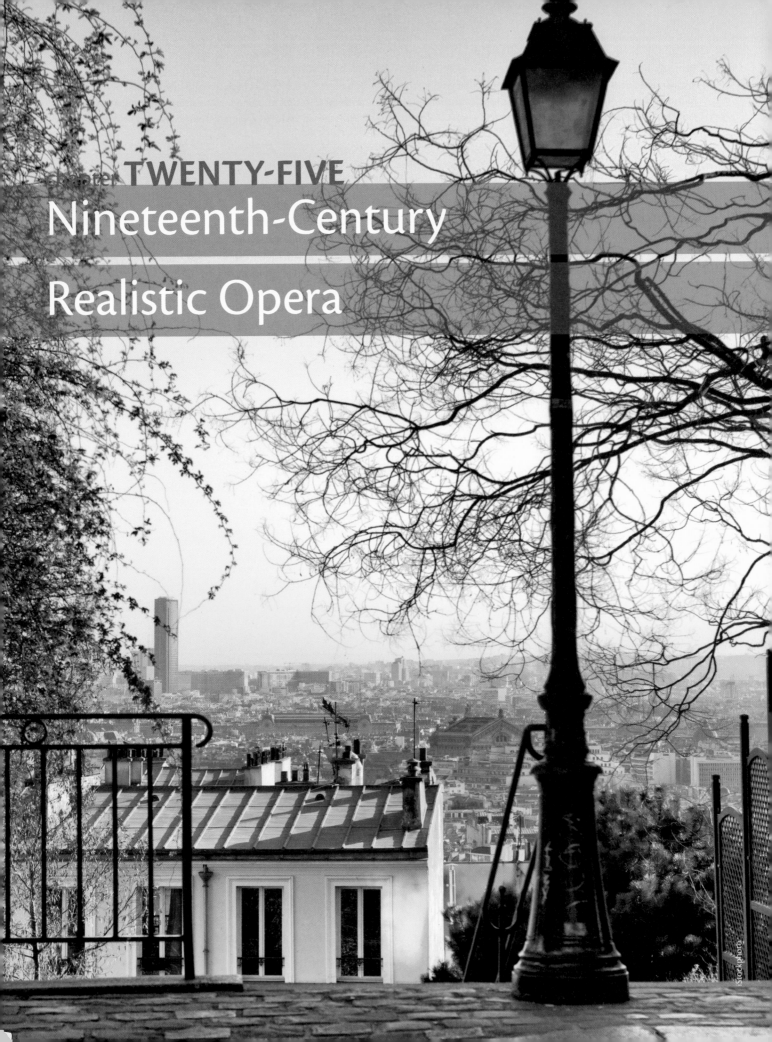

chapter **TWENTY-FIVE**

Nineteenth-Century

Realistic Opera

Romantic opera, much like contemporary film, is largely an escapist art. The stage is populated by larger-than-life characters or by the well-to-do, people of leisure untroubled by mundane concerns or financial worries. During the second half of the nineteenth century, however, a contrasting type of opera developed in Europe, one more in tune with the social truths of the day. It is called **realistic opera**, because the subject matter treats issues of everyday life in a realistic way. Poverty, physical abuse, industrial exploitation, and crime—afflictions of the lower classes in particular—are presented on stage for all to see. In realistic opera rarely is there a happy ending.

Realistic opera was part of an artistic reaction to the ill effects of the nineteenth-century Industrial Revolution, an economic transformation that brought with it great prosperity for some, but oppressive factory conditions and social disintegration for others. Science played a role here, too, for the nineteenth century witnessed the emergence of the theory of evolution. First popularized in Charles Darwin's *On the Origin of Species* (1859), evolutionary theory suggests a dog-eat-dog world in which only the fittest survive. Painters such as J.-F. Millet (1814–1875) and the young Vincent van Gogh (1853–1890) captured on canvas the life of the downtrodden (Fig. 25.1). Writer Charles Dickens (1812–1870) did the same in realistic novels such as *Oliver Twist* (1838) and *Bleak House* (1852). These artists aimed to transform the mundane and commonplace into art, to find the poetic and heroic in even the most ordinary aspects of human experience.

Must art imitate life? Composers of realistic opera thought so and thus embraced the gritty and unsavory facets of nineteenth-century society. The plots of their operas could read like tabloid headlines: "Knife-Wielding Gypsy Girl Arrested in Cigarette Factory" (Bizet's *Carmen*, 1875); "Jealous Clown Stabs Wife to Death" (Leoncavallo's *Pagliacci*, 1892); "Abused Singer Murders Chief of Police" (Puccini's *Tosca*, 1892). If traditional Romantic opera is usually sentimental, nineteenth-century realistic opera is sensational.

Hear Luciano Pavarotti sing "E lucevan le stelle" from Puccini's *Tosca*, in the iTunes playlist at CourseMate for this text.

Figure 25.1

Vincent van Gogh, *The Potato Eaters* (1885). During his youth, van Gogh chose to live and work in the coal-mining region of eastern Belgium. This grim painting records his impressions of life within a mining family and the evening meal of potatoes and tea.

Art Resource, NY

 ## Georges Bizet's *Carmen* (1875)

The first important realistic opera is *Carmen* (1875) by Georges Bizet (bee-SAY). Bizet (1838–1875), who spent his short life entirely in Paris, was primarily an opera composer, and *Carmen* is his masterpiece. Set in nineteenth-century Spain, the opera centers on a sensual young gypsy woman known only as Carmen. This sexually assertive, willful woman holds the populace in her sway. By means of her alluring dance and song, she seduces a naïve army corporal, Don José. Falling hopelessly in love, Don José deserts his military post, "marries" Carmen, and takes up with her gypsy bandit friends. But Carmen, who refuses to belong to any man, soon abandons Don José to give herself to the handsome bullfighter Escamillo. Having lost all for nothing, the humiliated Don José stabs Carmen to death in a bloody ending.

This violent conclusion highlights the stark realism of *Carmen*. The heroine is a woman of easy virtue available to every man, albeit on her own terms. She lives for the moment, surrounded by social outcasts (gypsies), prostitutes, and thieves. All this was shocking stuff for the refined Parisian audience of Bizet's day. During the first rehearsals in 1875, the women of the chorus threatened to quit because they were asked to smoke and fight on stage. Critics called the libretto "obscene." Bizet's producers asked him to tone down the more lurid aspects of the drama (especially the bloody ending)—to make it more acceptable as family entertainment—but he refused.

Carmen is full of alluring melodies, including the well-known Toreador Song and the even more beloved Habanera. In fashioning these tunes, Bizet borrowed phrases from several Spanish popular songs, folk songs, and **flamenco** melodies (songs of southern Spain infused with gypsy elements). The Habanera, which introduces the character Carmen, makes use of a then-popular Spanish song.

Literally, **habanera** means "the thing from Havana." Musically, it is a type of dance song that developed in Spanish-controlled Cuba during the early nineteenth century. African and Latin influences on its musical style can perhaps be seen in the descending chromatic scale, and certainly in the static harmony (the downbeat of every measure is a D in the bass), as well as in the insistent, repetitious rhythm (♩♫♩ | ♩♫♩). The infectious rhythm gives the habanera its irresistible quality—we all want to get up and join the dance. But the habanera is a sensual dance, like its descendant the tango, and this sensual quality contributes greatly to Carmen's seductive aura.

The structure of Bizet's Habanera is straightforward. At first, Carmen sings a descending chromatic line of four 4-bar phrases ("Love is like an elusive bird"). By their nature, highly chromatic melodies often seem to have no tonal center. This one, too, is musically noncommittal and slippery, just as Carmen herself is both ambiguous and evasive. The chorus immediately repeats the chromatic melody, but now Carmen glides voluptuously above it, singing the single word "*L'amour*" ("Love"). As her voice soars, like the elusive bird of love, the tonality brightens from minor to major. To this is then added a refrain ("Love is like a gypsy child") in which the melody alternates between a major triad and a minor one. Against this refrain, the chorus shouts, "Watch out!" warning of Carmen's destructive qualities. This same structure—a chromatically descending melody, followed by a triadic refrain with choral shouts—then repeats. Bizet wanted his Habanera to establish the character of Carmen as a sensual enchantress. In every way, the music *is* Carmen. And like Carmen, once this seductive melody has us in its spell, it will never let go.

Listening Guide

Georges Bizet, Habanera, from *Carmen* (1875)

Situation: The scantily clad gypsy woman Carmen, exuding an almost primeval sexuality, dances before Don José, soldiers, and other gypsies.

4/17

| 0:00 | 17 | Bass ostinato with habanera rhythm; minor mode |

Stanza 1

| 0:06 | Carmen enters with enticing descending melody. |

L'amour est un oiseau rebelle	Love is like an elusive bird,
Que nul ne peut apprivoiser;	That cannot be tamed;
Et c'est bien en vain qu'on l'appelle,	You call it in vain
S'il lui convient de refuser.	If it decides to refuse.
Rien n'y fait, menace ou prière,	Neither threat nor prayer will prevail;
L'un parle bien, l'autre se tait;	One man talks a lot, the other is silent;
Et c'est l'autre que je préfère	And it's the latter I prefer,
Il n'a rien dit; mais il me plaît.	He hasn't said a word, but he pleases me.

| 0:41 | Change to major mode; chorus repeats melody; Carmen soars above on "L'amour." |

| 0:57 | Carmen sings refrain. |

L'amour est enfant de Bohème,	Love is like a gypsy child,
Il n'a jamais connu de loi,	Who has never known constraint,
Si tu ne m'aimes pas, je t'aime;	If I love you, and you don't love me,
Si je t'aime, prends garde à toi!	Watch out!

| 1:14 | Chorus shouts, "Prends garde à toi!" |

| 1:37 | Chorus sings refrain with Carmen. |

| 2:14 | Bass ostinato with habanera rhythm |

Stanza 2

| 2:21 | Carmen enters with enticing chromatic melody. |

L'oiseau que tu croyais surprendre	The bird you thought you'd surprised
Battit de l'aile et s'envola;	Beat its wings and flew away;
L'amour est loin, tu peux l'attendre;	Love is far away, but expect it;
Tu ne l'attends plus, il est là!	You don't expect it, but there it is!
Tout autour de toi, vite,	All around you, quick!
Il vient, s'en va, puis il revient;	It comes, it goes, and then it returns;
Tu crois le tenir, il t'évite;	You think you've trapped it, it escapes;
Tu crois l'éviter, il te tient!	You think you've escaped it, it traps you!

| 2:55 | Change to major mode; chorus repeats melody; Carmen soars above on "L'amour." |

| 3:11 | Carmen, chorus (3:51), and then Carmen (4:09) again sing refrain. |

🔊 Listen to streaming music in an Active Listening Guide at CourseMate or in the eBook.

🔊 Take online Listening Exercise 25.1 and receive feedback at CourseMate or in the eBook.

To see Carmen in all her dangerous allure from a production of the Royal Opera House Covent Garden, go to the YouTube playlist at CourseMate for this text.

Figure 25.2

Beyoncé Knowles poses with the red dress that she wore in *Carmen: A Hip Hopera*.

At its premiere in Paris on March 3, 1875, *Carmen* was a flop—the realistic subject matter was thought too degrading. Despondent over this poor reception, composer Georges Bizet suffered a fatal heart attack exactly ninety days later.

As the nineteenth century progressed and theatrical subjects became increasingly realistic, however, the appeal of *Carmen* grew. Now arguably the world's most popular opera, *Carmen* has been recorded many times and has been transformed into nearly twenty films, including an early silent movie (1915) and an Academy Award–winning production (1984). In addition, the most popular melodies of *Carmen* serve as background music in countless TV commercials and cartoons, and are sometimes the object of parody (witness the Muppets' hilarious spoof of the Habanera). In an early episode of *The Simpsons*, the family goes to the opera, where it hears—what else?—*Carmen*, and Bart and Homer sing along. *Carmen* has also been refashioned into an African opera set in Senegal (*Karmen Gei*, 2001), an African American Broadway musical (*Carmen Jones*, 1954), and an MTV special (*Carmen: A Hip Hopera*, starring Beyoncé Knowles, 2001; Fig. 25.2). Not surprisingly for a realistic opera, *Carmen* is a work that transcends race and class, a quality that accounts in part for its lasting popularity.

See a video of the Muppets' Habanera performance, in the YouTube playlist at CourseMate for this text.

Great Opera for the Price of a Movie

The digital revolution has transformed the way we produce and consume music. Not every aspect of this technological change has been positive. With new media constantly clamoring for our attention, for example, it grows increasingly difficult to persuade children to take music lessons at home. There is little doubt, however, of one huge benefit: Classical music has become more accessible than ever. A case in point is the new series of HD broadcasts from the Metropolitan Opera. Some dozen times a year, the Met now streams live performances from New York to select theaters across the United States, Canada, and fifty-four other countries around the globe. The audio is of the highest quality (in Dolby Digital Surround Sound) and the video stunning (with multiple cameras for close-ups and zooms). Begun by general manager Peter Gelb, the aim of this initiative is to make opera more relevant to contemporary society and to stem the "graying of the audience." To appeal to a younger public, Gelb has borrowed a tactic from Hollywood: presenting singers who excel at acting and are telegenic. The result has been phenomenal. In 2011, some 3 million viewers in 1,600 theaters watched HD broadcasts, bringing $11 million in profit to the company—a sizeable sum in an era when most opera houses struggle to stay afloat. Such success is not surprising. The camera for the HD broadcasts is continually close to the performers, sometimes even shooting from backstage. This gives the viewer the equivalent of a front-row seat or better, a privilege that, in person, would cost about $450. If you don't have hundreds of dollars to spare for a ticket and a flight to New York, simply Google "Met live in HD + your local city" to find the what, when, and where of the broadcasts. The experience is breathtaking and the cost roughly that of a movie!

The rising superstar and Met HD favorite, Peruvian tenor Juan Diego Flóres

Giacomo Puccini's *La bohème* (1896)

Italian realistic opera of the late nineteenth century goes by its own special name, **verismo** opera (*verismo* is Italian for "realism"). Yet while it enjoys a separate name, *verismo* opera in Italy was little different from realistic opera elsewhere. Although many Italian composers wrote *verismo* operas, by far the best known today is Giacomo Puccini.

Giacomo Puccini (1858–1924) descended from four generations of musicians living in the northern Italian town of Lucca. His father and his grandfather had both written operas, and his forebears before them had composed religious music for the local cathedral. But Puccini, like Verdi, was no child prodigy. For a decade following his graduation from the Milan Conservatory, he lived in poverty as he struggled to develop a distinctive operatic style. Not until the age of thirty-five did he score his first triumph, the *verismo* opera *Manon Lescaut* (1893). Thereafter, successes came in quick order: *La bohème* (1896), *Tosca* (1900), and *Madama Butterfly* (1904). Growing famous, wealthy, and a bit complacent, Puccini worked less and less frequently. His last, and many believe his best, opera, *Turandot*, remained unfinished at the time of his death from throat cancer in 1924.

Puccini's best-known opera—indeed, the most famous of all *verismo* operas—is *La bohème* (*Bohemian Life*, 1896). The realism of *La bohème* rests in the setting and characters: The principals are bohemians—unconventional artists living in abject poverty. The hero, Rodolfo (a poet), and his pals Schaunard (a musician), Colline (a philosopher), and Marcello (a painter), inhabit an unheated attic on the Left Bank of Paris. The heroine, Mimi, their neighbor, is a poor, tubercular seamstress. Rodolfo and Mimi meet and fall in love. He grows obsessively jealous while she becomes progressively more ill. They separate for a time, only to return to each other's arms immediately before Mimi's death. If this sounds familiar, there may be a reason: The Pulitzer Prize–winning musical *Rent* (1996, produced as a motion picture in 2005) is a modern adaptation of this bohemian tale, but there the protagonist dies of AIDS in Greenwich Village, rather than of tuberculosis in Paris.

In truth, *La bohème* hasn't much of a plot, nor does it have much character development. Instead, the glorious sound of the human voice (*bel canto* singing) carries the day. Puccini continues the nineteenth-century tendency to lessen the distinction between recitative and aria. His solos typically start syllabically (no more than one note per syllable), as if the character is beginning a conversation. Gradually, the voice grows in intensity and becomes more expansive, with the strings doubling the melody to add warmth and expression. When Rodolfo, for example, sings of Mimi's frozen little hand in the aria "Che gelida manina" ("Ah, What a Frozen Little Hand"), we move imperceptibly from recitative to aria, gradually transcending the squalor of the Left Bank garret and soaring to a better world far beyond. The contrast between the dreary stage setting and the transcendental beauty of the music is the great paradox of realistic opera.

Figure 25.3

Giacomo Puccini

Tully Potter/Lebrecht Music and Arts Photo Library

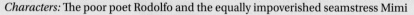
Giacomo Puccini, "Che gelida manina," from *La bohème* (1896)

5   2

4/18   2/12

Characters: The poor poet Rodolfo and the equally impoverished seamstress Mimi

Situation: Mimi has knocked on Rodolfo's door to ask for a light for her candle. Charmed by the lovely stranger, he naturally obliges. The wind again blows out Mimi's candle, and amidst the confusion, she drops her key. As the two search for it in the darkness, Rodolfo by chance touches her hand and then, holding it, seizes the moment to tell her about himself and his hopes.

Performer: The tenor here is the renowned Placido Domingo

0:00	Rodolfo begins conversationally, much as in recitative.	Che gelida manina se la lasci riscaldar. Cercar che giova? Al buio non si trova. Ma per fortuna è una notte di luna, e qui la luna l'abbiamo vicina.	Ah, what a frozen little hand, let me warm it up. What's the good of searching? We won't find it in the dark. But by good luck there is moonlight tonight, and here we have the moon nearby.
	(Mimi tries to withdraw her hand.)	Aspetti, signorina, le dirò con due parole	Wait, young lady, I will tell you in two words
1:03	Voice increases in range, volume, and intensity, as Rodolfo explains who he is and what he does.	chi son, e che faccio, come vivo. Vuole? Chi son? Sono un poeta. Che cosa faccio? Scrivo. E come vivo? Vivo!	who I am and what I do, how I live. Would you like this? Who am I? I'm a poet. What do I do? I write. How do I live? I live!
1:55	Return to conversational style	In povertà mia lieta scialo da gran signore rime et inni d'amore. Per sogni et per chimere e per castelli in aria, l'anima ho milionaria.	In my delightful poverty I grandiosely scatter rhymes and songs of love. Through dreams and reveries and through castles in the air, I have the soul of a millionaire.
2:27	Voice grows more expansive with longer notes and higher range; orchestra doubles voice in unison.	Talor dal mio forziere ruban tutti i gioelli due ladri: gli occhi belli. V'entrar con voi pur ora, ed i miei sogni usati e i bei sogni miei tosto si dileguar! Ma il furto non m'accora,	Sometimes from the strongbox two thieves steal all the jewels: two pretty eyes. They came in with you just now and my usual dreams, my lovely dreams vanish at once! But the theft doesn't bother me,
3:25	Orchestra sounds melody alone; then is joined by voice for climactic high note on "speranza!"	poichè v'ha preso stanza la speranza!	Because their place has been taken by hope!
3:47	As music diminishes, Rodolfo asks for a response from Mimi.	Or che mi conoscete, parlate voi, deh! parlate. Chi siete? Vi piaccia dir!	Now that you know who I am, Tell me about yourself, speak! Who are you? Please speak!

🔊 Listen to streaming music in an Active Listening Guide at CourseMate or in the eBook.

See the role of Rodolfo sung in 1990 by Luciano Pavarotti, arguably the greatest tenor of the twentieth century, in the YouTube playlist at CourseMate for this text. You can also hear a younger (and vocally better) Pavarotti sing a concert version of the same aria in 1964.

Key Words

realistic opera (295)   habanera (296)
flamenco (296)   *verismo* opera (299)

For a complete review of this chapter, see the Main Points, Chapter Quiz, Flashcards, and Glossary in CourseMate.

Join us on Facebook at **Listening to Music with Craig Wright**

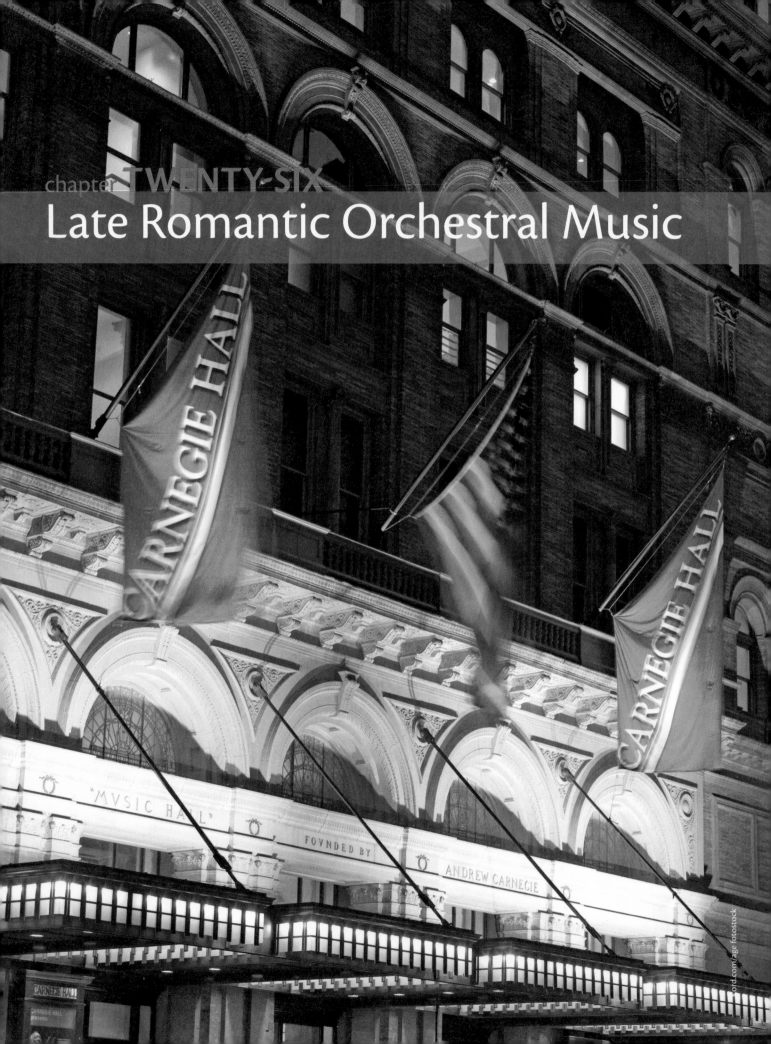

chapter **TWENTY-SIX**

Late Romantic Orchestral Music

The symphony orchestra reached its full glory in the late nineteenth century, developing into a colorful, powerful force of more than 100 players. But to hear it, listeners had to make a special trip to a large concert hall; computers, smartphones, and electronically amplified sounds were still far in the future. Today, of course, digital downloads of classical music are only a click away. But accessibility has come at a price; the recent revolution in electronically disseminated music has been accompanied by a general decline in the quality of sound that we hear. Listening to Beethoven or Wagner via compressed MP3 or M4A files gives only a vague approximation of the nineteenth-century original. To experience a symphony orchestra at its best, as did listeners in the late Romantic era, we must journey to a large concert hall with great architecture, ambience, and acoustics.

Romantic Values and Today's Concert Hall

The growth of the symphony orchestra coincided with the construction of large, "music-only" halls in Europe as well as the United States in the second half of the nineteenth century. Prior to 1850 the public concert hall was actually a multipurpose theater in which a concert of classical music one night would be followed by an opera the next, and then perhaps by a circus or horse show. (Recall, for example, Fig. 18.6, in which horses are seen on the very same stage where Beethoven's famous Symphony No. 5 premiered.) After 1850, however, prosperous cities around the globe began to erect auditoriums exclusively for classical concerts; the halls built about this time in Vienna (Musikverein, 1870), New York (Carnegie Hall, 1891; see chapter opener), and Boston (Symphony Hall, 1900) remain the finest ever constructed, notable especially for their excellent acoustics. The new Walt Disney Concert Hall in Los Angeles (2003) and the Schermerhorn Symphony Center in Nashville (2006) continue this tradition. Indeed, the Schermerhorn Center (Ch. 1 opener) copies many of the architectural features of the Viennese Musikverein (Fig. 26.1). All of these venues were built to be large halls—"temples" for classical music—seating 2,000 to 2,700 listeners.

JazzSign/Lebrecht Music & Arts

Figure 26.1

Vienna's Musikverein (Music Center) was initiated by admirers of Beethoven and often played host to Brahms. It set the standard throughout the Western world for a "music-only" environment and for quality acoustics.

Because classical music is a conservative art, what today's concertgoer experiences does not differ much from what listeners of the late Romantic era experienced. The concert hall is about the same size (average of 2,500 seats), and the symphony orchestra performing there includes about the same number of musicians (100 or more players at full strength). So, too, have the mainstays of the repertoire remained unchanged since the end of the nineteenth century; now, as then, the orchestral genres of symphony and concerto feature prominently on the concert program.

The Late Romantic Symphony and Concerto

The symphony orchestra is so called because it most often performs a genre of music called the symphony. Symphonic composers in the Romantic period generally continued to follow the four-movement format inherited from their Classical forebears—(1) fast, (2) slow, (3) minuet or scherzo, and (4) fast. Yet throughout the nineteenth century, the movements grew progressively in length. Perhaps as a consequence, composers wrote fewer symphonies. Schumann and Brahms composed only 4; Mendelssohn, 5; Tchaikovsky, 6; and Dvořák, Bruckner, and Mahler, 9 each. No one approached the 40-odd symphonies of Mozart, to say nothing of Haydn's 106.

Similarly for the concerto, with expanded length came a reduction in number. A Classical concerto may last twenty minutes, a Romantic concerto forty; Mozart gave us twenty-three piano concertos, but Beethoven only five. Beethoven, Mendelssohn, Brahms, and Tchaikovsky penned just a single violin concerto apiece, yet each is a substantial showpiece for the soloist. Despite its growing length, the Romantic concerto retained the three-movement plan established during the Classical period: fast, slow, fast. To sum up, although everything about an orchestral concert expanded in scope during the Romantic period—the hall, the audience, the performing forces, and the length of the pieces—the genres of symphony and concerto remained preeminent.

Johannes Brahms (1833–1897)

It took courage for a late Romantic composer such as Johannes Brahms even to contemplate the creation of a large, multimovement symphony or concerto. How could one possibly top the monumental works of Beethoven? Wagner asked why anyone after Beethoven bothered to write symphonies at all, given the dramatic impact of Beethoven's Third, Fifth, and Ninth. Wagner himself wrote only one, and Verdi none. Some composers, notably Berlioz and Liszt, turned to a completely different sort of symphony, the program symphony (see Ch. 21), in which an external scenario determined the nature and order of the musical events. Not until the late Romantic period—nearly fifty years after the death of Beethoven—did Johannes Brahms emerge to assume the role of Beethoven's successor.

Brahms was born in the north German port city of Hamburg in 1833. He was given the Latin name Johannes to distinguish him from his father, Johann, a street musician and beer-hall fiddler. Although Johannes's formal education never went beyond primary school, his father saw to it that he received the best training on the piano and in music theory, with the works of Bach and Beethoven given pride of place. While he studied these masters by day, by night Brahms earned money playing out-of-tune pianos in "stimulation bars" on the Hamburg waterfront. (During 1960–1962, The Beatles went to Hamburg to play in the descendants

Watch a video of Craig Wright's Open Yale Course class session 20, "The Colossal Symphony: Beethoven, Berlioz, Mahler, and Shostakovich," at CourseMate for this text.

Figure 26.2

Johannes Brahms in his early thirties. Said an observer of the time, "The broad chest, the Herculean shoulders, the powerful head, which he threw back energetically when playing—all betrayed an artistic personality replete with the spirit of true genius."

© The Art Archive/Historisches Museum (Museen der Stadt Wien), Vienna/Gianni Dagli Orti

of these strip joints.) To get his hands on better instruments, Brahms sometimes practiced in the showrooms of local piano stores.

Brahms first caught the public's attention in 1853, when Robert Schumann published a highly laudatory article proclaiming him a musical messiah, the heir apparent to Haydn, Mozart, and Beethoven. Brahms, in turn, embraced Robert and his wife, Clara (see Fig. 20.3), as his musical mentors. After Robert was confined to a mental institution, Brahms became Clara's confidant, and his respect and affection for her ripened into love, despite the fact that she was fourteen years his senior. Whether owing to his unconsummated love for Clara or for other reasons, Brahms remained a bachelor all his life.

Disappointed first in love and then in his attempt to gain a conducting position in his native Hamburg, Brahms moved to Vienna in 1863. He supported his modest lifestyle—very "un-Wagnerian," he called it—by performing and conducting. His fame as a composer increased dramatically in 1868 with performances of his *German Requiem,* which was soon sold to amateur choruses around the world. In this same year, he composed what is today perhaps his best-known piece, the simple yet beautiful art song *Wiegenlied,* known among English speakers as "Brahms's Lullaby" (see Ch. 3 and (intro)/20). Honorary degrees from Cambridge University (1876) and Breslau University (1879) attested to his growing stature. After Wagner's death in 1883, Brahms was generally considered the greatest living German composer. His own death, from liver cancer, came in the spring of 1897. He was buried in the central cemetery of Vienna, thirty feet from the graves of Beethoven and Schubert.

Vienna was (and remains) a musical yet conservative city, fiercely protective of its rich cultural heritage. That Brahms should choose it as his place of residence is not surprising—Vienna had been the home of Haydn, Mozart, Beethoven, and Schubert, and the conservative Brahms found inspiration in the music of these past masters (Fig. 26.3). Again and again, he returned to traditional genres, such as the symphony, concerto, quartet, and sonata, and to conventional forms, such as sonata–allegro and theme and variations. Most telling, Brahms composed no program music. Instead, he chose to write **absolute music**, chamber sonatas, symphonies, and concertos without narrative or "storytelling" intent. The music of Brahms unfolds as patterns of pure, abstract sound within the tight confines of traditional forms. Although Brahms could write lovely Romantic melodies, he was at heart a contrapuntalist, a "developer" in the tradition of Bach and Beethoven. Indeed, he was to be dubbed the last of the famous "three B's": Bach, Beethoven, and Brahms.

Alfredo Dagli Orti/The Art Archive at Art Resource, NY

Figure 26.3

Brahms's composing room in Vienna. On the wall, looking down on the piano, is a bust of Beethoven. The spirit of Beethoven loomed large over the entire nineteenth century (see also Fig. 18.2) and over Brahms in particular.

Violin Concerto in D major (1878)

In 1870, Brahms wrote, "I shall never compose a symphony! You have no idea how the likes of us feel when we hear the tramp of a giant like him behind us." That "giant," of course, was Beethoven, and Brahms, like other nineteenth-century composers, was terrified by the prospect of competing with his revered predecessor. But Brahms did go on to write a symphony—indeed, four of them, first performed, in turn, in 1876, 1877, 1883, and 1885. In the midst of this symphonic activity, Brahms also wrote his only violin concerto, which rivals the earlier violin concerto of Beethoven in scope and emotional impact.

How do you write a concerto for an instrument that you can't play? Can you possibly know how to make the instrument sound good and what to avoid? Brahms, by training a pianist and not a violinist, did as composers before and after him: He turned to a virtuoso on the instrument—in this case, his friend Joseph Joachim (1831–1907). When the concerto was premiered in 1878, Joachim played the solo part while Brahms conducted the orchestra. One technical trick that Joachim surely insisted Brahms employ is the art of playing **double stops**. Usually, we think of the violin as a monophonic instrument, capable of executing only one line of music at a time. But a good violinist can hold (stop) two and sometimes more strings simultaneously and sweep across them with the bow. This imparts a richer, more brilliant sound to the soloist's part. Example 26.1 shows how Brahms incorporates double stops into the melody of the last movement of his concerto.

EXAMPLE 26-1

Figure 26.4

American-born violin virtuosa Hilary Hahn, whose spirited and beautifully clear performance is heard in our recording, which she made at the age of twenty-two

When he arrived at the finale of his Violin Concerto, Brahms the conservative turned to a form traditionally used in the last movement of a concerto: the rondo. Recall that a rondo centers on a single theme that serves as a musical refrain. Here the refrain has the flavor of a gypsy tune, like the Hungarian dances Brahms often heard in Viennese cafés as he sipped beer and chatted with friends. What marks this refrain is its lively rhythm: ( ). Above this foot-tapping motive, the violin sometimes soars with difficult passage work (scales, arpeggios, and double stops). The makers of the Academy Award–winning *There Will Be Blood* (2007) chose this movement by Brahms to serve as the background music in their film—perhaps to represent the tug of war (concerto) between the greedy oil man and the landowners. Indeed, the nineteenth-century solo concerto was not only a "concerted" effort by all participants, but also a contest between soloist and orchestra. In Brahms's work, the orchestra sometimes supports the soloist and sometimes competes with it, running away with the rondo theme. Listen to this exciting movement and declare a winner: soloist, orchestra, or listener.

Listening Guide

Johannes Brahms, Violin Concerto in D major (1878)

Third movement, *Allegro giocoso, ma non troppo vivace* (fast and playful, but not too lively)

Genre: Concerto

Form: Rondo

5   2

4/19–21 2/13–15

WHAT TO LISTEN FOR: The give and take as soloist and orchestra wrestle over the refrain, as well as the heavy technical demands that Brahms places on a soloist such as violinist Hilary Hahn (see Fig. 26.4)

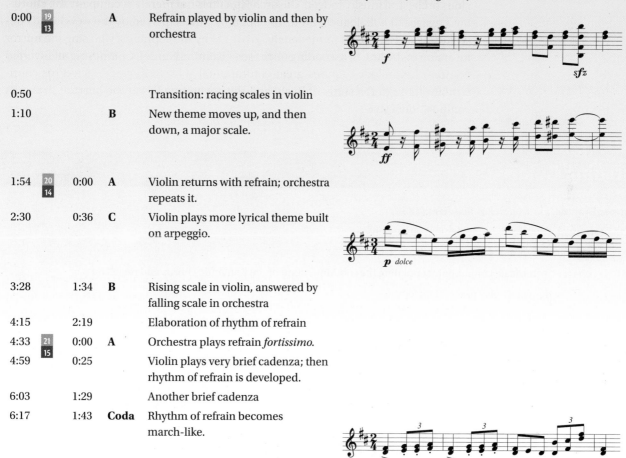

0:00	19 13		A	Refrain played by violin and then by orchestra
0:50				Transition: racing scales in violin
1:10			B	New theme moves up, and then down, a major scale.
1:54	20 14	0:00	A	Violin returns with refrain; orchestra repeats it.
2:30		0:36	C	Violin plays more lyrical theme built on arpeggio.
3:28		1:34	B	Rising scale in violin, answered by falling scale in orchestra
4:15		2:19		Elaboration of rhythm of refrain
4:33	21 15	0:00	A	Orchestra plays refrain *fortissimo*.
4:59		0:25		Violin plays very brief cadenza; then rhythm of refrain is developed.
6:03		1:29		Another brief cadenza
6:17		1:43	**Coda**	Rhythm of refrain becomes march-like.

🔊 Listen to streaming music in an Active Listening Guide at CourseMate or in the eBook.

🔊 Take online Listening Exercise 26.1 and receive feedback at CourseMate or in the eBook.

A Requiem for the Concert Hall: Brahms's *Ein Deutsches Requiem* (1868)

Though a conservative at heart, Brahms's output includes a number of innovative works. Notably, it was Brahms who brought the sacred Requiem Mass into the secular concert hall, using his skill as a choral composer to expand the boundaries of late romantic orchestral music.

When we think of a "Requiem," what first comes to mind is a Latin Mass, performed in the Catholic Church for the burial of the dead. In writing his *Deutsches Requiem* (*German Requiem*), however, Brahms created music for neither a Catholic Mass—nowhere is heard the voice of God on the Day of Judgment—nor a Protestant funeral service. Instead, Brahms composed an ecumenical work in his native German that could be performed in a concert hall. His *Deutsches Requiem* is a profession of faith that extends sounds of solace to all who have suffered the loss of a loved one. For Brahms personally, the inspiration for the work seems to have stemmed from the death of his mentor Robert Schumann and the more recent loss of his mother.

The emotional core of this hour-long, seven-movement work is found in its fourth movement. "Wie lieblich sind deine Wohnungen" ("How lovely is Thy dwelling place"), says the text of Psalm 84, and before us looms an image of the heavenly House of the Lord. Imitating the blissful souls in heaven, a four-part chorus sings praises to God in a skillful blend of homophonic and polyphonic textures. This is religious orchestral music. Indeed, the orchestra does not merely accompany the chorus, but engages in a dialogue with it. The opening phrase played by the woodwinds descends peacefully but is immediately answered by the sopranos, who sing the mirror inversion of the line in ascending form (see Listening Guide). Composing an inverted version of a melody requires great contrapuntal skill. Brahms perfected his counterpoint through the study of Bach, and this technique lies at the heart of Brahms's compositional style.

Listening Guide

Johannes Brahms, *Ein Deutsches Requiem* (1868)

Fourth movement, "Wie lieblich sind deine Wohnungen"

Text: Psalm 84, verses 1, 2, and 4

5
4/22–23

WHAT TO LISTEN FOR: Intricate counterpoint enriching the soothing sound of the Romantic chorus and orchestra

0:00 `22` Woodwinds play peaceful melody.

| 0:08 | Sopranos respond in same mood. | Wie lieblich sind deine Wohnungen, Herr Zebaoth! | How lovely is Thy dwelling place, O, Lord of Hosts! |

0:46 Tenors sing same text;
basses, altos, and sopranos
follow in imitative counterpoint.

| 1:26 | More imitative counterpoint is sung with strong accents in orchestra. | Meine Seele verlanget und sehnet sich nach den Vorhöfen des Herrn; | My soul longs and thirsts for the courts of the Lord; |

1:59		Chorus sings homophony with strong accents in orchestra.	Mein Leib und Seele freuen sich in dem Lebendigen Gott.	Mine body and soul rejoice in the living God.
2:26	23 0:00	Return of opening music in orchestra and then chorus	Wie lieblich . . .	How lovely . . .
3:15	0:49	Chorus quietly sings chordal homophony.	Wohl denen, die in deinem Hause wohnen,	Blessed are they who dwell in Thy house,
3:38	1:12	Chorus declaims its praise of the Lord in forceful imitative counterpoint.	die loben Dich immerdar.	Where they praise You ever after.
4:27	2:01	Return of opening music and text	Wie lieblich . . .	How lovely . . .

Listen to streaming music in an Active Listening Guide at CourseMate or in the eBook.

Antonín Dvořák (1841–1904)

"There is no doubt that he is very talented. He is also very poor." Thus Johannes Brahms wrote to the music publisher Simrock in 1876, describing then-unknown Czech symphonist Antonín Dvořák. The son of a butcher, Dvořák was a native of Bohemia, an area of the Czech Republic south of Prague. He, too, passed an apprenticeship to be a butcher, but a prosperous uncle saw musical talent in the teenager and sent him to study organ in Prague for a year. Thereafter, for nearly two decades, Dvořák eked out a living as a freelance violist and organist in Prague, playing in dance bands, the opera orchestra, and church. All the while he composed tirelessly—operas, symphonies, string quartets, and songs, almost all of which went unheard. When recognition came, it did so not through these learned forms, but rather through simpler music that could be played on the piano at home. Hoping to capitalize on a bit of musical nationalism (see Ch. 21), Simrock published Dvořák's *Slavonic Dances* (1878), a set of eight pieces for piano duet that incorporate the spirit of the folk dances of the Czechs (a subset of the Slavs). The pieces were wildly popular, and Dvořák was soon known throughout Europe. Now even his more ambitious "high art" works were given performances in London, Berlin, Vienna, Moscow, Budapest, and even the United States, in Cincinnati—which then included a large German and Czech contingent among its population.

In the spring of 1892, Dvořák received an offer he couldn't refuse. He was promised the astonishing sum of $15,000 per year (the equivalent of about $650,000 today) to become director of the newly founded National Conservatory of Music in New York City. And so, on September 17, 1892, Dvořák set sail for America and took up residence at 327 East 17th Street. Here he immediately began work on his "American" Quartet and his Symphony No. 9, "From the New World." Instead of returning to Prague that summer, Dvořák and his family traveled, mostly by train, to Spillville, Iowa. Spending three months among the mainly Czech-speaking people of this rural farming community, he finished his ninth and last symphony.

Symphony No. 9 in E minor, "From the New World" (1893)

The symphony "From the New World" proved to be the capstone of Dvořák's career and remains today by far his best-known work. It received a rousing premiere in New York at America's most prestigious new concert venue, Carnegie Hall (see chapter opener), on December 16, 1893. As Dvořák wrote to publisher Simrock the following week:

DR. DVORAK'S GREAT SYMPHONY.

"From the New World" Heard for the First Time at the Philharmonic Rehearsal.

ABOUT THE SALIENT BEAUTIES.

First Movement the Most Tragic, Second the Most Beautiful, Third the Most Sprightly.

INSPIRED BY INDIAN MUSIC.

The Director of the National Conservatory Adds a Masterpiece to Musical Literature.

Dr. Antonin Dvorak, the famous Bohemian composer and director of the National Conservatory of Music, dowered American art with a great work yesterday, when his new symphony in E minor, "From the New World," was played at the second Philharmonic rehearsal in Carnegie Music Hall.

The day was an important one in the musical history of America. It witnessed the first public performance of a noble composition.

It saw a large audience of usually tranquil Americans enthusiastic to the point of frenzy over a musical work and applauding like the most excitable "Italianissimi" in the world.

The work was one of heroic porportions. And it was one cast in the art form which such poet-musicians as Beethoven, Schubert, Schumann, Mendelssohn, Brahms and many another "glorious one of the earth" has enriched with the most precious outwellings of his musical imagination.

And this new symphony by Dr. Antonin Dvorak is worthy to rank with the best creations of those musicians whom I have just mentioned.

Small wonder that the listeners were enthusiastic. The work appealed to their sense of the æsthetically beautiful by its wealth of tender, pathetic, fiery melody; by its rich harmonic clothing; by its delicate, sonorous, gorgeous, ever varying instrumentation.

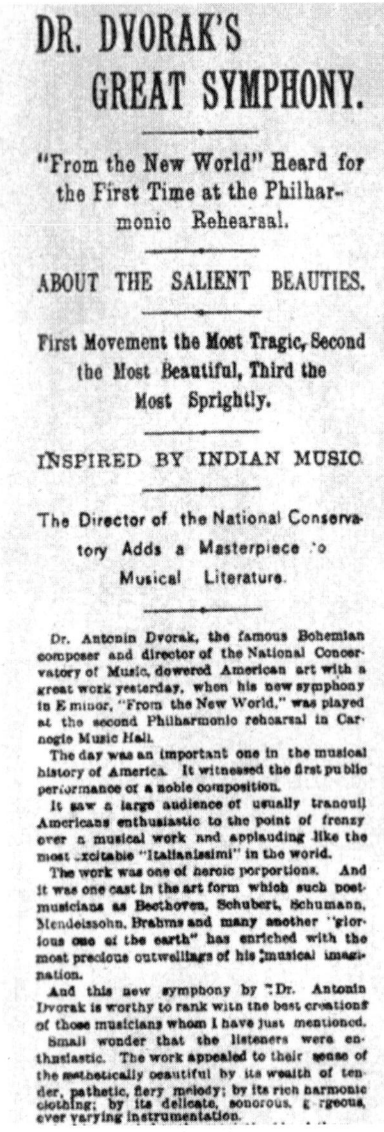

Figure 26.5

A review of the premiere of the symphony "From the New World" in the *New York Herald*, December 17, 1893. The author actually reviewed the dress rehearsal, a practice still common today.

The success of the symphony was tremendous. The papers write that no composer has ever had such a triumph [Fig. 26.5]. I was in a box. The hall was filled with the best New York audience. The people clapped so much that I had to thank them from the box like a king! You know how glad I am if I can avoid such ovations, but there was no getting out of it, and I had to show myself [to take bows] like-it-or-not.

The title Dvořák gave to this symphony, "From the New World," might suggest he placed within it musical elements that are distinctly American. Yet while Dvořák showed a keen interest in the indigenous music of African Americans and American Indians, none of the many tuneful melodies heard in the symphony has yet been identified as a preexisting folk song. At the very least, the composer seems to have re-created the spirit of his American experience, writing a moving tribute to the memory of some distant home.

Although an energetic and tuneful first movement and a powerful finale frame the symphony "From the New World," the slow second movement is the emotional soul of the work. A mood of calm strength envelops the opening, a memorable moment for players of brass instruments and listeners alike. Once this solidly serene atmosphere is established, a haunting melody emerges from the English horn (Fig 26.6). Throughout the Romantic period, the English horn was used to suggest feelings of distance and nostalgia—to create the effect of looking back on a time, place, and people (friends, relatives, countrymen) that existed no longer. Although the genesis of this theme remains unclear, we do know that it came to represent "home" in the psyche of many turn-of-the-century Americans; a publisher extracted this signature tune from the symphony and printed it as a song under the title "Goin' Home."

But to *whose* home? Is this a melody composed from scratch by Dvořák in the style of a folk song, or is it one taken from an African American colleague? Is it distinctly American or Czech? In truth, the melody (see Listening Guide) is built around a pentatonic scale (here $D\flat$ $E\flat$ F, $A\flat$ $B\flat$ which, as we have seen (Ch. 21), is characteristic of folk music around the world. But such is the power of music: Each listener can experience in this movement the memories and emotions of his own homeland, no matter where it may lie.

Craig Wright

Figure 26.6

A diplomatic facsimile of an autograph sketch of the famous English horn theme from the second movement of Dvořák's symphony "From the New World." The tempo was later changed from *andante* to *largo* and some of the notes altered to emphasize the pentatonic scale, a traditional signifier of "the folk." For example, compare the sketch to the final version in the Listening Guide, and notice that the G♭s. have been removed. In other words, the second note in the facsimile is different from the second note in the musical example.

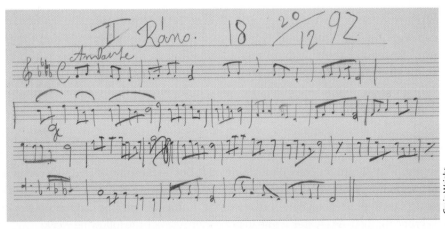

Antonín Dvořák, Symphony No. 9 in E minor, "From the New World" (1893)

Second movement, *Largo* (very slow and broad)

4/24–26

Form: **ABCA'**

WHAT TO LISTEN FOR: The initial fullness of the brass projecting a sense of a vast horizon, then the slow, mournful tune of the English horn, the signature song of the movement, seeming to recall a distant past

A Section

0:00	24	Solemn introductory chords in low brass choir, then timpani
0:40		English horn solo, the "Goin' Home" melody

1:06	Clarinet joins English horn, then strings join as well.
2:20	Introductory chords now played by high woodwinds and French horn, concluded by brasses and timpani
2:48	Strings repeat and extend "Goin' Home" melody.
3:44	Melody returns to English horn and is completed by woodwinds and strings.
4:25	French horn echoes the melody.

B Section

4:48	25	0:00	Faster tempo and new theme (**B1**) in flute and oboe

5:20	0:32	Second new theme (**B2**) in clarinets above bass pizzicato

6:10	1:22	Melody **B1** played more insistently by violins
7:25	2:37	Melody **B2** played more intensely by violins

C Section

8:28	3:40	Oboe introduces chirping of flute and clarinet.
8:54	4:06	Brasses play *fortissimo* recall of first theme of first movement.
9:10	4:22	Diminuendo and lovely transition back to **A**

A Section

9:23	26	0:00	English horn brings back "Goin' Home" melody.
9:47		0:25	Pairs of violins and violas play melody but break off, as if choked by emotion.
10:18		0:55	Solo cello and solo violin play melody, then full strings join.
10:54		1:31	Quiet soliloquy by violins
11:22		1:59	Final return and extension of opening chords

🔊 Listen to streaming music in an Active Listening Guide at CourseMate or in the eBook.

The Orchestral Song

The history of nineteenth-century music can be seen as a development of musical extremes: small-scale private music for the home (mostly piano character pieces and art songs) and large-scale public music for the opera house and concert hall (mostly symphonies and concertos). So great was the attraction of the large symphony orchestra, however, that a domestic genre, namely, the art song, gradually found its way to the concert hall, thereby producing a hybrid genre: the orchestral song. An **orchestral song** (or **orchestral *Lied***) is an art song in which the full orchestra replaces the piano as the medium of accompaniment. Because a large orchestra can add more color and a greater number of contrapuntal lines, the orchestral song grew longer, denser, and more complex than the piano-accompanied art song. The orchestral song provided the best of both worlds—an intimate poem full of Romantic sentiment as well as a powerful medium with which to express it. In the *Lieder* of Gustav Mahler, song and orchestra joined to yield a sound both extravagant and idiosyncratic. The extravagance is typical of late-nineteenth-century music; the idiosyncrasies derive from Mahler's unusual personality.

Gustav Mahler (1860–1911)

Gustav Mahler (Fig. 26.7) was born in 1860 into a middle-class Jewish family living in Moravia, now encompassed by the Czech Republic. As did many other gifted Czechs at that time, however, Mahler moved to a larger, more cosmopolitan German city to advance his career. At the age of fifteen, he enrolled in the prestigious Vienna Conservatory of Music, where he studied composition and conducting. Mahler felt that his mission in life was to conduct—to interpret—the works of the masters ("to suffer for my great masters," as he phrased it). Like most young conductors, he began his career in provincial towns, gradually working his way to larger and more important musical centers. His itinerary as resident conductor took him, among other places, to Kassel (1883–1884), Prague (1885–1886), Leipzig (1886–1888), Budapest (1888–1891), Hamburg (1891–1897), and finally back to Vienna.

In May 1897, Mahler returned triumphantly to his adopted city as director of the Vienna Court Opera, a position Mozart had once coveted. The next year he also assumed directorship of the Vienna Philharmonic, then and now one of the world's great orchestras. But Mahler was, in contemporary terms, a "control freak," a tyrant in search of an artistic ideal; he filled his scores with countless small expression marks and then insisted the orchestra do exactly as he prescribed. That he drove himself as hard as he pushed others was little comfort to the singers and instrumentalists who had to endure his wrath during rehearsals. After ten stormy but artistically successful seasons (1897–1907), Mahler was dismissed from the Vienna Opera. About this time, he accepted an offer from New York to take charge of the Metropolitan Opera, and eventually he conducted the New York Philharmonic as well. (The first season alone he earned $325,000 in today's money for three months' work.) Here, too, both acclaim and controversy coexisted. And here, too, at least at the Met, his contract was not renewed after two years, though he stayed on longer, until February 1911, with the Philharmonic. He died in Vienna in May 1911 of a lingering streptococcal infection that had attacked his weak heart—a tragic end to an obsessive and somewhat tormented life.

Figure 26.7

Gustav Mahler

Bettmann/CORBIS

Orchestral Song *Ich bin der Welt abhanden gekommen* (*I Am Lost to the World*; 1901–1902)

Mahler is unique among composers in that he wrote only orchestral songs and symphonies. Songs, however, seem to have come first, both chronologically and psychologically. He began his career as a composer setting various collections of poetry to music: *Lieder eines fahrenden Gesellen* (*Songs of a Wayfaring Lad,* 1883–1885), *Des Knaben Wunderhorn* (*A Youth's Magic Horn,* 1888–1896), *Kindertotenlieder* (*Songs on the Death of Children,* 1901–1904), and the *Five Rückert Songs* (1901–1902).

Friedrich Rückert was a German Romantic poet whose verse had been set previously by Schubert, as well as by both Robert and Clara Schumann. During the summers of 1901 and 1902, Mahler selected five of the many hundreds of Rückert's poems and created a group of orchestral songs—among his finest works in this genre. With the help of Rückert's verse, the composer was able to express perfectly his own outlook on life and on art.

Ich bin der Welt abhanden gekommen—the third of the *Five Rückert Songs*—speaks of the artist's growing remoteness from the travails of everyday life and his withdrawal into a private, heavenly world of music, here signified by the final word: "*Lied*" ("song"). Although the poem has three stanzas, Mahler chose not a strophic setting, but a through-composed one, which enabled him to depict the emotional progression of the text. The first strophe sets the mood of the song; a mournful English horn begins to play a halting melody, which is then picked up and extended by the voice. The second stanza moves to a faster tempo, with more rapid vocal declamation, as if the mundane world should be quickly left behind. The final strophe returns to a slow tempo. Here, the composer sets the notes of the bass on the beat and on the roots of triads, projecting a settled, satisfied feeling—the self-absorbed poet-composer has begun to withdraw into the peaceful realm of art. In the poignant closing measures of the song, Mahler neatly encapsulates the entire message of the poem. First, the strings (at 6:23) play an extended dissonance (F against E♭), which resolves to a consonance (E♭ against E♭). This gesture is repeated at the very end (at 6:39) by the English horn, "dying out expressively (*morendo*)," as the composer requests. The journey from the dissonant exterior world into the consonant sphere of art and self has been fulfilled.

Listening Guide

Gustav Mahler, *Ich bin der Welt abhanden gekommen*, from *Five Rückert Songs* (1901–1902)

5/1–2

Genre: Orchestral song

Form: Through-composed

WHAT TO LISTEN FOR: A mournful English horn, lush but languid strings, and the beautiful dissonance-consonance conclusion as the musician finds inner peace

0:00	1		English horn haltingly rises with melody.		
1:00			Voice enters and extends melody.	Ich bin der Welt abhanden gekommen, mit der ich sonst viele Zeit verdorben;	I am lost to the world, in which I've squandered so much time;
				sie hat so lange nichts von mir vernommen,	it has known nothing of me for so long,
1:56			English horn returns with melody.	sie mag wohl glauben, ich sei gestorben!	it may well think that I am dead!
2:34			Triplets in harp; faster tempo, recitative quality in voice	Es ist mir auch gar nichts daran gelegen, ob sie mich für gestorben hält. Ich kann auch gar nichts sagen dagegen, denn wirklich bin ich gestorben der Welt.	I don't really care, if it takes me for dead. Nor can I contradict, for really I am dead to the world.
3:39	2	0:00	Melody returns in English horn; slow, peaceful conclusion.	Ich bin gestorben dem Weltgetümmel und ruh' in einem stillen Gebiet! Ich leb' allein in meinem Himmel, in meinem Lieben, in meinem Lied.	I am dead to the world's commotion, and rest in a world of peace. I live alone in my own heaven, in my love, in my song.
5:47		2:08	English horn returns with melody.		

(continued)

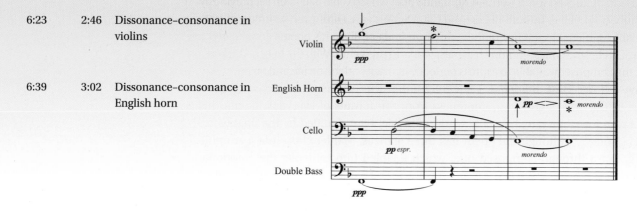

| 6:23 | 2:46 | Dissonance–consonance in violins |
| 6:39 | 3:02 | Dissonance–consonance in English horn |

🔊 Listen to streaming music in an Active Listening Guide at CourseMate or in the eBook.

So important was vocal writing to Mahler that when the composer turned to the traditional four-movement symphony, he did something unusual—he brought the song into the instrumental genre. Mahler's collection of single-movement songs served as a musical repository, or vault, to which the composer could return for inspiration while wrestling with the problems of a large, multimovement work for orchestra. His First Symphony (1889), though entirely instrumental, makes use of melodies already present in his song cycle *Lieder eines fahrenden Gesellen*. His Second (1894), Third (1896), and Fourth (1901) symphonies incorporate various portions of the *Wunderhorn* songs as solo vocal parts. Symphonies Five (1902) and Six (1904) are again purely instrumental, but once more borrow preexisting melodies from earlier songs. (In the former, *Ich bin der Welt abhanden gekommen* forms the basis of a beautiful slow movement.) Altogether, Mahler finished nine symphonies, seven of which make use of his own orchestral *Lieder* or other preexisting vocal music.

To Mahler though, a symphony was much more than just an extended orchestral *Lied*. "The symphony is the world; it must embrace everything," he once said. And so he tried to embrace every sort of music within his symphonic writing. Folk dances, popular songs, military marches, off-stage bands, bugle calls, and even Gregorian chant all sound at various points in his symphonies (Fig. 26.8). What results is a collage of sound on the grandest scale, one achieved, in part, by employing massive forces and a greatly extended sense of time. Mahler's Symphony No. 2, for example, calls for ten horns and eight trumpets, and lasts an hour and a half. And the first performance of his Symphony No. 8 in Munich in 1910 involved 858 singers and 171 instrumentalists! With good reason, it has been nicknamed the "Symphony of a Thousand."

Gustav Mahler was the last in the long line of great German symphonists that extends back through Brahms, Schubert, and Beethoven to Mozart and, ultimately, to Haydn. What had begun as a modest instrumental genre with a limited emotional range had grown in the course of the nineteenth century into a monumental structure, the musical equivalent, in Mahler's view, of the entire cosmos. As he said: "Try to imagine the whole universe beginning to ring and resound. These are no longer human voices, but planets and suns revolving."

Figure 26.8

A satire of Gustav Mahler conducting one of his colossal symphonies. As the cartoonist suggests, his symphonies contain the whole world of sound, from bird songs and nursery rhymes, to bells and whistles, to military music.

© Imagno/Getty Images

absolute music (305)   double stops (306)   orchestral song (orchestral *Lied*) (312)

For a complete review of this chapter, see the Main Points, Chapter Quiz, Flashcards, and Glossary in CourseMate.

Join us on Facebook at **Listening to Music with Craig Wright**

Checklist of Musical Style

Romantic: 1820–1900

REPRESENTATIVE COMPOSERS

Beethoven	Chopin	Dvořák
Schubert	Liszt	Tchaikovsky
Berlioz	Verdi	Musorgsky
Mendelssohn	Wagner	Mahler
Robert Schumann	Bizet	Puccini
Clara Schumann	Brahms	

A complete Checklist of Musical Style for the Romantic era can be found at CourseMate for this text.

PRINCIPAL GENRES

symphony	tone poem (symphonic poem)	solo concerto
program symphony	opera	character piece for piano
dramatic overture	art song (*Lied*)	ballet music
concert overture	orchestral song (orchestral *Lied*)	

Melody	Melody is more flexible and irregular in shape than in the Classical period; long, singable lines with powerful climaxes and chromatic inflections for expressiveness
Harmony	Greater use of chromaticism makes the harmony richer and more colorful; sudden shifts to remote chords for expressive purposes; prolonged dissonance conveys feelings of anxiety and longing
Rhythm	Rhythms are free and relaxed, occasionally obscuring the meter; tempo can fluctuate greatly (tempo *rubato*) and sometimes slows to a crawl to allow for "the grand gesture"
Color	The orchestra becomes enormous, reaching upward of one hundred performers: trombone, tuba, contrabassoon, piccolo, and English horn added to the ensemble; experiments with new playing techniques for special effects; dynamics vary widely to create extreme levels of expression; piano becomes larger and more powerful
Texture	Predominantly homophonic but dense and rich because of larger orchestras and orchestral scores; sustaining pedal on the piano also adds to density
Form	No new forms created; rather, traditional forms (strophic, sonata–allegro, and theme and variations, for example) used and extended in length; traditional forms also applied to new genres such as tone poem and art song

part SIX

Modern and Postmodern Art Music, 1880–Present

1880	1890	1900	1910	1920	1930	1940

MODERNISM AND POSTMODERNISM

- 1894 Claude Debussy composes *Prelude to The Afternoon of a Faun*

- 1905 Charles Ives finishes *Variations on America*

- 1907 Pablo Picasso paints *Les Demoiselles d'Avignon*

- 1912 Arnold Schoenberg composes *Pierrot lunaire*

- 1913 Igor Stravinsky composes *The Rite of Spring*

1914–1918 World War I

- 1924 Joseph Stalin takes control of Soviet government

- 1929 Crash of American stock market and beginning of Great Depression

- 1935 Sergey Prokofiev composes ballet *Romeo and Juliet*

- 1937 Dmitri Shostakovich composes Symphony No. 5

1939–1945 World War II

Although historians like things neat and tidy, the creative activity of humanity cannot be easily pigeonholed. Trends and styles overlap, making it difficult to identify the end of the old and the beginning of the new. Setting the dates of "Modernism" and "Postmodernism" is a particularly thorny task. Until recently, historians have usually referred to "modern" music simply as "twentieth-century" music. But modern musical idioms appeared in some Impressionist music of the late nineteenth century, whereas aspects of musical Romanticism continue to exist even today, particularly in film scores. Similarly, "Postmodernism" may have begun as early as the 1930s and continues to develop during our own times. Given that the terms "Modern" and "Postmodern" together connote a large, overlapping musical period, then, what are a few of the features that mark this epoch?

At the beginning of the twentieth century, composers increasingly turned against the warm sentimentality characteristic of nineteenth-century music, replacing this Romantic aesthetic with an increasingly harsh, percussive, impersonal sound. Melodies become more angular and harmonies more dissonant. Simultaneously, the massive compositions of the late Romantic period—perhaps best represented by Gustav Mahler's "Symphony of a Thousand" (1910)—yield to smaller, less extravagant works. The abstract, impersonal quality of modern music is most clearly evident in Arnold Schoenberg's rigid twelve-tone music. In the 1960s, a reaction against the formalism of Schoenberg and his disciples contributed to the increasing popularity of musical Postmodernism, which allowed for a diversity of musical genres—electronic music and chance music, for example—performed in unconventional ways. Modernism had turned and done battle with traditional musical styles. Postmodernism, on the other hand, dispenses entirely with conventional musical forms and processes, saying, in effect: "Any creator can have whatever artistic values he or she wishes."

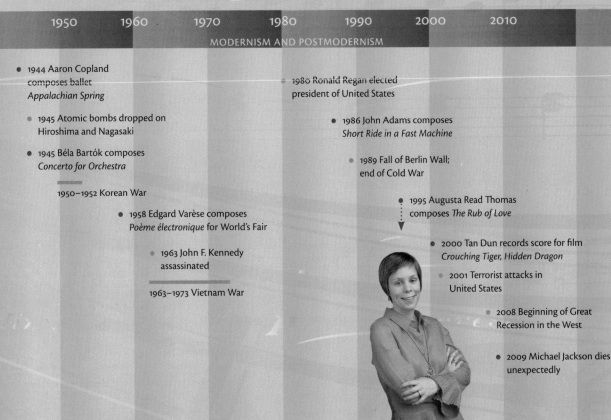

| 1950 | 1960 | 1970 | 1980 | 1990 | 2000 | 2010 |

MODERNISM AND POSTMODERNISM

1944 Aaron Copland composes ballet *Appalachian Spring*

1945 Atomic bombs dropped on Hiroshima and Nagasaki

1945 Béla Bartók composes *Concerto for Orchestra*

1950–1952 Korean War

1958 Edgard Varèse composes *Poème électronique* for World's Fair

1963 John F. Kennedy assassinated

1963–1973 Vietnam War

1980 Ronald Regan elected president of United States

1986 John Adams composes *Short Ride in a Fast Machine*

1989 Fall of Berlin Wall; end of Cold War

1995 Augusta Read Thomas composes *The Rub of Love*

2000 Tan Dun records score for film *Crouching Tiger, Hidden Dragon*

2001 Terrorist attacks in United States

2008 Beginning of Great Recession in the West

2009 Michael Jackson dies unexpectedly

Impressionism and Exoticism

mpressionism is a musical style midway between the lush sounds of Romanticism and the dissonant bombshells of Modernism. As we have seen, Romantic music reached its peak during the late nineteenth century in the grandiose works of Wagner, Tchaikovsky, Brahms, and Mahler. But by 1900, this German-dominated musical empire had started to crumble. Some composers outside the mainstream of Romanticism challenged the validity of the predominantly German style, epitomized by the music of Wagner. Not surprisingly, the most powerful anti-German sentiment was felt in France. (France and Germany went to war in 1870 and would do so again in 1914.) French composers began to ridicule German music as being too heavy, too pretentious, and too bombastic, like one of Wagner's Nordic giants. Meaningful expression, it was believed, might be communicated in more subtle ways, in something other than epic length and sheer volume of sound.

Impressionism in Painting and Music

The movement that arose in France in opposition to German Romantic music has been given the name **Impressionism**. We are, of course, more familiar with this term as a designation for a school of late-nineteenth-century painters working in and around Paris, including Claude Monet (1840–1926), Auguste Renoir (1841–1919), Edgar Degas (1834–1917), Camille Pissarro (1830–1903), and the American Mary Cassatt (1844–1926).

The chapter opener shows Claude Monet's *Impression: Sunrise* (1873), a painting that lent its name to an epoch. There, the ships, rowboats, and other elements in the early morning light are more suggested than fully rendered. In 1874, Monet submitted this painting for exhibition at the Salon of the French Academy of Fine Arts, but it was rejected. One critic, Louis Leroy, derisively said: "Wallpaper in its most embryonic state is more finished than that seascape." In the uproar that followed, Monet and his fellow artists were disparagingly called "impressionists" for the seemingly imprecise quality of their art. The painters accepted the name, partly as an act of defiance against the establishment, and soon the term was universally adopted.

French Impressionism, which once generated such controversy, is now, ironically, the most popular of all artistic styles. Indeed, if we judge by museum attendance and reproductions sold, almost limitless enthusiasm exists for the art of Monet, Degas, Renoir, and their associates—precisely the paintings that the artists' contemporaries mocked and jeered. But what quality about the Impressionist style initially caused such a furor?

The Impressionists saw the world as awash in vibrant rays of light and sought to capture the aura that sun-dappled objects created in the eyes of the beholder (Fig. 27.1). To accomplish this, they covered their canvases with small, dab-like brushstrokes in which light was broken down into spots of color, thereby creating a sense of movement and fluidity. Shapes are not clearly defined but blurred, more suggested than delineated. Minor details disappear. Sunlight is everywhere and everything shimmers.

As impressions and sensations became paramount for turn-of-the-century painters, not surprisingly, they showed an intensified interest in music. What art form is more elusive and suggestive? What medium allows the receiver—the listener—more freedom to interpret the sensations he or she perceives? Painters began to speak in musical terms. Paul Gauguin (1848–1903) referred to the harmonies of line and color as the "music of painting," and Vincent

Figure 27.1

Claude Monet, *Woman with Umbrella* (1886). The Impressionist canvas is not a finished surface in the traditional sense. Rather, the painter breaks down light into separate dabs of color and juxtaposes them for the viewer's eye to reassemble. Here, bold brushstrokes convey an astonishing sense of movement, freshness, and sparkling light.

Woman with Parasol Turned to the Left, 1886 (oil on canvas), Monet, Claude (1840–1926)/Musee d'Orsay, Paris, France/Giraudon/The Bridgeman Art Library

Figure 27.2

Claude Debussy at the age of twenty-four

Watch a video of Craig Wright's Open Yale Course class session 21, "Musical Impressionism and Exoticism: Debussy, Ravel, and Monet," at CourseMate for this text.

Figure 27.3

The poet Stéphane Mallarmé, author of "The Afternoon of a Faun," as painted by the great predecessor of the Impressionists, Edouard Manet (1832–1883). Mallarmé was a friend and artistic mentor of the composer Debussy.

van Gogh (1853–1890) suggested "using color as the music of tones." James Whistler (1844–1903), an American who worked in Paris in the 1860s and 1880s, created "nocturnes" and "symphonies." The painters envied the musicians' good fortune to work in a medium that changed continually, rather than one requiring the artist to seize one moment and fix it on canvas.

For their part, musicians found inspiration in the Impressionist art of the day. They, too, began to work with dabs of color. Claude Debussy, whose compositions most consistently displayed the Impressionist style in music, was delighted to be grouped with the Impressionist painters. "You do me great honor by calling me a pupil of Claude Monet," he told a friend in 1916. Debussy gave various collections of his compositions such artistic titles as *Sketches, Images,* and *Prints.* Composer Maurice Ravel (1875-1937) referred to painting by metaphor when he said: "The French composers of today work on small canvases, but each stroke of the brush is of vital importance." Rare are the moments in history when the aesthetic aims of painters and musicians were so closely aligned.

Claude Debussy (1862–1918)

Debussy was born in 1862 into a modest family living in a small town outside Paris. As neither of his parents was musical, it came as a surprise when their son demonstrated talent at the keyboard. At the age of ten, Debussy was sent to the Paris Conservatory for lessons in piano, composition, and music theory. Owing to his skill as a performer, he was soon engaged for summer work in the household of Nadezhda von Meck, a wealthy patroness of the arts and the principal supporter of Tchaikovsky (see Fig. 21.6). This employment took him, in turn, to Italy, Russia, and Vienna. In 1884, he won the Prix de Rome, an official prize in composition funded by the French government, one that required a three-year stay in Rome. But Debussy was not happy in the Eternal City. He preferred Paris with its bistros, cafés, and bohemian ambience.

Returning to Paris more or less permanently in 1887, the young Frenchman continued to study his craft and to search for his own independent voice as a composer. He had some minor successes, and yet, as he said in 1893: "There are still things that I am not able to do—create masterpieces, for example." But the next year, in 1894, he did just that. With the completion of *Prélude à l'Après-midi d'un faune (Prelude to The Afternoon of a Faun),* he gave to the public what has become his most enduring orchestral work. Debussy's later compositions, including his opera *Pelléas et Mélisande* (1902), the symphonic poem *La Mer* (*The Sea,* 1905), and his two books of *Préludes* for piano, met with less popular favor. Critics complained that Debussy's works lacked traditional form, melody, and forward motion—in other words, that they possessed characteristics of the Modernism that was to come. Illness and the outbreak of World War I in 1914 brought Debussy's innovations to a halt. He died of cancer in the spring of 1918, while the guns of the German army were shelling Paris from the north.

Prelude to The Afternoon of a Faun (1894)

Debussy spent more of his time in the company of poets and painters than musicians. His orchestral *Prelude to The Afternoon of a Faun,* in fact, was written to precede a stage reading of the poem "The Afternoon of a Faun" by his friend and mentor Stéphane Mallarmé (1842–1898; Fig. 27.3), the leader of a progressive group of poets called the **Symbolists**. The faun of Mallarmé's poem is not a young deer but a satyr (a mythological beast that is half man, half goat), who spends his days in lustful pursuit of the nymphs of the forest. On this afternoon, we see the faun, exhausted from the morning's escapades, reclining on the forest floor in the still air of the midday heat (Fig. 27.4). He contemplates future conquests while blowing listlessly on his panpipes. The following passage from Mallarmé's poem suggests the dream-like mood, vague and elusive, that Debussy sought to re-create in his musical setting:

No murmur of water in the woodland scene,
Bathed only in the sounds of my flute.
And the only breeze, except for my two pipes,
Blows itself empty long before
It can scatter the sound in an arid rain.
On a horizon unmoved by a ripple
This sound, visible and serene,
Mounts to the heavens, an inspired wisp.

Figure 27.4

Mallarmé's "The Afternoon of a Faun" created something of a sensation among late nineteenth-century artists. This painting by Pal Szinyei Merse (1845–1920) is just one of several such representations of the faun and woodland nymphs. Notice that he holds classical panpipes, which Debussy transformed into the sound of the flute.

Not wishing to compose narrative programmatic music in the tradition of Berlioz or Tchaikovsky, Debussy made no effort to follow closely the events in Mallarmé's poem. As he said at the time of the first performance in December 1894: "My *Prelude* is really a sequence of mood paintings, throughout which the desire and dreams of the Faun move in the heat of the midday sun." When Mallarmé heard the music, he, in turn, said the following about Debussy's musical response to the poem: "I never expected anything like it. The music prolongs the emotion of my poem and paints its scenery more passionately than colors could."

Note that both musician and poet refer to *Prelude to The Afternoon of a Faun* in terms of painting. But how does one create a painting in music? Here, a musical tableau is depicted by using the distinctive colors of the instruments, especially the woodwinds, to evoke vibrant moods and sensations. The flute has one timbre, the oboe another, and the clarinet yet a third. Debussy has said, in effect: "Let us focus on the sound-producing capacity of the instruments, let us see what new shades can be elicited from them, let us try new registers, let us try new combinations." Thus a solo flute begins in its lowest register (the pipes of the faun), followed by a harp glissando, then dabs of color from the French horn. These tonal impressions swirl, dissolve, and form again, but seem not to progress. No repeating rhythms or clear-cut meters push the music forward; instead of a singable melody as we know it, we hear a twisting, undulating swirl of sound. All is languid beauty, a music that is utterly original and shockingly sensual.

Listening Guide

Claude Debussy, *Prelude to The Afternoon of a Faun* (1894)

Genre: Symphonic poem

Form: Ternary (**ABA'**)

5/3–5 2/16–18

WHAT TO LISTEN FOR *(and what you won't hear):* How colors and textures are of primary importance, while clear-cut melodies and foot-tapping rhythms are largely absent

(continued)

A

0:00 `3` `16`   Solo flute plays undulating line.

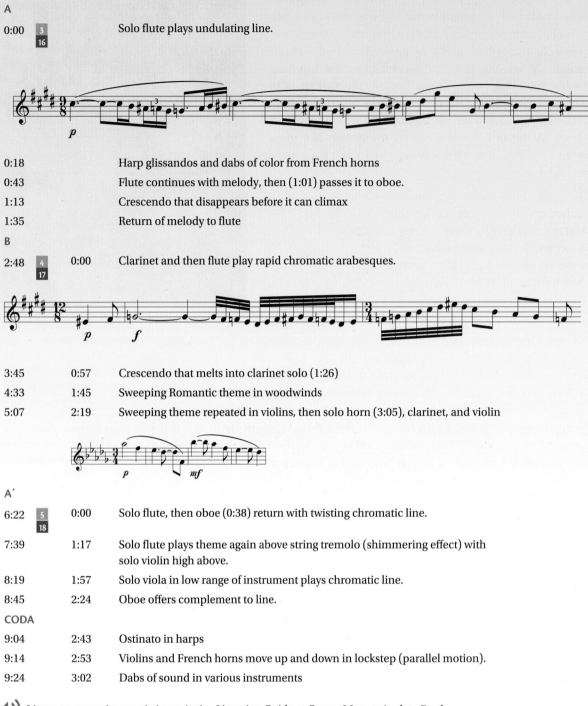

0:18   Harp glissandos and dabs of color from French horns

0:43   Flute continues with melody, then (1:01) passes it to oboe.

1:13   Crescendo that disappears before it can climax

1:35   Return of melody to flute

B

2:48 `4` `17`   0:00   Clarinet and then flute play rapid chromatic arabesques.

3:45   0:57   Crescendo that melts into clarinet solo (1:26)

4:33   1:45   Sweeping Romantic theme in woodwinds

5:07   2:19   Sweeping theme repeated in violins, then solo horn (3:05), clarinet, and violin

A'

6:22 `5` `18`   0:00   Solo flute, then oboe (0:38) return with twisting chromatic line.

7:39   1:17   Solo flute plays theme again above string tremolo (shimmering effect) with
                 solo violin high above.

8:19   1:57   Solo viola in low range of instrument plays chromatic line.

8:45   2:24   Oboe offers complement to line.

CODA

9:04   2:43   Ostinato in harps

9:14   2:53   Violins and French horns move up and down in lockstep (parallel motion).

9:24   3:02   Dabs of sound in various instruments

◀)) Listen to streaming music in an Active Listening Guide at CourseMate or in the eBook.

◀)) Take online Listening Exercise 27.1 and receive feedback at CourseMate or in the eBook.

Claude Debussy had clearly turned away from what he called the German "developmental agenda." Believing that music need not progress and evolve to be pleasing to the listener, Debussy created repetitive, ostinato-like melodies and harmonies that meander without a well-defined goal. He also demonstrated that music did not have to march along with a strong meter—it could just relax and enjoy the moment. Most important, Debussy replaced the German primacy of theme with an Impressionist primacy of color. For him, color might exist independent of melody and, perhaps, overshadow it.

Figure 27.5

Henri Matisse's *Red Studio* (1911). In a survey undertaken by *Time* magazine, this painting was voted No. 5 among the most influential works of modern art, owing primarily to the way the passionate red color escapes and overruns the linear boundaries of the objects.

Separating color from melodic line was a radical idea. Think back to the orchestral music of Beethoven, Brahms, and Tchaikovsky. In these earlier works, new themes are generally introduced by a new instrument or group of instruments. Instrumental color thus reinforces and gives profile to the melody. With Debussy, in contrast, instruments enter with a distinct color but no easily discernible theme. Thus, colors, and textures to some degree, begin to replace melody and harmony as the primary agents of musical expression. Debussy's approach was adopted by the revolutionary Modernists of twentieth-century music—among them, Charles Ives, Edgard Varèse, and John Cage (see Chs. 31 and 32)—who often generate musical form through colors and textures, rather than through thematic development. Not coincidentally, during the peak of Debussy's career (about the turn of the twentieth century), progressive painters began to separate color from line as well (Fig. 27.5).

Préludes for Piano (1910, 1913)

Debussy's last and most far-reaching attempt at evocative writing in music is found in the two books of *Préludes* for piano that he published in 1910 and 1913. In these pieces, the challenge to create musical impressions was all the greater, for the piano has a more limited musical palette than the colorful orchestra. The titles of some of these short pieces allude to their mysterious qualities: *Steps in the Snow, The Sunken Cathedral, What the West Wind Saw,* and *Sounds and Perfumes Swirl in the Night Air.*

Voiles (*Sails*), from the first book of *Préludes* of 1910, takes us to the sea (Fig. 27.6). As we hear a fluid descent, mostly in parallel motion, we imagine sails flapping listlessly in the breeze. The hazy, languid atmosphere is created in part by the special scale Debussy employs, the **whole-tone scale**, one in which all the pitches are a whole step apart:

EXAMPLE 27.1 Whole-Tone Scale

Because in the whole-tone scale each note is the same distance from its neighbor, no one pitch is heard as the tonal center—all pitches seem equally important. The composer can stop on any note of the scale, and it will sound no more central, or final, than any other note. The music floats without a tonal anchor. Then, as if impelled by

Figure 27.6

Claude Monet's *Sailboats* (1874). The rocking of the boats is suggested by the exaggerated reflections on the water.

Erich Lessing/Art Resource, NY

a puff of wind, the boats seem to rock on now-rippling waters. Debussy creates this gentle rocking sensation by inserting a four-note ostinato into the texture (Ex. 27.2). Frequently used by Impressionist composers, ostinatos help account for the often static, restful feeling in the harmony. By definition, ostinatos involve repetition and inertia rather than dramatic movement.

EXAMPLE 27.2 Ostinato

A new ostinato now appears in the upper register (right hand), while a succession of four-note chords sounds in the middle register (left hand) (Ex. 27.3). Notice that all four notes of each chord consistently move in what is called parallel motion. In **parallel motion**, all parts move together, locked in step, in the same direction.

EXAMPLE 27.3 Parallel Motion

left
hand

Parallel motion is the antithesis of counterpoint, the traditional musical technique in which two or more lines usually move in directions opposite to one another. Parallel motion was an innovation of Debussy, and it was one way he expressed his opposition to the German school of Wagner and Brahms, so heavily steeped in counterpoint.

Suddenly, a gust of wind seems to shake the ships as the pianist races up the scale in a harp-like glissando. This scale, however, is different from the preceding whole-tone one. It is a pentatonic scale (Ex. 27.4). The octave is divided into five notes, here corresponding to the black keys on the piano. We have seen before that the pentatonic scale is often found in folk music (see Ch. 21, Musorgsky, and Ch. 26, Dvořák). Debussy first encountered it in the Southeast Asian music he heard at the Paris World's Fair of 1889 (see box).

At the turn of the twentieth century, Paris was the cultural capital of the Western world, and its citizens were eager to turn their eyes and ears to the East. In 1889, the French government sponsored an *Exposition universelle* (World's Fair) which featured Far Eastern art. Here, painter Paul Gauguin (1848–1903) first became enamored with the tropical colors of the Pacific. Claude Debussy, too, made several visits. Not only did he see the newly completed Eiffel Tower and newfangled inventions like electric lighting and electric-powered elevators, but he also heard for the first time the exotic sounds of Southeast Asia. Colonial governments, including those of Cambodia, Vietnam, and Indonesia, had sent small ensembles of instrumentalists, singers, and dancers to perform in newly constructed pavilions. The Cambodian pagoda seems to have been the inspiration for a later piano piece called *Pagodes* (*Pagodas*, 1903). Debussy also encountered a colorful gamelan orchestra from Indonesia, as he recalled to a friend some years later: "Do you not remember the Javanese (Indonesian) music that was capable of expressing every nuance of meaning, even unmentionable shades, and makes our tonic and dominant sounds seem weak and empty?" This experience inspired Debussy to incorporate into his own music the sounds of the East: ostinatos, static harmonies, pentatonic and whole-tone scales, delicately layered textures, and shimmering surfaces. It also

The Cambodian pagoda at the World's Fair in Paris in 1889. Here Debussy heard the music of Cambodia, China, Vietnam, and Indonesia, and began to formulate a musical aesthetic different from the prevailing German symphonic tradition.

suggested to him that music did not always have to progress toward a goal—instead, it might simply exist for the moment.

EXAMPLE 27.4 Pentatonic Scale

Following this energized whirl around the pentatonic scale, the nautical scene regains its placid demeanor with the return of the whole-tone scale and, ultimately, the descending parallel thirds with which the piece began. At the end, Debussy directs the pianist to push down and hold the sustaining pedal (the rightmost of the three pedals). Once the sustaining pedal is pressed and held, all notes sounded thereafter will blur into vagueness, like the hazes and mists that envelop many Impressionist paintings (see chapter opener).

Listening Guide

Claude Debussy, *Voiles*, from *Préludes*, Book I (1910)

Form: Ternary (**ABA´**)

5/6

WHAT TO LISTEN FOR: How the composer has used different scales to differentiate the formal sections (**A** and **B**) but, more importantly, how he has created a new aesthetic, a sense of beauty very different in style from any German-tradition work we have heard

(continued)

0:00	6	A	Descending parallel thirds using whole-tone scale
0:10			Bass pedal point enters.
1:01			Ostinato enters in middle register.
1:38			Ostinato moves into top register; chords move in parallel motion in middle register.
2:09		B	Harp-like glissandos using pentatonic scale
2:23			Chords moving in parallel motion above pedal point
2:46			Glissandos now employing whole-tone scale
3:16		A´	Descending thirds return.
3:28			Glissandos blur through use of sustaining pedal.

))) Listen to streaming music in an Active Listening Guide at CourseMate or in the eBook.

Exoticism in Music

One of the magical qualities of music is its capacity to transport us to distant lands. Far-off places can be experienced in our minds, if only through the strange and mysterious sounds we associate with them. Composers at the turn of the twentieth century delighted in such vicarious journeys, and their music is brimming with the "exotic." Claude Debussy was strongly influenced by the art of the Far East (see box), and so, too, were the famous painters of the time. Impressionist Claude Monet lined the walls of his home in Giverny, France, not with his own canvases, but with prints and watercolors from Japan. Their influence can be seen in the startling portrait of his wife in traditional Japanese costume (Fig. 27.7). Modernists like Pablo Picasso (1881–1973) and Georges Braque (1882–1963) began collecting African art in Paris during the years 1905–1908. Some historians believe that the Cubist movement in painting (see Ch. 28) was born of Picasso's interest in African sculpture and ceremonial masks.

But what was the exotic in music? Briefly, **Exoticism** is a musical style communicated by any sound drawn from outside the traditional Western European musical experience, be it a non-Western scale, a folk rhythm, or a musical instrument. The opera composer Giacomo Puccini, for example, used a variety of techniques to transport his listeners to exotic locales: In *The Girl of the Golden West* (1910), he evokes the American West via references to native American Indian songs; and in *Madama Butterfly* (1904) he includes both American and Japanese melodies as these two cultures clash on the island of Japan. Puccini's exotic *tour de force* is his stunning *Turandot* (1926), in which listeners experience Chinese melodies, pentatonic scales, intervals moving in parallel motion, and traditional Chinese instruments, including gongs.

The Exotic of Spain: Ravel's *Bolero* (1928)

Although not as distant as China, Spain was nonetheless considered an exotic place by Northern Europeans in the late nineteenth and early twentieth centuries. The culture of southern Spain in particular, only thirty miles from the tip of North Africa, offered the mysterious allure of the New East. As French poet Victor Hugo (1802–1885) said: "Spain is still the Orient; Spain is half African, and Africa is half Asiatic." Like the poets and painters of France, French composers created art with a would-be Spanish character. Debussy composed an orchestral piece (*Ibéria,* 1908) and a piano work (*Evening in Grenada,* 1902) using Spanish melodies. Maurice Ravel wrote

Figure 27.7

Claude Monet, *La Japonaise* (*Madame Camille Monet in Japanese Costume*, 1876). Europe and America began to show an enthusiasm for things Japanese after the opening of trade with Japan in the 1850s. Fashionable Parisian women wore kimonos and furnished their homes with oriental furniture, prints, and *objets d'art*.

INTERFOTO/Fine Arts/Alamy

his first orchestral work (*Spanish Rhapsody,* 1907) and his last ballet (*Bolero,* 1928), as well as an opera (*The Spanish Hour,* 1911), on Spanish subjects. Yet ironically, neither Debussy nor Ravel ever set foot in Spain. As a friend of Ravel remarked: "He was the eternal traveler who never went there."

Indeed, Maurice Ravel (1875–1937) spent almost all of his life in Paris, a modest music teacher and composer earning a modest living. (Within his otherwise sedentary life of the imagination can be noted a single exception: a wildly successful tour of the United States undertaken in 1928.) For the most part, then, Ravel was content to conjure far-off lands through his exotic music, as he did in his final "voyage" to Spain—a modern-style ballet titled *Bolero.* A **bolero** is a sultry Spanish dance in a slow tempo and triple meter. For the first performance in Paris, on November 22, 1928, Ravel set the stage to look like a Spanish inn. A single light shone down on a female gypsy dancer, as in John Sargent's painting *Spanish Dancer* (Fig. 27.8). Around the room, male dancers sat listlessly, a few holding guitars as if to accompany the lone ballerina. In a style reminiscent of the seductive gypsy Carmen in the opera of that name (see Ch. 25), the female dancer begins, moving with ever-increasing passion. The men, one by one, rise and join in the dance of seduction. The sound gets louder and louder. With growing abandon, the entire company begins to sway to the repetitive, hypnotic music, moving inexorably toward a frenzied climax. After fourteen minutes, the melody suddenly rises in pitch, breaking the hypnotic spell, and the work comes to a crashing conclusion.

Most of the audience that first night in Paris cheered Ravel and his new work, but at least one woman yelled: "He's mad!" What excited the crowd's passions was that Ravel had written an extended work with only a single melody. The two versions of this theme—one a major-like form, the other minor-like—are repeated again and again. Ravel himself was somewhat ambivalent about his creation: "I have written only one masterpiece. That is the *Bolero.* Unfortunately, it contains no music." What Ravel meant by this paradoxical statement is that the piece has no development of the traditional German sort. The melody is entirely static. Instrumental color and the growing volume of sound are all it takes to make the listener want to join the spellbinding dance.

The Granger Collection, NYC

Figure 27.8

John Singer Sargent (1856–1925), *El Jaleo: Spanish Dancer.* Sargent was an American painter working in Paris who got caught up in the European enthusiasm for all things Spanish during the late nineteenth century.

Listening Guide

Maurice Ravel, *Bolero* **(1928)**

Genre: Ballet

Form: **AABBAABB** etc.

5

5/7

WHAT TO LISTEN FOR: By writing a two-part melody (**A** and **B**) that does nothing but repeat, Ravel forces the listener to concentrate on the kaleidoscopic changes of instrumental color. Note that space limitations on CD 5 preclude presenting the full recording there, but it can be heard in the downloads and streaming at CourseMate for this text.

0:00 **7** Snare drum (imitating castanets) and low strings begin two-bar rhythmic ostinatos.

(*continued*)

| 0:11 | Flute enters quietly with melody **A**. |
| 1:00 | Clarinet presents melody **A**. |

1:50	Bassoon enters with melody **B**, harp added to accompaniment.
2:40	High clarinet presents melody **B**.
3:25	Bassoon joins with snare drum in playing rhythmic ostinato.
3:31	Low oboe plays melody **A**.
4:20	Trumpet (with mute) and flute together play melody **A**.
5:10	Saxophone plays melody **B**.
6:00	High saxophone repeats melody **B**.
6:50	Two flutes, French horn, and celesta (keyboard instrument producing bell-like sound) together play melody **A**.
7:40	Several woodwind instruments play melody **A**.
8:29	Trombone plays melody **B**.
9:19	Woodwinds and French horn play melody **B** loudly.
10:02	Timpani added to accompaniment
10:08	First violins and woodwinds play melody **A**.
10:56	First and second violins and woodwinds play melody **A**.
11:44	Violins, woodwinds, and trumpets play melody **B**.
12:32	Violins, violas, cellos, woodwinds, and trumpets play melody **B**.
13:20	First violins, trumpets, and piccolos play melody **A**.
14:08	Same instruments, now with trombone added, play melody **A**.
14:50	Musical climax; melody **B** moves to higher pitch level and is extended.
15:11	Melody settles back down to original pitch level.
15:23	End: no melody, just rhythmic ostinato and cymbal crashes

Listen to streaming music in an Active Listening Guide at CourseMate or in the eBook.

Key Words

| Impressionism (319) | whole-tone scale (323) | Exoticism (326) |
| Symbolists (321) | parallel motion (324) | bolero (327) |

For a complete review of this chapter, see the Main Points, Chapter Quiz, Flashcards, and Glossary in CourseMate.

Join us on Facebook at **Listening to Music with Craig Wright**

Checklist of Musical Style

Impressionist: 1880–1920

REPRESENTATIVE COMPOSERS

Debussy   Ravel

PRINCIPAL GENRES

tone poem (symphonic poem)   orchestral song   character piece for piano
string quartet   opera   ballet music

A complete Checklist of Musical Style for the Modern era can be found at CourseMate for this text.

Melody	Varies from short dabs of sound to long, free-flowing lines; melodies are rarely tuneful or singable but instead twist and turn rapidly in undulating patterns
Harmony	Purposeful chord progressions replaced by static harmony; chords frequently proceed in parallel motion; use of nontraditional scale patterns (whole-tone, pentatonic) confuses sense of tonal center
Rhythm	Usually free and flexible with irregular accents, making it difficult to determine meter; rhythmic ostinatos used to give feeling of stasis rather than movement
Color	More emphasis on woodwinds and brasses and less on violins as primary carriers of melody; more soloistic writing to show that the color of the instrument is as important as, or more important than, the melody line it plays
Texture	Can vary from thin and airy to heavy and dense; sustaining pedal of the piano often used to create a wash of sound; glissandos run quickly from low to high or high to low
Form	Traditional forms involving clear-cut repetitions less frequent, although ternary form is not uncommon; composers try to develop a form unique and particular to each new musical work

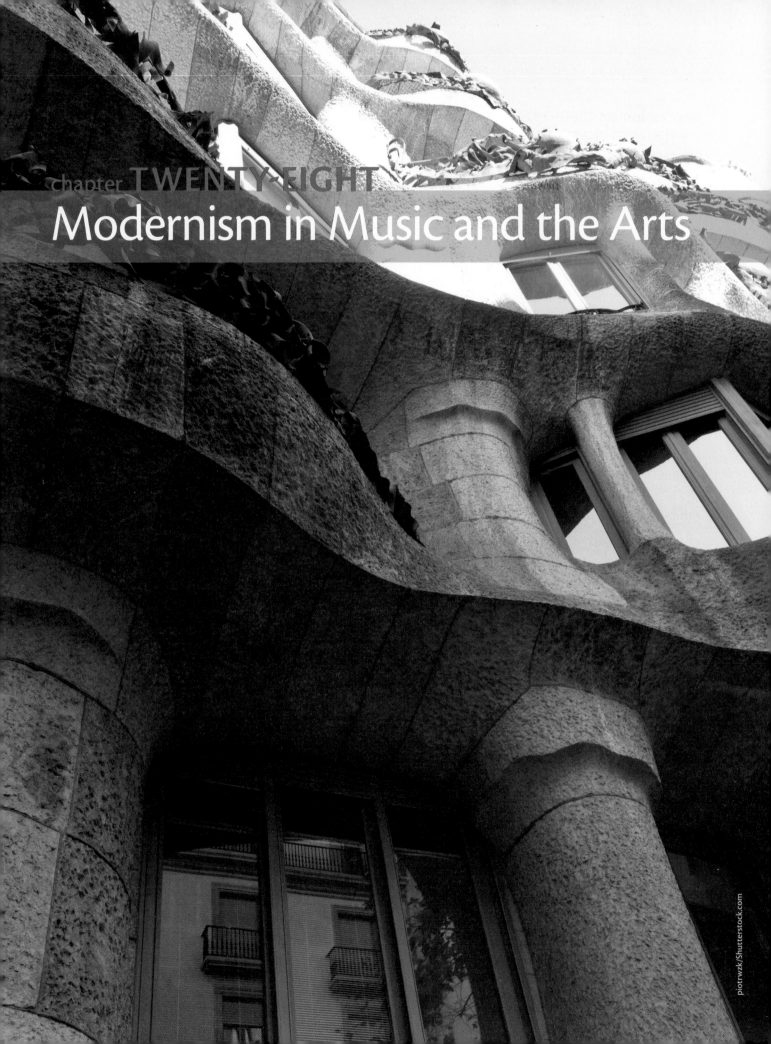

chapter TWENTY-EIGHT

Modernism in Music and the Arts

piotrwzk/Shutterstock.com

"A PIANO. If the speed is open, if the color is careless, if the selection of a strong scent is not awkward, if the button holder is held by all the waving color and there is no color, not any color."—Gertrude Stein, *Tender Buttons*

This verse about a piano was written by American poet Gertrude Stein (1874–1946) in 1914, while she was living in Paris. Can you make sense of it? Stein was a mentor of poet Ezra Pound (1885–1972) and novelist Ernest Hemingway (1899–1961); she also was the first to champion the works of Pablo Picasso (1881–1973) and Henri Matisse (1869–1954), thereby ushering in painting's Modernist age. **Modernism** is a bracing, progressive style that dominated classical music and the arts generally from the beginning to the end of the twentieth century. Today Modernist art is no longer "modern" in a chronological sense; some of it is now more than a hundred years old. But if "modern" means a radical departure from traditional values, then this description remains apt. It still shocks us more than the more recent art of the Postmodernist period (1945–present). Modernism took the usual expectations for a poem, for example—that it make sense as narrative or image, and possess proper grammar and syntax—and turned them upside down. So, too, with Modernist music: The concertgoer's expectations for what makes a good melody, pleasing harmony, and regular meter were confounded. Audiences of the early twentieth century were just as baffled by the Modernist sounds of Stravinsky and Schoenberg as they were by the poetry of Gertrude Stein that opens this chapter.

 ## Modernism: An Anti-Romantic Movement

Why did such a shockingly different kind of expression emerge shortly after 1900? In part because of a violent social disruption that shook Europe and (to a far lesser degree) North America: the run-up to, and outbreak of, World War I. For the Western world, the first two decades of the twentieth century constituted a social earthquake of the highest magnitude. World War I (1914–1918) left 9 million soldiers dead on the battlefields. Shocked by the carnage, intellectuals turned away from the predominantly idealistic, sentimental aesthetics of Romanticism—how could one think of love and beauty in the face of wholesale destruction? For writers, painters, and composers alike, disjunction, anxiety, and even hysteria became valid artistic sentiments that reflected the realities of the day.

Musicians of the early twentieth century did not turn away from the traditions of classical music. Instead, they confronted and altered them. They retained, for example, the genres of opera, ballet, symphony, concerto, and string quartet. They radically transformed, however, the elements of expression *within* these genres, creating new kinds of melody, harmony, rhythm, and tone color.

Radical experimentation in music began quietly enough in the music of the Impressionists—specifically, in Claude Debussy's early separation of color from line (see Ch. 27). But as World War I approached, a crescendo of protest could be heard in the music of the avant-garde. The progressives renounced the notion that music should be beautiful, pleasing, and expressive or that it should delight or comfort the listener. Instead, they distorted traditional musical practices, sometimes violently, with the intention of shocking audiences. Their compositions often achieved the intended effect: Arnold Schoenberg's early experiments with dissonance were received at first with hoots by a hostile public in Vienna in 1913; and Igor Stravinsky's dissonant chords and pounding rhythms caused a riot at the first performance of *Le Sacre du printemps (The Rite of Spring)* in Paris that same year. Such avant-garde composers sought to shake their listeners out of complacency, to yank them from the Romantic mists and back to harsh reality.

Watch a video of Craig Wright's Open Yale Course class session 22, "Modernism and Mahler," at CourseMate for this text.

Watch a film on Cubism as four-dimensional art in the YouTube playlist at CourseMate for this text.

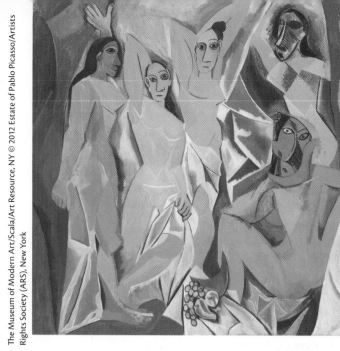

Figure 28.1

One of the first statements of Cubist art, Picasso's *Les Demoiselles d'Avignon* (1907). The ladies of the evening are depicted by means of geometric shapes on a flat, two-dimensional plane. Picasso had seen exhibitions of "primitive" African sculpture in Paris at this time and was much affected by its style, to which the mask-like faces of the women attest.

Figure 28.2

The aural dissonance heard in early-twentieth-century Modernism had its counterpart in the visual dissonances in avant-garde painting of that same time, as can be seen in Wassily Kandinsky's *Improvisation 28* (1909). We now call this style of painting—one emphasizing emotions to the exclusion of objects—abstract Expressionism (see Ch. 29).

One can see clear parallels between the music and visual art of this period: Early-twentieth-century painters also introduced radical distortions into their works, similarly offending conservative sensibilities. The increasingly angular melody and discontinuous rhythm of the new music found analogous expression in an artistic style called **Cubism**. In a Cubist painting, the artist fractures and dislocates formal reality into geometrical blocks and planes, as in the famous *Les Demoiselles d'Avignon* (Fig. 28.1), created in 1907 by Pablo Picasso, in which the female form has been recast into angular, interlocking shapes. Picasso seems to have found his musical counterpart in Stravinsky—the two friends admired each other's works and occasionally collaborated artistically. Schoenberg, a talented painter himself, found artistic camaraderie in the works of the German Expressionist painters (see Ch. 29), who so distorted formal reality that objects in their paintings were sometimes barely recognizable. Just as traditional (singable) melody disappeared from early Modernist music, so, too, the conventional figure vanished from avant-garde painting (see Fig. 28.2).

Early-Twentieth-Century Musical Style

The early twentieth century was a period of stylistic diversity and conflict. During these years, Gustav Mahler continued to write his massive symphonies in a predominantly Romantic idiom (see Ch. 26), while Claude Debussy composed in the Impressionist style (see Ch. 27), an early French forerunner of Modernism. At the same time, the most progressive composers of art music turned to unprecedented, indeed shocking, new ways of expressing melody, harmony, rhythm, and tone color.

Melody: More Angularity and Chromaticism

Unlike the melodies of the Romantic period, many of which are song-like in style and therefore easily sung and remembered, twentieth-century music has very few themes that the listener goes away humming. If Romantic melody is generally smooth, diatonic, and conjunct in motion (moving more by steps than by leaps), early-twentieth-century melody tends to be fragmented and angular, like a Cubist painting. The young avant-garde composers went to great lengths to *avoid* writing conjunct, stepwise lines. Rather than moving up a half step from C to D♭, for example, they were wont to jump down a major seventh to the D♭ an octave below. Avoiding a simple interval for a more distant one an octave above or below is called **octave displacement**, a feature of modern music. So, too, is the heavy use of chromaticism. In the following example by Arnold Schoenberg (1874–1951), notice how the melody makes large leaps where it might more easily move by steps and also how several sharps and flats are introduced to produce a highly chromatic line (Ex. 28.1).

EXAMPLE 28.1

could have been
written as

Harmony: The "Emancipation of Dissonance," New Chords, New Systems

Since the late Middle Ages, the basic building block of Western music had been the triad—a consonant, three-note chord (see Ch. 2, "Harmony"). A composer might introduce dissonance (a nontriad tone) for variety and tension, yet the rules of consonant harmony required that a dissonant pitch move (resolve) immediately to a consonant one (a member of the triad). Dissonance was subordinate to, and controlled by, the triad. By the first decade of the twentieth century, however, composers such as Arnold Schoenberg were using so much dissonance that the triad lost its adhesive force. Schoenberg famously referred to this development as "the emancipation of dissonance," meaning that dissonance was now liberated from the requirement that it resolve into a consonance.

At first, audiences rebelled when they heard Schoenberg's dissonance-filled scores, but the composer ultimately succeeded in raising the bar for what the ear might stand, thereby preparing listeners for a much higher level of dissonance in both classical and popular music. Indeed, the work of Schoenberg and like-minded composers paved the way, albeit indirectly, for the heavy dissonances of today's progressive jazz and the dissonant "metal" styles of Metallica, Slipknot, and others.

Early-twentieth-century composers created dissonance not only by obscuring or distorting the traditional triad but also by introducing new chords. One technique for creating new chords was the superimposition of more thirds above the consonant triad. In this way were produced not only the traditional **seventh chord** (a seventh chord spans seven letters of the scale, from A to G, for example) but also the **ninth chord** and the **eleventh chord**. The more thirds that were added on top of the basic triad, the more dissonant the sound of the chord:

EXAMPLE 28.2

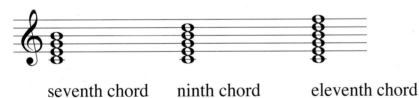

seventh chord   ninth chord   eleventh chord

The ultimate new chord was the **tone cluster**, the simultaneous sounding of a number of pitches only a whole step or a half step apart. Example 28.3 shows a tone cluster created by the American Modernist Charles Ives (1874–1954). But you, too, can create this high-dissonance chord simply by striking a group of adjacent keys on the piano with your fist or forearm. Try it.

EXAMPLE 28.3

Chromatic dissonance, new chords, and tone clusters all weakened the traditional role of tonality in music. Remember that triads had belonged to an interlocking system (key) and that each moved progressively toward a tonic (see Ch. 2,

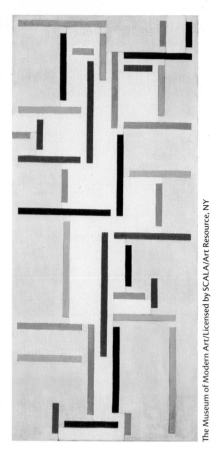

Figure 28.3

Lines of varying lengths can be seen as analogous to measures of different lengths caused by changing meters. Theo van Doesburg's *Rhythms of a Russian Dance* (1918) was surely inspired by the Russian sounds of Igor Stravinsky's *The Rite of Spring* (1913).

The Museum of Modern Art/Licensed by SCALA/Art Resource, NY

"Harmony"). As the triad disappeared, so, too, did the feeling of a key and the pull of a tonic. What were composers to do without triads, keys, and tonality, all of which had provided a structural framework for music? Simply said, they invented new systems to give structure to music. As we shall see in Chapter 29, Igor Stravinsky anchored much of his music in long ostinatos, while Arnold Schoenberg invented an entirely new type of musical structure called the twelve-tone method.

The "Emancipation of Rhythm": Asymmetrical Rhythms and Irregular Meters

As Arnold Schoenberg spoke of the "emancipation of dissonance," Igor Stravinsky might well have advocated the "emancipation of rhythm." For in the music of Stravinsky, above all others, rhythm and meter broke out from behind bars—or at least bar lines. Classical music created before 1900, as well as most pop and rock music down to the present day, is governed by regular patterns of duple ($\frac{2}{4}$), triple ($\frac{3}{4}$), or quadruple ($\frac{4}{4}$) meter. At the turn of the twentieth century, however, composers such as Stravinsky and Béla Bartók (see Ch. 30) began to write music that made it all but impossible for listeners to tap their feet to repeating rhythms or hear regular metrical patterns. Accents moved from one pulse to another, and meters changed from measure to measure. In abandoning the traditional framework of rhythm and meter, these composers mirrored the techniques of modern poets like Gertrude Stein (see beginning of this chapter) and T. S. Eliot (1888–1965), who dispensed with traditional poetic meters and repeating accents in favor of free verse.

Tone Color: New Sounds from New Sources

Twentieth-century composers created a brave new world of sound. This came about in large part because many musicians were dissatisfied with the string-dominated tone of the Romantic symphony orchestra. The string sound, with its lush vibrato, was thought to be too gentle, perhaps too mushy and sentimental, for the harsh realities of the modern world. So the strings, which had traditionally carried the melody, relinquished this role to the sharper, crisper woodwinds. Instead of playing a sweeping melody, the violinists might now be asked to beat on the strings with the wooden part of the bow or to take their hands and strike the instrument on its sound box.

The new emphasis on percussive effects was also reflected in the growing prominence of the percussion family. Entire pieces were written for percussion instruments alone. Instruments such as the xylophone, glockenspiel, and celesta were added to the group, and objects that produced an unfixed pitch, like the cowbell, brake drum, and police siren, were also heard on occasion. Finally, the piano, which in the Romantic era had been favored for its lyrical "singing" tone, came to be used more as a percussion instrument in Modernist scores, prized for the way the hammers could be made to bang the strings.

Introducing new instruments, or having traditional instruments make new sounds by means of novel playing techniques, was an important innovation. But a more sweeping development came about as composers began to think of musical color as a wholly independent expressive element. In his *Prelude to The Afternoon of a Faun* (Ch. 27), we heard how Debussy took a radically Modernist step by separating color (instrumental sounds) from line (melody). Similarly, we have seen Ravel's preoccupation with instrumental timbre in *Bolero* (Ch. 27) and in his colorful orchestration of Musorgsky's *Pictures at an Exhibition* (Ch. 21). Modernists such as Stravinsky (see Ch. 29) would bring bracing new orchestral colors to the traditional genres and forms of classical music. Postmodernists such as Varèse and Cage (see Ch. 32) would dispense with traditional genres and forms entirely, focusing instead on the possibilities of color and texture alone. The recognition that color and texture might elicit a strong emotional response from a listener or viewer was arguably the most significant development in the history of twentieth-century art.

Key Words

Modernism (331)	seventh chord (333)	eleventh chord (333)
Cubism (332)	ninth chord (333)	tone cluster (333)
octave displacement (332)		

For a complete review of this chapter, see the Main Points, Chapter Quiz, Flashcards, and Glossary in CourseMate.

Join us on Facebook at **Listening to Music with Craig Wright**

Early-Twentieth-Century

Modernism

Among the composers of the early twentieth century, no two had greater influence on the course of Western musical history than Igor Stravinsky and Arnold Schoenberg. Their ideas about Modernist music were very different, and, in the course of time, they developed contempt for each other. Yet so compelling were these artists' respective visions that they came to dominate the Modernist era. Stravinsky, after perfecting flamboyant Modernist ballet, moved on to a more restrained idiom called Neo-classicism, while Schoenberg began with uncompromising atonal music and ultimately developed the twelve-tone system of composition.

Igor Stravinsky (1882–1971)

For three-quarters of the twentieth century, Igor Stravinsky (chapter opener) personified the cultural pluralism and stylistic diversity of cutting-edge art music. He created Modernist masterpieces in many traditional genres: opera, ballet, symphony, concerto, church Mass, and cantata. His versatility was such that he could write a ballet for baby elephants (*Circus Polka*, 1942) just as easily as he could set to music a Greek classical drama (*Oedipus Rex*, 1927). Throughout his long life, he traveled with the fashionable set of high art. Although reared in St. Petersburg, Russia, where his father was a leading operatic bass, he later lived in Paris, Venice, New York, and Hollywood. Forced to become an expatriate by the Russian Revolution (1917), he took French citizenship in 1934, and then, having moved to the United States at the outbreak of World War II, he became an American citizen in 1945. He counted among his friends the painter Pablo Picasso (1881–1973), the novelist Aldous Huxley (1894–1963), and the poet T. S. Eliot (1888–1965). On his eightieth birthday, in 1962, he was honored by President John F. Kennedy at the White House and, later in the same year, by Russian Premier Nikita Khrushchev in the Kremlin. He died in New York in 1971 at the age of eighty-eight. Though working in the esoteric world of Modernist art music, Stravinsky achieved—and consciously cultivated—celebrity status.

Stravinsky rose to international fame as a composer of ballet music. In 1908, his early scores caught the attention of Sergei Diaghilev (1872–1929), the legendary **impresario** (producer) of Russian opera and ballet (Fig. 29.1). Diaghilev wanted to bring Russian ballet to Paris, at that time the artistic capital of the world. He sensed that the fashionable French, who were currently crazy about all things exotic (see Ch. 27, "Exoticism"), would clamor to see ballet full of Russian folklore and exotic "Orientalisms." To this end, Diaghilev formed a dance company he called the ***Ballets russes*** (Russian Ballets) and hired, over the course of time, the most progressive artists he could find: Pablo Picasso and Henri Matisse for scenic designs (see Figs. 27.5, 28.1, 29.2, and 29.3), and Claude Debussy, Maurice Ravel, and Stravinsky, among others, as composers. Stravinsky soon became the principal composer of the Diaghilev's "export company," and the *Ballets russes* became the focus of his musical activity for the next ten years. Accordingly, the decade 1910–1920 has become known as Stravinsky's "Russian ballet period."

With the onset of World War I and the temporary disappearance of large symphony orchestras in Europe, Stravinsky, along with others, developed a style called **Neo-classicism**, which emphasized classical forms and smaller ensembles of the sort that had existed in the Baroque and Classical periods. Stravinsky's Neo-classical period extended from 1920 until 1951, when he adopted the twelve-tone technique of Arnold Schoenberg (see "Arnold Schoenberg and the Second Viennese School" at the end of this chapter), which he continued to pursue until his death.

Although Stravinsky's style continually evolved over the course of his nearly seventy-year career, his particular brand of Modernism—the "Stravinsky sound"—is always recognizable. In simple terms, his music

Watch a video of Craig Wright's Open Yale Course class session 22, "Modernism and Mahler," at the text website.

Figure 29.1

Sergei Diaghilev in New York in 1916. Diaghilev's creation, the modern dance company he called *Ballets russes*, has been immortalized by the award-winning film *Ballets Russes* (2005).

Lebrecht Music and Arts Photo Library/Alamy

Figures 29.2 and 29.3

(top) Like Picasso, Henri Matisse was a proponent of Primitivism in art, to which the unadorned composition titled *Dance* (1909) attests. Here he achieves raw primitive power by exaggerating a few basic lines and incorporating a few cool tones. Two years later, he created an even more intense vision of the same scene. (bottom) In *Dance* (1911), Matisse uses greater angularity and more intense colors, and thereby inspires a more powerful reaction to this later version of a primitive dance scene.

is lean, clean, and bracing. Stravinsky does not write "homogenized" sounds, as occur when the winds and strings together join on a single line, but rather distinctly separate timbres. He downplays the warm strings, preferring instead the tones of piercing winds and brittle percussion. While his orchestra can be large and colorful, its sound is rarely lush or sentimental. Most important, rhythm is the vital element in Stravinsky's compositional style. His beat is strong, but often irregular, and he builds complexity by requiring independent meters and rhythms to sound simultaneously (see below). All of these stylistic traits can be heard in his ballet *The Rite of Spring*. This watershed of musical Modernism, Stravinsky's most famous work, stunned and angered the audience at its explosive 1913 premiere.

Le Sacre du printemps (The Rite of Spring, 1913)

Igor Stravinsky composed three important early ballet scores for Diaghilev's dance company: *The Firebird* (1910), *Petrushka* (1911), and *The Rite of Spring* (1913). All are built on Russian folk tales—a legacy of musical nationalism (see Ch. 21)—and all make use of the large, colorful orchestra of the late nineteenth century. Yet the choreography for these Russian ballets is not the elegant, graceful ballet in the Romantic tradition, the sort that we associate with Tchaikovsky's *Swan Lake* and *The Nutcracker*. These are modern dances with angular poses and abrupt, jerky motions. Dancers do not soar in tutus (see Fig. 21.7); wearing primitive costumes, they stomp the ground. Indeed, the aesthetic that Stravinsky uses here is called Primitivism, an artistic mode of expression also seen in the paintings of Paul Gauguin (1848–1903), Picasso (see Fig. 28.1), and Matisse (Figs. 29.2 and 29.3). **Primitivism** attempts to capture the unadorned lines, raw energy, and elemental truth of non-Western art and apply it in a Modernist context. In *The Rite of Spring*, Stravinsky expresses these elements through pounding rhythms, almost brutal dissonance, and a story that takes us back to the Stone Age.

THE PLOT

The plot of *The Rite of Spring* is suggested by its subtitle: *Pictures of Pagan Russia*. Part 1, "The Kiss of the Earth," depicts the springtime rituals of primitive Slavic tribes. In Part 2, "The Sacrifice," a virgin dances herself to death as an offering to the god of spring. Before the curtain rises on Part 1, the huge orchestra plays an Introduction. This music unfolds gradually but inexorably, from soft to loud, from one line to many, and from tranquil to cacophonous, suggesting the earth's flora and fauna coming to life with the beginning of spring. The first scene, "Augurs of Spring," features jarring accents (see Ex. 29.1) and ear-splitting dissonance (see Ex. 29.4). Yet lyrical, almost sensuous moments are found in the score, especially when Stravinsky incorporates folk music, whether quoting authentic Russian songs or (more commonly) composing his own melodies within this folk idiom. Despite the folkloric element, however, the bulk of the composition came from within. As Stravinsky declared, "I had only my ears to guide me. I heard and I wrote what I heard. I am the vessel through which *The Rite of Spring* passed."

Although *The Rite of Spring* has been called *the* great masterpiece of modern music, at its first performance it provoked not admiration, but a riot of dissent. This premiere, the most notorious in the history of Western music, took place on an unusually hot evening, May 29, 1913, at the newly built Théâtre des Champs-Élysées in Paris. *Le beau monde* (high society) packed the house, paying double the usual ticket prices. Yet from the very first sounds, many listeners voiced, shouted, and hissed their displeasure. Some, feigning auditory pain, yelled for a doctor, others for two. Arguments and flying fists abounded as opponents and partisans warred over this Russian brand of Modernist art. To restore calm, the curtain was lowered momentarily, and the house lights were turned on and off. All in vain. The musicians still could not be heard, and consequently, the dancers had difficulty following the pulse of the music. The disorder was experienced firsthand by a visiting critic of the *New York Press,* who reported as follows:

> I was sitting in a box in which I had rented one seat. Three ladies sat in front of me and a young man occupied the place behind me. He stood up during the course of the ballet to enable himself to see more clearly. The intense excitement under which he was laboring, thanks to the potent force of the music, betrayed itself presently when he began to beat rhythmically on the top of my head with his fists. My emotion was so great that I did not feel the blows for some time. They were perfectly synchronized with the beat of the music!

In truth, the violent reaction to *The Rite of Spring* was in part a response to the Modernist choreography by twenty-three-year-old Vaslav Nijinsky (1890–1950), which sought to obliterate any trace of classical ballet. Nijinsky's dance was just as "primitive" as Stravinsky's score. But what aspects, specifically, of Stravinsky's music shocked so many in the audience that night?

PERCUSSIVE ORCHESTRA

First, a new percussive—one might say "heavy metal"—approach to the orchestra is present. The percussion section is enlarged to include four timpani, a triangle, a tambourine, a guiro, cymbals, antique cymbals, a bass drum, and a tam-tam. Even the string family, the traditional provider of warmth and richness in the symphony orchestra, is required to play percussively, attacking the strings with repeated down-bows at seemingly random moments of accent. Instead of warm, lush sounds, we hear bright, brittle, almost brutal ones pounded out by percussion, heavy woodwinds, and brasses.

IRREGULAR ACCENTS

Stravinsky intensifies the effect of his harsh, metallic sounds by placing them where they are not expected, on unaccented beats, thereby creating explosive syncopations. Notice in the following example, the famous beginning of "Augurs of Spring," how the strings accent (>) the second, fourth, and then first pulses of subsequent four-pulse measures. In this way, Stravinsky destroys ordinary 1-2-3-4 meter and forces us to hear, in succession, groups of 4, 5, 2, 6, 3, 4, and 5 pulses—a conductor's nightmare!

EXAMPLE 29.1

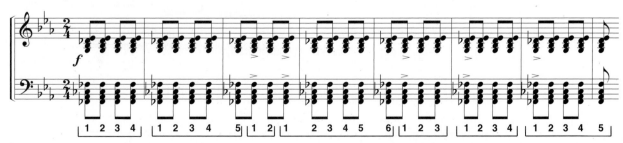

See what the riotous premiere of *The Rite of Spring* was like, in the YouTube playlist at CourseMate for this text.

POLYMETER

The rhythm of *The Rite of Spring* is complex because Stravinsky often superimposes two or more different meters simultaneously. Notice in Example 29.2 that the oboe plays in $\frac{6}{8}$ time, the E♭ clarinet plays in $\frac{7}{8}$, while the B♭ clarinet is in $\frac{5}{8}$. This is an example of **polymeter**—two or more meters sounding simultaneously.

EXAMPLE 29.2

To see a demonstration of how various meters can be combined, watch "Extreme Polymetric Ostinato Demonstration" in the YouTube playlist at CourseMate for this text.

POLYRHYTHM

Not only do individual parts often play separate meters, but they also sometimes project two or more independent rhythms simultaneously. Look at the reduced score given in Example 29.3. Every instrument seems to be doing its own thing! In fact, six distinct rhythms can be heard, offering a good example of **polyrhythm**—the simultaneous sounding of two or more rhythms.

EXAMPLE 29.3

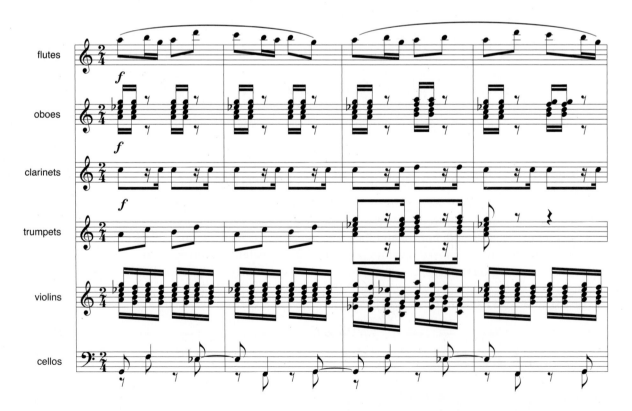

OSTINATO FIGURES

Notice also in Example 29.3 that most of the instruments play the same motive over and over at the same pitch level. Such a repeating figure, as we have seen, is called an ostinato. In this instance, we hear multiple ostinatos. Stravinsky was not the first twentieth-century composer to use ostinatos extensively—Debussy had done so earlier in his Impressionist scores (see Ch. 27). But Stravinsky employs them more often and for longer spans than did his predecessors. In *The Rite of Spring*, ostinatos with fast tempos give the music its incessant, driving quality.

DISSONANT POLYCHORDS

The harsh, biting sound heard throughout much of *The Rite of Spring* is often created by two triads, or a triad and a seventh chord, sounding at once. What results is a **polychord**—the simultaneous sounding of one triad or seventh chord with another (Fig. 29.4). When the individual chords of a polychord are only a whole step or a half step apart, the result is especially dissonant. In Example 29.4, the passage from the beginning of "Augurs of Spring," a seventh chord built on E♭ is played simultaneously with a major triad built on F♭.

See the Joffrey Ballet's re-creation of the original choreography and costuming for *The Rite of Spring*, in the YouTube playlist at CourseMate for this text.

EXAMPLE 29.4

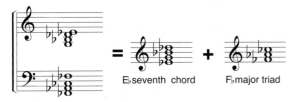

Remarkably, the sonic shockers of *The Rite of Spring* still sound outrageously inventive today, as musicians around the world discovered in 2013 when they celebrated the work's centenary. The opening salvo of the Modernist age has lost little of its vitality and daring in the hundred years since its creation.

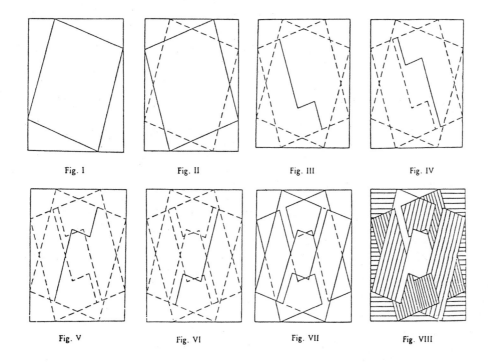

Figure 29.4

In his *Schemes of Painting* (1922), the artist Albert Gleizes demonstrates that a Cubist work can be created by rotating a figure or line against itself, and then again and again until visual dissonance results. Similarly, a polychord is created by placing two or more triads or seventh chords off center and against one another, thereby creating musical dissonance.

Igor Stravinsky, *The Rite of Spring* **(1913)**

Introduction and Scene 1

Genre: Ballet music

5   2

5/8–9   2/19–20

WHAT TO LISTEN FOR: Whatever you listen for, listen repeatedly, for by hearing this "difficult" music again and again, its beauty will become apparent.

INTRODUCTION

(Awakening of earth; curtain still down)

0:00	**8 19**	Bassoon writhing in high register
0:21		Other winds (bass clarinet, English horn, another bassoon, high clarinet) gradually enter.
1:40		Flutes play in parallel motion.
1:56		Writhing woodwinds continue.
2:40		Ostinato in bass supports gradual orchestral crescendo.
3:03		Bassoon melody returns; clarinet trills.

AUGURS OF SPRING: DANCES OF THE ADOLESCENTS

(Youthful dancers pound onto stage; male and female groups entice one another; attention shifts to more folk-like dances of girls.)

3:38	**9 20**	0:00	Elemental pounding of dissonant string chords punctuated by blasts from French horns and trumpets (see Ex. 29.1)
4:26		0:48	Bassoons and then trombones play stepwise motive.
4:57		1:19	*Fortissimo* chords and timpani blows
5:21		1:43	French horn plays folk-like melody.
5:43		2:05	Flute plays melody.
5:58		2:20	Trumpets play new folk-like melody.
6:32		2:54	Gradual orchestral crescendo

🔊 Listen to streaming music in an Active Listening Guide at CourseMate or in the eBook.

🔊 Take online Listening Exercise 29.1 and receive feedback at CourseMate or in the eBook.

Following the *succès de scandale* that attended the premiere of *The Rite of Spring*, Stravinsky extracted the music from the ballet itself and presented it as an independent orchestral suite. The music alone was now recognized as an important, if controversial, statement of the musical avant-garde. Later, in 1940, the score of *The Rite of Spring* furnished the music for an important segment of Walt Disney's hugely popular animated film, *Fantasia*, in which volcanoes explode and dinosaurs roam in a primitive landscape. Through Disney's *Fantasia*, musical Modernism took steps toward the mainstream.

See Walt Disney's visual rendering in *Fantasia* of the Introduction and opening scene of Stravinsky's *The Rite of Spring*, in the YouTube playlist at CourseMate for this text.

Arnold Schoenberg and the Second Viennese School

Ironically, the most radical shoot of musical Modernism took root in Vienna, a city with a long history of conservatism. In the early twentieth century, a trio of native Viennese musicians—Arnold Schoenberg (1874–1951), Alban Berg (1885–1935), and Anton Webern (1883–1945)—ventured to take high-art music in a completely new direction. The close association of these three innovative composers has come to be called the **Second Viennese School** (the first, of course, consisted of Mozart, Haydn, and Beethoven—see Ch. 13, "Vienna: A City of Music").

Arnold Schoenberg, the leader of this group, almost singlehandedly thrust musical Modernism upon a reluctant Viennese public. Schoenberg came from a Jewish family of modest means and was, as with many geniuses, largely self-taught. As a young man, he worked as a bank clerk during the day but studied literature, philosophy, and music at night, becoming a competent performer on the violin and cello. He came to know the music of Brahms, Wagner, and Mahler, mostly by playing their scores and attending concerts. Having "left the world of bank notes for musical notes" at the age of twenty-one, he earned a humble living by conducting a men's chorus, orchestrating operettas—the Viennese counterpart of our Broadway musicals—and giving lessons in music theory and composition. Eventually, his own compositions began to be heard in Vienna, though they were usually not well received.

Schoenberg's earliest works are written in the late Romantic style, with rich harmonies, chromatic melodies, expansive forms, and programmatic content. But by 1908, his music had begun to evolve in unexpected directions. Strongly influenced by Wagner's chromatic harmonies, Schoenberg started to compose works with no tonal center. If Wagner could write winding chromatic passages that temporarily obscured the tonality, why not go one step further and create fully chromatic pieces in which no tonality exists? This Schoenberg did, and thereby created what is called **atonal music**—music without tonality, without a key center (see also the boxed essay "Expressionism and Atonality").

Schoenberg's contemporaries found his atonal music difficult. Not only was a tonal center absent, but the melodies were highly disjunct, and the harmonies exceedingly dissonant (see Ch. 28, "Harmony: The 'Emancipation of Dissonance,' New Chords, New Systems"). Some performers refused to play his music, and when others did, the audience reaction could turn violent. At one concert on March 31, 1913, the police had to be called in to restore order. Despite this hostility, Schoenberg remained true to his own vision, offering this directive to all creative artists: "One must be convinced of the infallibility of one's own fantasy; one must believe in one's own creative spirit."

Expressionism and Atonality

Arnold Schoenberg and his students Alban Berg and Anton Webern were not alone in creating a radically new style of art. At precisely this same time, an important new movement appeared in the visual arts, called Expressionism. **Expressionism** was initially a German-Austrian development that arose in Berlin, Munich, and Vienna. It aimed not to depict objects as they are seen but to express the strong emotion they generated in the artist; not to paint a portrait of an individual but to express the subject's innermost feelings, anxieties, and fears. In Edvard Munch's early Expressionist pastel *The Scream* (1893), the subject cries out

(continued)

to an unsympathetic and uncomprehending world. Schoenberg's statement in this regard can be taken as a credo for the entire Expressionist movement: "Art is the cry of despair of those who experience in themselves the fate of all Mankind" (1910). Gradually, realistic representation gave way to highly personal and increasingly abstract expression. Schoenberg was himself a painter and exhibited his works with the Expressionists in 1912 (see Fig. 29.5). In fact, the music and art of this movement can be described in rather similar terms. The bold, clashing colors, disjointed shapes, and jagged lines of the painters have their counterparts in the harsh dissonances, asymmetrical rhythms, and angular, chromatic melodies of Schoenberg and his followers. It is surely not an accident that Schoenberg moved from tonality to atonality in music (1908–1912) at precisely the time that Munch and Kandinsky (see Fig. 28.2) turned from realistic representation to abstract expression.

The Scream, by Edvard Munch. Munch actually created this vision four times. In May 2012, one of the four sold at Sotheby's in New York for $120 million—the highest amount ever paid at auction for a work of art.

Pierrot lunaire (Moonstruck Pierrot, 1912)

Figure 29.5

Notice line 6 of the poem *Madonna* as set by Schoenberg in *Pierrot lunaire*: "Gleichen Augen, rot und offen" ("Like eyes, red and open"). This was the emotion that Schoenberg felt when he painted the Expressionist work *Red Gaze* in 1910. Expressionism aimed not to depict an object from the outside, but rather to project the internal feelings of the artist through a subject. As Schoenberg said, "One must express oneself! Express oneself directly!" Compare the similarly intent gaze of Igor Stravinsky in the chapter opener.

Pierrot lunaire (Moonstruck Pierrot), Schoenberg's best-known composition, is an exemplary work of Expressionist art. Schoenberg aimed to create an intimate chamber work for small ensemble and a female singer, who declaims twenty-one poems by Albert Giraud (1860–1929). Here we meet Pierrot, a sad clown from the world of traditional Italian pantomime and puppet shows. Yet in this Expressionist poetry, the clown has fallen under the sway of the moon and changed into an alienated modern artist. Pierrot projects his inner anxiety by means of **Sprechstimme** (speech-voice), a vocal technique that requires the vocalist to declaim the text more than to sing it (as indicated by the "x" in the example in the Listening Guide). The voice is to execute the rhythmic values exactly; but once it hits a pitch, it is to quit the tone immediately, sliding away in either a downward or an upward direction. This creates exaggerated declamation of the sort one might hear from a lunatic, which is appropriate for Pierrot, given the lunar spell cast upon him.

Poem 6 of *Pierrot lunaire* depicts the protagonist's tormented, hallucinatory vision of the suffering Madonna at the cross. Its poetic form is that of a rondeau, an ancient musical and poetic form marked by the use of a refrain (set in boldface type in the Listening Guide). Traditionally, composers had used the appearance of a textual refrain to repeat the melody as well, thereby creating musical unity (see Ch. 3, "Strophic Form"). However, Schoenberg the iconoclast repeats the text but not the music. Thus his music unfolds in an ever-varying continuum, like a stream of consciousness. Schoenberg was not alone in engaging in deep introspection at this time. As the composer toiled over *Pierrot lunaire*, a fellow Viennese resident, Sigmund Freud, was probing the human psyche in an equally revolutionary way—developing the theory of psychoanalysis.

Alban Berg, a pupil of Schoenberg, once posed the question: "Why is Schoenberg's music so difficult to understand?" One immediate answer is that it is highly disjunct and dissonant. Equally important is the fact that, because Schoenberg's lines unfold continually, no musical event is repeated and thus nothing becomes familiar. Imagine a journey through a landscape in which everything is constantly new and different—this would be very unsettling, indeed.

Similarly, the absence of familiar landmarks in a musical work can be aurally disorienting for the listener. Your first reaction to the dissonant continuum of sound in *Pierrot lunaire* may be decidedly negative. Yet with repeated hearings, the force of the jarring elements of the atonal style begins to lessen, and a bizarre, eerie sort of beauty emerges, especially if you are sensitive to the meaning of the text.

Listening Guide

Arnold Schoenberg, *Pierrot lunaire* (1912)

Number 6, *Madonna*

5 2
5/10 2/21

Ensemble: Voice, cello, clarinet, flute, and piano

Genre: Art song

WHAT TO LISTEN FOR: The eerie, almost scary sound of *Sprechstimme*. Does the initially offputting quality of the music reinforce the graphic image of the text? Don't bother trying to sing the tonic (home) pitch—this is atonal music!

(*Sprechstimme* — "speech-voice")

Steig, O Mut-ter al-ler Schmer-zen, auf den Al-tar mei-ner Ver-se!

10
21

Steig, O Mutter aller Schmerzen	**Arise, O Mother of all sorrows**
Auf den Altar meiner Verse!	**On the altar of my verse!**
Blut aus deinen magern Brüsten	Blood from your thin breast
Hat des Schwertes Wut vergossen.	Has spilled the rage of the sword.
Deine ewig frischen Wunden	Your eternally fresh wounds
Gleichen Augen, rot und offen,	Like eyes, red and open,
Steig, O Mutter aller Schmerzen	**Arise, O Mother of all sorrows**
Auf den Altar meiner Verse!	**On the altar of my verse!**
(1:15) In den abgezehrten Händen	In your thin and wasted hands
Hältst du deines Sohnes Leiche	You hold the body of your Son
Ihn zu zeigen aller Menschheit,	To show him to all mankind,
Doch der Blick der Menschen meidet	Yet the look of men avoids
Dich, **O Mutter aller Schmerzen**.	You, **O Mother of all sorrows**.

 Listen to streaming music in an Active Listening Guide at CourseMate or in the eBook.

Schoenberg's Twelve-Tone Music

When Arnold Schoenberg and his followers did away with tonal chord progressions and recurring melodies, they found themselves facing a serious artistic problem: how to write large-scale compositions in the new atonal style. For centuries, musical structures, like fugue and sonata–allegro form, had been laid out according to a clear tonal plan and the repetition of broad musical themes—repetition created form. But Schoenberg's chromatic, atonal, nonrepeating melodies made traditional musical forms all but impossible. What other formal plan might be used? If all twelve notes of the chromatic scale are equally important, as is the case in atonal music, why choose any one note over another at a given moment? For nearly a decade, Schoenberg's pen fell silent as he tried to devise a way out of this compositional impasse.

By 1923, Schoenberg had solved the problem of "formal anarchy"—the absence of form caused by total chromatic freedom. He discovered a new way of creating music that he called "composing with twelve tones." **Twelve-tone composition** is a method of writing that uses each of the twelve notes of the chromatic scale set in a fixed, predetermined order. The composer begins by arranging the twelve notes of the chromatic scale in a sequence of his or her choosing, forming a "tone row." Throughout the composition, these twelve notes must come in the same order. Music in which elements such as pitch, timbre, or dynamics come in a fixed series is called **serial music**. In twelve-tone music, the twelve-note series may unfold not only as a melody but also as a melody with accompaniment, or simply as a progression of chords, because two or more notes of the row may sound simultaneously. Moreover, in addition to appearing in its basic form, the row might go backward (retrograde), or upside down (inversion), or both backward and upside down at the same time (retrograde inversion). While such arrangements might seem wholly artificial and very unmusical, we should remember that composers such as Johann Sebastian Bach in the Baroque era and Josquin Desprez in the Renaissance subjected their melodies to similar permutations. The purpose of Schoenberg's twelve-tone method was to create musical unity by basing each piece on a single, orderly arrangement of twelve tones, thereby guaranteeing the perfect equality of all pitches so that none would seem like a tonal center.

See an excellent discussion of Arnold Schoenberg's twelve-tone system in the YouTube playlist at CourseMate for this text. To see a biting satire of Schoenberg's and Berg's twelve-tone music, watch "Twelve Tone Commercial" in the YouTube playlist.

Trio from *Suite for Piano*, Opus 25 (1924)

Schoenberg's first steps along this radical twelve-tone path were tentative, and the pieces he created were very short. Among Schoenberg's first serial compositions was his *Suite for Piano*, a collection of seven brief dance movements, including the Minuet and Trio to be discussed here. The tone row for the *Suite*, along with its three permutations, is as follows:

Row													Retrograde											
E	F	G	Db	Gb	Eb	Ab	D	B	C	A	Bb		Bb	A	C	B	D	Ab	Eb	Gb	Db	G	F	E
1	2	3	4	5	6	7	8	9	10	11	12		12	11	10	9	8	7	6	5	4	3	2	1

Inversion													Retrograde-inversion											
E	Eb	Db	G	D	F	C	F#	A	G#	B	Bb		Bb	B	G#	A	Fb	C	F	D	G	Db	Eb	E
1	2	3	4	5	6	7	8	9	10	11	12		12	11	10	9	8	7	6	5	4	3	2	1

Schoenberg allows the row or any of its permutations to begin on any pitch, as long as the original sequence of intervals is maintained. Notice in the Trio, for example, that the row itself begins on E but is also allowed to start on Bb (see Listening Guide). In the second part, measures 6–9, the exact serial progression of the row breaks down slightly. The composer explained this as a "justifiable deviation," owing to the need for tonal variety at this point. Notice that the rhythms in which the notes appear may also be changed for the sake of variety. As you listen to the Trio, see if you can follow the unfolding of the row and all its permutations. Listen many times—the piece is only fifty-one seconds long! Its aesthetic effect is similar to that of a constructivist painting of an artist like Theo van Doesburg (see Fig. 29.6). If you like the mechanical precision of the painting, you'll likely enjoy Schoenberg's twelve-tone piano piece as well.

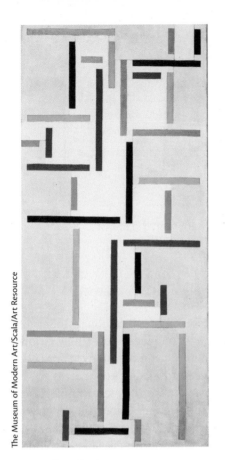

Figure 29.6

Artist Theo van Doesburg (1883–1931) often fashioned designs in retrograde motion, in which the pattern proceeding downward from the top left was the same as that upward from the bottom right. One can simulate the same effect by comparing his *Rhythms of a Russian Dance* (1918) in upright and rotated orientations.

Listening Guide

Arnold Schoenberg, Trio from *Suite for Piano* (1924)

Genre: Twelve-tone piano music

WHAT TO LISTEN FOR: Listen several times (it's a very short piece); with each hearing the disjunction and dissonance will recede, leaving a sense of an abstract sonic space, one free of emotional commitment.

 5/11

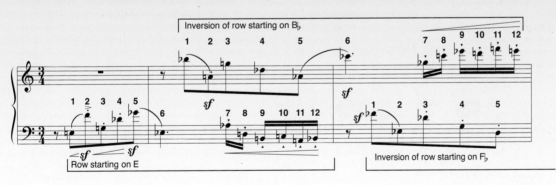

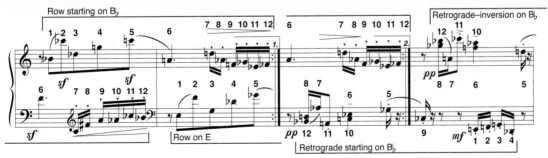

(continued)

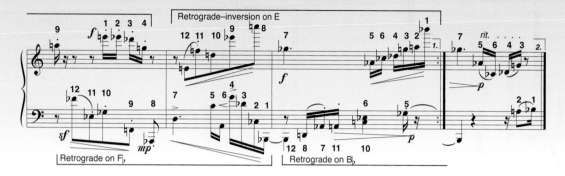

Retrograde–inversion on E

Retrograde on F♭

Retrograde on B♭

🔊 Listen to streaming music in an Active Listening Guide at CourseMate or in the eBook.

Although the twelve-tone process became the rage among Modernist composers—even Stravinsky came under its sway—audiences never fully embraced it. Why would anyone write music that is mechanistic and not pretty? For Schoenberg, "pretty" was not the point; as this piano piece proves, the job of art is to stimulate as well as satisfy. Nevertheless, most music lovers continued to find Schoenberg's twelve-tone style inaccessible. Oddly, here the listening public ultimately won out, for twelve-tone composition disappeared with the Modernist movement. Indeed, the twelve-tone system has been called one of the two great failed experiments of the twentieth century, the other being Communism. Schoenberg was philosophical about the public's general dislike of his music: "If it is art, it is not for all, and if it is for all, it is not art."

Key Words

impresario (337)	polyrhythm (340)	*Sprechstimme* (344)
Ballets russes (337)	polychord (341)	twelve-tone composition (346)
Neo-classicism (337)	Second Viennese School (343)	serial music (346)
Primitivism (338)	atonal music (343)	
polymeter (340)	Expressionism (343)	

For a complete review of this chapter, see the Main Points, Chapter Quiz, Flashcards, and Glossary in CourseMate.

f Join us on Facebook at **Listening to Music with Craig Wright**

Russian and Eastern European

Modernism

e naturally tend to assume that Western civilization has been shaped primarily by events taking place in the West itself. In the early twentieth century, however, several events of great importance to Western history occurred in Russia and Eastern Europe (Fig. 30.1). In 1917, the West was shaken by the **Russian Revolution**, the overthrow of the Russian tsar by the socialist Bolshevik Party. This upheaval paved the way for the establishment of a Communist-ruled Soviet Union in 1922, a development that led ultimately to the Cold War, which dominated Western foreign policy concerns for decades. We similarly tend to credit the military powers of the West with the defeat of Adolf Hitler and his Nazi regime in the Second World War. But although Western soldiers unquestionably played a vital role, the bulk of the fighting took place on the Russian Front. Apart from combat in the Pacific, fully 80 percent of soldiers killed in World War II died on the Russian Front—about 11 million Russians and 5 million Germans. Civilian casualties in the East likewise outnumbered those in the West. The number of civilian dead in Russia—victims of war, famine, and government purges—is estimated between 30 and 40 million. These horrors affected all segments of society, including artists, intellectuals, and musicians. Indeed, it is no exaggeration to say that the three composers discussed in this chapter had their lives ruined by the cataclysmic events that rocked Russia and Eastern Europe in these decades. We begin with Russia.

Progressive artists who worked in the Soviet Union during the dictatorship of Joseph Stalin (r. 1924–1953) did so under conditions that are incomprehensible today. During the 1920s and 1930s, the ruling Communist Party forcefully confiscated the wealth of the well-to-do and redistributed it collectively among the proletariat. Anything that smacked of "elitism"—anything that could not be immediately understood and enjoyed by the masses—was suspect. Heading the list of likely

Figure 30.1

Western Russia and Central and Eastern Europe, early twentieth century

"subversives" were the names of almost all Modernist artists, including composers, and especially those who wrote in the atonal or twelve-tone style. The Soviet regime encouraged patriotic compositions in which large choruses sang hymns of praise to the fatherland and to the working class—musical propaganda to promote the agenda of the Communist Party. Soviet authorities referred to Modernist music as **formalism** and branded it "antidemocratic." To be identified as a "formalist" was tantamount to a death sentence. The challenge for a composer working under Stalin was to remain true to a personal artistic vision, yet remain alive.

Sergey Prokofiev (1891–1953)

The career of Sergey Prokofiev is full of contradictions and ironies, caused in part by the place he occupied in Russian history. The son of a well-to-do farm administrator, he fled the Russian Revolution in 1917 but later returned to celebrate in music the most murderous of the revolutionaries, Joseph Stalin. Prokofiev was once known as the dissonant, atonal "bad boy" of the St. Petersburg Conservatory, where he received his musical education, but he later wrote such pleasantly benign works as *Peter and the Wolf* (1936). He thought of himself above all as a serious composer—the author of seven symphonies, six operas, six ballets, five piano concertos, and nine piano sonatas. Today, however, he is remembered mainly for his lighter works: the *Classical Symphony, Peter and the Wolf,* and the film scores *Lieutenant Kijé* and *Alexander Nevsky.*

The Russian Revolution (October 1917) has been called "the ten days that shook the world," and it certainly shook Prokofiev's world. With his family's wealth about to be confiscated, he took the Trans-Siberian Express eastward toward Japan and ultimately landed in San Francisco. After four years (1918–1922) as a composer–pianist in America, the vagabond Prokofiev moved to Paris, where for a time he worked as a ballet composer for Sergei Diaghilev and his *Ballets russes* (see beginning of Ch. 29). But his career languished. Eager to have illustrious expatriates return to the Soviet Union, and working through his secret police in Paris, dictator Joseph Stalin lured Prokofiev back home with the promise that a simpler, less dissonant musical style would bring both popular success and governmental approval.

Romeo and Juliet (1935)

Prokofiev's first official work as a Soviet composer was the ballet *Romeo and Juliet,* which he wrote for the famous Kirov Ballet of St. Petersburg during the summer of 1935. To conform to a Soviet artistic dictate of the day (no tragic endings), the composer revised Shakespeare and penned a happy conclusion. Before the work could be staged, however, a reign of cultural terror fell upon all Soviet artists in 1936, and Prokofiev withdrew the work. Not until five years later, in 1940, did the composer feel that the political environment was safe enough to allow the ballet to be performed.

What could possibly be controversial about *Romeo and Juliet*? Neither the age-old story nor the idea of romance, but rather Prokofiev's musical style. Prokofiev had been a dissonant and occasionally atonal composer before his return to the Soviet Union. Now his task was to meld his Modernist tendencies with the simple, melodious music the government demanded. As we listen to the ball scene ("Dance of the Knights") from *Romeo and Juliet,* we can hear this Modernist–populist dialectic at work. For a courtly dance, we would expect pleasant music. What we get is pleasing but not quite pleasant (invigorating would be more accurate). The initial music is dark (minor), somewhat disjunct melodically, and unstable tonally, sliding from one unexpected chord to another, which is the hallmark of Prokofiev's style. Yet the music has power and energy; we feel ourselves swaying to the beat of the regular, duple-meter bass line. As the *corps de ballet* exits to allow a *pas de deux* ("steps for two," here Paris and Juliet), the music becomes softer (high flutes), and the melody is strangely beautiful, owing to its slightly dissonant cast. Present everywhere is just enough hard edge and bite to Prokofiev's music to prevent this sentimental story from becoming sappy. Sentimentality had no place in the Modernist aesthetic.

Listening Guide

Sergey Prokofiev, "Dance of the Knights," from *Romeo and Juliet* (1935)

Genre: Ballet

Form: **ABCBA**

Situation: The ball scene as represented in Shakespeare's rendition, Act I, Scene 4. The young aristocrats of the Capulet clan dance; Juliet dances with Paris and is observed by an enthralled Romeo.

WHAT TO LISTEN FOR: How Prokofiev, like his countryman Tchaikovsky, excels at writing evocative tableaux (**A**, **B**, and **C**) that conform to the demands of the drama yet are short enough to accommodate the physical limitations of the dancers

0:00	**12** **A**	Heavy, ponderous, yet powerful music in the low register; grows in volume and rises in pitch as more dancers come forward	

1:21		Heavy music of dance continues.

| 1:46 | **B** | Light melody in triple meter for flutes accompanied by simple pizzicato strings |

| 2:29 | **C** | Balancing melody in duple meter for solo oboe |

| 3:07 | **B** | Return to contrasting flute melody |
| 3:48 | **A** | Return to heavy duple-meter dance led first by woodwinds (including saxophones) and then full orchestra and full corps of dancers |

 Listen to streaming music in an Active Listening Guide at CourseMate or in the eBook.

See "Dance of the Knights" as ballet in the YouTube playlist at CourseMate for this text.

Had you been general secretary of the Communist Party at this time, would *you* have banned the music you just heard because its Modernist sounds might cause social unrest? In fact, performances of Prokofiev's music were officially outlawed in 1948. That same year, his wife, Lina, was arrested by the secret police for "espionage" and sentenced to an exile of twenty years. With Prokofiev in ill health, his output dwindled to nothing. He died within a few minutes of his nemesis, Joseph Stalin, on the night of March 5, 1953. Yet news of Prokofiev's death was withheld for days to avoid deflecting attention from the deceased dictator. No flowers could be bought for the great composer's coffin; the funeral of Stalin had, without exaggeration, claimed them all.

Dmitri Shostakovich (1906–1975)

Prokofiev was not the only composer to suffer during Stalin's reign of terror. Dmitri Shostakovich (Fig. 30.2), a few years Prokofiev's junior, experienced even greater trauma.

Born into a musical family, Shostakovich showed exceptional promise from an early age. He had perfect pitch and could play through all of Bach's *Well-Tempered Clavier* by age eleven. In 1919, he entered the St. Petersburg Conservatory, where he studied harmony, orchestration, and composition. After mixed results in his courses at the Conservatory, Shostakovich achieved his first major success in 1925 with the completion and performance of his Symphony No. 1, which earned the composer international acclaim at the age of nineteen. In 1934, Shostakovich attracted widespread attention once again with his realistic opera *Lady Macbeth of the Mtsensk District*. In 1936, however, his career took a disastrous turn when Joseph Stalin attended a performance of his opera but walked out three-quarters of the way through. Two days later, Shostakovich's music was denounced in the official Soviet newspaper *Pravda*, in an article titled "Chaos Instead of Music." The review concluded: "This game might end very badly." A bad review is one thing, a veiled threat something else. Shostakovich told his friends that he expected arrest and imprisonment.

For the rest of the 1930s and the 1940s, Shostakovich's relationship with the Soviet government remained on shaky ground, as the official position on his work oscillated between reluctant acceptance and strict condemnation. On one hand, his symphonies were played not only at home but also throughout Europe and in the major cities of the United States and Canada; this international stature gave Shostakovich a measure of protection, making it difficult for Stalin to exile him to a work camp, or to execute him, as he did other intellectuals. In some years, Shostakovich was even "in favor" at home. In 1941, he received the Stalin Medal for service to the state and served as a model for the spirit of Russian resistance in the war with Hitler's Germany (Fig. 30.3). On the other hand, twice, in 1936 and 1948, his music was officially denounced as "formalistic." After each denunciation, Shostakovich hid his most progressive scores (those with atonal or twelve-tone content) and "toned down" the Modernist component in the little music that he did allow to be performed. This game of cat and mouse—with Shostakovich the mouse—continued until the composer died of a heart attack in 1975.

Figure 30.2

Dmitri Shostakovich

Figure 30.3

Shostakovich, the icon of Russian resistance to German aggression, as presented to Americans in 1942

Symphony No. 5 (1937)

In his Symphony No. 5, written the year following his first denunciation at the hands of Soviet authorities, Shostakovich felt compelled to keep his Modernist tendencies largely hidden from view. The work was a huge success when it premiered in November 1937. Here was music that the average listener—Stalin, for example—could understand. With its brilliant orchestration and expressive, emotional character, Symphony No. 5 reveals Shostakovich's debt to the Romantic spirit of Gustav Mahler (Ch. 26). Yet Shostakovich was fully a citizen of the twentieth century, intent on speaking with a fully modern voice. While the progressive voice is, of necessity, somewhat muted, it can still be heard in the heavy percussion, moderate (but not extreme) dissonance, ostinatos, and "sliding harmonies" of the sort found in Prokofiev's *Romeo and Juliet*. Shostakovich would go on to compose ten more symphonies.

While many of these are often performed today, the fifth remains his most popular. The exultant finale seems to signal the ultimate triumph of the human spirit. In light of the circumstances under which it was written, though, critics still ask: Was the "rejoicing" expressed here truly felt, or was it feigned—forced from the composer? Shostakovich himself suggested the answer when he said: "The majority of my symphonies are tombstones."

Listening Guide

Dmitri Shostakovich, Symphony No. 5 (1937)

Fourth movement, *Allegro non troppo* (fast, but not too fast)

Genre: Symphony

Form: Abbreviated sonata–allegro

WHAT TO LISTEN FOR: Ask yourself: Where are the moments of Modernism, and where are those of traditional Romanticism in this stirring symphonic finale?

5/13–15

EXPOSITION

0:00	13	Percussive sounds as low brasses play first theme
0:32		First theme unfolds continually in brass, strings, and winds.
2:08		Trumpet introduces second theme above swirling mass of strings.
2:33		Violins sweep along with second theme in heroic fashion.
3:04		Low brasses play transition.
3:18		French horn plays lyrical solo (variant of second theme).

DEVELOPMENT

| 3:51 | 14 | 0:00 | Strings and then winds quietly develop second theme and then fragments of first. |
| 4:57 | | 1:06 | Hints of first theme begin to appear in low strings and then low brasses. |

ABBREVIATED RECAPITULATION

| 6:38 | 15 | 0:00 | First theme returns quietly and somewhat altered with snare drum accompanying. |
| 7:30 | | 0:52 | First theme grows in intensity. |

CODA

| 8:11 | | 1:33 | Brasses play first theme slowly; intervals altered to change mode from minor to major. |
| 8:34 | | 1:56 | Harmony is static, holding on tonic pitch; timpani pounds dominant and tonic pitches. |

◀)) Listen to streaming music in an Active Listening Guide at CourseMate or in the eBook.

◀)) Take online Listening Exercise 30.1 and receive feedback at CourseMate or in the eBook.

Béla Bartók (1881–1945)

The music of the Hungarian composer Béla Bartók (Fig. 30.4) is decidedly Modernist, yet distinctly different in sound from that of Stravinsky or Schoenberg. While it can be atonal, like the music of Schoenberg, it is often exceptionally tuneful, making use of sweeping melodies. And while it is frequently percussive and highly rhythmic, like the motor-driven sounds of Stravinsky, Bartók's rhythmic force derives mainly from folk music. Bartók's creative imagination was fired by folk materials of his native Hungary (see Fig. 30.1). He saw a return to the simple, direct style of folk music as a way to counter the tendency in Romantic music toward ostentation and sentimentality. Ultimately, he came to use Hungarian folk music as a musical defense against expanding German nationalism, the Nazi threat that eventually overran Hungary.

The turbulent events that occurred in Eastern Europe during the first half of the twentieth century deeply affected the life of Béla Bartók. He was born in 1881 in Hungary, but in a part of that nation given over to Romania at the end of World War I. Throughout his life, he was an ardent Hungarian nationalist, and he chose to develop his obvious musical talents at the Academy of Music in Budapest rather than at the German-dominated Vienna Conservatory, to which he had also been admitted. As a student at the academy in Budapest, he studied composition and piano, quickly acquiring a reputation as a concert pianist of the highest quality. By the 1920s, he had achieved an international reputation both as a pianist and as a composer of Modernist music. His tours even carried him to the West Coast of the United States, where a local newspaper alerted the public to the approaching "danger" with the following headline: "Hungarian Modernist Advances upon Los Angeles." As both a Hungarian Modernist and nationalist, Bartók was an outspoken critic of the supporters of Nazi Germany, who gained control of the Hungarian government in the late 1930s. He called the fascists "bandits and assassins," cut off ties with the German firm that published his music, and banned the performances of his works in Germany and Italy, thereby losing considerable performance and broadcast fees. Ultimately, in 1940, he fled to the United States.

Béla Bartók is rare among musicians in that he was not only a composer but also an **ethnomusicologist**—a musical anthropologist who does field work gathering and studying the music of indigenous peoples around the world. Traveling from village to village, Bartók collected folk music in Hungary, Romania, Bulgaria, Turkey, and even North Africa, using the newly invented recording machine of Thomas Edison (Fig. 30.5). In this way, his ear became saturated with the driving rhythms and odd-numbered meters of peasant dances, as well as the unusual scales on which the folk melodies of Eastern Europe were constructed.

The musical heritage of Eastern Europe is heard throughout Bartók's music, from his first string quartet (1908) to his great final works for orchestra: *Music for Strings, Percussion and Celesta* (1936), *Divertimento for Strings* (1939), and *Concerto for Orchestra* (1943). This last-named piece was commissioned by the conductor of the Boston Symphony Orchestra for the then-substantial fee of $1,000.

Figure 30.4

Béla Bartók

Figure 30.5

Béla Bartók recording folk songs among Czech-speaking peasants in 1908. The performers sang into the megaphone of a wax-cylinder recording machine invented by Thomas Edison.

How did it come to pass that Bartók worked for the Boston Symphony Orchestra? During the 1930s, radical Modernists—not only in the Soviet Union but also in Fascist-controlled Europe—were under attack. Fearing for their lives, many artists fled, seeking safe harbor and employment in the United States. Stravinsky, Schoenberg, novelist Thomas Mann, and filmmaker Sergey Eisenstein (1898–1948) moved to Hollywood, where the movie industry was thriving. Bartók emigrated to New York City and took a minor position as a cataloger of folk music at Columbia University. The commission from the Boston Symphony signaled that the artistry of this displaced composer deserved support in difficult times. Momentarily free of financial concerns, Bartók created his best-known and most alluring composition.

Concerto for Orchestra (1943)

Normally, concertos are written for a single solo instrument—piano or violin, for example—pitted against an orchestra. In Bartók's *Concerto for Orchestra*, however, the composer encourages many instruments to step forward from within the orchestra to serve as soloists from time to time. The spotlight switches from one instrument to another or to a new combination of instruments, each displaying its distinctive tonal color against the backdrop of the full orchestra. The concerto comprises five movements. The first is "written in a more or less regular sonata form," as the composer says, and makes use of the folk-like pentatonic scale; the second is a colorful parade of pairs of instruments; the third is an atmospheric nocturne, an example of what is called Bartók's "night music," in which the woodwinds slither around chromatically above a misty tremolo in the strings; the fourth is an unusual intermezzo; and the fifth is a vigorous peasant dance in sonata-allegro form. Let's focus our attention on the fourth movement, *Intermezzo interrotto (Broken Intermezzo)*.

An **intermezzo** (Italian for "between piece") is a light musical interlude intended to separate and thus break the mood of two more serious surrounding movements. But here, as the title *Broken Intermezzo* indicates, the light intermezzo is itself rudely interrupted by contrasting music. At the outset of the movement, a charming theme in the oboe establishes a sophisticated mood (Ex. 30.1). As is usual for Bartók, this melody shows the influence of the Hungarian folk song both in its pentatonic construction (the five notes that make up the scale of the melody are B, C#, E, F#, and A#) and in the way the meter switches back and forth between an even $\frac{2}{4}$ and an odd $\frac{5}{8}$. As we have often seen (Ch. 21, "Musical Nationalism"), the pentatonic scale and irregular meters are marks of the folk.

EXAMPLE 30.1

After the tune is passed among several wind instruments, an even more ingratiating melody emerges in the strings (Ex. 30.2). It, too, has a Hungarian style. In fact, it is Bartók's idealized reworking of the song "You Are Lovely, You Are Beautiful, Hungary."

EXAMPLE 30.2

But the nostalgic vision of the homeland is suddenly interrupted by a new, cruder theme in the clarinet, and it also tells a tale (Ex. 30.3). Bartók had just heard Dmitri Shostakovich's Symphony No. 7, composed in 1942 as a programmatic work designed to stiffen Russian resistance to the German army, which had invaded the previous year. Shostakovich was a Russian hero at that moment (see Fig. 30.3), and Bartók borrowed the theme that Shostakovich had written to signify the invading Germans, believing its simple quarter-note descent to be appropriately heavy and trite.

EXAMPLE 30.3

Thus, Bartók's *Broken Intermezzo* can be heard as an autobiographical work in which, as the composer related to a friend, "the artist declares his love for his native land in a serenade which is suddenly interrupted in a crude and violent manner; he is seized by rough, booted men who even break his instrument." Bartók tells us what he thinks of these "rough, booted men" (the Nazis) by surrounding them with rude, jeering noises in the trumpets and sneering trombone glissandos. Ultimately, he brings back the idyllic vision of the homeland by returning to the two opening themes. As for the soloists in this movement of Bartók's *Concerto for Orchestra,* many have an opportunity to shine: oboe, clarinet, flute, English horn, and the entire section of violas.

Listening Guide

Béla Bartók, *Concerto for Orchestra* (1943)

Fourth movement, *Broken Intermezzo*

Genre: Concerto

Form: Rondo

5

5/16

WHAT TO LISTEN FOR: Melodies and rhythms that sound slightly askew, owing to scales that are neither major nor minor, and meters that are irregular, both characteristics of folk music

0:00	16		Four-note introduction
0:05		**A**	Oboe introduces folk-like theme.
1:00		**B**	Violas introduce theme "You Are Lovely, You Are Beautiful, Hungary."
1:43		**A**	Oboe briefly plays folk-like theme.
2:06		**C**	Clarinet introduces theme (borrowed from Shostakovich).
2:16			Rude noises in trumpets and trombones
2:29		**C**	Parody of theme in violins
2:37			More rude noises

(continued)

2:41	C	Theme played in inversion by violins
2:45		More rude noises
2:54	B	Hungarian song returns in violas.
3:28	A	Folk-like theme returns in English horn, flute (cadenza-like), oboe, bassoon, and piccolo.

◀)) Listen to streaming music in an Active Listening Guide at CourseMate or in the eBook.

As was true for Prokofiev and Shostakovich, Bartók's last years were not golden. He tried to supplement the meager income of his job at Columbia by composing and performing. But, aside from his *Concerto for Orchestra*, he had little success and ultimately died of leukemia in New York's West Side Hospital in 1945—a sad ending in an era that brought disillusionment, turmoil, and death to millions.

Key Words

Russian Revolution (350)   formalism (351)   ethnomusicologist (355)   intermezzo (356)

For a complete review of this chapter, see the Main Points, Chapter Quiz, Flashcards, and Glossary in CourseMate.

[f] Join us on Facebook at **Listening to Music with Craig Wright**.

American Modernism

The United States is a highly pluralistic society, home to recent and not-so-recent immigrants, as well as Native Americans. This cultural and ethnic diversity is reflected in the country's many popular musical traditions, including blues, ragtime, jazz, rock and roll, traditional Appalachian, bluegrass, and country and western. American art music of the past hundred years was equally variegated, exemplified by high-art Modernist music of the European type, Modernism with a distinctly American flavor, and, most recently, Postmodernist music. Unlike the suppressed European composers discussed in Chapter 30, twentieth-century American composers were free to create without governmental constraints. Offering both a "free market" for the exchange of artistic ideas and a safe homeland for ethnic groups from around the globe, the United States has come to enjoy the most diverse and vibrant musical culture in the world. In this chapter, we explore how three composers of art music refracted twentieth-century Modernism through the prism of the American experience.

Charles Ives (1874–1954)

Charles Ives was an American original, arguably the greatest—and certainly the most experimental—of American Modernist composers. He was born in Danbury, Connecticut, the son of George Ives (1845-1894), a bandleader in the Union army who had served with General Ulysses S. Grant during the Civil War. The senior Ives gave his son a highly unorthodox musical education, at least by European standards. True, the obligatory study of the three B's (Bach, Beethoven, and Brahms), instruction in harmony and counterpoint, and lessons on the violin, piano, organ, cornet, and drums were all included. But young Ives also learned, as he put it, to "stretch his ears." In one exercise, for example, he was made to sing "Swanee River" in E♭ while his father accompanied him on the piano in the key of C—a useful lesson in **polytonality** (two or more keys sounding simultaneously).

Because his forebears had gone to Yale, it was decided that Charles should enroll there, too. At Yale, he took courses in music with Horatio Parker (1863–1919), a composer who had studied in Germany. But Ives's youthful, independent ideas about how music should sound clashed with Parker's traditional European training in harmony and counterpoint. The student learned to leave his more audacious musical experiments—which included, for example, a fugue with a subject entering in four different keys—outside Parker's classroom. Ives became heavily involved in extracurricular activities, playing on the baseball team and joining a fraternity (Delta Kappa Epsilon), as he maintained a D+ average (a "gentleman's" mark before the days of grade inflation).

When he graduated in 1898, Ives decided not to pursue music as a profession, realizing that the sort of music he heard in his head was not the kind the public would pay to hear. Instead, he headed for New York City and Wall Street, and in 1907, he and a friend formed the company of Ives and Myrick, an agency that sold insurance as a subsidiary of Mutual of New York (MONY). Ives and Myrick became the largest insurance agency in the United States, and in 1929, the year in which Ives retired, the company had sales of $49 million.

But Charles Ives led two lives: high-powered insurance executive by day, prolific composer by night. During the twenty years between his departure from Yale (1898) and the American entry into World War I (1917), Ives wrote the bulk of his 43 works for orchestra (including 4 symphonies), 41 choral pieces, approximately 75 works for piano solo or various chamber ensembles, and more than 150 songs. Almost without exception, they went unheard. Ives made little effort to get his music performed—composition was for him a very private matter. By the 1930s, however, word of his unusual creations had spread among a few influential performers and critics. In 1947, he was awarded the

Figure 31.1

Young Charles Ives in the baseball uniform of Hopkins Grammar School, New Haven, Connecticut. A better ballplayer than student, Ives needed an extra year between high school and college to prepare for Yale.

the Pulitzer Prize in music for his Third Symphony, one he had written forty years earlier! Having become a gruff, grumpy eccentric, Ives told the members of the Pulitzer committee, "Prizes are for boys. I'm grown up."

Ives's Music

Charles Ives was an idiosyncratic man with an equally idiosyncratic aesthetic; his extreme Modernist music is unlike that of any other composer. Between 1898 and 1917, Ives independently devised the same radical compositional techniques—including atonality, polymeter, polyrhythm, and tone clusters—that had begun to appear in the works of Schoenberg, Stravinsky, and the other European Modernists. Moreover, Ives was the first composer to use polytonality extensively, and he even experimented with **quarter-tone music**—music in which the smallest interval is not the chromatic half step (the smallest division the modern piano can play) but *half* of a half step. Ives's music places great demands on performer and listener alike. It is full of grinding dissonances and dense, complex textures. At the same time, however, it contains many simple, popular-musical elements, incorporating patriotic songs, marches, hymns, dance tunes, fiddle tunes, rags, and football cheers; this was Ives's musical America. Ives often combines these familiar musical idioms with melodies of his own, piling one tune on top of another to form a new composite. What results is a jarring kind of **collage art**: art made up of disparate materials taken from very different places. In a manner akin to that of a progressive artist who reinterprets fragments of reality in surprising ways (Fig. 31.2), Ives takes the familiar and "defamiliarizes" it, thereby making the old sound very modern.

The Old Cupboard Door, 1889 (oil on canvas), Harnett, William Michael (1848–1892)/Sheffield Galleries and Museums Trust, UK/Photo © Museums Sheffield/The Bridgeman Art Library

Figure 31.2

William Harnett's *Music and the Old Cupboard Door* (1889) creates a satisfying collage of Americana by melding various objects from a closet and the world of music.

Variations on America (1892–ca. 1905)

Ives took an important step toward collage art in one of his earliest works, *Variations on America* for organ, which he began in 1892 at the age of seventeen. As the title indicates, this is a set of variations on the patriotic tune known in the United States as "America" or "My Country 'Tis of Thee" (in Canada and England as "God Save the Queen [King]").

The work opens with a conventional introduction, followed by a statement of the well-known theme. Variation 1 is filled with increasingly chromatic figuration in the right hand, but otherwise seems tame enough. Thereafter, however, Ives lets loose, building a "mashup" of outside musical references with the original melody. Variation 2 ends with the close chromatic harmony popular with turn-of-the-century barbershop quartets, while Variation 3, with its quick puffs of sound, is reminiscent of a calliope, or steam organ, at a village fair. Variation 4 introduces the most foreign element: a Polish polonaise (traditional dance). The fifth and final variation features a Bach-like walking bass to be played by the pedals "as fast as they can go." The collage in this piece, then, consists of a patriotic tune melded with allusions to a barbershop quartet, steam whistles, a Polish polonaise, and a Baroque organ toccata.

Sometime during the first decade of the twentieth century, during his time as an insurance agent in New York City, Ives revisited his *Variations on America* and inserted two interludes. Both are remarkable for their extensive use of polytonality. In the first interlude, for example, the right hand plays the melody in F major; against this the left hand and the pedal perform the same music, but in the clashing key of Db! The same theme is set against itself, as happens in the visual arts in the chapter opener, a 1958 collage created by Jasper Johns. Ives was the first composer in the history of music to employ polytonality consistently, and the result is bracingly dissonant. "America" had never sounded like this before! Indeed, America wasn't ready for Ives's ear-splitting sonorities. Not until 1949, more than fifty years after Ives began *Variations on America,* did he find a publisher willing to print it.

Charles Ives, *Variations on America* **(1892–ca. 1905)**

Genre: Organ work

Form: Theme and variations

WHAT TO LISTEN FOR: The discrepancy in sound between the variations

5/17–18

Introduction

0:00	17	Hints of theme to come
0:54		Theme "America" in chordal homophony

Variation 1

1:24	Theme in left hand as rapid figuration in right hand becomes increasingly chromatic

Variation 2

2:18	Dark, descending chromatic harmonies cover the theme.

Interlude 1

3:08	Dissonant polytonality; right hand plays tune in F major, and left hand and pedal play in D♭ major.

Variation 3

3:31	Meter changes from triple to duple.
4:01	New, fast-moving counterpoint added in left hand

Variation 4

4:32	18	0:00	Theme set as a snappy polonaise (Polish dance) in minor key and triple meter

Interlude 2

5:19	0:47	More polytonality; right hand in A♭, left hand in F major

Variation 5

5:32	1:00	Steady, Bach-like walking bass played rapidly in the pedal

Coda

6:25	1:53	Recall of introduction; pedal plays beginning of theme as final flourish.

 Listen to streaming music in an Active Listening Guide at CourseMate or in the eBook.

Aaron Copland (1900–1990)

Until the twentieth century, the United States was a cultural backwater of a European tide. European symphonic scores, for example, dominated the repertoire of symphony orchestras in New York, Boston, Cincinnati, and Chicago, among other places, in post–Civil War America. During the twentieth century, however, as the presence of the United States loomed increasingly large on the world stage, American composers provided this emerging nation with its own distinctive musical identity. Charles Ives pressed forward with his unique musical style, one full of American patriotic songs, marches, and hymn tunes. Aaron Copland (Fig. 31.3) did the same, but drew also on early jazz and cowboy songs. In contrast to his older contemporary, however, Copland set his bits of Americana not within a collage of dissonant polytonality, but instead against a conservative backdrop of generally consonant harmony.

Copland was born in Brooklyn of Jewish immigrant parents. After a rudimentary musical education in New York City, he set sail for Paris to broaden his artistic horizons. In this he was not alone, for the City of Light at this time attracted young writers, painters, and musicians from across the world, including Igor Stravinsky (1882–1974), Pablo Picasso (1881–1973), James Joyce (1882–1941), Gertrude Stein (1874–1946), Ernest Hemingway (1898–1961), and F. Scott Fitzgerald (1896–1940). After three years of study, Copland returned to the United States, determined to compose in a distinctly American style. Like other young expatriate artists during the 1920s, Copland had to leave his homeland to learn what made it unique: "In greater or lesser degree," he remarked, "all of us discovered America in Europe."

At first, Copland sought to forge an American style by incorporating into his music elements of jazz, recognized the world over as a uniquely American creation. Then, beginning in the late 1930s, Copland turned his attention to a series of projects with rural and western American subjects. The ballet scores *Billy the Kid* (1938) and *Rodeo* (1942) are set in the West and make use of classic cowboy songs like "Goodbye, Old Paint" and "The Old Chisholm Trail." Another ballet, *Appalachian Spring* (1944), re-creates the ambience of Pennsylvania farm country, and his only opera, *The Tender Land* (1954), is set in the Cornbelt of the Midwest. In 2009 Ken Burns featured Copland's music prominently in the soundtrack of his TV miniseries *The National Parks: America's Best Idea.* What could be more American than the wide-open sounds of Aaron Copland?

Copland evokes a sense of space in his music by means of a distinctive kind of orchestration called "open scoring." He typically creates a solid bass, a very thin middle, and a top register of one or two high, clear tones, such as those of the clarinet or flute. This separation and careful spacing of the instruments create the fresh, uncluttered sound so pleasing in Copland's music. Another characteristic element of Copland's style is the use of Americana; he incorporates American folk and popular songs to soften the dissonant harmonies and disjunct melodies of European Modernism. Copland's melodies tend to be more stepwise and diatonic than those of other twentieth-century composers, perhaps because Western folk and popular tunes are conjunct—have few skips—and are nonchromatic. His harmonies are almost always tonal and often change slowly in a way that can evoke the vastness and grandeur of the American landscape. The triad, too, is still important to Copland, perhaps for its stability and simplicity. What little dissonance is present unfolds gradually, rather than in a jarringly abrupt, Modernist fashion. Spatial clarity, folk songs, and a conservative approach to dissonance, then, mark Copland's most popular scores.

The clarity and simplicity of Aaron Copland's music is not accidental. During the Great Depression of the 1930s, he became convinced that the gulf between modern music and the ordinary citizen had become too great—that dissonance and atonality had little to say to most music lovers. "It made no sense to ignore them [ordinary listeners] and to continue writing as if they did not exist. I felt that

AP Photo/Martell

Figure 31.3

Aaron Copland

To get a sense of Paris as an artistic mecca in the 1920s, watch a clip from Woody Allen's *Midnight in Paris,* in the YouTube playlist at CourseMate for this text.

it was worth the effort to see if I couldn't say what I had to say in the simplest possible terms." Thus, he not only wrote appealing new tonal works like *Fanfare for the Common Man* (1942) but also highlighted simple, traditional tunes such as "The Gift to Be Simple," which he uses in *Appalachian Spring.*

Appalachian Spring (1944)

Appalachian Spring is a one-act ballet that tells the story of "a pioneer celebration of spring in a newly built farmhouse in Pennsylvania in the early 1800s." A new bride and her farmer–husband express through dance the anxieties and joys of life in pioneer America. The work was composed in 1944 for the great American choreographer Martha Graham (1893–1991), and it won Copland a Pulitzer Prize the following year (Fig. 31.4). It is divided into eight connected sections that differ in tempo and mood. Copland provided a brief description of each of these orchestral scenes.

SECTION 1

"*Introduction of the characters one by one, in a suffused light.*" The quiet beauty of the land at daybreak is revealed, as the orchestra slowly presents, one by one, the notes of the tonic and dominant triads.

EXAMPLE 31.1

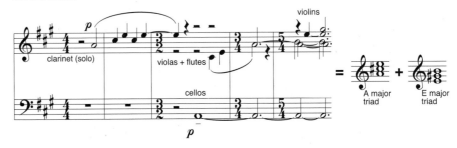

While this overlapping presentation of two triads constitutes a polychord, the effect is only mildly dissonant because of the slow, quiet way in which the notes of the two chords are introduced. The serene simplicity of the introduction sets the tone for the entire work.

SECTION 2

"*A sentiment both elated and religious gives the keynote of this scene.*" The early calm is suddenly broken by a lively dance with a salient rhythm played aggressively in the strings. The dance has all the modern rhythmic vigor of Stravinsky's music, but none of the extreme polymeter. As the dance proceeds, a more restrained hymn-like melody emerges in the trumpet.

SECTIONS 3–6

Section 3 is a dance for the two principals, a *pas de deux* accompanied by lyrical writing for strings and winds. Sections 4 and 5 are musical depictions of the livelier aspects of country life, with Section 4 including a toe-tapping hoedown, while Section 6 recalls the quiet calm of the opening of the ballet.

SECTION 7

"*Calm and flowing. Scenes of daily activity for the Bride and her Farmer–husband.*" For this section, Copland chose to make use of a traditional tune of the Shakers, an extreme religious sect that prospered in the Appalachian region in the early

Julie Lemberger/CORBIS

Figure 31.4

A scene from Martha Graham's ballet *Appalachian Spring*, with music by Aaron Copland. Here Katherine Crockett dances the role of the Bride (New York, 1999).

See the ballet as originally choreographed by Martha Graham, and filmed in 1944, in the YouTube playlist at CourseMate for this text.

nineteenth century and whose members expressed their spiritual intensity in frenzied singing, dancing, and shaking. Today this tune is famous, having been featured, among other places, in a piece John Williams composed for Barack Obama's inauguration in 2009. But the melody has become well known only because of Copland's *Appalachian Spring*. The composer plucked it from an obscure book of folk songs in 1944 because he thought the simple, diatonic tune (Ex. 31.2) fit well with the American character of the ballet, and because the text of the Shaker song is harmonious with what occurs on stage: "scenes of daily activity."

EXAMPLE 31.2

'Tis the gift to be simple,

'Tis the gift to be free,

'Tis the gift to come down where we ought to be,

And when we find ourselves in the place just right,

'Twill be in the valley of love and delight.

In the five variations that follow, "The Gift to Be Simple" is not so much varied as it is clothed in different instrumental attire.

SECTION 8

"*The Bride takes her place among her neighbors.*" Serenity returns to the scene as the strings play a slow, mostly stepwise descent, as Copland says, "like a prayer." The hymn-like melody from Section 2 is heard again in the flute, followed by the quiet "landscape music" from the beginning of the ballet. Darkness has again descended on the valley, leaving the young pioneer couple "strong in their new house" and secure in their community.

Listening Guide

Aaron Copland, *Appalachian Spring* (1944)

Sections 1, 2, and 7

Genre: Ballet music

5/19–21 2/22–24

WHAT TO LISTEN FOR: Section 1 demonstrates Copland's "open scoring"; Section 2 has percussive, Modernist dissonance; and Section 7 employs a bit of Americana—a Shaker hymn tune—in theme and variations form.

SECTION 1

0:00	19 / 22	Quiet unfolding of ascending triads by clarinet and other instruments
0:53		Soft melody descends in woodwinds and strings.
1:34		More ascending triads in woodwinds and trumpet, then flute melody (1:46)
2:01		Oboe and then bassoon solos
2:49		Clarinet plays concluding ascending triad.

(continued)

| 0:00 | **20** **23** | Percussive rhythm (♫ ♩ ♫ ♩) in strings and rising woodwinds |
| 0:17 | | Rhythm gels into sprightly dance. |

mf

| 0:43 | | Trumpet plays hymn-like melody above dance. |

ff

1:13		Rhythmic motive scattered but then played more forcefully
2:10		Hymn played quietly in strings, with flute counterpoint above
2:45		Rhythmic motive skips away in woodwinds.

SECTION 7

| 0:00 | **21** **24** | Clarinet presents Shaker tune. |

p

0:33		Variation 1: Oboe and bassoon play tune.
1:02		Variation 2: Violas and trombones play tune at half its previous speed.
1:49		Variation 3: Trumpets and trombones play tune at fast tempo.
2:12		Variation 4: Woodwinds play tune more slowly.
2:30		Variation 5: Final majestic statement of tune by full orchestra

🔊 🔊 🔊 Listen to streaming music in Active Listening Guides at CourseMate or in the eBook.

🔊 Take online Listening Exercise 31.1 and receive feedback at CourseMate or in the eBook.

By the end of the Second World War, American composers such as Charles Ives and Aaron Copland had taken European Modernism and given it a distinctly American voice. Consequently, American composers thereafter no longer felt obliged to forge a national style. Ellen Taaffe Zwilich, a Julliard-trained composer and the first woman to win the Pulitzer Prize in music, described the stylistic plurality that took hold in the United States after midcentury: "There was a time, in the 1920s with the music of Copland, for example, when we were searching for an American voice. Then we went beyond that stage. Our musical interests are now really quite all over the map."

Augusta Read Thomas (b. 1964)

Drawing on wide-ranging influences—from Bach to jazz to high Modernism—the output of Augusta Read Thomas (Fig. 31.5) exemplifies the stylistic diversity of art music in the contemporary United States. Thomas, born in Glen Cove, New York, was a child prodigy in composition. (Indeed, her parents seem to have preordained her to be a creator by giving her the initials ART.) Like Mozart, she began writing music at the age of five and did so prolifically. After formal study of composition at Northwestern and Yale, her scores eventually caught the ear of Leonard Bernstein (see Ch. 35, "*West Side Story*"), whose support strengthened her resolve "to continue pursuing a lifetime composing music." Between 1989 and 1994, Thomas won several prizes, including a Guggenheim Fellowship, and commissions flooded in from leading orchestras around the world. All was going well. But in 1994 Thomas took a radical step: She burned her autographs and asked her publisher to remove from circulation all of her previous works. ("Self-critical is my middle name," she says.) Only the twenty-three scores that she deemed worthy of recognition would remain, and to these she added carefully as the years proceeded.

The Rub of Love (1996): A Modernist Madrigal

Among the works that Augusta Read Thomas allowed to circulate was *The Rub of Love*. Like many composers of the twentieth century, Thomas frequently seeks inspiration in the music of the past, a strategy that is emphasized in this vocal piece from 1996. Engaging in a musical dialogue with previous periods in the history of music—whether the Middle Ages, Renaissance, Baroque, or Classical—is an exercise in Neo-classicism. In a Neo-classical composition, elements of Modernist music blend with and play against elements taken from an earlier style. The fun for the listener is to pick out which earlier style is referenced and when—"Do I hear medieval or Baroque here?" for example—and to determine which moments are antiquated and which are modern.

The subtitle of *The Rub of Love* gives the game away: "A short madrigal in twelve parts." The point of reference is the madrigal of the late sixteenth century. The work was commissioned in 1995 by the San Francisco-based a cappella ensemble Chanticleer, which specializes in Renaissance vocal music. Clearly, Thomas had the group's sound in mind when she wrote *The Rub of Love*, as she incorporates several distinctive features of the Renaissance style: First, the purely a cappella settings hearken back to the earlier period; next, the words "ha ha ha" echo the "fa la la" of light English madrigals and carols; and finally, word painting ("madrigalisms") recalls the treatment of the text common in the English music of the Renaissance (see Ch. 6, "The Madrigal"). But Thomas also liberally dabs the work with what she calls "twentieth-century perfume." The Modernist elements include dissonant tone clusters, highly chromatic vocal lines, and the disjunct (start-and-stop) flow of the music. In recalling how she composed this Modernist madrigal, Thomas walked over to a bookcase and pulled out the old volume that contained the poem, an anonymous verse from Greek antiquity.

> Whenever I start to compose, I read the text over and over. I feel I should be responsible to the text, so as to make the colors of the words stand out. When I read *The Rub of Love*, I started to laugh, thinking of the double entendre involved in "to rub" [to repeatedly touch, and also to be ironic, as in "there's the rub"]. The energy and imagery of the text began to convert into sonic material. I was having fun as I wrote—it all seemed so whimsical (tugging at the wings of Cupid and drinking him down).

Thomas's creative expression is based on the symbiotic relationship of poetry and music. In 2009, she was elected to the American Academy of Arts and Letters, joining a select group of just 250 famous artists, including Meryl Streep, Toni Morrison, Stephen Sondheim, Woody Allen, and Martin Scorsese. The citation for her work read "Augusta Read Thomas's impressive body of works embodies unbridled passion and fierce poetry, [making her] one of the most recognizable and widely loved figures in American Music."

Figure 31.5

Augusta Read Thomas

© Lebrecht Music & Arts/The Image Works

Augusta Read Thomas, *The Rub of Love* (1995)

Genre: Madrigal

WHAT TO LISTEN FOR: First, differentiate between the moments of Modernism and the references to the Renaissance. Then, listen more generally to the beautifully clear a cappella sound of the performing group Chanticleer, which commissioned this work. The album (*Colors of Love*), on which *The Rub of Love* appears, won a Grammy in 2000.

0:00	Modernist tone cluster	The rub of love.
0:24	Madrigalism: laughing on the words	Ha, ha, ha, ha!
0:30	Madrigalism: rubbing, a "tickling" of a neighboring pitch a half step away	Eros tickles me.
0:49	Madrigalism: spinning out a chromatic line on the word "plaiting" (weaving)	Once while plaiting a wreath I found Eros [Cupid] among the roses.
1:26	Modernist dissonance	I grabbed him by the wings and dipped him in the wine
1:47	Madrigalism: music descends on word "down."	and drank him down.
1:57	Modernist dissonance	Now inside my limbs
2:09	"Tickling" a neighboring pitch	he tickles me with his wings.
2:25	Modernist tone cluster ending	The rub of love.

As of our press date, *The Rub of Love* had not cleared for use on the CD sets, but it can be downloaded for 99 cents from the iTunes playlist at CourseMate.

Key Words

polytonality (360)   quarter-tone music (361)   collage art (361)

For a complete review of this chapter, see the Main Points, Chapter Quiz, Flashcards, and Glossary in CourseMate.

Join us on Facebook at **Listening to Music with Craig Wright**

Checklist of Musical Style

Modern: 1900–present

REPRESENTATIVE COMPOSERS

Stravinsky	Prokofiev	Copland
Schoenberg	Shostakovich	Thomas
Bartók	Ives	

A complete Checklist of Musical Style for the Modern era may also be found at CourseMate for this text.

PRINCIPAL GENRES

symphony	string quartet	ballet music
solo concerto	opera	choral music

Melody	Wide-ranging disjunct lines, often chromatic and dissonant, angularity accentuated by use of octave displacement
Harmony	Highly dissonant, marked by chromaticism, new chords, and tone clusters; dissonance no longer must move to consonance but may move to another dissonance; sometimes two conflicting, but equal, tonal centers sound simultaneously (polytonality); sometimes no audible tonal center is present (atonality)
Rhythm	Vigorous, often asymmetrical rhythms; conflicting simultaneous meters (polymeter) and rhythms (polyrhythm) make for temporal complexity
Color	Color becomes agent of form and beauty in and of itself; composers seek new sounds from traditional, acoustical instruments and innovative singing techniques from electronic instruments and computers, and from noises in environment
Texture	As varied and individual as the men and women composing music
Form	A range of extremes: sonata–allegro, rondo, theme and variations benefit from Neo-classical revival; twelve-tone procedure allows for almost mathematical formal control; forms and processes of classical music, jazz, and pop music begin to influence one another in exciting new ways

chapter **THIRTY-TWO**
Postmodernism

n the course of this book, we have discussed the music and culture of many different periods: from the Middle Ages to the Baroque, and from the Renaissance to the Romantic. But how can we describe the music being composed today? We are modern people, so we might first assume that our art belongs to the Modernist age. But Modernism, it turns out, is no longer cutting edge. In the years since World War II, it has been superseded by a new style, aptly called Postmodernism. While Modernists reacted to, and played against, the genres, forms, and procedures of the Western classical tradition, Postmodern artists do not labor under the "anxiety of influence" of any previous music.

Instead, Postmodernism is an all-inclusive, "anything goes" movement. For Postmodernists, art is for everyone, not just an elite few, and all art is of equal potential. Andy Warhol's famous paintings of Campbell's Soup cans or of Marilyn Monroe (chapter opener), for example, are just as meaningful as Picasso's creations. Consequently, there is no "high" or "low" art, only *art* (and maybe not even that). With respect to the proper subject for art, the acceptable boundaries have exploded in the Postmodern period. In 1952, Francis Bacon, whose paintings now sell for $20 million and more, attached slabs of beef to his torso and photographed himself; in 2010, Lady Gaga shocked crowds at the Video Music Awards by wearing a dress made entirely of raw meat. These adventurous artists aim to show that any object can be transformed into a bold creative statement. Finally, Postmodernism holds that we live in a pluralistic world in which one culture is as important as the next. Indeed, cultural distinctions are gradually disappearing because of globalization, a process of homogenization made inevitable by instant mass-media communication. Postmodernism is thus refreshingly egalitarian when it comes to sex and gender, affirming a belief that the creations of, say, gay living black women are just as important as those of straight dead white men.

Postmodernist principles apply to music as well as art and fashion. If all art holds equal potential, then it is no longer necessary to separate classical from popular music—the two styles can even coexist within one and the same composition, as they do, for example, in recent works by Paul McCartney and Wynton Marsalis. No longer, according to Postmodernism, need distinctions be made between "highbrow" and "lowbrow" music; all music—classical, country, hip hop, folk, rock, and all the rest—deserves to be prized in equal measure. John Williams's film soundtracks are as important as Igor Stravinsky's ballet scores; Madonna is as worthy of our attention as Mozart.

Finally, Postmodernism brings with it a new agenda for how to create music. Classical formal models, such as sonata–allegro and theme and variations, are no longer operative. Each musical composition must fashion its own unique form according to the demands and creative urges of the moment. Music no longer need be "goal oriented"; a particular piece does not have to work progressively to a defined point of arrival or climax. In today's musical culture, amplified instruments and electronic music are commonplace in symphony hall and rock arena alike. Traditional acoustic instruments must share the spotlight with newer electric and electronic ones. While Yo-Yo Ma's Stradivarius cello is a cultural treasure, so, too, is Jimi Hendrix's electric guitar. Postmodernism embraces an egalitarian, pluralistic musical world in which technology plays an important role.

Figure 32.1

Jeff Koons's figure of a bare-backed blonde hugging a toy Pink Panther provokes the argument: What is art? What makes a work of genius? While some may claim that Koons's porcelain figure *Pink Panther* (1988) is not art, it sold at auction on May 10, 2011, for $16.8 million. But do artistic and monetary values always equate? To think further about what makes great art, consider another sculpture shown in this book, Michelangelo's *David* (Fig. 6.2).

See Yo-Yo Ma participate in the creation of a Postmodernist piece embracing Bach, bluegrass, and the sounds of Beijing, in the YouTube playlist at CourseMate for this text.

Edgard Varèse (1883–1965) and Electronic Music

The origins of musical Postmodernism can be traced to the 1930s and the experimental compositions of Edgard Varèse (Fig. 32.2). Varèse was born in France but immigrated to the United States in 1915 in search of a less traditional artistic environment. After an

The application of modern technology to music began in 1877, when Thomas Edison patented the phonograph. About 1920, the sounds of the phonograph became harnessed to electromagnetic wave diffusion via the radio; the principal content of the radio broadcast was music, some live, but most played from phonograph records. The magnetic tape recorder appeared in 1936 as a tool for recording and transmitting music, but during the 1990s the cassette tape was replaced by the CD and it, in turn, by the downloadable MP3 and M4A files of today. Thus, the means of disseminating music has changed dramatically during the past hundred years. To hear music, it is no longer necessary to learn to play an instrument or go to a concert; one need only buy a digital download.

Technology has revolutionized not merely the dissemination of music but also its production. In the years since World War II, electronic sounds have played an increasingly important part in the creation of music, a process aided by the advent of the electronic synthesizer. Edgard Varèse (1883–1965), working in both New York and Paris, was one of the earliest practitioners of electronic music. Varèse's experimental compositions—including the landmark *Poème électronique* (1958)—combine music generated by a synthesizer with bits of *musique concrète*, or "found sound." **Musique concrète** is so called because the composer works not with sounds written for voice or musical instruments, but with those found naturally in the everyday world. A car horn, a person speaking in a room, or a dog's barking may be captured by recorder and doctored in some way—reassembled and repeated (mixed, and looped) to form an unexpected montage of sound.

The technological advances that so altered the classical music landscape were soon appropriated by pop artists, and with remarkable success. The Beatles' John Lennon used "tape looping" to create a novel background ambience for his song "Revolution 9" (1968). As Lennon recounted, "We were cutting up [tapes of] classical music and

Composer Danny Elfman seen here in an electronic recording studio, blends electronic music and traditional, acoustical sounds in his film scores, among them *Good Will Hunting, Milk, Terminator Salvation, Alice in Wonderland, Batman, Beetlejuice,* and *Men in Black (1, 11,* and *111).*

AF archive/Alamy

making different size loops, and then I got an engineer tape on which an engineer was saying, 'Number nine, number nine, number nine.' All those different bits of sound and noises were all compiled. . . . I fed them all in and mixed them live." Lennon also added *musique concrète* (found sound) to a few Beatles songs. "Strawberry Fields Forever," for example, has a piano crash followed by a dog's whistle played at 15,000 vibrations per second. Not to be outdone, the rock band Pink Floyd incorporated the sounds of a clanging cash register into their song, appropriately titled, "Money" (1973). And filmmakers, too, jumped on the electronic bandwagon. George Lucas used banging chains to create

Figure 32.2

Caricature of composer Edgard Varèse in a futuristic time capsule, surrounded by the unconventional musical instruments that became his signature

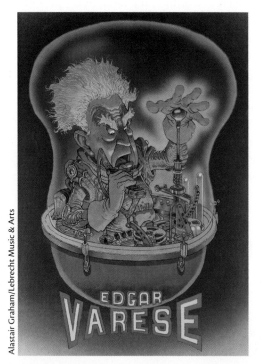

Alastair Graham/Lebrecht Music & Arts

accidental fire caused the loss of some scores he had brought from Paris, he destroyed the rest intentionally, thereby obliterating all traces of his European musical past. Already an extreme Modernist, Varèse showed himself eager to step beyond the boundaries of the Western musical tradition and embrace the Postmodernist age. But Varèse was a pioneer, in some ways ahead of his time, and musical Postmodernism was not to reach full force until the 1960s. Thus, as with many artistic and cultural eras, Modernism and Postmodernism overlapped for decades. Indeed, in many ways, the two styles still coexist today.

Significantly, Varèse titled his first work written in the United States *Amériques* (1921), suggesting not only a new geography but also a new world the sound of the Imperial Walkers for his *Star Wars* epics. To be specific, he recorded, and then modified and layered, the noise of a bicycle chain falling on a concrete floor—a literal example of the principle of *musique concrète*.

What began as esoteric experiments by a few avant-garde scientists and high-art composers thus transformed the world of popular entertainment. The technological development that made this possible was miniaturization. During the 1960s, the large-console tape machine was reduced to the portable tape recorder, and then, during the 1980s, microprocessors became small enough to power keyboard synthesizers. In more recent years, the increasing power, versatility, and availability of the personal computer have facilitated revolutionary changes in the way music is composed, produced, and recorded. Almost any aspiring composer or rock band can now own the hardware required to produce and manipulate their own sounds. Today's computer-driven synthesizer can generate sounds that are almost indistinguishable from those of a ninety-piece orchestra. Consequently, **computer music** has revolutionized the world of commercial music. The computer-equipped recording studio now generates much of the music we hear on radio and television. For example, the opening theme of the perennially popular *Desperate Housewives,* written by Danny Elfman (b. 1953), is electronically based computer music, but incorporates acoustic string sounds as well. Today, only two TV shows make use of a traditional acoustical orchestra to create the music soundtrack (*The Simpsons* and *Family Guy*); the remainder employ electronically processed music nearly exclusively.

Technology has also facilitated new processes for producing pop music. In the 1980s, rap and hip hop artists began using a technique called **sampling** whereby the rapper or producer extracts a small portion of prerecorded music and then mechanically repeats it over and over as a musical backdrop to the text that he or she raps. And in **scratching**, another technique popular in rap and hip hop, a creative DJ with one or more turntables manipulates the needles, scratching on the vinyl of the record while other prerecorded sounds loop continually in the background.

Musician Thom Yorke surrounded by some of the electronic equipment that gives his band Radiohead its distinctive "electronic" sound

Frank Micelotta/Getty Images

Perhaps no contemporary rock group has blended songwriting with the manipulation of electronic audio more extensively than Radiohead. For their albums and concert tours, they use not only analog and digital synthesizers but also special-effects pedals and distortion filters to re-form the audio of their voices and instruments. All these electronic devices and computer processes help give the music of Radiohead a disembodied, otherworldly quality.

of musical sound. Besides the usual strings, brasses, and woodwinds, the orchestra for *Amériques* also required a battery of new percussion instruments, including sirens and sleigh bells, most of which had never been heard in a symphony orchestra. In earlier centuries, composers had typically called on the percussion to provide accentuation. The thuds, bangs, and crashes of these instruments helped to delineate the outline of the musical structure. Like road signs, they pointed the way but did not constitute the essence of the musical journey. By the 1930s, however, Varèse had radically altered the traditional role of the percussion family. In *Ionization* (1931), the orchestra consists of nothing but percussion instruments, including two sirens, two tam-tams, a gong, cymbals, anvils, three different sizes of bass drum, bongos, various Cuban rattles and gourds, slap-sticks, Chinese blocks, sleigh bells, and chimes. Here, percussive sounds do not *reinforce* the music; they *are* the music.

To grasp the significance of an all-percussion orchestra, remember that most percussion instruments generate sounds of indefinite pitch, rather than one continuous frequency or musical tone. Without discrete tones, two essential elements of traditional music—melody and harmony—have been removed. All that remains is rhythm, color, and texture, which Varèse deployed in original ways. Yet, having created new percussive soundscapes in *Ionization,* Varèse wanted more. As he said in a lecture in 1936: "When new instruments allow me to write music as I conceive it, [then my shifting sound-masses] will be clearly perceived." Two decades later, the "new instruments" Varèse had envisioned—electronic instruments—became available.

Poème électronique (1958)

Most traditional music around the world is played on acoustic instruments (ones made of natural materials). Shortly after World War II, however, new technology led to the development of **electronic music** produced by a **synthesizer**—a machine that can create, transform, and combine (synthesize) sounds by means of electronic circuitry. Varèse's *Poème électronique* is an early landmark of electronic music. In this piece, the composer combined new electronic sounds generated by a synthesizer with bits of *musique concrète* (see boxed essay "Electronic Music: From Thomas Edison to Radiohead"), including taped sounds of a siren, a train, an organ, church bells, and a human voice, all altered or distorted in some imaginative way. Varèse created this "poem for the electronic age" to provide music for a multimedia exhibit inside the pavilion of the Philips Radio Corporation at the 1958 World's Fair in Brussels. Varèse's eight-minute creation was recorded on tape and then played back over 425 speakers, again and again, to the 15,000 to 16,000 people who walked through the structure daily. While the music played, a video montage was projected on the inside walls of the building.

Listening Guide

Edgard Varèse, *Poème électronique* (1958), (opening)

Genre: Electronic music

WHAT TO LISTEN FOR: A brave new sonic world comprising prerecorded sounds from everyday life (found sounds) manipulated electronically and new sounds generated by electronic means

5

5/22

0:00	22	Large bell, squibbles and zaps, sirens
0:41		Drip-like noise, squawks
0:56		Three-note chromatic ascent sounded three times
1:11		Low sustained noise with rattle, siren, more squawks
1:33		Three-note chromatic ascent, squawks and chirps
2:03		Percussion instruments, siren (2:12)
2:34		Large bell returns, sustained tones
2:58		More drips, large low crescendo, rattles and zaps

Listen to streaming music in an Active Listening Guide at CourseMate or in the eBook.

John Cage (1912–1992) and Chance Music

If all art is more or less of equal value, as the Postmodernists say, why not just leave it to chance? This is essentially what American composer John Cage decided to do. Cage was born in Los Angeles, the son of an inventor. He graduated valedictorian of Los Angeles High School and spent two years at nearby Pomona College before going to Europe to learn more about art, architecture, and music. Arriving in New York City in 1942, he worked variously as a wall washer at the YWCA, teacher of music and mycology (the science of mushrooms) at the New School for Social Research, and music director of a modern dance company.

From his earliest days as a musician, Cage had a special affection for percussion instruments and the unusual sounds they could create. His *First Construction (in Metal)* (1939) has six percussionists play piano, metal thunder-sheets, ox bells, cowbells, sleigh bells, water gongs, and brake drums, among other things. By 1941, he had collected 300 percussion objects of this kind—anything that might make an unusual noise when struck or shaken. Cage's tinkering with percussive sounds led him to invent the **prepared piano**—a grand piano outfitted with screws, bolts, washers, erasers, and bits of felt and plastic all inserted between the strings (Fig. 32.3). This transformed the piano into a one-person percussion band that could produce a great variety of sounds and noises—twangs, zaps, rattles, thuds, and the like—no two of which were exactly the same in pitch or color. In creating the prepared piano, Cage was merely continuing along the experimental trail blazed by his spiritual mentor, Edgard Varèse: "Years ago, after I decided to devote my life to music, I noticed that people distinguished between noises and sounds. I decided to follow Varèse and fight for noises, to be on the side of the underdog."

Cage's glorification of everyday noise began in earnest during the 1950s. Rather than engage in a titanic struggle to shape the elements of music, as had Beethoven, he decided to sit back, relax, and simply allow noises to occur around him. In creating this sort of intentionally purposeless, undirected music, Cage invented what has come to be called chance music, the ultimate Postmodernist experiment. In **chance music**, musical events are not carefully predetermined by the composer, but come instead in an unpredictable sequence as the result of nonmusical decisions, such as following astrological charts, tossing coins, throwing dice, or shuffling randomly the pages of music to be played. The musical "happening" that results is the sort of spontaneous group experience that was to flower during the 1960s. For example, in Cage's work *0′00″* (1962), performed by the composer himself that year, he sliced and prepared vegetables at a table on a stage, put them through a food processor, and then drank the juice, all the while amplifying and broadcasting the sound of these activities throughout the hall. Cage's declaration that the ordinary noise made by food processing can be "art" is virtually identical in intent to Andy Warhol's glorification of the Campbell's Soup can. Both styles typify the kind of radical art fashioned during the 1960s in New York City, then the epicenter of Postmodernism.

Naturally, music critics called Cage a joker and a charlatan. Most would agree that his "compositions," in and of themselves, are not of great musical value in traditional terms. Nevertheless, by raising profound questions regarding the relationships between human activity, sound, and music, his compositions eloquently articulate his own musical philosophy. By focusing on the chance appearance of ordinary noise, Cage aggressively asks us to ponder the basic principles that underlie most Western music: Why must sounds of similar range and color come one after the other? Why must music have form and unity? Why must it have "meaning"? Why must it express anything? Why must it develop and climax in some organized way? Why must it be goal-oriented, as is so much of human activity in the West?

4′33″ (1952)

The "composition" that causes us to focus on these questions most intently is Cage's *4′33″*. Here, one or more performers carrying any sort of instrument come on stage, seat themselves, open the "score," and play nothing. For each of the three carefully timed movements, no notated music exists, only the indication *tacet* ("it is silent"). But as the audience soon realizes, "absolute" silence is virtually impossible to attain. With no organized sound to be heard during the four minutes and thirty-three seconds that follow, the listener gradually becomes aware of the background noise in the hall—a creaking floor, a passing car, a dropped paper clip, an electrical hum. Cage

To hear the sounds of a prepared piano, listen to "John Cage Sonata V" in the YouTube playlist at CourseMate for this text.

See and hear a random performance of Cage's chance music *0′00″* in the YouTube playlist at CourseMate for this text.

Figure 32.3

John Cage "preparing" a piano. By putting spoons, forks, screws, paper clips, and other sundry objects into the strings of the piano, the composer changes the instrument from one producing melodic tones to one generating percussive impacts.

New York Times Co./Getty Images

asks us to embrace these random everyday noises, to tune our ears in innocent sonic wonder. Are these sounds not of artistic value, too? What is music? What is noise? What is art?

Needless to say, we have not filled your CDs or your downloads with four minutes and thirty-three seconds of background noise. You can create your own, and John Cage would have liked that. Sit in a "quiet" room for four minutes and thirty-three seconds, and notice what you hear. Perhaps this experiment will make you more aware of how important willful organization is to the art we call music. If nothing else, Cage makes us realize that music, above all, is a form of organized communication from one person to the next and that random background noise cannot be a medium of communication.

Listening Guide

John Cage, 4´33´´ (1952)

Genre: Chance music

WHAT TO LISTEN FOR: Nothing, except the ambient background noise of the room and whatever external noise may intrude by chance. Is there musical beauty in the environment?

0:00–0:30	First movement—silence (?)
0:31–2:53	Second movement—silence (?)
2:54–4:33	Third movement—silence (?)

Hear less experimental (that is, "real") music by Cage in *Nocturne for Violin and Piano* (1947) in the YouTube playlist at CourseMate for this text.

 ## John Adams (b. 1947) and Minimalism

Western classical music—the music of Bach, Beethoven, and Brahms—is typically constructed of large, carefully placed units. A movement of a symphony, for example, has themes, which come in a hierarchy of importance, and sections (development and coda, for example), which must be heard in a particular order. A compelling sequence of events leads to a desired end and conveys a message from composer to listener. But what would happen if composers reduced the music to just one or two simple motives and repeated these again and again? What would happen if they focused on what things *are,* rather than on what these things might *become*? Such is the approach taken by a group of American Postmodernist composers called the Minimalists.

Minimalism is a style of postmodern music, originating in the early 1960s, that takes a very small musical unit and repeats it over and over to form a composition. A three-note melodic cell, a single arpeggio, two alternating chords—these are the sort of "minimal" elements a composer might introduce, reiterate again and again, modify or expand, and then begin to repeat once more. The basic material is usually simple, tonal, and consonant. By repeating these minimal figures incessantly at a steady pulse, the composer creates a hypnotic effect; "trance music" is the name sometimes given to this music. The trance-like quality of Minimalist music has influenced rock musicians (The Velvet Underground, Talking Heads, and Radiohead) and has led to a new genre of pop music called "techno," or "rave," music. Minimalism, in both art and music, has

Figure 32.4

John Adams. In 2003, New York's Lincoln Center held an eight-week "Absolutely Adams" festival to go along with its annual "Mostly Mozart" program.

Ron Scherl/Redferns/Getty Images

been mainly an American movement. Its most successful musical practitioners are Steve Reich (b. 1936), Philip Glass (b. 1937), and John Adams (b. 1947).

John Adams (no relation to the presidents) was born in Worcester, Massachusetts, in 1947 and educated at Harvard. As a student there, he was encouraged to compose in the twelve-tone style of Arnold Schoenberg (see Ch. 29). But if Adams counted twelve-tone rows by day, he listened to The Beatles in his dorm room at night. Moving to San Francisco after graduation, Adams developed his own eclectic musical style that blended the learned with the popular and added increasing amounts of Minimalism, which was then gaining popularity in California. Some of Adams's early scores of the 1980s are strict Minimalist works, but later ones become more all-embracing; from time to time, an operatic melody or a funk bass line, for example, will creep into his constantly repeating, minimal sonorities. In 2003, Adams received the Pulitzer Prize in music for his *On the Transmigration of Souls,* which commemorated those killed in the World Trade Center terrorist attacks of 2001. Ironically, although Adams is a Minimalist composer, he has been able to extend his ever-repeating blocks of sound into lengthy operas. The best known of these are *Nixon in China* (1987) and *Doctor Atomic* (2005)— Minimalist operas that achieve maximum effect. His most recent composition, the oratorio entitled *The Gospel According to the Other Mary* (2012), runs nearly two and a half hours. As a creature of the Postmodernist age, Adams feels squeezed between the rich classical tradition and the all-powerful world of pop culture:

> I have bad days when I really feel that I'm working in an art form [classical music] that's just not relevant anymore, that had its peak in the years from Vivaldi to Bartók, and now we are just fighting over the crumbs. A really good recording of mine might sell 50,000 copies; that's very rare in classical music. For a rock group, 50,000 CDs sold would be a disaster. (*Harvard Magazine,* 24 July 2007)

Watch an expansive example of John Adams's minimalist style—from his opera *Nixon in China*—in the YouTube playlist at CourseMate for this text.

Short Ride in a Fast Machine (1986)

To experience Postmodern Minimalism quickly, we turn to an early work by Adams, one commissioned in 1986 by the Pittsburgh Symphony. *Short Ride in a Fast Machine* is scored for full orchestra and two electronic keyboard synthesizers. Example 32.1 shows how the music is composed of short (mostly four-note) motives that continually repeat. This work has five sections (we'll call them laps). In each lap, the machine seems to accelerate, not because the tempo gets faster but because more and more repeating motives are added. The effect created is that of a powerful, twentieth-century engine firing on all cylinders. As Adams has said about his Minimalist work, "You know how it is when someone asks you to ride in a terrific sports car, and then you wish you hadn't?"

EXAMPLE 32.1

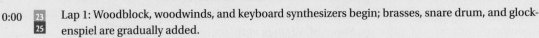
John Adams, *Short Ride in a Fast Machine* (1986)

Delirando (with exhilaration)

5/23   2/25

WHAT TO LISTEN FOR: To make a Minimalist suggestion: short, repeating motives

0:00 `23` `25` Lap 1: Woodblock, woodwinds, and keyboard synthesizers begin; brasses, snare drum, and glock-enspiel are gradually added.

1:04 Lap 2: Bass drum "backfires"; motives rise in pitch and become more dissonant.

1:43 Lap 3: Starts quietly with sinister repeating motive in bass; syncopation and dissonance increase.

2:30 Lap 4: Two-note falling motive in bass

2:53 Lap 5: Trumpets play fanfare-like motives (this is the "victory lap").

3:50 Musical vehicle begins another lap but suddenly breaks down.

◀)) Listen to streaming music in an Active Listening Guide at CourseMate or in the eBook.

◀)) Take online Listening Exercise 32.1 and receive feedback at CourseMate or in the eBook.

Tan Dun (b. 1957) and Globalization

The signs of **globalization**—the development of an increasingly integrated global economy—are everywhere. Computers, smartphones, MP3 players, and Facebook (all Western inventions) have brought Western, and particularly American, culture to the Far East. The youth of China, for example, can watch most of the newest American films and TV programs, and listen to the latest American music, as instantaneously as can students in the United States. Traditional Western musical culture has also infiltrated the Far East. Music students in conservatories in Japan, China, and Korea now study Western classical music as much as they do their native music. They learn, for example, how to play the piano, a uniquely Western instrument, performing Bach's fugues and Beethoven's sonatas. Today, nearly as many CDs of Western classical music are sold in China and Japan as in the United States. But commerce, as well as cultural influence, inevitably flows in two directions. The shorts, socks, and shoes we wear likely came from China, and the automobile in which we ride probably was made (or designed) in Japan. So, too, traditional Chinese music has also made inroads in the West, most emphatically with the Grammy Award–winning film score to *Crouching Tiger, Hidden Dragon* (2000) composed by Tan Dun (Fig. 32.5). As economic barriers are removed, the flow of ideas accelerates, and cultural distinctions begin to blur.

No one better personifies "musical globalization" than Tan Dun (Fig. 32.6). Tan was born in Hunan, China, in 1957 and raised in a rural environment full of music, magic, and ritual. During the **Cultural Revolution** (1966–1976) of Mao Zedong, he was sent to a commune to cultivate rice but was later summoned to play fiddle and arrange music for a provincial troupe of the Beijing Opera. He first heard Beethoven's Symphony No. 5 when he was nineteen and began to dream

Figure 32.5

A poster promoting the film *Crouching Tiger, Hidden Dragon*

of becoming a composer. In 1978, owing to his exceptional knowledge of Chinese folk music, Tan was admitted to the Central Conservatory in Beijing, China's most prestigious music school, where he remained for eight years. In 1986, he received a fellowship to study at Columbia University in New York, and at this time, he came under the sway of the most progressive styles of Modernism. Indeed, some of Tan's compositions of the 1980s have the sort of atonal, dissonant sound that would have made Arnold Schoenberg smile.

By the 1990s, however, the sounds of Tan's homeland had crept back into his scores: the pentatonic scale, microtonal pitch slides, scratchy string bowings, vibrant percussion sounds, and nasal timbres of the Beijing Opera style. Tan's own opera *Marco Polo* (1996) earned him the Grawemeyer Award, classical composition's most prestigious prize. Two years later, he wrote the music for the American thriller *Fallen*, starring Denzel Washington. To create his Oscar- and Grammy Award–winning score for *Crouching Tiger, Hidden Dragon*, Tan worked with Yo-Yo Ma (also of Chinese descent). Ma played the cello solos, which were recorded in New York; these were later patched into the full soundtrack, which was recorded in Shanghai by a Western-style orchestra supplemented by traditional Chinese instruments—a truly global enterprise! Most recently, Tan Dun has worked with Yo-Yo Ma on a series of concerts and recordings called *The Silk Road Project*, a continuing program designed to highlight and integrate the music and instruments of China with those of the Western tradition. In 2009, Google commissioned Tan to compose *Internet Symphony No. 1 "Eroica"* to be performed collaboratively by the YouTube Symphony Orchestra.

Figure 32.6

Tan Dun

To hear strains of Tan and Beethoven in *Internet Symphony No. 1 "Eroica,"* go to the YouTube playlist at CourseMate for this text.

Marco Polo (1996)

Tan Dun's opera *Marco Polo* is an excellent vehicle through which to experience his music and explore the process of musical globalization. It was financed and coproduced by opera companies in Amsterdam, Munich, and Hong Kong, where the first three "premieres" occurred simultaneously. Moreover, the subject of Marco Polo, an Italian explorer who traveled the Silk Road to China in the thirteenth century, offered Tan the opportunity to present the music of several different cultures: Western, Middle Eastern, Indian, Tibetan, Mongolian, and Chinese. In the scene "Waiting to Depart," Marco Polo stands before the sea, looking eastward. The figures of Water and Shadows beckon him to begin the journey of time and space. Marco exists in the present (Western Europe) but envisions the future (the Far East). This we know not from reading the sparse libretto, but from listening to the orchestra. What composer Tan has said about this opera in general applies particularly well to this scene: "I think sounds and different musical cultures guide my own development, leading me through a deeper journey. . . . From Medieval [Western] chants, from Western Opera to Beijing Opera, from orchestra to sitar, pipa (Chinese lute) and Tibetan ritual horns—the fusion of musical sounds from all corners of the globe is the definition of *Marco Polo* to me."

Tan Dun, "Waiting to Depart," from *Marco Polo* (1996)

Genre: Opera

Situation: Marco Polo stands at the edge of Piazza San Marco in Venice, about to embark on his physical and spiritual journey to the East.

0:00	Low string drone, like Tibetan chant, and then high woodwinds sliding between pitches
0:29	"Reedy" piccolo plays melody around outline of pentatonic scale (E, F#, G#, B, C#, E).
1:03	(Western) viola continues with melody based on same pentatonic scale.
1:42	Romantic-sounding (Western) French horn plays same pentatonic scale.
2:02	Voice of Water says, "Listen," accompanied by Chinese pipa (lute)
2:14	Voice of Marco says, "Maintain."
2:22	Voices of Water and two Shadows say, "Now journey; listen; now maintain; the journey onward."
3:07	Voice of Marco says, "Preserve; question; read; see."
3:23	Others repeat "Journey," in style of early Western parallel organum.
3:45	Drum and gong enter, then full chorus *fortissimo* with dissonant tone clusters: "Go; hurry; into; join."
4:34	Low string drone returns, suggesting mystery and vast distances of East.

Listen to streaming music in an Active Listening Guide at CourseMate or in the eBook.

Key Words

musique concrète (372)	electronic music (374)	Minimalism (376)
computer music (373)	synthesizer (374)	globalization (378)
sampling (373)	prepared piano (375)	Cultural Revolution (378)
scratching (373)	chance music (375)	

For a complete review of this chapter, see the Main Points, Chapter Quiz, Flashcards, and Glossary in CourseMate.

Watch a video of Craig Wright's Open Yale Course class session 23, "Review of Musical Style," at the text website.

Join us on Facebook at **Listening to Music with Craig Wright**

Checklist of Musical Style

Postmodern: 1945–present

REPRESENTATIVE COMPOSERS

Varèse

Cage

Glass

Reich

Adams

Tan

A complete Checklist of Musical Style for the Postmodern era may also be found at CourseMate for this text.

PRINCIPAL GENRES

no common genres; each work of art creates a genre unique to itself

Nearly impossible to generalize in terms of musical style; major stylistic trends not yet discernible

Barriers between high art and low art removed; all art judged to be of more or less equal value—symphony orchestras play video game music

Experimentation with electronic music and computer-generated sound

Previously accepted fundamentals of music, such as discrete pitches and division of octave into twelve equal pitches, often abandoned

Narrative music (goal-oriented music) rejected

Chance music permits random "happenings" and noises from the environment to shape a musical work

Introduction of visual and performance media into the written musical score

Instruments from outside the tradition of Western classical music (e.g., electric guitar, sitar, kazoo) prescribed in the score

Experimentation with new notational styles within musical scores (e.g., sketches, diagrams, prose instructions)

Glossary

absolute music: instrumental music free of a text or any preexisting program

a cappella: a term applied to unaccompanied vocal music; originated in the expression *a cappella Sistina,* "in the Sistine Chapel" of the pope, where instruments were forbidden to accompany the singers

accelerando: a tempo mark indicating "getting faster"

accent: emphasis or stress placed on a musical tone or a chord

accidental: a sharp, flat, or natural sign that alters the pitch of a note a half step

accompagnato: see *recitativo accompagnato*

acoustic instruments: instruments that produce sounds naturally when strings are bowed or plucked, a tube has air passed through it, or percussion instruments are struck

acoustic music: music produced by acoustic instruments

adagio: a tempo mark indicating "slow"

Alberti bass: a pattern of accompaniment whereby, instead of having the pitches of a chord sound all together, the notes are played in succession to provide a continual stream of sound

allegretto: a tempo mark indicating "moderately fast"

allegro: a tempo mark indicating "fast"

allemande: a stately dance in $\frac{4}{4}$ meter with gracefully interweaving lines

alto (contralto): the lower of the two female voice parts, the soprano being higher

andante: a tempo mark indicating "moderately moving"

andantino: a tempo mark indicating "moderately moving" yet slightly faster than *andante*

antecedent phrase: the opening, incomplete-sounding phrase of a melody; often followed by a consequent phrase that brings the melody to closure

anthem: a composition for chorus on a sacred subject; similar in design and function to a motet

aria: an elaborate lyrical song for solo voice

arioso: a style of singing and a type of song midway between an aria and a recitative

arpeggio: the notes of a triad or seventh chord played in direct succession and in a direct line up or down

Art of Fugue, The: Bach's last project (1742–1750), an encyclopedic treatment of all known contrapuntal procedures, set forth in nineteen canons and fugues

art song: a genre of song for voice and piano accompaniment with high artistic aspirations

atonal music: music without tonality; music without a key center; most often associated with the twentieth-century avant-garde style of Arnold Schoenberg

augmentation: the notes of a melody held for longer than (usually double) their normal duration

backbeat: a drumbeat or cymbal crash occurring regularly after a strong beat, as on beats 2 and 4 in a measure with four beats

ballet: an art form that uses dance and music, along with costumes and scenery, to tell a story and display emotions through expressive gestures and movement

ballet music: music composed to accompany a ballet, with short bursts of tuneful melody and captivating rhythm, all intended to capture the emotional essence of the scene

Ballets russes: a Russian ballet company of the early twentieth century led by Sergei Diaghilev

bandoneon: a square-cut woodwind instrument much like an accordion, except that it is played by pushing buttons rather than keys

bar: see *measure*

baritone: a male voice part of a middle range, between the higher tenor and the lower bass

Baroque: term used to describe the arts generally during the period 1600–1750 and signifying excess and extravagance

bas instruments: a class of soft musical instruments, including the flute, recorder, fiddle, harp, and lute, popular during the late Middle Ages

bass: the lowest male voice range

bass clef: a sign placed on a staff to indicate the notes below middle C

bass drum: a large, low-sounding drum struck with a soft-headed stick

basso continuo: a small ensemble of at least two instrumentalists who provide a foundation for the melody or melodies above; heard almost exclusively in Baroque music

bassoon: a low, double-reed instrument of the woodwind family

basso ostinato: a motive or phrase in the bass that is repeated again and again

bass viol: see *viola da gamba*

Bayreuth Festival: still controlled by the descendants of Wagner, a festival that continues to stage the music dramas of Wagner—and only Wagner—at the Bayreuth Festival Theater, an opera house built especially for that purpose

beat: an even pulse in music that divides the passing of time into equal segments

bel canto: (Italian for "beautiful singing") a style of singing and a type of Italian opera developed in the nineteenth century that features the beautiful tone and brilliant technique of the human voice

binary form: a musical form consisting of two units (**A** and **B**) constructed to balance and complement each other

bongo drum: a pair of small Afro-Cuban single-headed drums created in Cuba c. 1900; often heard in Latin American dance bands

Brandenburg Concertos: set of six concerti grossi composed by J. S. Bach between 1711 and 1720, and subsequently dedicated to Margrave Christian Ludwig of Brandenburg

brass family: a group of musical instruments traditionally made of brass and played with a mouthpiece; includes the trumpet, trombone, French horn, and tuba

bridge: see *transition*

bugle: a simple brass instrument that evolved from the valveless military trumpet

cabaletta: the concluding fast aria of any two- or three-section operatic scene; a useful mechanism to get the principals off the stage

cadence: the concluding part of a musical phrase

cadenza: a showy passage for the soloist appearing near the end of the movement in a concerto; usually incorporates rapid runs, arpeggios, and snippets of previously heard themes into a fantasy-like improvisation

canon (of Western music): a core repertoire, or the "chestnuts," of classical music performed at concerts continually since the eighteenth century

canon (round): a contrapuntal form in which the individual voices enter and each in turn duplicates exactly the melody that the first voice played or sang

cantata: a term originally meaning "something sung"; in its mature state, it consists of several movements, including one or more arias, ariosos, and recitatives; cantatas can be on secular subjects and intended for private performance (see *chamber cantata*) or on religious subjects such as those of J. S. Bach for the German Lutheran church

caprice: a light, whimsical character piece of the nineteenth century

castanets: percussion instruments (rattles) of indefinite pitch associated with Spanish music

castrato: a male adult singer who had been castrated as a boy to keep his voice from changing so that it would remain in the soprano or alto register

celesta: a small percussive keyboard instrument using hammers to strike metal bars, thereby producing a bright, bell-like sound

cello (violoncello): an instrument of the violin family but more than twice the violin's size; it is played between the legs and produces a rich, lyrical tone

chamber cantata: a cantata performed before a select audience in a private residence; intimate vocal chamber music, principally of the Baroque era

chamber music: music, usually instrumental music, performed in a small concert hall or private residence with just one performer on each part

chamber sonata: see *sonata da camera*

chance music: music that involves an element of chance (rolling dice, choosing cards, etc.) or whimsy on the part of the performers; especially popular with avant-garde composers

chanson: a French term used broadly to indicate a lyrical song from the Middle Ages into the twentieth century

character piece: a brief instrumental work seeking to capture a single mood; a genre much favored by composers of the Romantic era

chorale: the German word for the hymn of the Lutheran Church; hence a simple religious melody to be sung by the congregation

chord: two or more simultaneously sounding pitches

chord progression: a succession of chords moving forward in a purposeful fashion

chromatic harmony: harmony utilizing chords built on the five chromatic notes of the scale in addition to the seven diatonic ones; produces rich harmonies

chromaticism: the frequent presence in melodies and chords of intervals only a half step apart; in a scale, the use of notes not part of the diatonic major or minor pattern

chromatic scale: scale that makes use of all twelve pitches, equally divided, within the octave

church cantata: see *cantata*

church sonata: see *sonata da chiesa*

clarinet: a single-reed instrument of the woodwind family with a large range and a wide variety of timbres within it

classical music: the traditional music of any culture, usually involving a specialized technical vocabulary and requiring long years of training; it is "high art" or "learned" music that is enjoyed generation after generation

clavier: a general term for all keyboard instruments, including the harpsichord, organ, and piano

clef: a sign used to indicate the register, or range of pitches, in which an instrument is to play or a singer is to sing

coda: (Italian for "tail") a final and concluding section of a musical composition

collage art: art made up of disparate materials taken from very different places

collegium musicum: a society of amateur musicians (usually associated with a university) dedicated to the performance of music, nowadays music of the Middle Ages, Renaissance, and Baroque eras

col legno: (Italian for "with the wood") an instruction to string players to strike the strings of the instrument not with the horsehair of the bow, but with the wood of it

color (timbre): the character or quality of a musical tone as determined by its harmonics and its attack and decay

comic opera: a genre of opera that originated in the eighteenth century, portraying everyday characters and situations, and using spoken dialogue and simple songs

computer music: the most recent development in electronic music; it couples the computer with the electronic synthesizer to imitate the sounds of acoustic instruments and to produce new sounds

concertino: the group of instruments that function as soloists in a concerto grosso

concerto: an instrumental genre in which one or more soloists play with and against a larger orchestra

concerto grosso: a multi-movement concerto of the Baroque era that pits the sound of a small group of soloists (the concertino) against that of the full orchestra (the tutti)

concert overture: an independent, one-movement work, usually of programmatic content, originally intended for the concert hall and not designed to precede an opera or play

conga drum: a large Afro-Cuban single-headed barrel drum played in Latin American dance bands

conjunct motion: melodic motion that proceeds primarily by steps and without leaps

consequent phrase: the second phrase of a two-part melodic unit that brings a melody to a point of repose and closure

consonance: pitches sounding agreeable and stable

continuo: see *basso continuo*

contrabassoon: a larger, lower-sounding version of the bassoon

contrast: process employed by a composer to introduce different melodies, rhythms, textures, or moods in order to provide variety

cornet: a brass instrument that looks like a short trumpet; it has a more mellow tone than the trumpet and is most often used in military bands

cornetto: a woodwind instrument, developed during the late Middle Ages and early Renaissance, that sounds like a hybrid of a clarinet and trumpet

Council of Trent: two-decade-long (1545–1563) conference at which leading cardinals and bishops undertook reform of the Roman Catholic Church, including its music

counterpoint: the harmonious opposition of two or more independent musical lines

Counter-Reformation: movement that fostered reform in the Roman Catholic Church in response to the challenge of the Protestant Reformation and led to a conservative, austere approach to art

courante: a lively dance in $\frac{6}{4}$ with an upbeat and frequent changes of metrical accent

crescendo: a gradual increase in the volume of sound

cross stringing: a practice popularized by the Steinway Company whereby the lowest strings of the piano ride up and across those of the middle register, thereby giving the piano a richer, more homogenized sound

Cubism: early-twentieth-century artistic style in which the artist fractures and dislocates formal reality into geometrical blocks and planes

Cultural Revolution: Chairman Mao Zedong's social and political reformation of the People's Republic of China between 1966 and 1976

cymbals: a percussion instrument of two metal discs; they are made to crash together to create emphasis and articulation in music

da capo **aria:** an aria in two sections, with an obligatory return to and repeat of the first; hence an aria in ternary (**ABA**) form

da capo **form:** ternary (**ABA**) form for an aria, so called because the performers, when reaching the end of **B,** "take it from the head" and repeat **A**

dance suite: a collection of instrumental dances, each with its own distinctive rhythm and character

decrescendo (diminuendo): gradual decrease in the intensity of sound

development: the centermost portion of sonata–allegro form, in which the thematic material of the exposition is developed and extended, transformed, or reduced to its essence; often the most confrontational and unstable section of the movement

diatonic: pertaining to the seven notes that make up either the major or the minor scale

Dies irae: a Gregorian chant composed in the thirteenth century and used as the central portion of the Requiem Mass of the Catholic Church

diminished chord: a triad or seventh chord made up entirely of minor thirds and producing a tense, unstable sound

diminuendo: a gradual decrease in the volume of sound

diminution: a reduction, usually by half, of all the rhythmic durations in a melody

disjunct motion: melodic motion that moves primarily by leaps rather than by steps

dissonance: a discordant mingling of sounds

diva: (Italian for "goddess") a celebrated female opera singer; a prima donna

Doctrine of Affections: early-seventeenth-century aesthetic theory that held that different musical moods could and should be used to influence the emotions, or affections, of the listener

dominant: the chord built on the fifth degree of the scale

doo-wop: type of soul music that emerged in the 1950s as an outgrowth of the gospel hymns sung in African American churches in urban Detroit, Chicago, and New York; its lyrics made use of repeating phrases sung in a cappella (unaccompanied) harmony below the tune

dotted note: a note to which an additional duration of 50 percent has been added

double bass: the largest and lowest-pitched instrument in the string family

double counterpoint: counterpoint with two themes that can reverse position, with the top theme moving to the bottom, and the bottom to the top (also called *invertible counterpoint*)

double exposition form: a form, originating in the concerto of the Classical period, in which first the orchestra and then the soloist present the primary thematic material

double stops: a technique applied to string instruments in which two strings are pressed down and played simultaneously instead of just one

downbeat: the first beat of each measure; indicated by a downward motion of the conductor's hand and usually stressed

dramatic overture: a one-movement work, usually in sonata–allegro form, that encapsulates in music the essential dramatic events of the opera or play that follows

drone: a continuous sound on one or more fixed pitches

duple meter: gathering of beats into two beats per measure, with every other beat stressed

dynamics: the various levels of volume, loud and soft, at which sounds are produced in a musical composition

electronic instruments: machines that produce musical sounds by electronic means, the most widespread instrument being the keyboard synthesizer

electronic music: sounds produced and manipulated by magnetic tape machines, synthesizers, and/or computers

eleventh chord: a chord comprising five intervals of a third and spanning eleven different letter names of pitches

encore: (French for "again") the repeat of a piece demanded by an appreciative audience; an extra piece added at the end of a concert

English horn: an alto oboe, pitched at the interval a fifth below the oboe, much favored by composers of the Romantic era

Enlightenment: eighteenth-century period in philosophy and letters during which thinkers gave free rein to the pursuit of truth and the discovery of natural laws

episode: a passage of free, nonimitative counterpoint found in a fugue

"Eroica" Symphony: Beethoven's Symphony No. 3 (1803), originally dedicated to Napoleon but published as the "Heroic Symphony"

Esterházy family: the richest and most influential among the German-speaking aristocrats of eighteenth-century Hungary, with extensive landholdings southeast of Vienna and a passionate interest in music; patrons of Haydn

etude: a short one-movement composition designed to improve one aspect of a performer's technique

exoticism: use of sounds drawn from outside the traditional Western European musical experience, popular among composers in late-nineteenth-century Europe

exposition: in a fugue, the opening section, in which each voice in turn has the opportunity to present the subject; in sonata–allegro form, the principal section, in which all thematic material is presented

Expressionism: powerful movement in the early-twentieth-century arts, initially a German-Austrian development that arose in Berlin, Munich, and Vienna; its aim was not to depict objects as they are seen but to express the strong emotion that the object generates in the artist

falsetto voice: a high, soprano-like voice produced by adult male singers when they sing in head voice and not in full chest voice

fantasy: a free, improvisatory-like composition in which the composer follows his or her whims rather than an established musical form

fermata: in musical notation, a mark indicating that the performer(s) should hold a note or chord for an extended duration

figured bass: in musical notation, a numerical shorthand that tells the player which unwritten notes to fill in above the written bass note

finale: the last movement of a multimovement composition, one that usually works to a climax and conclusion

flamenco: a genre of Spanish song and dance, with guitar accompaniment, that originated in southernmost Spain and exhibits non-Western, possibly Arab-influenced, scales

flat: in musical notation, a symbol that lowers a pitch by a half step

flute: a high-sounding member of the woodwind family; initially made of wood, but more recently, beginning in the nineteenth century, of silver or even platinum

folk-rock: a mixture of the steady beat of rock with the forms, topics, and styles of singing of the traditional Anglo-American folk ballad

folk song: a song originating from an ethnic group and passed from generation to generation by oral tradition rather than written notation

form: the purposeful organization of the artist's materials; in music, the general shape of a composition as perceived by the listener

formalism: modern music, according to Soviet authorities in the 1920s and 1930s, who branded it as "antidemocratic"

forte (f): in musical notation, a dynamic mark indicating "loud"

fortepiano (pianoforte): the original name of the piano

fortissimo (ff): in musical notation, a dynamic mark indicating "very loud"

free counterpoint: counterpoint in which the voices do not all make use of some preexisting subject in imitation

free jazz: a style of jazz perfected during the 1960s in which a soloist indulges in flights of creative fancy without concern for the rhythm, melody, or harmony of the other performers

Freemasons: fraternity of the Enlightenment who believed in tolerance and universal brotherhood

French horn: a brass instrument that plays in the middle range of the brass family; developed from the medieval hunting horn

French overture: an overture style developed by Jean-Baptiste Lully with two sections, the first slow in duple meter with dotted note values, the second fast in triple meter and with light imitation; the first section can be repeated after the second

fugato: a short fugue set in some other musical form, such as sonata–allegro or theme and variations

fugue: a composition for three, four, or five parts played or sung by voices or instruments; begins with a presentation of a subject in imitation in each part and continues with modulating passages of free counterpoint and further appearances of the subject

full cadence: a cadence that sounds complete, in part because it usually ends on the tonic note

furiant: an exuberant folk dance of Czech origin in which duple and triple meter alternate

galliard: fast, leaping Renaissance dance in triple meter

genre: type of music; specifically, the quality of musical style, form, performing medium, and place of performance that characterize any one type of music

Gesamtkunstwerk: (German for "total art work") an art form that involves music, poetry, drama, and scenic design; often used in reference to Richard Wagner's music dramas

Gewandhaus Orchestra: the symphony orchestra that originated in the Clothiers' House in Leipzig, Germany, in the eighteenth century

gigue: a fast dance in $\frac{6}{8}$ or $\frac{12}{8}$ with a constant eighth-note pulse that produces a gallop-like effect

glissando: a device of sliding up or down the scale very rapidly

globalization: development of an increasingly integrated global economy

glockenspiel: a percussion instrument made of tuned metal bars that are struck by mallets

gong: a circular, metal percussion instrument of Asian origin

grave: a tempo mark indicating "very slow and grave"

great (grand) staff: a large musical staff that combines both the treble and the bass clefs

Gregorian chant (plainsong): a large body of unaccompanied monophonic vocal music, set to Latin texts, composed for the Western Church over the course of fifteen centuries, from the time of the earliest fathers to the Council of Trent (1545–1563)

ground bass: the English term for *basso ostinato*

guiro: a scraped percussion instrument originating in South America and the Caribbean

habanera: an Afro-Cuban dance song that came to prominence in the nineteenth century, marked by a repeating bass and a repeating, syncopated rhythm

half cadence: a cadence at which the music does not come to a fully satisfying stop but stands as if suspended on a dominant chord

half step: the smallest musical interval in the Western major or minor scale; the distance between any two adjacent keys on the piano

harmony: the sounds that provide the support and enrichment—the accompaniment—for melody

harp: an ancient, plucked-string instrument with a triangular shape

harpsichord: a keyboard instrument, especially popular during the Baroque era, that produces sound by depressing a key that drives a lever upward and forces a pick to pluck a string

hauts instruments: a class of loud musical instruments, including the trumpet, sackbut, shawm, and drum, popular during the late Middle Ages

Heiligenstadt Testament: something akin to Beethoven's last will and testament, written in despair when he recognized that he would ultimately suffer a total loss of hearing; named after the Viennese suburb in which he penned it

"heroic" period: a period in Beethoven's compositional career (1803–1813) during which he wrote longer works incorporating broad gestures, grand climaxes, and triadic, triumphant themes

hip hop: larger genre, encompassing rap music, in which the vocal line is delivered more like speech than like song and in which a wide variety of rhythmic devices are used

homophony: a texture in which all the voices, or lines, move to new pitches at roughly the same time; often referred to in contradistinction to polyphony

horn: a term generally used by musicians to refer to any brass instrument, but most often the French horn

hornpipe: an energetic dance, derived from the country jig, in either $\frac{3}{2}$ or $\frac{2}{4}$ time

humanism: Renaissance belief that people have the capacity to create many things good and beautiful; it rejoiced in the human form in all its fullness, looked outward, and indulged a passion for invention and discovery

idée fixe: literally, a "fixed idea"; more specifically, an obsessive musical theme as first used in Hector Berlioz's *Symphonie fantastique*

idiomatic writing: musical composition that exploits the strengths and avoids the weaknesses of particular voices and instruments

imitation: the process by which one or more musical voices, or parts, enter and duplicate exactly for a period of time the music presented by the previous voice

imitative counterpoint: a type of counterpoint in which the voices or lines frequently use imitation

impresario: renowned producer

Impressionism: late-nineteenth-century movement that arose in France; the Impressionists were the first to reject photographic realism in painting, instead trying to re-create the impression that an object produces upon the senses in a single, fleeting moment

incidental music: music to be inserted between the acts or during important scenes of a play to add an extra dimension to the drama

intermezzo: (Italian for "between piece") a light musical interlude intended to separate and thus break the mood of two more serious, surrounding movements or operatic acts or scenes

interval: the distance between any two pitches on a musical scale

inversion: the process of inverting the musical intervals in a theme or melody; a melody that ascends by step, now descends by step, and so on

invertible counterpoint: see *double counterpoint*

jazz: a lively, energetic music with pulsating rhythms and scintillating syncopations, usually played by a small instrumental ensemble

jazz-fusion: a mixture of jazz and rock cultivated by American bands in the 1970s

jazz riff: a short motive, usually played by an entire instrumental section (woodwinds or brasses), that appears frequently, but intermittently, in a jazz composition

key: a tonal center built on a tonic note and making use of a scale; also, on a keyboard instrument, one of a series of levers that can be depressed to generate sound

key signature: in musical notation, a preplaced set of sharps or flats used to indicate the scale and key

Köchel (K) number: an identifying number assigned to each of the works of Mozart, in roughly chronological order, by Ludwig von Köchel (1800–1877)

Kyrie: the first portion of the Ordinary of the Mass, and hence usually the opening movement in a polyphonic setting of the Mass

largo: a tempo mark indicating "slow and broad"

La Scala: the principal opera house of the city of Milan, Italy, which opened in 1778

leading tone: the pitch a half step below the tonic, which pulls up and into it, especially at cadences

leap: melodic movement not by an interval of just a step, but usually by a jump of at least a fourth

legato: in musical notation, an articulation mark indicating that the notes are to be smoothly connected; the opposite of staccato

leitmotif: a brief, distinctive unit of music designed to represent a character, object, or idea; a term applied to the motives in the music dramas of Richard Wagner

lento: a tempo mark indicating "very slow"

libretto: the text of an opera

Liebestod: (German for "love death") the famous aria sung by the dying Isolde at the end of Richard Wagner's opera *Tristan und Isolde*

Lied: (German for "song") the genre of art song, for voice and piano accompaniment, that originated in Germany c. 1800

Lisztomania: the sort of mass hysteria, today reserved for pop music stars, that surrounded touring Romantic-era pianist Franz Liszt

London Symphonies: the twelve symphonies composed by Joseph Haydn for performance in London between 1791 and 1795; Haydn's last twelve symphonies (Nos. 93–104)

lute: a six-string instrument appearing in the West in the late Middle Ages

lyrics: text set to music

madrigal: a popular genre of secular vocal music that originated in Italy during the Renaissance, in which usually four or five voices sing love poems

madrigalism: a device, originating in the madrigal, by which key words in a text spark a particularly expressive musical setting

major scale: a seven-note scale that ascends in the following order of whole and half steps: 1-1-½-1-1-1-½

marimba: Mexican percussion instrument similar in construction to the xylophone

Marseillaise, La: a tune written as a revolutionary marching song in 1792 by Claude-Joseph Rouget de Lisle and sung by a battalion from Marseilles as it entered Paris that year; it subsequently became the French national anthem

Mass: the central religious service of the Roman Catholic Church, one that incorporates singing for spiritual reflection or as accompaniment to sacred acts

mazurka: a fast dance of Polish origins in triple meter with an accent on the second beat

measure (bar): a group of beats, or musical pulses; usually, the number of beats is fixed and constant so that the measure serves as a continual unit of measurement in music

melisma: in singing, one vowel luxuriously spread out over many notes

melismatic singing: many notes sung to just one syllable

melodic sequence: the repetition of a musical motive at successively higher or lower degrees of the scale

melody: a series of notes arranged in order to form a distinctive, recognizable musical unit; most often placed in the treble

meter: the gathering of beats into regular groups

meter signature: see *time signature*

metronome: a mechanical device used by performers to keep a steady tempo

mezzo-soprano: a female vocal range between alto and soprano

middle C: the middlemost C on the modern piano

Minimalism: a style of modern music that takes a very small amount of musical material and repeats it over and over to form a composition

Minnesinger: a type of secular poet-musician that flourished in Germany during the twelfth through fourteenth centuries

minor scale: a seven-note scale that ascends in the following order of whole and half steps: 1-½-1-1-½-1-1

minuet: a moderate dance in $\frac{3}{4}$ though actually danced in patterns of six steps, with no upbeat but with highly symmetrical phrasing

mode: a pattern of pitches forming a scale; the two primary modes in Western music are major and minor

moderato: a tempo marking indicating "moderately moving"

Modernism: a bracing, progressive style that dominated classical music and the arts generally from the beginning to the end of the twentieth century

modified strophic form: strophic form in which the music is modified slightly to accommodate a particularly expressive word or phrase in the text

modulation: the process in music whereby the tonal center changes from one key to another—from G major to C major, for example

monody: a general term connoting solo singing accompanied by a *basso continuo* in the early Baroque period

monophony: a musical texture involving only a single line of music with no accompaniment

motet: a composition for choir or larger chorus setting a religious, devotional, or solemn text; often sung a cappella

motive: a short, distinctive melodic figure that stands by itself

mouthpiece: a detachable portion of a brass instrument into which the player blows

movement: a large, independent section of a major instrumental work, such as a sonata, dance suite, symphony, quartet, or concerto

music: the rational organization of sounds and silences as they pass through time

musical nationalism: see *nationalism*

music drama: a term used for the mature operas of Richard Wagner

musique concrète: music in which the composer works directly with sounds recorded on magnetic tape, not with musical notation and performers

mute: any device that muffles the sound of a musical instrument; on the trumpet, for example, it is a cup that is placed inside the bell of the instrument

nationalism: a movement in music in the nineteenth century in which composers sought to emphasize indigenous qualities in their music by incorporating folk songs, native scales, dance rhythms, and local instrumental sounds

natural: in musical notation, a symbol that cancels a preexisting sharp or flat

Neo-classicism: a movement in twentieth-century music that sought to return to the musical forms and aesthetics of the Baroque and Classical periods

New Age music: a style of nonconfrontational, often repetitious music performed on electronic instruments that arose during the 1990s

ninth chord: a chord spanning nine letters of the scale and constructed by superimposing four intervals of a third

nocturne: a slow, introspective type of music, usually for piano, with rich harmonies and poignant dissonances intending to convey the mysteries of the night

nonimitative counterpoint: counterpoint with independent lines that do not imitate each other

oboe: an instrument of the woodwind family; the highest-pitched of the double-reed instruments

octave: the interval comprising the first and eighth tones of the major and minor diatonic scale; the sounds are quite similar because the frequency of vibration of the higher pitch is exactly twice that of the lower

octave displacement: a process used in constructing a melody whereby a simple, nearby interval is made more distant, and the melodic line more disjunct, by placing the next note up or down an octave

Ode to Joy: *An die Freude* by poet Friedrich von Schiller, set to music by Beethoven as a hymn in honor of universal brotherhood and used in the finale of his Symphony No. 9

opera: a dramatic work in which the actors sing some or all of their parts; it usually makes use of elaborate stage sets and costumes

opera buffa: (Italian for "comic opera") a genre of opera featuring light, often domestic subjects, with tuneful melodies, comic situations, and happy endings

opera seria: a genre of opera that dominated the stage during the Baroque era, making use of serious historical or mythological subjects, *da capo* arias, and lengthy overtures

operetta: a light opera with spoken dialogue and numerous dances involving comedy and romance in equal measure

ophicleide: a low brass instrument originating in military bands about the time of the French Revolution; the precursor of the tuba

opus: (Latin for "work") the term adopted by composers to enumerate and identify their compositions

oral tradition: the process used in the transmission of folk songs and other traditional music in which the material is passed from one generation to the next by singing, playing, and hearing without musical notation

oratorio: a large-scale genre of sacred music involving an overture, arias, recitatives, and choruses, but sung, whether in a theater or a church, without costumes or scenery

orchestra: see *symphony orchestra*

orchestral dance suite: a dance suite written for orchestra

orchestral Lied: see *orchestral song*

orchestral score: a composite of the musical lines of all of the instruments of the orchestra and from which a conductor conducts

orchestral song: a genre of music emerging in the nineteenth century in which the voice is accompanied not merely by a piano but by a full orchestra

orchestration: the art of assigning to the various instruments of the orchestra, or of a chamber ensemble, the diverse melodies, accompaniments, and counterpoints of a musical composition

Ordinary of the Mass: the five sung portions of the Mass for which the texts are invariable

organ: an ancient musical instrument constructed mainly of pipes and keys; the player depresses a key, which allows air to rush into or over a pipe, thereby producing sound

organum: the name given to the early polyphony of the Western Church from the ninth through the thirteenth centuries

oscillator: a device that, when activated by an electronic current, pulses back and forth to produce an electronic signal that can be converted by a loudspeaker into sound

ostinato: (Italian for "obstinate") a musical figure, motive, melody, harmony, or rhythm that is repeated again and again

overtone: Extremely faint sound, in addition to the fundamental sound of an instrument, caused by fractional vibrations of a string or air column within a pipe

overture: an introductory movement, usually for orchestra, that precedes an opera, oratorio, or dance suite

parallel motion: a musical process in which all of the lines or parts move in the same direction, and at the same intervals, for a period of time; the opposite of counterpoint

part: an independent line or voice in a musical composition; also, a section of a composition

pastoral aria: aria with several distinctive musical characteristics, all of which suggest pastoral scenes and the movement of simple shepherds attending the Christ Child

"Pathétique" Sonata: one of Beethoven's most celebrated compositions for piano

pavane: slow, gliding Renaissance dance in duple meter performed by couples holding hands

pedal point: a note, usually in the bass, sustained or continually repeated for a period of time while the harmonies change around it

pentatonic scale: a five-note scale found often in folk music and non-Western music

phrase: a self-contained portion of a melody, theme, or tune

pianissimo (pp): in musical notation, a dynamic mark indicating "very soft"

piano (p): in musical notation, a dynamic mark indicating "soft"

piano: a large keyboard instrument that creates sound at various dynamic levels when hammers are struck against strings

pianoforte: the original name for the piano

piano transcription: the transformation and reduction of an orchestral score, and a piece of orchestral music, onto the great staff for playing at the piano

piccolo: a small flute; the smallest and highest-pitched woodwind instrument

pickup: a note or two coming before the first downbeat of a piece, intending to give a little extra push into that downbeat

pipa: an ancient, four-string Chinese lute

pitch: the relative position, high or low, of a musical sound

pizzicato: the process whereby a performer plucks the strings of an instrument rather than bowing them

plainsong: see *Gregorian chant*

point of imitation: a distinctive motive that is sung or played in turn by each voice or instrumental line

polonaise: a dance of Polish origin in triple meter without an upbeat but usually with an accent on the second of the three beats

polychord: the stacking of one triad or seventh chord on another so they sound simultaneously

polymeter: two or more meters sounding simultaneously

polyphony: a musical texture involving two or more simultaneously sounding lines; the lines are often independent and create counterpoint

polyrhythm: two or more rhythms sounding simultaneously

polytonality: the simultaneous sounding of two keys or tonalities

popular music: a broad category of music designed to please a large section of the general public; sometimes used in contradistinction to more "serious" or more "learned" classical music

prelude: an introductory, improvisatory-like movement that gives the performer a chance to warm up and sets the stage for a more substantive subsequent movement

prepared piano: a piano outfitted with screws, bolts, washers, erasers, and bits of felt and plastic to transform the instrument from a melodic one to a percussive one

prestissimo: in musical notation, a tempo mark indicating "as fast as possible"

presto: in musical notation, a tempo mark indicating "very fast"

prima donna: (Italian for "first lady") the leading female singer in an opera

Primitivism: artistic mode of expression that attempts to capture the unadorned lines, raw energy, and elemental truth of non-Western art and apply it in a Modernist context

program music: a piece of instrumental music, usually for symphony orchestra, that seeks to re-create in sound the events and emotions portrayed in some extramusical source: a story, a play, a historical event, an encounter with nature, or even a painting

program symphony: a symphony with the usual three, four, or five movements in which the individual movements together tell a tale or depict a succession of specific events or scenes

Proper of the Mass: the sections of the Mass that are sung to texts that vary with each feast day

qin: an ancient seven-string Chinese dulcimer played with two bamboo sticks

quadrivium: a curriculum of four scientific disciplines (arithmetic, geometry, astronomy, and music) taught in medieval schools and universities

quadruple meter: music with four beats per measure

quarter note: unit of musical duration that most often represents the beat; normally moves at roughly the rate of the average person's heartbeat

quarter tone: the division of the whole tone, or whole step, into quarter tones, a division even smaller than the half tone, or half step, on the piano

realistic opera: a general term for those operas of the nineteenth and early twentieth centuries that deal with everyday, gritty subjects; includes Italian *verismo* opera

rebec: a medieval fiddle

recapitulation: in sonata–allegro form, the return to the first theme and the tonic key following the development

recital: a concert of chamber music, usually for a solo performer

recitative: musically heightened speech, often used in an opera, oratorio, or cantata to report dramatic action and advance the plot

recitativo accompagnato: a recitative accompanied by the orchestra instead of merely the harpsichord; the opposite of simple, or *secco*, recitative

recorder: an end-blown wooden flute with seven finger holes, played straight out instead of to one side

relative major: the major key in a pair of major and minor keys; relative keys have the same key signature, for example, E♭ major and C minor (both with three flats)

relative minor: the minor key in a pair of major and minor keys; see *relative major*

repetition: process employed by a composer to validate the importance of a section of music by repeating it

rest: a silence in music of a specific duration

retransition: the end of the development section, where the tonality often becomes stabilized on the dominant in preparation for the return of the tonic (and first theme) at the beginning of the recapitulation

retrograde: a musical process in which a melody is played or sung, not from beginning to end, but starting with the last note and working backward to the first

rhythm: the organization of time in music, dividing up long spans of time into smaller, more easily comprehended units

Ring **cycle:** a cycle of four interconnected music dramas by Richard Wagner that collectively tell the tale of the Germanic legend *Der Ring des Nibelungen*

Risorgimento: the name given to the political movement that promoted the liberation and unification of Italy in the mid-nineteenth century

ritard: a gradual slowing down of the tempo

ritardando: in musical notation, a tempo mark indicating a slowing down of the tempo

ritornello form: form in a Baroque concerto grosso in which all or part of the main theme—the ritornello (Italian for "return" or "refrain")—returns again and again, invariably played by the tutti, or full orchestra

romance: a slow, lyrical piece, or movement within a larger work, for instruments, or instrument and voice, much favored by composers of the Romantic period

rondeau: see *rondo form*

rondo form: classical form with at least three statements of the refrain (**A**) and at least two contrasting sections (at least **B** and **C**); placement of the refrain creates symmetrical patterns such as **ABACA, ABACABA,** or even **ABACADA**

rubato: (Italian for "robbed") in musical notation, a tempo mark indicating that the performer may take, or steal, great liberties with the tempo

Russian Five: a group of young composers (Borodin, Cui, Balakirev, Rimsky-Korsakov, and Musorgsky) centered in St. Petersburg, whose aim was to write purely Russian music free of European influence

Russian Revolution: overthrow of the Russian tsar by the socialist Bolshevik Party in 1917

sackbut: a brass instrument of the late Middle Ages and Renaissance; the precursor of the trombone

Salzburg: mountain town in Austria, birthplace of Mozart

sampling: reusing (and often repeating) portions of a previous sound recording in a new song

Sanctus: the fourth section of the Ordinary of the Mass

sarabande: a slow, elegant dance in $\frac{3}{4}$ with a strong accent on the second beat

scale: an arrangement of pitches that ascends and descends in a fixed and unvarying pattern

scena: a scenic plan in Italian opera involving a succession of separate elements such as a slow aria, a recitative, and a fast concluding aria

scherzo: (Italian for "joke") a rapid, jovial work in triple meter often used in place of the minuet as the third movement in a string quartet or symphony

Schubertiad: a social gathering for music and poetry that featured the songs and piano music of Franz Schubert

score: a volume of musical notation involving more than one staff

scratching: sound processing that involves the rhythmical manipulation of a vinyl record

secco recitative: see *simple recitative*

Second Viennese School: a group of progressive modernist composers that revolved around Arnold Schoenberg in Vienna in the early twentieth century

sequence: a Gregorian chant, sung during the Proper of the Mass, in which a chorus and a soloist alternate; see also *melodic sequence*

serenade: an instrumental work for a small ensemble originally intended as a light entertainment in the evening

serial music: music in which some important component—pitch, dynamics, rhythm—comes in a continually repeating series; see also *twelve-tone composition*

seventh chord: a chord spanning seven letter names and constructed by superimposing three thirds

sforzando: a sudden, loud attack on one note or chord

sharp: a musical symbol that raises a pitch by a half step

shawm: a double-reed woodwind instrument of the late Middle Ages and Renaissance; the precursor of the oboe

simple recitative: recitative accompanied only by a *basso continuo* or a harpsichord, and not the full orchestra

sinfonia: (Italian for "symphony") a one-movement (later three- or

four-movement) orchestral work that originated in Italy in the seventeenth century

Singspiel: (German for "singing play") a musical comedy originating in Germany with spoken dialogue, tuneful songs, and topical humor

Sistine Chapel: the pope's private chapel within his Vatican apartments

snare drum: a small drum consisting of a metal cylinder covered with a skin or sheet of plastic that, when played with sticks, produces the "rat-ta-tat" sound familiar from marching bands

soft pedal: the left pedal of the piano, which, when depressed, shifts the keyboard in such a way that the hammers strike fewer strings, making the instrument sound softer

solo: a musical composition, or portion of a composition, sung or played by a single performer

solo concerto: a concerto in which an orchestra and a single performer in turn present and develop the musical material in the spirit of harmonious competition

solo sonata: a work, usually in three or four movements, for keyboard or other solo instrument; when a solo melodic instrument played a sonata in the Baroque era, it was supported by the *basso continuo*

sonata: originally, "something sounded" on an instrument as opposed to something sung (a "cantata"); later, a multi-movement work for solo instrument, or instrument with keyboard accompaniment

sonata–allegro form: a dramatic musical form that originated in the Classical period involving an exposition, development, and recapitulation, with optional introduction and coda

sonata da camera (chamber sonata): a suite for keyboard or small instrumental ensemble made up of individual dance movements

sonata da chiesa (church sonata): a suite for keyboard or small instrumental ensemble made up of movements indicated only by tempo marks such as *grave, vivace,* and *adagio;* originally intended to be performed in church

song cycle: a collection of several songs united by a common textual theme or literary idea

soprano: the highest female vocal part

Sprechstimme: (German for "speech-voice") a vocal technique in which a singer declaims, rather than sings, a text at only approximate pitch levels

staccato: a manner of playing in which each note is held only for the shortest possible time

staff: a horizontal grid onto which are put the symbols of musical notation: notes, rests, accidentals, dynamic marks, etc.

stanza: a poetic unit of two or more lines with a consistent meter and rhyme scheme

statement: presentation of important musical idea

step: the interval between adjacent pitches in the diatonic or chromatic scale; either a whole step or a half step

stomp: a piece of early jazz in which a distinctive rhythm, with syncopation, is established in the opening bars, as in the opening phrases of the "Charleston"

stop: a knob (or key) on a pipe organ that, when pulled (or pushed), allows a particular group of pipes to sound, thereby creating a distinctive tone color

string bass: see *double bass*

string instruments: instruments that produce sound when strings are bowed or plucked; the harp, the guitar, and members of the violin family are all string instruments

string quartet: a standard instrumental ensemble for chamber music consisting of a single first and second violin, a viola, and a cello; also, the genre of music, usually in three or four movements, composed for this ensemble

strophe: see *stanza*

strophic form: a musical form often used in setting a strophic, or stanzaic, text, such as a hymn or carol; the music is repeated anew for each successive strophe

style: the general surface sound produced by the interaction of the elements of music: melody, rhythm, harmony, color, texture, and form

subdominant: the chord built on the fourth, or subdominant, degree of the major or minor scale

subject: the term for the principal theme in a fugue

suite: an ordered set of instrumental pieces, usually all in one key, intended to be played in a single sitting (see also *dance suite*)

sustaining pedal: the rightmost pedal on the piano; when it is depressed, all dampers are removed from the strings, allowing them to vibrate freely

syllabic singing: a style of singing in which each syllable of text has one, and only one, note; the opposite of melismatic singing

Symbolists: group of poets in late-nineteenth-century Paris whose aesthetic aims were in harmony with those of the Impressionist painters; they worked to create a poetic style in which the literal *meaning* of the word was less important than its *sound* and the associations that that the particular sound might produce

symphonic poem (tone poem): a one-movement work for orchestra of the Romantic era that gives musical expression to the emotions and events associated with a story, play, political occurrence, personal experience, or encounter with nature

symphony: a genre of instrumental music for orchestra consisting of several movements; also, the orchestral ensemble that plays this genre

symphony orchestra: the large instrumental ensemble that plays symphonies, overtures, concertos, and the like

syncopation: a rhythmic device in which the natural accent falling on a strong beat is displaced to a weak beat or between the beats

synthesizer: a machine that has the capacity to produce, transform, and combine (or synthesize) electronic sounds

tambourine: a small drum, the head of which is hung with jangles; it can be struck or shaken to produce a tremolo effect

tam-tam: an unpitched gong used in Western orchestras

tango: a genre of popular urban song and dance originating in Cuba and Argentina in the nineteenth century; marked by a duple meter with syncopation after the first beat and a slow, sensuous feel

tempo: the speed at which the beats occur in music

tenor: the highest male vocal range

ternary form: a three-part musical form in which the third section is a repeat of the first; hence **ABA**

terraced dynamics: a term used to describe the sharp, abrupt dynamic contrasts found in the music of the Baroque era

texture: the density and disposition of the musical lines that make up a musical composition; monophonic, homophonic, and polyphonic are the primary musical textures

theme and variations: a musical form in which a theme continually returns but is varied by changing the notes of the melody, the harmony, the rhythm, or some other feature of the music

through-composed: a term used to describe music that exhibits no obvious repetitions or overt musical form from beginning to end

timbre: see *color*

time signature (*meter signature*): two numbers, one on top of the other, usually placed at the beginning of the music to tell the performer what note value is carrying the beat and how the beats are to be grouped

timpani (kettle drums): a percussion instrument consisting usually of two, but sometimes four, large drums that can produce a specific pitch when struck with mallets

toccata: a one-movement composition, free in form, originally for solo keyboard but later for instrumental ensemble as well

tonality: the organization of music around a central tone (the tonic) and the scale built on that tone

tone: a sound with a definite, consistent pitch

tone cluster: a dissonant sounding of several pitches, each only a half step away from the other, in a densely packed chord

tone poem: see *symphonic poem*

tonic: the central pitch around which the melody and harmony gravitate

transition (bridge): in sonata–allegro form, the unstable section in which the tonality changes from tonic to dominant (or relative major) in preparation for the appearance of the second theme

treble: the uppermost musical line, voice, or part; the part in which the melody is most often found

treble clef: the sign placed on a staff to indicate the notes above middle C

tremolo: a musical tremor produced on a string instrument by repeating the same pitch with quick up-and-down strokes of the bow

triad: a chord consisting of three pitches and two intervals of a third

trill: a rapid alternation of two neighboring pitches

trio: an ensemble, vocal or instrumental, with three performers; also, a brief, self-contained composition contrasting with a previous piece, such as a minuet or a mazurka; originally, the trio was performed by only three instruments

trio sonata: an ensemble of the Baroque period consisting actually of four performers, two playing upper parts and two on the *basso continuo* instruments

triple meter: gathering of beats into three beats per measure, with every third beat stressed

triplet: a group of three notes inserted into the space of two

trivium: a literary curriculum of three disciplines (grammar, logic, and rhetoric) taught in medieval schools and universities

trobairitz: female poet-musician of medieval southern France

trombone: a brass instrument of medium to low range that is supplied with a slide, allowing a variety of pitches to sound

troubadour: a type of secular poet-musician that flourished in southern France during the twelfth and thirteenth centuries

trouvère: a type of secular poet-musician that flourished in northern France during the thirteenth and early fourteenth centuries

trumpet: a brass instrument of the soprano range

tuba: a brass instrument of the bass range

tune: a simple melody that is easy to sing

tutti: (Italian for "all") the full orchestra or full performing force

twelve-bar blues: a standard formal plan for the blues involving a repeating twelve-measure harmonic support in which the chords can progress I-IV-I-V-I

twelve-tone composition: a method of composing music, devised by Arnold Schoenberg, that has each of the twelve notes of the chromatic scale sound in a fixed, regularly recurring order

unison: two or more voices or instrumental parts singing or playing the same pitch

upbeat: the beat that occurs with the upward motion of the conductor's hand and immediately before the downbeat

variation: process employed by a composer to alter melody or harmony in some way

vaudeville: an early form of American musical theater involving songs and dances, comedy skits, etc.; a precursor of the musical comedy of Broadway

verismo opera: "realism" opera; the Italian term for a type of late-nineteenth-century opera in which the subject matter concerns the unpleasant realities of everyday life

verse and chorus: strophic form; in successive strophes, new lines of text come at the beginning of each strophe followed by a textural refrain at the end; in group performance the verse is usually sung by a soloist and the chorus by the chorus, hence the name

vibrato: a slight and continual wobbling of the pitch produced on a string instrument or by the human voice

vielle: medieval fiddle

Viennese School: group of Classical composers, including Haydn, Mozart, Beethoven, and Schubert, whose careers all unfolded in Vienna

viola: a string instrument; the alto member of the violin family

viola da gamba (bass viol): the lowest member of the viol family; a large six- or seven-string instrument played with a bow and heard primarily in the music of the late Renaissance and Baroque eras

violin: a string instrument; the soprano member of the violin family

virtuosity: extraordinary technical facility possessed by an instrumental performer or singer

virtuoso: an instrumentalist or singer with a highly developed technical facility

vivace: in musical notation, a tempo mark indicating "fast and lively"

vocal ensemble: in opera, a group of four or more solo singers, usually the principals

voice: the vocal instrument of the human body; also, a musical line or part

volume: the degree of softness or loudness of a sound

walking bass: a bass line that moves at a moderate pace, mostly in equal note values, and often stepwise up or down the scale

waltz: a popular, triple-meter dance of the late eighteenth and nineteenth centuries

Well-Tempered Clavier, The: two sets of twenty-four preludes and fugues compiled by J. S. Bach in 1720 and 1742

whole step: the predominant interval in the Western major and minor scale; the interval made up of two half steps

whole-tone scale: a six-note scale each pitch of which is a whole tone away from the next

woodwind family: a group of instruments initially constructed of wood; most make their sound with the aid of a single or double reed; includes the flute, piccolo, clarinet, oboe, English horn, and bassoon

word painting: the process of depicting the text in music, be it subtly, overtly, or even jokingly, by means of expressive musical devices

xylophone: a percussion instrument consisting of tuned wooden bars, with resonators below, that are struck with mallets

Index